THE COMPLETE
CROSSWORD DICTIONARY

Compiled by Philip J. Montamble
and
Edited by Leila B. Gemme

Galahad Books • New York City

Library of Congress Number 73-91326
ISBN Number 0-88365-149-1

CONTENTS

Introduction	4
PART I Definitions	5
PART II Information by Subject	235
Geographical Gazetteer	236
Coins, Money	260
Weights and Measures	261
The Bible	263
Mythological Terms	266
Prefixes	269
Suffixes	270
Names of Famous Persons	272
Nobel Prizes	279
Religious Terms	284
Heraldic Terms	285
Chemical Elements	287
Presidents of the United States	289
PART III Word Finder	295
Two letter words	296
Three letter words	299
Four letter words	333

INTRODUCTION

The universal rationale of crossword puzzle solving is that, like most arts, it should begin in delight and end in wisdom. This dictionary is unique in that unlike other crossword puzzle dictionaries it does not call upon the corpus of American-English wordstock, namely several hundred thousand words, and through some semi-sophisticated computer technique deduce the words which might — or might not — be used in general crossword puzzle solving. The current dictionary is indigenous in the fact that the word choice has been culled from actual crossword puzzles appearing in American newspapers, books and magazines during the past forty years.

All crossword puzzle solving should be fun. If this dictionary helps you to find the first word or the last word, or some middle term in any crossword puzzle, then it has served its purpose.

For convenience the dictionary is divided into three parts. Part I is an alphabetical listing of terms and words commonly found in crossword puzzles. Included in each entry is a series of definitions calling upon all the parts of speech. The definitions are not restricted either grammatically or morphologically, but assume the widest latitude as do actual crossword puzzles in newspapers and magazines.

Part II of this dictionary lists information by subject. The subjects are found in almost every crossword puzzle and range from a geographical Gazetteer to Presidents of the United States. This section is encyclopedic in nature and can be used for general reference work on different subjects: geography, coins and money, the Bible, weights and measures, mythology, prefixes and suffixes, famous people, Nobel prizes, religion, heraldry, chemistry, and U.S. Presidents.

Part III of this dictionary is a spatial approach to crossword puzzle solving in that sections on two letter, three letter, and four letter words aid the solver in rapidly determining the answers to the most difficult clues. Specific instructions on how to use part III are found on page 295.

After many years in progress it is foolish to say this work is finished. To return to our original thesis, if this dictionary helps you to find a given word or term and to complete a crossword puzzle that you are solving, then it has more than done its service. Most of all, it aids the ever growing avocation of crossword puzzle solving.

Aaron's rod—MULLEIN
abalone—ORMER, SEA EAR, SNAIL
abalone shell—ORMER
abandon—ABDICATE, MAROON, WAIVE
abbess—AMMA
able—CAN, CAPABLE, CLEVER, COULD, COMPETENT, MAKE, MANAGE, QUALIFIED
abnormal—ABERRANT, IRREGULAR
abnormal desire—ONIOMANIA
abnormal mass of tissue—TUMOR, WART, WEN
abode—DWELLING, HABITAT, HABITATION, HOME, INN, LODGE, RESIDENCE
abode of ancient harp—TARA
abode of dead (Babyl)—AARU, ARALU
abode of human beings—MIGARD
abode of Morgan Le Fay—AVALON
abode of Oriental—DAR
abode of the blessed dead—ELYSIUM
abode of the dead—AARU, ARALU, ELYSIUM, HADES, SHEOL
abode of the gods—ASGARD
abode of the Grecian gods—OLYMPUS

abound—FLEET, SNEE, SWARM, TEEM
abounding—REPLETE, RIFE
about—ANENT, AROUND, AT, CIRCA, CONCERNING, OF ON, SOME
about as to dates—CIRCA
above—ABUNE, ALOFT, ATOP, HIGH, HIGHER, OER, OVER, PAST
above (dialect)—ABOON
above (poetic)—OER
above (prefix)—SUPER, SUPRA, EPI
above zero—PLUS
abraded—ERASED, FLAT, LEVEL, RAW, SCRAPED, SMOOTH
abrading tool—FILE, RASP
abrasive—BORT, EMERY, ERODENT, QUARTZ, SAND
abridgment—ABSTRACT, BRIEF, COMPENDIUM, EPITOME
abrogate—ANNUL, CANCEL, REPEAL, RESCIND
abrupt—BROKEN, BRUSQUE, CRAGGY, CURT, HASTY RUDE, SHORT, STEEP, SUDDEN
abscond—DECAMP, DESERT, ELOIGN, ELOPE, ESCAPE, FLEE
absence of blood poison—ASEPSIS

absence of government
—ANARCHY
absence of hair—ACOMIA
absence of order—ATAXIA
absence of taste—AGEUSIA
absolute—DEAD,
IMPLICIT, MERE,
PLENARY, PURE,
SHEER, STARK,
TOTAL, UTTER
absolve—ACQUIT, ASSOIL,
EXPIATE, FREE,
PARDON, REMIT
absorb—DRINK, ENGULF,
SOAK, SUCK
absorbed—ENGROSSED,
RAPT
abstain—CEASE, DENY,
DISUSE, REFRAIN,
SPARE, WAIVE
abstain from—AVOID,
ESCHEW, REFRAIN
abstract—BRIEF,
COMPEND, ENS,
ENTIA, EPITOME,
STEAL
abstract being—ENS,
ESSE, ENTIA
abstract (rare)—PRECIS
abstruse—DEEP,
ESOTERIC, HIDDEN,
RECONDITE
abundance (-ant)—AMPLE,
COPIOUS,
EXUBERANCE,
GALORE, PLENTY,
RIFE
abuse—DECEIVE,
MALTREAT, MAUL,
MISTREAT,
OUTRAGE, RAIL,
REVILE, SNASH,
abyss—DEPTH, GULF,
PIT, POT
academic—CLASSIC,
SCHOLASTIC
Acadian (French
descent)—CAJUN
acaudal—ANUROUS,
TAILLESS

accelerate—HASTEN,
SPEED, REV
accent—ICTUS, MARK,
STRESS
accenting syllable—ARSIS,
UPBEAT
accept—ADMIT, AGREE,
ALLOW, APPROVE,
BELIEVE, ENGAGE,
RECEIVE, TAKE
access—ADIT, ENTREE,
ENTRY, FIT
accessory—ABETTOR,
APPURTENANT,
AUXILIARY,
CONTRIBUTORY,
SUBSIDIARY
acclaim—ECLAT, LAUD,
PRAISE, EULOGIZE,
APPLAUSE
acclamation—CRY,
PLAUDIT, SHOUT,
VOTE
acclivity—HILL, SLOPE,
TALUS
accomplice—ABETTOR,
ALLY, BUDDY,
CHUM, PAL
accomplish—DO, EFFECT,
ENACT
accord—CONCERT,
UNANIMITY, UNITY,
ADJUST, AGREE,
CONCORD,
HARMONY, PROPER,
SUIT
according to—A LA, AUX,
PURSUANT
account—ASSIGN, DEEM,
RECITAL, RENDER,
REPORT, SAKE, TAB,
TAIL, TALE, WORTH
account entry—DEBIT,
ITEM
accouter—ARRAY, GIRD,
EQUIP
accumulate—ACCRUE,
AMASS, COLLECT,
FUND, HOARD,
STORE, GARNER

accuse—APPEAL,
ARRAIGN, BLAME,
CENSURE, CHARGE,
DELATE, IMPLEAD
accuse a public
officer—IMPEACH
accustom—INURE, HABIT,
TOUGHEN
ace—EXPERT, JOT,
ONE, PARTICLE, PIP,
TIB, TOP, UNIT
acerb—BITTER, HARSH,
SHARP, TART
acetic acid—ESTER, SOUR,
VINEGAR
acetone—KETONE
acetose—ACID, ACETOUS,
SOUR
ache—PAIN, PANG,
SMART, THROB,
THROE
achieve—ATTAIN, DO,
REALIZE, WIN,
EARN, GAIN,
OBTAIN, PERFORM,
REACH
acid—AMINO, BITING,
NITRIC, OLEATE,
SHARP, SOUR,
TART
acidity—ACERBITY,
ACOR
acknowledge—AVOW,
OWN, SIGN, THANK
acme—APEX, CAP,
CLIMAX, HEYDAY
acolyte—BOY, HELPER
acomia—BALDNESS
acquiesce—ACCEDE,
AGREE, CHIME
acquaint—APPRISE,
POSSESS, TELL
acquire—ATTAIN, EARN,
GAIN, GET, LEARN,
REAP, SECURE, WIN
acquit—CLEAR,
EXCULPATE,
EXCUSE, FREE
acrid—SHARP, SOUR

acrobat net—
TRAMPOLINE
acrobat of India—NAT
across—ATHWART,
OVER, TRAVERSE
action—ACT, AGENCY,
BATTLE, DEED,
FUNCTION
action (field)—ARENA,
STAGE
action (law)—RE, RES
action (noun suffix)—ENCE
action (to recover)—
TROVER
action (suffix)—URE
active—AGILE, ALIVE,
ASTIR, BRISK,
NIMBLE, QUICK,
SPRY
actress—DOER, PLAYER,
STAR, THESPIAN
acuity—EDGE, WIT
acute—CRITICAL,
INTENSE, KEEN,
POIGNANT,
POINTED, SHREWD,
TART
adage—AXIOM,
MAXIM, MOTTO,
PROVERB, SAW,
SAYING
adapt—ADJUST, ATTUNE,
CONFORM, FIT, SUIT
add—AFFIX, ANNEX,
APPEND, ATTACH,
AUGMENT,
INCREASE, TOTAL
add up—FOOT, SUM, TOT
addiction—HABIT,
PRONE, WAY,
WONT
addition—ADDEND,
ALSO, AND,
AUGEND, BESIDES,
ELSE, ELL, EKE,
MORE, PLUS, TOO
addition to contract—
RIDER
addition to a will—CODICIL

addle—MIRE, MUDDLE

adherent—AIDE, ALLY,
IST, ITE, DISCIPLE,
VOTARY

adhesive—CEMENT,
EPOXY, GLUE, TAPE

adjective ending—IL

adjective (suffix)—ALS,
ENE, ENT, IAN, IC,
ICAL, ILE, INS, ISH,
IVE

adjourn—DEFER, DELAY,
PROROGUE, RISE,
SUSPEND

adjust—ALIGN, FIX,
SETTLE

adjutant—AIDE

ado—FUSS, BOTHER

adolescence—PUBERTY,
TEENS, YOUTH

adorn—BEDECK, CREST,
DECK, DECORATE,
DRAPE, EMBELLISH,
FESTOON, GARNISH,
ORNATE, PINK,
TRIM

adrift—ASEA, DERELICT,
LOST

adroit—DEFT, HANDY

adult—GROWN,
MATURED

advance—COME,
FORWARD, GAIN,
PROGRESS,
PROMOTE, RISE

advance by degrees—
CREEP, INCH

advance guard—VAN

advance notice—WARNING

advantage—AVAIL,
BENEFIT, EDGE,
PROFIT

adventuress—DEMIREP,
GOLDDIGGER

adverb ending—LY

adviser—EGERIA,
MONITOR, NESTOR

advocate—PRO, ABETTOR,
APOLOGIST,
BACKER,
PARACLETE

affair—MATTER,
CONCERN

affair of
chance—LOTTERY

afar—AWAY, AT, OFF

affect—ACT, ATTACK,
INFLUENCE,
PRODUCE, TOUCH

affect deeply—IMPRESS,
PENETRATE

affected—FALLAL,
FEIGNED, POSEY

affliction—DISTRESS,
ILL, PAIN, SORE,
SORROW, WOE

affray—BATTLE,
COMBAT, FIGHT,
MELEE

aforesaid—ANTECEDENT
DITTO, PRIOR

afloat—BUOY, ASEA,
ADRIFT,
RAFT, SAIL,
SWIMMING

afreet—ARAB MYTH,
AFRIT, JINNEE

aft—ABAFT, ASTERN

after—BEHIND, LATER

after a while—ANON,
LATER

again—ANEW, ENCORE,
MOREOVER, OVER

against—CON, VERSUS,
ANTI

against (prefix)—ANTI

agalloch—AGAR, ALOES

agave—ALOE, MAGUEY,
SISAL

agave cordage—ISTLE

agave fiber—PITA, SISAL,
ISTLE

age—AEON, EON, EPOCH,
ERA, CENTURY,
LIFETIME,
SENIORITY, YEARS

age (at the same)—COEVAL

aged—ELDERLY, OLD,

SUPERANNUATED,
ANILE, NESTORIAN
aged rustic—GAFFER
agency—HAND, MEANS,
OPA
agent—CONSIGNEE,
BROKER, DEPUTY,
DOER, FACTOR,
MEDIUM,
PROMOTER, PROXY,
REPRESENTATIVE
agent (anglo ind)—WALLA
agglomerate—HEAP,
LUMP, MASS, SLAG
ago—PAST, SINCE, YORE
ago (poetic)—AGONE
agog—EAGER,
EXPECTANT,
WONDER
agony—GRIPE, PAIN,
PANIC, THROE,
TORTURE
agouti—PACA, RODENT
agree—CONCUR, GRANT,
JIBE, MATCH,
TALLY
agree to—CHIME,
CONCEDE, CONCUR,
HARMONIZE,
UNDERSTAND
agreeable—AMENE,
CONSONANT,
DULCET, LIEF,
SUAVE
agreement—ASSENT,
CONSENT,
ENTENTE, PACT,
RAPPORT, TREATY,
UNISON, UNITY
Ahab's daughter—
ATHALIE
aim (at)—ASPIRE,
DIRECT, INTENT,
OBJECTIVE, POINT,
TARGET
aimless—RANDOM
air—AER, ARIA,
ATMOSPHERE,
BREEZE, CARRIAGE,

DISPLAY, MANNER,
MIEN
air (comb form)—AER,
AERI, AERO
air (pertaining to)—AERO
aircraft—AERI, AERO,
AIRPLANE,
BIPLANE, BLIMP,
BOMBER, JET
aircraft shelter—HANGAR,
airplane—AIRCRAFT,
HELICOPTER,
PLANE, JET,
BOMBER
airplane climbing turn—
CHANDELLE
airplane device—RADAR
airplane part—FUSELAGE,
EMPENNAGE,
LONGERON, NOSE,
TAIL, WING
airplane type—BOMBER,
FIGHTER, JET,
LINER
airport area—APRON
airports—DULLES,
KENNEDY,
LAGUARDIA,
LOGAN, OHARE,
ORLY
SHANNON
airy—AERIAL,
ETHEREAL, LIGHT,
SPRIGHTLY
airy spirit—ARIEL
ait—EYOT, HOLM,
ISLAND, ILE, ISLE
akin—AGNATE, ALIKE,
ALLIED, RELATED,
SIB, SIMILAR
alarm—ALARUM, ALERT,
AROUSE,
FRIGHTEN,
STARTLE, TOCSIN
alas—ACH, HEU, OCH,
OCHONE, OHONE,
OIME, (greek)
OTOTOTOI
albatross, the

sooty—NELLY
Alcazar of the moorish kings
    at Granada——
    ALHAMBRA
alcohol—ETHAL, ETHYL,
    IDITE, STEROL
alcohol radical—AMYL
alcohols—BRANDY, GIN,
    MEAD, POSSET,
    RUM, RYE, SCOTCH,
    SLING, WINE,
    WHISKEY
Alcott heroine—AMY,
    BETH, JO, MEG
alcove—BAY, BOWER,
    NICHE, NOOK,
    ORIEL, RECESS
alder tree—ARN
alder yellow—SAGEROSE
ale—MUM
ale house—PUB
ale (kind)—ALEGAR, FLIP,
    MUM, PURL
alembic—CUP, RETORT,
    STILL, VESSEL
alewife—HERRING,
    WALLEYE
alfalfa—LUCERNE
Ali Baba's
    brother—CASSIM
Ali Baba's pass
    word—SESAME
alias—ELSE, EPITHET,
    NAME, OTHER, PEN
    NAME, TITLE
alien (ancient)—METIC
alien raider—INVADER,
    STRANGER
align—RANGE, TRUE
alike (comb form)—ISO
alkali land—USAR
alkaline—LIME, OXIDE
alkaline compound—SODA
alkaline solution—LYE
alkalinity—SALINITY
alkaloid—CURARE,
    ESERIN, SINAPIN,
    THRINE
all—ENTIRE, EVERY,

INDIVIDUALLY,
    QUITE, SOLELY,
    TOTAL, WHOLLY
all (comb form)—PAN
all creating—OMNIFIC
all (French)—TOUT
all (Latin)—OMNIS, TOTO
all (music)—TUTTI
all (prefix)—TOTI
allay—ASSUAGE,
    PALLIATE
allegiance—FEALTY,
    LOYALTY
allegory—ANAGOGE,
    FABLE, PARABLE,
    METAPHOR
alley—BLIND, LANE, MIG
alliance—AIX, ENTENTE,
    LEAGUE, TREATY
allied—AGNATE, AKIN,
    COGNATE, KIN,
    KINDRED, SIMILAR
allied by nature—AKIN
allot—CAVEL, DEAL,
    DISTRIBUTE, DOLE,
    GRANT, METE
allow—ADMIT, ENDURE,
    GRANT, LET,
    PERMIT
allowance—ARRAS,
    AUTHORIZATION,
    BOTE, DEDUCTION,
    DOLE, ODDS,
    RATION, SIZE,
    STINT, TARE, TRET
alloy—COMPOUND,
    AMALGAM, BLEND
allude (to)—ADVERT,
    HINT, IMPLY,
    REFER
allure—DRAW, ENTICE,
    LURE, TEMPT
alluvial deposit—DELTA,
    MUD, PLACER, SILT
alluvial fan—DELTA
alluvial matter—GEEST
alluvial river
    mouth—DELTA
ally—JOIN, LEAGUE,

PAL, UNION
almandine—SPINEL
almond-shaped—
    AMYGDALOID
almost—
    APPROXIMATELY,
    NEARLY, NIGH
alms—CHARITY, DOLES,
    HANDOUT,
aloe—AGAVE, ALOIN,
    PICRA, TAMBAC
alone—FORLORN, LONE,
    LORN, ONLY, SELF,
    SOLITARY, SOLO,
    SINGLY, SOLE,
    UNIQUE
aloof—ABACK, ADRIGH,
    COOL, FROSTY,
    REMOTE
alpha—CHIEF, DENEB,
    FIRST
alphabetic
    character—LETTER,
    RUNE, OGAM,
    OGHAM
also—AND, TOO,
    WITHAL, BESIDE,
    DITTO, EKE,
    HENCE, PLUS
altar—ARAS, BEMA
altar boy—ACOLYTE
altar Constellation—ARA
altar offering—ALTERAGE
altar screen—REREDOS
altar slab—MENSA
altar, top of—FRONTA,
    MENSA
alter—CHANGE, GELD,
    MUTATE, VARY
alternate—ELSE,
    INTERMITTENT,
    OTHER, VARY
although—ALBEIT, EEN,
    HOWEVER
alveolate—
    HONEYCOMBED,
    PITTED
always—AYE, EVER,
    EVERMORE
always (poetic)—EER

amadou—TINDER
amalgamate—BLEND,
    COMBINE, MERGE,
    UNITE
amateur—DABBLER,
    DILETTANTE,
    LOVER, TYRO
amatory—EROTIC,
    LOVING
amaze—ASTONISH,
    STAGGER, STUN
ambages—DEVIOUS,
    ROUNDABOUT,
    WINDING
ambassador—LEGATE,
    AGENT, DIPLOMAT,
    ENVOY, MINISTER
ambergris—PERFUMERY
amend—ATONE,
    EXPIATE,
    RECONCILE,
    REDEEM, REDRESS,
    REPAIR
amino acid—ALANINE,
    LEUCINE
ammonia compound—
    AMIDE, AMINE
ammonia
    derivative—AMIDE,
    AMINE, ANILIDE
ammunition—AMMO,
    AMMY, SHOT
ammunition
    wagon—CAISSON
among—ALONG, AMIDST,
    IN, MID
amount—EFFECT,
    FIGURE, NUMBER,
    QUANTITY, RATAL,
    REACH,
    SUBSTANCE, SUM,
    VOLUME
amphibian order—ANURA
ample—ABUNDANT,
    ENOW, FULL,
    GALORE, PLENTY
amplify—ADD, ENLARGE,
    EXPAND, INCREASE,
    WIDEN
amulet—CHARM, FETISH,

MERIAT, PERIAPT,
SCARAB, TALISMAN
amusing—COMIC,
DIVERTING, DROLL,
FARCICAL, RISIBLE
an (Scot)—AE
anathematize—CURSE
anchor—CAT, CRAMP,
GRAPNEL,
GRAPPLING,
KEDGE, MOOR
anchor lift—CAT,
CAPSTAN, DANDY
anchor part—ARM, BILL,
CROWN, FLUKE,
PALM, RING,
SHANK, STOCK,
THROAT
anchovy—SPRAT
ancon—ELBOW
and—ALSO
and (French)—ET
and (Latin)—ET
and not—NOR
and others—ETAL
and so forth—ETCETERA,
ETC
andiron—FIREDOG,
HESSIAN
anesthetic—
CHLOROFORM,
ETHER, GAS,
NOVOCAIN
angel—AZRAEL, BELIAL,
AEBLIS, CHERUB
MAH, SERAPH
angel of bottomless
pit—APOLLYON
angel of death—AZRAEL
angel of light—CHERUB
angel of Persia—MAH
angel of the moon—MAH
angelic—CHERUBIC,
SAINTLY
anger—CHOLER,
DUDGEON, FURY,
GALL, IRE, PIQUE,
RAGE, RILE
angry—CRANKY, IRATE,

IRRITATED, MAD,
SORE (sl.), RABID,
WROTH
anguish—AGONY,
DOLOR, PAIN,
REMORSE, SORROW,
TRAVAIL
angular—BENT, FORKED,
CROOKED, ZIGZAG
aniline dye—BENZOLE,
MAGENTA
animal life of area—FAUNA
animate—ALIVE, DASH,
ENLIVEN,
INVIGORATE, LIVEN
animation—LIFE, PEP,
SPIRIT, VIVACITY
animosity—ANGER, IRE,
RANCOR, SPITE
ankle—TARSAL,
TARSI, TARSUS
ankle bone—ASTRAGAL,
ASTRAGALUS,
TALUS, TARSAL
ankles—HOCK, TALI,
TALUS, TARSI,
TARSUS
anneal—FUSE, HEAT,
SMELT, TEMPER,
TOUGHEN
annex—ADD, ATTACH,
EL, ELL, EXTEND,
EXTENSION, JOIN,
SUBJOIN
annotate—COMMENT,
NOTE
annotation—
COMMENTARY,
FOOTNOTE,
GLOSSARY, RUBRIC
announce—BROADCAST,
BRUIT, DIVULGE
HERALD, PROCLAIM
announcement—BANNS,
BULLETIN, NOTICE,
PROCLAMATION,
TIDINGS
annoy—IRK, NAG,
PESTER, RILE,

TEASE, TRY, VEX
annual—BOOK, ETESIAN,
MASS, PLANT,
YEARLY
annul—ABOLISH,
ABROGATE,
CANCEL, ELIDE,
NULLIFY, REPEAL,
RESCIND, REVOKE
anoint—ANELE, CHRISM,
CONSECRATE,
HALLOW, OIL,
SANCTIFY
anon—AGAIN,
IMMEDIATELY,
SOON
answer—REPLY,
RESPOND, RETORT,
SOLUTION
antagonist—ENEMY, FOE,
RIVAL
antecedent—PRECEDENT,
PRIOR
antenna—AERIAL,
FEELER, HORN
anti-aircraft
artillery—FLAK,
ACKACK
anti-aircraft missile—NIKE,
ZEUS
antidote—EMETIC,
REMEDY, SERUM
antique red—CANNA
antitoxin—ANTIGEN,
SERA, SERO, SERUM
antler parts—PRONG,
TINE
antler types—CROWN,
ROYAL, BROW
antrum—CAVERN,
CAVITY, SINUS
anvil—INCUS, TEEST
anxiety—CARE, QUALM,
WORRY, PANIC
any—ALL, SOME
aorist (a verb
tense)—ACTION
aoudad—ARGALI, ARUI,
SHEEP
apart—ALOOF, ASIDE,

ASUNDER, ENISLED,
SEPARATE,
SEPARATELY,
PLACE, ALONE
apart (prefix)—DIS
apartment—DUPLEX,
FLAT, ROOMS,
SUITE
ape—BABOON, COPY,
CHIMPANZEE,
GIBBON, GORILLA,
JACKO, IMITATE,
LAR, MIME, MIMIC,
MOCK, ORANG
aperture—BOLE, BORE,
CLEFT, PORE,
BREACH, SLIT,
ORIFICE, STOMA,
VENT
apex—ACME, APOGEE,
POINT, TIP, TOP,
SUMMIT, VERTEX
aphorism—ADAGE,
DICTUM, EPIGRAM,
GNOME, MAXIM,
SAW
apocalyptic—
PROPHETIC,
PROPHET
apocrypha—(book of)
MACCABEES
apoplexy—STROKE
apoplexy (plant)—ESCA
apostate—RENEGADE,
TURNCOAT,
RECREANT,
DESERTER
apparatus—DEVICE,
APPLIANCE,
GADGET, TOOL,
GEAR, EQUIPMENT
apparent—CLEAR,
DISTINCT, PATENT
apparition—EIDOLON,
GHOST, SHAPE,
SPECTER, VISION
appellation—EPITHET,
NAME, TITLE
appendage—ADDENDA,
ADJUNCT, ARISTA,

RIDER, TAB, TAG,
TAIL
appendix—ADDENDUM
appetite—GUSTO, ZEST,
HUNGER, PALATE,
PENCHANT
appetizer—APERITIF,
CANAPE, OLIVE,
RADISH, SALAD
applaud—CHEER, CLAP,
HURRAH, HUZZA,
ROOT, PRAISE,
EXTOL, LAUD,
WHISTLE
applause—BRAVO, ECLAT,
ENCORE, HAND,
HURRAH, HUZZA,
ROOT
apple acid—MALIC
apple juice—CIDER
applelike fruit—
POMEGRANATE,
QUINCE
appleseed—PIP, PIT
apple tree—SORB
appoint—ASSIGN, NAME,
EQUIP, ORDAIN, SET
apportion—DEAL, DOLE,
METE, SPREAD,
DISTRIBUTE
apprehend—FEAR, GRASP,
INTUIT, NAB,
CATCH
apron—BRAT, PINAFORE,
RUNWAY, TOP, BIB
arbiter—JUDGE,
REFEREE, UMPIRE
arbitrary—CAPRICIOUS,
DESPOTIC,
PREEMPTORY
arbor—BOWER, PERGOLA
arboreal—SYLVAN
arc—ARCH, BOW, OVER,
COVE, SPAN
arcade—CLOISTER,
VAULT, ARCH
DOME, PASSAGE
arch—OGIVE, COVE,
DOME, SPAN,

VAULT, CUNNING,
SLY
archangel—RAPHAEL,
URIEL, MICHAEL,
SATAN, GABRIEL
arched passage—ARCADE
archer—BOWMAN,
CUPID, TELL,
BOWER, CLIM,
CLYM
archetype—MODEL,
IDEAL, PATTERN
architecture
(type)—BAUHAUS,
BAROQUE,
BOURBON, CLASSIC,
COPTIC, DORIC,
EMPIRE, GOTHIC,
GREEK, IONIC,
LANCET, LATIN,
MOORISH, MOSLEM,
NORMAN, ROCOCO,
ROMAN, TUDOR,
TUSCAN
architectural column—
PILASTER
architectural design—
SPANDREL
architectural drop-like
marking—GUTTA
architectural
ornament—DENTIL,
CORBEIL, OVE
architectural pier—ANTA
architectural screen—SPIER
architectural type of
molding—OGEE,
TORUS
architectural type of
roof—PEDIMENT
arctic—FRIGID, POLAR,
NORTHERN,
GALOSH
ardent—EAGER, FIERY,
FERVID, INTENSE,
ZEALOUS,
PARTISAN,
DEVOTED
ardor—ELAN, SPIRIT,

FERVOR
area—EXTENT, RANGE,
    REGION, SECTION,
    SITE, SPACE, TRACT,
    AREOLA, PURLIEU
arenaceous—SANDY
arenose—SANDY
Argonaut's leader—JASON
argot—SLANG, CANT,
    DIALECT, JARGON,
    PATOIS, JIVE, LINGO
argue—DEBATE,
    QUIBBLE, QUARREL,
    REBUT, SPAR
argument—DEBATE,
    FUSS, HASSLE,
    POLEMIC, ROW,
    SPAT, TIFF, WORDS
aria—AIR, MELODY,
    SONG, SOLO
arid—BARREN, DRY,
    PARCHED, SEC,
    WATERLESS,
    JEJUNE, STERILE,
    VAPID
ark—ASYLUM, COFFER,
    SHIP, CHEST, BOAT
ark builder—NOAH, NOE
ark landing
    place—ARARAT
arm—BRANCH, FORTIFY,
    MAN, MIGHT,
    EQUIP
arm bone—RADIUS,
    ULNA, HUMERUS
arm chair—FAUTEUIL
arm covering—SLEEVE
arm muscle—FLEXOR
arm of crane—GIB
arm of the sea—ARMLET,
    BAY, ESTUARY,
    FIRTH, GULF,
    INLET, STRAIT
armpit—ALA, AXILLA
armed band—POSSE
armed fleet—ARMADA,
    NAVY
armed force—ARMY,
    BATTALION,
    DETACHMENT,

PLATOON,
    REGIMENT, TROOP
armed galley of
    northmen—AESC
armed guard—SENTINEL,
    SENTRY
armed merchantman—
    RAIDER
armed power—
    ARMAMENT
armed private vessel—
    PRIVATEER
armed with a noose—
    LAQUEARIAN
army—HOST, LEGION,
    TROOPS
army chaplain—SKYPILOT,
    PADRE
army detachment—SQUAD,
    UNIT
army follower—SUTLER
army group—CADRE
army host—HORDE, U.S.O.
army peddler—SUTLER
army section—DIVISION,
    CORPS
army unit—BATTALION,
    BRIGADE,
    PLATOON,
    REGIMENT, TROOP
aroid (bot)—ARAD,
    ARUM
aromatic—FRAGRANT,
    PUNGENT, SPICY
aromatic bark—SINTOC
aromatic beverage—MATE
aromatic condiment—SPICE
aromatic evergreen
    shrub—LAUREL
aromatic gum
    resin—MYRRH
aromatic herb—ANISE,
    BASIL, CARAWAY,
    CHERVIL, FENNEL,
    MINT, SPEARMINT,
    TARRAGON
around—CIRCA, NEAR
around (prefix)—PERI
arouse—ACTUATE,
    ALARM, EXCITE,

STIR, WAKE,
ANIMATE, REVIVE,
SUMMON
arouse to action—RALLY
arraign—ACCUSE,
CHARGE, INDICT,
CENSURE
arrange—ADJUST,
DEPLOY, DISPOSE,
FETTLE, PLACE,
PLAN, PREPARE
arrange troops—DEPLOY
arrange for
exhibition—STAGE
arrangement—DISPOSAL,
ORDER, PLAN,
SETUP, SYSTEM,
COLLOCATION,
FOLE
array—ATTIRE, CLOTHE,
DECK, MARSHAL
arrow body—STELE
arrow case—QUIVER
arrow dart—BARB
arrow feather—VANE
arrow fit to string of
bow—NOCK
arrow poison—ANTIAR,
CURARE, CURARI,
INEE, UPAS
arrowroot—ARUM,
ARARAO, PIA,
CANNA
arsenic disulphide—
REALGAR
art—APTITUDE
FACILITY, KNACK,
SCIENCE, WILE
art (Latin)—ARS
art in general—SKILL,
TECHNIC
art principle—TECHNIC
art style—DADA, OP, POP
artery—AORTA
Arthurian Eden—
AVALON
Arthurian knight—BORS,
GARETH,
PERCIVALE,

GALAHAD,
LAUNCELOT
Arthurian lady—ELAINE,
ENID
article—A, AN, ITEM,
THE, THING
article (French)—LA, LE,
LES, UN, UNE
article in a
document—CLAUSE
article of
commerce—STAPLE
article of faith—TENET
atricle of virtu—CURIO,
BIJOUTERIE, BIJOU
artificial—FEIGNED,
FICTITIOUS,
SYNTHETIC,
UNREAL, ERSATZ,
FAKE, SHAM
artist—ARTISAN,
ARTISTE, JOCOSE,
SCHEMER
artist's medium—
TEMPERA, OIL
artist's mixing
board—PALETTE
artist's stand—EASEL
arum plant—ARAD,
AROID, LILY,
CALLA
aryan—MEDE, SLAV
as—LIKE, QUA, SIMILAR,
SUPPOSE, THUS,
WHILE
asbestos—AMIANTHUS
ascent—RISE, LIFT,
SURGE, CLIMB,
STEEP, SLOPE
ascertain—LEARN, SEE
ascetic—ESSENE, STOIC,
YOGI, AUSTERE,
HERMIT
ascorbic acid—VITAMIN C
ash—CHAR, EMBER
ashes of seaweed—KELP
ashes (Scot)—ASE
ask—BEG, BID, INQUIRE,
INVITE, REQUEST,

SOLICIT
ask (Scot)—SPERE
ask payment—DUN
aspect—ANGLE, FACET,
    PHASE, FORM, VIEW
asphyxia—APNEA
assay—ANALYSIS, TEST,
    TRY
assemble—
    CONGREGATE,
    CONVENE,
    CONVOKE, MASS,
    MEET, MUSTER
assembly—AGORA, DIET
assembly hall—AULA
assert—AFFIRM, ALLEGE,
    ATTEST, AVER,
    AVOUCH, AVOW,
    CONTEND,
    DECLARE,
    VINDICATE, POSIT,
    PREDICATE,
    PRONOUNCE,
    STATE, UTTER
assess—TAX, ESTIMATE,
    LEVY
assessment
    amount—RATAL
assign—ALLOT, APPOINT,
    NAME,
    NOMINATE, REFER
association—CABAL,
    CARTEL, CLUB,
    GUILD, LODGE,
    UNION
assume—ADOPT, AFFECT,
    DON, FEIGN,
    POSSESS, PRETEND,
    SUPPOSE, USURP,
    WEAR
astern—ABAFT, REAR
asteroid—PALLAS
astringent—ALUM,
    STYPTIC, TANNIN,
astronomical—URANIAN
astronomical halo—
    CORONA
astronomical
    instrument—ABA,
    ARMIL, ORRERY,

SECTOR
astronomy muse—URANIA
asylum—ALTAR, GRITH,
    HAVEN, SHELTER,
    TEMPLE
atheist—INFIDEL
athletic contest—AGON,
    MEET, OLYMPICS,
    TOURNAMENT
athletic prize—AGON,
    MEDAL, RIBBON,
    TROPHY
Atlantic shark—GATA
atmospheric—AERIAL,
    AIRY
atmospheric conditions
    —CLIMATE
atmospheric
    disturbance—FOG,
    HURRICANE,
    STORM, STATIC,
    TORNADO,
    TYPHOON, WIND
atmospheric gas—ARGON,
    XENON
atoll center—LAGOON
atoll in Marshall
    Islands—ENIWETOK
atoll island—BIKINI,
    TARAWA
atom—ION, IOTA,
    JOT, MONAD,
    PARTICLE, PROTON
atom part—NUCLEI
attach—AFFIX, APPEND
attempt—ASSAY, EFFORT,
    ENDEAVOR, STAB,
    STRIVE, TEST, TRIAL,
    TRY
attendant—AIDE, CLERK,
    HELPER, PAGE,
    SERVER, WAITER
attendant of a
    lord—THANE
attendant of the sea
    god—TRITON
attentive—ALERT, EARED,
    INTENT, WARY
attic—GARRET, LOFT,
    DORMER

attraction—ALLURE,
GRAVITATION,
MAGNET, PULL
attractive—CHARMING,
ENGAGING,
TAKING, CUTE
auditory—OTIC
auditory organ——EAR
auger—BORER, GIMLET,
TERRIER, WIMBLE
author—BARD, CREATOR,
POET, WRITER
authoritative—
ASSERTIVE,
OFFICIAL
authority—
DOMINANCE,
DOMINION,
EXPERT
authorize—ACCREDIT,
DELEGATE,
LICENSE
authorize (letter)—BREVE
autocrat—DESPOT,
MOGUL, RULER,
TSAR, TYRANT
autocracy—TYRANNY
automaton—GOLEM,
ROBOT
auxiliary—ALAR, ALLY,
ANCILLARY,

ASSISTANT,
HELPING
aversion—DISLIKE,
DISTASTE, HATE,
HATRED
aversion to
exertion—INERTIA
aviary—ORNITHON
await—ATTEND, BIDE,
EXPECT
await settlement—PEND
award—ASSIGN, BESTOW,
METE, PRIZE
award of valor—MEDAL
away—ABSENT, ASIDE,
BEGONE, FAR, FRO,
OFF, OUT,
REMOVED
away from—OFF, FRO
awn—ARISTA, BEARD,
BRISTLE
awn of grain—ARISTA,
BEARD
ax handle—HELVE
ax shaped stone—CELT
axelike tool—ADZE
azure—CERULEAN
azygous—ODD, SINGLE
azyma (Latin)—BREAD
azymous—
UNLEAVENED

-B-

Baalite—IDOLATER
babble—BLAB, CHATTER,
GIBBER, GOSSIP,
TATTLE, PURL
Babel—DIN, UPROAR,
HUBBUB, RACKET,
TOWER (loc. in Shinar)
baby—HUMOR, INFANT,
INFANTILE
baby carriage—GOCART,
PRAM, STROLLER
baby food—PAP
baby heelless shoes—CASKS
baby kangaroo's

cradle—SAC
bacchan cry—EVOE
bacchante—MAENAD,
MAENADIC,
MENAD, MENADIC
back—BACKWARD, FRO,
REAR, SUPPORT,
UPHOLD

backbone—CHINE,
RACHIS, SPINE
backbone of
animal—CHINE,
DORSUM
back door—POSTERN

back gate—POSTERN
back (go)—REGRESS,
    RETURN
back of a book—SPINE
back of the head—INION
back of the neck—NAPE
back out—BLENCH,
    FUNK, QUAIL,
    RECOIL, RETREAT
back part of the
    skull—OCCIPUT
back payment—ARREARS
back (prefix)—UN, ANA,
    RE, RETRO
back water in
    rowing—SHEAVE
backbite—MALIGN,
    SLANDER, VILIFY
bacon cut—RASHER
bacteria—COCCUS, GERM,
    BACILLI, MICROBE
bacteria culture—AGAR
bad—DECAYED,
    DEFECTIVE, EVIL,
    FAULTY, HURTFUL,
    SORRY, UNFIT,
    WICKED
badge—EMBLEM,
    EPAULET, INSIGNE,
    PIN, PLAQUE,
    TOKEN
badge of honor—MEDAL
badge worn on the
    arm—BRASSARD
badger—BAUSON
    HECKLE, NAG,
    NEEDLE, PESTER,
    TAUNT, TWIG
badly—ILLY
badly (prefix)—MAL
badminton
    shuttlecock—BIRD
bag—ASCUS,
    CAPTURE, CATCH,
    CYST, ENTRAP,
    GRIP, MUSETTE,
    POUCH, PURSE,
    SACK, SATCHEL,
    SUITCASE, VALISE
bagatelle—GAME, VERSE,

TRIFLE
bagpipe—DRONE
bagpipe sound—SKIRL
bagpipe music—PIBROCH
bail—BOND, DIPPER,
    LADLE, SCOOP,
    SPOON, SURETY
bailiff—GEREFA,
    MAGISTRATE,
    REEVE, SHERIFF
baker's implement—PEEL
baker's kneading
    trough—BRAKE
baking chamber—OAST,
    OVEN, KILN
baking dish—RAMEKIN
baking pit—IMU
baking soda—SALERATUS
balance—BALLAST,
    EVEN, FLUCTUATE'
    PAR, POISE,
    REMAINDER, REST,
    SANITY, SCALE,
    WAVER, WEIGHT
balcony—GALLERY,
    TERRACE
balcony railing—PARAPET
balcony with
    windows—GAZEBO
baldness—ALOPECIA,
    ACOMIA
balk—BAFFLE, FOIL,
    FRUSTRATE,
    IMPEDE, THWART
ball—BEAD, DANCE,
    GLOBE, PELLET,
    SPHERE
ball of thread—CLEW,
    CLUE
ball of the
    thumb—THENAR
ball (to hit)—BUNT, LOB,
    SWAT
ballad—DERRY, LAY,
    SONG, SONNET
ballast—BRACE,
    BRACKET, SUPPORT
ballet dance for
    two—ADAGIO
ballet dancer—CORYPHEE

ballet skirt—TUTU
ballet term—ARABESQUE,
  BOUREE, COUP,
  GLISSADE, PAS, PLIE
balloon—AIRSHIP, BLIMP,
  GONDOLA
balloon part—CAR,
  NACELLE
balm—ANODYNE,
  BALSAM,
  OINTMENT, SALVE,
  UNGUENT
Balm of Gilead—BALSAM,
  POPLAR
balsam—BALM, TOLU
bamboo grass—REED
bamboo shoot—ACHAR
banana cluster—HAND
bananalike fruit—PAPAW,
  PLANTAIN
band—BELT, COMPANY,
  CREW, FETTER,
  FILLET, GIRDLE,
  GROUP, STRAP,
  STRIP, SPECTRA
bandage—FASCIA,
  LIGATE, SWATHE
bank—BRINK,
  MOUNT, PILE,
  RIDGE, RIPA,
  RIPARIAN, ROW,
  TIER
banker (Ind.)—SARAF,
  SHROFF
bankrupt—BREAK,
  FAILURE,
  INSOLVENT,
  QUISBY, SMASH
banquet—MEAL, REPAST,
  FEAST, SPREAD
banter—CHAFF, JOSH,
  TWIT
baptismal vessel—FONT
baptismal water—LAVER
bar—BANK, CAKE,
  COURT, ESTOP,
  EXCEPT, EXCLUDE,
  LEVER, PRY, RAIL,
  STRIPE

bar in weaving—EASER
bar for holding cutting
  tools—ARBOR
bar for lifting—JIMMY,
  PRY
bar of balance—BEAM
bar of cast metal—INGOT
bar legally—ESTOP
bar of soap frame—SESS
bar supporting a top
  mast—FID
bar to transmit
  force—LEVER, PRY
barb—ARROW, DART,
  HOOK, FLUE, JAG,
  NAG, SPINE
barb of a
  feather—PINNULA,
  HARL, RAMUS
barb of a spear—GAFF
barbarian—GOTH, HUN
barbarian ruler—ODOACER
barbarian tribe—GOTHS
barber—FIGARO,
  SHAVER, TONSOR
bard—DRUID,
  MINSTREL, POET,
  RUNER, SCOP,
  SKALD
bargain—BUY,
  CONTRACT, DEAL,
  DICKER, HAGGLE,
  PACT, STEAL
barge—ARK, BOAT,
  DORY, LUNGE,
  LURCH
bark—BAY, CLAMOR,
  DIN, RIND, YELP,
  YAP, SKIN
bark cloth—TAPA
bark exterior—ROSS
bark layer—BAST
bark of East Indian
  tree—NIPA
bark of the paper
  mulberry—TAPA
barker—SPIELER, TOUT
barking—LATRANT
barometric line—ISOBAR

barony—FIEF
barracks—BILLET,
  BIVOUAC
barrel—CASK, KEG, TUN
barrelside piece—
  STAVE
barrel maker—COOPER
barren—ARID, DESERT
  (land), STERILE
barrier—BAR, POLE,
  FENCE, LIMIT
base—ABJECT, BED,
  ESTABLISH,
  IGNOBLE, LOW,
  MEAN, PEDESTAL,
  PLINTH, SNIDE,
  SORDID, UNCOUTH,
  VILE
base for cultures—AGAR
baseball terms—BAG,
  PLATE, SACK,
  SLUGGER
baseball positions—
  LEFTFIELD,
  RIGHTFIELD,
  SHORTSTOP
basin—FONT, PAN,
  STOUP
basis—BASE,
  FOUNDATION,
  GROUNDWORK,
  PRINCIPLE, ROOT
basis (conclusion)—
  PREMISE
basis of assessment—RATAL
basket—CORBEIL, CORF,
  CREEL, DOSSER,
  HAMPER, PANNIER,
  CRESSET
basketry rod—OSIER
battering instrument—RAM,
  RAMMER
battery plate—GRID
battle—COMBAT,
  CONFLICT,
  ENCOUNTER,
  ENGAGEMENT,
  FIGHT, WAR
battle of 1775—CONCORD

battle of
  1815—WATERLOO
battle of 1870—SEDAN
battle of 1941—BATAAN
battle formation—
  ECHELON
battleaxe—GISARME
battlement
  embrasure—CRENEL
bauble—GEWGAW,
  ORNAMENT,
  TINSEL, TOY,
  TRINKET
bay—BIGHT, COVE,
  INLET, SINUS
bay color—ROAN
bay horse—BAYARD,
  ROAN
bay window—MIRADOR,
  ORIEL
bazaar—AGORA,
  BARGAIN, FAIR,
  GINZA, MART
beacon—ALARM, ALERT,
  GUIDE, PHAROS,
  TOWER
bead—DROP, GLOBULE
bead (string of)—
  CHAPLET,
  NECKLACE,
  ROSARY
beak—BILL, NEB, NIB,
  PROW
beak membrane—CERE
bean—GOA, HARICOT,
  LEGUME, LIMA,
  NAVY, PINTO, SOY,
  SOYA, STRING
bean eyes—HILA
bear—ABIDE, BRUIN,
  CARRY, ENDURE,
  LAST, STAND,
  SUFFER, TOLERATE,
  URSA
bear (female)—URSA
bearlike—URSINE
bearlike animal—PANDA
beard—ARISTA, AWN,
  GOATEE, WHISKERS

beard lichen—USNEA
beard of grains and
    grasses—ARISTAE,
    AVELS, AWNS
bearded—ARISTATE,
    BARBATE
bearing—AIR, CARRIAGE,
    MIEN
beast—ANIMAL, BRUTE,
    LOUT, SAVAGE
beat—BEST, CONQUER,
    DEFEAT, DRUM,
    FLAIL, FLOG, LAM,
    LASH, MIX,
    MYSTIFY, POUND,
    RAIN, STRIKE,
    SWINDLE, THRASH,
    THROB, TREAD
bear back—REPEL,
    REPULSE
beat hard—HAMMER
beat hemp—TAW
beat into plate—
    MALLEATE
beat soundly—LARRUP
beat to (Scot)—TOWEN
beater—DASHER, RAB
beautiful—BONNY,
    COMELY,
    HANDSOME,
    LIVELY, PRETTY
beaver—CASTOR
become—BEFIT, GET,
    GROW, SUIT, WAX
becket—COIL, EYE,
    GROMMET, ROPE
bed—BASE, BASSINET,
    COT, COUCH, CRIB,
    MATRIX, PALLET,
    STRATUM, STEAD,
    STOCK
bedeck—ADORN, BEDO,
    GRACE, ORNATE
bedlam—UPROAR
bee colony—HIVE
bee house—APIARY, HIVE,
    SKEP
bee male—DRONE
beer—ALE, LAGER

beer ingredient—HOPS,
    MALT
beer mug—SEIDEL, STEIN
beer (spiced)—FLIP
beetle—AMARA,
    CANTHARIS, DOR,
    ELATER,
    OVERHANG,
    SCARAB, CHAFER,
    WEEVIL, LARVA,
    GRUB
befall—BECOME, BETIDE,
    HAP, HAPPEN, TIDE
befit—BECOME, SUIT
begin—COMMENCE,
    LEAD, INITIATE,
    OPEN, SETOUT,
    START
beginning—ALPHA,
    COMMENCEMENT,
    DAWN, DEBUT,
    FRONT, INITIAL,
    NASCENT, ONSET,
    ORIGIN, START
behind—ABAFT, AFTER,
    ASTERN, PAST,
    REAR
behind a vessel—AFT,
    ASTERN
behind another—LAG,
    REAR, SLOW
behind (nautical)—ABAFT,
    AFT
behold (Latin)—ECCE
being—ENS, ENTITY,
    ESSE, EXISTENCE,
    HUMAN, LIVING
belief—CREDO, CREED,
    CREDENCE,
    DOCTRINE, FAITH,
    IDEA, ISM, TENET,
    TRUST
believe—CREDIT, OPINE,
    THINK, SUPPOSE
believer in all
    religions—OMNIST,
    IST, DEIST
bell—FLARE, GONG
bell clapper—TONGUE

bellflower—
CAMPANULA
belong—INHERE,
PERTAIN
below—ALOW, BENEATH,
INFERIOR, INFRA,
NEATH, SOTTO
belt—BAND, CORDON,
CESTUS, CINGLE,
CUMMERBUND,
ENCIRCLE, GIRDLE,
OBI, SASH, STRAP,
SURROUND, ZONE
bench—BANC, BAR, PEW,
SEAT
bend—ARCH, BOW,
CROOK, CURVE,
FLEX, LEAN, NOD,
SAG, STOOP, TREND
benediction—BLESSING,
SHEMA
berry—ACINI, BACCA,
CUBEB
berserk—AMOK
ENRAGED,
FRENZIED, MAD
berth—BED, BILLET,
BUNK, DOCK, JOB,
SLIP
beside another—ALONG
beside (prefix)—PAR, PARA
best—ACE, CREAM,
DEFEAT, FINEST,
LARGEST, MOST,
OUTSTRIP,
OVERCOME,
OVERMATCH
bestow—AWARD,
CONFER, ENDOW,
GIVE, GRANT,
IMPART, RENDER
bet—ANTE, BAS, HEDGE,
GAMBLE, POT,
PARLAY, WAGER
betake—GO, HIE,
JOURNEY, MOVE,
REPAIR
betel—ARECA, ITMO, SIRI
betray—ACCUSE, BLAB,
PEACH, SELL,

SING, SQUEAL,
TRAP, TRICK
betrayer—JUDAS, RAT,
SEDUCER, SKUNK,
TRAITOR
betroth—AFFIANCE,
ASSURE, ENGAGE,
PLIGHT
better—AMEND, EMEND,
EXCEL, MEND,
REFORM, TOP
between—AMID, AMONG,
BETWIXT, ENTIRE,
JOINING, MESNE
beverage—ADE, ALE,
BEER, CIDER,
COFFEE, COCOA,
DRINK, EGGNOG,
GIN, LAGER,
LEMONADE,
LIQUOR, MALT,
MILK, NEGUS,
PORTER, TEA,
TODDY, WINE
bevy—BATCH, BROOD,
COVEY, DROVE
FLOCK, GAGGLE,
GROUP, HERD,
PACK, SWARM
bewail—CRY, GRIEVE,
KEEN, LAMENT,
MOAN, RUE, WEEP
beware—AVOID, HEED,
ESCHEW, SHUN
bewilder—ABASH,
ADDLE, AMAZE,
DAZE, FOIL, FOG
bewitch—CHARM,
ENCHANT,
ENSORCEL, HEX
beyond—ABOVE, ACROSS,
FARTHER,
HEREAFTER,
LATER, OVER, PAST,
YONDER
bicker—CAVIL, QUIBBLE,
SPAT, SPAR, TIFF
bight—BAY, COVE,
INLET, GULF, LOOP
bilk—CHEAT, COZEN,

FLEECE, GYP,
HOAX, TRICK
billiard shot—BRICOLE,
CAROM, MASSE
bind—BAND, BANDAGE,
CONFINE, COHERE,
FASTEN, HOLD,
LINK, PROTECT,
SECURE, SWATHE,
TAPE, TIE, TRUSS,
UNITE
Bingo—KENO, LOTTO
biography—LIFE,
MEMOIR, VITA
birthmark—BLAIN, MOLE,
NAEVI, NAEVUS,
NEVUS
birthright—HERITAGE
bishop—ABBE
bishop's headdress—HURA,
MITER, MITRE
bishop's jurisdiction—
DIOCESE, SEE
bishop's official
chair—CATHEDRA
bishop's staff—CROZIER
bishop weed—AMMI,
GOUT
bit—ACE, ATOM, IOTA,
JOT, MITE, MORSEL,
MOTE, SMIDGE
bite—CHAMP, CHEW,
GNASH, GNAR,
GNAW, MORSEL,
SNACK
bitter—ACERB, ACRID,
ASTRINGENT, GALL
bitter drug—ALOE
bitter vetch—ERS, OO
bivalve—CLAM,
MOLLUSK, MUSSEL,
PIDDOCK, OYSTER
bivouac—CAMP, ETAPE,
WATCH
bizarre—DAEDAL, QUEER,
ODD, OUTRE
black—EBON, FOUL,
INKY, HOSTILE, JET,
MELANIC, NEGRITO,
NEGRO, RAVEN,

SABLE, SOOTY,
TARRY, WICKED
black and blue—LIVID
blacksmith—FARRIER,
SMITHY
blade—EDGE, LEAF, OAR,
SPIRE (grass), SWORD
blain—BLISTER, BULLA,
SORE
blame—ASCRIBE,
CENSURE, GUILT,
ONUS, ODIUM
bland—BENIGN, MILD,
SUAVE
blast—BLIGHT, BOMB,
DETONATION,
DESTROY,
EXPLOSION, RUIN,
SHRIVEL
blast furnace—SMELTER
blatant—COARSE, GLIB,
GROSS, VOCAL,
VULGAR
blemish—BLUR, BRUISE,
FLAW, MACULE,
MAR, STIGMA
blend—COALESCE, FUSE,
JOIN, MERGE, MIX
blessing—BENEFICE,
BENISON, BOON,
GIFT, GRACE
blind—DECOY, SEEL,
SHADE, SHUTTER
blind alley—IMPASSE,
CULDESAC
blindness—ANOPSIA,
CECITY
blood—GORE, HEMAL,
(pert. to) PLASMA,
SERA, SERUM
blood deficiency—ANEMIA
bloom—HEYDAY, PRIME
blow—BOAST, GALE,
INFLATE, MELT,
MOVE, PANT, PUFF,
RAP, SLAP, STROKE,
THUMP, WAFT
blue—DEPRESSED,
DISMAL, GLOOMY,
GLUM, LOW, SAD

blunder—BLOW, BONER,
 BOTCH, BUNGLE,
 ERR (OR), GAFFE
blunt—ASSUAGE,
 DEADEN, DULL,
 GRUFF, OBTUSE,
 OUTSPOKEN, RUDE
blush—FLUSH, REDDEN,
 TINGE
boast—BRAG, CROW,
 EXTOL, GAB,
 VAUNT
boat—ARK, BARGE,
 BARK, BRIG,
 CANOE, CORACLE,
 CAT, DORY,
 FREIGHTER, GIG,
 LINER, OILER,
 PUNT, SCOW,
 SCHOONER, SLOOP,
 STEAMER
boatman—CHARON,
 GONDOLIER
bodice—BASQUE,
 CORSET, WAIST
bodkin—AWL, DAGGER,
 EYELETEER,
 NEEDLE, PIN,
 STILETTO
body—BULK, CADAVER,
 CARCASS, CORPSE,
 CORPUS, MASS,
 SOMA, STEM, TORSO,
 TRUNK
body of men—ARMY,
 CORPS, FORCE,
 POSSE
bodyguard—ESCORT,
 RETINUE, THANE
bodily—SOMATIC, SOMAL
bog—FEN, MARSH,
 MIRE, MOOR,
 MORASS, MUSKEG,
 SWAMP
boil—BUBBLE,
 FURUNCLE, RAGE,
 SEETHE, SIMMER,
 STEW, STY, TEEM
bolt—BAR, CLOSE,

ELOPE, FASTEN,
 LOCK, PIN
bolus—CLOD, CUD,
 LUMP, MASS
bomb—BOMBARD, DUD,
 EGG, FLOP,
 PROJECTILE, SHELL
bomb (kind)—ATOM, GAS,
 GRENADE
bombard—ATTACK,
 BATTER, SHELL,
 STRAFE
bombast—BLUSTER, GAS,
 RAGE, RANT, RAVE,
 TYMPANY
bond—BAIL, DUTY,
 ESCROW, NEXUS,
 PLEDGE, TIE, VOW
book—BIBLE, CANTO,
 DIARY, FOLIO,
 LIBER, LOG,
 MANUAL, MISSAL,
 MSS., OPUS,
 PSALTER, PRIMER,
 TEXT, TOME,
 VOLUME
boom—BUMP, JIB, SPAR,
 SPRIT, SUPPORT
boon—FAVOR, GRANT,
 JOVIAL
border—ABUT, BRIM,
 BRINK, EDGE,
 FRINGE, HEM,
 LIMIT, LIP, MARGIN,
 RAND, RIM, SIDE,
 SKIRT, VERGE
bore—ANNOY, DRILL,
 ENNUI, IRK, PALL,
 WEARY
born—NASCENT, NATIVE,
 NATURAL, NEE
borrow—ADOPT, COPY,
 LOAN, STEAL, TAKE
boss—BAAS, KNOB,
 MASTER, STUD
bottle—COSTREL, CRUET,
 FLASK, GOURD,
 MAGNUM
 PHIAL, VIAL

bottom—BASE, BED,
BEDROCK, DREGS,
FLOOR, GROUND,
NADIR, SOLE
bough—ARM, BRANCH,
LIMB, SPRIG,
SHOOT, TWIG
bounce—EJECT, FIRE,
LEAP, SACK, SPRING
boundary—LIMIT, LINE,
MERE, METE, SIDE,
TERMINUS
bow—ARC, ARCH, AVE,
BEND, CURTSEY,
CURVE, DEFER,
NOD, PROW,
SALAAM, STOOP,
SUBMIT, YIELD
bowl—ARENA, BASIN,
BEAKER, TUREEN,
VESSEL
bowling term—SPARE,
SPLIT, STRIKE
box—BIN, BINN,
CARTON, CASE,
CHEST, CIST, CRATE,
LOGE, SPAR, STOW
boxing term—BOUT,
KAYO, KO, MATCH,
TKO
boy—BUB, GROOM, LAD,
SHAVER, TOT,
YOUTH
boycott—AVOID, DEBAR,
BLACKBALL,
BLACKLIST,
OSTRACIZE, SHUN
brace—CRUTCH, GIRD,
LEG, PAIR, PROP,
SHORE, STAY,
STIFFEN
braid—LACET, PLAIT,
PLAT, TRIM, TRESS
brain—GYRI, INTELLECT,
LURA, MIND, OBEX,
PIA, PYLA
branch—ARM, BOUGH,
FORK, LIMB,
RAMUS, SPRIG,

TWIG
brave—BOLD,
COURAGEOUS,
DARE, DARING,
DAUNTLESS,
EMBOLDEN,
EXCELLENT,
MANLY, SUPERIOR,
VALIANT
brazen—BRASS,
CALLOUS, CHEEKY,
HARSH, MERRY,
PERT, SASSY
breach—CHASM, CLEFT,
CRACK, GAP, RENT,
RIFT, RUPTURE,
SLAP
bread—BUN, CUSH,
LOAF, MATZOS,
PAIN, PANADA,
PONE
break—CAESURA,
CRACK, HIATUS,
HINT, RUIN,
RUPTURE
breast bone—STERNA,
'STERNUM
plate—ARMOR, URIM
work—FORT,
PARAPET, RAMPART
breath—ANDE, GASP,
HALITUS, HUFF,
LIFE, PANT
breathe—INFUSE, PANT,
PAUSE, PUFF,
RESPIRE, UTTER,
WHEEZE
breed—BEGET,
GENERATE, ILK,
KIND, ORIGINATE,
PRODUCE,
PROGENY,
PROPAGATE RACE,
RAISE, REAR, SIRE,
STOCK
breeze—AIR, AURA,
BLOW, GALE, GUST,
STIR, ZEPHYR
breve—MARK, NOTE,

ORDER, WRIT
breviary—DIGEST,
  EPITOME, ORDO,
  PORTAS
brew—ALE, BEER,
  CONCOCT, DEVISE,
  FOMENT, HATCH,
  MIX
bribe—BUY, GREASE,
  HIRE, LEAVINGS,
  PRICE, SCRAP, SOP
bric a brac—BIBELOT,
  CURIO,
  KNICKKNACK
brick—ADOBE, DOOK,
  TILE
brick carrier—HOD
 furnace—KILN, OAST
bridal—NUPTIAL
bride—KALLAH
bridge—GANTRY, PONS,
  PONTOON, SPAN,
  TRESTLE, VIADUCT
bridge term—BID, BOOK,
  BYE, CHICANE,
  SLAM, SET, SUIT,
  TRICK, TRUMP,
  VOID
brief—CONCISE, CURT,
  LACONIC, TERSE
brigand—BANDIT,
  LADRONE, OUTLAW,
  PIRATE, YEGG
bright—APT, FIT,
  GARNISH, NITID,
  RIANT, ROSY,
  SMART, STARRY,
  SUNNY
brightness—ACUMEN,
  ECLAT, FLAME,
  NITOR, SHEEN
brilliance—ECLAT,
  GLITTER, GLORY,
  LUSTER
brilliant—DAZZLING,
  DIAMOND, GEM,
  RADIANT, SHINING
brim—EDGE, LIP, RIM
bring—BEAR, CARRY,

FETCH, INDUCE,
  PREFER (as charges)
brink—DITCH, EDGE,
  END, MARGE,
  VERGE
brisk—ALERT, ALLEGRO,
  SPRY
brittle—CRISP, FEEBLE,
  FRAIL, WEAK
broker—AGENT,
  DEALER, FACTOR,
  JOBBER
bronze—BUST, STATUE,
  TAN
brooch—CAMEO, CLASP,
  FIBULA, SHIELD
brood—BEVY, COVEY,
  FRY, INCUBATE,
  LITTER, PONDER,
  SET, SIT, TEAM
brook—BOURN, BOURNE,
  RILL, RILLET,
  RIVULET, RUNNEL
broom—BESOM, MOP,
  SWAB
brother—BILLY, CADET,
  FELLOW, FRA,
  FRERE, FRIAN,
  SIBLING
brow—BRAE, BREE,
  CREST, EDGE,
  RIDGE, TOP
brown—BEIGE, COOK,
  DUN, SEPIA, TAN,
  TAWNEY, TENNE,
  TOAST, UMBER
browse—BRUT, CROP,
  FEED, FORAGE,
  GRAZE, NIBBLE,
  PASTURE
bruise—BRASH, BRAY,
  CONTUSE, CRUSH,
  DENT, HURT, MAUL
bruit—CLAMOR, FAME,
  HEARSAY, NOISE,
  RALE, REPORT,
  RUMOR, TELL
brush—CLEAN, COMB,
  COPSE, FIGHT,

FRAY, SKIM
brusque—ABRUPT, BLUFF,
CURT, GRUFF,
RUDE, TERSE
bubble—AIR, BEAD,
BLAIN, BLISTER,
BOLL, GLOB,
SEETHE
buccaneer—CORSAIR,
FREEBOOTER,
PICAROON, PIRATE
bucket—BAIL, SCOOP,
SKEEL, TUB
buckle—BIND, BOW,
CURL, WARP
bucolic—IDYL,
PASTORAL, RURAL,
RUSTIC
bud—BEGIN(NING),
BLOSSOM, CION,
GERM, GRAFT,
SPROUT
Buddha—FO, GAUTAMA
budget—BAG, BUNCH,
PACK(ET), PLAN,
PROGRAM
buffet—BEAT, BLOW,
BLUFF, BOX,
COUNTER, CUFF,
SLAP, TOSS
bugaboo—BETENOIR,
BOGLE, BOGY,
GOBLIN, SPECTER
bugle call—RETREAT,
REVEILLE,
TANTARA, TAPS,
TATTOO
build—FORM, RAISE,
REAR
building—CASA, EDIFICE,
PILE
building addition—ELL
lot—SITE
part—APSE, EAVE,
FLOOR, ROOF
WALL, WING
bulb—BUD, CORM,
LAMP, SWELL,
TUBER

bulge—BAG, BUG, HUMP,
KNOB, LUMP,
SWELL
bulging—BOWED,
CONVEX, FULL,
GIBBOUS
bull—APIS, BOBBY, COP,
OX, PEELER,
TAURUS
bullet—BALL, LEAD,
MISSILE, PELLET,
SHELL, SHOT, SLUG,
TRACER
bullfighter—MATADOR,
PICADOR,
TOREADOR,
TORERO
bully—BEEF, BUCKO,
HECTOR, JOVIAL,
RUFFIAN, SCARE
bulrush—REED, RUSH,
SEDGE, TULE
bulwark—BAIL,
BASTION, CITADEL,
FORT, WALL
bumpkin—CASK, CLOD,
CUR, GAWK, LOUT,
OAF, RUBE, YAHOO,
YOKEL
bunch—BALE, CLUSTER,
CROWD, FAGOT,
HUMP, TUFT, WAD,
WISP
buoy—BELL, CAN, DAN,
FLOAT, MARKER,
NUN
burglar—LOOTER,
PILFERER, ROBBER,
THIEF, YEGG
burial place—AHU,
CHARNEL, CRYPT,
GOLGOTHA, GRAVE,
SEPULCHER, TOMB
burlap—FABRIC, GUNNY
burlesque—COMEDY,
FARCE, PARODY,
REVUE, SATIRE,
TRAVESTY
burn—ASH, BROOK,

CAUTERIZE, CENSE,
CHAR, CONSUME,
CREMATE,
INCINERATE, SEAR,
SERE

burning—ABLAZE, AFIRE,
ARDENT, EAGER,
FIERY, TORRID

burr—BRIAR, CIRCLE,
CORONA, HALO,
KNOT, NUT, WHIR

burrow—DIG, HOLE,
MINE, MOIL,
NUZZLE

burst—ERUPT, POP,
SALLY, VOLLEY

bushman—SAAN, SAN,
WOODSMAN

bushy—DUMOSE,
SHAGGY

business—AFFAIR,
CHORE, ERRAND,
FEAT, FIRM, LINE,
STINT, TRADE

bustle—ADO, BOTHER,
FUSS, HUBBUB,
POTHER, STIR, TOD

busy—DILIGENT,
ENGAGED, HIRED,
OCCUPIED,
WORKING

busybody—FACTOTUM,
MEDDLER,
QUIDNUNC

butter—BEURRE, FIRKIN,
FULWA, GHEE, GHI,
OLEO, SPREAD

buttery—LARDER,
PANTRY, SPENCE

button—BADGE, BOSS,
BUD, CATCH, HOOK,
KNOB

buyer—AGENT, CHAP,
EMPTOR, PATRON,
VENDOR

buzzer—ALARM, BEE,
BELL, SIGNAL

by—AGO, ALONG,
ASIDE, AT, BESIDE,
CAUSE, CLOSE,
NEAR, PAST, PER,
SIDE, VIA

-C-

caama—ASSE, FOX,
HARTEBEEST

cab—HACK, TAXI

cabal—BLOC, CLIQUE,
INTRIGUE, JUNTA,
PLOT

cabbage—COLE,
COLLARD, KALE

cabin—BERTH,
CABANA, COACH,
HOVEL, LODGE,
SHED

cabinet—ALMIRAH,
BUHL, BUREAU,
MINISTRY,
WHATNOT

cable—BOOM, COAXIAL,
CORD, GUY, LINK,
ROPE, WIRE

cacao—BEAN, BROMA,
CHOCOLATE,
COCOA

cache—BURY, HIDE,
STORE, STOW

cachet—SEAL, STAMP,
WAFER

cactus—MESCAL,
COCHAL, CACTOID

cadence—LILT, METER,
METRE, PACE,
RHYTHM, TONE

cadet—JUNIOR,
PLEDGE, SON,
YOUTH

cadge—BEG, MOOCH,
SPONGE

caduceus—INSIGNE,
SCEPTER, STAFF,

SYMBOL
Caesar's foe—BRUTUS,
   CASSIUS
cafe—BARROOM,
   BEANERY, BISTRO,
   CABARET,
   RESTAURANT
caffeine—ALKALOID,
   STIMULANT,
   THEIN(E)
cage—AVIARY, BRAKE,
   HUTCH, PEN
cahoots—COLLUSION,
   LEAGUE, PARTNERS
caisson—BOX, CHAMBER,
   CHEST, PONT,
   WAGON
caitiff—BASE, COWARD,
   MEAN, VILE,
   WICKED
cake—BAR, BUN,
   HARDEN, SCONE,
   TORTE, WAFER
calculate—AIM,
   COMPUTE, FRAME,
   RATE, RECKON,
   TALLY
calendar—ALMANAC,
   DIARY, DOCKET,
   JOURNAL, LOG,
   ORDO
calf (pert to.)—SURAL,
   VEAL
caliph—ABUBEKR, AGA,
   ALI, CALIF, HARUN,
   IMAM, MANSUR,
   OTHMAN
calk—CLOSE, COPY, STOP
call—BID, CITE,
   CONVOKE,
   DENOMINATE, DUB,
   ELICIT, ENTITLE,
   INVITE, MUSTER,
   NAME, PAGE,
   PHONE, STYLE,
   SUMMON, TERM,
   VISIT
callous—HARD, THORNY
calorie—THERM(E)

calyx—HUSK, LEAF,
   SEPAL
cam—COG, LOBE,
   TRIPPET, WIPER
camel driver—SARWAN
   hair cloth—ABA, ARA
   like animal—LLAMA
   two-humped—
   BACTRIAN
camera part—EYE,
   FINDER, LENS,
   SHUTTER, TRIPOD
camp—BIVOUAC, ETAPE
campus—FIELD,
   GROUNDS, QUAD
canal—CHANNEL,
   CONDUIT, DUCT,
   STRAIT
cancel—ANNUL, BLOT,
   DELE, EFFACE,
   ERASE, OMIT,
   POSTMARK, REMIT,
   REPEAL, REVOKE,
   VOID
candle—BOUGIE, CIERCE,
   DIP, LUMINARY,
   TAPER, TEST, WAX

candle holder—
   GIRANDOLE,
   LAMPAD, SCONCE
candy—BONBON,
   CARAMEL,
   CHOCOLATE,
   CONFECTION,
   FONDANT,
   NOUGAT, PRALINE,
   SWEETS, TAFFY
cane—FLAY, FLOG,
   MALACCA, PUNISH,
   RATTAN, ROD,
   STAFF, STEM, STICK
canine—CANIS, CUR,
   DOG, FANG, FOX,
   PUG, PUP
canon—AXIOM, CODE,
   HYMN, LAUD,
   SONG, TENET
canonical—ORTHODOX
canonical hours—

COMPLIN,
LAUD, MATIN,
NONE, PRIME, SEXT,
TERCE, VESPERS
canopy—AWNING, COPE,
DAIS, FINIAL,
SHRINE, SKY,
TESTER, THRONE
canto—AIR, FIT,
MELODY, PACE,
PASSUS
canvas—DUCK, SAIL,
SAILCLOTH, SCRIM,
TARP, TENT
canyon—ABRO, ARROYA,
CAJON, CHASM, GAP
cap—BERET, COIF,
CORK, COVER,
CROWN, EXCEL,
FEZ, TAJ, TAM, TOP
cap-shaped—PILEATE
cape—AMICE, COD,
FICHU, MANTLE,
MAY, NECK, NESS,
RAS, TALMA
caper—ANTIC, CAVORT,
DIDO, FRISK,
GAMBOL, LEAP,
ROMP
caprice—FAD, IMPULSE,
KINK, QUIRK,
VAGARY, WHIM
capstan—CYLINDER,
DRUM, HOIST,
LEVER, WINDLASS
capsule—CACHET,
PEARL, PILL, POD,
SHEATH, THECA
captain—AHAB, BLIGH,
SKIPPER
captious—CRAFTY,
CARPING, SEVERE,
TESTY
caput—FINISHED, HEAD,
TOP
caravan—CAFILA,
CARAVANSARY,
CHOULTRY,
HOSTEL, IMARET,

INN, SAFARI, SERAI,
TREK
card (as wool)—ROVE,
TEASE
card game—BASSET,
BEZIQUE,
BLACKJACK,
BOSTON, BRAG,
BRIDGE, CANASTA,
CASINO, COONCAN,
EUCHRE, EUCRE,
FANTAN, FARO,
GLEAK, HEARTS,
LOTTO, LOO, LU,
MONTE, NAPOLEON,
NEW MARKET,
NELLO, OMBRE,
PAM, PEDRO,
PINOCHLE, POKER,
SKAT, SETBACK,
STUD, STUSS, VINT,
WHIST
careen—CANT, HEEL,
KEEL, LIST, TIP,
TILT
care—CARK, HEED,
RECK, TEND
careless—COOL, EASY,
LAX, REMISS
caress—CODDLE,
COSSET, HUG,
NUZZLE
carnation—PICOTEE
carom—REBOUND,
RICOCHET, SHOT
carouse—BOOZE, REVEL
carp—CAVIL, CENSURE,
FISH, HARP, NAG
carpel—LEAF, PISTIL,
SOREMA
carpenter—ANT, FRAMER,
JOINER, WRIGHT
carpenter's tool—AWL,
ADZE, HAMMER,
LEVEL, PLANE, SAW
carriage—AIR, BEARING,
CALASH, CHARIOT,
CLARENCE,
DEARBORN, GIG,

LANDAU, MIEN,
POISE, RIG, SHAY
cartel—PACT, POOL,
TRUST
cartoonist—ARNO, BUELL,
CAPP, DISNEY,
NAST, SCHULZ
carve—CHISEL, INCISE,
SCULPT, SHAPE
carved figure—GLYPH
cascade—CATARACT,
FIREWORK,
PITFALL,
WATERFALL
case—ABLATIVE,
DATIVE, ETUI,
ETWEE,
NOMINATIVE,
SHEATH, TRIAL,
TROUSSE,
VOCATIVE
cash—DOUGH, LETTUCE,
MONEY, MOOLA,
SPECIE
cask—BARECA, BARREL,
CADE, FIRKIN, KEG,
TIERCE, TUN, TUB,
VAT
casket—BOX, CIST,
COFFER, PYX, TYE
cast—EJECT, MOLD,
MOLT, SPEW, TILT,
TOSS
caste—BANIAN,
BRAHMAN, CLASS,
DIVISION, MAGI,
VARNA
castle—ALCAZAR,
BASTILLE,
CHATEAU,
CITADEL,
ELSINORE, FORT,
FORTRESS, ROCK,
WINDSOR
castle part—DONJON,
KEEP, MOAT,
TOWER
castor—BEAN, BEAVER,
CRUET, HAT, STAR

castrate—ALTER,
EMASCULATE,
EUNUCH, GIB,
GELD, NEUTER,
PRUNE, SPAY
catafalque—BIER,
SCAFFOLD
catalogue—CANON,
CENSUS, FILE,
INDEX, ROLL,
ROSTER, ROTA
catch—BAG, CLUTCH,
COP, CORNER,
DETENT, ENGAGE,
ENTRAP, GRASP,
HASP, HITCH, HOOK,
SEIZE, SNAP, STOP,
TRAP
catchword—BYWORD,
CUE, PHRASE,
SLOGAN, TAG
category—CLASS, GENRE,
GENUS, RANK,
RUBRIC, SPECIES
cater—FEED, HUMOR,
PANDER, PROVIDE,
PURVEY, SERVE,
TREAT
catgut—CORD
cathedral—CANON,
CHARTRES,
CHURCH, DOM,
LATERAN
catkin—AMENT, RAG,
SPIKE
catspaw—CULLY, DUPE,
GULL, STOOGE,
TOOL
cattle—BEEF, BOVINES,
COWS, KINE,
NEWT, OXEN,
STOCK
cattle dealer—DROVER,
HERDER, RANCHER
caucasian—ARYAN, IMER
caucasian language—AVAR,
UDIC
native—IMER
cauldron—BOILER,

KETTLE, POT, VAT
caustic—ACRID, ACID,
  ALUM, BITING,
  ERODENT, LYE,
  TART
caution—ADMONISH,
  CARE, CAVEAT,
  HEED, PRUDENCE,
  WARINESS
cautious—BEWARE,
  CAREFUL, CANNY,
  CHARY, FABIAN,
  SHY, WARY
cavalier—BRUSQUE,
  CURT, GALLANT,
  KNIGHT, PROUD
cavalry—LANCERS
cavalryman—DRAGOON,
  HUSSAR, LANCER
cave—ANTRUM,
  CAVERN, CAVITY,
  DEN, GROTTO, LAIR,
  RECESS
cave dweller—BAT,
  SPELEAN, TAURI,
  TROGLODYTE
  researcher—
  SPELUNKER
cease—CESSATE, DESIST,
  HALT, PAUSE,
  PETER, QUIT, REST,
  STAY, STOP
cede—AWARD, FOREGO,
  GRANT, LEAVE,
  WAIVE, YIELD
celebrity—ECLAT, LION,
  NAME, STAR, VIP
celestial—ANGELIC,
  DIVINE, HOLY,
  URANIC
cell—CYTODE, EGG,
  GAMETE, GERM,
  NEURON, SPORE
cell destruction—LYSIS
  division—AMITOSIS
cement—GLUE, PASTE,

PUTTY, SOLDER
cemetery—NECROPOLIS
cenobite—ANCHORITE,

ESSENE, HERMIT,
  MONK, NUN,
  UNMARRIED
censure—ACCUSE,
  ASPERSE, BLAME,
  CONDEMN,
  REPROVE, SLATE,
  TAUNT
center—CENTRAL, CORE,
  HEART, HUB, MID,
  MIDDLE, NAVE,
  NUCLEUS, PIVOT
  (away from)—DISTAL
  (toward)—ENTAD,
  MESIAL
centerpiece—EPERGNE
central—AXIAL, BASIC,
  CHIEF, DOMINANT,
  HUB, MID, NAVE
cerate—LARD,
  OINTMENT, SALVE,
  WAX
ceratoid—HORNY
cereal—BRAN, FARINA,
  GRASS, GRITS,
  HOMINY, MAIZE,
  MILLET, OAT,
  OATMEAL, RICE,
  RYE, WHEAT
ceremony—FETE, FORM,
  POMP, RITE, RITUAL
certain—ASSURED,
  DESTINED, FIXED,
  POSITIVE,
  RELIABLE,
  SETTLED, SURE,
  TRUE
certainly
  (archaic)—CERTES,
  IWIS
certificate—DEBENTURE,
  DIPLOMA, SCRIP,
  STOCK, VOUCHER
certify—ATTEST, AVOW,
  DEPOSE, EVINCE,
  VERIFY, VOUCH
cess—SCOT, TAX
cessation—DEATH,
  FAILURE, LULL,
  PAUSE, STOP

cetacean—DOLPHIN,
GRAMPUS, INIA,
ORC, WHALE

chafe—ABRADE, FRET,
IRK, RUB, VEX

chaff—BANTER, BRAN,
HULLS, HUSK, PUG,
TRASH

chaffer—BARGAIN,
DICKER, HAGGLE,
HIGGLE, MARKET,
SIEVE

chain—CATENA,
COLLAR, FETTER,
RESTRAIN

chair—ROCKER, SEAT,
SEDAN, STOOL,
SPEAKER, PULPIT

chair part—RUNG, SPLAT

chalcedony—
AGATE, ONYX,
SARD

chalice—AMA, BOWL,
CALIX, GRAIL,
GOBLET
 (cover)—PALL
 (veil)—AER, AIR

chamber—CAISSON,
CAMERA, KIVA,
LOCHLUS, ODA

champagne—AY

champion—ACE, AONE,
BACK, ESPOUSE,
HERO, PALADIN,
PROTAGONIST,
VICTOR

chance—FATE, FORTUNE,
HAPPENSTANCE,
KISMET

chancel part—ALTAR,
BEMA, SEDILA,
SEDILE

change—ALTER, AMEND,
CONVERT, EMEND,
FLUX, MODIFY,
MUTATE,
MUTATION,
OBVERT, SHIFT,
TRANSFER, VARY
 (course)—REVERSE

 (direction)—TURN,
VEER

channel—CHUTE, DUCT,
FLUME, GAT,
MEDIA, PASSAGE,
STRAIT, VALE, WAY

chant—CANTICLE,
DRONE, INTONE,
INTROIT

chaos—ABYSS, BABEL,
CHASM, GULF,
HAVOC, MESS, VOID

chaotic—FORMLESS,
MUDDLED, SNAFU

chapel—BETHEL,
CHANTRY, CHOIR,
SERVICE, VESTRY

chaperon—DUENNA,
ESCORT

chaplet—ANADEM,
FILLET, GARLAND,
NECKLACE,
ROSARY, WREATH

character—ETHOS,
NATURE, QUALITY,
REPUTE, ROLE,
RUNE, STAMP, TONE

charge—ACCUSE,
ARRAIGN, COST,
DEBIT, FARE, FEE,
LIEN, LOAD, PRICE,
RATE, TOLL

charger—HORSE, MOUNT,
PLATE, PLATTER,
STEED, WARHORSE

chariot—ESSEDA,
ESSEDE, RATHTAJ

charioteer—DRIVER, HUR,
PILOT

charitable—BENIGN,
ELEEMOSYNARY,
HUMANE

charity—ALMS, DOLE,
LARGESS, MERCY

charlatan—EMPIRIC,
FAKE(R), QUACK

charm—AMULET,
ENAMOR,
ENCHANT, FETISH,
GRIGRI, JYNX,

MAGIC, MOJO, OBI,
PERIAPT, SCARAB,
TALISMAN
chart—DIAGRAM, PLAN,
MERCATOR,
SCHEMA, TABLE
charter—DEED, HIRE,
RENT, LEASE,
PATENT, PERMIT
chassis—BODY, FRAME
chatter—BABBLE, BLAT,
CARP, GIBBERISH,
JABBER, PATTER,
PRATE, YAP
chauvinist—JINGOIST,
PATRIOT
cheap—NOMINAL,
PALTRY, SHODDY,
TAWDRY, TINNY,
VILE
cheat—BAM, BILK,
CHISEL, CLIP, CON,
COZEN, DEFRAUD,
DUPE, FLEECE,
FOB, FRAUD, GYP,
HOCUS, MULCT,
RENEGE, SHAM,
SWINDLE
check—ARREST, BLOCK,
BRIDLE, CURB,
INHIBIT, NIP,
REPRESS, RESTRAIN,
REIN, STAY, STEM,
TAB, TEST
checkered—MOSAIC,
PLAID, PIED, VAIR
checkers—DRAUGHTS
(terms)—CROWN, KING
checkmate—BAFFLE,
DEFEAT, DRAW,
FRUSTRATE,
SCOTCH, STOP,
STYMIE
cheek—BRASS, BUCCA,
CHAP, GALL, JOWL,
NERVE, SAUCE
(pert. to)—GENAL,
MALAR, MOLAR,
BUCCAL
cheer—APPLAUD, CLAP,

ELATE, HURRAH,
LAUD, OLE, PRAISE,
ROOT
cheerful—BLITHE,
GENIAL, JOYFUL,
ROSY, SUNNY
cheese—BRIE, CHEDDAR,
DILSIT, DUNLOP,
EDAM, GOUDA,
GRUYERE,
LIMBURGER,
MYSOST,
PARMESAN,
ROQUEFORT,
STILTON, TILSITER
chemical compound—
AMIDE, AMINE
BORIDE, ESTER,
IMID,
ISOMER, KETONE,
PURINE, SUCRATE
chemist—ANALYST,
APOTHECARY,
DRUGGIST
chemist implement—
ALUDEL, BEAKER,
PESTLE, PHIAL
PITOT, UDELL
cherish—DOTE, ESTEEM,
FOSTER
cheroot—CIGAR
cherry—AMARELLE,
CHOKE, GEAN,
MOREL, MORELLO,
OXHEART
chess move—DEBUT,
GAMBIT
pieces—BISHOP,
CASTLE, HORSE,
KING, KNIGHT,
MAN, PAWN,
QUEEN, ROOK
chest—ARCA, ARK, CASE,
CIST, COFFER,
LOCKER, SAFE,
THORAX
chestnut—BROWN,
CHINQUAPIN,
HORSE, JOKE
chevron—MARK, RANK,

STRIPE
chevrotain—DEERLET,
KANCHIL, NAPU
chew—BITE, CHAMP,
GNAW,
MANDUCATE,
MASTICATE,
MUNCH, QUID
chic—DAPPER, MODISH,
NIFTY, SMART,
STYLISH
chicanery—ARTIFICE,
CAVIL, FEINT,
INTRIGUE, RUSE,
WILE
chicken—BROILER,
CAPON, COCK,
FOWL, FRYER, HEN,
POULTRY
chicle—GUM, LATEX
chief—AMEER, AMIR,
ARCH, CAPITAL,
CENTRAL, ELDER,
FIRST, HEAD,
HEADMAN, KHAN,
MAIN, PARAMOUNT,
PRIMAL, PRIME,
PRINCIPAL, STAPLE,
chilblain—KIBE
child—BABE, BABY,
BRAT,
DESCENDANT, IMP,
INFANT, LAD,
MOPPET, PROGENY,
SIB, TAD, TIKE, TOT,
TYKE, YOUTH
chill—AGUE, ALGOR,
COOL, FROST,
GELID, ICE, NIP,
RIGOR
chimney—FLUE, PIPE,
SMOKESTACK,
TEWEL, TUBE, VENT
chimney piece—MANTEL,
PAREL
china—CERAMIC,
CROCKERY, DELFT,
DISHES, LIMOGES,
PORCELAIN,
POTTERY, WARE

chink—BORE, CRACK,
CRANNY, CREVICE,
FISSURE, GAP, RIFT,
RIME
chipmunk—CHIPPY,
HACKEE
chisel—CHEAT, CUT,
DROVE, GAD,
GOUGE, PARE
chit—BABE, INFANT,
IOU, VOUCHER
chloroform—ACETONE,
ANESTHETIC,
KETONE, KILL
chocolate—CANDY,
COCOA
(powder)—PINOLA
choice—BEST, CREAM,
DAINTY, ELEGANT,
ELITE, FINE,
OPTION, PICK,
PRIME, RARE,
SELECT, SELECTION
choke—DAM, GAG,
PLUG, STIFLE
choler—ANGER, BILE,
FURY, IRE, RAGE,
SPLEEN, TEMPER,
WRATH
choose—CULL, ELECT,
OPT, PICK, PREFER,
SELECT, SELECTION,
VOTE
chop—AXE, BITE,
CARVE, CHIP, CUT,
HACK, HEW, JAW,
LOP, MINCE, SLICE
chord—HARMONY,
TRIAD
chorda filum—SEALACE
chorus—ACCORD,
ASSENT, CHOIR,
UNISON
Christ—MESSIAH
Christian—GENTILE,
GILLIE, KINDLY
Christmas—NOEL, XMAS,
YULETIDE
chronicle—ACCOUNT,
ANNAL, ARCHIVE,

DIARY, JOURNAL,
RECORD
chrysalis—PUPA, PUPAE
church—BASILICA,
BETHEL,
CATHEDRAL,
CHAPEL, DOM,
KIRK, MISSION,
MOSQUE, PAGODA,
TEMPLE
(part)—ALTAR, APSE,
CHANCEL, GALILEE,
NAVE, PEW,
SANCTUARY, SPIRE,
STEEPLE,
TRANSEPT, VESTRY
(office)—BEADLE,
BISHOP, DEACON,
ELDER, PASTOR,
PRIEST, POPE,
SACRISTAN,
SEXTON, VICAR
(land)—GLEBE
(law)—CANON
churl—BOOR, CARL,
KNAVE, LOUT, OAF,
VILLAIN
cicada—CICALA, LOCUST
cigar—CHEROOT, CLARO,
CORONA, MADURO,
PANETELA,
PERFECTO, STOGIE,
TOBY
cigarette—BIRI, CIG, FAG,
GASPER, REEFER,
SMOKE
cinder—ASH, CLINKER,
DROSS, EMBER,
GRAY, LAVA, SLAG
cinnamon bark—CASSIA
cion—BUD, SCION,
SHOOT, SPROUT,
TWIG
circle—ARC, CIRCLET,
HALO, LOOP, ORB,
RING, RINGLET
circlet—BRACELET,
HEADBAND,
NECKLACE, RING,
WREATH

circuit—AMBIT, CYCLE,
DETOUR, EYRE,
LAP, ORBIT, ROUT,
TOUR, ZONE
circuitous—CROOKED,
DEVIOUS, MAZY,
circular—BILL, CYCLOID,
DISCOID, ROUND,
ROUNDABOUT
circumference—AMBIT,
EDGE, GIRTH,
VERGE
circus—BIGTOP,
CARNIVAL, CIRCLE,
COLISEUM,
HIPPODROME
cirque—CORRIE,
EROSION, RECESS
citadel—ALAMO,
CASTLE, FORT,
FORTRESS,
STRONGHOLD,
TOWER
cite—ADDUCE, CALL,
QUOTE, SUMMON
citizen—BURGHER, CIT,
DENIZEN, DEMOS,
NATIONAL, NATIVE,
OPPIDAN,
RESIDENT, SUBJECT
citron—CEDRAT, LEMON,
LIME, ORANGE,
TANGERINE,
YELLOW
civet—CAT, GENET,
NANDINE, RASSE
civic—CIVIL, LAY,
POLITE, SECULAR,
URBANE
civil—CIVIC, HEND(E),
POLITE, SUAVE,
URBANE
civilian dress—MUFTI
claim—ALLEGE,
ARROGATE, ASSERT,
DEMAND, LIEN,
MAINTAIN,
REQUIRE, TITLE
clamp—BOLT, BRACE,
CLASP, LUG, NIP,

PIN, VISE
clan—CASTE, CLIQUE,
FAMILY, GENOS,
SET, SIB
clandestine—FOXY,
FURTIVE, PRIVY,
SECRET, SLY
clarify—CLEAR,
DEPURATE, FREE,
RENDER
clasp—BROOCH, BUCKLE,
CINCH, HASP, HUG,
PIN, TACHE
class—CASTE, DIVISION,
GENUE, GENUS,
GRADE, GROUP,
ILK, KIND, RANK,
SECT, SET, SORT
classical—ATTIC, CHASTE,
GREEK, PURE,
ROMAN
clause—PLANK, PROVISO,
RIDER,
STIPULATION
clay—ADOBE, ARGIL,
BRICK, BOLE,
KAOLIN, LATERITE,
LOAM, LOESS,
MARL, MUD,
OCHRE, TILE
clayey—BOLAR, LUTOSE,
MALMY, MARLY
clean—APINOID, BREAM,
CHASTE, KOSHER,
TRIM
clear—ABSOLVE,
ACQUIT, CLARIFY,
CRYSTAL, EVIDENT,
EXONERATE,
GRAPHIC, LUCID,
OBVIOUS, PLAIN,
PURE, RID
clearing—(AS)SART
GLADE
cleat—BATTEN, BLOCK,
BOLLARD, CHOCK,
WEDGE
cleave—ADHERE, BISECT,
CLING, COHERE,

SLIT, STICK,
SUNDER, REND, RIP
clergyman—ABBE,
CANON, CLERIC,
CURATE, DEAN,
DOMINIE,
MINISTER, PADRE,
PARSON, PASTOR,
PRIEST, PRIOR,
RABBI, RECTOR,
VICAR
cleric's house—MANSE,
PARSONAGE,
RECTORY,
VICARAGE
clever—ABLE, APT,
ASTUTE, CANNY,
CUTE, DEFT,
DEXTEROUS,
FACILE, HABILE,
HEND (E), SHREWD,
SLICK, SMART,
TALENTED
click—AGREE, CATCH,
DETENT
click beetle—ELATER,
ELATERID
cliff—BLUFF, CRAG,
HILL, SCARP
climax—ACME, APEX,
APOGEE,
CULMINATION,
SUMMIT, ZENITH
climb—ASCEND, ASCENT,
RISE, SCALE, SHIN,
SPEEL
cling—ADHERE, HUG,
RELY, STICK, TRUST
clique—CABAL, CLUB,
COTERIE, GANG,
JUNTA
clock—CLEPSYDRA,
DIAL, INDICATOR,
NEF, TIME, WATCH
close—CALK, DENSE,
ENDS, FINALE,
MUGGY, NEAR,
NIGH, OCCLUDE,
SEAL, SEAM, SHUT,

STINGY
closet—AMBRY, CUDDY,
  EURY, LOCKER,
  PANTRY, SAFE
clot—COAGULATE, DOT,
  EMBOLUS, GEL,
  GOB, JELL, LUMP,
  MASS
clothes—APPAREL,
  ATTIRE, DRESS,
  DUDS, GARB, HABIT,
  RAIMENT, REGALIA,
  TOGS, TOGGERY,
  VESTURE, WEAR
cloud—CIRRI, CIRRUS,
  CUMULI, CUMULUS,
  NIMBO, NIMBUS,
  STRATUS, SCUD,
  VAPOR
cloudy—CONFUSED,
  FILMY, FUZZY,
  GRAY, HAZY,
  NEBULAR,
  NIMBOSE, OBSCURE,
  OPAQUE, OVERCAST
clover—LOTUS,
  LUCERNE,
  MELILOT, TREFOIL
cloven—BIFURCATE,
  CLEFT, SPLIT
clown—BUFFOON, GOFF,
  HOB, JESTER, MIME,
  OAF, PUNCH,
  RUSTIC, STOOGE,
  ZANY
club—BAT, CANE,
  LODGE, MACE,
  ORDER, STAFF
  (famous)—ELKS,
  FRIARS, KIWANIS,
  LAMBS, MASONS,
  MOOSE, ROTARY
clubfoot—TALIPES
clubshaped—CALVATE
clump—BUNCH, MOTT,
  PATCH, TUFT
clumsy—AWKWARD,
  GAUCHE,
  GRACELESS, INEPT,
  OAFISH

cluster—BUNCH, CYME,
  CORYMB, FLOCK,
  GROUP, GROVE,
  NEP, PLUMP, SORUS,
  THICKET, TUFT
coachman—DRIVER,
  JEHU, PILOT, WHIP
coagulant—GELATINE,
  RENNET, STYPTIC
coagulate—CAKE, CLOD,
  CLOT, CONGEAL,
  GEL, POSSET, SET
coal—ANTHRACITE,
  BASS,
  BLACKDIAMOND,
  CANNEL, CARBON,
  CHARCOAL,
  CINDER, COKE,
  FUEL, LIGNITE,
  SMUT, SWAD
  (box)—HOD, SCUTTLE
  (refuse)—ASH, CINDER,
  CLINKER, COKE,
  COOM, CULM, DUST,
  SLAG, SMUT
  (size)—EGG, NUT, PEA,
  STOVE
coarse—BRUTISH, CRASS,
  GROSS, OBSCENE,
  PLAIN, RIBALD,
  RUDE, ROUGH,
  THICK, VULGAR
coast—BANK, BEACH,
  GLIDE, LAND, RIPA,
  SHORE, SLIDE
coastal—LITTORAL,
  ORARIAN,
  RIPARIAN
coat—COVER, FUR,
  MANTLE, OVERLAY,
  PAINT
cobble—BOTCH, DARN,
  MEND, PATCH,
  PAVE
cock—FOWL, FAUCET,
  HEAP, PILE, TAP
cockade—BADGE, KNOT,
  ROSETTE
cocker—CUDDLE, DOG,
  FONDLE, PET.

SPANIEL
cockle—BOAT, GITH,
    KILN, OAST, SHELL
cockpit—ARENA, CABIN,
    RING, RINK
coconut fiber—COIR,
    COIRE, KOIR, KYAR
    (meat)—COPRA
    (palm)—COCO, NIOG,
    SIRI
cocoon—CLEW, DELL,
    POD, SHELL
code—CIPHER, DIGEST,
    ETHICS, KEY, LAW,
    RULE, SIGNALS
codicil—RIDER, SEQUEL
coffee (kind)—BRAZIL,
    JAVA, MOCHA, RIO,
    SANTOS, SUMATRA
coffer—ARK, CAISSON,
    CASKET, CHEST,
    DAM, THORAX,
    TRUNK
coffin—BIER, CASKET,
    CHEST, CIST,
    SARCOPHAGUS
cog—CAM, CHEAT,
    COZEN, LIE, TENON,
    TOOTH, WEDGE,
    WHEEL
cognomen—EPITHET,
    SURNAME
coil—ANSA, CLEW,
    CURL, HELIX,
    QUERL, TWINE,
    TWIST, WHORL,
    WIND
coin—BRASS, CASH,
    INVENT, MAKE,
    MINT, SPECIE
cold—ALGID, CHILLY,
    FRIGID, FROSTY,
    GELID, ICY
collaborator—QUISLING
collar—CATCH, FICHU,
    RING, RUCHE,
    RUFF, TORQUE
    (bone)—CLAVICLE
collect—ACCUMULATE,
    AMASS, BAG,
    COMPACT,
    COMPILE,
    GARNER, GATHER,
    GLEAN, HOARD,
    LEVY, PRAYER,
    POOL
collection—
    ACCUMULATION,
    ANA,
    ASSEMBLAGE,
    BOODLE,
    CABOODLE, HEAP,
    LOT, OLIO, PILE,
    RAFT, SET, SORITE
colleen—DAMSEL, GIRL,
    LASS, LASSIE,
    MAIDEN, MISS
college—ACADEMY,
    INSTITUTION,
    LYCEE, SCHOOL,
    UNIVERSITY
    (grounds)—CAMPUS,
    LAWN, QUAD
    (officers)—BEADLE,
    BURSAR, DEAN,
    DON, PREXY,
    PROCTOR, REGENT,
    REGISTRAR
collide—BUMP, CLASH,
    CRASH, HIT,
    HURTLE, STRIKE
colonizer—ANT, OECIST,
    SETTLER
colorless—ALBINO,
    ACHROMIC, DRAB,
    DULL, PALE,
    PALLID, WAN
Columbus's birthplace—
    GENOA
    (port of embarkation)—
    PALOS
    (ships)—NINA, PINTA,
    SANTA MARIA
column—ANTA, DORIC,
    FUST, IONIC,
    PILASTER, PILLAR,
    SHAFT, STELE
coma—LETHARGY,

STUPOR, TORPOR
comb—BRUSH, CARD,
CREST, CURRY,
RAKE, RIDGE,
TEASE
combat—BATTLE, COPE,
DUEL, FIGHT, FRAY,
JOUST, MEET,
OPPOSE, SKIRMISH,
STRUGGLE
combination—
ALLIANCE,
CABAL, CARTEL,
CLIQUE, JUNTO,
MERGER, TRUST,
UNION
combine—ADD, MARRY,
MERGE, MIX, POOL,
SPLICE, UNITE, WED
come—ACCRUE,
APPROACH, ARRIVE,
EMERGE, ENSUE,
REACH
(ashore)—LAND
(before)—PRECEDE,
PREVENE
(forth)—EMANATE,
EMERGE, GUSH,
ISSUE, SPEW
(out)—EMERGE,
SPRING
comedian—ANTIC, BUFF,
BUFFOON, CARD,
COMIC, CLOWN,
JESTER, JOKER,
WAG, WIT
comedy—BURLESQUE,
FARCE, REVUE,
SLAPSTICK,
TRAVESTY
comely—BONNY,
DECENT, FAIR,
NICE, PRETTY
comic—DROLL,
FARCICAL, FUNNY,
RISIBLE
coming—ADVENT,
ARRIVAL, DUE,
NEXT, IMPENDING
command—BADE, BECK,

BEHEST, BID,
DICTATE, EDICT,
ENJOIN, FIAT,
MANDATE, ORDER
commander—AGHA,
CHIEF, CID,
LEADER
commandment—
DECALOGUE, LAW,
ORDER, PRECEPT,
RULE
commend—COMMIT,
EXTOL, LAUD, PAT,
PRAISE
comment—ASIDE,
CRITICIZE, GLOSS,
NOTE, POSTIL,
WORD
commentary—
EXEGESIS, GLOSS,
MEMOIR, TREATISE
comminute—CRUSH,
GRIND, MILL,
PULVERIZE
commiseration—
CONDOLENCE
EMPATHY, PITY
SYMPATHY
commission—BREVET,
BREVIT, CHARGE,
DEPUTE, ERRAND,
ORDAIN, PROXY,
TASK
commit—ALLOT, ASSIGN,
CONNECT,
CONSIGN, ENTRUST,
INTRUST, REFER,
TRUST
common—BANAL,
COARSE, FAMILIAR,
GENERAL,
HABITUAL, JOINT,
LOW, MUTUAL,
ORNERY, PLAIN,
PLEBEIAN,
POPULAR, PUBLIC,
TRITE, VULGAR
commonplace—BANAL,
DAILY, HUMDRUM,
PROSAIC, STALE,

TRITE, USUAL
commonwealth—
  COMMUNITY,
  DEMOS,
  REPUBLIC, RES
  PUBLICA, STATE
commotion—ADO,
  AGITATE, BUSTLE,
  FLARE, FRAY, FUSS,
  HUBBUB, NOISE,
  POTHER, RIOT, STIR,
  TODO, WELTER
commune—ARGUE
  DEBATE, IMPART,
  KIBBUTZ,
  MIR, SHARE,
  TOWNSHIP
communion—CREED,
  EUCHARIST, FAITH,
  HOST, MASS,
  RAPPORT, SECT
community—BURG, MIR,
  TOWN, VILLAGE
compact—BOND,
  CONDENSE, DENSE,
  ETUI, FAST, HARD,
  SOLID, TERSE,
  TIGHT, TRIG,
  TREATY
companion—ALLY,
  BUDDY, COMRADE,
  CONSORT, CRONY,
  ESCORT, MATE,
  MATEY, PAL,
  PLAYMATE, PEER,
  SPOUSE
company—BAND,
  BATTERY, BEVY,
  FIRM, PARTY,
  PHALANX,
  RETINUE, SOCIETY,
  TROUPE
comparative—EQUAL,
  RELATIVE
compare—COLLATE,
  CONTRAST, LIKEN,
  MATCH, SEMBLE,
  VIE
comparison—ANALOGY,
  ESTIMATE,

PARABLE,
  QUANTITY,
  RELATION, SIMILE
compass—AMBIT,
  ATTAIN, ENCLOSE,
  GAMUT, GYRO,
  REACH, SWEEP
compass part—AIRT(H),
  BINNACLE, GIMBAL,
  NEEDLE, RHUMB,
  VANE
compass point—ENE, ESE,
  NE, NNE, NNW, NW,
  SE, SSE, SSW, SW,
  WNW, WSW
compassion—GRACE,
  MERCY, PITY, RUE,
  SYMPATHY
compel—DRAGOON,
  DONE, DRIVE,
  FORCE, IMPEL,
  OBLIGE,
  OVERPOWER, PRESS
compendium—APERCU,
  BRIEF, DIGEST,
  EPITOME, PRECIS,
  SUMMARY, SURVEY,
  SYLLABUS
compensation—
  DAMAGES,
  FEE, HIRE,
  PAYMENT,
  RECOMPENSE,
  REDRESS, UTU
compete—CONTEND,
  COPE, EMULATE,
  MATCH, RACE,
  STRIVE, VIE
competent—ABLE, ADEPT,
  APT, CAPABLE,
  FIT, SANE, SMART
competition—CONTEST,
  MATCH, RIVALRY,
  STRIFE
complain—BEEF, CARP,
  CROAK, FRET, FUSS,
  GRIPE, GRUMBLE,
  GROAN, GRUNT,
  KICK, LAMENT,
  MOAN, WHINE,

YAMMER
complaint—GRAVAMEN,
ILLNESS, LAMENT
complaisant—AFFABLE,
CIVIL, EASY, KIND,
OBLIGING, SUAVE
complexion—BLEE,
COLOR, HUE,
TINGE, TINT
complicate—BEWILDER,
INTORT, PERPLEX,
TANGLE, WORSEN
complication—NODE,
NODUS, SNARL
compliment—EULOGY,
EXTOL, FLATTER,
LAUD, PRAISE
component—ELEMENT,
FACTOR,
INGREDIENT,
INTEGRAL,
MATERIEL, PART,
UNIT
comport—ACT, AGREE,
ACCORD, BEHAVE,
CONDUCT, CARRY,
DEMEAN, SUIT
composition—CENTO,
ESSAY, OPUS, PIECE,
THEME, VERSES
composure—BALANCE,
MIEN, POISE, QUIET,
REPOSE, SERENITY
compound—AMIDE,
AMALGAM,
FARRAGO, MIX,
MIXTURE, OLIO,
OXIDE
comprehend—CONTAIN,
EMBRACE,
FATHOM, GET,
GRASP, INCLUDE,
REALIZE, SEE,
SENSE, TRAMMEL
compunction—
PENITENCE,
PRICK, QUALM
REGRET, REMORSE,
RUE, SCRUPLE,
STING

comrade—ALLY, BUDDY,
CHUM, CRONY,
FRATER, MATE,
PAL, PEER
concave—ARCHED,
HOLLOW, VAULTED,
VOID
conceal—CACHE, CLOAK,
FEIGN, HIDE, MASK,
PALLIATE, PALM,
SECRETE, VEIL,
WRY
concealed—
CLANDESTINE,
DOGGO, LATENT,
PERDUE, VEILED
concede—
ACKNOWLEDGE,
ADMIT
AGREE, GRANT,
SURRENDER, YIELD
conceit—CAPRICE, EGO,
FLAM, IDEA, PRIDE,
VAGARY, VANITY
conceited—ARROGANT,
CLEVER, EGOTISTIC,
PRIGGISH
concerning—ABOUT,
ANENT, ASTO, FOR,
INRE, OF, ON, RE
concert hall—ACADEMY,
LYCEUM, ODEON,
ODEUM
conch—COCKLE,
MUSSEL, SHELL
conclude—CLOSE,
DEDUCE,
DETERMINE, END,
FINISH, INFER,
REST, SETTLE,
TERMINATE
conclusion—CODA, END,
EPILOGUE, FINIS
conclusive—COGENT,
FINAL, TELLING,
VALID
concoct—BREW, COOK,
DIGEST, HATCH,
MIX, REFINE
condemn—AMERCE,

BAN, BLAME,
CENSURE,
CRITICIZE, DECRY,
DENOUNCE, DOOM,
FILE, SENTENCE
condense—COMPRESS,
CUT, DECOCT,
DIGEST, LESSEN
condescend—DEIGN,
FAVOR, FEIGN,
STOOP
condition—COVIN,
ESTATE, FACET,
FETTLE, IF, PHASE,
PLIGHT, PROVISO,
STATE, STATUS,
TERM
conduce—AID, EFFECT,
LEAD, TEND
conduct—ACTION,
CONVEY, DEMEAN,
DEPORTMENT,
DIRECT, ESCORT,
LEAD, MANAGE,
PRESIDE, RUN,
TRANSACT
conductor—CAD,
CICERONE,
CONVEYOR, GUIDE,
IMPRESARIO,
LEADER, MAESTRO
conduit—ADIT,
CHANNEL, DRAIN,
DUCT, MAIN, PIPE
cone—CONOID, FUNNEL,
STROBILE
confection—BONBON,
CIMBAL, COMFIT,
DAINTY, DESSERT,
FONDANT, JAM,
MARCHPANE,
MARZIPAN,
PRALINE
confederate—ABETTOR,
ALLY, BAND,
LEAGUE, PARTNER,
REBEL
confer—BESTOW, DUB,
ENDOW, GRANT,
IMPART, PARLEY,

VEST
conference—COLLOQUY,
CONFAB, HUDDLE,
PALAVER, SYNOD,
TALK
confess—ADMIT, AVOW,
CONCEDE, OWN,
REGRET, REPENT,
REVEAL, RUE,
SHRIVE
confession—
ADMISSION,
AVOWAL, CREDO,
CREED, SHRIFT
conflict—BATTLE,
BOUT, CONTEND,
CONTEST, CLASH,
DISCORD, FRAY,
STRUGGLE, WAR
conform—ADAPT,
AGREE, COMPLY,
YIELD
confuse—ABASH, BEFOG,
BEFUDDLE,
DERANGE,
DISCONCERT,
DISTRACT,
FLUSTER, JUMBLE,
MUDDLE, NONPLUS,
PERPLEX, STUPEFY
confused—ADDLED,
ASEA, CHAGRINED,
CHAOTIC,
FLUSTERED,
FUDDLED,
MUDDLED, MUSSY,
RATTLED
confusion—ADO, BABEL,
BOTHER, CHAOS,
DIN, DISORDER,
MESS, MOIL, SNAFU,
TURMOIL, WELTER
congeal—CURDLE,
FREEZE, GEL,
HARDEN, ICE, JELL,
PECTIZE, SET
conic section—ELLIPSE,
PARABOLA
conifer—CEDAR, FIR,
LARCH, PINE,

PINALE, SPRUCE,
TORREY, YEW
connect—AFFIX, ALLY,
BIND, CHAIN,
COUPLE, LINK,
MARRY
connection—BOND, LINK,
NEXUS, RELATION
connoisseur—CRITIC,
EXPERT,
GOURMAND,
GOURMET, JUDGE,
TASTER
connubial—CONJUGAL,
DOMESTIC,
MARITAL
conquer—BEAT, BEST,
LICK, MASTER,
ROUT, SUBDUE
conqueror—HERO,
VICTOR, WINNER
consecrate—ANOINT,
BLESS, HALLOW,
SAIN, TABOO, VOW
consecrated—HALLOW,
OBLATE, SACRED,
VOTIVE
consider—DEEM, HEED,
MULL, MUSE,
REFLECT
consolation—BOOBY
PRIZE, SOLACE, SOP
consonant—ATONIC,
DENTAL, FORTIS,
HARMONIC, LENE,
LENIS, SPIRANT,
SURD
conspicuous—BLATANT,
CLEAR, OBVIOUS,
OVERT, PATENT,
POINTED, SALIENT,
SIGNAL
conspiracy—CABAL,
COUP, INTRIGUE,
JUNTO, PLAN, PLOT,
RING, SCHEME
conspire—ABET,
COLLUDE,
COMPLOT, PLOT,
SCHEME

constable—BAILIFF,
BEADLE, BULL, COP,
WARDEN
constant—CHRONIC,
CONTINUAL,
FAITHFUL, LOYAL,
REGULAR,
STAUNCH, STILL
Constantine's
birthplace—NIS, NISH
constitution—CANON,
CHARTER, CODE,
HEALTH, HUMOR,
MAKEUP
constrict—ASTRINGE,
CRAMP, NARROW
consummate—ARRANT,
ACHIEVE, IDEAL,
RIPE, SHEER
consumption—DECAY,
PHTHISIS, USE,
WASTE
contagion—MIASMA,
POX, TAINT, VIRUS
contain—CHECK,
ENCLOSE, HOLD,
SUBSUME
container—BAG, BASKET,
BOX, CAN, CARTON,
CASE, CRATE,
CRUET, CUP, GLASS,
HOLDER, PAIL, POT,
POUCH, RECEIVER,
SACK, TUB, URN,
VAT, VIAL
contaminate—CORRUPT,
DEFILE, POLLUTE,
SOIL, STAIN, SULLY,
TAINT
contemporaneous—
COEVAL, CURRENT,
LIVING
content—GIST, HAPPY,
SATED, REPLETE
contest—AGON, ARGUE,
BATTLE, BOUT,
CONFLICT, COPE,
DISPUTE, GAME,
JOUST, LITIGATE,
OPPOSE, RACE, SUE,

SETTO, TOURNEY
continent—ATLANTIS,
    CASCADIA, CHASTE,
    CONTENT,
    MAINLAND, SOBER
continue—ABIDE,
    ENDURE, LAST
continued—CHRONIC,
    PROTRACTED,
    SERIAL
contort—COIL, DEFORM,
    GNARL, TWIST,
    WARP
contour—FIGURE, LINE,
    LINEAMENT,
    OUTLINE,
    PERIPHERY,
    PROFILE, SHAPE,
    SILHOUETTE
contract—INCUR,
    INDENTURE, LEASE,
    PLEDGE, SHRIVEL,
    STRAITEN
contradict—BELIE, DENY,
    FORBID, GAINSAY,
    IMPUGN, NEGATE,
    REBUT, REFUTE
contraction—CRAMP,
    ELISION, FIST, ILL,
    SPASM, STRICTURE
contrary—AVERSE,
    CONTRA, OPPOSED,
    ORNERY, REVERSE
control—CHECK, CURB,
    DEMEAN,
    DOMINATE,
    GOVERN, MANAGE,
    POWER, REIGN,
    REGIMEN, RULE,
    STEER, SWAY,
    WIELD
controversial—ERISTIC,
    ERISTICAL,
    POLEMIC,
    POLEMICAL
controversy—DEBATE,
    DISPUTE, SPAT, SUIT
conundrum—ENIGMA,
    PUN, PUZZLE,

RIDDLE
convent—ABBEY,
    CLOISTER,
    NUNNERY, PRIORY
conventional—FORMAL,
    NOMIC, ORTHODOX,
    PROPER
conversation—CAUSERIE,
    CHAT, DIALOGUE,
    PALAVER,
    PARLANCE, TALK
convert—ANSAR, ALTER,
    CHANGE, DECODE,
    PROSELYTE,
    TRANSMUTE
convex—ARCHED,
    BULGING, GIBBOUS
convey—BEAR, BRING,
    CARRY, CEDE,
    DEED, GRANT,
    SELL, TOTE,
    TRANSFER,
    TRANSPORT
conveyance—CART, DEED,
    DEMISE, DRAY, GIG,
    WAFTAGE
convict—CONDEMN,
    FELON, LIFER,
    PRISONER, TERMER
convulsion—FIT, SHRUG,
    SPASM, SPASTIC,
    THROE
cook—CHEF, FRY,
    GRILL, ROAST,
    SHIRR, STEAM,
    STEW
cooking (art of)—CUISINE,
    MAGIRICS
cool—CALM, CHILL,
    COLLECTED,
    COMPOSED, GELID,
    ICE, NERVY,
    NONCHALANT,
    SOBER
coop—CAGE, COTE,
    HUTCH, JAIL, MEW,
    PEN, STY
cop—BOBBY, BULL,
    GENDARME,

PEELER,
POLICEMAN
copal—ANIME, RESIN
copious—AMPLE, LUSH,
PLENTY, PROFUSE,
REPLETE
copper—BOBBY,
CAULDRON, CENT,
CUPRUM, PENNY,
POLICEMAN
(alloy)—BRASS,
OROIDE, RHEOTAN
copse—ATOLL,
MEDREPORA,
PINK, RED, REEL
cord—AEA, AGAL, LINE,
STRING. TORSADE,
TENDON, TWINE,
WELT
core—AME, CENTER,
GIST, HEART,
MATRIX, NOWEL,
NUT, PITH
cork—BOBBER,
PLUG, SHIVE,
STOPPER, STOPPLE
corn—CALLUS, CLAVUS,
MAIZE, SALT
(meal)—HOMINY,
MASA, PONE
corner—ANGLE, CANT,
CLEW, COIGN,
HERNE, INGLE,
NICHE, NOOK, TREE
cornice—ASTRAGAL,
DRIP
corolla—BELL, GALEA,
PERIANTH, PETAL(S)
corollary—ADJUNCT,
PORISM
corona—AUREOLE,
SCYPHUS
coronet—ANADEM,
CIRCLET, CORONAL,
CROWN, DIADEM,
FILLET, TIARA
WREATH
corporeal—BODILY,
HYLIC, SOMATIC
corpse—CADAVER,

CARCASS, MUMMY,
STIFF
corral—ATAJO, PEN,
POUND, STY
correct—ADJUST,
AMEND, CHASTEN,
EDIT, OK, REDRESS
corrode—BURN, CANKER,
EAT, ERODE, EROSE,
GNAW, RUST
corrosive—ACID, BITING,
CAUSTIC, MORDANT
corsair—FREEBOOTER,
PICAROON,
PIRATE, PRIVATEER
corset—BUSK, CAMISOLE,
STAYS
cortex—BARK, PEEL,
PERIDIUM, RIND
cosmetic—CERUSE,
CREAM, HENNA,
LOTION, MASCARA,
PAINT, ROUGE
cosmic cycle—EON,
OLGOS
cosmos—EARTH, GLOBE,
HARMONY, ORDER,
REALM, WORLD
cosset—FONDLE, LAMB,
PAMPER, PET
costa—BORDER, RIB,
RIDGE, VEIN
costume—ATTIRE, DRESS,
GETUP, RIG, TOG
coterie—CAMARILLA,
CIRCLE, CLIQUE,
JUNTO, SET
cottage—BARI, CABIN,
CHALET, COSH, HUT
couch—BED,
DAVENPORT,
DIVAN, LAIR,
SETTEE, SOFA
cougar—CATAMOUNT,
PANTHER, PUMA
cough—BARK, HACK,
TUSSIS
council—CABAL,
CABINET,
CAMERAL, DIET,

JUNTA, SENATE,
SYNOD, WITAN
counsel—ADVICE,
LAWYER, LORE,
REDE
count—CENSUS, EARL,
GRAF, RECKON,
SCORE, TALLY,
TELL, TOTE
countenance—ABET, AID,
BROW, DEMEANOR,
FACE, VISAGE
counterfeit—BASE,
BOGUS, FAKE,
FALSE, FORGE,
FORGERY, PHONY,
PASTICHE, SHAM,
SIMULATE
countermand—ANNUL,
CANCEL, RESCIND,
REVOKE
counterpart—COPY,
DOUBLE, IMAGE,
PARALLEL
countersink—BEVEL,
CHAMFER, REAM
country—LAND, NATION,
PAYS, REGION,
SOIL, VALE,
WEALD
coup—PUTSCH, SCOOP,
STRATAGEM,
STROKE, UPSET
course—CAREER, CIRRU,
DIRECTION,
ENTREE, HEAT, LAP,
LEG, PATH, ROAD,
ROTE, ROUTE, RUN,
TRAIL, WAY
court—ALLURE, AREA,
ATTRACT, BAR,
BEADLE, CLERK,
CRIER, CROWD,
EYRE, INVITE,
PALACE, PARVIS,
PATIO, SOLICIT,
SPARK, WOO
courtly—AULIC,
ELEGANT, HEND,

POLITE
couturier—CARDIN,
CASSINI, CHANEL,
DESIGNER, DIOR,
PUCCI
cover—CAP, COAT,
ENVELOP, HIDE,
LAP, LID, PRETEXT,
SCREEN, SHEATHE,
SHELTER, THATCH,
TOP, TREE
covered—AWASH,
CAPPED, HID,
TREED
covering—ARMOR,
CRUST, HUSK, LID,
TEGUMEN, TILE
covet—ACHE, CRAVE,
ENVY, PINE
covey—BEVY, BROOD,
FLOCK
cow—BOSSY, BOVINE,
BULLY, BROCK,
BROWBEAT, DAUNT,
DEPRESS,
INTIMIDATE, KINE,
LOP, OVERAWE,
POLL, VACH
coward—CHICKEN,
CRAVEN,
POLTROON
cowboy—GAUCHO,
HERDER, LLANERO,
PUNCHER,
VAQUERO
coxcomb—BUCK, DUDE,
FOB, NOB, SWELL
coy—ARCH, CHARY, SHY
coypu—NUTRIA,
RODENT
cozy—CHATTY,
COVERING, HOMEY,
QUILT, SNUG
crab—ARACHNID,
FIDDLER, MAIAN,
MOLLUSK, UCA
crack—CHAP, FLAW,
GAG, JEST, JIBE,
RIFT

cradle—CADRE, CRECHE, CUNABULA, SLEE, SOLEN

craft—ART, CUNNING, GUILE, METIER, SKILL, TALENT, TRADE, VESSEL

craftsman—ARTISAN, NAVVY, WRIGHT

crafty—ASTUTE, SLY, WILY, WISE

crag—ARETE, BRACK, CLIFF, SCAR, STEEP, TOR

cramp—CRICK, KINK, PAIN

crane—DAVIT, DERRICK, GIB, GRUS, HERON, JIB, JINNY, WADER

cranium—CEREBRUM, HEAD, PAN, SKULL

crater—CALDERA, CONE

crave—ASK, BEG, HANKER, LONG, YEARN

craw—CROP, MAW, STOMACH

crawl—CREEP, FAWN, INCH, SLITHER

crayon—CHALK, GRAPHITE, PENCIL

crazy—AMOK, BATTY, DAFFY, DAFT, DEMENTED, DOTTY, LOCO, LOONY, INSANE, MAD, MANIC, REE, UNSOUND, WACKY

cream—CREME, ELITE, EMULSION, FROTH

creator—AUTHOR, DESIGNER, GOD, MAKER

creature—BEAST, DEPENDENT, MINION, WRETCH

credit—BELIEF, FAITH, HONOR, IMPUTE, TICK, TRUST

creed—APOSTLES, CREDO, CULT, FAITH, ISM, NICENE, SECT, TENET

creek—ARROYO, BAYOU, ESTERO, KILL, RIA, RIO, RIVULET, STREAM

creep—CRAWL, FAWN, GROVEL, INCH, SKULK, SLINK, STEAL

creeper—IVY, SNAKE, VINE, WORM

creeping—REPENT, REPTANT, SERVILE

cremate—BURN, CALCINE, INCREMATE

crescent—LUNAR (shaped)—BICORN, CUSP, LUNAR, LUNATE, LUNE, MOONY

crest—ARETE, COMB, COP, COPPLE, CROWN, PEAK, PLUME, RIDGE, SUMMIT, TOP, TUFT

crested—CORONATED, CRISTATE, PILEATE

crevice—CRANNY, FISSURE. SEAM, VEIN

crib—BIN, BUNKER, CRATCH, CRECHE, MANGER, PONY, RACK, STEAL

cribbage term—NOB, PEG

cricket—GRIG, GAME (term)—BYE, ONS, OVER, OFF, YORKER

crime—ARSON, EVIL, FELONY, SIN, VICE

criminal—CONVICT, CROOK, CULPRIT, FELON, INMATE, NOCENT

crimsom—CARMINE,
DYE, LAC, RED

cringe—FAWN, KNEEL,
QUAIL, SUBMIT,
TRUCKLE

cripple—HALT, IMPAIR,
INJURE, LAME,
LAMITER

crisp—BRITTLE,
FRANGIBLE,
FRIABLE, RUMPLED

criterion—CANON,
JUDGING, MODEL,
NORM, RULE,
STANDARD, TEST,
TYPE

critic—BOOER, CARPER,
CAVILER, CENSOR,
LITERATOR,
NOMUS, ZOILUS

critical—ACUTE,
CAPTIOUS,
CAVILING, EDGY

criticize—CARP, FLAY,
NAG, PAN, RAP,
REBUKE, ROAST

crochet—HOOK, KNIT,
LOOP, TRICOT,
WEAVE

crone—BELDAM, HAG,
WITCH

crook—BEND. CHEAT,
CROSIER, CURVE,
KNEE, PEDUM,
TURN

crooked—ASKEW, AWRY,
BENT, RENT

crop—CRAW, GEBBIE,
GIZZARD, HARVEST,
MAW, PRODUCE,
REAP, SPROUT

cross—ANGRY, ANKH,
CELTIC, CORSE,
CROSSBREED,
CRUX, GO, HYBRID,
INTERSECT,
MALTESE,
OBSTRUCT,
PEEVISH, ROOD,

SURLY, SWASTIKA,
TRACE

crossbeam—GIRDER,
TRAVE

crosspiece—BUCK, RUNG,
SPAR, YOKE

crossthreads—WEFT,
WOOF

crow—AGA, BRAG, CAW,
DAW, RAVEN,
ROCK, VAUNT

crowbar—JIMMY, LEVER,
PRY

crowd—CRAM, DROVE,
HERD, POSSE,
SERRY

crown—CAP, CORONA,
CORONAL,
CORONET, DIADEM,
PATE, TIARA

crucial—FINAL, SEVERE
(point)—CRISIS, CRUX,
PIVOT

crucible—CRUSET,
RETORT

crucifix—CROSS, PAX,
ROOD

crude—BALD, CRASS,
COARSE, RAW,
ROUGH, RUDE

cruel—BRUTAL, FELL,
FIERCE, MEAN,
MERCILESS,
OGRISH, PITILESS,
RAW, SAVAGE,
TYRANNIC

cruet—AMA, AMPULLA,
CASTOR, CRUSE,
VIAL

crumbly—BRASHY,
FRIABLE

crusader—PILGRIM,
TEMPLAR
(enemy)—SALADIN,
SARACEN, TURK

crush—MASH, QUASH,
QUELL, SUBDUE

crust—CAKE, HULL,
RIND, SHELL

cry—BOOHOO, CAW,
HUE, MEWL, MOAN,
PULE, SCREAM,
SHOUT, SNIVEL,
SOB, WEEP

crystal—CLEAR,
DIAMOND, FROST,
LUCID

cube—DICE, DIE

cubicle—ALCOVE,
BOOTH, CARREL,
CELL, NICHE, ROOM

cucumber—CONGER,
GHERKIN, PEPO

cud—CHEW, QUID,
RUMEN

cudgel—BAT, CANE,
STAVE

cull—DUPE, GLEAN, OPT,
PLUCK, SIFT,
WINNOW

culmination—ACME,
APEX, APOGEE,
CLIMAX, NOON,
VERTEX, ZENITH

cult—CLAN, FAD, ISM,
MANIA, SECT

cultivate—GROW,
HARROW, HOE,
NURSE, PLOUGH

culture—AGAR, ART,
POLISH,
REFINEMENT

cunning—ARCH, CRAFTY,
DAEDAL, FOXY,
SLY, STEALTHY

cup—AMA, CHALICE,
CRUSE, DOP,
GOBLET, GRAIL,
NOGGIN, TASS

cupbearer—HEBE

cupboard—AMERY,
BUFFET, LARDER

cupid—AMOR, DAN,
EROS, LOVE

cupola—DOME,
FURNACE,
LANTERN, TURRET,
VAULT

curare—OORALI, POISON

curate—ABBE,
CLERGYMAN,
DOMINIE,
MINISTER, PRIEST

curd—CASEINE,
CONGEAL, CURDLE

cure—CORN, HEAL,
PRESERVE, REMEDY

curio—BIBELOT, RELIC,
VIRTU

curl—BEND, COIL, KINK,
RINGLET, TRESS

currants—RIBES

current—EDDY, FLOW,
FLUX, RAPID, RIFE,
TIDE

curse—ANATHEMA,
BAN, BANE, HEX,
MALIGN, OATH,
REVILE, SWEAR

curt—BLUFF, BRIEF,
BRUSQUE, CONCISE,
CRISP, SHORT

curtain—DRAPE, SCREEN,
SHROUD, VEIL

curtsy—BOB, BOW,
CONGE, DIP,
SALAAM

curve—ARC, ARCH,
BEND, BOW, CROOK,
ELLIPSE, ESS, LOOP,
OGEE, PARABOLA,
TURN, TWIST, WIND

curved—ARCHED,
ARCIFORM,
ARCUATE, BENT,
BOWED, CONCAVE,
CONVEX, CROOKED,
TURNED, TWISTED,
WOUND

cushion—BOLSTER,
BUFFER, HASSOCK,
MAT, PAD

custody—CHARGE,
DURANCE, TRUST

custom—HABIT,
MANNER, MODE,
MORE, MORES, RITE,
USAGE

customs—DUTY, IMPOST,
  LEVY, TARIFF, TAX,
  TOLL
cut—BOB, CARVE,
  CLEAVE, CLIP, DICE,
  FELL, GASHED,
  HEWED, INCISE,
  INCISION, LANCE,
  LESION, LOP, MOW,
  NIP, SEVER, SHEAR,
  SLICE, SNIP
  (in half)—BISECT,
  HALVE, SECANT
  (off)—CROP, ELIDE,
  ROACH, SHAVE,
  SNIP
cutlass—DUSACK,
  TESACK, SWORD
cutting—ACUTE.

CAUSTIC, INCISIVE,
  MORDANT, SECANT,
  SCION
cycle—AGE, BIKE,
  CIRCUIT, EON, ERA,
  ROUND, WHEEL
cyclone—TORNADO,
  TWISTER, TYPHOON
cylinder—GABION,
  PLATEN, ROLL,
  ROLLER, SPOOL,
  TUBE
cylindrical—CENTRIC,
  ROUND, TERETE
cymbal—TAL, ZEL
cynic—ASCETIC,
  DOGLIKE, EGOTIST,
  TIMON

-D-

dabbler—DILETTANTE,
  MESSER, SCIOLIST,
  TRIFLER
dado—BASE, DIS,
  SOLIDUM,
  WAINSCOT
dagger—BAYONET,
  BODKIN, DIRK,
  DRIS, PANADE,
  PONIARD, SKEAN,
  SNEE, STILETTO
daily—ADAY, DIURNAL,
  QUOTIDIAN
dairy—CREAMERY,
  LACTARIUM
dais—ESTRADE,
  PLATFORM,
  PODIUM, ROSTRUM,
  TABLE, TRIBUNE
daisy—GERBERA,
  GOWAN, MORGAN,
  OXEYE
dale—DELL, DINGLE,
  GLEN, VALE
dam—BLOCK, CHECK,
  DIKE, GARTH, MAR,
  PARENT

damp—DANK, HUMID,
  MOIST, WET
dance—BALL, BALLET,
  DANDLE, FRISK,
  GAVOT, HOP,
  PARTY, POLONAISE,
  PROM, TOE
dancer—ALMA, ALMEH,
  BALLERINA,
  CHORINE, DEGAS
dandruff—DANDRIFF,
  SCURF
dandy—BEAN, BEAU,
  BUCK, DUDE, FINE,
  FOP, JAKE, SWELL,
  TOFF
danger—HARM, HAZARD,
  PERIL, RISK
dangerous—CRITICAL,
  DIRE, FERAL,
  INSECURE,
  OMINOUS,
  PARLOUS,
  PERILOUS, RISKY
dank—DAMP, HUMID,
  MOIST, WET
dapper—CHIC, NATTY,

NEAT, TRIM
dapple—FLECK,
  FRECKLE, SPOT
dare—BRAVE, DEFY,
  OSSE, RISK,
  VENTURE
dark—BLACK, DIM,
  DISMAL, DUSKY,
  EBON, GLOOMY,
  MELANIC, JOYLESS,
  OCCULT, SWARTHY,
  UNLIGHTED
darling—CHERI, DEAR,
  HONEY, JO,
  MOPPET, PET
dart—ARROW, BARB,
  BOLT, BOUND,
  ELANCE, FLIT,
  JACULATE,
  JAVELIN, LICK,
  MISSILE, SCOOT,
  SHOOT, SPEAR
dash—ENERGY, ELAN,
  HURL, HYPHEN,
  SOUPCON, RACE
data—FACTS,
  INFORMATION,
  MATERIAL
date—COURT, EPOCH,
  ERA, OUTMODE
daub—BLOB, COAT,
  COVER, GAUM,
  MUD, PAINT,
  PLASTER, SMEAR,
  SOIL, SULLY, TEER
daunt—AWE, COW,
  DAW, FAZE
davit—CRANE, SPAR
dawdle—DALLY. IDLE,
  LAG, LINGER, POKE,
  POTTER, TRIFLE
dawn—AURORA,
  DAYBREAK, DEW,
  EOS, EXPAND,
  SUNUP, UPRISE
day—DATE, DIES, TIME,
  YOM
daze—ASEA, BEMUSE,
  BLOW, DAZZLE,
  FEAR, GRIEF, FOG,

MAZE, STUN,
  TRANCE
dead—BARREN, CEASE,
  DECEASED,
  DEFUNCT,
  EXPIRED, EXTINCT,
  FEY, FLAT, GONE,
  MORT, NAPOO, OBIT
deaden—BLUNT, DAMP,
  MUTE, OPIATE,
  STUN
deadlock—DRAW,
  IMPASSE,
  STALEMATE. TIE
deadly—FATAL, LETHAL,
  MORTAL
  (sins)—ANGER,
  COVETOUSNESS,
  ENVY, GLUTTONY,
  LUST, PRIDE, SLOTH
deafness—ADDER,
  SMUSIA, SURDITY
deal—ALLOT,
  APPORTION,
  BARGAIN, BESTOW,
  DISTRIBUTE, SALE,
  TRADE
dealer—AGENT, BROKER,
  DRAPER, JOBBER,
  MONGER, TRADER,
  VINTNER
dean—ELDER, SENIOR
dearth—DEARNESS,
  DROUGHT, FAMINE,
  LACK, PAUCITY,
  WANT
death—CESSATION,
  DECEASE, DEMISE,
  EVANISHMENT,
  EXTINCTION, OBIT,
  MORT, PESTILENCE,
  PRIVATION
debar—ESTOP, EXCLUDE,
  HINDER,
  PRECLUDE,
  SECLUDE, TABU
debase—ABASE, ALLOY,
  CORRUPT, DEFILE,
  DEGRADE,
  DEMEAN, LOWER,

REDUCE, SINK,
VITIATE
debatable—MOOT
debate—AGON, ARGUE,
CANVASS, DISCUSS,
MOOT, PALAVER,
PLEAD, REASON,
TALK
debauch—BINGE, BOUT,
CORRUPT, DEBASE,
DISAFFECT, ORGIE,
SEDUCE
debauchee—RAKE, ROUE,
SATYR
debility—ATONE,
FRAILTY, LANGUOR
debris—DETRITUS,
RUBBISH, SCREE,
TRASH
debt—ARREARS, DUTY,
FAULT, IOU,
LIABILITY
decay—DECOMPOSE,
DISINTEGRATE,
PUTREFY, ROT,
SPOIL
decanter—CARAFE, EWER
deceased—DEAD,
DEFUNCT,
DEPARTED, GONE
deceit—COZEN, CRAFT,
FRAUD, RUSE,
SHAM, WILE
deceive—BILK, BLIND,
BLUFF, COZEN,
HOODWINK
deceiver—FAKER,
IMPOSTER,
SHARPER, TREPAN
decent—COMELY,
DECOROUS,
HONEST, MODEST,
PROPER, SEEMLY
deception—FAKE, FRAUD,
GAFF, HOAX, RUSE,
SHAM, WILE
deceptive—HOLLOW,
ILLUSIVE, SIRENIC,
VAGUE
decide—CERN,

DETERMINE, OPT,
RESOLVE, SETTLE
decimal—REPETEND,
TEN
deck—ADORN, ARRAY,
DIZEN, ENRICH,
GILD, ORLOP, POOP,
TIFF
declaim—BLAZON,
BLEEZE,
HARANGUE,
HERALD, MOUTH,
ORATE, PERORATE,
SPEAK, SPOUT,
RANT
declare—AFFIRM,
ALLEGE, ASSERT,
AVER, AVOW,
MELD, PUBLISH,
PROCLAIM,
PRONOUNCE, SAY,
STATE
decline—ABATE,
DETERIORATE,
DIE, DIP, DROOP,
EBB, FALL, FAIL,
REFUSE, REJECT,
SLUMP, WANE
decorate—ADORN, DECK,
EMBELLISH,
FESTOON, MINIATE,
ORNATE, PAPER,
TITIVATE
decoration—MEDAL,
RIBBON
decorous—DECENT,
MODEST, PROPER,
SEEMLY, STAID
decoy—ALLURE,
CALLER, ENTICE,
ENTRAP, LURE,
SHILL,
STOOLPIGEON
TOLE
decree—ACT,
ADJUDGE, ARRET,
EDICT, ENACT,
FIAT, IRADE, LAW,
ORDAIN, TENET,
UKASE

deduce—DEEM, ELICIT,
  INFER
deduct—BATE, CURTAIL,
  DOCK, REBATE
deed—ACT, ACTION,
  ESCROW, EVENT,
  FEAT, GEST,
  RECORD, REMISE
deep—ABYSMAL, BASS,
  DARK, GRAVE,
  HIDDEN, OBSCURE,
  PROFOUND,
  SOLEMN, TRICKY
deer—CERVINE,
  DAMINE, DOE, ELK
defame—CALUMNIATE,
  LIBEL, MALIGN,
  SLANDER
default—DEFICIT, FAIL,
  LACK, LOSS,
  NEGLECT
defeat—BEAT, BEST,
  CONQUER, FOIL,
  MATE, ROUT, SET
defect—FLAW, BLEMISH,
  BUG
defendant—APPELLEE,
  REUS
defense—ALIBI,
  BULWARK, PLEA,
  PROTECTION,
  SEPIMENT
deference—FEALTY,
  HOMAGE, RESPECT
deficiency—LACK,
  SCARCITY,
  SHORTAGE,
  ULLAGE, WANT
defile—DEBASE, PASS,
  POLLUTE, SOIL,
  SULLY, SMUT,
  TAINT
deflect—DIVERT, PARRY,
  SWERVE
deform—DEFACE, MAIM,
  MAR, WARP
defraud—BILK, CHEAT,
  COZEN, DECEIT,
  FLEECE, GULL, ROB,
  SWINDLE, TRICK

deft—ADROIT, APT,
  CLEVER,
  DEXTEROUS,
  PROFICIENT
defy—BEARD, BRAVE,
  DARE, FLOUT
degree—CLASS, DIVISION,
  EXTENT, GRADE,
  HONOR, RANK,
  RATE, STAGE, STEP
  (academic)—B.A., B.S.,
  D.D., PH.D., LITT.D.,
  LL.B, LL.D, M.A.,
  M.D., M.S.
dejected—AMORT,
  DEPRESSED,
  DROOPY, GLUM,
  LOW, SAD
delay—BELATE,
  DALLY, DEMUR,
  DETAIN, HINDER,
  LAG, LINGER,
  LOITER, STALL
delegate—AUTHORIZE,
  DEPUTIZE, DEPUTY,
  LEGATE,
  REPRESENTATIVE
delete—DELE, EFFACE,
  ERASE, EXPUNGE,
  REMOVE
deletion—APOCOPE,
  EXCISION, DELE
delicacy—CATE, DAINTY,
  FINESSE, KNACK,
  TACT, TIDBIT
delicate—CHOICE,
  DAINTY, FINE,
  FRAGILE, FRAIL,
  MINIKIN
delight—BLISS,
  DELECTATE, ELATE,
  ENTRANCE, GLEE,
  JOY, MIRTH,
  PLEASE, REGALE,
  REVEL
delineate—
  DESCRIBE,
  DRAW, LIMN,
  OUTLINE, PICTURE
delirious—FRANTIC,

MAD, MANIC,
RAVING
deliver—REDEEM,
RELEASE, RENDER,
RESCUE, RID, SENT
dell—DALE, DENE,
DINGLE, GLEN,
RAVINE, SLADE,
VALE
deluge—FLOOD, SWAMP,
INUNDATE
delusion—MIRAGE,
MOCKERY,
PHANTASM, RUSE
delve—DIG, DIP, MINE,
PLUMB, PROBE
demand—ASK, CLAIM,
CRY, DUN, ELICIT,
EXACT, INSIST,
NEED, REQUIRE
demented—CRAZY,
INSANE, LOONY,
LUNY, MAD,
UNSOUND
demolish—LEVEL, RAZE,
RUIN, WRECK
demon—ATUA, CLOOT,
CLOOTIE, DEUCE,
DEVIL, FIEND, IMP,
OGRE, RAHU,
SUCCUBUS, SATAN
demure—COY, MIM,
MODEST, PRIM, SHY,
STAID
den—CAVE, CAVEA,
CAVERN, DIVE,
HAUNT, LAIR, NEST
SANCTUM
denomination—CLASS,
CULT, SECT, TITLE
denote—INDICATE,
MARK, MEAN,
SIGNIFY, SHOW
dense—CLOSE, CRASS,
OBTUSE, POPULOUS,
THICK
dent—DINGE, DINT,
HOLLOW, INDENT,
NOTCH, TOOTH

dental—ORAL,
ORTHODONTICS
denture—BRIDGE, PLATE,
TEETH
deny—ABJURE,
ABNEGATE, DEBAR,
DISAVOW, DISOWN,
GAINSAY, NEGATE,
REFUSE
depart—DEATH, DIE,
EGRESS, GO, LEAVE,
MOSEY, SCRAM,
VAMOOSE
departure—EXIT,
EXODUS, HEGIRA
dependent—CLIENT,
HANGERON,
MINION, SPONGER,
SUBJECT
depict—DELINEATE,
LIMN, SKETCH
depilate—PLUCK, SHAVE,
STRIP
depilatory—RUSMA
deplore—BEWAIL,
LAMENT, REGRET,
RUE
deport—BANISH, EXILE,
EXPEL
deportment—CONDUCT
depose—AVER, OUST,
OVERTHROW,
SWEAR, UNSEAT
deposit—ALLUVIA, BED,
CACHE, DELTA,
DREGS, LAY,
LEAVE, LOESS,
MARL, PLACE,
OOZE, PUT,
SEDIMENT, SET,
SILT
depository—CACHE,
OSSUARY, SAFE,
VAULT
depot—GARE, STATION,
STOP
depression—BLUES, COL,
DENT, DINT, DIP,
ENNUI, FOSSA, PIT,

TROUGH, VAPORS
deprive—BEREAVE,
DEBAR, DESTROY,
DIVEST, HINDER,
MULCT, TAKE
deprived—AMERCED,
REFT, SHORN
derelict—ABANDONED,
CASTAWAY. TRAMP,
WAIF, WRECK
deride—BELITTLE,
FLEER, GIBE, JEER,
JIBE, MOCK,
RIDICULE. SCOFF,
SCORN, SNEER,
TAUNT
derive—CONCLUDE,
DEDUCE, DESUME,
DRAW, EDUCE,
EVOLVE. GET,
INFER. OBTAIN,
TRACE
derma—CORIUM
dermal filament—HAIR
dervish—FAKIR, HERMIT,
MONK
descendants—BREED,
LITTER, POSTERITY,
PROGENY, SCION,
OFFSPRING. SONS
describe—DEFINE,
DELINEATE,
DEPENCIL, DEPICT,
NAME, POINT,
RELATE, STATE
descry—ESPY, KEN,
DETECT, SEE. SIGHT
desert—ABANDON.
ABSCOND, DUE,
EMPTY,
FORSAKE, MERIT,
RENEGE, RAT,
WASTELAND
deserter—ABANDONER,
ABSCONDER, RAT,
RENEGADE,
TURNCOAT
design—AIM, FORM,
INTENTION,
MODEL, MOTIF,

PATTERN, PLAN,
PURPOSE
desire—ASPIRE, CARE,
COVET, CRAVE
EYE, HEART, HOPE,
LONGING, LUST,
YEN
desk—AMBO. LECTERN,
PEW, PULPIT
desolate—ALONE, BLEAK,
DREARY, LORN,
RUIN, SACK, WASTE
despoil—DIVEST,
FLEECE, INJURE,
PLUNDER, REAVE,
RIP, ROB. SPOIL
despot—AUTOCRAT,
SATRAP, TSAR,
TYRANT
dessert—
BLANCMANGE,
CAKE, COURSE,
FRUIT, MOUSSE. PIE,
PUDDING, SNACK
destiny—DOOM. EURE,
FATE, KARMA, LOT
destroy—DEMOLISH,
RAZE, SACK,
WRECK
destroyed—KAPUT
detach—DISJOIN, SEVER,
UNFASTEN
detain—ARREST, CHECK,
INTERN, STAY, STOP
detective—BEAGLE,
SLEUTH, SPOTTER,
SPY, TAILER, TEC
detent—CATCH, CLICK,
DOG, RATCHET
devil—AZAZEL, BELIAL,
BEELZEBUB,
CLOOT, CLOOTIE,
DEUCE, DICKENS,
DULE, DEMON,
FIEND, IMP,
LUCIFER, SATAN
devotee—BUFF, FAN,
ZEALOT
devotion—ARDOR,
FIDELITY,

LOYALTY, NOVENA,
VOTARY
dewlap—FOLD, PALEA
diadem—CROWN, TIARA
diagonal—BIAS
diagram—CHART, EPURE,
GRAPH, MAP, PLAN
dialect—ARGOT, CANT,
IDIOM. JARGON,
LINGO, PATOIS,
SLANG, SPEECH
TONGUE
diameter—BORE,
BREADTH, CALIBER,
CIRCLE, MODULE,
PI, WIDTH
diamond—ADAMANT,
GEM, STONE
diary—JOURNAL, LOG,
RECORD
diaskeuast—CRITIC,
EDITOR
diatribe—CRITICISM,
HARANGUE,
SCREED, TIRADE
dice—BONES, CHOP,
CRAP. CUBE, DIE,
MINCE
dictionary—CALEPIN,
GRADUS, LEXICON,
ONOMASTICON
didactic—MENTORIAL,
MORALISTIC,
PREACHY,
TEACHING
dido—ANTIC, CAPER,
PRANK, TRICK
die—DADO, DICE, DOD,
EXPIRE, MOLD,
PERISH, PRINT,
SICCA, STAMP
diet—CONGRESS, FARE,
FAST, RATION,
REGIMEN
difference—CLASH,
DISPUTE, ODDS,
NUANCE
different—DIVERS,
OTHER. SUNDRY,

UNLIKE
difficult—HARD,
KNOTTY, RUB
SNAGGY
difficulty—CAVIL,
DILEMMA, FIX,
HARDSHIP, KNOT,
PICKLE. RIGOR,
RUB. SCRAPE, SNAG,
STRAIT
dig—BURROW, DELVE,
EXCAVATE, JAB,
MINE, PION, SPADE,
UNEARTH
digest—ABSORB. APERCU,
CODIFY, EPITOME,
PANDECT, PRECIS
digestion—EUPEPSIA,
PEPSIS
digit—CIPHER, FIGURE,
FINGER, INTEGER,
NUMBER. TOE, UNIT
dignified—AUGUST,
DECOROUS,
ELEVATED, SEDATE,
STATELY,
TOGATED
dike—CAUSEWAY,
DITCH, GAP. GULF,
JETTY, LEVEE,
MOUND
dilate—DISTEND,
EXPAND, EXTEND,
SPREAD, SWELL,
WIDEN
dilatory—FABIAN, LAX,
REMISS, SLOW,
TARDY
dilemma—FIX, JAM,
PICKLE, QUANDARY
dilettante—ADMIRER,
AMATEUR,
DABBLER
dill—ANET, FENNEL
dilute—DIMINISH.
RAREFY, THIN,
WEAKEN
dim—BLEAR, BLUR,
CALIGINOUS. DARK,

DULL, ECLIPSE,
FAINT, INDISTINCT,
OBSCURE, OBTUSE,
TARNISHED
diminish—ABATE, BATE,
CURTAIL,
DECREASE. EBB,
FADE. LESSEN,
LOWER, PETER,
TAPER, WANE,
WAVE
diminutive—BANTAM,
DWARF, PETITE,
RUNTY, SMALL,
WEE
dining room—CENACLE,
MESSHALL,
REFECTORY, SALON
dingle—DALE, DELL,
GLEN, VALE
diocese—BISHOPRIC,
SEE
dip—BAIL, DAP,
DECLINE,
DEPRESSION,
DOUSE, DROP,
IMMERSE, INCLINE,
LADE, PITCH,
PLUNGE, SINK, WET
dipthong—AE, AO, EA, IE,
OI
diplomacy—
DEXTERITY,
FINESSE,
TACT
diplomat—ATTACHE,
AMBASSADOR,
CONSUL, DEAN,
EMISSARY, ENVOY,
MINISTER, NUNCIO
dire—BANEFUL,
DREADFUL, EVIL,
FATAL, FEARFUL
direct—AIM, ADDRESS,
BOSS. DRIVE,
GOVERN, GUIDE,
LEAD, MANAGE,
MARSHAL, REFER,
STEER

direction—COURSE,
GUIDANCE, TREND
directory—LIST,
PHONEBOOK,
REGISTER
dirge—CORONACH,
GRIEF, HEARSE,
LAMENT, SONG,
THRENODY
dirigible—BALLOON,
SHENANDOH
dirk—DAGGER,
PONIARD, SNEE,
SNY
disable—BREAK, GRUEL,
LAME, MAIM, SAP
disappear—EVANESCE,
FLEE, VANISH
disaster—BALE, BLOW,
MISHAP, STROKE
disavow—ABJURE, DENY,
DISOWN, RECANT
disbeliever—ATHEIST,
HERETIC, SKEPTIC
discard—ABANDON,
CHUCK, JUNK,
SCRAP, SLUFF
discharge—ABSOLVE,
BLAST, DISMISS,
EMIT, EXUDE, FIRE,
FREE, QUIETUS,
RELIEVE, RID,
SALVO, SHOOT,
SPEED
disciple—ADHERENT,
APOSTLE, PUPIL,
SCHOLAR
disclaim—ABJURE, DENY,
DISAVOW, DISOWN
discolored—LIVID,
STAINED, TINGED
discomfort—DISTRESS,
EMBARRASS,
UNEASE
disconcert—ABASH,
DAUNT, FAZE,
RATTLE
discount—AGIO, BATTA,
IGNORE, REBATE,

REDUCE

discourse—CARP,
EULOGY, HOMILY,
ORATE, PRELECT,
SERMON

discover—DETECT,
DISCERN, ESPY,
EXPOSE, UNEARTH

discriminate—
DEMARCATE,
PERCEIVE

discus—DISK, QUOIT,
TRENCHER

discuss—AIR, DEBATE,
MOOT, TREAT

disease—AFFECTION
AILMENT,
DISCOMFORT,
GOUT, MALADY,
MEASLES, POX,
RINGWORM
of animal—ANTHRAX,
DISTEMPER,
MANGE, NAGANA
SURRA, SURRAH
of cattle—ANTHRAX,
GARGET, HOOVE,
NAGANA
of cereals—SMUT
of children—MEASLES,
POX
of chickens—PEROSIS,
PIP, ROUP
of citrus trees—
TRISTELA
of dog—DISTEMPER,
MANGE
of eye—IRITIS
of fowls—PIP, ROUP
of grapes—COLEUR,
ESCA
of grain—ICTERUS
of horses—CARNEY,
HOOVES, MALIS,
SPAVIN
of joints—GOUT
of kidneys—UREMIA
of livestock—NAGANA
of nerves—PELLAGRA,
TIC

of plants—ERGOT, ROT,
SCAB, SMUT
of rye—ERGOT
of silkworm—UJI
of swine—GARGET

disembark—ALIGHT,
DEBARK, DEPLANE,
DETRAIN, LAND

disentangle—DETACH,
FREE, RAVEL,
RELEASE, SLEAVE,
UNRAVEL

disgrace—ABASE,
INFAMY, ODIUM,
SCANDAL, STIGMA

disguise—HIDE, MASK,
VEIL

dish—BOAT, BOWL,
CHARGER, CRUSE,
CUP, PATINA,
PLATE, PLATTER,
SAUCER, TUREEN,
UTENSIL, VESSEL

dishearten—AMATE,
DAUNT, DETER,
UNNERVE

disinfectant—
GERMICIDE,
IODIN(E), PHENOL

disinter—EXHUME,
UNBURY, UNEARTH

disk—ATEN, DIAL,
HARROW, MEDAL,
RECORD, SEQUIN

dislike—ANTIPATHY,
AVERSION,
HATRED, LOATHE,
ODIUM

dislocate—DISJOINT,
LUXATE, SPLAY

dismay—APPALL, DAUNT,
DREAD

dismiss—AMAND,
CASHIER, DEMIT,
DISCHARGE, EJECT,
GATE, OUST,
RELEGATE, REMUE,
SHELVE

dismissal—CONGE

dismount—ALIGHT, AVALE

dispute—ARGUE, BICKER,
CHAFFER,
CONTEST, DEBATE,
DISCUSS, DISSENT,
HAGGLE, SPAR,
SPAT, WRANGLE

disputed—MOOT

dissenter—HERETIC,
NONCONFORMIST,
RECUSANT

dissertation—ESSAY,
LECTURE, SERMON,
THEME, TRACT,
TREATISE

dissipate—DIFFUSE,
SCATTER, SPEND,
WASTE

dissolute—IMMORAL,
LAX, LAWLESS,
LEWD, LOOSE,
RAKISH

dissolve—DISBAND, END,
FADE, MELT, THAW

dissonant—ATONAL,
CACOPHONOUS,
GRATING, JARRING

distance—MILEAGE,
SPACE, STEP

distant—AFAR, ALOOF,
COLD, FAR,
FORMAL, FOREIGN,
REMOTE, UTMOST,
YON

distilling device—ALEMBIC

distort—ASKEW, AWRY,
CROOKED

distress—AGONY, AIL,
GRIEF, MISERY,
PAIN, SUFFERING

distribute—ALLOT, DEAL,
DOLE, METE, SORT

disturb—AGITATE, AIL,
ANNOY, HECKLE,
MOLEST, RILE, ROIL,
AVALE

disparaging—ABUSE,
DECRY, MALIGN,
SLUR

dispatch—DISPOSE,
HASTE, KILL,
MESSAGE, POST,
SEND, SLAY

dispel—BANISH,
DISPERSE. EJECT,
OUST, SCATTER

dispensation—
ABSOLUTION,
EXEMPTION

dispense—DOLE, EXCUSE,
EXEMPT, FOREGO

display—AIR. EVINCE,
EXPOSE, FLAUNT,
MANIFEST,
PARADE, POMP,
SCENE, SHOW,
SPLURGE. STAGE,
WEAR

displease—ANGER,
ANNOY, MIFF,
OFFEND

disposed—BENT, PRONE,
TENDING

disposition—ANIMUS,
BENT, BIAS, MIEN,
MOOD. MORALE,
NATURE

dispossess—DEPRIVE,
DIVEST, EJECT,
EVICT, OUST

disprove—DISALLOW,
NEGATE, REBUT,
REFUTE
ROUST, RUFFLE,
STIR

disturbance—BRAWL,
FRACAS, HUBBUB,
RIOT, ROW,
TUMULT

ditch—ACEQUIA, DIKE,
ENTRENCH, FOSS,
FOSSE, MOAT, RUT,
SAP, TRENCH

diurnal—DAILY,
EPHEMERAL,
JOURNAL

divan—COUCH,
LEEWAN, LOUNGE,
SALOON, SETTEE,
SOFA

dive—DEN, DROP,

GAINER, HEADER,
JACKKNIFE, SWAN
diverge—DEVIATE,
DIFFER, VARY
divert—AMUSE,
BEGUILE, DEFLECT,
RELAX
divest—BARE, DENUDE,
DOFF, REFT, STRIP
divide—BISECT, CLEAVE,
FORK, HALVE, LOT,
REND, RIVE,
SEPARATE, SHARE,
SEVER, SUNDER
divided—APART, CLEFT,
PARTITE, REFT
dividend—BONUS, PLUM,
SHARE
divination—AUGURY,
CAPNOMANCY,
DOWSING, OMEN
divinity—DEITY,
THEOLOGUMENON
division—CLASS,
DICHOTOMY, PART,
PARTITION, SCHISM,
SECTION, SHARE
SQUADRON
divorce law—TALAK
dizziness—VERTIGO,
WHIRL
dock—BANG, BASIN,
JETTY, PIER,
WHARF
(worker)—
LONGSHOREMAN,
STEVEDORE
doctrine—BELIEVE,
CALABA, CREED,
DOGMA, GOSPEL,
HEDONISM, ISM,
LOGIC, LORE,
TENET
dogdays—CANICULE
dogma—DOCTRINE,
SEPT, TENET
dole—ALMS, GRATUITY,
GRIEF, METE,
PITTANCE, RELIEF,
SHARE, SORROW

doleful—DISMAL, DREAR,
SAD, SORROWFUL
doll—RAG, MAMA, MOP,
PUPPET, TOY
dollar—BILL, BEAN,
BUCK, SIMOLEON,
SKIN
dolphin—BOUTO,
DORADO, INIA,
PORPOISE
dolt—ASS, CLOD,
CLODPATE, DUNCE,
FOOL, LOON,
NINNY, OAF,
SIMPLETON,
NINCOMPOOP
domain—BARONY,
BOURNE, DEMESNE,
EMPIRE, ESTATE,
REALM, SCOPE
dome—CAP, CUPOLA,
PATE, ROOF
domestic—BUTLER,
DOMAL,
ENCHORIAL,
HOMEY, LOCAL,
MAID, MENIAL,
SERVANT, TAME,
VALET
dominate—CONTROL,
MASTER, OVERTOP,
RULE, SWAY
dominion—COLONY,
DUCHY, EMPIRE,
REIGN,
SOVEREIGNTY
domino—AMICE, DICE,
CLOAK, IVORY,
MASK, TILE
donate—BESTOW, GIVE,
PRESENT
donkey—ANE, ASS,
BURRO, NED,
ONAGER
doom—CONDEMN,
DESTINE, DESTINY,
FATE, LOT,
SENTENCE
door—ACCESS, JANUA,
PORTAL, POSTERN

(part)—JAMB, KNOB,
LINTEL, STILE
doorkeeper—
CONCIERGE, HASP,
OSTIARIUS,
OSTIARY, PORTER,
TILER
dormant—ASLEEP,
INACTIVE, INERT,
LATENT,
QUIESCENT, TORPID
dorsal—BACK, NEURAL,
NOTAL, TERGAL
dose—BOLUS, POTION
dot—DOWRY, IOTA,
PERIOD, POINT,
SCATTER, SPECK,
STIPPLE
dote—ADORE, BESTOW,
ENDOW, LOVE
dotted—PIEBALD, PINTO,
SEME
double—BINARY,
BINATE, DUAL,
DUPLEX, TWAIN,
TWIN
doubt—DISTRUST,
MISTRUST, QUERY,
SUSPECT,
UNCERTAIN
dough—BATTER, DUFF,
LEAVEN, MONEY,
NOODLE, PASTE,
SPUD
doughnut—CRULLER,
SINKER
dove—COO, CULVER,
CUSHAT, INCA,
NUN, PIGEON,
TUMBLER
dower—BEQUEST,
DONATION, DOS,
ENDOW, GRANT
down—EIDER, FUZZ,
NAP, PILE
downfall—DESCENT,
REVERSE, RUIN
downright—BLUNT, FLAT,
STARK
downy—PILLAR,
VILLOUS
dowry—DOS, DOT, GIFT,
MONEY
draft—CONSCRIPT,
POTION, PROTOCOL,
SKETCH
drag—HAUL, HALE, LUG,
TOW
dragnet—TRAINEL,
TRAWL, WEB
dragon—DRAKE,
KETU, MONSTER,
ORC, RAHAB
drama—DIORAMA,
KABUKI, MIME,
OPERA, PLAY
drape—ADORN,
CURTAIN, HANG,
COVER
draw—ATTRACT,
DEPICT, DRAFT,
DRAG, EXTRACT,
HAUL, LIMN, LURE,
PULL, TOG, TOW
drawback—DEFECT,
RESILE, WINCE
drawn—ETIOLATED,
HOVE, TIED
dread—AWE, FEAR,
GRISE, HORROR,
TERROR
dream—FANCY,
IMAGINE, REVERIE,
ROMANCE, VISION
dredge—DRAG, RAISE,
SIFT
drench—DOUSE, HOSE,
IMBUE, SATURATE,
SOAK, SOUSE
dress—ALIGN, ARRAY,
ATTIRE, CLOTHE,
DECK, DIGHT,
FROCK, GARB,
GOWN, RIG, TOG
dresser—BUREAU, CHEST,
LEVANTER, TABLE
dribble—GUSH, SPOUT,
TRICKLE
drift—AIM, CRESCENT,
COURSE, CURRENT,

FLOAT, INTENT,
IMPORT, PILE,
PURPORT, SAG,
TENDENCY, TENOR,
TREAT, TREND
drill—AUGER, BORE,
EXERCISE,
PERFORATE,
PIERCE, PRACTICE,
REHEARSE, TRAIN
drink—ADE, ALE,
BEVERAGE, COLA,
DRAM, GIN, IMBIBE,
NECTAR, NIP, NIPA,
PANAL, POTABLE,
QUAFF, SIP, TODDY
drip—DROP, LEAK, SEEP,
SILE, TRICKLE
drive—FORCE, IMPEL,
PROPEL, RIDE,
ROUST, SLOG, URGE
drivel—DOTE, DROOL,
MAD, SLAVER
driver—JEHU, MOTORIST,
WHIP
droll—AMUSING,
BUFFOON, COMIC,
WAGGISH,
WHIMSICAL, ZANY
dromedary—CAMEL,
DESERTSHIP
drone—HUM, IDLER,
SNAIL
drool—DRIVEL,
SLOBBER, SLAVER
droop—DECLINE, FADE,
FAG, LANGUISH,
LOP, LULL, PINE,
SAG, SLOUCH, WILT
drooping—NUTANT,
SAGGING
drop—BEAD, BLOB, DRIP,
FALL, GOUT, OMIT,
PLUMMET, REMIT,
SINK, TRAPDOOR
dropsy—ASCITES, EDEMA
dross—DREGS, REFUSE,
SCORIA, SCOBS,
SCUM, SLAG, SPRUE

drought—ARIDITY, NEED,
THIRST
drove—ATAJO, CHISEL,
CROWD, FLOCK,
HERD, HORDE,
RODE
drowse—DOVER, DOZE,
NAP, NOD, SLEEP
drowsiness—LETHARGY,
OSCITANCE
drudge—FAG, HACK,
LABOR, LABOUR,
MOIL, PLOD, SLAVE
drug—ALOES, ATROPINE,
COCAINE, DOPE,
HEROIN, OPIUM,
SENNA, STUPEFY,
TONGA
drugget—MAT, RUG
druggist—
APOTHECARY,
CHEMIST,
GALLIPOT,
PHARMACIST
drum—ATABAL, BASS,
BEAT,
KETTLEDRUM,
RUNDLE, SNARE,
TABOR, TOMTOM,
TYMPANUM
(call)—RAPPEL,
RATAPLAN, TATTOO
drunkard—DIPSOMANIAC,
LUSH, SOT
TIPPLER, TOSSPOT,
TOPER
drupelet—ACINUS,
NUTLET, TRYMA
dry—ARID, AERIFY,
BRUT, DULL,
PARCH, SEC, SERE,
SICCATE, TED,
THIRSTY, WIPE
dryad—DEITY, NYMPH
duad—DUAL, DYAD,
TWO
duct—CANAL, PASSAGE,
PIPE, RACE, TUBE,
VAS

dude—DANDY, FOP
duel—COMBAT,
    CONTEST, TILT
dull—BLUNT, BLUR,
    DEADEN, DIM,
    DINGY, DRAB, DRY,
    DUN, HUMDRUM,
    INERT, LEADEN,
    LOGY, JEJUNE,
    MATTE, OBTUSE,
    PALLING, PROSY,
    SLOW, SLUGGISH,
    STODGY, STOLID,
    VAPID
dumb—MUTE, SILENT,
    STILL, STUPID
dummy—PEL, SHAM,
    SUBSTITUTE
dun—ANNOY, ASK,
    URGE
dunce—ASS, COOT, DOLT,
    FOOL, GOONY,
    IGNORAMUS, OAF
dupe—DECEIVE, FOOL,
    FOX, GULL, TOOL,
    VICTIM
duplicate—BIS, COPY,
    DOUBLE, DUPLEX,
    REPLICA,
    REPLICATE, TWIN
durable—FIRM, LASTING,
    STOUT, TOUGH
dusky—DARK, DIM,
    MURKY, SWARTHY,
    TAWNY, UMBRA
dust—BRISS, PILM, STIVE
duty—CHORE, DEVOIR,
    EXCISE, IMPOST,
    LASTAGE, OFFICE,
    TARIFF, TASK, TAX,
    TOLL
dwarf—BANTAM, ELF,
    GNOME, MANIKIN,
    MIDGET, PYGMY,
    RUNT, STUNT,
    TROLL
dwell—ABIDE, BIDE,
    HINDER, LINGER,
    LIVE, LODGE,
    RESIDE, TARRY
dwelling—DAR, FLAT,
    QUARTERS,
    RESIDENCE
dye—AAL, AN(N)ATTO,
    ARCHIL, AZARINE,
    AZOBLUE, COLOR,
    EOSIN, EOSINE,
    FUGUS, HENNA,
    IMBUE, KINO, LIT,
    ORCHAL, ORCHIL,
    STAIN, TINGE, TINT
dynamite—DUALIN, TNT
dynamo—GENERATOR
dynasty—KINGSHIP,
    LORDSHIP, REALM

-E-

eager—AGASP, AGOG,
    AFIRE, ANXIOUS,
    APT, ARDENT, AVID,
    DESIROUS, EARNEST,
    INTENT, KEEN,
    SHARP, THIRST
eagerness—ARDOR
eagle—BERGUT, ERN,
    ERNE, GIER, HARPY,
    JOVE
ear—AURICLE, HARKEN,
    HEED, LUG, PINNA,
    SPIKE
early—BETIMES,
    MATUTINAL, SOON
earn—ACHIEVE, ADDLE,
    ATTAIN, DESERVE,
    EKE, ETTLE, GAIN,
    MERIT, RATE, WIN
earnest—EAGER,
    SERIOUS, SOBER,
    ZEALOUS
earth—CLAY, DIRT, ERD,
    GEAL, GLOBE,
    LAND, LOAM,
    MARL, SOD, SOIL,

TERRA, WORLD
earthen jar—OLLA
earthenware—CROCK,
CROCKERY, DELFT,
JASPER, PORCELAIN
earthflax—AMIANTHUS
earthling—TELLURIST
earthquake—
SEISM, TREMOR
earthwork—AGGER, DIKE,
FORT, TUMP
earthy—GROSS, LOW,
MUNDANE, PACE,
TERRENE,
WORLDLY
ease—ALLAY, COMFORT,
FACILITATE,
LIGHTEN, MOLLIFY
RELIEF, RELIEVE,
REPOSE, SOOTHE
easily—DEXTEROUSLY,
READILY, SLEEK,
SMOOTHLY
easy—COMFORTABLE,
FACILE, GENTLE,
GLIB, SIMPLE
eat—CORRODE,
DEVOUR, DINE,
FEED, GNAW,
MANAGE, RUST,
SUP
eatable—EDIBLE,
ESCULENT
eaten away—ERODED,
EROSED
eavesdrop—HEARKEN
ebb—DECLINE,
DECREASE, NEAP,
RECEDE, REFLUX,
SINK, SUBSIDE,
WANE
eccentric—CRANK,
ERRATIC, ODD,
TIKE, STRANGE
ecclesiastical area—PARISH
attendant—ACOLYTE
benefice—GLEBE
banner—LABARUM
cap—BIRETTA

cape—CAPPA
close fitting
vestment—RACHET
council—SYNOD
court—CLASSIS, ROTA,
RUNA
degree—CANON,
DECRETAL
headdress—MITER
hood—AMICE
law—CANON
linen cloth—FANON
metropolitan—EPARCH
octave of a feast—UTAS
plate—PATEN
reader—LECTOR
residence—MANSE
scarf and vest—ORALE
seat—DEANERY,
SEDILE
skull cap—BIRETTA,
CALLOTE
surplice—CETTA
title—DOM, FATHER,
FRA, PADRE
unit—PARISH
vestment—ALB, AMICE,
CHASUBLE, COPE,
ORALE, STOLE,
VAGAS
echo—APE, IMITATE,
ITERATE, RESOUND,
REPEAT
eclat—ACCLAIM, GLORY,
NOTORIETY,
PRAISE, RENOWN,
SPLENDOR
eclipse—OBSCURE, STAIN,
SURPASS
ecology—BIONOMICS
economize—HUSBAND,
RETRENCH
SAVE, SCRIMP,
STINT
ecru—BEIGE, TAN,
YELLOW
ecstasy—BLISS, RAPTURE,
TRANCE
ecu—COIN, SHIELD

eddy—BORE, GULF, POOL, SWIRL, VORTEX, WHIRLPOOL, WREATHE

edema—DROPSY, SWELLING, TUMOR

eden—GLORY, HEAVEN, PARADISE

edge—BORDER, BRIM, BRINK, HEM, LIP, MARGIN, RAND, RIM, SELVEDGE, VERGE

edible—COMESTIBLE, ESCULENT

edict—ACT, ARRET, ASSIZE, DECREE, ESCRIPT, MANDATE, UKASE

edit—EMEND, REVIEW, REVISE

editor—DIASKEUAST

education—LITERACY, TUITION

educator—ANGELL, ADLER, BARNES, FROEBEL, MANN, PATRI, RABBITT

eel—ANGUILLA, CONGER, MORAY, MURAENA, SIREN

eerie—MACABRE, SCARY, UNCANNY, WEIRD

effervesce—AERATE, BUBBLE

effigy—DOLL, GUY, FACSIMILE, ICON, IMAGE

effort—ATTEMPT, CONATUS, ESSAY, EXERTION, STRAIN, STRUGGLE, TUG

egest—EXCRETE, VOID

egg—ABET, GOAD, INCITE, NIT, OVA, OVULE, OVUM, ROE, URGE

ego—ATMAN, JIVATMA, PAST, SELF

egress—EXIT, ISSUANCE, OUTLET

egret—AGAMI, AIGRETTE, HERON, STILT, STORK, TERN, TERNE

eidolon—APPARITION, ICON, IMAGE, PHANTOM

eight—OCTA, OCTAVE, OCTET

eject—DISLODGE, ELIMINATE, EMIT, EVICT, EXPEL, OUST, PUT, SPEW, VOID

elbow—ANCON, ANGLE, BEND, SQUEEZE

elder—DEAN, OLDER, PRIOR, SENIOR, SIRE

eldest—EIGNE

electric capacity— OHMAGE, VOLTAGE

car—TRAM

circuit—LOOP

current—AC, DC

device—AMPLIFIER, CODER, COIL, DYNAMO, FAN, GENERATOR, HEATER, MOTOR, RADIO

force—ELOD

light—ARC, BULB

particle—ION

unit—AMPERE, FARAD, HENRY, MHO, OHM, PERM, REL, VOLT, WATT

electrode—ANODE, CATHODE

elegance—BEAUTY, GRACE, LUXURY, POLISH, REFINEMENT

elegy—FUNERAL, LAMENT, NENIA, REQUIEM

element—COMPONENT,

CONSTITUENT,
METAL
elementary—BASIC,
INCHOATE,
PRIMARY
elephant—BULL, CALF,
COW, MASTODON,
PACHYDERM
elevation—BANK, HILL,
MOUND, RISE
elf—EFT, FAIRY, FAY,
GNOME, HOB, IMP,
NEWT, MIX, OAF,
OUPHE, PERI
elfin—FEY
elicit—EDUCE, EVOKE,
EXTRACT, STRETCH
elide—DELE, OMIT, SKIP
elixir—ARCANUM,
PANACEA, SPIRIT
elk—ALCE, ELAND,
MOOSE, SAMBUR,
STAG, WAPITI
elliptic—OBLONG, OVAL,
OVATE
elongated—LANK,
LINEAR, PROLATE
elusive—BAFFLING,
EELY, EQUIVOCAL,
EVASIVE, SLICK,
SLIPPERY, SUBTLE
elysium—EDEN,
PARADISE
emaciation—ATROPHY,
TABES
emanation—AURA,
EFFLUX, NIDOR
emancipate—FREE,
MANUMIT,
RELEASE
embankment—BUND
DIGUE, DIKE,
LEVEE, QUAY
embellish—ADORN,
BEAUTIFY, BEDECK,
EMBOSS, DRESS,
GARNISH, GILD,
ROUGE
ember—ASH, CINDER,

COAL, IZLE
embezzle—DISSIPATE,
SQUANDER, STEAL
emblem—BADGE, BAR,
DESIGN, IMAGE,
INSIGNE, MACE,
REGALIA, SIGN,
STANDARD,
SYMBOL, TYPE
embodiment—AVATAR,
EPITOME
embrace—ACCOLADE,
ACCOLL, ADOPT,
CARESS, CLASP,
COMPRISE,
CONTAIN, FOLD,
HUG, INCLUDE
embrocation—ARNICA,
LINIMENT
embroider—EMBOSS,
LACE, TAT
embryo—BLASTULA,
FETUS, LARVA,
OVUM
emery—ABRASIVE,
CORUNDUM
emetic—EVACUANT,
IPECAC
emissary—AGENT,
LEGATE, SCOUT,
SPY
emit—DISCHARGE,
EJECT, ERUPT,
EXHALE, EXUDE,
ISSUE, PLUFF,
RADIATE, SHED,
UTTER, VOICE
emmet—ANT, PISMIRE
emotion—ANGER,
CHERISH, FEELING,
IRE, PASSION,
PATHOS, TREMOR
emotionless—APATHETIC
UNFEELING
emperor—CZAR.
IMPERATOR, INCA,
KAISER, TSAR
employ—ENGAGE, HIRE,
OCCUPY, USE

employer—BOSS, HIRER,
MANAGER
empty—BARE, CLEAR,
DEPLETE, IDLE.
INANE, VACANT,
VAIN, VOID
emulate—APE, COPY,
RIVAL, VIE
enact—DECREE, ENJOIN,
ORDAIN, PASS,
PERFORM. PLAY
enamel—GLAZE, GLOSS,
PAINT, SLICK
encamp—BIVOUAC,
SIEGE, TENT
enchantress—CIRCE,
MEDEA, SIREN,
WITCH
encircle—BELT, ENCLASP,
ENFOLD,
ENSPHERE,
ENVIRON, GIRD,
GIRDLE, HOOP,
INARM, ORB, RING,
SASH
enclose—CORRAL, COOP,
ENCLAVE, HEM,
PEN, SURROUND
enclosure—BAWN, CAGE,
COOP, PEN,
STOCKADE. YARD
encomium—ELOGE,
EULOGY.
PANEGYRIC,
TRIBUTE
encore—AGAIN, BIS,
REPEAT
encourage—ABET, AID,
BOOST, EGG,
FOSTER, IMPEL,
URGE
end—AIM, CEASE,
CLIMAX, CLOSE,
DESIST, FINALE,
FINIS, FINISH,
LIMIT, OMEGA,
OUTCOME, TAIL,
TOE
endless—CONTINUAL,

ETERNAL,
EVERLASTING,
INFINITE,
PERPETUAL
endowment—
APPANAGE, DOWER,
FUND, GIFT, GRANT,
TALENT
endue—CLOTHE, ENDOW,
TEACH
endure—ABIDE, BEAR,
BROOK, CONTINUE,
DREE, LAST, LIVE,
STAND, SUFFER,
SUSTAIN,
TOLERATE
enemy—ADVERSARY,
FOE, HATER, RIVAL
energy—BENT, ERG, PEP,
VIGOR, VIM
engage—AFFIANCE,
BETROTH, BOOK,
ENLIST, HIRE, JOIN,
MESH
engine—DIESEL, GIN,
MOGUL, MOTOR,
TURBINE
engrave—CARVE, CHISEL,
CUT, ETCH, INCISE,
INFIX, STIPPLE
engraver's ink pad—
DABBER
machine—ROUTER
of stone—LAPIDARY
tool—BURIN
enigma—CONUNDRUM,
PUZZLE, REBUS,
RIDDLE
enlarged—DILATED,
EXPANDED,
MAGNIFIED,
REAMED
enmity—AVERSION,
ANIMUS,
MALEVOLENCE,
RANCOR
enough—AMPLE, BASTA,
FULLY, QUITE
enroll—ENTER, ENLIST,

IMPANEL, JOIN,
MATRICULATE,
POLL, RECORD

ensign—
ORIFLAMME

ensnare—BENET, BITE,
CATCH, ENTRAP,
NET, NOOSE, TRAP,
TRICK, WEB

entertain—AMUSE,
BEGUILE, DIVERT,
FETE, HARBOR,
REGALE, TREAT

entertainer—ACTOR,
COMEDIAN,
COURTESAN,
HOSTESS

enthusiasm—ELAN,
VERVE, ZEAL, ZEST

enthusiast—DEVOTEE,
FAN, FANATIC, IST,
ZEALOT

entice—ALLURE,
ATTRACT, CHARM,
DECOY, INVEIGLE,
INVITE, LURE,
TEMPT, TOLE, WIN

entity—BEING, ENS,
THING, UNIT

entomb—INTER, INURN

entrance—ADIT, CHARM,
DELIGHT, DOOR,
DOORWAY, ENTRY,
GATE, GATEWAY,
INGRESS, INLET,
PORTAL, POSTERN,
WAY

entry—ACCESS,
EGRESS,
ENTRANCE, ITEM,
HALLWAY,
PASSAGE,
VESTIBULE

envelope—BURR, CASE,
SHROUD, VESICLE,
WRAPPER

environment—MILIEU,
SURROUNDINGS

environs—EXURBS, HEM,
OUTSKIRTS,
VICINITY

envy—COVET, RANKLE,
SPITE

enzyme—ASE, DIASTASE,
MALTASE, PAPAIN,
PEPSIN, PTYALIN,
UREASE

eon—AGE, ERA, CYCLE,
TIME

epic—GRAND, HEROIC,
NOBLE, POEM, SAGA

epicure—
GLUTTON,
GOURMAND,
GOURMET,
SYBARITE

epidemic—FLU, PEST,
PLAGUE, POX,
PESTILENCE

epithet—AGNOMEN,
APPELLATION,
NAME,
NOUN

epoch—AGE, EON, ERA,
TIME

equal—ADEQUATE,
BOTH,
COORDINATE,
EVEN, ISO, PAR,
PEER, RIVAL,
SAME, TIE

equality—EQUITY,
PARITY

equine—ASS, BURRO,
HORSE, MARE,
MULE, STEED

equip—APPOINT, GIRD,
OUTFIT, RIG

equivocate—DODGE,
EVADE, FENCE,
HEDGE, LIE, SHIFT

era—AGE, CYCLE, DATE,
EON, EPOCH,
PERIOD, TIME

erase—BLOT, CANCEL,
DELE, DELETE,
EFFACE, EXPUNGE

ermine—FUR, STOAT,
WEASEL

err—LAPSE, MISS, SIN,

SLIP
error—BLUNDER,
    BONER, ERRATA,
    GAFFE, LAPSE,
    MISCUE, MISSTEP,
    MISTAKE, SIN, SLIP,
    TYPO
escape—AVOID, ELOPE,
    EVADE, FLEE,
    INNER, LAM,
    SECRET
eschew—ABSTAIN,
    FOREGO, SHUN
escort—BEAU,
    CHAPERONE,
    CONVOY, DUENNA
escutcheon—ARMS, CREST
esoteric—ARCANE,
    INNER, MYSTIC,
    SECRET
essay—ATTEMPT, CHRIA,
    EFFORT, PAPER,
    TEST, THEME,
    TRIAL, TRY
essence—ATTAR, GIST,
    MARROW, NATURE,
    PERFUME, PITH,
    NUB, SOUL, YOLK
essential—ABSOLUTE,
    CARDINAL,
    INHERENT,
    NECESSARY, VITAL
establish—BASE, FIX,
    FOUND, INSTITUTE,
    PLANT, RADICATE,
    REAR, SET, SETTLE,
    VERIFY
estate—ALOD, FIEF,
    LEGACY, MANOR,
    PROPERTY
ester—SILICATE,
    STEARIN, TROPATE
estrade—DAIS,
    PLATFORM
estuary—FIORD, FIRTH,
    FRITH, INLET
etagere—WHATNOT
eternal—AGELESS,
    CEASELESS,
    DEATHLESS,

ENDLESS,
    EVERLASTING,
    TIMELESS
eternity—AEON, INFINITY
ether—AIR, SKY, SPACE
ethereal—AERIAL, AERY,
    AIRLIKE, AIRY,
    BODY, SOUL
eucharist box—PIX, PYX
    vessel—AMA, AMULA,
        PATEN
eucharistic plate—PATINA
    spoon—LABIS
    wine—KRAMA
    cup—AMA, CHALICE
eulogy—ELOGE,
    ENCOMIUM, PRAISE
evade—AVOID, BILK,
    DODGE, ELUDE
evanescent—CURSORY,
    EPHEMERAL,
    EVASIVE, FLEETING
evangelist—APOSTLE,
    GRAHAM,
    MCPHERSON,
    PREACHER,
    SUNDAY
even—BALANCE,
    EQUABLE,
    EQUALIZE, FLUSH,
    LEVEL, PLANE,
    PLUMB, SMOOTH,
    TIED, UNVARIED
evening—SUNSET, DUSK,
    GLOAMING,
    SHADES, SOIREE,
    TYING, VESPER
ever—AYE, ALWAYS,
    ANON, ONCE
evergreen—ABELMOSK,
    BARETTA, PINE,
    SPRUCE, TARARA
    shrub—BOX, GALAX,
        FURZE, HEATH,
        HOLLY, OLEANDER,
        PRIVET, SAVIN,
        TOYON
everlasting—AEONIAN,
    AGELONG,
    ENDLESS, ETERNE,

ETERNAL,
UNENDING
evict—EJECT, EXPEL,
OUST, SACK
evident—CLEAR,
GLARING,
PALPABLE, PATENT,
VISIBLE
evil—BAD, BANE,
CORRUPT,
HARMFUL, ILL,
INIQUITY, SIN,
SINFUL, VICE
ewer—CROCK, JUG, URN
exacerbate—EMBITTER,
ENRAGE, PROVOKE,
IRK
exact—ACCURATE,
DEMAND, ESTREAT,
JUST, LITERAL,
MINUTE, PRECISE,
STRICT
exaggerated—
EXCEPTIONAL,
OUTRE,
OVERDONE,
OVERSTATED,
OVERTOLD
exalt—ELEVATE, EXTOL,
HONOR, LAUD,
RAISE
examination—ASSAY,
ESSAY, INQUEST,
INQUIRY, QUIZ,
TEST, VERBAL
examine—APPOSE,
EXPLORE, PERUSE,
PORE, TEST, TRY
example—CASE, NORM,
PARADIGM,
SAMPLE
excavation—CAVITY,
CUT, HOLE, MINE,
MUCK, PIT
excellence—ARETE,
CLASS, MERIT,
VIRTU
excellent—AONE, BRAVE,
CAPITAL, FINE,
GOOD, PRIME,

SELECT
except—BESIDES, BUT,
BAR, EXCLUDE,
OMIT, SAVE,
UNLESS
excess—NIMIETY, OVER,
PLETHORA, PLUS,
SURPLUS
exchange—AGIO, BANDY,
BARTER, BOURSE,
RAP, TRADE, SWAP
exchequer—FISC, PURSE
excite—AGITATE, FIRE,
FOMENT, PIQUE,
SPUR
excited—AGOG,
FEVERED, MANIC
excitement—ADO, FUROR,
STIR
exclamation—AH, AHA,
AHEM, ALAS, BAH,
EGAD, EVOE,
EXPLETIVE, FIE,
HEIGH, HIP, HO,
HAH, HEY, OHO,
OUCH, OW, PAH,
PHEW, PHO, RATS,
TUT, UGH, WOW,
YAH
excoriate—ABRADE,
FLAY, GALL
exclusive—SELECT,
SINGLE, SOLE,
UNIQUE
excrete—DEFECATE,
EGEST, EVACUATE
excuse—ALIBI, APOLOGY,
CONDONE, PARDON,
PLEA, PRETEXT,
REASON
execute—ACT, HANG,
KILL, MURDER,
SPEED
exercise—LESSON,
PRACTICE
exhibit—AIR, EVINCE,
SHOW, STAGE,
STATE
exist—ALIVE, AM, ARE,
BE, ESSE, IS

exit—DEPART, DOOR,
EGRESS, LEAVE,
OUTLET
exodus—FLIGHT,
HEGIRA,
MIGRATION
expand—ENLARGE,
DILATE, DISTEND,
FLAN, GROW,
SPLAY,
SPREAD, STRETCH
expect—DEEM, HOPE,
WAIT, WEEN, WISH
expedition—CARAVAN,
CRUSADE, DRIVE,
FORAY, JAUNT,
SAFARI, TREK
expert—ACE, ADEPT,
ADROIT, DEFT,
WHIZ
expiate—ATONE, PURGE
explicit—CLEAR, EXACT,
LUCID, OPEN, PLAIN
explode—BACKFIRE,
BURST, DETONATE,
FULMINATE
explorer—BALBOA, BYRD,
CABOT, DRAKE,
DESOTO,
HUDSON, PIZARRO
explosion—BLAST,
OUTBURST, POP
explosive—AMATOL,
AMMO, CAP, CERIA,
DYNAMITE,
MAXIMITE,
NITRO,
ROMITE, TETRYL,
TNT, TONITE,
TROTYL
expose—BARE, DETECT,
DISPLAY, OPEN,
REVEAL, UNMASK
express—AIR, BROACH,
UTTER, VOICE
expression—ASPECT,
LOCUTION, MEANS,
MODE, PHRASE,
SAYING, TERM,
TOKEN
expressive—ELOQUENT
extend—DEPLOY, EKE,
EXPAND, JUT, LIE,
PROTRACT, REACH,
RENEW, SEIZE,
SPAN, SPREAD,
STRETCH
extent—AMBIT, AREA,
DEGREE, LENGTH,
LIE, LIMIT, RANGE,
SEIZURE, SCOPE,
SPAN, SPACE
exterior—ECTAL,
EXTERNAL,
EXTRINSIC,
FOREIGN, OUT,
OUTER, OUTSIDE,
OUTWARD,
SURFACE
external—CORTICAL,
OUT, OUTER,
OUTSIDE
extinct—DEAD,
EXTINGUISHED,
QUENCHED
extinguish—ANNUL,
DOUSE, QUELL,
QUENCH
extirpate—DELE, ERASE,
EXCISE
extort—BLEED, COMPEL,
EXACT, MILK,
WREST
extra—MORE, OVER,
SPARE, SURPLUS,
ULTRA
extract—CITE, DRAW,
ELICIT, ESTREAT,
EXCERPT
extraneous—ALIEN,
EXOTIC, EXTRA,
FOREIGN
extravagance—E LA,
WASTE
extreme—DIRE, END,
INTENSE, LAST,
LIMIT, RADICAL,
RANK, SORE,

ULTRA, UNDUE
exude—DISCHARGE,
EMIT, FLOW, OOZE,
REEK, SEEP
eye—OBSERVE, OGLE,
OPTIC, ORB,
REGARD, SIGHT,
UTA, VIEW, VISION,
WATCH
cavity—ORBIT, SOCKET
coat—RETINA
colored portion—IRIS
coloring—MASCARA
disease—GLAUCOMA,
IRITIS

dropper—PIPETTE
flap—BLINDER,
BLINKER, PATCH,
VISOR
glass—LENS,
LORGNON,
MONOCLE
lashes—CILIA
of bean—HILA, HILUM
opening—PUPIL
part—IRIDE, STRALE,
UVEA
pert. to—IRIAN, OPTIC
shield—PATCH
strings—TENDONS

-F-

fable—ALLEGORY,
APOLOGUE,
LEGEND, LIE,
MYTH, STORY
fabric—ATLAS, BAIZE,
CHIFFON, COTTON,
DENIM, FAILLE,
FELT, FLANNEL,
LANSDOWNE, LENE,
MOIRE, MOREEN,
PARAMATTA, RAS,
RAYON, SILK, TOILE,
VOILE, ETAMINE
fabricate—COIN,
CONCOCT,
CONTRIVE, DEVISE,
FORM, MINT
face—ANSWER,
CONFRONT, DARE,
DIAL, FRONT,
GRIMACE, MAP,
MEET, MOUE, MUG,
PRESTIGE, PUSS
facet—BEZEL, CULET,
PHASE
facile—ABLE, APT,
DEFT, EASY,
QUICK
facsimile—COPY, MATCH,
REPLICA
fact—DATA, DATUM,

DEED, FEAT, FIAT,
KEYNOTE, REALITY,
TRUTH
faction—BLOC, CABAL,
CLIQUE, JUNTO,
PARTY, SECT, SIDE
factor—AGENT, BROKER,
ELEMENT, GENE,
MANAGER
faculty—ABILITY, BENT,
GIFT, KNACK,
TALENT
fad—CRAZE, FANCY,
HOBBY, RAGE,
WHIM
fade—DIM, PALE,
PETER, VANISH,
WANE, WILT
fail—DEFAULT, DEFECT,
DISAPPOINT, EBB,
FLOP, FLUNK, LOSE,
MISS, PETER
failure—DUD, FIASCO,
FLOP, FOIL, LACK
faint—DIM, PALE,
SWELTER,
SWOON, WEAK
fainting spell—SYNCOPE
fair—AVERAGE,
BAZAAR, BLOND,
COMELY, CANDOR,

CLEAN, DECENT,
ELEGANT,
HONESTY,
IMPARTIAL. JUST,
LIGHT, OPEN, PURE,
SMOOTH. SPOTLESS,
UNBIASED

fairy—EFT, ELF. ELFKIN,
ELVE. FAY, GNOME,
LEPRECHAUN,
NEWT. PERI, PIXY,
SPRITE

  king—OBERON
  queen—MAB, TITANIA,
  UNA

faith—BELIEF, CREED,
CONFIDENCE,
CREDIT, CULT,
TROTH. TRUST

faithful—DEVOTED,
FAST, LEAL, LIEGE,
LOYAL, SWEAR,
TRUE

fake—FALSIFY, FEIGN,
FRAUD, PHONIE,
PHONY, SHAM

fakir—DERVISH,
MENDICANT,
MONK, YOGI

falcon—EAGLE, HAWK,
KESTREL,
LANNERET,
PEREGRINE,
SORAGE

fall—DROP, PLOP,
PLUMMET, RUIN,
SIN, SLIP, SUBSIDE,
TUMBLE

fallacy—ERROR, IDOLUM

falls—CASCADE,
CATARACT

false—BOGUS, FAKE,
PSEUDO, SHAM,
SOPHISTRY,
SPURIOUS, TALE,
UNRELIABLE

falsehood—CANARD,
FLAM, FRAUD, LIE,
PERJURY, TALE

falsify—BELIE, DISTORT,
FORGE, GARBLE,
PERVERT

fame—GLORY, KUDOS,
NOTE, RENOWN,
REPUTE

famed—EMINENT,
NOTED,
NOTORIOUS,
FAMOUS

familiar—BOLD, CLOSE,
COMMON, HOMELY

family—CLAN, GENS.
ILK, LINE, LINEAGE,
STIRPS, TRIBE

famous—CELEBRATED,
EMINENT, NAMED,
NOTABLE, NOTED

fan—BUFF, COOL,
DEVOTEE, FOMENT,
ROOTER, VOTARY,
WINNOW, ZEALOT

fanatic—BIGOT,
ENTHUSIAST,
FRANTIC, LUNATIC,
MAD, PHRENETIC,
ZEALOT

fancy—CAPRICE,
DREAM, FAD, IDEA,
IDEATE,
IMAGINATION,
MEGRIM, WHIM

fane—BASILICA, SHRINE,
SANCTUARY,
TEMPLE

fantasy—DREAM, FANCY,
IDEA, IMAGINE

far—AWAY, ADVANCED,
OFF, REMOTE,
WIDELY

farce—COMEDY,
MOCKERY,
PARODY, SKIT,
STUFFING

fare—DIET, FOOD,
PASSENGER, PAY,
PROSPER, RATE,
TRY

farewell—ADIEU, ADIOS,

ALOHA, AVE,
BONVOYAGE,
CONGE, TATA, VALE
farinaceous—MEALY,
STARCHY
farm—COTLAND, CROFT,
CULTIVATE,
GRANGE, PLOW,
RANCH, RANGE,
TILL
animal—BULL, COW,
DOG, EWE,
GOAT, HORSE,
MARE, MULE, OX,
PIG, PONY, RAM,
SHEEP, SOW,
STALLION, STEER,
SWINE
building—BARN,
GRANARY, COOP,
SILO, SMOKEHOUSE,
STABLE
horse—DOBBIN
farm machine—BALER,
BINDER,
CULTIVATOR,
CHURN, DISK,
HAYFORK,
HARROW, MILKER,
MOWER, PLANTER,
PLOW, RAKE,
RAKER, REAPER,
SEEDER,
SEPARATOR,
SHOCKER, TEDDER,
THRESHER, TILLER,
TRASNER, WEEDER
out buildings—STEADING
tenant—COTTER
tool—AXE, BRANDER,
FENCER, FLAIL,
FORK, HAYFORK,
HOE, NIPPERS,
PLOW, RAKE
farmer—CULTIVATOR,
GRANGER,
PLANTER, SEEDER,
RYOT, YEOMAN
fashion—CRAZE, DESIGN,
MODE, MODEL,

RAGE, SHAPE,
STYLE, VOGUE
fat—ADIPOSE, ADEPS,
CORPULENT, ESTER,
FLESHY, LARD,
LIPA, OBESE,
PINGUID, PLUMP,
PORTLY, OILY, SUET
fatal—DEADLY, LETHAL,
MORTAL, OMINOUS
fate—DESTINY, DOOM,
KISMET, LOT
father—ABBA, ABBE,
ABU, BEGET, DAD,
DADDY, PA, PADRE,
PAPA, PARENT,
PERE, SIRE
fathom—DELVE, GRASP,
PROBE, SOLVE
fatuous—INANE, SILLY,
WITLESS
faucet—COCK, SPIGOT,
TAP, VALVE
fault—BLEMISH, CAVIL,
CULPA, DEFECT,
FOIBLE, LAPSE,
OFFENCE, SLIP
fault finder—CARPER,
MOMUS
faultless—IDEAL,
IMPECCABLE,
PARAGON,
PERFECT, RIGHT
faun—DEITY, SATYR
faux pas—BONER, ERROR,
GAFFE, MISSTEP,
SLIP
favorite—DEAR, MINION,
PET
fawn—BUCK, CRINGE,
DEER, GROVEL,
KOWTOW, TOADY
fear—AWE, DREAD,
PANIC, PHOBIA,
TERROR
of being burned alive
—TAPHEPHOBIA
of crossing road—
DROMOPHOBIA
of darkness—

NYCTOPHOBIA
of drafts—AEROPHOBIA
of fire—PYROPHOBIA
of lightning—
  TROPHOBIA
of number 13—
  TRISKAIDEKA-
  PHOBIA
of open spaces—
  AGORAPHOBIA
of pain—
  ALGOPHOBIA
of poisons—
  TOXIPHOBIA
of strangers—
  XENOPHOBIA
fearful—CAUTIOUS,
  DIRE, TIMID
feast—REVEL, BANQUET,
  FETE, LUAU, SEDER
feat—ACT, DEED,
  EXPLOIT, STUNT
feather—DOWN, EIDER,
  QUILL, PENNA,
  PINNA, PLUME,
  REMEX
federation—LEAGUE,
  UNION
fee—BRIBE, CHARGE,
  FIEF,
  HONORARIUM,
  PAYMENT,
  RETAINER, PRICE,
  TIP, WAGE
feeble—ANILE, DOTTY,
  LAME, PUNY, WEAK
feed—FODDER, GORGE,
  REPAST
feeding box—MANGER
feel—AIL, GROPE, PALP,
  SENSE, SUFFER,
  TOUCH
feeler—ANTENNA, PALPI,
  PALPUS, TENTACLE
feet (having)—DIPODY
  number—FOOTAGE
  pert. to—PEDAL,
  PODAL
  without—APODAL
feign—ACT, ASSUME,

DISSEMBLE, FAKE,
  GARBLE,
  PRETEND,
  SIMULATE, SHAM
feint—BLIND, FETCH,
  PRETENSE, RUSE,
  SHIFT, TRICK
feline—CAT, CATLIKE,
  JAGUAR, MOUSER,
  SLY, STEALTHY,
  TIGER, TOM, WILY
fellow—BLOKE, BO,
  CHAP, CUSTOMER,
  LAD, MATE, PEER,
  PERSON
fen—BOG, MARSH,
  MOOR, MORASS,
  SUMP, SWAMP
fence—BULWARK,
  FAGIN, PALISADE,
  RAIL, SCRIME
fencing breast
  plate—PLASTRON
  cry—HAI, SASA,
  TOUCHE
  dummy—PEL
  foot tap—APPEL
  hit—PUNTO
  movement—VOLT
  posture—CARTE, PEL,
  SEPTIME, SECONDE
  redoubling of an
  attack—REPRISE
  stroke—APPEL, BUTT
  sword—EPEE, FOIL,
  RAPIER, SABRE
  term—GARDE, HAI,
  PALING, PARRY,
  QUARTE, RIPOSTE,
  TIERCE, TOUCHE
  thrust—CARTE,
  FOIBLE, FORTE,
  PUNTO, REMISE,
  RIPOST, RIPOSTE
feral—DEADLY, FERINE,
  SAVAGE, WILD
ferment—BARM, BREW,
  FRET, LEAVEN,
  SEETHE, YEAST
fermented drink—ALE,

BEER, MEAD, WINE
fern—BRACKEN, BRAKE,
  NARDEE, NEVE,
  SORI, SPORES, TARA
ferrum—IRON
ferry—PONT, SCOW,
  TRAJECT
fertilizer—COMPOST,
  GUANO, MARL,
  NITRATE
fester—ABSCESS,
  PUSTULE, RANKLE
festival—BEE, CARNIVAL,
  FAIR, FEAST, FEIS,
  FETE, FIESTA, GALA
festoon—GARLAND,
  LEI, SWAG
fetch—BRING, RETRIEVE
fetid—FUSTY, NOISOME,
  OLID, PUTRID,
  RANCID, RANK
fetish—GRIGRI, JUJU,
  MASCOT, OBEAH
fetter—BAND, BIND,
  BOND, CHAIN,
  GYVE, HOBBLE,
  IRONS, MANACLES,
  SHACKLE
feud—BROIL, FRAY,
  VENDETTA
feudal castle—CHATEAU
  estate—FEOD, FIEF
  tax—TAILAGE,
    TALLAGE
  tenant—SECAGER,
    VASSAL
  tribute—HERIOT
fever—AGUE, ARDOR,
  DENGUE, ENECIA,
  PYREXIA
fez—BERET, BUSBY,
  CAFTAN, CAP,
  SHAKO, TARBOOSH,
  TURBAN
fiat—ACT, DECREE,
  EDICT, ORDER,
  SANCTION
fiber—BAST, HAMP,
  NOIL, RAMIE, SISAL,
  STRAND, THREAD

fickle—DIZZY,
  FAITHLESS, FALSE,
  UNSTABLE,
  VOLATILE
field—ACRE, ARENA,
  CROFT, GLEBE,
  GRID, LEA, RANGE,
  ROWEN
fiery—ANGRY, ARDENT,
  HOT, IGNEOUS,
  INTENSE,
  METTLESOME
fig—ELEME, ELEMI,
  FICO, PIPAL
fight—BATTLE, COMBAT,
  DUEL, FEUD, FRAY,
  MELEE, RIOT,
  SCRAP, SETTO,
  STRIVE
figure—BODY,
  CALCULATE,
  COMPUTE, DIGIT,
  DOLL, ENTAIL,
  FORM, SYMBOL,
  TYPE
figure of speech—
  ECPHONESIS,
  IRONY, LITOTES,
  METAPHOR, SIMILE,
  TROPE
filament—DOWL, HAIR,
  HARL, STRAND,
  THREAD
file—CABINET, DOSSIER,
  ENTER, FOLDER,
  LIST, QUANNET,
  ROLL, ROW, RUB
fill—CHOKE, DILATE,
  FEED, SATE,
  SATURATE, STUFF
fillet—ORLE, REGULA,
  RIBBON, SNOOD,
  SOLA, TAENIA
fillip—EXCITE, SNAP,
  STIMULUS
filly—COLT, FOAL, GIRL
film—BRAT, HAZE,
  LAYER, NEGATIVE,
  PATINA, PELLICLE,
  SCUM, VEIL, WEB

final—DECISIVE, LAST,
   ULTIMATE
finale—CLOSE, CODA,
   COMPLETION, END,
   ENDING, FINISH,
   SONG, SWAN,
   TERMINATION
finch—FRINGILLA,
   LINNET, REDPOLL
   SERIN, SISKIN,
   SPINK, TERIN
  American—
   CHEWINK,
   JUNCO, TOWHEE
canary-like—SERIN
copper—CHAFFINCH
  gold—DRAWBIRD
  North Africa—MORO
  yellow—SERIN, TARIN
find—DISCOVER,
   LOCATE
fine—AMERCE, DAINTY,
   KEEN, MULCT,
   NICE, SCOT, THIN
finger—DACTYL, DIGIT,
   POINTER
fingerprint mark—ARCH,
   LOOP, LUNULE,
   WHORL
finial—CANOPY, KNOT,
   TEE, TOP
fire—CHAR, DISCHARGE,
   FLAME, IGNIS,
   IGNITE, INFLAME,
   KINDLE, SHOOT
firearm—GAT, GUN,
   PIECE, RIFLE
fireman—STOKER, VAMP
fireplace—HEARTH,
   INGLE
firewood—BILLET,
   FAGGOT, LENA
fireworks—FIZGIGS,
   GIRANDOLE, GERB,
   RIPRAP, ROCKETS,
   SERPENTS
first—CHIEF, ERST,
   FOREMOST, INITIAL,
   MAIDEN. ORIGINAL,
   PRIMAL, PRIMUS

fish—ALBACORE,
   ALEWIFE, AWA,
   BASS, BARACUDA,
   ANCHOVY,
   BLACKFISH,
   BLENNY, BLUEFISH,
   BONITO. BLEAK,
   BLOWFISH, BREAM,
   BURGOT, CARP,
   CATFISH, CERO,
   CHUB, CISCO, COD,
   CUSP, DAB, DACE,
   DARTER, DRUM,
   DOGFISH, EEL,
   EELPOUT,
   FLOUNDER, FLUKE,
   GAR, GADOID,
   GOBY,
   GRAMPUS,
   GROUPER,
   HADDOCK, HAKE,
   HALIBUT, HERRING,
   IDE, KILLY,
   LING, LORO,
   MACKEREL,
   MARLIN, MINNOW,
   MOLA, MORAY,
   MULLET, OPAH,
   PARR, PERCH, PIKE,
   PICKEREL,
   PIRANHA,
   POMPANO, POUT,
   RAY, RENA,
   REMORA, ROACH,
   RUDD, SALMON,
   SARDINE, SCAD,
   SCROD, SCUP,
   SEABASS, SHAD,
   SERGEANT, SHARK,
   SMELT, SMOLT,
   SNAPPER, SOLE,
   SPET, SPOT, SPRAG
   SPRAT, STURGEON,
   TAI, TARPON,
   TENCH, TILEFISH,
   TROUT, TUNA,
   TUNNY, TURBOT,
   WAHOO, WALLEYE,
   WRASSE
  Amer. fresh

water—DARTER
Amer. hyodon
　(genus)—MOONEYE
aquatic
　mammal—MANATEE
arctic—BIB
bait—KILLY, LURE,
　PLUG, SPINNER,
　WORM
barracuda—SENNET,
　SPET
bin for salting—KENCH
bivalve—SCALLOP
bleak—BLAY
bonito—SKIPJACK
broken bellied—THOKE
brook trout—CHAR,
　CHARR
burbot—EELPOT, LOTA
butter—GUNNEL
butterfly—BENNIE
carangoid—CHAD,
　RUNNER, SCAD
caribe—PIRAYA
carp family—CHUB, IDE,
　LOCAH, RUD
cat (electric)—RAAD
catch—SHACK
cephaloptera—MANTA
chopped—CHEM
cigar—SCAD
climbing—ANABAS,
　SKIPPER
coal—PAAR
cobia—SERGEANT
cod—BACALAO, TORSK
cod-like—GADOID,
　CUSK, LING
condiment—PASTE
cow—MANATEE
crab and fiddler—UCA
Cuban—ESCOLAR,
　PALU
cuttle—SEPIA, SQUID
cyprinoid—BARBEL,
　CHI, DACE, ID, IDE,
　TENCH, UIT
devil—MANTA, RAY
dog—HOUND,
　SCYLLIUM

dolphin—COWFISH,
　INIA
East Indian—ARCHER,
　DARTER. DORAB,
　GOURAMI
edible—BASS, COD,
　HADDOCK, ID,
　LOACH, TAUTOG,
　TILE. TUNA,
　WEEVER, WRASSE
eel bright
　colored—MORAY,
　OPAH
eel conger—ELVER
eel marine—CONGER
eel like—APOD, LANT
eggs—CAVIAR, ROE
elasmobranch—
　SAWFISH
Europe—BARBEL,
　BOCES. DOREE,
　DORY, PICAREL,
　TENCH, TIRU
female—RAUN
flat—DAB, PLAICE,
　SKATE, SOLE,
　TURBOT
flying—SAURY
food—BAYA, CARP,
　CERO, GROUPER,
　HAKE, MEAGRE,
　MULLET, PLAICE,
　POMPANO,
　SARDINE, SCUP,
　SESELE, SHAD,
　SMELT, TARPON,
　TROUT, TUNA,
　WRASSE
fresh water—ANABAS,
　BURBOT, CRAPPIE,
　DARTER, LOACH,
　REDEYE. TROUT
frog—ANGLER
game—MARLIN,
　SALMON, SWORD,
　TARPON, TROUT
ganoid, large—DIPNOI,
　GAR. STURGEON
gig—SPEAR
globe—DIODON

gobioid—LOTER
gobylike—DRAGONET
grampus—ORC
grunt—CREAKER,
   RONCO
half beak—IHI
hawk—OSPREY
herring—ALEWIFE,
   ALOSA, SPRAT
herring barrel—CADE
herring
   family—PILCHARD
herring-like—
   ANCHOVY, CISCO
hook—GAFF, SPROAT
hook money—LARI
hound—GARFISH
jelly—ACALEPH,
   MEDUSA
kind—ORFE, ORF,
   ROCK, THOSSE
ladder—DAM
little—MINNOW,
   SARDINE, SMELT
mackerel—TONNY,
   TUNNY
marine—BLENNY,
   CHOPA, CUSK,
   GRUNT, LING,
   MENHADEN, SCUP,
   TARPON
maskalonge—LONGE
milk—ANGED, AWA,
   SABALO
mollusk—OCTOPUS,
   SQUID
mutton—SAMA
net—FYKE, SAGENE,
   SEINE, TRAWL
net bagging—BUNT
net support—METER
New Zealand—IHI
ornamental—
   PARADISE
oyster—TAUTOG
parrot—LANIA, LIRO,
   SCAR
perch-like—DARTER
pike—DORE, GED,
   LUCE

pike-like—
   ARAPAIMA, GAR,
   LUCE, ROBALO
place—WARREN
porgy—SCUP
pork—SISI
Polynesian tagalog—ISDA
porpoise—DOLPHIN,
   INIA
poison—FUGU
ray—DOM, MANTA,
   SEPHEN, SKATE
red—CLEE, FATHEAD
redmouth—GRUNT
remora—PEGA
river ascending—
   ANADROMOUS
rock (Calif.)—RENA,
   REINA
rod reel—PIRN
sailor's choice—PORGY
salmon
   (adult)—GULLING
salmon (Jap.)—MASU

salmon (second
   year)—SPROD
salmon
   (young)—ALEVIN,
   PARR
salmonoid—POWAN,
   TROUT
sandshark—BONEDOG
sardine (India)—LILE
sauce—ALEC,
   ANCHOVY, SOY
scabbard—GANOID
shad (Europe)—ALOSE
shadlike—ALEWIFE
shark—MAKO, TOPE
shark family—ANGEL
sheat—SOM
shell—ABALONE,
   LIMPET, SCALLOP
shiner—ROACH
shiny—GANOID
silvery
   (Samoan)—SESELE
slender—GAR, SAURIES,
   SAURY

smelt family—CAPELIN
snapper (black fin)—SESI
soap—JABON
soup—CHOWDER
S. Amer.—ACARA,
    CARIBE
spade—PORGY
sparoid—NAPA,
    PORGY, SAR,
    SARGO, TAI
spear—GIG
sperm—MILT
spotted trout—MALMA
squirrel—MARIAN
sturgeon—STERLET
surf—ALFIONA
synodontoid—TIRU
tail—ANALFIN
tarpon family
    (genus)—ELOPS
teleost—APODA, EEL
tench—TINCA
terrapins
    (genus)—EMYDEA,
    EMYS
threadfin—BARBUDO
trap—FYKE, WEIR
toad—SAPO
tropical—
    BARRACUDA,
    CHRONID, PACO,
    ROBALO, TYNOSA
trout family—CHAR,
    EQUASSA
whale or
    sturgeon—BELUGA
whale order—CETE
whiting—GWYNIAD
wolf—LUPIN
young—ALEVIN, FRY,
    PARR
fisherman—ANGLER,
    EELER, SEINER,
    SQUAM
fish hook—ANGLE, BARB,
    SPROAT
fishing—ANGLING,
    SNELLING, SPILLET,
    WHALING
fissure—CHINK, CLEFT,

CRACK, CRANNY,
    CREVICE, LEAK,
    RENT, RIFT, RIMA,
    SEAM, SLIT, SPLIT
fist of hand—NEAF, NEIF,
    NIEVE
fit—ADAPT, APT,
    COMPETENT,
    CORRECT, DUE,
    ELIGIBLE, GEE,
    MEET, PAT, SPASM,
    SPELL, TANTRUM,
    TEMPER
fix—ADJUST, AMEND,
    CORRECT,
    DILEMMA, MEND,
    POSED, REPAIR, SET,
    SETTLE
fixed allowance—RATION
    charge—FEE, RATE,
    RENTAL, TAX
    course—ROTE
    ratio—RATE
    routine—RUT
    salary—STIPEND
    time—ERA, FAST, RUT,
    TERM
    value on—ASSESS
flag—BANDEROLE,
    BANNER, BUNTING,
    DROOP, ENSIGN,
    GONFALON,
    GUIDON,
    SIGN,
    PENNANT, PENNON,
    STANDARD, WEAK
flagon—CANTEEN,
    CARAFE,
    DEMIJOHN, EWER,
    JUG, STOUR
flail—BEAT, SWINGLE,
    THRASH, THRESH
flaky—LAMINAR, SCALY,
    SQUAMOUS
flambeau—CRESSET,
    TORCH
flank—LEER, LOIN, SIDE,
    THIGH
flannel—LANA, LANO
flap—FLUTTER, LOMA,

SLAT

flask—BETTY, CANTEEN,
CARAFE, CRUSE,
EWER, FLAGON,
OLPE

flat—APARTMENT,
BANAL, BROKE,
EVEN, INSIPID,
LEVEL. LOW,
MOLLE, PLANE,
SHOAL, SIMPLE,
STALE, PRONE,
TAME. VAPID

flatter—ADULATE,
BLAND. CARESS,
CHARM, BYE, OIL,
PALP. PLEASE,
SMOOTH

flattery—BLARNEY,
BULL. BUNK,
CAJOLERY, OIL,
PALAVER

flavor—AROMA, ANISE,
FRAGRANCE,
GUSTO,
SALT, SAUCE,
SAVOR, TANG,
TASTE

flax—CARD, HURDS, LIN,
LINEN, LINT, RET

flea—CHIGOE, CYCLOPS,
PULEX

flee—AVOID, ELOPE,
ESCAPE, HASTEN,
RUN, SHUN, VANISH

fleece—CHEAT,
DESPOIL, MULCT,
NAP, PILE, SHEAR,
SKIN, SWINDLE,
WOOL

fleshy—ADIPOSE,
CORPULENT, FAT,
OBESE, PLUMP

flex—BEND, CURVE,
DEFLECT

flexed—BENT, CURVED,
DEFLECTED,
TURNED, TWISTED

flexible—ELASTIC,
LIMBER, LISSOME,
LITHE, LITHESOME,
PLIABLE, PLIANT,
WILLOWY

flicker—BLAZE, FLARE,
GLARE, WAVER,

flight—ABSCOND,
AVIATION, EXODUS,
HEGIRA. SOARING,
VOLITATION

flinch—BLENCH, FEAR,
QUAIL, RECOIL,
SWERVE, WINCE,
WONDE

flint—CLINT, CHERT,
SILEX

float—BUOY, CORK,
DRIFT, LURE, RAFT,
RIDE, SAIL, SELL,
SWIM, WAFT,
WATCH

floating—AWASH,
NATANT

flock—BANK, BEVY,
COVEY, HERD,
HIRSEL, GAGGLE,
POD, SEDGE, SKEIN,
RAFT

flog—BALEISE, BEAT,
CANE, CAT,
LARRUP, LASH,
TAN, TROUNCE,
WALE, WELT, WHIP,
YANK

flood—BORE, CATARACT,
CATACLYSM,
DELUGE, EAGRE,
FRESHET,
INUNDATE,
OVERFLOW, SEA,
SPATE, TORRENT

floodgate—HATCH,
SLUICE

floor—BOTTOM, DOWN,
PAVE, OVERTHROW,
STORY

florid—ORNATE, RED
RUDDY

flounder—DAB. FAIL,
GROVEL, PLAICE,
TOSS. TURBOT,

WELTER
flourish—BLOOM, BOOM,
    BRANDISH,
    FANFARE, GROW,
    PARAPH, PROSPER,
    ROULADE, THRIVE,
    WAVE. WIELD
flow—ABUNDANCE,
    ISSUE, OOZE, POUR,
    RECOVER. RUN,
    SPOUT, STREAM,
    WELL
flower—algae
    (genus)—NOSTOC
anemone (sea)—CRASSE
apetalus
    (genus)—TREMA
aromatic—CAMOMILE
august—POPPY
avens (yellow)—
    BENNET
border—PLATBAND
branch—SPRAY
buckwheat (fragrant)—TITI
bud—GEMMA, KNOT
burr—TEASEL
butterfly
    lily—MARIPOSA
cardinal—LOBELIA
center—EYE
cluster—UMBEL,
    CORYMB, CYME,
    RACEME
delicate
    pink—RHODORA
dry—AZALEA
dust—POLLEN
Egypt (sacred)—LOTUS
emblem of Wales—LEEK
envelope—PERIANTH
erica (genus)—HEATH
extract—ATTAR, OTTO
fancier—ROSARIAN
felwort—GENTIAN
field—GOWAN
fragrant—JASMINE
full bloom—ANTHESIS
garden—FREESIA,
    GREENERY
genus—ADONIS,

ROSA, VIOLA
head—PANICLE,
    TEASEL
heath—ERICA
hibiscus (E.
    Indies)—CAMAS
indigo—ANIL
iris—ORRIS
(Jap.)—UDO
jasmine (Arab.)—BELA
leaf—BRACT, PETAL
lily—ARUM, LOTUS,
    SEGO
marigold—COWSLIP
meadow—BLUET
nightshade—TRILLIUM
orchid—ARETHUSA
pansy—PENSE
part—ANTHER, BRACT,
    COROLLA,
    PERICARP, PETAL,
    PISTIL, SEPAL,
    STAMEN
passion—MAYPOP
pinks—SILENE
pistil—CARPEL
ragwort—JACOBY
reseda—MIGNONETTE
rootstock—TARO
rose of sharon—LOTUS
seed—HERB. OVULE
sheath—SPATHE
sifter—BOLTER
spicule (star-
    shaped)—ASTER
spike—AMENT, SPADIX
spring—HYACINTH
stalk—KEMP,
    PEDUNCLE,
    PETIOLE, SCAPE
stand—EPERGNE
starwort—ASTER
(Swiss)—EDELWEISS
(Syrian)—RETEM
syringa—LILAC
turban—TULIP
unfading—AMARANTH
water lily—LOTUS
white weed—DAISY
willow bed—OSIERIE

wind—ANEMONE
wood sorrel—OXALIS
fluctuate—SWAY, VEER,
　　VIBRATE
fluid—AIR, FLUX,
　　FLUME, GORSE,
　　LIQUID, SAP, STEAM
flume—CHUTE, GORGE,
　　RACE, SLUICE
flush—BLUSH, ELATE,
　　EVEN, REDDEN
fly—AVIATE, FLIT,
　　GNAT, HASTEN,
　　SOAR, TSETSE,
　　WHEW, WHIR, WING
foam—BARM, BOIL,
　　FROTH, LATHER,
　　RAGE, SCUM,
　　SPUME, SUDS
fodder—ALFALFA,
　　ENSILAGE, GRASS,
　　HAY, SILAGE,
　　STOVER
fog—AEROSOL, BRUME,
　　HAAR, HAZE, MIST,
　　OBSCURE, ROKE,
　　SMOG, SMOKE,
　　VAPOR
fold—CREASE, CRIMP,
　　EMBRACE, FLAP,
　　LAP, LOOP, PLAIT,
　　PLEAT, PLICATE,
　　PLY
follow—CHASE, DOG,
　　ENSUE, HEED,
　　IMITATE, OBEY,
　　TAG, TAIL, TRACE,
　　TRAIL
follower—ADHERENT,
　　APER, BUFF,
　　DEVOTEE, DISCIPLE,
　　FAN
folly—DOTAGE,
　　LUNACY, SIN
fond—ATTACHED, DOTE,
　　DOTING, LOVING,
　　PARENTAL
fondness—AFFECTION,
　　LOVE, TASTE
food—ALIMENT, BREAD,

DIET, FARE, MEAT,
　　NOURISHMENT,
　　NUTRIMENT, ORT,
　　PAP, PEMMICAN,
　　PABULUM, VIANDS,
　　VICTUAL
fool—ASS, DECEIVE,
　　CLOWN, DOLT,
　　DOTARD, DUNCE,
　　DUPE, IDIOT,
　　JESTER, NINNY,
　　RIDICULE, SPOOF,
　　ZANY
foolish—ASININE, DAFT,
　　DAFFY, HARISH,
　　INEPT, MAD,
　　UNWISE
foot—ANAPEST,
　　IAMB, IAMBUS,
　　PAW, SOLE, TOTAL
foot and mouth
　　disease—MURRAIN
football field—GRID
footed (large)—MEGAPOD
footless—APOD, APODAL,
　　FREE, NOMADIC
footlike part—PEDATE,
　　PES
footman—FLUNKY,
　　LACKEY, SERVANT,
　　VALET
footpad—
　　HIGHWAYMAN,
　　THUG
footprint—STEP, TRACE,
　　TRACK
footstalk—PEDICEL
forage—FOOD, MARAUD
　　MILLET, PLUNDER,
　　RAID
foray—INCURSION,
　　INROAD, PILLAGE,
　　RAID
forbid—BAN, DEBAR,
　　DENY, ENJOIN,
　　TABU
force—COMPEL, DINT,
　　DURESS, DRIVE,
　　ENERGY, IMPEL,
　　POWER, PRESSURE,

URGE, VIM, VIS
foreboding—AUGURY,
MENACE, OMEN
forecasting—ORACULAR
forecaster—DOPESTER,
NOSTRADAMUS,
SEER, TOUT
forefather—
PROGENITOR
forefoot—PAW, PUG
forefront—VAN,
VANGUARD,
foregoing—ABOVE, PAST,
PREFIX
forehead—BROW,
SINCIPUT
foreign—ENDEMIC,
EPIGENE, FORANE,
PEREGRINE
foreigner—ALIEN,
GRINGO, HAOLE,
TRAMONTANE
forerun—ANTECEDE,
HERALD
forest—ARDEN, GAPO,
GLADE, GROVE,
SILVA, WOLD
foretell—AUGUR, BODE,
FORECAST,
PREDICT, PRESAGE,
PROPHESY, READ,
forever—AYE,
CONTINUAL,
ETERNE
forge—IMITATE, MAKE,
MINT, SMITH
forgetfulness—
AMNESTY, LETHE
fork—DIVIDE, GRAIP,
PRONG, TINE
forked—FURCATE
form—CAST, CEREMONY,
CHIC, CONTOUR,
CREATE, FRAME,
MAKE, MOLD,
RITUAL, SHAPE,
STYLE, VARIETY
formal—CEREMONIAL,
CONVENTIONAL,
DISTANT, PRECISE,

REGULAR, STIFF,
SOLEMN
formation—FILE, FORM,
RANK, STRUCTURE
former—ERST, EX,
LATE, OLD, OLDER,
ONCE, PASSED,
PREVIOUS,
QUONDAM,
SOMETIME, WHILOM
formerly—AT ONE TIME,
AGO, ERSTWHILE,
NEE, ONCE,
ONETIME, THEN
formless—ANIDIAN,
ARUPA
formula—LAW, LURRY,
MAXIM, RITUAL,
RULE
fortification—ABATIS,
RAVELIN, REDAN,
REDOUBT
fortress—ALCAZAR,
BASTILE, CASTLE,
CITADEL, DONJON,
FORT, KEEP,
RAMPART
fortunate—DEXTER,
FAUST, HAPPY,
LUCKY
fortune—CHANCE,
DOOM, ESTATE,
FATE, HAP, LOT,
STARS
foster—BREED, CHERISH,
CULTIVATE, FOOD,
NURSE, PROMOTE,
REAR
foul—DIRTY, RANK,
UNFAIR
foundation—BASE, BASIS,
BASIC, BED,
BEDROCK, BOTTOM,
ROOT
fountain—AQUA, FOUNT,
GENESIS, HEAD,
SPA, SPRING, SYKE,
WELL
fowl—CAPON, COCK,
DOVE, GOOSE, HEN,

POULT

fox—CUB, REYNARD,
TOD, VIXEN
(African)—ASSE,
FENNEC
(Asiatic)—ADIVE
female—VIXEN
killer—VULPICIDE
like—VULPINE
(Russian)—CORSAK,
KARAGAN
(Scot)—TOD
(variant)—RENARD
fraction—BIT, DECIMAL,
PART, SEGMENT
fragment—BIT, CHIP,
CRUMB, ORT, RELIC,
SCRAP, SHARD,
SHRED, SNATCH,
SNIP, REMNANT,
TATTER, WISP
fragrant—AROMATIC,
ODOROUS, OLENT,
REDOLENT, SWEET,
SPICED
frame—ADJUST, BIN,
CARCASS, CHASSIS,
COMPOSE, DEVISE,
FASHION, FORGE,
FORM, RACK, SHAPE
franchise—GRANT,
LICENSE, SOCAGE,
VOTE
frank—BLUNT, CANDID,
FREE, HONEST,
MARK, OPEN
fraud—FAKE, RUSE,
SHAM, WILE
freckle—LENTIGO, SPOT
free—ABSOLVE, CLEAR,
DELIVER, GRATIS,
LAX, LIBERATE,
LIBRE, LOOSE,
MANUMIT,
RELEASE, RESCUE,
RID
freedman—THANE
freedom—IMMUNITY,
LATITUDE, LIBERTY,
LICENSE,

UNRESTRICTED
frenzy—AMOK, BERSERK,
ENRAGED,
FRANTIC,
FRENETIC, FUROR
frequent—HABITUAL,
OFT, PERSISTENT
fresh—BREEZY, BRIGHT,
NEW, NOVEL, RAW
freshet—FLOOD, SPATE,
STREAM, TIDE,
TORRENT
freshman—FROSH,
NOVICE, PLEBE
fret—ABRADE, AGITATE,
ANNOY, CHAFE,
CORRODE, FUME,
FUSS, HERPES,
IRRITATE, NAG,
STEW, VEX, WHELK,
WORRY
friar—ABBOT, FRA,
FRATER, LISTER,
MINOR, MONK
friction—CHAFE,
ERASURE, RUB
friday—FRIGGA (Norse)
friend—ALLY, AMI,
AMIE, AMICUS,
CHUM,
COMPANION,
CRONY, FOLK,
QUAKER
friendly—AMICABLE,
KIND, KINDLY
fright—ALARM, AWE,
FEAR, FRAY, GHAST,
OGRE, PANIC,
TERROR
frill—FURBELOW, JABOT,
RUCHE, RUFFLE
fringe—BORDER,
EDGING, LOMA
frisk—BRISK, CAPER,
FROLIC, GAMBOL,
SEARCH
frog—ANURA, ANURAN,
PEEPER,
POLLYWOG, RANI,
RANA

frolic—BINGE, CAPER,
    FUN, GAMBOL,
    FRISK, LARK, PLAY,
    PRANK, ROMP,
    SPREE
front—FACADE, FACE,
    FORE, FORNENT,
    OBVERSE, PROW,
    VAN
frontier—BORDER,
    BOUNDARY
frost—FOAM, HOAR, ICE,
    RIME
frown—GLOOM,
    GLOWER, LOWER,
    SCOWL
frozen—CHILLY, GELID,
    GLACE, ICY
fruit—ACHENE, APPLE,
    BANANA,
    CHERRY, DATE,
    GAGE, OLIVE,
    ORANGE, PAPAW,
    PAPAYA, PEACH,
    PEAR, PEPO, PLUM,
    POME, TANGERINE,
    TOMATO
frugal—CHARY,
    PROVIDENT,
    SAVING, SPARE,
    THRIFTY
fry (lightly)—SAUTE
    (out fat)—RENDER
frying pan—SKILLET,
    SPIDER
fugitive—DESERTER,
    EMIGRE, EXILE,
    FLEEING,
    ITINERANT,
    REFUGEE,
    RUNAGATE
fugue—DIATONIC,
    THEMES, TONAL
full—AMPLE,
    BOUFFANT, LADEN,
    OROTUND,
    PLENARY, REPLETE,
    SATED, SRO
fume—ANGER, INCENSE,
    RAGE, RAVE, REEK,
    RUFF, SMOKE,
    STEAM, VAPOR
fun—CHAFF, GAME,
    GIG, JEST, JOKE,
    PLAY, SPORT
function—ACTION, DUTY,
    FESTIVITY,
    OCCASION
funeral—EXEQUIES,
    OBSEQUIES
    attendant—MUTE
    car—HEARSE
    hymn—DIRGE
    notice—OBIT
    oration—ELOGE,
        EULOGY
    pile—PYRE
    poem—ELEGY
    pyre—PILE, SUTTEE
    song—DIRGE, ELEGY,
        NENIA, REQUIEM,
        THRENODY
    stand—BIER
fur—FITCH, KARAKUL,
    PELAGE, PELT,
    PELTRY, PLATINA,
    SKIN, VAIR
furnace—CALDRON,
    FORGE, HEATER,
    KILN, OVEN,
    SMELTER
furnish—AFFORD,
    CATER, ENDOW,
    EQUIP, INDUE,
    LEND, PROVIDE,
    RENDER, RIG
furniture—EQUIPAGE,
    GOODS, GRAITH
furor—CRAZE, FLURRY,
    FRENZY, MANIA,
    RAGE, TUMULT
furrow—GROOVE,
    INTRENCH, LINE,
    PLOW, RUT, STITCH,
    STRIA
furrowed—RIVOSE,
    RUTTED, SULCATE
further—ABET, AID, AND,
    MORE, PROMOTE,
    REMOTE, YET

furtive—ARCH, COVERT,
SKULKING, SLY,
SNEAKY,
STEALTHY, WARY
fury—ANGER, FRENZY,
IRE, RAGE, WRATH
fuse—ANNEAL,
LIQUEFY, MELT,
MIX, SMELT,
SOLDER
fuss—ADO, BOTHER,
BUSTLE, FIKE,
FRET, FUME, TODO
futile—IDLE, OTIOSE,
USELESS, VAIN
future—STILL, TO BE,
YET

-G-

gall—BILE, CHAFE, FELL,
HARASS, IRRITATE,
SOW, SPITE, VEX
gallant—BRAVE,
CAVALIER,
CICISBEO, HERO,
KNIGHT, SPARK
galleon—ARGOSY,
gabelle—EXCISE, TAX
gable—AILERON, PINION
gad—GALLIVANT,
GOAD, ROVE
Gaelic—CELTIC, ERSE,
SCOTCH
gaff—GAMBLE, HOOK,
SPAR, SPUR
gag—CHOKE, HOAX,
JOKE, RETCH,
SILENCE
gaily—MERRILY
gain—ACQUIRE,
ADVANCE,
APPROACH,
ATTAIN, EARN, GET,
IMPROVE, LUCRE,
NET, REAP, OBTAIN,
PROFIT
gainsay—DENY, DISPUTE,
FORBID, IMPUGN,
OPPOSE
gait—AMBLE, CANTER,
GALLOP, LOPE,
PACE, RACK,
SHAMBLE, STEP,
STRIDE, TROT,
WALK
gaiter—PUTTEE, SPAT,
STRAD
gala—FESTAL, FESTIVE,
FESTIVITY, FIESTA,
POMP
CARACK, CARRACK
gallery—ALCOVE,
ARCADE, BALCONY,
LOFT, LOGGIA,
PIAZZA, VERANDA
galley—KITCHEN, PROOF,
TRIREME
gambler—DICER,
PLAYER, SHARK,
SHILL
gambling—GAMING,
WAGERING
  house—CASINO
gambol—CAPER,
CURVET, FRISK,
FROLIC, ROMP
game—CONTEST,
DIVERSION,
GAMBLE, FUN, JEST,
LAME, MOCKERY,
PLAY, PLUCKY,
SPORT
gamin—ARAB,
MUDLARK, SERF,
TAD, URCHIN
gammon—BACON, BOSH,
HAM
gamut—RANGE, SCALE
gander—GOOSE,
WANDER
gangster—GOON, THIEF,
THUG, WHYO, YEGG
gap—BREACH, CHASM,
CLEFT, FAULT,
HIATUS, LACUNA,
NOTCH, OPENING,
SHARD, SPLIT

gape—DEHISCE, OGLE,
OPE, OSCITATE,
YAWN
garden—CULTIVATE,
EDEN, HOE, PATCH
garland—ANADEM,
CHAPLET, FESTOON,
LEI, ROSARY,
WREATH
garlic root—MOLY,
RAMSON
garment—ABA, APPAREL,
DRESS, ROBE,
STOLE, VESTURE
garnet—APLOME,
ESSONITE,
HESSONITE,
MELANITE, PYROPE,
RED
garnish—ADORN,
BEDECK,
DECORATE,
EMBELLISH, TRIM
garret—ATTIC,
COCKLOFT, LOFT,
MANSARD
gas—FREON, NEON,
PETROL, PROPANE,
RADON
gate—BAB, DAR,
ENTRANCE,
PASSAGEWAY,
PORTAL, POSTERN
gateway—DAR, GOPURA,
TORAN, TORANA
gather—ACQUIRE,
AMASS, ASSEMBLE,
BREW, COLLECT,
FOLD, FULL,
GARNER, GLEAN,
REAP, SHIRR
gaunt—BONY,
HAGGARD, LANK,
RAWBONED
gauze—CREPE, HAZE,
LENO, LISSE
gazelle—AHU, ARIEL,
CHIKARA, CORA,
CORINNE, DAMA,
GOA, KEVEL, KUDU,
MOHR, ORYX,
SPRINGBOK
gear—CAM, CLOTHING,
HARNESS, OUTFIT,
RIG, TACKLE,
TOOLS, TRAPPINGS
gelatin—AGAR, ASPIC,
COLLOID
gem—AGATE, BERYL,
DIAMOND,
JADE, JEWEL,
ONYX, OPAL,
PEARL, RUBY,
SAPPHIRE, TOPAZ
facet—CULET
gender—BREED, BEGET,
ENGENDER,
NEUTER, SEX
genealogy—ACCOUNT,
HISTORY, LINEAGE,
PEDIGREE, TREE
general—COMMON,
GROSS, USUAL,
VAGUE
gentle—DOCILE, EASY,
KIND, MEEK, MILD,
SOFT, TAME,
TENDER
gentleman—KNIGHT,
MISTER, SAHIB,
SENOR, SIR,
YOUNKER
genuflect—CURTSY,
KNEEL
genuine—REAL,
SIMONPURE,
SINCERE, STERLING,
TRUE
geometric body—CONE,
CUBE, LUNE,
PRISM, PYRAMID
geometrical—CIRCLE,
ELLIPSE,
RECTANGLE,
RHOMBUS, SHAPE,
SQUARE
germ—BACTERIA, BUD,
MICROBE, SEED,
SPORE, VIRUS
gesture—ACT, BEAR,

BEHAVE, GEST,
MOTION
get—ACQUIRE, BEGET,
BETAKE, CAUSE,
CAPTURE, DERIVE,
EARN, GAIN,
OBTAIN, PROCURE,
RECEIVE, WIN
ghastly—CADAVEROUS,
HORRIBLE, LURID,
PALLID, SHOCKING
ghost—BOGIE, DAEMON,
EIDOLON, HAUNT,
KER, LARVA,
PHANTOM, SHADE,
SPECTRE, SPOOK,
WRAITH
giant—ANAK, ETEN,
HUGE, MAMMOTH,
OGRE, TITAN,
TROLL
gibbon—APE, LAR,
SIAMANG,
WOUWOU
gift—ALMS, BOON,
DONATION, ENAM,
ENDOW, LEGACY,
PRESENT, TALENT
giggle—CHUCKLE,
SNICKER, TEHEE,
TITTER
gilded—ADORNED, GILT
gill—COLLAR, WATTLE
gin—NET, SLOE, SNARE,
TRAP, TRICK
giraffe—CAMELOPARD
girasol—OPAL,
SUNFLOWER
girder—BEAM, BINDER,
TRUSS
girdle—BAND, BELT,
CEST, CINCTURE,
CINGLE, CORSET,
OBI, SASH, ZONE
girl—DAMSEL, LASS,
LASSIE, MAIDEN,
MINX, MISS, SIS
gist—CHAT, CORE, CRUX,
ESSENCE, NUB,
PITCH, PITH, POINT,

PURPORT, TREND
give—BESTOW, CONFER,
CONTRIBUTE,
DONATE, HAND,
IMPART, PRESENT,
PROFFER, RENDER
glacial—ICY
deposit—ESKER,
MORAINE, PLACER
fragment—SERAC
hills—KAMES
ice—FIRN, NEVE
laminated structure
—CIPELLINO
ridge—ESKAR, ESKER,
KAME, OS, OSAR
silt—MORAINE
snow—NEVE
waste
deposit—ALLUVIUM
glad—DELIGHTED,
ELATED, FAIN,
GRATIFIED, HAPPY,
JOYFUL, MERRY,
PLEASED
glad tidings—EVANGEL,
GOSPEL, JOY, NEWS
glade—DELL, GAP,
VALLEY
gladly—FAIN, FREELY,
LIEF, READILY
glance—EYE, GLEAM,
LEER, OGLE
gland—CAROTID,
LYMPH
glass—BEAKER, BOTTLE,
GOBLET, LENS,
MIRROR,
PHOSPHATES,
TUMBLER
glaze—COAT, ENAMEL,
VENEER
gleam—BEAM, FLASH,
GLOW, RAY, SHEEN
glide—SAIL, SKID, SKIP,
SLIDE, SLIP,
SLITHER
globule—BLOB, DROP,
MINIM, PILL, TEAR
gloomy—DARK, DIM,

DOLESOME, DREAR,
DREARY, EERIE,
GLUM, LURID,
MOROSE, MURKY,
SAD, STYGIAN,
TENEBROUS,
WAN
glorify—ADORE, BLESS,
EXALT, LAUD,
PRAISE, WORSHIP
glory—AUREOLA, ECLAT,
FAME, HALO,
HONOR, KUDOS,
PRIDE, RENOWN,
SPLENDOR
gloss—EXCUSE, LUSTER,
LUSTRE, PALLIATE,
SHEEN
glossy—GLACE,
LUSTROUS, NITID,
SHEENY, SHINY,
SILKEN, SLEEK,
SLICK
glove—CESTUS, CUFF,
GANT, GAUNTLET,
MIT, MITT, SUEDE
glowing—BURNING,
CANDENT,
CANDESCENT,
RADIANT
glucose—DEXTROSE,
glut—CLOY, FEED,
PAUNCH, SATE,
SATIATE, SURFEIT
glutton—
GORMANDIZER,
gnaw—CORRODE, EAT,
NIBBLE, PECK
gnome—BOGIE, GOBLIN,
IMP, MAXIM, NIS,
SPRITE
gnu—ANTELOPE
go—BETAKE, DEPART,
FARE, GAE, GANG,
LEAVE, SALLY,
WEND
goad—ANKUS, EGG,
PIQUE, PROD, SPUR
goal—AIM, AMBITION,
END, FATE, HOME,

MECCA, META,
OBJECT, TARGET
goat—ALPACA, BEZOAR,
GORAL, JEMLAN,
TAHR
antelope—CHAMOIS,
SEROW
bezoar—PASAN
female—CAPRA
goblet—CHALICE, CUP,
GLASS, HANAPER,
SKULL, TASS,
TUMBLER
goblin—BARGHEST,
BHUT, BOGIE, ELF,
GNOME, OUPHE,
SPRITE, TROLL
god—FATHER, SPONSOR
goggler—SCAD
gold--AUR, AURUM,
GILT, ORO
golden—AUREATE,
AURIC, YELLOW
golf approach
shot—RUNUP
club—BRASSIE,
BULGER, CLEEK,
DRIVER, HOSEL,
IRON, MASHIE,
MIDIRON, NIBLICK,
SPOON, PUTTER,
SOCKET
course—LINKS
course parts—FAIRWAY,
GREEN, TEE, TRAP
hazard—TRAP
mount—TEE
obstacle—BUNKER
position—STANCE
score—BOGEY, PAR,
STROKE
shot—CHIP, DRIVE,
PUTT, SCLAFF
stroke—BAFF, CHIP,
DRIVE, FOOZLE,
PUTT, SHOT, SLICE,
SCLAFF
term—ACE, BAFF,
BOGEY, CHIP,
DIVOT, EAGLE, PAR,

PUTT, SCLAFF,
SLICE, TEE, TRAP
gone—AGO, LOST,
NAPOO, OFF, PAST
good—AMPLE,
AGREEABLE, BEAU,
BON. PLEASANT,
PROPER, UP, VALID,
WEAL
goods—FEE, JETSAM,
WARES, WRACK
goon—ROUGH, THUG
goose—ANSER,
BERNICLE, BRANT,
GREYLAG, SOLAN
gore—BLOOD, CRUOR,
GUSSET, PIERCE,
STAB
gorge—BOLT, CANYON,
CHASM, GLUT,
POUCH, RAVINE,
SATE, STRID
Gorgon—EURYALE,
STHENO
gorse—FURZE, JUNIPER
gospel—DOCTRINE,
EVANGEL, SPELL,
TIDINGS
gossip—CAT, CHAT,
CHITCHAT, CLAVER,
NORATE,
ONDIT, RUMOR,
SLANDER, TATTLE
gourd—CALABASH,
CUCURBIT, FLASK,
MELON, PEPO,
SQUASH
gourmand—EPICURE,
GLUTTON,
gourmet—EPICURE,
TASTER
govern—BRIDLE,
CONTROL, DIRECT,
LEAD, REGULATE,
REIGN, RULE, RUN
government—POLITY,
REGIMEN, SWAY
governor—DYNAST,
PILOT, REGENT,
VICEROY

gown—FROCK,
SOUTANE, SULTANE
grace—ADORN, CHARM,
ENHANCE, ESTE,
FAVOR. GARB,
HONOR
graces—AGLAIA,
EUPHROSYNE,
THALIA
mother—AEGLE
graceful—EASY,
ELEGANT, FEAT,
SYLPH
graft—IMP, INARCH, ICE
grain—ATOM, CEREAL,
CORN, GRANULATE,
IOTA, KERNEL, OAT,
WHIT
beard—ARISTA, AWN
black—URD
bristle—AWN
cereal—BRAN, OAT,
RICE, RYE,
WHEAT
disease—ICTERUS,
SMUT
husk—BRAN, GLUME
refuse—PUG
shock—COP
sorghum—HEGARI,
MILO
stalk—STRAW
grampus—ORC, ORCA,
WHALE
granary—BIN, GOLA,
GRANGE, LOFT,
SILO
grand—AUGUST, EPIC,
GREAT, HOMERIC
grandchild—OY, OYE
grandfather—AIEL,
PATRIARCH
(pert. to)—AVAL,
AVITAL
grandfather's grandfather
—TRESAYLE
grandmother—AVIA,
BELDAM,
GRANDAM
grandson—NEPOTE

grant—ADMIT, ALLOW,
  APPANAGE,
  APPEASE, BESTOW,
  CEDE, CONFER,
  ENAM, GIFT, LEND,
  LOAN, PERMIT,
  YIELD
grape—ACINI, ACINUS,
  CATAWBA,
  CONCORD,
  DELAWARE,
  ISABELLA,
  MALAGA, MUSCAT,
  NIAGARA, TOKAY,
  UVA
  body—CORESE
conserve—UVATE
  disease—COLEUR,
    ESCA, MELANOSE
  dried—RAISIN
  drink—WINE
  fruit—POMELO,
    SHADDOCK
  juice—DIBS, MUST,
    SAPA, STUM
  like—UVIC
parasite—PROCRIS
pomace—RAPE
preserve—UVATE
refuse—MARC
seeds—ACINI
  stone—ACINI
  sugar—DEXTROSE,
    MALTOSE
  sun dried—PASA
  vine disease—ERINOSE
  white—NIAGARA
graphite—LEAD,
  PLUMBAGO, SOOT
grapple—ATTACK, BIND,
  CLUTCH, FASTEN,
  LOCK, KNIT,
  WRESTLE
grappling iron—CRAMPON,
  GRAPNEL
grasp—FIST, GRAB,
  HENT, HOLD, SEIZE
grass—FODDER, GRAMA,
  GRAZE, HERB,
  PASTURE, POA,

REED, RYE, SEDGE,
  SPART, SWARD
Amer.—GAMA,
  RYE, SESAME
arrow—ESPARTO
Asiatic—COIX
Austrian
  beach—MARRAM
bamboo-like—REED
barn—ANKEE
beach—MAT
Bengal—MILLET
Bermuda—DOOB
blade—SPEAR
blue june—POA
bract—PALEA
bull—GAMA
burden's—REDTOP
carpet—SMUT
cattail—TIMOTHY
cereal—MILLET, OAT,
  RICE, RYE
cloth plant—RAMIE
coarse—GAMA
corn—KAFFIR, SEDGE
couch—BROME
country—VELDT
  covered earth—SOD
  creeping beard—FESCUE
  darnel—TARE
  devil's—COUCH
  ditch—ENALID
  dried—HAY
  edible—GRAIN
  esparto—ALFA
  feather—STIPA
  flyaway—BENT
  forage—MILLET,
    REDTOP
  gama—SESAME
  goose—LOVEMAN,
    SPEAR
  Guatemala—TEOSINTE
  hunger—FOXTAIL
husk—GLUME
  Indian cereal—RAGEE
  jointed stem—CULM
  Kentucky blue—POA
  kind—BARLEY,
    BROME, EEL, GAMA,

NARD, TAPE
leaf—BLADE
lemon—COCKSPUR
Louisiana—BENA
lyme—HASSOCK
marsh—SEDGE
mesquite—GRAMA,
　NEEDLE
Mexican—OTATE,
　TEOSINTE
moor—HEATH
oat—AVENA
poison rye—DARNEL
quitch—COUCH
reedy (Algerian)—DISS
rye—MARCITE
salt—ALKALI
scale—PALEA
sedge—BROOM
seneca—VANILLA
silt—KNOT
So. African—VELDT
Spanish—ESPARTO
stem—CULM, REED
swamp—SEDGE
tuft—TUSSOCK
Virginia lyme—TERRELL
grassland—LEA,
　MEADOW, SWARD
grate—ABRADE, CHARK,
　GRILL, GRIND,
　GRIT, IRRITATE,
　RASP, RUB, SCRAPE
gratify—ARRIDE,
　CONTENT, HUMOR,
　INDULGE, LUST,
　OBLIGE, PLEASE,
　SATE, WREAK
gratuity—BONUS,
　CUMSHAW, FEE,
　PENSION, PILON,
　PRESENT
grave—DEMURE, FOSSE,
　SOBER, SOLEMN,
　SOMBER, SUANT,
　TOMB, URN
gravel—BEACH,
　CALCULI, PUZZLE
gravy—SAUCE
gray—ASHEN, ASHY,

DISMAL, HOARY,
　LEADEN, TAUPE
grease—AXUNGE, BRIBE,
　FAT, LARD,
　LUBRICANT,
　LUBRICATE, MORT,
　OIL
great—BIG, EMINENT,
　GRAND, HUGE,
　IMMENSE, LARGE,
　NOBLE, PLENARY,
　SUBLIME, VAST
green—CALLOW,
　CHLORINE, FRESH,
　RAW, UNRIPE,
　VERDANT, WREATH
greenhorn—IKONA,
　NOVICE, ROOKIE
greenroom—FOYER
greet—ACCOST,
　ADDRESS, HAIL,
　SALUTE,
　WELCOME
greeting—ACCOIL, AVE,
　HAIL, HELLO, HI,
　HOLLA, HOW, NOD,
　SALUTE,
　SALUTATION
grief—DISTRESS, DOLE,
　DOLOR, RUE, SIGH,
　SORROW, TRIAL,
　WOE
grill—BROIL, GRATE,
　GRIDIRON
grimace—MOE, MOP,
　MOUE, MOW, SHAM
grind—BRAY, CRUSH,
　DIG, GRATE,
　MASTICATE, MULL
grinding stone—METATE,
　MULLER
　substance—ABRASIVE,
　EMERY
grit—BRAVERY, GRATE,
　GRAVEL, NERVE,
　SAND
groove—CHASE, FLUTE,
　FURROW, RABBET,
　RUT, SCORE, SLOT,
　STRIA, SULCATE

grooved—
CANALICULAR,
STRIATE, SULCATE
grotesque—BAROQUE,
BIZARRE, CLOWN,
FREAK, ODD,
UNIQUE
grotto—CATACOMB,
CAVE, CAVERN,
VAULT
ground—CLAY, CLOD,
GRITTED, LAND,
SOIL, TERRAIN
group—BAND, BUNCH,
BEVY, CLASS,
HANK, SET, SQUAD,
SWARM, TEAM
grouse—PTARMIGAN
grow—ACCRUE,
BECOME, DEVELOP,
ENLARGE, EXPAND,
INCREASE,
MATURE, RAISE,
THRIVE, WAX
growl—GIRN, GNAR,
GNARL, RUMBLE,
SNARL
growth—ACCRETION,
INCREASE, SHOOT,
STATURE, TUMOR
grub—DRUDGE, LARVA,
MAGGOT, MATHE
gruesome—GRISLY,
MACABRE
guarantee—ASSURE, BAIL,
BOND, ENSURE,
SECURITY
guard—FEND, FENDER,
KEEPER, PATROL,
PICKET, PROTECT,
SENTINEL, TEND
guardian—ANGEL,
ARGUS, CERBERUS,
HELPER, MONITOR,
PATRON, TRUSTEE,
TUTELAR, WARDEN
guest—CALLER, LODGER,
PATRON, VISITANT,
VISITOR
guide—CLEW, CLUE,

COURIER, DIRECT,
LEAD, LEADER,
PILOT, KEY, STEER,
TEACH
guiding—DIRIGENT,
POLAR
guilty—CULPABLE,
NOCENT, WICKED
gulf—BAY, BIGHT,
CHASM
gull—COB, DUPE, LARID,
MEW, PEWEE,
PEWIT, PIRR,
SEEDBIRD, SKUA,
TEASER, TRICK,
XEME
gully—ARROYO,
COULOIR, GUT,
SIKE, WADI
gum—AMRA, ASA,
CHICLE, CONIMA,
RESIN, ULA
gumbo—OCRA, OKRA
gun—BAZOOKA, KRUPP,
MORTAR, PISTOL,
RIFLE, ROD,
SPRINGFIELD
African—ROER
caliber—BORE
chamber—GOMER
leather case—HOLSTER
lock catch—SEAR
pointer device—DOTTER,
SIGHT
sight—BEAD
gush—JET, POUR, RAIN,
SPOUT, SPURT,
STOUR
gutter—DITCH, EAVES,
gutteral—BURR, DRY,
HUSKY, THROATY,
VELAR
gymnastic feat—KIP
gypsum—ALABASTER,
SELENITE
gypsy—CALE, ROM,
ROMANY
gyrate—CIRCLE, COIL,
ROTATE, SPIN,
TURN, TWIRL

gyrator—PILOT, TOP
gyre—CIRCLE, RING

gyves—FETTER, IRON,
SHACKLE

-H-

h-shaped—ZYGAL
habit—ATTIRE, CUSTOM,
MORES, ROUTINE,
RUT, USAGE,
USANCE, WONT
habitat—ABODE,
ENVIRONMENT,
ECO
habituate—ADDICT,
ENURE, USE
hacienda—CROFT, FARM,
GRANGE,
PLANTATION
hack—COUGH, TAXI,
WRITER
hackneyed—BANAL,
CLICHE,
COMMONPLACE,
THREADBARE, SAW,
STALE
Hades—ABADDON,
ABYSS, ADES,
ARALU, ACHERON,
ORCUS, PIT, SHEOL,
TARTARUS
haft—BAIL, DUDGEON,
HANDLE, HILT
hag—BELDAME, CRONE,
HARRIDAN,
JEZEBEL, VIXEN,
WITCH
haggard—BONY,
GAUNT
LANK, LEAN
hail—AHOY, AVE,
ACCOST, CALL,
GREET,
SALUTE, SIGNAL,
SLEET
hair—BRISTLE,
FILAMENT, TRESS
braid—CUE, PIGTAIL
cloth—ABA, CILICE
comb. form—PILO, PIL
covering—PELAGE

disease—MANGE,
XERASIA
dressing—POMADE
dye—HENNA
false—FRONT,
PERUKE, TETE, WIG
fillet—SNOOD
lock—LOVELOCK,
TRESS
loss of—ALOPECIA
net—LINT, SNOOD
ornament—COMB,
RIBBON
less—BALD,
GLABELLA,
GLABROUS, PELON
pad—RAT
pert. to—CRINAL,
LINUS, NOIL, PILAR
piece—PERUKE,
SNOOD, TOUPEE,
WIG
plant—PILUS, PUBES
remover—EPILATE
strips—EPILATES
wooly—SHAG
halberd—AX, FRAME,
GLAIVE
half—ARF, DEMI, EN,
HEMI, MIDWAY,
MOIETY, SEMI
witted—IMBECILE,
SILLY
hall—ATRIUM, AULA,
CORRIDOR, ENTRY,
FOYER, LYCEUM,
SALON
halo—ARC, AUREOLA,
BROUGH, CORONA,
CIRCLE
hamlet—ALDEE, CASALE,
DORP, THORP
hammer—BEAT, BEETLE,
MALLET, MARGE,
MAUL, OLIVER,

PLEXOR, POUND,
SLEDGE
hamper—BASKET,
CRAMP, CRATE,
ENCUMBER, HALT,
HANAPER, HOPPLE,
IMPEDE, MAUND,
SEROON
hand—FIST, GIVE,
MANUS, PAW,
POINTER, PROFFER,
TILL
handbill—DODGER
handbook—CODEX,
MANUAL, TOME
handcuffs—BRACELETS,
FETTERS,
MANACLES, DARBY,
DARBIES
handle—ANSA, HAFT,
HANK, HEFT,
HELVE, HILT,
MANAGE, TREAT,
WIELD
hang—CLING, DANGLE,
DRAPE, HOVER,
PEND, SUSPEND,
SWAG
hanging—DORSAL,
DOSSER, DRAPE,
PENDENT, PENSILE,
SESSILE
hangman's noose (pert.
to)—HEMPEN
hank—RAN, SKEIN
happen—BEFALL,
BETIDE, CHANCE,
EVENT, FARE,
OCCUR
happening—EVENT,
INCIDENT, NEWS,
TIDINGS, SPORADIC
harass—ANNOY, BAIT,
BESET, BOTHER,
CHASE, DISTRACT,
FRET, GALL, HAZE,
IRK
harbinger—HERALD,
INFORMANT, OMEN,
PRECURSOR, USHER

harbor—COVE, HAVEN,
HOLD, PORT
hard—ADAMANT,
ARDUOUS,
AUSTERE, CALLOUS,
DOUR, IRON,
RENITENT, SET,
SOLID, STEELY,
STONY, STERN,
harden—ENURE, GEL,
INURE, KERN,
OSSIFY, SEAR, SET,
STEEL
hare—CONY, RODENT,
SCUT
 female—DOE
 genus—LEPUS
 male—BUCK
 ragout—CIVET
 S. Amer.—TAPETI
 young—LEVERET
harem—SERAGLIO, SERAI
 female slave—
 ODALISQUE
 room—ADA, ODA
harlequin—
 CLOWNISH
harmful—BANEFUL,
MALEFICENT,
NOCENT, NOISOME,
NOXIOUS
harmless—INNOCUOUS
harmonize—AGREE,
ATTUNE, BLEND,
CHIME, KEY, TONE,
TUNE
harness—ARMOR, GEAR,
GRAITH
harp—ITERATE, KOTO,
LYRE, NANGA
harpsichord—
 CLAVECIN,
 SPINET
harsh—ACERB, ASPERITY,
CRUEL,
DISCORDANT,
DURE, GRATING,
GRIM, RASPY,
ROUGH, SEVERE,
STERN, VENOMOUS

HALE, LUG, PULL,
TOW, TREK

haunt—DEN, LAIR, NEST,
OBSESS, RESORT,
VISIT

have—HOLD, OWN,
POSSESS

haven—ASYLUM,
HARBOR, HITHE,
PORT, REFUGE

hawk—ASTUR,
BUZZARD,
CARACARA,
COOPERI, ELANET,
EYAS, FALCON,
HARRIER, OSPREY

hawkweed—DINDLE

hawser—ROPE

haycock—COB, COIL

haystack—MOW, RICK

hazard—DANGER, LOT,
PERIL, RISK, STAKE

haze—FILM, FOG, MIST,
SMOG, VAPOR

head—CAPUT, COP,
DIRECTOR, LEAD,
LEADER, NOG, NOB,
PATE, POLL

headdress—ALMICE,
CAPELINE, CUPEE,
PINNER, TIARA,
WIG

headland—CAPE, KOP,
NESS, RAS

heal—CURE, MEND,
PACIFY, REMEDY

heap—AMASS, COP,
MASS, PILE, SORITE,
STACK, TUMP

hear—HARKEN, HEED,
LISTEN, REGARD

hearing—AUDITION

hearsay—BRUIT, GOSSIP,
REPORT, RUMOR,

hartebeest—CAAMA,
CAANA, ASSE,
LECAMA, TORA

harvest—CROP, FRUIT,
GATHERING, REAP,
YIELD

hassock—CUSHION,
TUFT

hasten—
AMAIN, APACE,
FLY, HIE, HURRY,
RACE, RUN,
SCAMPER, SCUD

hasty—ABRUPT, BRASH,
CURSORY, EAGER,
IMPATIENT,
IMPULSIVE, RASH,
SUDDEN

hat—BERET, BIRETTA,
BONNET, CHAPEAU,
CAP, DERBY,
FEDORA, FELT,
TAM, TOPPER

hate—DETEST, LOATHE

haul—BOUSE, CART,
DRAG, DRAW,
TALK

heart—CARDIA, COR,
CORE, COURAGE,
SPIRIT

heat—ARDOR, CALOR,
CALORIC, FIRE,
ZEAL

heath—BENT, GRIG,
MOOR, PLAIN

heathen—GENTILE,
GODLESS, INFIDEL,
PAGAN, PAYNIM

heaven—ARCADIA, CIEL,
EDEN, ELYSIUM,
ETHER,
FIRMAMENT,
PROVIDENCE, SKY

heavenly—ANGELIC,
CELESTIAL, DIVINE,
SUPERNAL,
URANIAN

hedge—BOMA, HAW,
RADDLE

heed—CARE, GOME,
HEAR, LISTEN,
MIND, NOTE,
NOTICE, RECK

heel—BOUNDER, CAD,
CANT, INCLINE,
TILT

height—ALT, ALTITUDE,
APEX, ELEVATION,
STATURE, SUMMIT,
TOP
heir—HERITOR,
LEGATEE,
PARCENER,
POSTERITY, SCION
helical—SPIRAL
hell—INFERNO, LIMBO,
PIT
helm—RUDDER, STEER,
TIMON, TILLER
helmet—ARMET, GALEA,
MORION, SALLET,
TOPEE, TOPI
help—ABET, AID,
AIDANCE, ASSIST,
ATTEND, BENEFIT,
CURE, STEAD,
SUCCOR
helper—AIDE, ANSAR,
ASSISTANT,
SERVANT,
TEAMMATE
hem—BORDER, MARGIN,
RESTRICT
hemp—CORDILLA, PITA,
TOW
　fiber—AGAVE, FLAX,
　SISAL, TOW
　Indian—BHANG
　loose—OAKUM
　Manila—ABACA
hence—ERGO, SO, THEN,
THEREFORE
henchman—GROOM,
PAGE, SQUIRE
henna—ALCANA, DYE,
ORCHANET
herald—BLAZON, CRIER,
MESSENGER,
PRECURSOR
herb—ANISE, CARAWAY,
CATNIP, LOVAGE,
MOLY, PARSLEY,
RUE, SAGE, SEDGE,
SEDUM, TELLIMA,
THYME
　genus—ARUM, CANNA,

CASSIA, CROTON,
GAURA, LIATRIA,
RUTA, SEDUM,
VINCA
herd—DROVE, FLOCK,
FLOTE, MOB,
RABBLE
herdsman—COWBOY,
GAUCHO, SENN,
VACHER, VAQUERO
hereditary—ANCESTRAL,
LINEAL
heretic—DISSENTER,
SCHISMATIC
hermit—ANCHORITE,
ASCETIC, CENOBITE,
EREMITE, RECLUSE
hero—DEMIGOD, IDOL,
STAR,
VALIANT, WARRIOR
heroic—BOLD, BRAVE,
EPIC, EPICAL
VALIANT, VIKING
heron—AIGRET, ALBA,
BITTERN, CRANE,
EGRET, HERLE,
HERN, RAIL
　brood—SEDGE
　family—ARDEA,
　CRANE,
　flock—SEDGE
　night—QUA, QUAWK,
　SOCO
　No. Amer.—EXILIS
　small—BITTERN
herring—ALEWIFE,
CISCO, RAUN, SPRAT
　genus—ALOSA
　young—BRIT, COB,
　MATIE, SILE
hesitate—DEMUR,
FALTER, HALT,
HAW, LAG, PAUSE,
WAVER
hex—BEWITCH, HAG,
JINX, SPELL
hiatus—BREAK, COL,
FISSURE, GAP,
LACUNA, PAUSE
hickory—SHAGBARK

No. Amer.—PECAN
nut—KISKATOM,
  PECAN
wattle—ACACIA
hidden—ARCANE,
  COVERT, CRYPTIC,
  DEEP, INNER,
  LATENT, PERDU,
  SECRET
hide—CACHE, CLOAK,
  CONCEAL,
  CONCEDE, COVER,
  ENSCONCE, HOOD,
  PELT, SCREEN,
  SECRETE, SKIN,
  SKULK, STOW, VEIL,
  WRAP
high—AERIE, ALOFT,
  ALT, ELA,
  ELEVATED, LOFTY,
  TALL, UP
highlander—GAEL, KILT,
  SCOT, TARTAN
hike—TOSS, TRAMP,
  WALK
hill—BARROW, BUTTE,
  MOUND, TOR,
  TUMULUS
hilt—HAFT, HANDLE
hind—HEARST,
  PEASANT, ROE
hinder—ARREST, BACK,
  BAR, CRAMP,
  CUMBER, DELAY,
  DETER, DETAIN,
  EMBAR, ESTOP,
  HAMPER, HARASS,
  IMPEDE, LET,
  OBSTRUCT, REAR,
  RETARD
hinge—DEPEND, JOINT,
  PIVOT
hint—ALLUDE,
  ALLUSION, CLUE,
  CUE, EYEWINK,
  GLANCE, IMPLY,
  REFER, TIP
hip—COXA, HUCK,
  HUCKLE
  bones—HUGGIN, ILIA

pert. to—SCIATIC
muscle—ILIOPSOAS
hired—CHARTERED,
  ENGAGED, HACK,
  SIGNED
hireling—ALLOWE, ESNE,
  SLAVE, VENAL
hirsute—HAIRY
adornment—BEARD,
  GOATEE,
  MUSTACHE,
  SIDEBURNS
hiss—BOO, SISS
hissing—FIZZ, SHISH,
  SIBILANT, TST
historian—ANNALIST,
  ARCHIVIST,
  CHRONICLER
history—ANNALS,
  DRAMA, ERA,
  MEMOIR, PAST
hit—ACE, BAT, BUNT,
  BOP, BUFFET,
  COLLIDE, FLICK,
  KNOCK, SLOG,
  SLUG, SMITE, SWAT
hive—APIARY, BOX,
  STORE,
  SWARM
hoar—WHITE
frost—RIME, RAG
hoax—BAM, BILK,
  CANARD, COD,
  SPOOF
hobby—AVOCATION,
  BICYCLE, DOLLY,
  FAD, FALCON
hobgoblin—BOGIE, BOGY,
  BUGABOO, BUGGER,
  BUGBEAR, ELF, IMP,
  PUCK, PUG, SCRAT,
  SPRITE
hockey—HURLEY,
  SHINDY
ball—NUR, ORR, PUCK
cup—STANLEY
goal—CAGE
stick—SHINNY
hocus—CHEAT, DRUG,
  DECEIVE, FRAUD

hodge podge—CENTO,
GALLIMAUFRY,
MEDLEY, MESS,
MELANGE, OLIO,
MIXTURE, STEW
hog—BOAR, PIG, SHOAT,
SHOTE, SOW
ground—MARMOT
like mammal—TAPIR
hogshead—CASK,
MEASURE, PIPE
hoist—BOOST, CAT,
HEAVE, LIFT, RAISE,
REAR, WINCH
hold—CLUTCH, HARBOR,
HAVE, KEEP,
RETAIN, SUPPORT
holder—CONTAINER,
OWNER, PAYEE,
TENANT
hole—APERTURE,
CAVITY, DEN,
EYELET, GOURD,
ORIFICE,
PERFORATION,
SLOT
holiday—FIESTA, FERIA,
FERIE, VACATION
hollow—CAPSULAR,
CAVAL,
CAVERNOUS,
CONCAVE, DENT,
FALSE, GORE,
SCOOP
holly—ASSI, HOLM,
HULL, ILEX, OPACA
holy—BLESSED,
HALLOW, CHASTE,
NUN, SACRED,
VESTAL
home—ABODE, ASTRE,
HABITAT, KERN,
NEST
honeycombed—
ALVEOLATE,
FAVOSE
honeydew—MELIGO,
NECTAR
honeyed—
MELLIFLUOUS,

SUGARY
honor—EXALT, FAME,
HOMAGE,
OBEISANCE, PROW,
RENOWN, RESPECT,
REVERE
hood—AMICE,
BURNOOSE,
CAPOTE, CLOAK
hooded—CUCULLATE
hoof—CLEE, CLUVE,
PASTERN, UNGULA
hook—CROOK, DECOY,
HAMULE, SNARE,
TRAP
hooked—ADUNC,
AQUILINE,
HAMATE, HAMOSE,
UNCINATE
hoop—BAIL, ENCIRCLE,
LOOP, RING
hop—CAPER, DANCE,
FRISK, GAMBOL,
HIP, LEAP, SPRING,
TRIP
hope—ANTICIPATE,
ASPIRE, DESIRE,
EXPECTATION,
OPAL, OPTIMISM,
TRUST, WISH
hopeless—FORLORN,
SARDONIC
hopscotch stone—PEEVER
horde—ARMY, CROWD,
SWARM, THRONG,
TRIBE, TROOP
horizon—LIMIT, SEARIM
horizontal—FLAT, LEVEL,
PLANE
hormone—ADRENALIN,
CORTISONE,
ESTROGEN,
ESTRONE,
PROLACTIN
horn—ANTLER, CORNU,
RHYTON, SIREN
hornless—ACEROUS,
DODDED, MULY,
POLLED, POLEY
hors d'oeuvre—

ANTIPASTO,
APPETIZER,
RELISH

horse—ARAB, BIDET,
GENET, MARE,
MILER, NAG,
PACER, STEED,
STUD, TRESTLE,
TROTTER

ankle—HOCK
barbary—BARB
chestnut—BUCKEYE
color—PIED, PINTO,
ROAN

command—GEE, HAW,
WHOA

dealer—COPER
disease—CALORIS,
CARNEY, FARCY,
GLANDERS, LAMPAS,
SPAVIN, SURRA

fancier—
EQUESTRIAN
fennel—SESELI
fly—BOTFLY,
TABANID
fodder—HAY, OATS
foot part—FETLOCK,
CORONET, PASTERN
gait—CANTER,
GALLOP, PACE,
RACK, TROT
genus—EQUUS
male—GELDING,
STALLION
round up—RODEO
shackle—TRAMMEL
small—BIDET,
BRONCO, COB,
GENET, NAG, PONY,
TIT
spirited—COURSER,
STEED
swift—PACOLET
tender—GROOM
trotting—COB,
MORGAN
wheel—POLER
winker—BLINDER,
BLINKER

worthless—CROCK,
JADE, SHACK
host—ARMY, HORDE,
PYX, SERVER,
THRONG
hostelry—
CARAVANSARY,
HOTEL, INN
hostler—GROOM
hotel—FONDA, HAVEN,
HOSTEL, INN,
MOTEL, TAVERN
hound—CERBERUS,
OTTER
hunting—HARRIER,
POINTER, SETTER
pert. to—SKIRTER
small—BASSET,
BEAGLE
wolf—ALAN
hourly—FREQUENT,
HORAL
house—ABODE, CASA,
CASINO, COTE,
DOMICILE,
GRANGE, HOME,
LODGE, PENT,
RESIDENCE
household—FAMILY,
MENAGE
hovel—CABIN, DEN,
DUGOUT, HUT,
HUTCH, SHACK,
STACK
however—BUT, FAR,
MUCH, YET
howl—LAMENT, ROAR,
ULULATE, WAIL
hub—CENTER, CORE,
NAVE
huge—ENORMOUS,
GIANT, GIGANTIC,
MASSIVE, TITANIC,
VAST
hull—COVERING, HUSK,
POD, SHED
hum—BOMBINATE,
BOOM, BUZZ,
CROON, DRONE,
TUNE, WHIZZ

human—ADAMITE,
FINITE, MAN,
MORTAL
humble—ABASE,
CHASTISE, DEMIT,
DISGRACE, LOW,
LOWER, MEEK
humbug—BOSH, CHEAT,
DECEIVE, FLAM,
FRAUD, HOAX,
IMPOSTURE, PAH
humid—DAMP, DANK,
MOIST, WET
humiliate—ABASE,
ABASH, DEBASE,
MORTIFY, NITHER,
SHAME
humming bird—AVA,
BLUET, COLIBRI,
COSTA,
RACKETTAIL,
RUFOUS, SAPPHO,
SYLPH
humor—BABY, CAPRICE,
CATER,
COMICALITY,
GRATIFY, MOOD,
QUIRK, WHIM, WIT
humorist—DROLL, WAG,
WIT
Hun—GERMAN, VANDAL
leader—ATTILA
hundred—CENTI, HECTO
hunger—BANE, LONG,
STARVATION, WANT
hungry—ACORIA, AVID,
BARREN, EAGER,
YAP
hunt—CHASE, DIG,
SCOUR, SEARCH,
SEEK, TRAIL
hunter—ACTAEON,
JAGER, NIMROD,
ORION, TRAPPER
hunting—PURSUIT
huntress—ARTEMIS
Greek—ATALANTA,
DIANA

hurl—CAST, FLING,
PELT, PITCH, SLING,
THROW, TOSS
hurry—CHASE, HASTE,
HASTEN, HIE, RUSH,
SESSA, SPEED
hurt—DAMAGE, DREE,
HARM, HARRY,
INJURE, INJURY,
PAIN, PAINED
hurtful—MALEFIC,
NOCENT, NOISOME,
SORE
husband's brother—LEVIR
hush—ALLAY, APPEASE,
CLAM, HIST, PST,
STILL
husk—BRAN, LEAM,
SHELL, SHUCK
hut—CABIN, HOVEL,
ISBA, SHACK,
SHANTY, SKEO
hybrid—CATTALO,
CROSS, MULE
hydrocarbon—CARANE,
coal tar—PYRENE
ethyl—CETANE
gaseous—FLUORINE
inflammable—BUTANE
liquid—CUMOL,
NONANE, TOLUOL
oily—ETHERIN,
radical—AMYL
solid—CRYSENE
solvent—XYLENE
unsaturated—OLEFINE
volatile—BENZENE,
TETROL
wax—MONTAN
hydrophobia—LYSSA,
RABIES
hymn—CANTICLE,
PAEAN, PSALM
hypnotic—MESMERIC,
ECTENIC, SLEEPY,
TRANCE
hysteria—FITFUL,
NERVES

-I-

ice—CHILL, CONGEAL,
    COOL, FREEZE,
    FROST
  mass—BERG. FLOE
idea—BELIEF, CONCEPT,
    FANCY,
    IMPRESSION,
    INTENTION,
    NOTION, OPINION,
    THEORY. THOUGHT
ideal—AIM, FAULTLESS,
    LIMIT, MENTAL,
    PERFECT,
    PARAGON,
    STANDARD,
    UTOPIAN
identical—EQUAL, ONE,
    SAME. SELF
ideology—DOGMA, ISM
idiocy—ANOESIA,
    FATUITY
idiom—DIALECT,
    DICTION,
    PECULIARITY,
    PHRASE
idle—FUTILE. GAMMER,
    LAZY, LOAF,
    LOITER, OTIOSE,
    USELESS, VAIN
idler—DAWDLER, DRONE,
    LAZER. LOAFER,
    LOUNGER,
    ROUNDER
idol—GOD, HERO, ICON,
    IMAGE, SYMBOL,
    ZEMI
if not—ELSE, NISI
igneous rock—BASALT,
    BATHOLITE. BOSS,
    DACITE, DIABASE,
    FELSITE, GABBRO,
    PORPHYRY,
    TONALITE
ill—AILING, BAD,
    BANEFUL, EVIL,
    HARMFUL, POORLY,
    SICK, WOE
illegal—CONTRABAND,

FOUL, ILLICIT
image—COPY, EFFIGY,
    EIKON, EMBLEM,
    EIDOLON, ICON,
    IDOL, IKON,
    PICTURE, PORTRAY
imaginary being—ELF,
    SYLPH
imbecile—ANILE,
    BUFFOON, CRETIN,
    DOLT, DUPE, FOOL,
    IDIOT, MORON,
    SIMPLETON,
    STUPID, WITLESS
imbecility—AMENTIA,
    ANOESIA, FATUITY,
    IDIOCY, MORIA
imbue—DYE, INFUSE.
    INGRAIN, LEAVEN,
    PERMEATE,
    PERVADE,
    SATURATE, STEEP
imitate—APE, COPY,
    ECHO, EMULATE,
    MIMIC, MIME,
    MOCK,
    MODEL, RESEMBLE
imitation—APISM,
    COPYING, MIMESIS,
    MIMICRY, PARODY,
    PASTE, SHAM
immature—CALLOW,
    CRUDE. GREEN,
    PREMATURE, RAW
    UNRIPE, YOUNG,
    YOUTHFUL
immediately—ANON.
    NOW, PRESTO, SOON
immense—ENORM,
    ENORMOUS, FINE,
    GIGANTIC. GREAT,
    INFINITE, TITANIC,
    VAST
immerse—DIP, DOUSE,
    ENGROSS, SOUSE,
    SUBMERGE
immigrant—ALIEN,
    FOREIGNER

immortal—PERPETUAL,
UNDYING
immure—CLOISTER,
CONFINE, ENTOMB,
WALL
imp—BRAT, DEMON,
ELF, FAY, FAIRY,
SPRITE
impact—BRUNT,
CONTACT, CRAM,
FORCE, STROKE
impair—DAMAGE, MAR,
RUIN, WEAR,
VITIATE
impartial—EQUAL,
EQUITABLE, JUST,
UNBIASED
impasse—CULDESAC,
DEADLOCK,
STALEMATE
impassive—CALM,
SERENE, STOIC
impatient—FIDGETY,
HASTY, ITCHING,
NERVOUS, RESTIVE,
RARES
impede—BLOCK, CLOG,
ESTOP, HINDER,
OBSTRUCT, RETARD
impediment—BAR,
BARRIER, CLOG,
HITCH, REMORA,
SNAG
impel—COMPEL,
CONSTRAIN, DRIVE,
FORCE. INCITE,
INDUCE, PUT, SPUR,
URGE
imperfect—ERRABLE,
FALLIBLE, FRAIL
imperial—MAJESTIC,
REGAL, SUPREME
impertinent—
MEDDLESOME,
OFFICIOUS,
SASSY, SAUCY
implement—
APPLIANCE, DATER,
FULFILL,
INSTRUMENT, KIT,

TOOL. UTENSIL
imply—ARGUE,
CONNOTE, DENOTE,
HINT, INDUCE,
INFER, INTIMATE,
MEAN, SUPPOSE
import—DRIFT, INTENT,
SENSE, TOUR,
VALUE
impose—ENTAIL,
INFLICT, LAY,
LEVY, OBTRUDE,
SUFFER
impost—DUTY, LEVY,
TASK, TAX, TOLL,
TRIBUTE
impostor—CHARLATAN,
DECEIVER, FRAUD,
QUACK
impress—AWE. DENT,
MARK, PRINT,
STAMP, STEAD
imprison—BOND. CAGE,
CONFINE, IMMURE,
INCARCERATE,
INTER, JAIL
improve—AMEND,
BETTER. EMEND,
GAIN, REVISE
impudent—AIRS, BOLD,
BRASSY, CHEEKY,
INSOLENT,
MALAPERT, PERT,
RUDE, SASSY,
SHAMELESS
impulse—DRIFT, FORCE,
IMPETUS, MOTIVE,
URGE
in—AMONG, AT, INTO
inactive—DORMANT,
FAINEANT, IDLE,
INDOLENT, INERT
inane—EMPTY,
FATUOUS, INEPT,
PUERILE, SILLY,
STUPID, VOID,
TRIVIAL
inarticulate—APHONIC,
DUMB, MUTE
inaugurate—AUSPICATE,

OMEN

inborn—CONNATURAL,
INBRED, INNATE,
NATIVE, NATURAL,
ORGANIC

incarnation—AVATAR,
EMBODIMENT

incense—ANGER,
ENRAGE,
MYRRH,
TACAMAHAC

incentive—CALL,
GROUND, MOTIVE,
SPUR, STIMULUS

incident—ACT, EPISODE,
EVENT,
HAPPENING

incidentally—OBITER

incipient—INCHOATE,
INITIAL

incite—ABET, AGITATE,
BUZZ, EDGE, EGG,
EXHORT, FOMENT,
GOAD, IMPEL, SPUR,
URGE

inclination—BEVEL, BOW,
CONATUS, GRADE,
NISUS, NOD, RAKE,
SLANT, TILT,
VERSANT

incline—ALIST, DIP,
ATILT, GRADE,
LEAN, RAMP,
SLANT, SLOPE,
TEND, TILT, TREND

inclined—APT, LEANT,
PRONATE, PRONE,
PROPENSE

inclosure—CAGE,
CORRAL, SEPIMENT,
SEPT

income—PORT, RENTE,
SALARY, USANCE

incorrect—BASE,
SOLECISTIC, WRONG

increase—ACCRETE, ADD,
AUGMENT, ASCENT,
DEEPEN, EKE,
ENLARGE, GROW,
RISE, WAX

incursion—ASSAULT,
FORAY, INROAD

incus—ANVIL, HAMMER

indeed—REALLY, TRULY,
YEA

indefinite—
AMBIGUOUS,
VAGUE,
UNMEASURED

indehiscent fruit—PEPO,
SAMARA

indentation—BOWED,
CRENEL, DINGE,
HOLLOW, JAB,
NOTCH

index—CATALOG, FILE,
LIST

indicate—BETOKEN,
BODE, CITE,
CONNOTE, DENOTE,
DOMINATE, READ,
SIGNIFY

indicator—
ANNUNCIATOR,
ARROW, DIAL,
VANE

indict—ACCUSE,
ARRAIGN, CHARGE,
IMPEACH, PANEL

indifferent—
APATHETIC,
BLASE, COOL,
NEUTRAL, SUPINE

indigenous—EDAPHIC,
ENDEMIC, INNATE,
NATIVE, NATURE

indigo—ANIL, BLUE
bale—SEROON
berry—RANDIA
derivative—KETOLE
genera—WOAD
source—ANIL, ISATIN

indite—DICTATE, PEN,
WRITE

individual—BION, EGO,
ONE, PERSON, SELF,
SINGLE, SOLE

induce—DRAW, INFER,
LEAD, TEMPT

indulge—HUMOR,

PAMPER, PLEASE,
YIELD
industrialist—
MAGNATE,
MOGUL, SHOGUN,
TYCOON
inert—INACTIVE,
INDOLENT,
LATENT. LIFELESS,
SLUGGISH, SUPINE,
TORPID
infant—BABE, BAIRN,
BAMBINO, TOT
infatuate—BEFOOL,
BESOT, CHARM
infect—CORRUPT, TAINT
inference—
ASSUMPTION,
CONCLUSION,
CONSEQUENCE,
SURMISE
inferior—BAD, DICKY,
LESS, LOW, LOWER,
MENIAL, MINOR,
PETTY, POOR,
WORSE
infernal—DEVILISH,
DIABOLIC,
FIENDISH,
MALIGNANT,
FLAGUY,
TARTAREAN
inferno—ABYSS, HADES,
HELL
infidel—AGNOSTIC,
ATHEIST, DEIST,
SARACEN
infinity—ETERNITY,
OLAM
infirm—ANILE, FEEBLE,
SENILE
inflame—ENRAGE, FIRE,
INCITE. RANKLE
inflammable—
ACCENDIBLE,
PICEOUS
inflammation of
bone—OSTEITIS
of iris of eye—IRITIS,
UVEITIS

of the breast—MASTITIS
of the
intestines—COLITIS,
ENTERITIS
of the shoulder—OMITIS
inflexible—ADAMANT,
DOUR, HARD, RIGID
inflict—ADD, DEAL,
IMPOSE, WREAK
inflorescence—CYME,
RACEME, WHORL
influence—AFFECT, BIAS,
IMPEL, INTEREST,
PRESTIGE, PULL,
SWAY, WIN
information—AVISO,
DATA, LORE,
NEWS, WORD
informer—AFFIRMER,
DELATOR, NARK,
SPY
infuse—IMBUE, INSTILL,
SATURATE, TINGE
infusion—ADMIXTURE,
DECOCTION, TEA,
TINCTURE
ingot—GAD, PIG, SYCEE
ingress—ACCESS,
ENTRANCE, ENTRY,
PORTAL
ingredient—
COMPONENT,
ELEMENT,
MATERIAL
inhabitant—CIT, CITIZEN,
DENIZEN, INMATE,
ITE, LODGER,
RESIDENT
inhale—RESPIRE, SMELL,
SNIFF
inheritance—
BENEFACTION,
BEQUEST,
HERITAGE, LEGACY
inhibit—CHECK,
PROHIBIT,
RESTRAIN
initiate—BEGIN,
INSTITUTE, START
injunction—BAN

MANDATE, ORDER,
PRECEPT
injure—DAMAGE,
GRIEVE, HARM,
HURT, IMPAIR,
LAME, MAIM, MAR,
SCATHE, WRONG
injury—DAMAGE, EVIL,
HARM, LESION,
TRAUMA,
WOUND
inlaid work—BUHL,
MOSAIC
inlet—ARM, BAY, BIGHT,
COVE, FIORD,
ORIFICE, PORE,
RAE, RIA, SUMP
inn—ABODE, CABARET,
FONDA, HOSTEL,
HOSTELRY, HOTEL,
MOTEL, TAVERN
innate—HIDDEN,
INBORN,
INGRAINED,
INHERENT, NATIVE,
NATURAL
inner—ESOTERIC,
INSIDE, INTAL,
INTERNAL,
OBSCURE, WITHIN
inquisitive—NOSEY,
PEERING, PRYING
insane—BATTY, CRAZY,
DEMENTED,
FRANTIC, LUNY,
MAD
insanity—AMENTIA,
MANIA, VESANIA
inscribe—DEDICATE,
DEPENCIL,
ENGRAVE, IMPRESS,
LETTER, PEN,
WRITE
insect—ANT, ANTLION,
APHID, APHIS, BEE,
BEETLE, BUG,
CRICKET, DOR,
EARWIG, ERI,
DIPTERA, FLEA,
FLY, GNAT, LERP,

MANTIS, MIDGE,
MITE, MOTH, NIT,
SPIDER, SPITTLE,
TERMITE, TREMEX,
WASP
antenna end—CLAVA
back—NOTUM
comb. form—STRIGIL
dipterous—MOSQUITO
egg—NIT
exudation—LAC
eyes—OCELLI
feeler—ANTENNA
four winged—BEETLE
genus—CICADA,
CICALA, EMESA,
NEPA, TERMES,
THRIPS
hard covering—CHITIN
immature—LARVA
in final stage—IMAGO
larva—GRUB, MAGGOT
leg—PROLEG
lepidopterous—MOTH
like—ENTOMOID
mature—IMAGO
middle
division—THORAX
migratory—LOCUST
molting—ECDYSIS
nests—NIDI, NIDUS
order—CRICKET, KOR,
LOCUST, SPIDER,
TREMEX
parisitic—TURCATA
powder—PYRETHRUM
resin—LAC
small—APHID, BUG
social—ANT, BEE
state of life—INSTAR,
PUPA
sting—ICTUS
stinging—GADFLY
wing spot—ISLE
wingless—APTERA
insert—ENCLOSE, ENTER,
INGRAFT, PANEL,
PUT
inset—INFLOW, INFLUX,
INLAY, PANEL

insignia—BADGE, BAR,
REGALIA, STAR
insignificant—LITTLE,
MINOR, NULL,
PETIT, PUNY,
SMALL, TRIFLING,
TRIVIAL
inspect—EXAMINE,
PRY,
SCRUTINIZE
inspire—ANIMATE,
IMPART, INHALE,
UPLIFT
instigate—ABET, EGG,
FOMENT, INCITE,
SPUR, STIR,
STIMULATE,
SUBORN
institute—ESTABLISH,
FOUND, INITIATE,
ORGANIZE
instrument—AGENT,
IMPLEMENT,
ORGAN, TOOL
insulate—ISOLATE,
QUARANTINE
insult—AFFRONT, FIG,
FLOUT,
OFFEND, RUFFLE,
SLAP, SLUR
insurance—TONTINE
insurgent—COM, REB,
REBEL, RED,
MUTINEER, PIRATE,
REVOLTER,
TURNCOAT
intellect—BRAIN, INWIT,
MENTALITY, MIND,
NOEMICS, SENSE
intense—ACUTE,
ARDENT, DEEP,
EXTREME, FIERCE,
FERVID,
INTENSIFIED
inter—BURY, ENTOMB,
INHUME, INURN
interdict—BAN, DEBAR,
ENJOIN, VETO
interest—BEHALF,
SHARE, SAVOR,
USURY, WEAL
interference—NOISE,
SNOW, STATIC
interior—INNER, INSIDE
interlude—ENTRACTE,
OVERTURE, BREAK
intermediate—MESNE
interpret—CONSTRUE,
DECODE, READ,
REDE, RENDER,
OPEN, SCAN
interpreter—
DRAGOMAN,
EXEGETE,
LATINER
interstice—APERTURE,
AREOLA, AREOLAE,
CHINK, CRACK,
CREVICE, PORE
interval—GAP, INTERIM,
LAPSE, PITCH,
RESPITE, REST,
SPACE, SPAN, TIME
intervening—BETWEEN,
INTERJACENT,
MESNE
interweave—BRAID, LACE,
MAT, PLAIT, PLAT,
PLASH, RADDLE,
SPLICE
intimate—CHIEF, CRONY,
PACK, SECRET, SIB
intimidate—ABASH, COW,
DAUNT, OVERAWE
intoxicated—HEADY,
LIT, DRUNK, SOT,
SOSH
intricate—COMPLEX,
DAEDAL, DEDAL,
GORDIAN, MAZY
intrigue—AMOUR,
BRIGUE, CABAL,
CHEAT,
COMPLICATE,
CONTRIVE, PLOT,
PUZZLE
intrinsic—IMMANENT,
INHERENT, REAL
introduce—BROACH,
HERALD, IMMIT,

INFUSE, INSERT,
PRESENT, USHER
introduction—DEBUT,
ENTREE,
INSERTION,
PREAMBLE,
PREFACE,
PRELUDE, PROEM,
PROLOGUE
introductory cry—HEAR,
OYEZ
intuitive—NOETIC,
PERCEIVING,
SEEING
inundation—ALLUVION,
FLOOD
inure—ACCUSTOM,
BENEFIT, HARDEN,
SEASON, TOUGHEN,
USE
invade—ENCROACH,
INFRINGE,
INTRUDE, RAID,
TRESPASS
invalid—INADEQUATE,
INFIRM, NULL,
SICK, VOID, WEAK
investigate—INDAGATE,
INQUIRE, PROBE,
SIFT, WASH
invite—ASK, BEG, BID,
ENTICE, ORDER,
SOLICIT, SUE, TRY
invoke—BEG, IMPLORE,
PRAY
involve—ENGAGE,
ENTAIL, EVINCE,
IMPLICATE, LAP,
TANGLE, WRAP
inward—ENTAD,
INTERNALLY,
SECRET
iodine—ANTISEPTIC,
EIGON, IATROL
  compound—IODATE
  source—KELP
iota—ACE, ATOM, DOT,
JOT, WHIT
ipecac (genus)—EVEA
irascible—ANGERED,

BRASH, CHOLERIC,
CRANKY, CROSS,
IREFUL, TECHY,
TOUCHY
irate—ANGRY, HOT,
MAD, WRATH,
WROTH
iris—FLAG, GODDESS,
IXIA, ORRIS,
RAINBOW
irk—ANNOY, BORE,
CHAFE, NETTLE,
VEX
irksome—DISGUSTING,
PAINFUL, TEDIUM,
TEDIOUS
iron—FERRUM, FETTER,
FIRM, FIRMNESS,
HARD, MANACLE,
MITIS, PRESS
irrational number—SURD
irregular—ABNORMAL,
ANOMALOUS,
ATACTIC, ATYPIC,
EROSE, ERRATIC
irritable—FIERY,
IRACUND, SPLEENY,
TECHY
irritate—ANGER, CHAFE,
FRET, GALL,
GRATE, IRE,
NEEDLE, NETTLE,
PEEVE, RILE, VEX
isinglass—AGAR,
CARLOCK, HUSO,
MICA
islet—AIT, ALT, BAY,
CAY, COVE, KEY
ism—BELIEF, DOGMA,
TENET
isolated—ENISLED,
EXILED,
QUARANTINED,
SEPARATED
issue—ARISE, EMANATE,
EMERGE, EMIT,
END, ERISTIC,
EDITION, OUTCOME,
PRINT, TERM
itch—PRURITUS, PSORA,

RIFF, SCABIES
item—AGENDUM,
ARTICLE, ASSET,
DETAIL, ENTRY,
MAXIM,
PARAGRAPH

itself—(Latin)—IPSO
ivory—DENTINE, TUSK
ivy (genus)—HEDERA
  ground—HOVE, HOVEA
  pert. to—HEDERAL

-J-

jab—DIG, POKE, PUNCH,
THRUST
jabber—BABBLE,
CHATTER, GABBLE,
PRATE, SPUTTER
jack—CLOWN, JUG,
KNAVE, TANKARD
jacket—BIETLE, BOLERO,
ETON, PEEL,
REEFER, SKIN
jade—HUSSY, NAG,
NEPHRITE, PLUG,
TIRE
jai alai—
PELOTA
  player—PELOTARI
  racquet—CESTA
jail—BRIG, BRIDEWELL,
COOLER, GAOL,
IMPRISON, LIMBO,
LOCKUP
jar—AMPHORA, CODUS,
CROCK, CRUSE,
EWER, HYDRIA,
OLLA, TERRINE
jargon—
ABRACADABRA,
ARGOT, CANT,
DIALECT, LINGO,
PATTER, RANE,
SLANG, AIRCON
jaunty—AIRY, COCKY,
PERKY, STYLISH
javelin—ASSAGAI, DART,
LANCE, PILE, SPEAR
jaw—CHAP, CHOKE,
GONIA, MAW,
WANG
  comb. form—GNATHO
  lower—MANDIBLE

  muscle—MASSETER
  upper—MAXILLA
jeer—BOO, DERIDE,
FLOUT, GIBE, HOOT,
JAPE, JIBE, SCOFF,
SNEER, TAUNT
jejune—ARID, BANAL,
DRY, MEAGER,
STALE
jelly—JAM, PRESERVE
  fish—ACALEPH,
MEDUSA, QUARL,
HYDROID
  grape—SAPA
  meat dish—ASPIC
jerk—BOB, NIDGE, TIC,
TWEAK, TWIST,
TWITCH, YANK
jest—BUTT, GAME, GEST,
JAPE, JOKE, MOT,
QUIP, TALE, TRIFLE,
STORY, WIT
jester—BUFFOON,
CLOWN, JAPER,
MIME, WAG, ZANY
jet—BLACK, COAL,
EBON, EBONY,
GUSH, JUT, SPOUT,
SPURT, SPRAY,
STREAM
jewel—BIJOU,
BRILLIANT, GEM,
JOY, NAIF, OPAL,
STONE, TRINKET
jewelry—LOGIES,
BIJOUTRY, QUOIN
  alloy—OROIDE
  cheap—PASTE, STRASS,
TOMBAC
jib—BALK, BOOM,

JOYFUL, MERRY
jostle—ELBOW, JAR, JOG,
RUSH, SHAKE,
SHOCK
jot—ACE, ATOM, BIT,
IOTA, ITEM, MINIM,
MITE, PARTICLE,
POINT, TITTLE,
WHIT
journal—DIARY, PAPER,
RECORD, REGISTER
journey—FARE, RUN,
TOUR, TRAVEL,
TREK, TRIP,
VOYAGE, WEND
joust—BOUT, COMBAT,
CONTEST, SPAR,
TILT, TOURNEY
joy—BLISS, ECSTASY,
GLAD, GLEE,
PLEASURE
joyous—BAUD, ELATED,
FESTAL, FESTIVE,
GLAD, HAPPY,
MERRY, RIANT,
VESTAL
judge—ARBITER,
ARBITRATOR,
DECIDE, DEEM,
CONSIDER,
ESTIMATE,
OFFICIAL,
REFEREE, UMPIRE
bench—BANC
chamber—CAMERA
circuit—ITER
gavel—MACE
in circuit—EYRE
judgment—AWARD,
DOOM, OPINION,
SENSE, SENTENCE,
VERDICT, WISDOM
jug—BUIRE, CRUSE,
EWER, FLAGON,
CHORE, SINECURE
jingle—CLINK
DOGGEREL, TINGLE
jitters—DITHERS,
NERVES
jockey—CAVALIER, DISC,

ARCARO,
SHOEMAKER
jog—DUNCH, JOSTLE,
MOG, NUDGE, PUSH,
REMIND, TROT
join—ADD, ALLY,
ANNEX, CONNECT,
COALESCE, ENTER,
LOCK, MEET, MELD,
MERGE, PIN,
SOLDER, WELD
joint—ELBOW, HINGE,
HIP, SEAM, TENON
cavity—BURSA
in stem—NODE
lubricator—SYNOVIA
of the arm—ELBOW
of the door—HINGE
of the leg—KNEE
of the plant stem—
PHYTOMER
joke—GAG, JEST, JAPE,
QUIP, SALLY
joker—CARD, DOR,
MISTIGRIS, WAG,
WIT
jolly—CHEER, BUXOM,
CROUSE, JOVIAL,
OLPE, TOBY
juice—CIDER, SAP, STUM,
WINE
jumble—BLEND,
DISPLACE, HASH,
MEDLEY, MIX,
RAFF, ROG
jumbled type—PI, PIE, SAN
jump—HOP, LEAP, LOPE,
START
junction—MEETING,
SEAM, UNION
juniper—CADE, CEDAR,
GORSE, RAETAM,
RETEM, SAVIN
junto—CABAL, CLIQUE,
FACTION
jurisdiction (law)—SOE
jury—ASSIZE, PANEL,
VENIRE
juvenile—IMMATURE,
UNDEVELOPED,
YOUNG, YOUTHFUL

-K-

kangaroo—BOOMER,
    JEROBA,
    MACROPODIAN
  female—DOE, GIN
  male—BILBI, BOOMER
  rat—POTOROO
  young—JOEY
keel—ABEAM, CAREEN,
    LIST, TILT, UPSET
keen—ACUTE, ASTUTE,
    BITTER, FINE,
    GARE, NICE,
    PUNGENT, SHARP,
    SNELL, SHREWD,
    TART
keenness—ACIES, EDGE,
    PUNGENCY
keep—CASE, DONJON,
    HOLD, MAINTAIN,
    RETAIN
keeper—CUSTODIAN,
    GUARD, LOCKNUT,
    WARDEN
keepsake—MEMENTO,
    TOKEN, RELIC,
    SOUVENIR
keg—CADE, CASK,
    BARREL, FIRKIN,
    TUN, VAT
kelp—ASH, SEAWEED,
    VARIC, WRACK
kernel—CAUSE, CORE,
    GIST, GRAIN,
    ENDOCARP, HEART,
    MEAT, NUT, PITH,
    SEED
ketch—JACK, SAIC, SHIP
ketone—ACETONE,
    BUTYRONE
kettle—CAULDRON,
    SIROP
kettledrum—ATABAL,
    ANACARA, NAKER,
    TIMBAL, TIMPANI,
    TIMPANO, TYMPAN
key—CAY, CLAVIS,
    CLEW, COTTER,

ISLET, PITCH,
    SOLUTION, WHARF
keystone—SAGITTA,
    SUPPORT, WEDGE
kick—BOOT,
    CALCITRATE, FUNK,
    KEVEL
kid—BANTER, JOSH
kidnap—ABDUCT, SEIZE,
    STEAL, TAKE
kidney—BEAN, BON,
    ORGAN
  disease—UREMIA
  shaped—RENIFORM
  stone—JADE,
    NEPHRITE
kill—BLAST, BURKE,
    OCCIDE, SLAY
killing—CARNAGE,
    FATAL, GAROTE,
    SLAYING
kiln—FURNACE, OAST,
    OST, OVEN, TILER
kin—FOLKS, GERMANE,
    SIB
kind—CLASS, GENRE,
    GENUS, GENTLE,
    FRIENDLY,
    HUMANE, ILK,
    SORT, STYLE
kindle—BURN, FIRE,
    FUME, IGNITE,
    LIGHT, LUME,
    ROUSE
kindly—BENIGN, BLITHE,
    GRACIOUS,
    HUMANE
kindred—ALLIED, AKIN,
    BLOOD, COGNATE,
    GENS, KINSHIP,
    KITH, SIB, TIE
kingly—AUGUST,
    GRAND, LEONINE,
    NOBLE, REGAL,
    ROYAL
kink—KNOT, SNARL,
    TWIST, WHIM

kinship—AFFINITY,
  NASAB
kiss—BASIATE, BUSS,
  OSCULATE, SMACK
kitchen gadget—CORER,
  DICER, MASHER,
  OPENER, PEELER,
  STRAINER
  garden—OLITORY
  naut.—GALLEY
kite—ELANET, GLEDE,
  MILAN
knack—APTNESS, ART,
  DEVICE,
  DEXTERITY, EASE,
  FEAT, HANG, MOCK,
  SKILL, TRICK
knave—LOREL, LOSEL,
  RASCAL,
  RAUTENER, ROGUE,
  SCAMP, VARLET
knee bone—DIB
  cap—PATELLA
  flexure—GENU
  inflammation—
    GONITIS
  joint—HOCK
  to bend—GENUFLECT
kneeling desk—PRIEDIEU
knicknack—GIMCRACK,
  TRIFLE
knife—MACHETE
  Burmese—DAH
  comb. form—DORI
  curved—KUKRI
  handle—HAFT, HILT
  Irish—SKEAN
  Malay—CREESE
  Maori—PATU
  moro—BARONG
  Philippines—ITAC
knight—CAVALIER,
  EQUES, EQUITE,
  GALLANT, LOVER,
  SIR, TEMPLAR

knighthood—
  ACCOLADE,
  , CHIVALRY, HOST
knit—COUPLE, ICNUTE,
  JOIN, SEAM
knitting—BROCADE,
  CROCHET, UNION
  stitch—PURL
knob—CAPET, KNOT,
  KNURL, LUMP,
  NODE, NODUS, NUB,
  UMBO
  in wood—NUR
  medicinal—TUBERCLE
  ornamental—BOSS,
    KNOB, STUD
  pert. to—ORLET
  pointed—FINIAL
knot—ENTANGLE,
  GNARL, MAT, NODE,
  NODULE, NOOSE,
  SNAG, TIE, TUFT
knotted—NODATED
  lace—TATTING
know—INTUIT, KEN,
  REGARD, REVEAL,
  WIS, WOT
knowledge—COGNITION,
  KEN, DITH, LORE,
  OLOGY, SCIENTIA,
  WISDOM
knuckle—SUBMIT, YIELD
kobold—BROWNIE,
  GNOME,
  HOBGOBLIN, NIS,
  NISSE
Koran—MUSLIM HOLY
  BOOK
  chapter—SURA
  division—ALCORAN,
    SURA, SURO
  scholar—ULEMA
  soldier—ROK
kosher—CLEAN
kulak—FIST

-L-

label—BAND, LAPPET,
  STICKER, TAG

labor—MOIL, TASK, TOIL,
  TRAVAIL, STRIVE,

WORK
organization—
AFL, CIO,
UAW, ULGWU, UMW
laborer—FELLAH, PEON,
SERF, TOILER,
TOTY, WORKER
labyrinth—CIRCUIT,
DAEDAL, MAZA,
MAZE
lace—BRAID,
EMBROIDERY,
FILIGREE, GIN, NET,
SHOESTRING,
SNARE, TAT,
THREAD
lacerate—CUT, MANGLE,
REND, RIP, RIVE,
TEAR
lachrymal drop—TEAR
lack—DEARTH, NEED,
REQUIRE, WANT
lacking—BARREN,
PALLID, SHORT, SHY
laconic—BRIEF, CONCISE,
TERSE
lacquer—ENAMEL, LAC,
JAPAN, SHELLAC,
VARNISH
ladder—ESCALADE, RUN,
SCALADO, STEE,
STY
ladle—BAIL, DIP, DIPPER,
GEAT, SCOOP,
SPOON
lady—BURD, DAME,
DONA, FEMALE,
MADAM, MAID,
MISTRESS, WOMAN
laity—FOLD, LAYMEN,
PEOPLE
lame—BILT, CRIPPLE,
HALT, HOBBLING,
INFIRM, LIMPING,
MAIM
lament—BEWAIL,
BEWEEP, DIRGE,
ELEGIZE, MOAN,
PINE, PLANGOR,
REPINE, RUE, WAIL

lamentation—ELEGIAC,
GROT, SIGH, TEARS
laminated—SLATY,
SPATHIC, TABULAR
rock—FISSILE, GNEISS,
SHAUL, SHALE
lamp—CRUSIE, ETNA,
FLASH, LANTERN,
LIGHT, LUCERN,
LUCIGEN, TORCH
lamplighter—SPILL
lampoon—IAMBIC, LIBEL,
RIDICULE, SATIRE,
SKIT, SQUIB
lamprey—EEL
lance—CUT, DART,
JAVELIN, OPEN,
PIERCE, SPEAR
lancer—HUSSAR,
TROOPER, UHLAN
landed—ALIT, PRAEDIAL,
TITHES
estate—DOMAIN,
MANOR, MANSION
property—ESTATE
proprietor—LAIRD
landing place—AIRPORT,
PIER, QUAY, WHARF
landlord—BONIFACE,
HOST, OWNER
landmark—CAIRN, COPA,
MILESTONE, SENAL
landscape—DEPICT,
PAYSAGE, SCENE,
SCENERY
landslide—EBOULEMENT
language—DIALECT,
IDIOM, LIP, TONGUE
languor—BOREDOM,
DEBILITY, ENNUI,
KAIL
lap—CIRCUIT, ENFOLD,
FOLD, TRUNCATE,
UNFOLD
lapel—COLLAR
lapse—ERR. ERROR,
MISSTEP, SLIP,
TARDY
larch—TAMARACK
lariat—LASSO, NOOSE,

REATA, RIATA,
ROPE
lark—ADVENTURE,
FROLIC, PRANK
larva—BOT, CHIGGER,
GRUP, LOA
early stage—PUPA,
REDIA
final stage—CHRYSALIS
footless—MAGGOT
lash—BERATE, FLOG,
QUIRT, RATE,
SCOLD, SCOURGE,
SMITE, SPLICE, TIE,
WHIP
lass—GIRL, MAID,
MAIDEN
lasso—CABESTRO,
LARIAT, LASH,
REATA, ROPE
last—CONTINUE,
ENDURE, FINAL,
LOWEST, OMEGA,
ULTIMATE, UTMOST
late—DEAD, DEEP,
DELAYED, NEW,
RECENT, TARDY
later—AFTER,
POSTERIOR, PUISNE
lattice—CANCELLI,
GRILLE, TRELLIS
laud—EXALT, EXTOL,
GLORIFY, PRAISE,
SING
laugh—CHORTLE,
CHUCKLE, GIGGLE,
GUFFAW, ROAR
laughable—COMIC,
DROLL, RISIBLE
laughing—MERRY,
RIANT, RIDENT
laughter—MIRTH, RISUS
laurel—BAY, DAPHNE,
IVY
lava—AA, ASH,
BASALTIC, LATITE,
TAXITE,
TRACHYTIC
lavender—ASPIC
lavish—FREE, GIVE,

LUSH, PRODIGAL,
PROFUSE,
SQUANDER, TIP
law—ACT, CANON,
CODE, DROIT,
JUSTICE, RULE,
STATUTE, TORA
lawlessness—ANARCHY,
VICIOUS, LICENSE,
MUTINY, RIOT,
UNRULY
lawn—BATISTE, GLADE,
GRASS
lawsuit—ACTION, CASE,
LEGE, LITIGATION
lawyer—ATTORNEY,
BARRISTER,
COUNSEL,
COUNSELOR,
JURIST, LEGALIST,
LEGIST
laxative—APERIENT,
PURGATIVE
lay—BALLAD, DITTY,
PAVE, PLACE, PUT,
SONG
layer—BED, COAT,
LAMINA, PLY, ROW,
STRATA,
THICKNESS, TIER
lazy—FAINEANT,
INDOLENT, OTIOSE,
SLOTHFUL, SLOW,
SLUGGISH
lead—CARRY, DIRECT,
GUIDE, HEAD,
LODE, STEER
leader—CHIEF, COCK,
DUCE, DUX,
ETHNARCH,
FUHRER
leading—CHIEF, MAIN
leaf—LAMINA, PAGE,
PETAL, SPATHE,
TENDRIL
bud—GEMMA
curvature—EPINASTY
disease—ERINEA
hinged—FLAP
large—FROND

manna—LERP
midrip—PEN
modified—BRACT
network—AREOLA
leaflet—PINNA
leafy—FOLIOSE,
 LAMINATE
league—ALLIANCE,
 BOND, COMBINE,
 FEDERATION,
 HANSE, UNION
lean—BARE, DEPEND,
 GAUNT, LANK,
 POOR, RELY, SLIM,
 SPARE, TILT, TIP,
 TRUST
lean-to—ROOF, SHACK,
 SHED
leap—BOUND,
 CAPRIOLE, DIVE,
 HOP, JUMP, LUNGE,
 RAMP, SALTO,
 SPRING, VAULT
learned—ERUDITE,
 LETTERED,
 MASTERED,
 SCHOLARLY, WISE
learning—ART, CULTURE,
 KEN, LORE,
 PHILOMATH, WIT
lease—CONTRACT,
 CHARTER, DEMISE,
 HIRE, LET, REMISE,
 RENT, TENURE
leash—CORD, JESS,
 LUNE, STRAP,
 TETHER
leather—COWHIDE,
 HORSEHIDE, KID,
 KIP, LEVANT,
 OXHIDE, NAPA,
 ROAN
leave—DEPART, GO,
 PERMISSION, QUIT,
 RETIRE
leaven—BARM, ENZYME,
 YEAST
leaves—FOLIAGE, PAGES
leavings—CULLS, DREGS,

LEFT, ORTS,
 REFUSE, REST,
 WASTE
ledge—BERM, CAY,
 LODE, REEF, RIDGE,
 SHELF
lee—COVER, SHELTER
leech—GILL, PARASITE,
 WORM
leer—EYE, OGLE, OVEN,
 SCOFF, SNEER,
 STARE, VOID
left—PART, LARBOARD
leg—CRURAL, GAM,
 HOOF, LIMB, SHANK
legal—LAWFUL, LEAL,
 LICIT, VALID
legend—CAPTION, EDDA,
 FABLE, MYTH,
 SAGA, TALE
legging—COGGER,
 GAITER, GAMBADE,
 PUTTEE, STRAD
legislative
 assembly—ASSIZE,
 DIET, HOUSE,
 SENATE
legislator—DEPUTY,
 SENATOR, SOLON
legislature (both
 branches)—BICAM-
 ERAL
legume—BEAN, CASEIN,
 LENTIL, LOMENT,
 PEA, POD, UVA
leisure—EASE, OTIOSE,
 TIME, TOOM
lemon—CITRUS
 grass—RUSA, SIRI
 product—CIRRIC
lemur—AYEAYE,
 GALAGO, LORI,
 LORIS, MACACO,
 MONKEY, SEMIAPE
 Asian—LORIS
 flying—COLUGO,
 GALAGO
 Madagascan—INDRI,
 MONGOOSE

ruffed—MACACO,
MAKI, VARI
lens—BIFOCAL, GLASS,
TORIC, UNAR
leopard—CHEETAH,
JAGUAR, OCELOT,
PARD
leper—LAZAR, LEPRA,
LEPROSY, OUTCAST
leprechaun—ELF, GOBLIN,
PIGMY, SPRITE
less—FEW, FEWER,
MINOR, MINUS,
SMALLER
lessen—ABATE, BATE,
DEPLETE,
DIMINISH, EASE,
LOWER, MINCE,
PALLIATE, TAPER
let—ALLOW, HINDER,
HIRE, LEASE,
PERMIT, RENT
lethargic—COMA,
COMATOSE, DULL,
INERT, PASSIVE,
SLEEPY, TORPID
letter—BREVE, CHAIN,
ELL, EPISTLE, ESS,
INSCRIBE, MEMO,
MISSIVE, TEE
lettuce—COS, MINION,
ROMAINE, SALAD
genus—LACTUCA
sea—ALGA, LAVER,
ULVA
levee—DIKE, DURBAR,
QUAY, RIDGE
level—AIM, EVEN, FLAT,
GRADE, PLANE,
RASE, RAZE
lever—CRANK,
CROWBAR, JIMMY,
PEAVY, PRISE, PRY,
TAPPET
levin—FLASH, LIGHTEN,
LIGHTNING
liable—APT, BOUND,
EXPOSED, PRONE,
SUBJECT
liar—ANANIAS, CHEAT,

FALSIFIER, FIBBER,
WERNARD
libel—CALUMNY,
MALIGN, LAMPOON,
ROORBACK,
SLANDER
liberal—AMPLE, BROAD,
ECLECTIC, FRANK,
GENEROUS
liberate—FREE,
MANUMIT, REDEEM
license—GRANT, PATENT,
PERMIT
lichen—MOSS, PARELLA,
USNEA
apothecium—TRICA
deriv. of—MOSS,
LITMUS
licit—DUE, JUST,
PERMITTED,
LAWFUL, LEGAL
licorice—ABRIN,
ABSINTHE
lid—BRED, CAP, CAWE,
COVER, ROOF, TILT
lie—FALSEHOOD, FIB,
LIGE, MENDACITY,
PALTER,
PREVARICATE,
REST
lien—CLAIM,
MORTGAGE
lieu—PLACE, STEAD
life—DAYS, HOURS, VIE
lifetime—AGE, DAYS,
WORLD
lift—AID, ELEVATE,
ELEVATOR, HEAVE,
HELP, HOIST, PERK,
PRY, RAISE, RISE
lifting apparatus—CRANE,
DAVIT, HOIST, JACK,
LEWIS
ligament—BAND, BOND
light—AERY, AIRY, FINE,
ILLUMINE, GLEAM,
LAMP, LEGER,
LUME, LUMEN,
SHINE, SUN, TORCH
light house—BEACON,

FINAL, PHARE,
PHAROS
like—ADMIRE, ALIKE,
AS, COPY, ENJOY,
EQUAL, PLEASING,
PREFER, RELISH,
SIMILAR
likeness—ANALOGY,
COPY, EFFIGY,
GUISE, ICON, IMAGE
likewise—ALSO, DITTO,
EKE, TOO
lily—ALOE, ARUM,
CALLA, IXIA, LIS,
LOTUS, TULIP,
WOKAS, YUCCA
butterfly—MARIPOSE,
SEGO
daffodil (genus)—
NARCISSUS
day—NIOBE
encrinite—PALEON
family—ALOE,
BELLWORT,
BESSERA, CAMAS,
SQUILL
gold-banded—
AURATUM
palm—TI, TOI
leaf—PAD
sand—SOAPROOT
water—CASTALIA,
LOTUS, NYMPHAEA
limb—BOUGH, BRANCH,
LEG
limber—AGILE, LIMP,
LITHE, PLIANT
limbo—HELL, JAIL,
PRISON
lime—CALX, CATCH,
LEASH
limestone—CALP, CAULK,
CHALK, MALM,
MARBLE, OOLITE
limit—AMBIT,
BOUNDARY,
BOURN, CONFINE,
END, EXTENT, FIX,
MERE, PALE, SPAN,
STINT, TERM

limn—DEPICT, DRAW,
PAINT
limp—CLOP, FAIL,
FLABBY, FLACCID,
HALT, HOP, LAX,
LIMBER, SOFT
linder (genus)—LIN, TIEL,
TILIA
line—CERIPH, CORD,
COURSE, FILE,
ISOBAR, MARK,
ORLE, RANK, REIN,
ROW, ROUTE, RULE,
SEAM, SERIF,
STRING, TOME
lineage—ANCESTRY,
BLOOD, KINDRED,
PEDIGREE, LINE,
RACE, STOCK,
STRAIN, TRENE
linen—BARRAS, CRASH,
DOWLAS, GULIX,
LINGERIE
linger—DAWDLE, DELAY,
DWELL, HOVER,
LAG, LENG, LOITER,
STAY, TARRY, WAIT
link—ATTACH, COUPLE,
NEXUS,
TIE, YOKE
lint—FLAX, FLUFF,
HEMP, NAP, TENT
lip—BRIM, EDGE,
LABIUM
liqueur—ANNISETTE,
COGNAC, CREME,
CURACAO, MARC,
RATAFIA
liquify—DISSOLVE, FUSE,
MELT
liquor—ELIXIR, GROG,
HYDROMEL,
NOYAU, RUM, RYE,
TIPPLE
lissome—AGILE, LIMBER,
LITHE, NIMBLE,
SLENDER, SUPPLE,
SVELTE
list—AGENDUM, CANT,
CAREEN, CATALOG,

HEEL, ITEMIZE,
REGISTER, ROLL,
ROSTER, TABLE, TIP
listen—ATTEND, EAR,
EAVESDROP, HARK,
HARKEN, HEAR,
LEST
listless—ACEDIA, ENNUI,
INDIFFERENT,
LANGUID
litany—COLLECT,
EKTENE, ORISON,
ROGATION
literary—BLUE,
LETTERED,
LITERATE, VERSED
litter—BIER, CABIN,
CLUTTER, COFFIN,
DOOLEE, JUMBLE,
MESS, STRETCHER
little—BIT, DARLING,
MODICUM, PETTY,
PUNY, SMALL, TINY,
WEE
liturgy—
CONSUETUDINARY,
RITE, RITUAL
live—ARE, BREATHE,
BRISK, DWELL,
EXIST, QUICK,
RESIDE, SUBSIST
liveliness—ACTIVITY,
ANIMATION, BRISK,
BRISKLY, LILT,
RAPID, VIVACITY
lively—AGILE,
ANIMATED, BRISK,
CADENCE, GAY,
GRIG, NIMBLE,
PERT, SPRY, VIVID
liver disease—CIRRHOSIS
living—BEING, EXTANT,
FILE, QUICK
lixiviate—ALKALI, LEACH
lizard—ADDA, AGAMA,
AGUANA, ANOLE,
ANOLI, EFT,
CHAMELEON,
GALLIWASP,
GECKO, GILA,

IGUANA, LACERTA,
MOLOCH, MONITOR,
NEWT,
SALAMANDER,
SAURIAN, SEPS,
SKINK
llama—ALPACA,
GUANACO,
KECHUA, VICUNA
load—BURDEN, CARGO,
CARK, DOPE,
FREIGHT, JAG,
LADE, ONUS,
ONERATE, SADDLE
loaf—IDLE, LOITER,
LOUNGE
loam—CLAY, DIRT,
EARTH, MARL, SOIL
loath—ABHOR,
ABOMINATE,
AVERSE,
DETEST, HATE,
HOSTILE,
RELUCTANT
lobby—CORRIDOR,
FOYER, HALL,
lobster chela—PINCER
  claw—CHELA, NIPPER
    TRANCE,
    VESTIBULE
  eggs—CORAL, ROE
  part—THORAX
  rel. to—BARNACLE,
    CRAB, SHRIMP
  row—CORAL
  trap—CREEL, CORF,
    POT
  small—JOE, PAWK

local—EDAPHIC,
EPICHORIC, LODGE,
NEWSPAPER,
PLACE, SQUAT,
UNION
locale—IDIOM, SCENE,
VENUE
locality—AREA, PLACE,
SITUS, SPOT
location—AREA, PLACE,
SEAT, SITE, SPOT

loch—LINCTURE, LIN,
    LAKE, NESS, POND
lock—BOLT, COTTER,
    FASTEN, HASP,
    RINGLET, STECKLE,
    TRESS, TUFT
loco—CRAZY, INSANE,
    MAD
locomotive—CAB,
    ENGINE, MOGUL,
    PILOT
locust—ACACIA, CICADA,
    CICALA,
    GRASSHOPPER
lodge—CABIN, HOUSE,
    HOVEL, HUT, HALL,
    IMPLANT, LAY, LIE,
    ORDER, ROOM,
    TEPEE
lodging cars—DOLLIES,
    PULLMANS
  establishments—
    HOTEL, HOSTEL,
    HOSTELRY, INN,
    LODGE, MOTEL
lofty—AERIE, AERIAL,
    AERY, ANDEAN,
    ELEVATED,
    EMINENT, EYRY,
    TALL, TOWERING
log—RECORD, TIMBER
logarithmic unit—BEL
logic—REASONING
logograph—ANAGRAM,
    PHONOGRAM,
    RIDDLE
loin cloth—MARO, PAGNE
long—CRAVE, HANKER,
    HONE, LENGTHY,
    PROLIX, YEARN,
    YEN
longshoreman—DOCKER,
    STEVEDORE,
    STOWER
look—APPEAR, BODE,
    CON, DISCERN, EYE,
    GLANCE, GAZE,
    KEN, LEER, LO, PRY,
    SEE
loom—APPEAR, AIR,

MIEN, SEEM
loon—DIVER, GREBE,
    WABBY
loop—ANSA, BRIDE,
    CIRCLE, CURVE,
    FOLD, NOOSE,
    PICOT, TAB, TERRY
loophole—MEUSE, OILET,
    PLEA
loose—FREE, LAX,
    RELEASE, SLACK,
    UNBOUND
loot—BOOTY, PILLAGE,
    PLUNDER, ROB,
    SACK, SPOILS
lop off—PRUNE, SNED,
    SNIP
lope—CANTER
loquat—BIWA
lord—BARON, DUKE,
    EARL, GRANDEE,
    JEHOVAH, LIEGE,
    MARQUIS, MASTER,
    PEER, VISCOUNT
lose—FORFEIT,
    MISS, ESTRANGE,
    MISPLACE, SPILL,
    STRAY, WASTE
loss—DEFEAT, FAILURE,
    FORFEITURE,
    HARM, LEAK, RUIN
lost—ASEA, DESTROYED,
    GONE, MISLAID,
    LORN, RUINED,
    WASTED
lot—DESTINY, DOOM,
    FATE, FORTUNE,
    HAZARD, MUCH,
    PORTION, SCAD,
    SHARE
lottery—CHANCE,
    PRIZES, RAFFLE,
    TERN
loud—CLAMOROUS,
    NOISY
louse egg—NIT
lout—BOOR, BOWN,
    BLOCKHEAD,
    BUMPKIN, GAWK,
    LOOBY, LURK,

LOON, OAF, YAHOO
love—AFFECTION,
  AMORE, AMOUR,
  CHARITY, FANCY,
  FONDNESS, GRA,
  WOO
lover—AMI, BEAU,
  FRIEND, MINION,
  PARAMOUR,
  ROMEO, SWAIN
loving—AMATIVE,
  AMOROUS, ARDENT,
  EROTIC, FOND
low—BASE, HUMBLE,
  INFERIOR, MOO,
  ORRA, SNEAKY,
  SOFT, SOFTLY,
  RUMBLE, SNIDE
lower—ABASE, BATE,
  DEBASE, DEGRADE,
  DIM, DIP, GROWN,
  HUMBLE, LESSEN,
  SINK
lowland—HILM,
  MOLEHILL, SPIT
loyal—FAITHFUL, LEAL,
  LIEGE, STANCH,
  TRUE
loyalist—TORY
loyalty—FEALTY,
  FIDELITY, HOMAGE
lozenge—PASTIL,
  PASTILLE, TABLET,
  TROCHE
luck—CHANCE, HAP,

FATE, FORTUNE,
  FORTUITY,
  SWASTIKA
lucre—EMOLUMENT,
  GAIN, PELF, PROFIT
lull—CALM, HUSH,
  LULLABY,
  MITIGATE, ROCK,
  QUIET, RESPITE,
  STILL
lumberman—LOGGER,
  SAWYER, SCORER
lump—CLOT, GOB, KNOB,
  LOB, MASS,
  NODULE, NUB
lurch—CAREEN, BILK,
  CHEAT, FILCH,
  JOLT, LURK,
  PROWL, ROLL,
  STAGGER, SWAG
luster—GLORY, GLOSS,
  NAIF, SHEEN, SHINE
lying—DECUMBENT,
  FALSE
  prone—PASSIVE,
  SUPINE
lynx—CARACAL,
  CATAMOUNT,
  COUGAR, LOSSE,
  LUCERN, WILDCAT
lyre—ASOR, HARP,
  SHELL, TRIGON
lyric muse—ERATO
  poem—EPODE, MELIC

-M-

macabre—EERIE,
  GHASTLY, GRIM,
  GRUESOME, LURID
macaw—ARA, ARARA,
  ARARAUNA,
  MARACAN
mace bearer—BEADLE,
  MACER
machine—
  AUTOMATON,
  DEVICE, ENGINE,

MOTOR, PARTY,
  SYSTEM
macintosh—APPLE, COAT
mackerel—MACULATUS,
  SCAD
  genus—SCOMBER
mad—FRANTIC,
  FRENETIC, INSANE,
  IRATE, MANIACAL,
  RABID, WILD
madam—DONNA, FRAU,

HUSSY, LADY,
SENORA
magazine—ARSENAL,
CHAMBER,
GRAINARY,
EPHEMERIS,
STOREHOUSE,
TABLOID
maggot—GRUB, MATHE,
MAWK
magi—BALTHASAR,
CASPAR, MACHIOR
magic—ART, FAIRY,
OBEAH, SHOW,
SORCERY, SPELL,
VOODOO
magician—CONJURER,
FAMULUS, MAGE,
NECROMANCER,
SORCEROR, WIZARD
magistrate—ALCALDE,
BAILIE, EPHOR,
PUISNE, SYNDIC
magpie—MADGE,
PIANET, PICA, PIET,
TALKER
mahogany—RATON,
RATTEEN
male—HE, MAN, MANLY,
STAMINAL, VIRILE
malediction—
ANATHEMA,
BAN, CURSE,
MALISON, THREAT
malicious—CATTY, EVIL,
FELONIOUS,
SPITEFUL
malign—ASPERSE,
DEFAME, EVIL,
LIBEL, REVILE,
VILIFY
malignant—ILL, EVIL,
HEINOUS, VICIOUS
malleable—PLASTIC, SOFT
mammal—APE, BEAR,
ECHIDNA, LORI,
MAN, PRIMATE,
aquatic—DUGONG
Australian—
maid—DOMESTIC, GIRL,

LASS, NYMPH
maiden—COLLEEN,
GIRL, LASS,
VIRGIN
mail—CONSIGN, DAK,
DAWK, POST
maim—CRIPPLE,
DISABLE, INJURE,
LAME, MUTILATE
main—CHIEF,
FOREMOST, OCEAN,
PRIME, PRINCIPAL,
SEA
maize—CORN
genus—ZEA
So. Afr.—MEALIES
major domo—SENESCHAL,
STEWARD
malaria—ANOPHELES,
MIASM, MIASMA
fever—AGUE,
PALUDISM
KANGAROO
carnivorous—PANDA
catlike—MONGOOSE,
OCELOT
gnawing—MOUSE, RAT
marine, large—SHARK,
WALRUS
nocturnal—LEMUR,
RATEL
man—FACTOTUM,
FORTIFY, HOMBRE,
HOMO, HOMO
SAPIENS, MALE,
PERSON, SOMEONE,
VIR, WER
manacle—FETTER, IRON,
SHACKLES
manage—ADMINISTER,
CONTRIVE,
CONTROL, DIRECT,
DIGHT, ENGINEER,
MAN, TEND, WIELD
manager—BOSS,
DIRECTOR, FACTOR,
GRIEVE, OPERATOR,
STEWARD
managerie—ZOO
manakin—DWARF,

MODEL, PIPRA
mandate—BEHEST,
  COMMAND, EDICT,
  INJUNCTION, ORDER
mandatory—DIRECTORY,
  PRECEPTIVE
mange—FODDER, ITCH
manger—BIN, BUNKER,
  CRIB, RACK, STALL,
  TROUGH
mangle—CUT, HACK,
  IRONER, MAGG,
  MAR
manifest—ATTEST,
  CLEAR, DISPLAY,
  EVIDENT, EVINCE,
  OPEN, OVERT,
  PLAIN, PATENT
maniple—HANDFUL,
  ORALE
mankind—ADAM, FOLK,
  HUMANITY, MAN,
  WORLD
manna—FOOD, LAAP,
  LERP
manner—AIR, CUSTOM,
  MEANS, MIEN,
  MODE, SORT, STYLE,
  WAY
manor—DEMESNE,
  ESTATE, HALL,
  MANSION
mantle—CAPE, CLOAK,
  FOAM, PALLIUM,
  ROBE, SPREAD
  kind—COPE, OCREA,
    PALL
  worn over
    armor—TABARD
manuscript—CODEX,
  FOLIO
  marks—DORSO, OBELI
  unpublished—INEDITA
many (prefix)—MULT,
  MULTI
map—ATLAS, CHART,
  DESIGN, DIAGRAM
maple (genus)—ACER
marabou—ARGALA,
  STORK

marble—AGATE, ALLEY,
  BASALT, DOLOMITE,
  MIB, MIG, SHOOTER,
  TAW
march—FILE, IDES, HIKE,
  PARADE, TRAMPLE,
  TREAD
mare—HORSE, JADD,
  MEARE, YAUD
marine—GYRENE,
  MARITIME,
  NAUTICAL,
  OCEANIC, SEADOG
mariner—JACKY, SALT,
  SAILOR, SEAMAN,
  TAR, WATERMAN
mark—BRAND, DOT,
  LABEL, LANE,
  NOTE, STAIN,
  SYMBOL, TAB,
  TARGET, TRACE,
  TRACK, TRAIT
marker—CHIP, COUNTER,
  ETCHER, PEG,
  SCORER, TAB
market—FORA, MART,
  RIALTO, SALE,
  SELL, STORE
  place—AGORA,
    EMPORIUM, MART,
    RIALTO, PLAZA
marl—GREENSAND,
  MALM, MARLITE
marmalade—
  CONFECTION,
  SAPOTE
marmoset—MONKEY,
  SAGOIN, TAMARIN
marmot—BOBAC,
  GROUNDHOG,
  RODENT,
  WOODCHUCK
marriage—CONNUBIAL,
  MARITAL,
  MATRIMONY,
  UNION, WEDLOCK
  broker—SCHATCHEN
  comb. form—GAMO
  dot—DOWER
  hater—MISOGAMIST

notice—BANNS
song—HYMENEAL
marriageable—NUBILE
married—MATED,
    WEDDED
marrow—ESSENCE,
    MEDULLA, PITH
marsh—BOG, FEN,
    LERNA, MIRE,
    MORASS, QUAG,
    SWALE, SWAMP
marshal—ALINE, ARRAY,
    GUIDE, RANGE,
    USHER
marshy—BOGGY, FENNY,
    PALUDAL,
    PALUDIC, WET
marsupial—BANDICOOT,
    DIPROTODON,
    KOALA, MARTEN,
    OPOSSUM,
    TAPOATAEA,
    WOMBAT
marvel—MIRACLE,
    PRODIGY, WONDER
masculine—LUIS, MALE,
    MAS, VIRILE
mask—CLOAK,
    CONCEAL,
    DISGUISE, DOMINO,
    VEIL, VISOR
mass—ASSEMBLE, BULK,
    CLOTURE, GOB,
    HEAP, LUMP, PAT,
    THRONG, WAD
massacre—CARNAGE,
    DECIMATE, HAVOC,
    POGROM
mast—ACORNS,
    NUTS, POLE, SPAR,
    SPRIT, STUFF
master—BEST, CHIEF,
    CONQUER, LORD,
    MAN, MIAN,
    PALRONE, RAB,
    RABBI, SUBDUE
matador's garment—CAPE
    staff—MULETA
    sword—ESTOQUE
match—CAP, COPE,

COPY, FUSEE,
    LUCIFER, MATE,
    PAIR, PEER, PIT,
    TALLY, TEAM,
    TWIN, VESTA
mate—FERE, MARINER,
    MARRY, PAIR
material—DATA,
    CORPOREAL,
    FABRIC, HYLIC,
    PLASMA, REAL,
    STUFF, SUBSTANCE
mathematical arbitrary
    number—RADIX
  arc—RADIAN
  constant—PARAMETER
  diagram—GRAPH
  function and ratio—
    COSINE, PI, SINE
  instrument—NABLA,
    QUATERNION,
    SECTOR, VERNIER
  irrational number—SURD
  line in space—VECTOR
  pure number—SCALAR
  surface—NAPPE
  symbol—DIGIT,
    FACIEND, OPERAND
  table—LOGARITHM
  term—COSH, COSINE,
    LOGARITHM, PI,
    SINE
matinee—LEVEE, PARTY,
    SALON, SOIREE
matrass—BOTTLE,
    CARAFE, FLASK,
    TUBE
matrix—BED, CAST,
    FORM, MOULD
matter—AFFAIR, BODY,
    COPY, CONCERN,
    ELEMENTS, IMPORT,
    PITH, SUBSTANCE
mattress covering—TICK
  filling—BATTS, KAPOK
mature—AGE,
    COMPLETE, DIGEST,
    GROW, MELLOW,
    RIPE, RIPEN,
    SEASON

mau—TSETSE
maul—ABUSE, BEETLE,
  GAVEL, MALLET,
  MOTH
maverick—CALF, DOGIE
maw—CRAW, CROP,
  STOMACH
maxim—ADAGE, AXIOM,
  DICT, GNOME,
  ITEM, MORAL,
  MOTTO, PRECEPT,
  PROVERB, TENET
meadow—BAAN,
  GRASSLAND, LEA,
  MEAD, SWALE
meager—ARID, BARE,
  LENTEN, SCANT,
  SCANTY, SLIM
meal—MESS, POWDER,
  RATION, REPAST,
  TIFFIN
mean—AVERAGE, BASE,
  BRUTAL, CRUEL,
  DENOTE, INTEND,
  IMPLY, MEDIAL,
  SENSE, SNIDE
meantime—INTERIM,
  INTERVAL
measles—MORBILLI,
  RUBEOLA
meat—FLESH, FOOD,
  MORSEL, VENISON
mechanical—DOOMED,
  INVOLUNTARY
median—AVERAGE,
  MESNE, MEAN
medical—CURATIVE,
  IATRIC
meditate—BROOD,
  CONTEMPLATE,
  MULL, MUSE,
  PONDER, PORE,
  RUMINATE, STUDY
medium—AVERAGE,
  MEAN, PSYCHIC,
  ORACLE
medley—ARIA,
  FARRAGO,
  MELANGE, OLIO,
  HODGEPODGE,

POTPOURRI, SONG
medulla—MARROW, PITH
meet—ASSEMBLE,
  CONFER,
  CONFRONT,
  CONVENE, EQUAL,
  FIT, JOIN, MATCH,
  SEEMLY
meeting—ASSEMBLAGE,
  CONCLAVE,
  JUNCTION, MALL,
  PARLEY, RALLY,
  SYNOD, TRYST
melancholy—ATRABILE,
  BLUE, DREAR,
  GLOOM, RUEFUL,
  SAD
mellow—AGE, LOAMY,
  MALM, MATURE,
  RIPE, SOFT
melody—AIR, ARIA,
  CANTILENA,
  CAVATINA, CHARM,
  CHIME, LAY, MUSIC,
  SONG, RHYTHM
melon—CASABA, GOURD,
  MUSK, PEPO
melt—DISSOLVE, FUSE,
  LIQUIFY, SWALE,
  THAW
member—LIMB, ORGAN,
  PART
membrane—CAUL, PIA,
  SKIN, TELA, WEB
memorandum—CHIT,
  MINUTE, NOTE
memorial—RECORD,
  TROPHY
memory—MIND,
  REMINISCENCE,
  ROTE
  loss of—AMNESIA,
  LETHE
  partial loss—APHASIA
  pert. to—CON,
  MNEMONIC
mend—COBBLE, DARN,
  HEAL, PATCH,
  REPAIR, SEW
mendicant—BEGGAR,

FAKIR
mental—IDEAL,
INTELLECT
mention—CITE, MIND,
NAME, REFER
mercenary—HACK,
HIRED, HIRELING,
HESSIAN, SORDID,
VENAL
merchandise—GOODS,
TRADE, WARES
merchant—DEALER,
SELLER, TRADER,
VENDER
merganser—
GOOSANDER,
HARLE, HERALD,
NUN, SHELDRAKE,
SMEE, SMEW
meridian—APEX, NOON,
NOONDAY, ZENITH
merit—DESERVE, EARN,
MEED, RATE,
WORTH
merry—BLITHE, GAY,
HAPPY, HILARIOUS,
JOCOSE, JOLLY,
JOYFUL, JOVIAL,
SUNNY
mescal—CACTUS,
PEYOTE
mesh—MITOME, NET,
TISSUE
mesquite—ALGAROBA,
PACAY, PROSOPIS
message—BODE, BREVET,
EVANGEL, NOTE,
TIDINGS, WORD
messenger—APOSTLE,
CARRIER, ENVOY,
HERALD, IRIS,
PAGE, TOTY
metal—BRASS, BRONZE,
COBALT, COPPER,
GOLD, IRON, LEAD,
NICKEL, SILVER,
STEEL, TANTALITE,
TIN, ZINC
bar—INGOT
bearing vein—LODE

casting—PIG
clippings—SCISSEL
coarse—MATTE
cymbals—TAL
disk—MEDAL, PATEN,
SEQUIN
dross—SLAG
eyelet—GROMMET
filings—LEMEL
fissure—LODE
ingot—GAD
leaf—FOIL
lightest—LITHIUM
mass—INGOT, PID
plate—DISC, PATEN,
PLATEN, SHIM
refuse—SLAG
shaper—SWAGE
thread—WIRE
trademark—MONEL
ware—TOLE, REVERE
worker—RIVETER,
SMITH, WELDER
metallic alloy—BRASS,
NICKEL, SOLDER
meteor—ANTLID, BIELID,
FIREBALL, LEONID
meter—MEASURE,
RHYTHM
method—ORDER, PLAN,
PROCESS, RULE,
SYSTEM,
TECHNIQUE, WAY
metric—ANAPEST, IAMB,
IAMBUS
metrical—POEM, ODE,
POESY, POETICAL
mezzanine—ENTRESOL
microscope thread—FILAR
middle—CENTRAL,
CENTER, MEDIAL,
MEDIAN, MESIAL,
MESNE, MID, MIDST
middling—AVERAGE,
SOSO
midshipman—PLEBE,
REEFER
mien—AIR, ASPECT,
BEARING,
CARRIAGE,

CUSTOM, HABIT,
GUISE, LOOK,
MANNER, SORT
might—ARM, POWER
migrant worker—OKIE,
WETBACK
mild—BENEDICT,
BLAND, GENTLE,
MEEK, SOFT, TAME
mildew—BLIGHT, MOLD,
MOULD, MUST
military—MARTIAL
milk—DRAIN, LAC,
NURSE
coagulator—RENNET
curd—CASEIN, ZEIGA
curdled—CLABBER
mill—BOX, FACTORY,
QUERN
millet—CENCHRINE,
KODA, PEARL
million thousand—
MILLIARD
millpond—DAM, DIKE,
DITCH
millstone part—INK,
RYND
mime—ACTOR,
BUFFOON, CLOWN,
COPY
mimic—APE, APER,
IMITATE, MIME,
MOCK
mince—CUT, DICE, HASH,
SLASH
minced oath—BEGAD,
DRAT, EGAD, ODS
mind—MOOD, NOUS,
OPINION, PURPOSE,
SYNONYM, THINK
mine—BURROW, DIG,
MY, PIT, SAP, VEIN
entrance—ADIT
miner's chisel—GAD
lamp—DAVY
mineral—ANKERITE,
CROCIDOLITE,
DANALITE,
ERINITE, IOLITE,
RUTILE, SPINEL,

TANTALITE,
TANTALUM
amorphous—PINITE
bed—SEAM
black—GRAPHITE,
URANITE
carbonate—TRONA
crystalline—FELSPAR
dark green—URALITE
deposit—LODE, ORE,
PLACER, SINTER
gray white—TRONA
hard—ALALITE,
SPINEL
matter mix—MAGMA
oil—COLZA
pale yellow—EPIDOTE,
PYRITE
pitch—ASPHALT,
BITUMEN
pulp—TALC
rare brittle—EUCLASE,
THORITE
salt—ALKALI, ALUM
silicate—MICA
spring—SPA
tar—MALTHA, BREA
water—SELTZER
wax like—OZOCERITE
whitish—BARITE,
SPALT
yellow green—EPIDOTE
mingle—ADMIX, BLEND
COALESCE, MELT,
MERGE, MIX, STIR,
WEAVE
minister—ANGEL,
ATTEND, CLERIC,
DIVINE, DOMINIE,
ENVOY, PARSON,
PREACHER, PRIEST,
RECTOR, SERVE,
TEND
minor—LESS, SMALLER,
YOUTH
minority—NONAGE,
PUPILAGE
minstrel—BARD,
GLEEMAN, HARPER,
PIERROT, POET,

RIMER
mint—CHIA, COIN,
HYSSOP, MONEY,
RAMONA
minuet (rel. to)—SCHERZO
minute—ITEM, MITE,
NOTE, ROTIFER,
SMALL, TRIFLING,
WEE
minx—COLLEEN, DOLL,
FILLY, GIRL, JADE,
MISS, SIS
miracle—ANOMY,
MARVEL, PLAY,
WONDER
mirage—ILLUSION,
SERAB, VISION
mire—ADDLE, BOG,
GLAR, MOIL, MUD,
MUCK, OOZE, SLUD,
STALL
mirror—CRYSTAL,
GLASS, REFLECT,
REFLECTOR,
SPECULUM
mirth—FUN, GLEE,
GAIETY, HILARITY,
JOLLITY
miscellany—ANA, OLIO
mischief—BANE,
DAMAGE, ILL,
KNAVERY, WRACK
mischievous—ARCH,
DEVILISH, ELFIN,
ELFISH, EVIL, SLY
miser—HOARDER,
HUNKS, NABAL,
NIGGARD
misery—DISTRESS,
GRIEF,
HEARTACHE,
PANDORA, WOE
missile—ARROW,
BULLET, DART,
GRENADE, LANCE,
LETTER, OUTCAST,
SHAFT, SPEAR
mist—BEDIM, BRUME,
DIM, FOG, HARR,
HAZE, MISLE,

SEREIN, SMUR
mistake—BARNEY,
BLUNDER, BONER,
BULL, ERR, ERROR,
FAULT, SLIP
mite—ACE, ATOM,
ACARID, ACARINA,
ACARUS, BIT, MOTE,
JOT, TICK, WEE
miter—CIDARIS, FILLET,
FRANK, GUSSET,
TIARA
mix—BLEND, CONSORT,
JUMBLE, MINGLE,
STIR
mixture—AMALGAM,
BLEND, HASH,
MELANGE,
MISCUE, OLIO,
POTPOURRI, SALAD
moan—CRY, COMPLAIN,
GROAN, LAMENT,
SUUM, WAIL
moat—CANAL, DITCH,
FOSS, FOSSE,
GRAFFE
mob—CANAILLE,
DROVE, GANG,
HERD, POPULACE,
RABBLE, ROUT,
THRONG
moccasin—LARRIGAN,
MAKAK, PAC,
SNAKE, LOAFER
mock—APE, COPY, DEFY,
DERIDE, FLEER,
FLOUT, GIBE,
IMITATE, LEER.
MIMIC, SCOFF,
SNEER, TAUNT
mockery—CRONY,
DELUSION, FARCE,
GAME, IRONY,
RUSE, SHAM, SPORT,
TRAVESTY
mocking—FLEERING,
GAB, JEERING
mode—FAD, FASHION,
FLAIR, MANNER,
STYLE, VOGUE

model—EXEMPLAR,
DESIGN, GAUGE,
NORM, PARADIGM,
PARAGON,
PATTERN,
PROTOTYPE, SHAPE,
SITTER, TYPE
modern—LATE, NEO,
NEOTERIC, NEW,
RECENT
modest—CIVIL, COY,
DECENT, DEMURE,
PRIM, RETIRING,
SHY
modify—ALTER,
CHANGE, MASTER,
VARY
mogul—LORD,
MONGOLIAN,
NABOB
moil—DRUDGE,
DRUDGERY,
MEDDLE, SOIL,
TAINT, TOIL
moist—DAMP, DANK,
DEWY, HUMID, WET
moisten—ANOINT,
BEDEW, MOIL,
SPARGE
molar—CHOPPER,
GRINDING, TEETH,
TOOTH
molasses—THERIACA,
TREACLE
mold—CAST, DIE, FORM,
FASHION, HUMUS,
KNEAD, MILDEW,
MODEL, MUST,
MOULAGE, MATRIX,
PLASM
molding—CAVETTO,
GULA, OGEE,
OVOLO, TORUS
  edge—ARRIS
  convex—REEDING
  small square—LISTEL
  tool—FLANGE
mole—BLES,
BREAKWATER,
MOLECULE, PIER,
QUAY, STARNOSE,
TALPA, TOUPE
molecule—MONAD,
PARTICLE
  component—ATOM,
  ION
mollusk—ABALONE,
CLAM, LIMPET,
MUSSEL, OYSTER,
SCALLOP,
SHELLFISH, SNAIL
  bivalve—LEDA,
  VENERIDA
  double shell—LIMPET
  edible—ASI, MUSSEL
  eight armed—OCTOPUS
  fresh water—CHITON,
  ETHERIA
  gastropod—
  ABALONE, SLUG
  genus—ASTARTE,
  BUCCINUM,
  CHAMA, MUREX
  gills—CERATA
  large part of—MANTLE
  larval—VELIGER
  sea—ABALONE, SALP
moment—SECOND,
FLASH, JIFF,
INSTANT, POINT,
TRICE
monarch—EMPEROR,
KING, RULER,
SACHEM,
SOVEREIGN, TSAR
monastery—ABBEY,
CONVENT, FRIARY,
HOSPICE
monastic—MONACHAL,
MONKLY, OBLATE,
ORDER
  garb—HABIT
  haircut—TONSURE
  house—PRIORY
  order—CALOYER,
  CELIBATE,
  BENEDICTINE,
  CISTERCIAN
  superior—PRIOR
mongoose—

ICHNEUMON, LEMUR,
URVA
mongrel—CUR, HYBRID,
MIXED, MUT, MUTT
monitor—IBIL, MENTOR,
PREPOSTER
monk—ABBOT,
CELIBATE, FRA,
FRIAR, PADRE
monkey—APE, ARABA,
GRIVET, GUENON,
CHIMP, LANGUR,
MARMOSET, MONA,
MONO, NISNAS,
PINCHE, QUAKARI,
SAI, SIME, TITI,
TOTA, VITOE, WAAG
arboreal—POTTO
Asiatic—MACAQUE
bearded—ENTELLUS
Brazilian—SAI, TEETER
capuchin—SAPAJOU,
SAI
Ceylonese—MAHA,
TOQUE
grivet—TOTA
house—APERY
howler—ARABA,
MONO, STENTOR
longtailed—LANGUR,
PATAS
proboscis—KAHA,
NOSEAPE
sacred of India—RHESUS
squirrel—SAMIRI
monotonous—DRAB,
DREARY, DRONE,
DULL, HUMDRUM,
SAME, TEDIOUS,
THRUM
monster—CHIMERA,
CENTAUR, GIANT,
GORGON, HILA,
OGRE, OGRESS,
SPHINX
moo—LOW, MENHIR,
OBELISK
moon—CYNTHIA,
DIANA, LUNA,
LUNAR, LUNE,

PHOEBE, SATELLITE
moon picture—
SELENOGRAPH
point farthest from
earth—APOGEE
position—OCTANT
valley—RILL
moonshine—
FLUMMERY,
FUSTIAN
moonstone—
FELDSPAR,
HECATOLITE
moor—ALGERINE,
ANCHOR, BERBER,
FASTEN, FEN,
MARSH, MORO
moose—ALCE, ELAND,
ELK
female—COW
genus—ALCES
male—BULL
pouch—BEL
moral—EPIMYTH,
ETHICAL, GOOD,
MAXIM, NOBLE,
RIGHTEOUS,
TEACHING
moray—CONGER, EEL,
HAMLET
morbid—DISEASED,
GRISLY,
GRUESOME,
HORRID,
OFFENSIVE,
SHOCKING
morning—AURORA,
DAWN, FORENOON,
EOS, MATIN, MORN
morose—GLOOMY,
GLUM, MOODY,
SOUR, SPLENETIC,
SULLEN
morsel—BIT, BITE,
CRUMB, ORT, PIECE,
SNACK, SCRAPS,
TIDBIT
mortal—DEADLY,
DEATH, FATAL,
HUMAN, LETHAL,

MAN

mortar—BOWL, CANNON,
CEMENT, HOBIT,
TROUGH
mortise—LAW,
AMORTIZE
mortuary—
CINERARIUM,
MORGUE
mosaic—INCRUST
gold—ORMOLU
law—TORA, TORAH
squares—TESSERAE
mosquito—ANOPHELES,
AEDES, CULEX,
CULICID,
GALLINIPPER,
IMAGO, STEGOMYIA
moss—BOG, LICHEN
moth—AM, ARRINDA,
EGGER, LAPPET, IO,
REGAL, TINEA
motion—ACT, AESTUS,
GAIT, GESTURE,
MOVEMENT,
REQUEST
motionless—INANIMATE,
INERT, STAGNANT,
STILL
motive—ARIA, CAUSE,
INCENTIVE, MOTIF,
PRESS, PRETEXT,
REASON, SAKE
mottled—MARBLED,
PIED, PINTO
motto—ADAGE, GNOME,
GRUNT, MOT,
MUTTER, POESY,
REASON, SLOGAN
mountaineer—AARON,
MONTE
mountains,
science—OROLOGY
study—OROGRAPHY
mourn—ERME, ERN,
GRIEVE, LAMENT,
RUE, SIGH, SORROW,
WAIL
mournful—DISMAL,
FUNEREAL,
PLAINTIVE, SAD,
SORROWFUL,
THRENODIC
mouse—VOLE
like mammal—
BAT
meadow—
VOLE
old world—
JERBOA
shrew—ERD
tiny—HARVEST
mouth—APERTURE,
LORRIKER, MUN,
ORIFICE, OS
move—AGITATE,
ACTUATE, BUDGE,
DRIVE, GEE, IMPEL,
KELTER, MOG,
SKIRR, SNEAK
movement—ACTION,
MOTION, TREND
movie (comb. form)—CINE
moving—ASTIR, MOBILE,
MOTILE, NOMADIC,
TRANSIENT
mow—CUT, DESS, MATH,
MEW, SHORTEN
mud—GOBBET, GOO,
MIRE, MUCK, SILT,
SLIME, SLUDGE,
SLOSH
muddle—ADDLE,
CONFUSE, MESS,
SOSS
muddled—ASEA,
BURBLED, CHAOS,
CHAOTIC, MUZZY,
REE, SLIMED
muddy—BESPATTER,
GOTE, MIRY, MOIST,
ROILY, SLAKY,
SLUDGY
mug—CUP, FACE, NOG,
NOGGIN, POT,
TOBY, STEIN
mulberry—AAL, ACH, AL,
AWL, RUBRA
mulct—AMERCE, BILK,
CHEAT, FINE,

PUNISH, SCOT,
STEAL
mule—ASS, HINNY,
HYBRID, MUTE
mullet—GOATFISH, LIZA,
SUCKER
multitude—CROWD, HOST,
GALAXY, MOB,
SHOAL, THRONG
mummy—CADAVER,
CORPSE, RELIC
murder—BURKE,
HOMICIDE, KILL,
SLAY
murderer—ARAM,
CAINKILLER,
SLAYER
murmur—COO, CURR,
GRUMBLING, HUM,
MUTTER, PURL,
REPINE
muscle—BRAWN,
INCISOR, LACERT,
SINEW, TENSOR,
TERES, THEW
muscular—BRAWNY,
BULKY, BURLY,
HUSKY, MIGHTY,
STRONG, THEWY,
TOROSE
muse—COGITATE,
DREAM, MEDITATE,
MULL, PONDER,
REVE, RUNE
mushroom—AGARIC,
FUNGUS, MISY,
MOREL, TRUFFLE
cap—STIPE
disease—FLOCK
part—GILLS
superior—MOREL
umbrella shaped
part—PILEUS
music—MELODY
aftersong—EPODE
all together—TUTTI
Anglo-Ind.
melody—RAGAS
as it stands—STA
at once—SUBITO

B flat—ZA
bright—ANIME
but—MA
canto—PASSUS
change—MUTA
character—CLEF, KEY
composition—FUGUE
concluding
passage—CODA
direction—ANIME,
POCO, STA, TACET
disconnected—
STACCATO
duet—DUO
emotionally—AGITATO
fast movement—
ALLEGRO,
PRESTO
first note—ROTE
flat—MOLLE
flourishes—CADENZAS
grace note—SANGLOT
half major
tone—SEMITONE
note—MINIM
step lower—
MORDENT
hall—GAFF, ODEUM
high—ALT
increasing—
CRESCENDO
independent
passage—CODA
in major—DUR
in time—ATEMPO
kettledrums—TIMPANI
leap in—SALTO
less—MENO
like—SIMILE
line across staff—BAR
lively—ANIMATO
loud—FORTE
major—DUR
scale—GAMUT
thirds in—DITONES
mark—SLUR
measured—MOTO,
PULSE
melodious—ARIOSE,
ARLOSO

melodic
  phrase—LEITMOTIF
metrical
  composition—POEM
minor—LESSER
moderately
  slow—ANDANTE
morning
  concert—AUBADE
more—PIU
movement—MOTO
much—MOLTO
muse—EUTERPE
mute—SORDINO
nine piece composition—
  NONET
ninth in—NONA
non concerted—SOLO
noble in
  style—GRANDIOSE
not too much—TANTO
organ—MELODIA
parts of measure—ARSES
pedal coupler—TIRASSE
potato—OCARILA
rapid in tempo—VELOCE
repeat—REPRISE
set of bells—PEAL
set of verses—DERRY
sextuplet—SESTOLE,
  SESTOLET
short song—ODE
sign in—SEGNO
silent—TACET
simple song—AIR, LAY,
  TUNE
slow—ADAGIO,
  LARGHETTO,
  LARGO, LENTO,
  TARDO
slower—
  ALLARGANDO, RIT
small tabor—TABRET
so much—TANTO
soft—DOLCE
soprano—CANTO
stately—LARGO
sustained—
  SOSTENUTO
sweet—DULCE

tempo—RUBATO
thrice—TER, TRIAD
time—GIUSTO, TEMPO
triplet—TERCET
turning—VOLTA
twice—BIS
upbeats—ARSES
very—ASSAI, MOLTO
vocal flourishes—
  ROULADES
wind instrument of oboe
  class—SAHWM
musical—
  HARMONIOUS, LYRIC,
  LYRICAL, MELIC,
  MELODIOUS
air—MELODY, SONG,
  TUNE
aria—SOLO
bells—CHIMES
character—CLEF, NOTE,
  REST, SHARP
coda—FINALE
comedy—REVUE
composition—
  ARIOSO, BALLADE,
  CANTATA,
  CONCERTO, FUGUE,
  GLEE, NOCTURN,
  OPERA, OPUS,
  ORATORIO, RONDO,
  SERENADE, SEXTET,
  SONATA, SONG,
  TRIO
direction—ACAPRICCIO,
  LENTO, SOLI,
  STA, TACET
drama—CANTATA
exercise—ETUDE
group—BAND, COMBO,
  ORCHESTRA
half globes—CYMBALS
horns—CORNI
instruments—ASER,
  BANDORE, BANGO,
  BANJO, BUGLE,
  CELLO, CALLIOPE,
  CLARINET,
  CLAVIER,
  CONCERTINA.

CORNET, CYMBAL,
DRUMS, FIFE,
FLUTE, GORA,
GUITAR, HARP,
LUTE, LYRE,
MARIMBA,
MANDOLIN,
MELODEON, OBOE,
NOVACHORD,
OCARINA, ORGAN,
PIANO, REBEC,
REED, ROTE,
SAXOPHONE, SITAR,
SPINET, TRIANGLE,
TROMBONE, TUBA,
UKE. VIOL, VIOLIN,
ZITHER
interlude—VERSET
interval—OCTAVE,
  REST, SECOND,
  TRITONE
key—MONOR
line—TIE
medley—CENTO, OLIO,
  RONDO
mutes—SOURDINES
nocturne—SERENADE
note,
  sharpening—ECBOLE
performance—CONCERT,
  RECITAL, REVUE
pipe—OAT, REED
pitch—TONE
play—OPERA,
  OPERETTA, REVUE
program—RECITAL
rattle—SISTRUM
response—ANTIPHON
scale—GAMUT. GRADO
score—CELESTA,
  NOTATOR
shake—TREMOLO,
  TRILL
show—REVUE
signs—ISON, SEGNO
sound—NOTE,
  SONANCE, TONAL,
  TONE
study—ETUDE
syllable—RE, SI, TRA

symbol—CLEF, REST
term—ANDANTIDO,
  MESE
theme—ETUDE,
  MOTET, TEMA
third—TIERCE
tone—CHORD
triplet—TERCET
up beat—ARSIS
wave—TREMOLO
work—OPUS
musket—FUSIL, HAWK
muslin—ADATI, MOSAL,
  MULL, NAINSOOK,
  SEERHAND, SHELA,
  TARLATAN
muss—CHAOS,
  CRUMBLE,
  DISHEVEL, LITTER,
  MESS, MUDDLE,
  RUMPLE
mussel, fresh
  water—NAIAD, UNIO
genus—MYTILUS
large—HORSE
part—BYSSUS
river—UNIO
must—JUICE, MILDEW,
  SAPA, STUM
mustard—CHARLOCK,
  SENVY, WOAD,
  SINAPIS
muster—GATHER, LEVY,
  MARSHAL, SUMMON
musty—BAD, FETID,
  FUSTY, HOAR,
  MOLDY,
  RANCID,
  SNUFF
mute—LENE, DUMB,
  MUFFLE, SILENT,
  SPEECHLESS,
  SURD, TACITURN
mutilate—DEFORM,
  GARBLE, GELD,
  INJURE, MAIM,
  MAR, MANGLE
mutiny—PUTSCH,
  REBELLION,
  REVOLT, TUMULT

mutter—GRUMBLE,
    MAUNDER,
    MUMBLE, MURMUR,
    MUSSITATE,
    PATTER, THREATEN
mutton—CABOB, KABOB,
    SHEEP
muzzle—COPE, GAG,
    NOSE, SNOUT
myrtle—GUAVA,
    PERIWINKLE
mysterious—CRYPTIC,
    MYSTIC. OCCULT,
    ORACULAR, RUNIC,
    SECRET, SPHINXINE
mystery—ARCANUM,
    CABALA, CRAFT,
    ENIGMA, ESOTERY,
    MAGIC, RUNE,
    SECRET
mystic—EPOPTIC,
    ORPHIC, RUNIC
mystical—IMAGINARY,
    LEGENDARY,
    OCCULT

-N-

nabob—DIVES, MIDAS,
    PLUTOCRAT
nacre—PEARL
nag—HECTOR,
    HENPECK, HORSE,
    IRK, PESTER,
    PLAGUE, RILE,
    SCOLD, TEASE, TWIT
nail—BRAD, CLINCH,
    FASTEN, GARRON,
    HOB, SECURE, SPAD,
    SPIKE, STUD, TACK
naive—ARTLESS,
    GUILELESS, NATURAL
naked—BARE, BARREN,
    EXACT, LITERAL
    NUDE, PLAIN,
    SIMPLE,
    UNPROTECTED
name—CALL
    DUB,
    ENTITLE,
    ENUMERATE,
    MENTION, TERM,
    TITLE
namely (law)—SILICET
namesake—EPONYM,
    HOMONYM
nap—DOZE, PILE,
    SIESTA, SNOOZE,
    SLEEP, SLUMBER,
    WINK
nape—NIDDICK, SCRUFF,
    SCURF, TURNIP
napkin—BIB, DIAPER,
    DOILIE, DOILY,
    SERVETTE
narcotic—ANODYNE,
    BHANG. COCAINE,
    DOPE. DRUG, HEMP,
    HEROIN, OPIATE,
    OPIUM
narrative—CONTE,
    FABLE, TALE
    poem—EPIC, EPOS,
    EPOPEE
narrow—AUGUST, CLOSE,
    CONTRACT, LIMIT,
    MEAGER, SCANT,
    STRAIT
nasal—NARINE, RHINAL
native—ABORIGINAL,
    ENDEMIC,
    INDIGENOUS, ITE,
    NATAL, SON, TAO
natural—ARTLESS, BORN,
    INBORN, INNATE,
    LIFELIKE, NORMAL,
    NAIVE
nature—
    CHARACTER,
    CREATION,
    ESSENCE, LUND,
    MOOD, SORT, TYPE
nautical—MARINE,
    MARITIME, NAVAL,

NAVIGATION,
OCEANIC
naval—MARINE,
MARITIME,
NAUTICAL
nave—HUB, NAVEL
extension—AISLE
of a church—BODY,
NEF
of a wheel—HOB, HUB,
navigation system—LORAN,
SHORAN, SONAR
navy ship—BATTLESHIP,
CRUISER,
DESTROYER,
MINELAYER,
MINESWEEPER
near—AT, BY,
CLOSE
DEAR, NIGH,
NEARBY, WITHIN
neat—NATTY, SPRUCE,
TRIM
neb—BEAK, BILL, FACE,
SNOUT
nebulous—CLOUDY,
HAZY, MISTY,
NEBULAR, VAGUE
neck—CERVIX, CRANE,
SWIRE
necklace—BEADS,
BALDRIC, RIVIERE,
TORQUE
necktie—ASCOT, CRAVAT,
SCARF, TIE
nectar—DRINK,
HONEY, HONEYDEW
MEGLIO, MEL
need—DEMAND,
LACK,
NECESSITATE,
POOR, POVERTY
REQUIRE, STRAIT,
THARF, WANT
needle—BODKIN,
OBELISK
negative—FILM, DENIAL,
ANE, ANY, NO, NOR,
NOT
negligee—PEIGNOIR

neophyte—
CATECHUMEN,
CONVERT,
NOVICE, TYRO
nephew—NEPOTE
nerve—COURAGE,
ENERGY, PLUCK,
STRENGTH, VIGOR
nest—AERIE, DEN,
HAUNT, NIDE,
NIDUS, RETREAT
nestle—CUDDLE,
PET, SETTLE,
SNUGGLE
nestling—BIRD, EYAS
of a pigeon—SQUAB
place—JUG
net—CLEAR, GAIN, GIN,
MESH, SEINE,
SNARE, TOIL, TRAP,
TRAMMEL, WEIR,
YIELD
nettle—ANNOY,
IRRITATE, PIQUE,
PROVOKE, VEX
network—FRET, MESH,
MOKE, PLEXUS,
RETE, RETIA,
RETICULUM, WEB
nevus—BIRTHMARK,
TUMOR
new—FRESH, LATE,
MODERN, NEO,
NEOTERIC, NOVA,
UNTRIED, UNUSED,
RECENT
news—TIDINGS, WORK
agency—AP, TASS, UPI
beat—SCOOP
monger—GOSSIP
stand—KIOSK
newspaper—NEWS, PRESS,
SHEET
item—ADS, HEADLINE,
OBIT
official—EDITOR,
REDACTOR
newt—EFT, EVET,
SALAMANDER,
TRITON

next—IMMEDIATE,
  NEIST, THEN
nice—AGREEABLE, FINE,
  FINICAL, GENTEEL,
  NEAT, PLEASANT,
  SOCIABLE, TICKLE
nickel alloy—INVAR,
  KONEL
nickname—AGNOMEN,
  AGNOMINA, LEN,
  MONIKER, UGO
night—BELATED,
  DARKNESS, EVE,
  CONCEALMENT,
  GABE, GABI,
  NIGHTFALL
nimble—AGILE, ALERT,
  DEFT, FLIT, GLEG,
  LISH, LISSOME,
  SPRY, VOLANT
nimbus—AUREOLA,
  GLORIA, HALO
ninny—BLOCKHEAD,
  DOLT, DUNCE,
  FOOL, LOUT,
  SAMMY, SIMPLETON
nip—BLAST, BLIGHT,
  CHILL, CLAMP,
  CLIP, CUT, GIBE,
  PECK, PINCER,
  PINCH
nitrogen—AZOTE
nobel—BARON, EDEL,
  EPIC, EPICAL,
  GRAND, PEER,
  SUBLIME, SUPERB
nobleman—BARON, EARL,
  GRANDEE,
  LORD,
  MARQUIS, PEER,
  PRINCE, THANE
nobody—JACKSTRAW,
  NONENTITY
node—KNOB, KNOT,
  PROTUBERANCE,
  SWELLING
nodule—KNOT, LUMP,
  MASS, TUBERCLE
noise—BLARE, CHANG,
  CHORTLE, CLAMOR,

DIN, HUBBUB,
  RACKET, RATTLE,
  ROAR
noisy—BLATANT,
  CLAMOROUS,
  CREAKY, LOUD,
  STREPATANT
nomad—ARAB, BEDOUIN,
  GYPSY, LURI,
  ROVER, SARACEN,
  WANDERER
nominal—PAR, TITULAR
nominate—APPOINT,
  CALL, ENTITLE,
  NAME
none—NARY, NAE, NIN,
  UN
nook—ANGLE, CANT,
  CORNER, COVE,
  NERNE, RECESS
noose—ENTRAP,
  HALTER, LASSO,
  LOOP, SNARE
norm—AVERAGE,
  MODEL, PATTERN,
  RULE, STANDARD
normal—JUST, MEAN,
  NATURAL, PAR,
  REGULAR, SAME,
  SANE, STANDARD
nose—CONK, NASUS,
  NEB, NOZZLE,
  SCENT, SNIFF,
  SPOUT
nosegay—ODOR, POSY
nostalgia—HOMESICK,
  NOSTOMANIA
nostril—NARE, NARI,
notch—DENT, GAP,
  INDENT,
  INDENTURE, JAB,
  JAG, SCORE,
  SERRATE
notched—CRENATED,
  EROSE, SERRATED
note—BILLET, HEED,
  MARGINAL,
  MINUTE, OBSERVE,
  REMARK
nothing—LUKE, NICHIL,

NIHIL, NIL,
NOUGHT, ZERO
notice—HEED,
MARK, OBSERVE,
QUOTE, SEE, SIGN,
SPOT
notion—FAD, IDEA,
OMEN, VIEW,
WARES, WHIM
notorious—ARRANT,
INFAMOUS,
FAMOUS
noun—APTOTE,
INDECLINABLE
novel—DIFFERENT,
FRESH, NEW, RARE,
ROMANCE,
STRANGE,
UNUSUAL
novice—ACOLYTE,
AMATEUR,
BEGINNER, PUNY,
TIRO, TYRO,
YOUNKER
noxious—BANEFUL,
EVIL, ILL, MIASMIC,
NOCENT, NOISOME,
PERNICIOUS
nuisance—ANTS, BANE,
PEST
null—CIPHER, INVALID,
VOID
number—COUNT, DIGIT,
ENUMERATE,
SCALER, SURD
nun—MONIAL, PIGEON,
SISTER, SMEW,

TERESA, TITMOUSE
nunnery—CLOISTER
nurse—AMAH, AYAH,
BOONE, FOSTER,
NANA, NORICE,
NURTURE, TEND
nursery—CRECHE,
GREENHOUSE
nut—FRUIT, KERNEL,
MEAT, PROBLEM
confection—
MARCHPANE,
MARZIPAN,
NOUGATS, PRALINE
kind—ALMOND, BEN,
BETEL, BRAZIL,
CASHEW, COBNUT,
COCO, FILBERT,
HAZEL, HICKORY,
JUVIA, KOLA,
PECAN, SHAGBARK,
WALNUT
tree—BEECH, CASHEW,
HAZEL, HICKORY,
KOLA, PECAN,
WALNUT
nutmeg—SEED, SPICE
husk—MACE
nuzzle—BURROW,
CHERISH, NESTLE,
NURSE, POKE,
SNUG, SNUFF
nymph—EGERIA,
GALATEA, HYADES,
HOURI, MAIA,
NEREID, OREAD,
SYLPH

-O-

oaf—BOOR, DOLT,
DUNCE, IDIOT,
LOUT, OUPH
oak—ALDER,
BLACKJACK,
BRAVE, CLUB,
STRONG
oar—PADDLE, PLY,

SCULL, SPOON
part—LOOM, PALM
oasis—SPRING, WADI
oast—KILN, OVEN
oath—AITH, BEDAD,
CURSE, DRAT,
GOSH, SERMENT,
VOW

obedient—AMENABLE,
DOCILE, DUTEOUS,
DUTIFUL,
TRACTABLE
obeisance—BINGE,
CURTSY, HOMAGE,
NONOR, SALAAM
to make—BOW,
CONGEE, CURTSY,
SALAAM
obelisk—GUGLIA,
NEEDLE, PYLON
obese—FAT, FLESHY,
LIPAROUS, PUFFY,
PURSY, TURGID
obey—COMPLY, EAR,
HEAR, MIND,
SUBMIT, YIELD
obi—CHARM, FETISH,
SASH
obit—DEATH, RELEASE,
REST
obituary—NECROLOGY,
NOTICE
object—AIM, DEMUR,
END, EVICT, GOAL,
INTENTION,
PROTEST, TARGET,
THING
objurgate—CHIDE, JAW,
REPROVE, SCOLD
obligation—BOND, DEBT,
DUE, DUTY, OATH,
ONUS, OWED,
PROMISE, TIE, VOW
oblique—AWRY, BEVEL,
LATERAL,
SIDELONG, SKEW,
SLANT
oblivion—ANNESTY,
LETHE, LIMBO
oboe, small—HOUTBOY,
MUSETTE, REED
obscure—BLUR, DARKEN,
DEEP, DIM, ECLIPSE,
FOG, FOGGY,
INDISTINCT,
MURKY
observation—ASSERTION,
ESPIAL, IDEA,
PROEM, REMARK
obsolete—ARCHAIC,
DISUSED, EFFETE
obtain—DERIVE, EARN,
FANG, GAIN, GET,
PROCURE, SECURE,
WIN
obvious—EVIDENT,
GROSS, OVERT,
PATENT
occasion—BREED,
ENGENDER, EVENT,
NONCE, ONCE,
SELE, TIME
occident—SUNSET, WEST
occult—CRYPTIC,
HIDDEN, MYSTIC,
MAGIC
occultism—CABALA,
MYSTERY
occupation—BUSINESS,
CALL, CAREER,
METIER, NOTE,
PURSUIT, TENURE,
TRADE
occupy—DWELL,
ENGAGE, FILL,
INTEREST, OVERSIT,
USE
occur—BEFALL, BETIDE,
COME, HAPPEN,
LIGHT, PASS
ocean—BRIM, BRINE,
DEEP, MAIN, POND,
MER, SEA
octave—EIGHT
octopus—HEE, POULPE,
SQUID
odd—AZYGOUS,
ECCENTRIC, EXTRA,
ORRA, QUAINT,
QUEER, RARE,
STRANGE
odious—HATEFUL,
ODIUM
odor—AROMA, FETOR,
FRAGRANCE,
NIDOR, NOSE,
SCENT, SMELL
off—AGEE, ASIDE,

AWAY, BEGONE,
DOFF,
INACCURATE,
MISTAKEN
offend—CAG, DISPLEASE,
INSULT, MIFF,
MORTIFY, PIQUE,
RASP, RASS, SIN
offender—CULPRIT
offense—FELONY, GRIEF,
MALUM, SIN
office—FUNCTION, POST,
STATION, WIKE
officer—ADJUTANT,
BAILIFF,
CONSTABLE,
DIRECTOR, MASTER,
POLICEMAN,
SHERIFF, TINDAL
official—BASHAW,
FORMAL, MAGNATE
offshoot—BRANCH,
ISSUE, ROD, SCION,
SON, SPRIG
offspring—
DESCENDANTS,
FRUIT,
PROGENY, SON
ogle—EYE, GAZE,
GLANCE, LEER,
MARLOCK
oil—ANOINT, ASARUM,
BEN, BREASE,
LUBRICATE, OLEIC,
OLEO, OLIUM,
PETROLEUM
oily—COMPLIANT, GLIB,
OLEIC, OLEOSE,
SEBACEOUS,
UNCTUOUS
ointment—BALM,
BALSAM, CERATE,
CEROMA, GREASE,
NARD, POMADE,
SALVE, UNGUENT
old—AGED, ANCIENT,
ANTIQUE, ARCHAIC,
AULD, DATED,
FORMER, GRAY,
SENILE, STALE

olive—OLEA, OLEASTER,
ESCUTCHEON
omen—ABODANCE,
FORBODE,
PORTENT, PRESAGE,
SIGN, TOKEN
omission—BALK, CARET,
OVERSIGHT
omit—BATE, CUT,
DELETE, ELIDE,
EXCEPT, IGNORE,
MISS, NEGLECT,
SKIP, SPARE
once—ANEW, ENE, ERST,
EVER, FORMERLY,
OCCASION, SINGLY,
YANCE
one—ACE, AN,
ANYBODY, ITE,
PERSON, SMAE,
SINGLE, UNIT,
UNITED, UNITY,
UNO
onion—BOLL, CEPA,
CIBOL, INGRAN,
LEEK, RARERIPE
bulb—SET
genus—ALLIUM
like plant—LEEK,
SHALLOT
small—ESCHALOT,
SCALLION
only—ALONE, LONE,
MERE, SOLE,
SOLELY
onyx—NICOLO,
ONICOLO, TECALI
ooze—EXUDE, LEAK,
MIRE, SEEP, SLIME,
SPEW, WESE
opal—HYALITE, PITCH,
RESIN
fire—GIRASOL
precious—NOBLE
reddish—HARLEQUIN
variety—
CACHOLONG,
MENILITE
open—AGAPE, APERT,
BARE. BLAND,

EXPOSED, FRANK,
OVERT, PATULOUS,
UNDO, UNLOCK
opiate—ANODYNE,
BAY, EYELET,
FISSURE, FORAMEN,
GAP, HIATUS, HOLE,
LOOP, PORE,
MEATUS, RIMA,
RIFT, SLOT
operate—MANAGE, RUN,
WORK
opiate—ANADYNE,
DOPE, DRUG, HEMP,
LAUDANUM,
NARCOTIC, OPIUM
opine—CONSIDER,
DEEM, JUDGE,
SUPPOSE, THINK
opinion—CONCEPT,
CREDO, DOOM,
IDEA, JUDGMENT,
REPUTE, THOUGHT,
VIEW, WENE
opium—DOPE, DRUG,
NARCOTIC
  alkaloid—CODEIA
  derivative—MECONIC
  Egypt—THEBAINE
  extract—CHANDOO
  paste—DOPE
  poppy seed—MAW
  source—POPPY
opossum, mouse—
  MARMOUSE
  So. Amer.—QUICA,
  SARIQUE
  water—YAPOK
oppose—FACE, REPEL,
RESIST, WITHSTAND
opposed—ANTI, AVERSE,
COPED, FRONTED,
MET
opposite—ANTONYM,
CONTRARY,
FACING, HOSTILE,
OTHER, POLAR
oral—ALOUD, MOUTH,
PAROL, SAY,
SPOKEN, VERBAL,

VOCAL
orange, Chinese—
  MANDARIN
  dye—CHICA, HENNA,
  MANDARIN
  flower oil—NEROLI
  genus—CITRUS
  kind—HEDGE, MOCK,
  OSAGE, NAVEL
  peel—ZEST
  red—CORAL
  red chalcedony—SARD
  red dyestuff—ALGA,
  CORALLINE
  red gum
  resin—GAMBOGE
  seed—PIP
  seedless—NAVEL
  tincture—TENNE
orangutan—APE, MIAS,
  PONGO, SATYR
orb—CIRCLE, EYE,
  GLOBE, RING,
  SPHERE
orbit—AUGE, ELLIPSE,
  PATH
orbital point—APOGEE,
  APSIS, PERIGEE
orc—GRAMPUS, WHALE
orchid—ARETHUSA,
  FAHAM, POGONIA
  appendage—
  CAUDICAL
  egg—OOSPHERE
  meal or root—SALEP
  part—ANTHER
  pods, derived—VANILLA
ordain—CALL, DEGREE,
ENACT, SEND, WILL
ordeal—CRUCIBLE,
GAFF, JUDGMENT,
TRIAL
order—ARRAY, BADE,
BID, CLASS,
COMMAND,
DECREE, DIRECT,
MANDATE, SYSTEM,
WILL
orderly—METHODICAL,
NEAT, REGULAR,

TRIM
ordinance—ASSIZE,
    DECREE, LAW, RITE,
    STATUTE
ordinary—AVERAGE,
    MEDIOCRE, NOMIC,
    NORMAL, PROSY,
    RUCK, USUAL,
    VULGATE
ore—IRON, MINERAL,
    TIN
  box—FLOSH
  earthy looking—PACO
  deposit—BED, LODE,
    VEIN
  fusing establishment—
    SMELTERY
  horizontal layer—STOPE
  impure—SPEISS
  iron used as
    pigment—OCHER,
    OCHRE
  loading platform—PLAT
  method of cleansing—
    VANNIN
  mill roller—
    EDGESTONE
  of lead—GALEN
  refiner—SMELTER
  sluiced—TRUNKED
  small bunches—NEST,
    SQUAT
  trough for
    washing—STRAKE
  vein—LODE, SCRIN,
    STOPE
  worthless—MATTE
organ, bass note—PEDAL
  desk—CONSOLE
  flutter
    device—TREMOLO
  interlude—VERSET
  keyboard—CLAVIER
  kind—ACCORDION,
    MELODIAN
  part—REED
  pedal—TIRASSE
  pipe—FLUTE, REED
  pipe voicer—TONER
  small—REGAL

  stop—BASSOON,
    CELESTA,
    DULCIANA, GAMBA,
    OBOE, ORAGE,
    PYRAMIDON, VIOLA
organic—INHERENT,
    STATE, VITAL
organism—AMOEBA,
    ANIMAL, PLANT,
    SOMA, SOMAS
organization—CADRE,
    POLITICS, SETUP,
    UNIT
orgy—BINGE,
    CAROUSAL, FROLIC,
    LARK, REVEL
orifice—HOLE, MOUTH,
    OPENING, PORE,
    OSTIOLE
origin—ALPHA, BIRTH,
    FOUNT, GENESIS,
    GENETIC, NATURE,
    NEE, PARENTAGE,
    ROOT, SEED,
    SOURCE
original—FONTAL,
    INITIAL, NATIVE,
    PRIMITIVE,
    PRISTINE, RADICAL
oriole, golden—LORIOT,
    PIROL
  genus—ICTERUS
ornament—ADORN,
    AMULET, GUTTA,
    DECOR, PIN,
    ROSETTE, SPANGLE,
    TRINKET
ornamental—BOW, BEAD,
    DECORATIVE,
    FANCY
ornate—ADORN,
    DECORATED,
    ELABORATE,
    FANCY, FLORID,
    GAY, SHOWY
ostentatious—GAUDY,
    PRETENTIOUS,
    SHOWY
ostrich—EMU, ANADU,
    RHEA

other (comb. form)—ALLO
otherwise—ALIAS, ELS,
 ELSE, OR
otter—ANNOTTO
 genus—LUTRA
 of sea—KALAN
ottoman—FOOTSTOOL,
 POUF, STOOL, TURK,
 TURKISH
out—AWAY, EJECT,
 EGRESS, EX,
 EXTERNAL,
 FORTH, FROM,
 ODDS, OUTSIDE
outbreak—ERUPTION,
 RASH, RIOT
outburst—ACCESS,
 FLAFE, GALE, RIOT,
 STORM
outcast—DERELICT,
 LEPER, PARIAH,
 RONIN
outcome—
 DENOUEMENT,
 END, ISSUE,
 RESULT, SEQUEL,
 UPSHOT
outdo—CAP, EXCEL,
 SURPASS, TRUMP
outfit—EQUIP, KIT, RIG
outlandish—BIZARRE,
 STRANGE
outlaw—BANDIT,
 FUGITIVE,
 BRIGAND,
 MARAUDER,
 PROSCRIBE,
 ROBBER, THIEF,
 YEGG
outlet—EGRESS, EXIT,
 ISSUE, OUTCAST,
 VENT
outline—ADUMBRATE
outlook—FRONTAGE,
 PURVIEW, SCOPE,
 VIEW, VISTA,
 WATCH
outmoded—PASSE
output—TURNOUT,
 YIELD

outspoken—BLUNT,
 CANDID, FRANK,
 FREE
outstrip—BEST, EXCEL,
 OUTDO
outward—ECTAD,
 EXTRINSIC
outwit—EUCHRE, BALK,
 BEST, FOIL
ouzel—BLACKBIRD,
 PIET, WHISTLER
oven—BAKER, KILN,
 OAST
over—ABOVE, AGAIN,
 ACROSS, ALSO,
 BEYOND,
 COMPLETED, DONE,
 ENDED, EXTRA,
 PAST
ovule—EGG, EMBRYO,
 SEED
owl—EAL, LULU, RURU,
 ULLET, TUTM,
 WAPACUT
 barn—MADGE, POUIE
 hawk—SURN
 like—STRIGINE
 short eared—MOMO
 small—AZIOLA, UTUM
 to hoot as—ULULU
 wailing—HOOT, ULLET
own—ADMIT, AVOW,
 CONFESS, HAVE,
 NAIN, POSSESS
oxen—BISONS
 kind—NEAT, NOWT
 of the Celebes—ANOAS
oxidize—CALCINE, RUST
oxygen—OZONE
oyster—BIVALVE,
 REEFER
 farm—CLAIRE, PARC,
 PARK
 gatherer—TONGMAN
 outer shell—TEST
 ova—SPAWN
 rake—TONG
 shell—HUSK, SHUCK
 spawn—CULTCH
 species—MOLLUSCA

young—SET, SPAT

-P-

pace—AMBLE, GAIT,
LOPE, RACK, RUN,
STEP, STRIDE,
TRACE, TROT
pachyderm—ELEPHANT,
RHINOCEROS
pack—CRAM, EMBALE,
GANG, STEEVE,
STOW, TRUSS
package—BALE, BOX,
CRATE, PAD,
PARCEL
pact—AGREEMENT,
COVENANT,
TREATY
pad—MAT, QUILT,
TABLET, TRAMP
paddle—OAR, ROW,
SCULL, SPOON
paddock—FIELD, FROG,
GARSTON, TOAD
pagan—HEATHEN,
IDOLATER, PAYNIM
page—BOY, CAHIER,
CHILD, LEAF
pagoda—PAGOD, TAA,
ATE, TEMPLE
pain—ACHE, AGRA, AIL,
DISTRESS, HURT,
MISERY, PANG,
STING, THROE
paint—COLOR,
DECORATE, LIMN,
PIGMENT, ROUGE,
STAIN
painter—ARTIST,
ENAMELER,
LIMNER
pair—BRACE, DUO,
DYAD, MATCH,
TEAM, TWAIN, TWO
paired—GEMINATE,
GEMEL, MATED,
TEAMED
palate—TASTE, UVULA,

VELEM
pale—ASHEN, ASHY,
BLANCH, DIM,
FAINT, MEALY,
PALLID, SALLOW,
WAN, WHITE
pallet—BED, LIP, PATE,
PLACHER
palliate—CONCEAL,
EXCUSE,
EXTENUATE,
GLOSS, MITIGATE,
SALVE, TEMPER
palm—ARECA, ASSAI,
ATAP, BETEL,
COCO, DATE, ENG,
ERYTHEA,
FANLEAF, GOMUTI,
NIPA, PIASSAVA,
TALIPOT
palms, genus—ARECA,
ATTALEA, BACABA
pamper—CODDLE,
COSHER, COSSET,
PET, HUMOR, SPOIL
panacea—CATHOLICON,
CURE, CUREALL,
ELIXIR, NEPENTHE,
SOLACE
pangolin—ANTEATER,
AARDVARK,
ECHIDNA,
TAMANDUA
pannier—BASKET,
DOSSER, OVERSKIRT
panther—COUGAR,
LEOPARD, PARD,
PUMA
parade—CAVALCADE,
FILE, FLAUNT,
MARCH, REVIEW,
STRUT, TOP, WALK
paragon—IDEAL, MODEL,
NONPAREIL,
PALADIN, TYPE

parasite—DRONE, LICE,
　LOUSE, SPONGE,
　TOADY
parcel—BUNDLE, BOX,
　CRATE, PAD, PACK,
　PACKET, PACKAGE
parent—DAD, ELDER,
　FATHER, GENITOR,
　MAMA, MOM,
　MOTHER, PAPA,
　PATER, POP, SIRE
parody—CARICATURE,
　SATIRE, SKIT,
　TAKEOFF,
　TRAVESTY
paroxysm—ANGER,
　EMOTION, FIT,
　SPASM, THROE
parrot—ARA, ARARA,
　COCKATOO, KEA,
　LORIE, LORY,
　MACAW, TIRIBA,
　VASA, VAZA
　African—JAKO
　Australia—CORELLA
　green—CAGIT
　hawk—HIA
　long tailed—MACAW
　of New Guinea—
　　LORIKEET,
　　LORY
　owl—KAPAO
　pert. to—ARINE
　small—LORILET,
　　PARAKEET
　species—
　　COCKATEEL,
　　COCKATOO, KEA,
　　LORIKEET,
　　LOVEBIRD, MACAW
parry—AVERT, ELUDE,
　EVADE, FEND,
　PREVENT
parson—MINISTER,
　PASTOR
part—BIT, DIVISION,
　FRAGMENT,
　MEMBER, PIECE,
　PORTION, ROLE,
　SECTION, SEVER

partial—BIASED,
　FAVORABLE, HALF
particle—ATOM, GRAIN,
　IOTA, JOT, MITE,
　MOTE, SHRED,
　SPECK, TITTLE
particular—ITEM, SINGLE,
　SOLE
partisan—GUERRILLA,
　SIDE, ZEALOT
partitions—SEPTA,
　SEVERANCES,
　WALLS, WITHES
partridge—CHUKOR,
　SEESEE, TITAL,
　YUTU
　kind—GROUSE,
　　QUAIL, TETUR,
　　TINAMOU
　noise—CHURR
　food—PUPAE
party—CLIQUE,
　COMPANY,
　DETACHMENT,
　FAID,
　ORGANIZATION,
　PERSON, SECT,
　SQUAD, TEA
parvenu—ABRIVISTE,
　ARRIVE, ATTAIN,
　SNOB, SUCCEED,
　UPSTART
pass—ADOPT, APPROVE,
　CIRCULATE,
　DEFILE, DEVOLVE,
　ELAPSE, ENACT,
　FARE, GO, OCCUR
passage—ADIT, AISLE,
　ATRIUM, AVENUE,
　CANAL, DEFILE,
　ENTRY, TRANSIT,
　TRAVEL, VOYAGE
passageway—AISLE,
　ALLEY, ARCADE,
　DOOR, GATE, RAMP
passion—ANGER, ARDOR,
　FEELING, EMOTION,
　IRE, LUST, PAIN,
　RAGE, WRATH, YEN
passover—PASCH

past—AFTER, AGO,
AGONE, BY, DEAD,
OVER, SINCE, YORE
paste—AME, ADHESIVE,
CEMENT, DOUGH,
FASTEN, GLUE, PAP,
STICK, STRASS
pastoral—DRAMA, IDYL,
POEM, RURAL,
RUSTIC
pastry—CAKE, ECLAIR,
PIE, STRUDEL, TART
pasture—AGIST, GRASS,
GRAZE, LEA, POA,
RIE, SEDGE, SWARD
pat—APT, BUTTER,
CARESS, FIT, PALP,
TAP, TIMELY
patch—BREACH, MEND,
PARCEL, PLOT,
REPAIR,
STRENGTHEN,
TRACT
paten—DISC, PLATE
path—BERM, COURSE,
FOOTWAY, LANE,
RODDIN, ROUTE,
ORBIT, TRACT,
TRAIL
patriarch—
BENEFACTOR,
CLIENT, FACTOR,
GUEST, MASTER,
PROTECTOR
pattern—BYSEN, DESIGN,
FORMAT, MODEL,
NORM, PARADIGM,
PARAGON, SEME,
TEMPLATE
pave—COVER, PATH,
TAR, TILE
pavilion—MARQUEE,
TABERNACLE, TENT
pawl—CLICK, COG,
DETENT, TONGUE
pawn—GAGE, HOCK,
PEACOCK, PLEDGE
pay—COMPENSATE,
DEFRAY, DISBURSE,
FEE, REMUNERATE,
REWARD, STIPEND,
TIP
paymaster—BAKSHI,
OFFICER, PURSER
pea, chick—CICER, GRAM
peace—CALM, CONCORD,
PAX, QUIET,
REPOSE, REST,
SERENITY, SILENCE
peaceful—CALM,
HALCYON, IRENIC,
IRENICAL, SERENE
peach—CRAWFORD,
ELBERTA,
NECTARINE
peacock—MOA, PAWN,
PAVO, PO, POO
blue—PAON
butterfly—IO
fan—FLABELLUM
female—PEAHEN
fish—WRASSE
genus—PAVO
kind—PAWN
like—PAVONINE, VAIN
peak—ACME, ALP, APEX,
CONE, CREST,
CROWN, CUSP,
SLINK, SUMMIT,
TOP, TOR
peanut—BUR,
EARTHNUT,
EARTHPEA,
GOOBER, MANI,
PINDA
pear—BERGAMOT,
POME, BARTLETT,
COMICE,
JARGONELLE
cider—PERRY
late autumn—BOSC
prickly—NOPAL, TUNA
pearl—GEM, PARGARITE,
ONION
peasant—BOOR, CARL,
CARLOT, COTTAR,
HIND, KNAVE,
RUSTIC, RYOT,
SWAIN, TILLER
peat—GOR

bog—CESS, MOSS
pebble—SCREE
pecan—HICKORY,
NOGAL, NUT
peculiar—ERRATIC, ODD,
PROPER, QUEER,
SINGULAR,
STRANGE, VERY
peddler—COSTER,
HAWKER
pedestal—ANTA, BASE,
SUPPORT
pedigree—ANCESTRY,
DESCENT, LINEAGE,
RACE
peel—BARK,
DECORTICATE,
PARE, REMOVE,
RIND, SKIN, SLIPE,
STRIP
peer—EARL, EQUAL,
FERE, GLANCE,
GAZE, LOOK,
MATCH, NOBLE,
NOBLEMAN, PEEK,
LORD
peg—DOWEL, MARKER,
NOB, PIN
pelt—FUR, HIDE, HURL,
PEPPER, SKIN,
THROW, WOOLFELL
pen—CAGE, CONFINE,
COOP, COTE,
ENCLOSE, HUTCH,
INDITE, QUILL, STY,
WRITE
penalty—AMAND, CAIN,
FINE, LOSS,
PUNISHMENT,
RONCE
pendant—
AGLET,
BOB,
EARRING,
ORNAMENT, TAG,
TASSEL
penitent—CONTRITE,
REPENTANT, SORRY
pennant—BANNER,
ENSIGN, FLAG,

STREAMER
penny—COPPER, CENT,
GROAT, SALTEE
penthouse—AERIE,
LEANTO, PENTICE
peon—ATTENDANT,
LABORER, SERF,
SOLDIER,
TRAVELER
people—DEMOS, FOLKS,
KIN, LAITY,
MONDE, NATION,
ONES, POPULATION
RACE
pepper—AVA,
BETEL,
CAPSICU, CAYENNE,
CHILIKAVA,
MANGO, PIMIENTO
perceive—APPREHEND,
FREDE, NOTICE,
REALIZE, SENSATE,
SENSE
perch—AERIE, ROD,
ROOST, SIT
percolate—MELT, OOZE,
SEEP, STRAIN
percussion
instrument—BELLS,
DRUM, GONG,
TRAP, TRIANGLE,
XYLOPHONE
perfect—COMPLETE,
FLAWLESS, IDEAL,
INVIOLATE, SOLE,
SPHERAL
perforate—BORE, DRILL,
EAT, GRID, PIERCE,
POUNCE, PUNCH,
RIDDLE,
TEREBRATE
perform—ACT, DO,
ENACT, EXECUTE,
PLAY, LABOR, TOIL,
TRAVAIL, WORK
performer—ACTOR,
ARTIST, PLAYER,
SHINE, STAR
perfume—ATAR, ATTAR,
CENSE, ESSENCE,

ESTER, NOSE,
FRANGIPANI,
SCENT
perhaps—BELIKE, HAPLY,
PERCHANCE
peril—DANGER,
HAZARD,
JEOPARDY,
MENACE, RISK
period—AGE, DOT, ERA,
POINT, TIME,
TRACK
periodic—ANNUAL,
ERAL, ETESIAN
periodical—ETESIAN,
JOURNAL,
MAGAZINE, PAPER,
PRESS, RECURRING
perish—DECAY, DIE,
EXPIRE, ROT, RUIN
permission—
AUTHORIZATION,
CONSENT,
GRACE, LEAVE,
LICENCE
permit—ALLOW,
CONSENT, GRANT,
LET, LICENSE,
PERMISSION,
WARRANT
pernicious—EVIL,
NOISOME, NOXIOUS,
VICIOUS
perpendicular—SHEER,
SINE, VERTICAL
perpetual—CONSTANT,
ENDLESS, LASTING,
PERMANENT
perplex—BESET, BOTHER,
CONFUSE, CRUXE,
HARASS, PUZZLE
persecute—ANNOY,
BADGER,
DRAGOON, HARRY,
INJURE, OPPRESS,
PURSUE, WRONG
person—BEING,
CHARACTER, LION,
ONE, SOUL, URF,
WIGHT

personal—INTIMATE,
PRIVATE
persuade—COAX,
CONVINCE, ENTICE,
INDUCE,
INFLUENCE,
REASON, URGE
pert—BOLD, BRASH,
DAPPER, CLEVER,
IMPUDENT, KEEN,
LIVELY, SHORT
pervade—FILL, IMBUE,
PERMEATE,
EXTEND, SPREAD
perverse—AWKWARD,
CRANKY,
OBSTINATE, WOGH
pest—BANE, BORE,
EPIDEMIC, PLAGUE
pester—ANNOY,
BADGER, HARASS,
HARRY, NAG, RILE
pestle—BRAYER,
MASHER, MULLER
pet—CADE, CARESS,
CODDLE, COSSET,
DANDLE, DARLING,
FONDLE, PAMPER
petal—CARPEL, LEAF
petition—ASK, BEG, PLEA,
PRAY, SOLICIT, SUE,
SUIT
petticoat—BALMORAL,
GIPON, JUPON,
KIRTLE, SLIP
petty—INFERIOR,
LITTLE,
MINUSCULE,
PREGALL, SMALL,
TRIFULE, TRIVIAL
phantasm—EIDOLON,
IDOLU, VAPOR
phantom—DELUSION,
EIDOLON, ENOS,
IDOLON, ILLUSION,
GHOST, SPECTER
phase—APPEARANCE,
ASPECT, FACET,
SIDE, STAGE
pheasant—MONAL,

PUKRAS, RINGNECK
Asian—TRAGOPAN
brood—NIDE, NYE
native—LEIPOA
nest—NIDE
philippic—SCREED,
  TIRADE
phosprate—PALAITE
photograph—
  HELIOGRAPH, MUG,
  PICTURE,
  PRINT, SNAP
physician—CURER,
  DOCTOR, GALEN,
  HEALER, MEDICO
piano, early—SPINET
  keyboard—CLAVIER
  like instrument—
  CELESTA
picked—CHOSEN,
  CULLED, ELITE
pickpocket—DIP
pickle—ACHAR, ALEC,
  BRINE, CORN,
  MARINADE, MESS,
  PREDICAMENT,
  SOUSE
picnic—GYPSY, JUNKET,
  OUTING, PLAY
picture—DEPICT, ICON,
  IMAGE, PASTEL,
  PHOTO, PROFILE,
  SCENERY, TABLEAU
piece—BIT, CHIP,
  FRAGMENT, LUMP,
  MISSEL, MORSEL,
  PART, PATCH,
  PORTION, SECTION
piece out—EKE
pied—PIEBALD, PINTO,
  VARIEGATED
pier—ANTA, DOCK,
  JETTY, MOLE,
  PILLAR, POST,
  SOCLE, STILT,
  WHARF
pierce—ENTER, GORE,
  LANCE,
  PENETRATE,
  PUNCTURE, STAB,

STICK
pig—BACON, DOO, FAR,
  HAM, HOG, PORK,
  CROCK, SOW, SWINE
African—AARDVARK
deer—BABIROUSSA
female—ELT, GILT,
  SOW
male—BOAR
young—FARROW,
  GRICE, SHOTE,
  SHOAT, SWINE
pigeon—BARB, CUSHAT,
  DOVE, CULVER,
  FANTAIL, GOURA,
  ISABEL, NUN,
  HOMER, JACOBIN,
  PIPER, POUTER,
  RUNT, TRUMPETER,
  TUMBLER, TURBIT
Australian—WONGA
carrier—HOMING,
  HOMER
dwarfed—RUNT
extinct—DODO
genus—COLUMBA
house—COLUMBARY,
  DOVECOT, EAVES
nestling—SQUAB
variety—CULVER, NUN,
  JACOBIN, RUFF,
  TUMBLER
pigment—OCHRE, PAINT,
  SIL
pigmy—DWARF, MINIM,
  SHORT
pigtail—BRAID, PLAIT,
  QUEUE
pike—DORE, ESOX, GED,
  HIGHWAY, LUCE,
  PICK, POULANE
pilaster—ANTA, ANTAE,
  COLUMN
pile—HEAP, LOAD, MASS,
  NAP, SHAG, SPILE,
  STACK
pilgrim—CRUSADER,
  WAYFARER
pill—BALL, BOLUS,
  PELLET, PILULE

pillage—FORAY, FLAY,
    HARRY, LOOT,
    PLUNDER,
    RANSACK, RAPINE,
    RAVAGE, RIFLE,
    SACK
pillar—LAT, OBELISK,
    POST, SHAFT, STELA
pillow case—BERE, SHAM,
    SLIP, TYE
pilot—AVIATE, AVIATOR,
    FLYER, GUIDE,
    GUIDER, LEAD,
    STEER, STEERER,
    STEERMAN
pin—BADGE, BOLT,
    COTTER, FASTEN,
    NOG, PEG, RIVET,
    SKITTLE
pincer—FORCEPS,
    PLIERS, TEW, TONG
pinch—CRAMP, GRIPE,
    NIP, PUGIL, RUB,
    SNAPE, TWEAK
pine—ARAR, CONIFER,
    DEAL, FRET,
    GRIEVE, HONE,
    KAURI, LAMENT,
    LANGUISH, LIN,
    MOPE, SULK,
    YEARN
pink—CORAL, DANDY,
    FOP, PAW, ROSE,
    ROSY, STAB, WINK
pinnacle—ACME, APEX,
    CREST, EPI, SPIRE,
    SUMMIT, TOP
pip—ACE, HIT, PAIP,
    SEED, SPOT
pipe—BRIER, CINCH,
    FLAGOLET, FLUE,
    HOSE, REED, TUBE
pipefish—SNACOT
pirate—BUCCANEER,
    CORSAIR,
    FREEBOOTER,
    LAFITTE,
    PICAROON,
    PRIVATEER, ROVER
pismire—ANT, EMMET

pistol—DAG,
    DERRINGER, GAT,
    ROD
pit—ABYSS, BONE, CAVE,
    CAVITY,
    ENDOCARP,
    EXCAVATION,
    FOSSA, GRAVE,
    HOLE, SUMP
pitch—GIST, KEY, TAR,
    THROW, TONE, TOSS
pitcher—CROCK, EWER,
    GORGE, HURLER,
    OLLA, OLPE, TOBY,
    TOSSER
pitfall—DANGER, DECOY,
    DIFFICULTY,
    ERROR, SNARE,
    TRAP
pith—CORE, ESSENCE,
    GIST, JET, MARROW,
    NUB, PULP
pithy—COGENT,
    CONCISE, FORCIBLE,
    LACONIC, SAPPY,
    SUTRA, SUTTA,
    TERSE
pixy—ELF, FAIRY,
    GOBLIN, SPRITE
place—ARRANGE,
    BOUND, DEPOSIT,
    LAY, LOCALE, LIEU,
    POSIT, PUT, SET,
    SEAT, STEAD
places—LOCI, LOCA,
    POSTS, SITES
placid—CALM,
    PEACEFUL, QUIET,
    SERENE, SUANT,
    UNDISTURBED,
    UNRUFFLED
plague—DUN, HARRY,
    HECTOR, PEST,
    PESTILENCE,
    TAUNT, TEASE,
    TORMENT, TWIT
plaid—TARTAN
plain—APPARENT, BARE,
    CLEAR, EVIDENT,
    HEATH, MERE,

MOOR, PAMPAS,
WOLD
plait—BRAID, FOLD,
PLAT, PLEAT,
WIMPLE
plan—ARRANGE,
DESIGN, DEVISE,
DRAFT, ETTLE,
CONTRIVE, INTENT,
PLAT, SCHEME
plane—AERO, EVEN,
LEVEL
planet—ASTEROID,
HESPERUS, JUPITER,
LUCIFER, MARS,
MERCURY, MOON,
NEPTUNE, PLUTO,
SATURN, STAR,
URANUS, VENUS
plaster—DAUB, PARGET,
SMEAR, STUCCO
plastic—FICTILE, GESSO,
LABILE
   clay—PUG
   fiber—SARAN
   ingredient—UREA
   material—LIGNIN
plate—DISC, DISH, GRID,
PATEN, PLATTER,
SAUCER, URIM
platform—DAIS,
ESTRADE, PODIA,
ROSTRUM, STAGE
play—ACT, CAVORT,
DRAMA, ENACT,
FEIGN, FROLIC,
MELODRAMA,
ROMP, SPORT, TOY
player—ACTOR,
BARNSTORMER,
GAMBLER,
THESPIAN
plaything—BAUBLE,
DOLL, MARBLE,
HOOP, PUZZLE,
SWING, TOP, TOY
pleasure—DELIGHT,
ENJOYMENT, GLEE,
GRACE, MIRTH,
SPORT

pledge—BET, COMMIT,
EARNEST,
GUARANTEE,
PROMISE, SEAL,
SWEAR, TOAST,
TRUCE, VOW
plenty—ABUNDANT,
FULL, GALORE
plod—DIG, DRUDGE,
SLOG, TOIL,
TRUDGE
plot—AREA, ACRE,
BREW, CABAL,
CHART, CONSPIRE,
INTRIGUE, PLAN,
SCHEME, WEB
plover—DOTTEREL,
KILLDEER,
SANDPIPER,
TURNSTONE
plow—FURROW, PLUCK,
TILL
pluck—COURAGE, GRIT,
NERVE, PICK,
SPUNK
plug—BOTT, BUNG,
ESTOP, SLOG, SPILE,
STOPPER, STOPPLE
plum—GAGE, SLOE
   kind—AMBRA,
CHESTON, DAMSON,
PERSIMMON, SLOE
plumage of bird—ROBE
plume—CREST, EGRET,
FEATHER,
PANACHE, PREEN
plump—BLUNT,
CLUSTER, CHUBBY,
CLUMSY, FAT,
FLOCK, OBESE,
PLOT, ROUNDED
plunder—BOOTY,
DESPOIL, GUT,
LOOT, MARAUD,
PILFER, PILLAGE,
RAID, ROB, STEAL
ply—BIAS, FOLD,
HANDLE, LAYER,
THICKNESS, URGE,
WIELD

pneumonia—
    BRONCHIAL,
    CATARRHAL,
    CROUPOUS, LOBAR,
    LOBULAR
pocket—BAG, BIN, CASE,
    ETUI, POUCH,
    PURSE
pod—ARIL, BOLL,
    CAROS, KID, SHUCK
poem—BALLAD, DIT,
    ELEGY, EPOPEE,
    EPIC, EPODE, EPOS,
    LAY, LYRIC, ODE,
    SONNET, VERSE
poet—BARD, ELEGIST,
    LYRIST, IDYLIST,
    METRIST, ODIST,
    RIMER, SCOP
poignant—ACUTE, KEEN,
    MOVING, PUNGENT,
    STING
point—AIM, APEX,
    APIECE, DOT,
    FOCUS, GIST, JOT,
    NIB, PERIOD,
    PRICKLE
pointed—ACUTE, AIMED,
    ACUATE, CONICAL,
    CUSP, SHARP, TERSE
points—FOCI
poison—ANTIAR,
    ARSENIC, ATROPIN,
    ATROPINE, BANE,
    BRUCINE, CONINE
poisonous—LOCO, TOXIC,
    VENOMOUS,
    VIRULENT
poke—BAG, DAWDLE,
    GORE, HOOK, JAB,
    JAM, PROD, SLAM
poker chip—DIB
    stake—ANTE, POT
    to call—SEE
pole—AXLE, MAST,
    POLISH, TERMINAL,
    TONGUE
policeman—BOBBY, COP,
    GENDARME,
    OFFICER, PEELER

polite—CIVIL,
    COURTEOUS,
    DEBONAIR,
    GENTEEL,
    GRACIOUS,
    MANNERLY,
    URBANE
poltroon—COWARD,
    CRAVEN, DASTARD,
    SCARAMOUCH
pome—APPLE, PEAR
pommel—FLAP,
    FLAT, KNOB
pomp—GALA,
    PAGEANT, SHOW,
    STATE
pompous—AUGUST,
    BUDGE,
    GRANDIOSE,
    PODSNAP, STILTED,
    TURGID
pond—LAGOON, POOL,
    PUDDLE
ponder—BROOD,
    CONSIDER,
    MEDITATE, MUSE,
    MULL, PORE,
    REFLECT,
    RUMINATE, TURN
pony—BRONCO, NAG,
    PIEBALD, PINTO,
    SHELTY, TAT,
    TATTOO
poodle—BARBET,
    BEAGLE, GUNDOG,
    PET, PUG
pool—GAME, FUND,
    LINN, MERE, PLASH,
    PUDDLE, TARN
poor—BAD, DEJECTED,
    FEEBLE, INDIGENT,
    INFERIOR, LEAN,
    NEEDY, SCANTY,
    WEAK
pope—BISHOP, FATHER,
    PRIEST
poplar—ABELE, ALAMO,
    ASPEN, BAHAN,
    COTTONWOOD,
    TULIP

Arab—GARAB
balsam—LIARD
species—BAHAN
poppy—FOXGLOVE,
    PAPAVER
cock—BOSH, ROT
corn—PONCEAU,
    RHOEAS
  field—CANKER
  genus—PAPAVER
  seed—MAW, PIP
popular—COMMON,
    DEMOTIC,
    EPIDEMIC, PLAIN,
    PREVALENT
porcelain—CLAY, CHINA,
    KAOLIN
porch—DINGLE,
    ENTRANCE, LANI,
    PLAZA, PORTICO,
    STOA, VERANDA
porcupine—HEDGEHOG,
    URSON
pore—CON, OPENING,
    PONDER, STOMA,
    STUDY
porgy—BREAM, PAGRUS,
    SCUP, TAI
porous—LEACHY
porpoise—DOLPHIN,
    INIA, PELLOCK
  genus—PHOCAENE
porridge—ATOLE, BROSE,
    GRUEL, GROUT,
    POTTAGE
port—GATE, HARBOR,
    HAVEN, LARBOARD,
    PORTAL
portable bridge—BAILEY,
    PONTOON
porter—ALE, BEER,
    BERMAN, CARRIER,
    JANITOR, HAMAL,
    REDCAP, SUISSE
portico—ARCADE,
    PORCH, STOA
portion—BIT, DAB, DOLE,
    HALF, PART, PIECE,
    SAMPLE, SHARE,
    SOME, TASTE

portray—ACT,
    DELINEATE,
    DEPICT, DRAW,
    FORM, LIMN, PAINT,
    PICTURE
pose—AFFECTATION,
    AIR, ATTITUDE,
    MANNERISM,
    POSTURE, SIT
poser—FACER, PUZZLE,
    PRETENDER,
    STICKER
positive—CERTAIN,
    CONFIDENT,
    CONSTANT,
    DOGMATIC, PLUS,
    SURE, THETIC
post—BITT, DAK, MAIL,
    MALL, MARKER,
    NEWEL, PICKET,
    PILLAR, STAKE
poster—BILL, BULLETIN,
    CARD, PLACARD,
    STICKER
posture—ATTITUDE,
    ORANT,
    POSE, STANCE
pot—KETTLE, JUG, MUG,
    OLLA, STAKE
potato—MURPHY, OCA,
    SPUD, TATIE,
    TUBER, YAM
potential—LATENT,
    MOOD, POWER
pottery—BLANC,
    CERAMIC, DELFT,
    CELADON, UDA
pouch—BAG, BURSA,
    GORGE, MAILBAG,
    POD, SAC, SACK
poultry, breed—ANCONA,
    BANTAM, DORKING,
    SHANHAI
  disease—PIP, ROUP
  dish—GALANTINE
  farm—HENNERY
pound—BEAT, HAMMER,
    RAM, THUMP,
    WEIGHT
pour—DECANT, DRAIN,

EMPTY, FLOOD,
FLOW, GUSH,
STREAM, TEEM
poverty—DEARTH, ILLTH,
INDIGENCE, LACK,
NEED, PAUCITY,
PENURY, WANT
powder—COSMETIC,
DUST, GRININGS,
PULVERIZE, TALC
power—ABILITY, DINT,
ENERGY, FORCE,
GIFT, MIGHT, JET,
STEAM, STRENGTH,
SWAY, VIGOR
powerful—COGENT,
DRASTIC, LEONINE,
POTENT, STRONG
practice—DRILL,
REHEARSE, USE
prairie—BAY, CAMAS,
MEADOW
praise—ACCLAIM,
ADULATE, BLESS,
EXALT, EXTOL,
FLATTER, LAUD,
PLAUDIT, TRIBUTE
prance—CAPER, CAVORT,
SPRING, STIR
prank—ANTIC, CAPER,
DIDO, ESCAPADE,
FROLIC, JIG, SHINE,
TRICK
prate—BABBLE,
CHATTER, GAB,
PRATTLE, RANT
prayer—AVE, BEAD,
ENTREATY,
LITANY, PLEA, SUIT
preacher—EVANGELIST,
HOMOLIST, PRIEST,
PULPITEER,
TEACHER
precede—FORERUN,
LEAD
precept—INSTRUCT,
LAW, MAXIM, RULE,
TEACH, WRIT
precious—COSTLY, DEAR,
GOLDEN, RARE

precipice—BLUFF, CLIFF,
CRAG, LINN, PALI
precipitous—HASTY,
SHEER
predicament—FIX,
DILEMMA, JAM,
PICKLE, PLIGHT,
QUANDARY,
SCRAPE
preen—DRESS, PLUME,
TRIM
preface—FORWARD,
FRONT, HERALD,
PRELUDE, PREMISE,
PROEM
prehistoric cutting
tool—CELT
prejudice—BIAS, HARM,
MISCHIEF,
PREDILECTION
prejudiced—BIASED,
BIGOT, PARTIAL
prelude—DEBAR,
OVERTURE,
PREFACE, PROEM
premium—AGIO, BONUS,
STAKE
prepare—ARRANGE,
PRIME, READY, SET
preposition—AT, BY, FOR,
IN, INTO, ON, OF,
OFF, ONTO, OUT,
THROUGH, TIL,
UPON, WITH
presage—BODE, DIVINE,
FORETIDE, OMEN,
PORTEND
prescribe—ALLOT,
DEFINE, ORDAIN,
SET
present—ATTEND,
BESTOW, BOOM,
BOON, DONATE,
GIFT, GIVE,
INTRODUCE, NOW,
POSE
presently—ANON, NOW
preserve—CAN, CURE,
MAINTAIN,
MARINATE, SAVE,

SPARE
press—CRAM, CLOSET,
CROWD, ENJOIN,
FORCE, IMPEL,
IRON, SQUEEZE,
URGE, WEDGE
presser—IRONER,
SADIRON
pressure—FORCE,
INSTANCY,
INFLUENCE,
STRESS, URGENCY,
WEIGHT
pretense—ACT, CANT,
CLAIM, EXCUSE,
FEINT, PLEA,
POSTIC, PRETEXT,
SHAM, STUDY
pretty—COMELY,
BEAUTIFUL, FAIR,
ELEGANT, FINE,
GOOD,
MODERATELY,
NEAT
prevail—DOMINATE,
EXIST, FOLD,
INDUCE, OBTAIN,
REIGN, SUCCEED,
TRIUMPH, WIN
prevent—AVERT, BLOCK,
DEBAR, DETER,
FORESTALL, STOP,
WARN
previously—BEFORE,
ERST, PRIOR, SUPRA
prey—BOOTY, LOOT,
PLUNDER, QUARRY,
SPOIL, VICTIM
prickly—BRAMBLY,
ECHINATE,
MURICATE,
PRICKLING,
STINGING
pride—ARROGANCE,
CONCEIT, GLORY,
VANITY
priest—CURE, DRUID,
ELDER, FLAMEN,
MINISTER, OBLATE,
ORATORIAN, PADRE

prig—BEG, CAD,
HAGGLE, PRUDE,
THIEF
prim—DEMURE,
MODEST, NEAT,
PRUDISH, SMELT,
SMUG
primal—CHIEF,
ELEMENTAL, FIRST
prime—CHIEF, CHOICE,
FIRST, FOREMOST,
PREPARE
primer—BOOK,
HORNBOOK,
READER,
TEXTBOOK, TYPE
primitive—EARLY, NAIVE,
PRISCAN, PRISTINE,
QUAINT
primrose—COWSLIP,
OXLIP, PRIMULA
primp—DRESS, PREEN,
PRINK
principal—ARCH,
CAPTAIN, CAPITAL,
CREDO, IDEAL,
MAXIM, REASON,
TENET
printed—COPIED,
ENGRAVED,
LETTERED, SPELL,
SPELT
prior—BEFORE, ERE,
FORMER, LEAD,
PREVIOUS
prison—BRIDEWELL,
CAGE, CLINK,
GAOL, JAIL, JUG,
QUOD,
PENITENTIARY
private—COVERT,
ESOTERIC, SECRET,
SOLDIER
privateer—CAP, CAPER,
CORSAIR, KIDD,
PIRATE
privet—HEDGE, IBOTA
prize—AWARD, BONUS,
ESTEEM, MEED,
PALM, STAKE,

TREASURE,
TROPHY, VALUE
probe—ENTER, INQUIRY,
INVESTIGATE,
SEARCH, TENT
problem—CRUX, KNOT,
MYSTERY, NUT,
PUZZLE
proboscis—NOSE, SNOUT,
TRUNK
proceed—ARISE, GO,
PLOW, SPRING
process—ADVANCE,
CONDUCT, MAKE,
PROJECTION,
SUBJECT,
TREATMENT, WRIT
proclaim—CALL,
ENOUNCE, HERALD,
MANIFEST, PUBLISH
proclamation—BANDO,
BLAZE, EDICT, FIAT,
NOTICE
procure—ACQUIRE,
EFFECT, FANG,
GET, OBTAIN,
PROVIDE
prod—EGG, GOAD,
NUDGE, POKE,
PUNCH, URGE
produce—BREED, CARRY,
CAUSE, CREATE,
CROP, ENGENDER,
GENERATE, STAGE,
WAGE
product—CROP, FRUIT,
HEIR, GROWTH,
SUM
profession—CAREER,
METIER,
OCCUPATION,
TRADE, VOCATION
proficient—ADEPT, APT,
EXPERT, SKILLED,
VERSED
profit—ADVANTAGE,
AVAIL, BENEFIT,
GAIN, LUCRE, NET,
PROGRESS
profound—DEEP,

INTENSE,
RECONDITE,
THOROUGH
progenitor—
FOREFATHER,
PARENT,
PRECURSOR, SIRE
progeny—BREED, ISSUE,
OFFSPRING, SEED,
STRAIN
progress—ADVANCE,
GAIN, GROWTH,
MOTION, MOVE,
PROCEED,
ONWARD, SUCCESS
prohibit—BAN, BAR,
DEBAR, ESTOP,
FORBID,
INTERDICT, STOP
project—BEETLE,
CONTRIVE, JET, JUT,
PLAN, PROTRUDE,
SCHEME
prolong—DEFER,
EXTEND,
LENGTHEN,
PROTRACT
promenade—ALAMEDA,
GALLERY, MALL,
MARINA, WALK
promote—ABET, AVAIL,
ADVANCE, FOSTER,
INCREASE,
FURTHER, NURSE,
SERVE
promontory—CAPE,
HEADLAND,
MOUNT, NESS,
PROJECTION,
PROTUBERANCE
prompt—ADVISE, EARLY,
EASY, SOON, TELL,
YARE
prone—APT, DISPOSED,
DOWNWARD, FLAT,
HORIZONTAL,
PROSTRATE, SUPINE
prong—FORK, NIB, PEG,
TINE
proof—EVIDENCE, TEST,

TRIAL
proofreader's
mark—CARET, DELE,
STET
prop—BRACE, GIB, LEG,
NOG, SPRAG, STAY,
STAFF, STANCHION,
SUPPORT
property—ASSET,
ATTRIBUTE,
ESTATE, HOLDINGS,
REALTY, TRAIT
proposition—
COROLLARY,
OFFER, PORISM,
SUGGESTION,
THESIS
proscribe—BAN, BAR,
CONDEMN,
DENOUNCE,
INTERDICT,
FORBID, OUTLAW,
PROHIBIT
proselyte—CONVERT,
LEARNER,
NEWCOMER
prospect—
ANTICIPATION,
EXPOSURE,
FORETASTE,
OUTLOOK, SCENE,
VIEW, VISTA
prosperity—BOOM, HAP,
SUCCESS, UPS,
WEAL, WELFARE
prosy—DRY, DULL,
JEJUNE, PROSAIC,
TEDIOUS
protect—ARMOR, BLESS,
DEFEND, GUARD,
PRESERVE,
SHELTER, SHIELD
protection—ARMOR,
APRON, BIB,
DEFENSE, EGIS,
HAVEN, LEE,
RESTRAIN, SUPPORT
protector—DEFENDER,
GUARD, PATRON,
REGENT, SOLDIER

protest—AFFIRM,
ASSERT, AVER,
COMPLAINT,
DEMUR, DISSENT,
PLAINT
protozoan—AMOEBA,
LOBE, LOROSA,
MONER
protract—DRAW, EKE,
EXTEND, PROLONG,
SPIN, STRETCH
protuberance—BULGE,
HUNCH, LOBE,
NODE, NUB, SNAG,
WART, WEN
prove—ESSAY,
EXPERIENCE,
EVINCE, NURSE,
TEST, TRY
proverb—ADAGE,
APHORISM, AXIOM,
MAXIM, SAW,
SAYING, VERIFIER
provide—AFFORD,
AGREE, CATER,
FURNISH, LOOK,
PURVEY, STORE,
SUPPLY, YIELD
provision—CATE, CHOW,
GRIST, FOOD,
LARDER, RATION,
STORE
pry—LEVER, MOUSE,
NOSE, PEEP, PEER,
SNOOP
pseudo—BOGUS, FALSE,
SHAM, SPURIOUS
pseudonym—ALIAS,
ANONYM
public—EXOTERIC,
NATIONAL, OVERT,
UNIVERSAL
publish—DELATE, EDIT,
ISSUE, PRINT,
RADIO, TV, VENT
pucker—BULGE, CREASE,
FOLD, PURSE,
WRINKLE
puerile—BOYISH,
CHILDISH, FEEBLE,

INFANTILE
puff—BLOW, DRIVE,
EMIT, EXPEK,
FLAM, PANT ,WAFF
pull—DRAW, HAUL, LUG,
PLUCK, TOW, TUG,
YANK
pulp—CHYME, FLESH,
PAP
pulpit—AMBO, BEMA,
DESK, ROSTRUM
pulsate—BEAT, THROB,
VIBRATE
pulverize—ATOMIZE,
BRAY, FINE, GRIND,
MULL, PESTLE,
POWDER, STAMP
pump—EJECT, CEMIT,
ELICIT, FILL, FORK,
QUIZ
pumpkin—POMPION,
POMPON, PEPO,
POPON
punch—DOUSE, GAD,
JAB, PASTE,
PERFORATE,
PRITCHEL, PROD
punctilious—EXACT,
NICE, STRICT
punctuation mark—CARET,
DASH, DOT,
HYPHEN, PERIOD
puncture—HOLE,
PERFORATE,
PIERCE, PRICK,
STAB
pundit—LEARNED,
NESTOR, SCHOLAR
pungent—ACRID, BITTER,
KEEN, PEPPERY,
PIQUANT, RACY,
SHARP, TEZ
punish—AVENGE,
CASTIGATE,
CHASTEN,
CHASTIZE,
CORRECT,
DISCIPLINE, FRAP
pupil—NEOPHYTE,
SCHOLAR,

STUDENT, TYRO
puppet—DOLL, GUY,
MARIONETTE,
MAUMET
puppy—DOG, FOP,
SHARK, WHELP
purchase—ACATE,
ACHATE, ACQUIRE,
BUY, OBTAIN,
PURSUE
pure—ABSOLUTE,
CANDID, CHASTE,
CLEAN, CLEAR,
INVIOLATE, VESTAL
purgatory—EREBUS,
LIMBO
purify—EPURATE,
LUSTRATE, SPURGE,
CLEAN, CLEANSE,
FILTER, REFINE
purl—EDDY, FRILL,
MURMUR, RIB,
PURFLE
purple—LILAC,
MAGENTA, MAUVE,
PURPORE, TYRIAN,
VIOLET
purse—BAG, BURSE,
POCKETBOOK,
POUCH
pursue—BOUND, CHASE,
FOLLOW, HUNT,
PLY, STEER, TRACE
pursuit—CHASE, QUEST,
SCENT, WORK
push—IMPEL, JOSTLE,
NUB, PING, POSSE,
SHOVE, URGE
pussy—KITTEN, PUSS
put—DEPOSIT, INSERT,
LAY, PLACE, SET
puzzle—ACROSTIC, CAP,
CHARADE, CRUX,
ENIGMA, GRIPH,
PERPLEX, POSE,
REBUS
pygmy—ATOMY, ANT,
ATOMIES, BATWA,
DWARF, DOKO,
MANAKIN, RUNT,

SHORT
python—BOA, COBRA, CONSTRICTOR, DRAGON, SERPENT

-Q-

quack—CHARLATAN,
CROCUS,
MOUNTEBANK
quadrangle—
COURTYARD,
QUOD,
TETRAGON
quadrat—EM, EN, SPACER
quadrate—AGREE,
ADAPT, CONFORM,
SQUARE
quadrille—CARDS,
DANCE, LANCER
quadruped—BEAST, DEER,
GOAT, HORSE,
MULE, OX, SHEEP
quagmire—BOG, FEN,
LAIR
quahog—CLAM,
QUAHAUG
quail—BLENCH,
BOBWHITE, COLIN,
COWER, FLINCH,
MASSENA
quake—DIVER,
EARTHQUAKE,
SHAKING,
SHUDDER,
TREMBLE, TREMOR,
VIBRATE
quaker—CANNON,
FRIEND, HERON,
MOTH
quality—CALIBER,
ENTITLE, FEATURE,
NATURE, STRAIN,
TRAIT
quantity—AMOUNT, ANY,
DOSE, KITTY, LOT,
SCAD, SPATE
quarrel—AFFRAY,
CHISEL, BICKER,
FEUD, FIGHT,
FRACAS, MISS, ROW,

SPAT, TIFF
quarry—CHASE, DELF,
GAME, PREY
quarter—CANTON,
LODGE, PLACE,
POST, SHELTER,
SPAN
quartz—AGATE,
ADINOLE, FLINT,
OGATE, ONYX,
PRASE
queer—ERRATIC, FAINT,
FUNNY, ODD,
PECULIAR, RUM,
SINGULAR
quell—ALLAY, DESTROY,
END, PACIFY,
REPRESS, STIFLE,
SUBDUE, SUPPRESS
quench—COOL, END,
EXTINGUISH, SATE,
SLAKE
question—CAVIL, DOUBT,
QUERY, QUIZ, POSE,
WAVER
quick—ACTIVE, AGILE,
APACE, APT, DEFT,
GAY, FAST, RAPID,
SPEEDY, SUDDEN
quickly—APACE,
DEFTLY, FLIT, LIVE,
PRESTO, PRONTO,
PROMPT,
QUICKNESS
quicksand—SYRT, SYRTIS
quid—CUD, FID
quiet—ALLAY, CALM,
EASE, GENTLE,
HUSH, LULL, INERT,
MEM, PEACE,
PLACID, STILL
quill—COP, PEN
quilt—CADDOW,
COVERLET, DUVET,

PATCHWORK
quite—ALL,
  COMPLETELY,
  POSITIVELY,
  REALLY, ENTIRELY
quiver—CASE, FLUTTER,
SHAKE, SHUDDER,
TREMOR, TWITCH
quoit—DISC, DISCUS
quota—CITE, NUMBER,
  SHARE, WHO

-R-

rabbit—BUNNY, CONY,
  HARE, LAPIN,
  LEPORID, RODENT,
  TAPETI
  burrow—CLAPPER
  fever—TULAREMIA
  genus—LEPUS
  fur—CONEY, CONY,
    LAPIN
  kind—CONY,
    COTTONTAIL, JACK,
    TAPETI
  like mammal—PIKA
  shelter—HUTCH
  swamp—TAPETI
  tail—SCUT, FUD
rabble—CROWD, MOB,
  POPULACE, RAFF
rabid—FANATIC,
  FURIOUS, MAD,
  RAGING, RAMPANT,
  VIOLENT
rabies—LYSSA, LYTTA,
  RAGE
racoon—COATI, COON
race—CASTE, CONTEST,
  HASTEN, LINEAGE,
  PEOPLE, RUN,
  SPECIES, SPEED
racecourse—HEAT, LAP,
  TRACT
racetrack—ASCOT,
  CIRCUS, OVAL, RING
racing boat—SCULL,
  SHELL
rack—AGONY, CRIB, GIN,
  PAIN, SKIN
radial—QUADRANT, RAY
radical—EXTREME,
  FULL, ORGANIC,
  SURD, ULTRA,
  WHOLE

radio—WIRELESS
radius—EXTENT, RADIX,
  SPOKE,
  SEMIDIAMETER
raft—CATAMARAN,
  COLLECTION,
  FLOAT, LOT
rag—REMNANT, SHRED,
  TATTER
rage—FUME, FRENZY,
  FUROR, FURY, IRE,
  RANT, STORM,
  VIOLENCE, WRATH
ragged—JAGGED, HARSH,
  ROUGH, SCOURY,
  SHREDDY
ragout—HARICOT,
  GOULASH, HASH,
  PATOUN, TUCKET
raid—ATTACK, FORAGE,
  FORAY, INCURSION,
  INVADE, MARAUDE,
  SIEGE, TALA
rail—BAR, COURLAN,
  CRAKE, FENCE,
  HERON, RANT,
  SCOFF, SCOLD, SORA
railroad, flare—FUSEE
  sleeping car—
    WAGONLIT
  switch—FROG
rain—SHOWER
  bow—ARC, ARCH, IRIS
  cloud—NIMBUS
  coat—PONCHO
  gauge—HYETOMETER,
    PLUVIOGRAPH,
    UDOMETER
  spout—RONE
  storm—DOWNPOUR
  tree—GENISARO,
    SAMSN, ZAMIA

raise—BOOST, BREED,
　　　EMBOSS, ERECT,
　　　EXALT, EXCITE,
　　　GROW, HOIST, REAR
raised—CONVEX,
　　　ELEVATED, BRED,
　　　EXCITED, GREW,
　　　REARED, UPLIFTED
rajah's wife—RANEE,
　　　RANI
rake—LECHER, RAFF,
　　　ROUE, SATYR, TOOL
rally—BANTER,
　　　COLLECT, JOKE,
　　　JOIN, PROCESS,
　　　REDUCE, REVIVE
ram—ARIES, BATTER,
　　　BUTT, CRAM, PUN,
　　　STRIKE, STUFF,
　　　TAMP, TUP
ramble—GAD, MEANDER,
　　　PROWL, RANGE,
　　　ROAM, ROVE,
　　　SAUNTER, STROLL
rampart—BULWARK,
　　　ESCARP, LINE,
　　　MOUND, PARAPET,
　　　REDAN, WALL
ranch—CASA, ESTANCIA,
　　　FARM, HACIENDA
rancid—FROWZY,
　　　MUSTY, OFFENSIVE,
　　　RANK, STALE,
　　　UNPLEASANT
rancor—ENMITY, GALL,
　　　HATRED, SPITE
range—AREA, EXTENT,
　　　GAMUT, ORBIT,
　　　RAMBLE, RANK,
　　　ROAM, SCOPE,
　　　STOVE, SWEEP
rank—CASTE, CLASS,
　　　DEGREE, ESTATE,
　　　ESTIMATE, FILE,
　　　FOUL, GRADE,
　　　RANCID, RATE
rankle—FESTER,
　　　INFLAME, PAINFUL
ransack—PILLAGE, RAKE,
　　　RIFLE

ransom—REDEEM,
　　　RESCUE
rant—BOMBAST, BOAST,
　　　DECLAIM, RAGE,
　　　RAIL, RAVE, REVEL,
　　　RIOT, STEVEN,
　　　TURGID
rapid—FAST, FLEET,
　　　QUICK, SPEEDY,
　　　SWIFT
rapids—NARROWS,
　　　DALLES, RIFT
rapier—BILBO, EPEE,
　　　SWORD, VERDUN
rapt—ABSORBED,
　　　ECSTATIC, HEED,
　　　INTENT, LIFTED,
　　　TRANSPORTED
rare—CHOICE,
　　　INFREQUENT, ODD,
　　　SCARCE, TENUOUS,
　　　UNIQUE, UNUSUAL
rascal—CAD, LOON,
　　　KNAVE, ROGUE,
　　　SCAMP, SCOUNDREL
rash—GIDDY,
　　　HEADSTRONG,
　　　ICARIAN,
　　　IMPUDENT, MAD,
　　　SCAMP, WANTON,
　　　WILD
rashness—ACRISY,
　　　FOLLY, TEMERITY
rasp—AFFECT, ABRADE,
　　　FILE, GRATE,
　　　OFFEND, SCRAPE
rat—APOSTATE.
　　　BANDICOOT,
　　　DESERTER,
　　　HAIRPIECE,
　　　LEMMING,
　　　MUSKRAT
ratchet—CLICK, DETENT,
　　　LATCH, PAWL
ratify—AMEN, CONFIRM,
　　　CONSENT,
　　　ENDORSE,
　　　PASS, SANCTION,
　　　SEAL
ratio—PI, PIE,

PROPORTION,
QUOTIENT
ration—ALLOT,
ALLOWANCE,
APPORTION, DIET,
FOOD, QUANTITY,
SHARE, SUPPLY
rational—AGREEABLE,
INTELLIGENT,
SANE, SENSIBLE,
SOUND, WISE
rattan—CANE, LASH,
NOOSE, REED, SEGA,
THONG, WHIP
rattle—AGITATE, CLACK,
CLATTER,
CONFUSE,
EMBARRASS, NOISE,
PRATTLE, RALE
ravel—ENTANGLE,
FRAY, SLEAVE,
UNKNIT, UNRAVEL
ravine—CANYON,
CLOUGH, DELL,
DALE, GORGE,
GULCH, LIN,
NULLAH
raw—BLEAK, CRUDE,
NATURAL, RUDE
ray—BEAM, DAY,
GLEAM, RADIATE,
SHINE, SKATE,
VISION
raze—CUT, DEMOLISH,
DESTROY, EFFACE,
ERASE, LEVEL,
OBLITERATE,
SCRAPE, SHAVE
re—ANENT, ABOUT,
CONCERNING
reach—ADVENE,
ARRIVE, ATTAIN,
ASPIRE, COME,
EXTEND, SPAN
reaction—PRECESS,
RECIPROCAL,
RESPONSE, TROPISM
read—ADVISE, COUNSEL,
GUESS, LEARN,
PERUSE, PORE,

RELATE, SKIM
reading—LECTION,
PERUSAL,
VARIATION
ready—ALERT, APT,
BAIN, FIT, HERE,
PREPARED, PRET,
PROMPT, RIPE,
WILLING, YARE
real—ACTUAL,
CONCRETE,
FACTUAL,
GENUINE, TRUE
realize—ACCOMPLISH,
CONCEIVE, GAIN,
KNOW, PERCEIVE,
SEE, SENSE, WIN
realm—EMPIRE,
DOMAIN, NATION,
SPHERE
reamer—BAR, BORER,
CHERRY,
MANDREL,
WIDENER
reap—GARNER, GATHER,
HARVEST
rear—BACK, BEHIND,
BREED, ELEVATE,
ERECT, HIND,
POSTERIOR
reason—ARGUE, CAUSE,
INTELLECT,
MOTIVE
rebel—ANARCH,
INSURGENT, RESIST,
TURNCOAT
rebellion—
INSURRECTION,
MUTINY,
REVOLT, TREASON,
UPRISING
recall—ANNUL, ENCORE,
REMEMBER,
REMIND, RENEW,
RETRACT, REVIVE
receptacle—BIN, BOX,
CARTON, CONE,
CONTAINER,
HANAPER, TANK,
TRAY

reception—INFARE,
LEVEE, OVATION,
RECEIVING, SOIREE,
TEA
recess—ALA, ALCOVE,
BAY, CRYPT, NICHE,
NOOK, SINUS
recipe—DISH, FORMULA,
PREPARATION,
RECEIPT, REMEDY
recipient—CONFERREE,
DONEE, LEGATEE,
RECEIVER
recital—CONCERT,
MUSICALE,
NARRATIVE, SAGA
recite—CANTILLATE,
NARRATE, RELATE,
REPEAT, REPORT,
SPEAK
reckless—BOLD,
DESPERATE,
HEADLONG,
HOTSPUR, MAD,
MADCAP, PERDU,
RASH
reckon—CALCULATE,
COMPUTE, DATE,
IMPUTE, OPINE,
RATE, RELY, TALLY
recline—LIE, LOLL,
REPOSE, REST
recluse—ANCHORET,
EREMITE, HERMIT,
MONK
recognize—
ACKNOWLEDGE,
ADMIT, AVOW,
KNOW, PERCEIVE
recoil—BLENCH, FLINCH,
FUNK, KICK, QUAIL,
RETREAT, SHRINK,
SHY, WINCE
reconcile—ADAPT,
ADJUST, ATONE,
PACIFY, RESIGN,
SETTLE, WEAN
record—ANNAL, ENROLL,
ENTER, ENTRY,
ESTREAT, FILE,

LEGEND, LOG,
NOTATE, PEN
recreation—
AMUSEMENT,
ENTERTAINMENT,
FUN, GAME,
LAUGHTER, PLAY,
PASTIME
rectify—AMEND, ADJUST,
ATONE, CORRECT,
DISTILL, EMEND,
PURIFY, REFINE
red—CARMEN,
CARMINE, CERISE,
CORAL, CRIMSON,
ERIC, ERUBESCENT,
FLUSHED, GULES,
HENNA, MAGENTA,
NACARAT, OEONY,
ROSEATE, ROSET,
ROSY, ROUGE,
SCARLET
reddish—ROSEATE
blue—MAGENTA
brown—AUBURN, BAY,
CHESTNUT, HENNA,
RUSSET, SEPIA,
SORREL
yellow—AGATE
wine—CLARET, PORT
redeemer—ATONER,
DELIVERER,
FULFILLER,
RESCUER, SAVIOUR
redolent—AROMATIC,
BALMY,
FRAGRANT,
IMBUED, OROROUS,
SCENTED
reduce—ABATE, DERATE,
DIMINISH, LESSEN,
LOWER, PARE,
PULL, THIN
reef—CAY, CAYO, KEY,
LODE, SHOAL
reefer—CIG, CIGARETTE,
ETON, MIDSHIPMAN
reel—BOBBIN, DANCE,
FALTER, ROCK,
SPIN, SPOOL,

STAGGER, SWAY
refer—ALLUDE,
APPEAL, ASCRIBE,
CITE,
DIRECT, IMPUTE,
MENTION, RECUR,
RELEGATE
referee—ARBITER,
ARBITRATOR,
JUDGE,
MODERATOR,
OFFICIAL, UMPIRE
reference—ALLUSION,
RELATION, RESPECT
refine—CULTIVATE,
NEAT, NICE, PURE,
SMELT, URBANIZE
reformer—AMENDER
refractory—INDOCILE,
INTRACTABLE,
OBSTINATE, REBEL,
RESTIVE, STUBBORN
refrain—ABSTAIN,
CHORUS, DITTY,
FOREGO, PHRASE,
VERSE
refuge—ARK, ASYLUM
DOORN, HAVEN,
PORT, ROCK,
RETREAT
refuse—CULM, DECLINE,
DENY, DROSS,
MARC, ORT, REJECT,
SCUM, TRASH,
VETO, WASTE
regal—IMPERIAL,
KINGLY, ROYAL,
STATELY
regale—DIVERT,
ENTERTAIN, FEAST,
TREAT
regard—CARE,
CONSIDER, DEEM,
ESTEEM,
ESTIMATION, EYE,
HEED, HONOR,
RATE
regent—DICTATOR,
GOVERNOR, LORD,
MONARCH,

PALATINE,
PRESIDENT. RULER
regiment—ALAI,
BATTERIES,
BRIGADE,
COMPANIES,
SQUADRON, TROOPS
region—AREA, CLIME,
DISTRICT,
ELECTORAL,
LOCALITY, REALM,
TERRAIN, ZONE
register—CARTULARY,
ENTER, ENLIST,
LIST,
MATRICULATE,
ROLL, ROTA, SLATE,
TALLY
regret—ARUE, DEPLORE,
LAMENT, MOURN,
PENITENCE,
REPENT, RUE
regular—CANONIC,
NATURAL,
NORMAL, PERIODIC,
STATED
regulate—ADJUST,
DIRECT, GOVERN,
MANAGE, ORDER,
SETTLE
reins—CHECKS, CURBS,
HAUNCHES,
LEASHES, LINES,
LOINS, RESTRAINS
reject—DENY, REFUSE,
REPEL, SPURN,
VETO
related—AKIN, AIM,
GERMAN, KIN,
INHERE, TOLD
relax—EASE, LOOSEN,
OPEN, REMIT, REST,
SLACKEN, SLEEP,
UNBEND
release—DELIVER, FREE,
LIBERATE, LOOSEN,
RELET, TRIP,
UNBIND, UNDO
relic—CURIO, CORPSE,
MEMENTO,

MEMORIAL,
RESIDUE,
SOUVENIR,
VESTIGE, WIDOW
religion—FAITH, PIETY,
TRUST, WORSHIP
relinquish—ABDICATE,
CEDE, GO, LEAVE,
RESIGN, WAIVE
reliquary—APSE, ARCA,
CHEST
relish—CANAPE, CHAW,
FLAVOR, GUSTO,
LIKE, OLIVE,
SAUCE, SAVOR,
TASTE, ZEST
rely—BANK, COUNT,
DEPEND, TRUST
remain—ABIDE,
CONTINUE, LEAVE,
LODGE, STAY,
TARRY, THOLE
remainder—ARREAR,
BALANCE, LAST,
MONITOR, ORT,
RECALL, RELIC,
RESIDUE, REST
remains—ASHES, CORPSE,
RUINS
remedy—AID, ANTACID,
BOTE, CURE,
CORRECT, HEAL,
NOSTRUM,
PANACEA
remnant—DREG, END,
ODDMENT, RAG,
RESIDUE, SCRAG
remote—AFAR, DISTANT,
FAR, FORANE, OLD,
SECLUDED,
ULTERIOR
remove—AVOID, BAIL,
CONVEY, DEBUNK,
DELE, DELETE,
DOFF, ELIDE, OUST,
PARE, RID
rend—CHOP, CLEAVE,
RIP, RIVE,
RUPTURE, SPLIT,
TEAR, WREST

render—BESTOW,
CONTRIBUTE,
DELIVER, FURNISH,
GIVE, MAKE,
SUNDER, TRANSMIT
rendezvous—
APPOINTMENT,
BENCH,
MEETING, REFUGE,
RETREAT, RESORT,
TRYST
renegade—APOSTATE,
DESERTER, RAT,
REBEL, TRAITOR,
TURNCOAT
renew—REFRESH,
REJUVENATE,
RENOVATE,
RESTORE,
RESUME
REVIVE
renounce—ABJURE,
DENY, REJECT,
RENEGE,
REPUDIATE, WAIVE
renown—CELEBRITY,
FAME, GLORY,
HONOR, REPORT,
RUMOR
rent—HIRE, LEASE, LET,
RIP, TEAR
reparation—AMEND,
ATONE, REDRESS
repast—DINNER, FEAST,
LUNCH, MEAL,
TIFFIN, TREAT
repeat—ECHO, ITERATE,
PARROT, RECUR,
RETELL
repel—OPPOSE, REJECT,
REPULSE, WARD
repent—ATONE,
CONTRITION,
GRIEVE, REGRET,
RUE
repetition—ECHO,
ENCORE, ITERANCE,
ITERATION,
REITERATE, ROTE
repine—COMPLAIN,

FRET, GRUMBLE
replica—BIS, COPY,
DUPLICATE,
FACSIMILE, IMAGE,
REPRODUCTION
reply—ANSWER, ECHO,
RESPONSE
report—BROADCAST,
BRUIT, CANARD,
DILATE, POP,
RUMOR
repose—DEPOSIT, EASE,
LAY, LIE, PEACE,
PLACE, RELY, REST,
SIT, SLEEP
representative—AGENT,
DELEGATE, LEGATE
repress—CRUSH, CURB,
QUELL, REIN,
RESTRAIN, STIFLE
reprimand—ADMONISH,
LESSON, REBUKE,
REPROVE, SCOLD,
SLATE
reproach—BLAME,
CHIDE, ODIUM,
REPROVE, SLUR,
TAUNT, UPBRAID
reprove—CENSURE,
FLAY, LEVY,
REBUKE, REFUTE
reptile—ALLIGATOR,
CROCODILE,
LIZARD, SNAKE,
TOAD, WORM
edible—TURTLE
scale—SCUTE
reputation—CREDIT,
DISTINCTION,
FAME, HONOR,
NAME, REPUTE,
STAMP
request—ASK, BEG,
ENTREAT,
ENTREATY, PARY,
PETITION, SOLICIT
require—CLAIM,
DEMAND, LACK,
NEED, REQUEST
requite—ATONE,

AVENGE, PAY,
REPAY, RETALIATE,
REVENGE,
REWARD, WAR
rescind—ABROGATE,
CANCEL, REPEAL,
RETRACT, RECALL,
REVOKE
rescue—AID,
DELIVER, FREE,
RANSOM, RECLAIM,
REDEEM, SUCCOR,
SAVE
reserve—BACKLOG,
KEEP, RETAIN,
SPARE
reserved—ALOOF, COY,
DISTANT, OFFISH,
SHY, SILENT,
TAKEN
reside—ABIDE, BIDE,
DWELL, LIVE,
LODGE, PRESENT,
VESTED
residence—DWELLING,
HOME, HUT,
PALACE, SEAT
resident—CITIZEN,
DWELLER,
INHERENT,
OCCUPANT
residue—ASHES, DOTTLE,
DREG, LEES, ORT,
OVER, REMAINS
resin—AMBER, ANIME,
COPAL, ELEMI,
ELEMIN, GUM, LAC,
KAURI
resist—FEND, OPPOSE,
REBEL, REPEL,
STEM,
WITHER,
WITHSTAND
resort—BETAKE, DIVE,
GO, HAUNT,
PURLIEU,
RECOURSE, SPA
resound—CLANG, ECHO,
PEAL, PLANGENT,
REVERBERATE,

RING, TOLL
resource—ASSETS,
  FUNDS, MEANS,
  MONEY, RESORT,
  STOPGAP
respect—AWE,
  DEFERENCE,
  ESTEEM, HOMAGE,
  HONOR,
  REVERENCE
respire—BREATHE,
  EXHALE, INHALE
respite—DELAY,
  INTERVAL, LULL,
  PAUSE, REST,
  REPRIEVE,
  POSTPONE
respond—ANSWER, PEAL,
  REACT, REPLY
rest—DESIST, DOZE,
  EASE, LEAN, PAUSE,
  RECLINE, RELY,
  REPOSE,
  REMAINDER, SIT
restless—
  DISCONTENTED,
  RESTIVE,
  TOSSING, UNEASY
restrict—CRAMP, DAM,
  HEM, LIMIT,
  CONFINE,
  RESTRAIN, STINT,
  TIE
result—EFFECT, END,
  ENSUE,
  EVENTUATE,
  FOLLOW, ISSUE,
  OUTCOME, TOTAL,
  UPSHOT
retard—DELAY, HINDER,
  IMPEDE, LATEN,
  SLOW, TRASH
retinue—CORTEGE,
  CREW, ESCORT,
  SUITE, TRAIN
retired—ABED, INACTIVE,
  SECLUDED,
  SOLITARY
retort—ALEMBIC, QUIP,
  REPARTEE, REPLY,

RIPOSTE
retreat—ASYLUM, DEN,
  HOTEL, LAIR, NOOK,
  RETIRE, ROUT,
  SANCTUM
retribution—AVENGE,
  NEMESIS, PAY,
  REQUITAL,
  REVENGE
return—RECUR,
  REGRESS, RESTORE,
  REVERT, WIND
reveal—BARE, BID,
  DISCLOSE, EXHIBIT,
  EXPOSE, JAMB,
  SHOW, TELL,
  UNVEIL, WRAY
revel—DELIGHT, FEAST,
  ORGY, RIOT, SPREE
revelation—
  DISCLOSURE,
  ORACLE
revenant—EIDOLON
revenue—INCOME,
  RENTAL, RENTS,
  YIELD
reverence—AWE, HONOR,
  PIETY, REVERE,
  VENERATE,
  WORSHIP
reverie—DAYDREAM,
  DREAM, FANTASY,
  MUSING, NOTION,
  RAVE, THEORY
review—CONSIDER,
  CRITIQUE, PARADE,
  REVISE, SURVEY
revile—ABUSE, ASPERSE,
  MALIGN, RAIL,
  SCOFF, VILIFY
revise—AMEND,
  CHANGE, EDIT,
  EMEND,
  PROOFREAD,
  REVIEW
revision—RECENSION,
  VERSION
revive—FRESHEN,
  RALLY,
  REANIMATE,

REFRESH, RELIVE,
RESPIRE, RENEW,
RESUSCITATE

revoke—ABJURE, ADEEM,
ANNUL, CANCEL,
RENEGE, REPEL,
REPEAL, RESCIND

revolt—INSURRECTION,
MUTINY, PIRACY,
REBEL, REBELLION,
RISE, UPRISING

revolution—CYCLE,
GYRE, REBELLION,
ROTATION, TURN

revolve—AYRATE, PIRL,
PONDER, ROLL,
ROTATE, SPIN,
TURN

revolver—DERRINGER,
GAT, PISTOL,
REPEATER,
FIREARM, GUN

reward—BONUS,
COMPENSATION,
GUERDON, MEDAL,
MEED, OSCAR,
PRIZE, UTU, YIELD

rhinoceros—ABADA
  black—BORELE
  2 horns—KEITOLA,
  REEM

rhythm—BEAT,
CADENCE, LILT,
MEASURE, METER,
METRE, TEMPO

rhythmic—CADENT,
METRICAL

ria—ENTRANCE, INLET,
RECESS

rialto—BRIDGE,
DISTRICT,
EXCHANGE,
MARKET, MART

riant—AIRY, BRIGHT,
GAY, LAUGHING,
SMILING

rib—NAP, PURL, VEIN,
VERTEBRA, TWIT

ribald—ATELLAN,
COARSE, LOW,

SCURRILOUS

ribbed—COSTATE,
RIDGED

rich—AFFLUENT,
COPIOUS, COSTLY,
FRUITFUL,
OPULENT,
PLEASING,
WEALTHY

riches—LUCRE,
MAMMON,
OPULENCE,
WEALTH

riddle—CRUX, ENIGMA,
HONEYCOMB, PUN,
REBUS, SIFT

ridge—RIB, WALE

ridicule—ASTEISM,
BANTER, DERIDE,
FOOL, JAPE, JEER,
JEST, LAMPOON,
MOCKAGE

ridiculous—ABSURD,
FARCICAL, FUNNY,
GROTESQUE, IRONY

rifle—CARBINE,
FIREARM, GARAND,
GUN, MAUSER,
PILLAGE, RANSACK,
ROB, STRIP

rift—BREAK, CLEFT,
FISSURE, GAP, LAG,
RIMA, SPLIT

rig—ATTIRE, BEDIZEN,
CARRIAGE, DRESS,
EQUIP, GEAR,
LATEEN, TACKLE,
TOOLS

right—CORRECT, DROIT,
EMEND, JUST,
PROPER, TITLE

rigid—AUSTERE, FIRM,
HARD, SET, SEVERE,
STARK, STIFF,
STRICT, STRINGENT

rigorous—DRASTIC,
INCLEMENT,
SEVERE, SPARTAN,
STERN, STIFF,
STRAIT

rill—BROOK, RILLET,
STREAMLET
rim—BRIM, BRINK,
BORDER, EDGE,
FLANGE, HEM,
LEDGE, LIP, VERGE
rime—HOAR,
HOARFROST, ICE
rind—BARK, CRUST,
EPICARP, PEEL,
SKIN
ring—ANNULET, ARENA,
BAGUE, CIRCLE,
COTERIE,
ENCIRCLE, HOOP,
KNELL, PEAL,
RINGLET
ringlet—CURL, CIRCLE,
RING, TENDRIL,
TRESS
rinse—ABSTERGE,
CLEANSE, DOUCHE,
LAVE, WASH, WET
riot—BRAWL, ORGY,
REVEL, REVELRY,
UPROAR, TUMULT
riotous—LUXURIANT,
RIAD, WANTON
ripe—CONSUMMATE,
MATURE, MELLOW,
READY
ripple—ACKER, EAGRE,
FRET, LAP, PURL,
RIFF, RUFFLE,
WAVE, WAVELET
rise—ASCENT, ELEVATE,
GROW, LEVITATE,
MOUNT, REBEL,
REVOLT, SOAR,
TIDE
risible—ABSURD, COMIC,
FUNNY,
LAUGHABLE
risk—CHANCE, DANGER,
DARE, HAZARD,
PERIL, PLIGHT,
STAKE, VENTURE
risque—HAZARDOUS,
RACY, RIBALD
ritual—CEREMONY,

CULT, LITURGY,
NOVENA, PRAYER,
SALAT
rival—COMPETITOR,
EMULATE,
EMULATOR, EVEN,
FOE, MATCH, PEER,
VIE
rivet—BOLT, FASTEN
rivulet—BROOK,
COCYTUS, CREEK,
RILL, RILLET, SIKE,
STREAMLET
road—AGGER, COURSE,
HIGHWAY, ITER,
ROUTE, STREET,
WAY
roam—ERR, GAD,
RAMBLE, RANGE,
ROVE, WANDER
roar—BELLOW, BOOM,
DIN, HOWL,
SCREAM, YELL
roast—ASSATE, BANTER,
PARCH
rob—BURGLE,
DEFRAUD, DESPOIL,
LOOT, PILFER,
PLUNDER, RIFLE,
STEAL, SWAG
robber—BURGLAR,
LOOTER, PILFERER,
PIRATE, THIEF,
YEGG
robe—ARRAY, ATTIRE,
MANTLE, TALAR
robot—AUTOMATON,
GOLEM
robust—HALE, HARDY,
RUGGED, SOUND,
STRONG, VIGOROUS
rock—DIAMOND,
DISTAFF, GEM,
LULL, PEBBLE,
QUIET, SHAKE,
STONE, TEETER,
TOTTER, SHALE,
SLATE
rocky—CLIFFY, DIZZY,
SHAKY, WEAK

rod—AXLE, BAR, BATON,
    EYEBAR, FERULE,
    GAT, POLE,
    SPINDLE, STAFF,
    TWIG, WAND
rodent—AGOUTI,
    BEAVER, CAVY,
    CHIPMUNK, COYPU,
    DEGU, GERBIL,
    HARE, MARMOT,
    MOUSE, PIKE, PACA,
    RABBIT, RAT,
    SQUIRREL, TUCAN,
    UTIA
  aquatic—BEAVER,
    MUSKRAT
  Belgian—LEPORIDE
  bushy tailed—MARMOT
  European—CONEY,
    CONY, LEROT
  genus—MUS
  gnawer—MOLE, MUA
  jumping—DIPUS
  nocturnal—SEWELLEL
  So. Amer.—AGOUTI,
    DEGU, MOCA, PACA
roe—CAPRET, EGGS,
    OVA, RA, SPAWN
rogation—LITANY,
    SUPPLICATION
rogue—BEGGAR, HEMP,
    IMP, KITE, KNAVE,
    PICAROON, RASCAL,
    SCAMP,
    SCOUNDREL, WAG
roguish—ARCH,
    ESPIEGLE,
    KNAVISH,
    MISCHIEVOUS,
    PAWKY, SLY
roil—DISTURB,
    IRRITATE, MUD,
    MUDDY, RUFFLE,
    RUST, VEX
roister—BLUSTER, BRAG,
    RUDE, SWAGGER,
    VIOLENT
roll—BUN, FURL, LIST,
    LURCH, REGISTER,
    REVOLVE, ROSTER,
    ROTA, TROLL
romance—DREAM,
    NOVEL
romp—FROLIC, GAMBOL,
    PLAY, SPORT,
    TOMBOY
rood—CROSS, CRUCIFIX
roof—CUPOLA, DOME,
    FIG, GAMBREL
rook—CASTLE, CHEAT,
    CHESSMAN, CUB,
    SHARPER
room—AULA, CHAMBER,
    GARDEROOM,
    LODGE, QUARTER,
    SALA, SCOPE, SPACE
roost—JOUK, LODGE,
    PERCH, POLE, SET,
    SIT
root—BASIS, BOTTOM,
    ORIGIN, RADICES,
    RADIX, SOURCE
rope—BOWLINE, CORD,
    HAWSER, JEFF,
    LANYARD, LARIAT,
    LASSO, LONGE,
    RATLINE, RIATA,
    TYE
rosary—BEADS, CHAPLET
rose—RHODA
  apple—POMAROSA
  bud fruit—HIP
  beetle—CHAFER
  bush spine—THORN
  colored
    lily—AMARYLLIS
  dye—EOSIN
  essence—ATTAR
  genus—ACAENA, ROSA
  family—AVENS,
    ROSACEAE
  like—ROSEATE
  red dye—EOSIN,
    EOSINE,
    RHODAMINE
  shaped
    ornament—ROSETTE
  wild—EGLANTINE
roster—LEET, LIST, ROLL,
    ROTA, SLATE

rostrum—DAIS, STAGE, TRIBUNE

rosy—AURORAL, BLOOMING, BLUSHING, PINK, RED, ROSACEOUS, ROSEATE

rot—DECAY, DECOMPOSE, DEGENERATE, RET

rotate—ALTERNATE, BIRL, GYRATE, RABATTE, ROLL, ROTE, REVOLVE, SPIN, TURN, WHIZ

roue—DEBAUCHEE, RAKE

round—CIRCLE, CIRCULAR, GLOBE, ORBED, RING, SPHERICAL

roundabout—AMBIENT, INDIRECT

rouse—AWAKEN, BESTIR, EXCITE, HIE, KINDLE, SPUR, STIR, WAKE, WAKEN

rout—BELLOW, CROWD, DEBACLE, DEFEAT, MOB, ROOT, SNORE, UPROAR

rove—DRAW, GAD, PROWL, RANGE, RAMBLE, SWERVE, WANDER

rover—NOMAD, PILGRIM, PIRATE, WAIF

row—ARGUMENT, BRAWL, BROIL, LAYER, LINE, OAR, FILE, QUARREL, RANK, SPAT, TIER

rowdy—GOON, HOOD, HOODLUM, LARRIKIN

rowel—PRICK, SPUR, URGE, WHEEL

royal—AUGUST, BASIL, KINGLY, IMPERIAL, MAJESTIC, REGAL, SAIL

rub—ABRADE, CHAFE, ERASE, FRET, GRATE, MASSAGE, POLISH, SCOUR, SCRAPE, SMEAR

rubber—CAOUTCHOUC, CEARA, ELASTIC, ERASER, GUM, LATEX, PARA

rubbish—ATTLE, DEBRIS, DROSS, OFFAL, REFUSE, ROT, TRASH, WASTE

rudder—HELM, TEMON

ruddy—FLORID, FLOWERY, RED

rude—BOORISH, CRUDE, HARSH, HOIDEN, IMPOLITE, ROUGH, SAVAGE, UNCIVIL, VIOLENT

ruminant—ALPACA, ANTELOPE, BISON, CAMEL, COW, DEER, GIRAFFE, GOAT, LLAMA, SHEEP, YAK

rumor—BRUIT, GOSSIP, HEARSAY, NOISE, REPORT, REPUTATION, SCUTTLEBUTT

run—BROOK, CONDUCT, EXTEND, FLOW, GAD, HIE, LOPE, OPERATE, RACE, SCUD, SPEED, SPRINT

runnel—BROOK, CHANNEL, RIVULET

runner—COURIER, FUGITIVE, MILER, OPERATOR, RACER, SKI, SPEEDER, STOLO, STOLON

runt—CHIT, DWARF, ELF, PYGMY

runway—AIRSTRIP, FILE, RAMP

rupee—ANNA, CRORE,
LAC, LAKH

rural—AGRESTIC,
ARCADIAN,
BUCOLIC, GEORGIC,
PASTORAL, RUSTIC

ruse—ARTIFICE,
DETOUR, DODGE,
FOOL, MANEUVER,
PRANK,
STRATAGEM, TRICK

rush—CATTAIL,
CHARGE, HURRY,
PRESS, SPATE,
SPEED, SURGE

rust—AERUGO,
CORRODE, EAT,
ERODE, IDLENESS,
INACTION,
VERDIGRIS

rustic—AGRESTIC, BOOR,
BUCOLIC, CARL,
CHURL, DORIC,
GEOPONIC, RUBE,
RURAL

rutilate—GLITTER, GLOW,
SHINE

-S-

S curve—OGEE

S shaped—SIGMATE,
SIGMOID

sable—BLACK, DARK,
EBON, PELLET

sac—ASCUS, BAG,
BURSA, CYST,
POUCH, SACK,
THECA, VESICLE

saccharine—HONEYED,
SUGAR, SUGARY,
SWEET

sachet—BAG, PAD,
PERFUME, SAC

sack—BAG, HAVOC,
LOOT, PILLAGE,
POKE, POUCH

sacrament—RETE, RITE

sacred—BALEFUL,
HALLOWED, HOLY,
RELIGIOUS

sacrifice—ATONEMENT,
HOLOCAUSE,
LIBATION, LOSS,
OBLATION

sad—BAD, DEJECTED,
DESPONDENT, DIRE,
DOLEFUL,
DOWNCAST,
GLOOMY,
MOURNFUL

saddle, bag—ALFORJA

blanket—CORONA,
TILPAH

boot—GAMBADO

bow—ARSON, POMMEL

cloth—PANEL,
SHABRACK

girth—CINCH

horses—PALFREYS,
REMUDA

light—PILCH, PILLION

loop—STIRRUP

pad—PANEL

pommel—CRUTCH,
TORE

strap—GIRTH, LATIGO

saddler—COZIER,
LORIMER

sadness—DOLOR,
DEPRESSION,
GLOOM,
MELANCHOLY,
PATHOS, SORROW

safe—CUPBOARD,
SECURE,
TRUSTWORTHY,
UNHURT, VAULT

saffron—YELLOW

sag—BEND, DROOP,
DRIFT, SINK, WILT

saga—EPIC, LEGEND,
MYTH, TALE

sagacity—ACUMEN, KEN,

WISDOM
sage—PROPHET,
  PRUDENT, SALVIA,
  SAPIENT, SEER,
  SOLON, WISE
sail—CRUISE, JIB,
  LATEEN, LUFF,
  LUG, NAVIGATE,
  TACK, VOYAGE
sailor—GOB, MARINER,
  MIDDY, SALT,
  SEAMAN, LASCAR,
  SHIPMAN, TAR,
  TOTY
salaam—BEND, BOW,
  CONGE, NOD
salad—GREENS
  corn—MACHES
  green—CRESS, ENDIVE,
    LETTUCE
  herb—COS, CRESS,
    ENDIVE, LETTUCE,
    TARRAGON
  kind—CAESAR, GREEN,
    TOMATO, WALDORF
  plant—COS, CRESS,
    ENDIVE, LETTUCE
salamander—BRASIER,
  EFT, EVET, FAY,
  NEWT, OLM, POKER,
  URODELA
salary—EARNINGS,
  EMOLUMENT, PAY,
  STIPEND, WAGES
sale—AUCTION,
  BARGAIN, BARTER,
  BAZAAR, DEAL,
  HANDSEL, MARKET,
  VEND
saline—SALINA, SALTY
  solution—BRINE
saliva—PYTALISM,
  RHEUM, SPITTLE
sally—GUSH, ISSUE, JEST,
  LEAP, SORTIE,
  START
salmon—GILLING,
  NERKA, MORT,
  SMOLT, SPROD
saloon—BAR,

DRAMSHOP,
  GROGGERY
salt—ALUM, FLAVOR,
  HALITE, HUMOR,
  MARINATE, SAL,
  SALINE, SAVOR,
  SEASON
saltworks—SALINA,
  SALTERY
salted—ALAT,
  MARINATED,
  SEASONED
saltpeter—NITER,
  NITRATE,
  ROCKSALT, NITRE,
  ANATRON
salty—BRINY, SALINE
salutation—ALOHA, AVE,
  BOW, GREETING,
  HELLO, PROSIT,
  SALAAM
salute—AVE, CURTSY,
  GREET, HAIL,
  HALSE, KISS, SALVO
salve—BALM, CURE,
  OINTMENT,
  PALLIATE,
  PLASTER, TRETE
salver—SAVE, TRAY,
  WAITER
same—ALIKE, COGNATE,
  DITTO, EQUAL,
  IDEM, IDENTICAL,
  ILK, ONE, SIMILAR
sameness—ANALOGY,
  IDENTITY,
  MONOTONY,
  PARITY
sample—INSTANCE,
  PATTERN, SLIP,
  SPECIMEN, TASTE,
  SWATCH
sanction—ABET, AMEN,
  APPROVAL, ASSENT,
  DUENESS,
  ENDORSE, FIAT,
  INFLUENCE,
  RATIFY
sanctuary—ALTAR, ARK,
  BEMA, CELLA,

CHURCH, FANE,
HAVEN, HOME,
TEMPLE
sanctum—ADYTUM, DEN,
JOCOSE, REFUGE,
SANCTUARY
sand—BEACH, GRIT,
SILICA
sandal—BUSKIN, CLOG,
SHOE, SLIPPER
sandpaper—
EMERYCLOTH
sandpiper—DUNLIN,
KNOT, PLOVER,
PUME, RUFF, STIB,
TATTLER, TEREK
sap—DRAIN, ENERVATE,
EXHAUST, JUICE,
LYMPH, MINE,
SAPOR, TRENCH,
WEAKEN
sappy—JUICY, LUSH,
SUCCULENT
sarcastic—BITING,
IRONIC, MORDANT,
SARDONIC, SATIRIC
sash—CUMMERBUND,
GIRDLE, OBI,
SCARF, TOBE, TOGA
sat—ADJUSTED,
PERCHED, POSED,
RESTED,
SUPPORTED
Satan—ARCHENEMY,
ARCHFIEND,
BELIAL,
BEELZEBUB, DEVIL,
LUCIFER, TEMPTER
satchel—BAG, HANDBAG,
RETICULE, VALISE
sate—FILL, FLUT,
SATIATE, SURFEIT
sated—ASAD, BLASE,
FULL
satellite—COMPANION,
ECHO, FOLLOWER,
LUNA, MOON,
PLANET
satire—IRONY,
LAMPOON,
MEDLEY, RIDICULE,
SCORN, SKIT, WIT
satirical—ABUSIVE,
CAUSTIC, IRONIC
satisfaction—AMENDS,
COMFORT, DUEL,
PAYMENT, TREAT
satisfy—ATONE,
CONTENT, PAY,
REQUITE, SATE,
SATIATE, SERVE,
STAKE, SUIT
satrap—DESPOT, MIR,
PRELATE, RULER,
SULTAN
sauce—ALEC, CURRY,
FLAVOR, GRAVY,
INSOLENCE,
PERTNESS, SASS,
SOY, TARTAR
saucepan—HORN,
POSNET, SKILLET
saucy—BRASH, COCKY,
INSOLENT,
MALAPERT, PERT,
PIET, SASSY
sausage—BOLOGNA,
HOTDOG, POLISH,
PORK, SALAMI
saute—FRY
savage—FERAL, FIERCE,
UNTAMED, WILD,
YAHOO
savin—CEDAR, JUNIPER
savior—DELIVERER,
REDEEMER, SAVER
savor—FLAVOR, ODOR,
RELISH, SAPIDITY,
SMACK, TASTE
savory—AROMATIC,
GUSTABLE, SAPID,
TASTY
savvy—SABE,
UNDERSTAND,
COMPREHEND
saw—ADAGE, MAXIM,
REDE, SPOKE
say—AVER, CITE, STATE,

UTTER, VOICE
saying—ADAGE, DIT,
    MOT, SAW
scab—CRUST, ESCHAR,
    MANGE, RAT,
    SCHAB
scabbard—PILCHER,
    PARA, SHEATH
scabies—ITCH, MANGE
scad—OODLE, SAUREL,
    SKATE
scald—BURN, STEAM
scale—CLIMB, FLAKE,
    GAMUT, MOUNT,
    PARE, RUNG,
    RUSTRE, STEPS,
    TONES
scallop—CRENA,
    MOLLUSK, QUIN
scaly—BASE, MEAN,
    LAMINAR, LEPROSE,
    STINGY
scamp—CAD, RASCAL,
    ROGUE, ROUE,
    SCALAWAG, SKIMP,
    SLIGHT
scanty—BARE, LITTLE,
    MEAGER, NARROW,
    NIGGARDLY, POOR,
    SCARCE, SPARING
scar—ARR, BLEMISH,
    CICATRICE, CLIFF,
    SEAM, SHORE
scarcity—DEARTH,
    FAMINE, PAUCITY,
    THIN, WANT
scare—ALARM, COW,
    DAUNT, FRIGHT,
    FRIGHTEN, PANIC,
    STARTLE
scarf—ASCOT, BOA,
    MUFFLER,
    NECKTIE, ORALE,
    PENDENT, SASH,
    SHAWL, STOLE,
    TIPPET
scat—BOO, SHOO, TAX,
    TRIBUTE
scatter—BEGONE,

BESTREW, DISBAND,
    DISPEL, DISPERSE,
    DEAL, LITTER,
    SPRAY, TED
scattering—DIASPORA,
    DIVIDING,
    LITTERING,
    SPRAYING
scene—EPISODE,
    LANDSCAPE,
    OUTLOOK, VIEW,
    VISTA
scent—AROMA, AURA,
    FLAIR, NOSE, ODOR,
    PERFUME, SMELL
scented—OLENT,
    SMELLING
scepter—BATON, MACE,
    STAFF, WAND
scheme—AIM, CABAL,
    CADRE, CONSPIRE,
    PLAN, PLOT,
    PROJECT, OUTLINE
schism—DISSENT,
    DIVISION, RENT,
    SEPARATION, SPLIT
scholar—PEDANT, PUPIL,
    SAVANT, STUDENT
school—EDUCATE,
    INSTRUCT, LEARN,
    TEACH, TRAIN,
    TUTOR
science—ART,
    KNOWLEDGE,
    PRACTICE,
    PROFICIENCY,
    SKILL
scoff—DERIDE, FLEER,
    GIBE, JEER, MOCK,
    RAIL, REVILE,
    SCORN, SNEER
scold—BERATE, CHIDE,
    JAW, NAG,
    OBJURATE, RAIL,
    RANT, REPROVE
sconce—BULWARK,
    CANDLESTICK,
    ENTRENCH, HEAD,
    SCREEN, SHELTER,

TRICK
scoop—LADLE, SHOVEL
scope—AREA, EXTENT,
LATITUDE,
MARGIN, RANGE,
TETHER
scorch—BLISTER, CHAR,
PARCH, SEAR,
SINGE, TOAST
score—CHALK, GOAL,
POINT, RUN,
SCRATCH, TALLY,
TICK, TWENTY
scorpion—LIZARD,
SCOURGE, WHIP
Scot—CALEDONIAN,
CELT, GAEL, PICT,
TAX
scoundrel—CAD, IMP,
KNAVE, RASCAL,
ROGUE, VARLET,
VILLAIN
scour—BURNISH, POLISH,
ROVE, RUB, SAND,
SCRUB
scourge—BANE, FLOG,
LASH, PUNISH,
WHIP
scrap—BIT, END,
EXTRACT, FIGHT,
FRAGMENT, MELEE,
MORSEL, ORT,
SHRED
scrape—ABRADE, GRATE,
RASP, RUB
scrappy—AGGRESSIVE,
BITTY, COMBATIVE,
DETERMINEDLY,
FRAGMENTARY
scratch—CLAW, GRATE,
MAR, RIST, RIT,
SCORE, SCRAPE
screen—BLIND, CLOAK,
COVER, GRILLE,
HIDE, PAVIS,
RIDDLE, REREDOS,
SHADE, SIEVE
screw—DISTORT, SPIRAL,
TWIST

scribe—AMANUENSIS,
SCRIVENER
scud—FLY, RUN, SLAP,
SPANK
scuff—ANPE, SHUFFLE
scull—PADDLE, OAR,
SHOAL, SPOON
scum—DROSS, REFUSE,
SILT
scurry—HIE, RUN,
SCAMPER, SCUTTLE,
SKELTER
scuttle—BUSTLE, HOD,
RUN, SINK
scythe—SY, SYE
handle—SNATH,
SNATHE, SNEAD,
SNEED
sea—MAIN, OCEAN,
WAVE
seal—CACHET, CERE,
CONFIRM, OTARY,
PLEDGE, RATIFY,
SIGIL, SIGNET,
STAMP, URSAL
seals—(genus)—OTARIA,
PHOCA
pert. to—PHOCINE
seam—JUNCTURE,
STRATUM, SUTURE
seamaid—MERMAID,
NYMPH, SIREN
seaman—JACKY,
NAUTILUS, SALT,
TAR
SALT, TAR
sear—BLAST, BRAISE,
BRAND, BURN,
CHAR, DRY, PARCH,
SCORCH, SERE
search—FERRET, GROPE,
HUNT, INQUIRY,
PROBE, QUEST,
RAKE, RUMMAGE,
SURVEY
season—AGE, AUTUMN,
FALL, INURE,
MATURE, PEPPER,
SALT, SPICE,

SPRING, SUMMER,
WINTER
seasoned—AGED, CURED,
MATURED, RIPE,
SPICED
seat—CHAIR, BENCH,
INSTALL, MASTABA,
PEW, PERCH, SELLA,
SETTEE, SITE,
STOOL
seaweed—AGAR, ALGA,
CARRAGEEN,
DULSE, KELP,
LAVER, ORA, ORE,
VAREC, WRACK
secluded—CLOISTRAL,
COVERT,
ISOLATED, LONELY,
PRIVATE, REMOTE
second—ABET,
ASSISTANT,
BACKER, MOMENT,
TRICE
secondary—BYE,
DERIVATIVE, LESS,
NEXT
secret—ARCANUM,
CONCEALED,
COVERT, DERN,
ESOTERIC, ELIXIR,
HIDDEN, KEY,
MYSTIC, PRIVATE
secretary—
AMANUENSIS,
CLERK,
CONFIDANT, DESK,
OFFICER
sect—CLASS, CULT,
FACTION, GROUP,
DENOMINATION,
PARTY, RELIGION
section—AREA,
DIVISION, FEN,
PANEL, PART,
PARTITION, PIECE,
SEGMENT, SLICE
secular—LAIC, LAICAL,
LAY, LAYMAN,
PERIODIC, PROFANE
secure—ACQUIRE, FAST,

FASTEN, FIRM, FIX,
GET, MOOR, NAIL,
OBTAIN, PIN, SAFE
security—BAIL, BOND,
GUARANTEE, GAGE,
PLEDGE, PAWN,
SAFETY, SHELTER,
WARRANTY
sedate—CALM,
MATRONLY, QUIET,
SETTLED, SOBER,
STAID, STILL,
TRANQUIL
sedative—ALDOL,
ANODYNE,
BARBITAL,
BARBITURATE,
BROMIDE, LUMINAL
sediment—DREG, LEES,
GREAVES, MAGMA,
SILT
seductive—ALLURING,
ENTICING, LURING,
TEMPTING
see—BEHOLD, DESCRY,
DISCERN, ESPY, LO,
LOOK, KNOW,
NOTICE, VIEW,
WITNESS
seed—GERM, GRAIN, PIP,
PIT, PLANT, OVULE,
PROGENY, SEMEN,
SOW
seek—ASPIRE, CRAVE,
COURT, EXPLORE,
HUNT, SEARCH
seep—LEAK, OOZE,
PERCOLATE,
TRANSUDE
seeress—PHOEBAD, SAGA,
SIBYL
seesaw—CROSSRUFF,
TEETER, TILT
seethe—BOIL, BULLER,
COOK, SOB, SOAK,
STEW
segment—CANTLE,
TELSON
seine—FARE, NET,
SAGENE, TRAP

seize—ARREST, CATCH, CLASP, CLUTCH, GRAB, GRASP, GRIP, NAB, REAVE

select—CHOOSE, CULL, ELITE, GOOD, OPT, PICK, TAKE

self—EGO, PERSON

sell—BARTER, CANT, DELIVER, DISPOSE, MARKET, TRADE, VEND

Semite—ARAB, HEBREW, JEW

send—DELIVER, DISPATCH, FORWARD, REMAND, REMIT, TRANSMIT

senile—AGED, OLD

senility—DOTAGE

senior—ELDER, ELDEST, OLDER

sensational—EMOTIONAL, LURID, MELODRAMATIC

sense—COMPREHEND, FEEL, FLAIR, INTUIT, MEANING, SAPIENCE, SIGHT, SMELL, WIT

senseless—DEFICIENT, FATUOUS, FOLLY, INANE, INEPT, MEANINGLESS, STUPID, ILLOGICAL

sensitive—LIABLE, SORE, TENDER

sentence—ADAGE, CONDEMN, DOOM, JUDGMENT, POSY

sentiment—MAXIM, OPINION, TOAST

sentimental—ROMANTIC, TENDER

sentinel—BIDET, GUARD, PICKET, SENTRY, VIDETTE

sentry—GUARD, KITE, SOLDIER, WATCH

separate—ALIENATE, APART, ASIDE, DISCRETE, DIVIDE, DIVORCE, ISOLATE, PART

separated—ALONE, FREE, ROULETTED, SHREDDED

separation—DIVORCE, SCHISM

sepulcher—ENTOMB, INTER, TOMB, VAULT

sequence—SERIES, STRAIGHT, TRAIN

seraglio—HAREM, SERAI

sere—DRIED, DRY, SEC, WITHER

serf—BONDMAN, COLONA, ESNE, ETA, HELOT, PEASANT, PEON, SLAVE, THRALL

series—SEQUENCE, SETS, VOLUMES

serious—DEMURE, EARNEST, GRAVE, GRIM, RAPT, SEVERE, SOBER, SOLEMN, STAID

sermon—ADDRESS, DISCOURSE, HOMILY, ORATION

serpent—ABOMA, ASP, ADDER, BOA, BASILISK, COBRA, NAGA, PYTHON, SNAKE

serpentine—SINUOUS, SNAKY, SUBTLE, ZIGZAG

servant—BATA, BILDAR, CHELA, DOMESTIC, GYP, MENIAL, SERVITOR, SLAVE, VASSAL

serve—ATTEND, BESTEAD, DEAL, DO, MINISTER,

RENDER, SATISFY,
WAIT

service—BENEFIT, RITE,
RITUAL, USE, WAGE

servile—ABJECT, BASE,
MENIAL, SLAVISH,
SYCOPHANTIC

session—COUNCIL, MEET,
SEANCE, SIT,
SITTING, VESTRY

set—ALLOT, APPOINT,
ADJUST, BROOD,
CLIQUE, CONGEAL,
COTERIE, FIT, FIX,
GEL

settle—DECIDE, FIX,
NEST, SEAT, SINK

settled—ADJUSTED,
AGREED,
COLONIZED,
DECIDED, LIT,
REGULATED,
SEDENTARY

settler—COLONIST

settling—DRED, GOOT,
LEE, SEDIMENT

seven—HEPDOMAD,
HEPTADE

sever—BREAK, CUT,
DISJOIN, DISUNITE,
LOP, PART, REND,
SEPARATE

severe—ACUTE,
CRUCIAL, DRASTIC,
DURE, HARD,
HARSH, RIGID,
SPARTAN, STRICT

sew—BASTE, MEND,
PREEN, STITCH,
SUTURE

sewer—DITCH, DRAIN,
DUCT, PIPE, VAS

sex—GENDER

shabby—MANGY, RATTY,
SCOURY, SEEDY,
TACKY, WORN

shack—CABIN, COE, HUT,
SHED, TRAMP

shad—ALEWIFE,
ANTONIO

shade—BLIND, CAST,
COLOR, HUE,
NUANCE, SCREEN,
SHADOW, TINGE,
TINT, TONE

shadow—DARKEN, DOG,
GLOOM, IMAGE,
SHADE, SHEPHERD,
SPECTER, TAIL,
UMBRA

shady—ADUMBRAL,
ELMY, HIDDEN

shaft—ARROW,
FLAGSTAFF,
GROOVE, LANCE,
MISSILE, POLE,
SPEAR, STEM,
VERGE

shaggy—BUSHY, NAPPY,
ROUGH, UNKEMPT

shake—AGITATE, BOB,
CONVULSE,
DODDER, JAR, JOLT,
RATTLE, SHIVER,
TREMBLE

shaking—ASPEN, AGUE,
EARTHQUAKE,
CONVULSION,
SPASM, TREMOR

shallot—ESCHALOT,
ONION, PLANT,
SCALLION

sham—ARTIFICIAL, APE,
DUMMY, FAKE,
BOGUS, FALSE,
FEIGN, IMPOSTURE,
PRETEND

shame—ABASEMENT,
ABASH, CHAGRIN,
DISGRACE,
HUMILIATE,
MORTIFY

shameful—GROSS,
INDECENT, VILE

shameless—ARRANT,
BAREFACED,
BRAZEN, IMPUDENT

shampoo—MASSAGE,
TRIPSIS, RINSE,
WASH

shank—CRUS, GAMB,
   SHIN
shape—CONTOUR, CUT,
   DESIGN, FORM,
   FRAME, GUISE,
   MODEL, MOULD,
   PLAN
shapeless—
   AMORPHOUS,
   CRUDE
share—BIT, DIVIDE,
   DOLE, IMPART, LOT,
   PART, PARTAKE,
   PORTION, QUOTA
shark—GATA, MAKO,
   TOPE
sharp—ACERB, ACUTE,
   BITING, BITTER,
   EDGED, EDGY,
   KEEN, NIPPY,
   PUNGENT, SOUR,
   TART
sharpen—{
   CACUMINATE,
   EDGE, HONE,
   KEEN, POINT,
   STROP, WHET
sharpshooter—
   MARKSMAN,
   SNIPER
shatter—BREAK, DASH,
   DISPERSE, SMASH,
   SPAND
shave—CUT, CHEAT,
   PARE, STRIP, SHEAR
shawl—MUFFLER,
   PAISLEY, WRAP
sheaf—EAR, GRAIN,
   HYPERPENCIL,
   KERN, OMEN, OMER
shear—CLIP, NIP, POLL,
   SHAVE, TRIM
sheath—CASE, ENCASE,
   OCREA, SCABBARD,
   SLEEVE, THECA
shebang—AFFAIR, SHOP,
   THING
shed—CAST, COTE,
   DISCARD, EMIT,

   LEANTO, MOLT,
   SPILL
sheen—BRIGHTNESS,
   GLOSS, LUSTER,
   POLISH
sheep—EWE, OVIS, RAM,
   SNA, TYP, UDAD
   brand—RUDDLE, SMIT
   breed—ARGALI,
   CHEVIOT,
   CORRIEDALE,
   COTSWOLD,
   DORSET, DUMBA,
   HAMPSHIRE,
   LEICESTER,
   LINCOLN,
   MOUFLON,
   OXFORD, ROMNEY,
   SUFFOLK
   coat—FLEECE, WOOL
   disease—ANTHRAX,
   BANE, BLAST,
   BRAXY, COE, CORE,
   GIT, ROT, SCRAPIE
   female—EWE, SHEDER
   fold—COTE, REE
   genus—OVIS, BOS
   fleece—KET
   fly—FAG
   head—JIMMY
   leader of a flock—
   BELLWETHER
   male—BUCK, HEDER,
   RAM, TYP, WETHER
   mange—SCAB
   mountain—IBEX,
   RASSE, SHA, SNA,
   URIAL
   shelter—COTE, DRAAL,
   OVIL, PEN, REE,
   REEVE
   theft of—ABIGEAT
   Tibetan—SHA, SNA,
   URIAL
sheer—ABRUPT, BRANT,
   DEVIATION, MER,
   PURE, THIN,
   UNMIXED
sheet—BEDDING,

NEWSPAPER,
PAPER, SHROUD
shelf—BINK, LEDGE,
REEF, SHOAL
shell—BOMB, CARAPACE,
CARTRIDGE,
COWRY, HUSK,
LORICA, POD,
SHARD, SHOT,
TUNICA
shelter—ABRI, ASYLUM,
COTE, COVER,
COVERT, DUGOUT,
HAVEN, LEE, PORT,
SHED, TENT
shepherd—HERDER,
PASTOR
shepherd's club—MULLEIN
sheriff—GRIEVE, JAILER
sherry wine—JEREZ,
OLOROSO, SOLERA,
XERES
shield—AEGIS, AVERT,
BLAZON, BUCKLER,
DEFEND, ECU, EGIS,
PAVIS, REGIS,
SCUTA
shift—BAFFLE, CHANGE,
DEVIATE,
EXCHANGE, FEND,
GIBE, TYBE, JIBE,
PLEA, VEER
shin—CLIMB, SHANK
shine—AID, BEAM,
GLEAM, GLISTEN,
GLITTER, GLOSS,
GLOW, LUSTER,
POLISH, RADIATE
shiner—BLACKEYE,
CHUB, MINNOW
shining—AGLOW,
LUCENT, RADIANT,
GLARY, GLOSSY,
NITID
ship—BOAT, GALLEY,
LINER, STEAMER,
TANKER, TENDER,
VESSEL, WHALER
shirk—AVOID, EVADE,

SHUN
shirker—RUNAWAY,
TRUANT
shirt—BLOUSE,
CAMISOLE, SARK,
SKIVVY
shoal—BAR, CROWD,
DRAVE, FLAT,
ROOF, SHALLOW
shock—BRUNT, JAR,
STARTLE
shoe—BALMORAL,
BLUCHER, BOOT,
BROGAN, CLOG,
OXFORD, PUMP,
SANDAL, SLIPPER
shoemaker's awl—ELSEN
nail—BRAD, SPARABLE
oil stone—SLIP
patron saint—CRISPIN
tool—AWL, HAMMER,
SKIVER
shoot—BAG, CHIT,
COTTON, DART,
DISCHARGE, CION,
FIRE, POT, RATOON,
SPRIG, TWIG
shore—BEACH, COAST,
LAND, MARGE,
PLAYA, PROP, SAND,
STRAND
short—ABRUPT, BRIEF,
CURT, FRIABLE,
PERT, SUCCINCT
shortage—DEFICIT,
ULLAGE
shorten—ABRIDGE,
CURTAIL, CUT, DOC,
DOCK, LESSEN, LOP,
RETRENCH
shoulder—AXILLA
shout—BAWL, CRY,
HOOT, HURRAH,
ROOT, YELL
shovel—HAT, SCOOP,
SPADE
show—ARRAY, DENOTE,
DISPLAY, EVINCE,
EXHIBIT, PARADE,

REVEAL
shower—DROW, MISLE,
  RAIN, RASH, SCAT
showy—ARTY,
  CLAPTRAP, DRESSY,
  GARISH, GAUDY,
  GAY, POMP,
  POMPOUS, SPORTY
shred—FRAGMENT,
  PARTICLE, RAG,
  RIP, SCRAP, SNIP,
  STRIP, TAG,
  TATTER, WISP
shrew—ERD, SCOLD,
  TARTAR,
  TERMAGANT,
  VIRAGO, VIXEN,
  XANTIPPE
shrewd—ASTUTE, ACUTE,
  CANNY, CLEVER,
  CLUTE, KEEN,
  KNOWING, POLITIC,
  SAGE, SLY
shrewdness—ACUMEN
shrill bark—YAP, YELP
shrink—CONTRACT,
  COWER, CRINGE,
  LESSEN, RECOIL,
  SHRIVEL, WINCE
shroud—CEREMENT,
  COWL, ENVELOPE,
  KELL, MASK,
  SCREEN
shrouded—CLOAKED,
  HID
shrub—ALDER, ALEM,
  ARUM, BUSH,
  ELDER, HALESIA,
  LAUREL, LILAC,
  MYRTLE, SALAL
  Adam's needle—YUCCA
  aromatic—ARALIA,
  LAVENDER
  Asian—BAGO, CHE,
  DEUTZIA, TCHE,
  TEA, WEIGELA
  bean family—BROOM,
  ILEX
  berry bearing—ELDER,

SALAL
bushy—CADE, SAVIN,
  TOD
Calif.—SALAL
Central Afr.—IBOGA
cherry—CERASUS
climbing—BIGNONIA,
  CLEMATIS, LIANA,
  RUBUS, VITIS
creeping—PYXIE
cytisus—BROOM
dogwood—CORNUS
E. Ind. medicinal—
  MUDAR, SOMA
elder—ELLEN
evergreen—
  ABELMOSK,
  AZARA, BOX,
  BUXUX, CAMELLIA,
  CISTUS, ERICA,
  FATSIA, HEATH,
  ILEX, JASMINE,
  LAUREL, MYRTLE,
  OLEANDER, PEPINO,
  SAVIN, TITI, YEW
euphorbiaceous—ALEM
fence—HEDGE,
  HEDGEROW
genus—BIYA, RHUS,
  SUMAC
Hawaii—AKAI, OLONA
Japan—AUCUBA,
  KERRIA
larch family—ALDER
liliaceous—TI
New Zealand—
  RAMARAMA,
  TUTU
olive—OLEA
oriental—HENNA
parisitic—MISTLETOE
pepper—KAVA
periwinkle—VINCA
Peruvian—MATICO,
  SHAMSA
prickly—BRAMBLE
rutaceous—
  JABORANDI
sambucus—ELDER

So. Amer.—CEIBO
spiny—FURZE, GORSE,
  ULEX
stunted—SCRAB
thick foliage—TOD
tropical—ABELIA,
  ABRUS, ASIS,
  LANTANA, OLACAD
W. Ind.—ANIL,
  CASSAVA, EBOE
yielding cocaine—COCA
shuffle—MIX, RUSE,
  SCUFF, TRICK
shun—AVOID, ESCHEW,
  EVITE, EVADE,
  .FLEE, RUN
shut—CLOSE, EXCLUDE,
  SLAM
shy—BASHFUL, COY,
  DEMURE, MODEST,
  SQUAB, SWERVE,
  TIMID
sickle—CROOK, HOOK,
  RISH, SIVE
side—ASPECT, BORDER,
  CHEEK, FACTION,
  FLANK, COSTAL,
  JAMB, LATUS,
  LATERAL, SECT
sidetrack—DISTRACT,
  SHUNT
sidewise—ASKANCE,
  ATHWART,
  LATERAL
siege—BESET,
  BLOCKAGE, SEAT,
  THRONE
siesta—LULL, MIDDAY,
  NAP, REST
sieve—BOLT, BOLTER,
  RIDDLE, SEARCH,
  SILE, TAMIS
sift—LUE, REE, SCREEN,
  SORT
sigh—GROAN, LAMENT,
  MOAN, SITHE, SOB,
  SUSPIRE, TWANK
sigmoid—CURVE, ESS
sign—MARK, NOTE,
  NOTICE, OMEN,

PARAPH,
  PARAGRAPH,
  SIGNAL, SYMBOL,
  TOKEN, TRACE
signal—ALARM,
  MESSAGE,
  NOTICEABLE, SIGN,
  WARNING
signature—HAND, PEN,
  SEAL, SIGIL
signet—SEAL, SIGIL
signify—DENOTE,
  IMPORT, INDICATE,
  MATTER, MEAN,
  SIGNAL
silent—MUM, MUTE,
  NOISELESS, TACIT,
  TACITURN
silicate—WELLSITE
  hydrous—
    CERITE
  MICA, OPAL
silk—GROS, IKAT, SATIN,
  TULLE
  and wool fabric—
    LANSDOWNE
  brown—MUGA
  corded—CRIN, FAILLE
  fabric—ALAMODE,
    PONGEE, SAMITE,
    SATIN, SURAH
  kind—ERIA, MOIRE
  material—PANG,
    SANDAL, TULLE
  net—TULLE
  raw—GREGE
  reeling—FILATURE
  watered—MOIRE,
    TABBY
silken—GLOSSY, SERIC
silkworm—ERI, ERIA, ESS,
  TUSSAH
  China—AILANTHUS,
    TUSSUR
  envelope—COCOON
silly—APISH, ASININE,
  DECIPIENT. DOTE,
  FATUOUS, INANE,
  SAPPY
silver—ARGENT,

ARGENTUM, LUNA,
PLATE
similar—AKIN, ALIKE,
ANALOGOUS,
MONOGEN, LIKE,
RESEMBLE, SAME,
SUCH, UNIFORM
simmer—BOIL, BRAISE,
SEETHE, STEW
simoon—SAMIEL,
TEBBAD, WIND
simple—EASY,
ELEMENTARY,
MERE, MUTE,
OAFISH, PLAIN
simpleton—ASS, BOOB,
BUMPKIN, COOT,
DAW, DOLT,
DUNCE, FOOL,
GABY, GAWK,
GEEDE, GOWK,
GUMP, IDIOT,
LOON, LOUT,
MORON,
MUGGINS,
NINCOMPOOP,
NINNY, NOODLE,
OAF, SAP, SIMP,
YAHOO, ZANY
simulate—ACT, APE,
FEIGN, IMITATE,
PRETEND, SHAM
sin—CRIME, ERR, EVIL,
INIQUITY,
OFFENSE,
MISDEMEANOR,
PECCANCY,
TRANSGRESS, VICE
since—AGO, AS,
BECAUSE, FOR,
HENCE, SITH, SYNE
sincere—EARNEST,
GENUINE, HONEST,
INTENSE, OPEN,
PURE
sinecure—SNAP
sinew—MUSCLE,
TENDON, THEW
sinful—EVIL, WICKED

sing—CAROL, CHANT,
CROON, INTONE,
LILT, WARBLE,
YODEL
singer—BARD, CAROLER,
DESCANTER
singers—CHOIR, DIVAS,
TENORS, VOCALISTS
single—ACE, ALONE,
BILL, LONE, ODD,
ONE, ONLY, SOLO,
SPORADIC, UNAL,
UNIQUE
singly—ALONE, APART,
INDIVIDUALLY,
KITHLESS, ONCE,
SINGLE, SOLO
sinister—EVIL, LEFT,
OMINOUS
sink—DEBASE,
DESCEND, DIP,
DROP, DRAIN, EBB,
ENGULF, FALL,
FOUNDER, LOWER
sinus—BAY, BEND,
CURVE
sip—GULP, LAP, PEG,
SUCK, SUP, TASTE
sire—BEGET, HORSE,
MALE, LORD
siren—ALARM,
CHARMER, CIRCE,
ENTICER,
FOGHORN,
LORELEI, LURER
sirius—CANICULA,
DOGSTAR,
PROCYON
sister—NUN, NURSE, SIB,
SIS
sit—BROOD, COVER,
INCUBATE, PERCH,
POSE, REST, REPOSE,
ROOST
site—AREA, LOCALITY,
SEAT, SITUATE,
SITUS, STANCE,
TOWN
sitting—CONVOCATION,

SEANCE, SEATED,
SEDENT, SESSION
six—SENARY, SESTET
size—AREA, BULK,
EXTENT,
MEASUREMENT,
TRUE
skein—HANK, MESH,
RAP, WEB
skeleton—ATOMY, BONES,
CAGE, FRAME,
MUMMY, RAME,
REMAINS
skeptic—APORETIC,
DOUBTER,
DISBELIEVER
sketch—ANA, DRAFT,
DRAW, DRAWING,
IDEA, LIMN, MAP,
OUTLINE, PAINT,
SKIT
skill—ART, CRAFT,
VERSE
skilled person—ARTISAN,
EXPERT,
OPERATOR, PRO
skillful—APT, ADEPT,
ADROIT, CLEVER,
DEDAL, DEFT,
HABILE
skim—FLIT, RIND,
SCOON, SCOOP,
SCUD
skin—BARK, DERM,
DERMA, EPIDERMIS,
HIDE, PEEL, PELT,
RIND, SUEDE
skinflint—CHEAT,
PELTER, SCREW
skip—CAPER, DAP,
FRISK, GAIT, HIP,
MISS, OMIT,
RICOCHET, TRIP
skirmish—BATTLE,
BRUSH, CLASH,
FEUD, FRAY,
MELEE
skit—CAPER, JOKE,
LAMPOON, PARODY,
PLAY, PLAYLET,

QUIP, SKETCH
skittles—GAME,
NINEPINS
skoal—CUP, HEALTH,
SKAL, SLAINTE,
TOAST
skull—CRANIUM, SCAP,
VOMER
skunk—ANNA,
CONEPATE,
POLECAT, SEGANKU
slack—CARELESS,
CHAFF, FRESE, LAX,
LISTLESS, LOOSE,
NEGLIGENT, SLOW,
SLUGGISH
slag—DROSS, LAVA,
SCORIA
slam—BANG, CLOSE,
IMPACT, SHUT
slander—ASPERSE, BELIE,
CALUMNIATE,
DEFAME, HIT,
LIBEL, MALIGN
slang—ARGOT, BLAH,
CANT, JARGON,
LINGO
slant—BEVEL, BIAS,
CANT, INCLINE,
LEAN, SKEW, SLOPE,
TILT
slate—BLAE, ENROLL,
RAG, SCHIST
slattern—BUNGLER,
MOPSY, SLUT,
TROLLOP
slaughter—BUTCHER,
BUTCHERY,
KILLING,
MASSACRE
slave—BONDMAN,
CHATTEL, DRUDGE,
ESNE, HELOT,
LASCAR, MINION,
SERF, THRALL, TOIL
slaver—DRIVEL, DROOL,
FAWN
slay—DESTROY, KILL
MURDER,
SLAUGHTER, SPOIL

sled—SLEDGE, SLEIGH,
TOBOGGAN, TODE
sleep—DOZE, NAP, NOD,
REST. SLUMBER,
SOPOR, WINK
sleeper—BEAM, DRONE,
SUPPORT, TIE
sleeping—DORMANT,
DOZING, NAPPING,
SLUMBERING
sleeve—ARM, CHEVRON
slender—FEEBLE, FINE,
FRAIL, LANK,
REEDY, SLIM,
SVELTE, THIN
sleuth—DETECTIVE,
HAWKSHAW, TEC
slice—CARVE, CUT,
GLISSADE, GASH,
LAYER, SHAVE,
SLAB, SPLIT
slide—SKID, SLEW, SLUE
slight—FAINT, FLIMSY,
FRAIL, IGNORE,
MEAGER, NEGLECT,
SCANT, SNUB
slime—GLEET, ICHOR,
LIMAN, OOZE, MUD,
SILT
slingshot—CATAPULT,
SLAPPY
slip—BONER, ERR,
ERROR, FAULT, IMP,
LAPSE, SKID, SLIDE,
SLIME
slipper—MULE, NEAP.
PINSON, SANDAL
slippery—EELY, ELUSIVE,
FICKLE, GLIB.
SHIFTY, SHUTTLE,
SLY
slogan—CATCHWORD,
CRY, MOTTO,
SHIBBOLETH
slope—BEVEL, CANT,
CLIVITY, DIP,
GRADE, HADE,
INCLINE, RAMP,
SCARP, SPLAY

sloth—AI, ACEDIA,
INDOLENCE,
INERTIA, LAZINESS,
UNAU
slovenly—FROWZY,
SLIPSHOD, SLOY
slow—DELAY,
DILATORY,
GRADUAL, INERT,
LATE, POKY,
RETARD, SLUGGISH,
TRAILY
slug—BULLET, DRONE,
SNAIL
sluggish—DRONY, DULL,
FOUL, INERT,
LEADEN, SLOW,
SUPINE
slur—ASPERSION, BLUR,
INNUENDO,
MACKLE,
REPROACH, SOIL,
TRADUCE
sly—ARCH, ARTFUL,
CAGEY, CRAFTY,
CUNNING, FOXY,
FURTIVE, WARY,
WILY, WINK
smack—BUSS, BLOW,
CRACK, HIT, KISS,
PUMP, SLAP,
STRIKE, TANG,
TASTE
small—ATOMIC, FEW,
LESS, LITTLE,
MINIATURE,
MINUSCULE,
MINUTE, PETITE,
TINY, WEE
smaller—LESS
smallest—LEAST, MINIM,
PETITE, WEE, WHIT
smart—ACUTE, APT,
ASTUTE, BRIGHT,
CHICK, CHIC,
CLEVER, DASHING,
SHREWD, TRIG
smear—BEDAUB, DAUB,
GAUM, GLAIR,

GORM, PLASTER,
SIMPER, SMIRCH,
SMIRK, SMUDGE
smell—AROMA, FETOR,
ODOR, OLID, REEK,
SCENT
  offensive—BAD, FETOR,
  FOUL, OLID
  loss of—ANOSMIA
smelt—FUSE, PRIM,
SCORIFY
smile—FAVOR, GRIN,
LAUGH, SMIRK,
SNEER
smiling—AGRIN, MERRY,
RIDENT
smoke—AEROSOL, CURE,
FLOC, FUME, LINT,
REEK, SMUDGE
smooth—BLAND, EASE,
EVEN, GLASSY,
GLIB, GREASY,
IRON, LENE, LEVEL,
OILY, PAVE, PLANE,
PREEN, SAND,
SLEEK, SNOD,
SUANT, URBANE
smother—BEFOG,
MUFFLE, STIFLE
smudge—BLOT, SMEAR,
SMOKE, SPOT
smug—CLEAN, CORRECT,
NEAT, SMART,
SPRUCE, TIDY, TRIM
snaffle—BIT, BRIDLE,
CURB, GAG
snail—DRONE, HELICID,
HELIX,
PERIWINKLE, SLUG,
WINKLE
  marine—
  ABALONE, TRITON,
  WELK, WHELK,
  WILK
snake—ADDER, ASP,
ABOMA, BOA,
CONSTRICTOR,
REPTILE, VIPER
  Asian—BONGAR,
  DABOIA, JESSUR
  black—RACER
  deity—ZOMBI
  eater—MONGOOSE
  Egypt—ASP
  eyes—AMBSACE
  Florida—MOCCASIN
  of Cent. Am.—FER DE
  LANCE
  of India—COBRA,
  DABOIA, DABOYA,
  KRAIT
  poisonous—ASP,
  COBRA, HABU,
  KULAMBA, MAMBA,
  MOCCASIN, KRAIT,
  RATTLER, REPTILE,
  VIPER
  python—
  ANACONDA,
  BOA, BUSHMASTER,
  CONSTRICTOR
  So. Amer.—ABOMA,
  BOM, LORA
snap—BITE, CLIP,
COOKY, CRACK,
CRACKLE,
FASTENER, FLIP,
WAFER
snapper—FASTENER,
PARGO, SESI,
TAMURE, TURTLE
snare—BENET, CATCH,
DRUM, ENTANGLE,
ENTRAP, GIN, GUM,
MESH, NET, NOOSE,
TRAP, WEB
snark—BOOJUM
snarl—GNAR, GROWL,
KNOT, NARR,
GNARR, SNAG,
SNAR, TANGLE, YAR
snarled—CONFUSED,
MUDDLED, SNAFU,
SNAGGED,
TANGLED
snatch—GRAB, NAB,
SEIZE, TWITCH,
WRAP, WREST

sneak—CREEP, CRINGE,
LURK, SLINK,
SNOOP, SPY
sneaky—FURTIVE,
SNOOPY
snee—DAGGER, DIRK
sneer—DERIDE, FLEER,
GIBE, GIRD, MOCK,
SCOFF, SCORN,
TAUNT
sneeze—CONTEMPT,
NEESE, SNUFF
snide—BASE, INFERIOR,
MEAN, TRICKY
sniff—NOSE, SCENT,
SNUFF, SMELL,
SNOOK
snivel—CRY, MUCUS,
SOB, WEEP, WHINE
snot—KNOBSTICK,
PARVENU, RAT
snobbish—ARROGANT,
PROUD, UPISH
snood—FILLET,
HAIRNET, SNELL
snoop—LURK, PROWL,
PRY, SLINK, SLY
snore—RALE,
RHONCHUS, SNIFF
snoring—STERTOR,
STERTOROUS
snout—FRONT, NOSE,
NOZZLE, ROSTRUM
snow—FIRN, NEVE,
PASH, SNA, WHITEN
snow runner—SKATE,
SKEE, SKI, SLED
snowy—NIVAL,
NIVEOUS
snub—CHECK, CHIDE,
REBUFF, REBUKE,
SLIGHT
snuff—MACCABOY,
NOSE, RAPPEE
snug—COMFORTABLE,
COSY, COZY,
MODEST, NEAT,
SNUGGLE, TIDY,
TRIM
snuggle—CUDDLE, CURL,

NESTLE
soak—BATE, DIP,
DRENCH, IMBUE,
RET, SATURATE,
SOG, SOP, SOUSE,
STEEP, WET
soaked—DRENCHED,
IMBUED,
SATURATED,
SOUSED, STEEPED
soap—AMOLE, BORAX,
BRIBERY, CLEANER,
DETERGENT, RUB,
SAPO, SUDS
soar—ASCEND, FLY,
HOVER, MOUNT,
RISE, SAIL, TOWER,
WING
sober—ABSTINENT,
CLEANSE, DEMURE,
GRAVE, SEDATE,
SERIOUS, SOLEMN,
STAID
society—ASSOCIATION,
COMMUNITY,
COMPANIONSHIP,
CONGREGATION,
GUILD, ORDER
socket—MORTISE, ORBIT,
PAN, POD
sod—DIRT, EARTH,
GLEBE, PEAT, SAND,
SEETHE, SOIL,
SWARD, TURF
soda—POP, SALERATUS,
SOFTDRINK
sodium—SAL, SALT
  carbonate—ANATRON,
  TRONA
  chloride—SAL, SALT
  nitrate—NITER, NITRE
  oxide—SODA
  symbol—NA
sofa—CANAPE,
CAUSEUSE, DIVAN,
LOUNGE
soft—BLAND, EASY,
GENTLE, LENIENT,
MILD, MELLOW,
MALLEABLE, LOW,

PLIABLE, TENDER,
WAXY
soften—ALLAY,
MACERATE,
MELLOW,
MITIGATE, RELAX,
TEMPER, THAW
softly—LOW
soggy—DAMP, DULL,
HEAVY, SOAKED,
SODDEN, WET
soil—BEGRIME, CLAY,
DEFILE, DIRT,
EARTH, GLEBE,
GUMBO, HUMUS,
LAND, LOAM, MIRE,
MOIL, MAUL, MESS,
SLUR, SMIRCH, SOD,
SULLY, TARNISH
soldering—BRAZING,
CEMENTING,
FUSING, PATCHING,
UNITING
soldier—CADET,
CHASSEUR, GI,
GUFFY, MILITANT,
VET, WARRIOR
sole—ALONE, HEIR,
ISOLATED, FISH,
LONE, MERE, ONE,
ONLY, SINGLE
solemn—AUGUST,
FORMAL, GRAVE,
SERIOUS, SOBER,
SOMBER, SPLENDID,
STAID
solicit—APPLY, ASK, BEG,
BEQUEST, CANVAS,
COURT, PETITION,
PLEAD, REQUEST
solid—COMPACT, FIRM,
HARD, PRISM, RIGID
solitary—ALONE,
HERMETICAL, LONE,
LONELY, ONLY,
SINGLE, SOLE
solo—ALONE, ARIA,
ARIAD, LONE, SOLE,
SINGLE
solution—ANSWER,

BREACH, CRISIS,
KEY, MELTING,
MIXTURE
somersault—FLIP, JUMP,
LEAP
somewhat—DEGREE,
PART, RATHER
song—AIR, BALLAD,
CANTICLE, CAROL,
DITTY, LAY, LILT,
MELODY, MELOS,
NOEL, ODE, RON,
TROLL
soon—ANON, BETIME,
EARLY, ERELONG,
IMMEDIATE,
PROMPTLY,
PRONTO, SHORTLY
sooner—ERE, ERST, FIRST
soot—CARBON, COOM,
COOMB, CROCK,
GRIME, SMUT, SOTE,
STUP
sooth—AUGURY, SWEET,
TRUTH
soothing—ANODYNE,
BALMY, BLAND,
EASING, LENITIVE
soothsayer—AUGUR,
CHALDEAN,
DIVINER, PROPHET,
SEER, TELEMUS,
WEIRD
sooty—BLACK,
BLACKEN,
FULIGINOUS
sophisticated—BLASE
sopor—CARUS, COMA,
LETHARGY
sora—CRAKE, RAIL
sorcerer—CONJURER,
MAGI, WIZARD
sorceress—CIRCE, HELIOS,
LAMIA, MEDEA,
MEDIA, SIBYL,
WITCH
sorcery—ART, MAGIC,
OBE, OBEAH, OBI
sordid—BASE, FILTHY,
GROSS, MEAN,

NIGGARDLY, VILE
sore—ANGRY,
DISTRESSING,
GRIEVOUS,
PAINFUL, TENDER,
ULCERATED
sorghum—FODDER,
GRAIN, GRASS,
SIRUP
sorrow—ANGUISH, BALE,
DOLOR, GRIEF,
GRIEVE, MOURN,
PINE, REPINE,
SADNESS, WOE
sorrowful—BLUE,
CONTRITE, DOLENT,
MOURNFUL, SAD,
SADDEN, WOE
sorry—DISMAL,
GLOOMY, MEAN,
PITY, POOR,
REGRET, SAD
sort—BLEND, CLASS,
CULL, GRADE,
GROUP, ILK, KIND,
MANNER, SPECIES,
TYPE, VARIETY
sortie—FORAY, MISSION,
RAID, SALLY
sot—BIBBER, DRUNK,
DRUNKARD,
TIPPLER, TOPER
soul—AME, ANIMA,
ATMA, ATMAN,
EGO, ESPRIT,
ESSENCE, KA,
PERSON, PNEUMA,
SPIRIT
sound—BLARE, DRONE,
HEALTHY, FIRM,
LEGAL, NOISE,
SANE, RUSTLE
sounded—BLARED,
SHRILLED
soup—BISQUE, BROTH,
POTAGE, POTTAGE,
PUREE
sour—ACERB, ACIDIC,
ACETIC, ACRID,
ACETOSE, BITTER,

MOROSE, RANCID,
TART
source—FONT,
FOUNTAIN, ORIGIN,
RISE, ROOT, SEED,
SPRING
souvenir—MEMENTO,
RELIC
sovereign—CHIEF,
DOMINANT, LIEGE,
MONARCH, PRINCE,
ROYAL, RULER,
SUPREME
sow—DISSEMINATE,
GILT, PIG, PLANT,
SCATTER, SEED,
STREW, SWINE
spa—EMS, BATH, BADEN,
BILIN, PAX, SPRING
space—AREA, AREOLA,
CONCOURSE,
EXTENT, KIND,
OPEN, DISTANCE,
ROOM, TIME, VOID
spade—DIG, LOY,
IMPLEMENT, PARE,
SPUD
spall—CHIP, GALLET,
SPLINTER
span—CROSS, EXTENT,
FORD, INTERVAL,
REACH, TEAM
spangle—GLEAM,
GLITTER,
PAILLETTE
spar—BOOM, BOX, GAFF,
MAST, POLE, SPRIT,
YARD
spare—DESIST,
DISPOSABLE,
EXTRA, GAUNT,
LEAN, RESERVE,
SCANT, SLIM
sparing—CHARY,
CAREFUL,
PROVIDENT,
THRIFTY
sparkle—CORUSCATE,
FLASH, GLEAM,
GLISTEN, GLITTER

sparrow—PHILIP,
WEAVERBIRD
spasm—CONVULSION,
FIT, GRIP, JERK,
THROE, TIC
spasmodic—
EXCITABLE,
FITFUL,
INTERMITTENT,
SPASTIC, TETANIC
spat—GAITER,
MOLLUSK, OYSTER,
QUARREL, ROW,
SLAP, TIFF
spathic—LAMELLAR,
SPARRY
spawn—CLUTCH, EGGS,
OVA, ROE
speak—ADDRESS,
ACCOST, BARK,
CARP, CONVERSE,
DECLAIM, LISP,
MOOT, ORATE, SAY
speaker—
ELOCUTIONIST,
ORATOR
speaking—
ADDRESSING,
ORATORY
spear—ARROW, DART,
HARPOON, JAVELIN,
LANCE, PIKE
special—CONCRETE,
ESPECIAL,
INDIVIDUAL,
PARTICULAR,
RESPECTIVE,
SPECIFIC
speciality—FORTE,
PARTICULARS,
TALENT
species—CLASS, FORM,
GENRE, KIND, SORT
specimen—CAST, COPY,
EXAMPLE,
INSTANCE
spectacle—DISPLAY,
PAGEANT, PARADE,
SCENE, SHOW,
SIGHT

specter—BOGIE,
EIDOLON, GHOST,
MARE, MANES,
SHADE, SHADOW,
SPECTRE, WRAITH
spectral—EERY,
GHOSTLY, IDOLUM
speech—
CONVERSATION,
DIALECT,
DISCOURSE, LIP,
ORATION, SONANT,
TONGUE
speed—EXIGENCY,
FAVOR, FLY, HASTE,
HIE, PACE, POST,
RACE, RUN, RUSH
speedy—APACE, FAST,
RACING, SPRINTING
spell—ABRACADABRA,
CHARM, BEWITCH,
FASCINATION,
HENCE, IMPORT,
RELIEVE, TRANCE
spelling—GLOSSIC,
HETERIC, NOMIC,
TALE
spelt—ADOR, EMMER,
FAR, WHEAT
spend—COST, DISBURSE,
EXERT, EXPEND,
EXHAUST, WASTE
spent—EFFETE, EVANID,
EXHAUSTED,
PETERED, SAPPED
sphere—ARENA, BALL,
GLOBE, ORB,
PLANET, MOON,
STAR, SUN
spherical—GLOBOSE,
GLOBULAR,
OBICULAR, ROTUND
spicy—AROMATIC,
FLAVORED,
PIQUANT,
PUNGENT,
SAVORING
spider—ACERA,
ARACHNID, MITE,
SCORPION, SKILLET,

SNARE, SPINNER,
TARANTULA
genus—AGALENA
nest—NIDUS
study of—
ARANEOLOGY

spigot—ANTLER, BROB,
EAR, GAD, NAIL,
SPADIX, SPICULE,
TINE
spill—DOWNPOUR, SHED,
SPILE, SPLASH,
SLOP, TELL
spin—BIRL, GYRATE,
PIRL, PROLONG,
PROTRACT,
REVOLVE, ROTATE,
SPURT, TROLL
spinach—GOOSEFOOT,
POTHERB
spinal—RACHIDIAN
spindle—ARBOR, AXLE,
HASP, MANDREL
spine—ACICULA, AXIS,
AXON, BACKBONE,
CHAETA, CHINE,
NEEDLE, SETA,
SPICULE, THORN
spinet—CLAVICHORD,
PIANO
spinner—FAIRING,
BLADE, LURE,
SPIDER, TOP
spinning—AWHIRL,
BIRLING,
REVOLVING,
ROTATING,
TURNING
spiral—COIL, COILED,
HELIC, HELICAL,
HELIX, HELIXE
spire—CURL, EPI, STAG,
STEEPLE, SUMMIT,
WHORL
spirit—ANIMATION,
BA, DASH, DEMON,
ELAN, ELF, GHOST,
HEART, LIKE,
MORALE, SOUL,

SPECTER, VIM
spirited—FELL, FIERY,
FERVENT, GAMY,
LIVELY, RACY
spiritless—AMORT,
DEJECTED, DULL,
MOPE, VAPID,
WOODEN
spiritlike—ETHEREAL,
GHOSTLY
spirits, Arab—JIN, HINNI
Babylon—IGIGI
guardian—GENII
spiritual—HOLY,
INWARD, PURE,
SACRED
spit—EJECT,
EXPECTORATE,
IMPALE, LIGHT,
RAIN, ROD, SALIVA,
SPITTLE
spite—MALICE, PIQUE,
RANCOR, THWART,
VENOM
spiteful—CATTY,
MALICIOUS
spitfire—NIPPER
spitter—BROCK, DEER
splash—BESPATTER,
BLOT, BLOTCH,
DAUB, LABBER,
SPATTER, SPLATTER
spleen—MALICE,
MELANCHOLY,
MILT
splendid—AUREATE,
GLORIOUS,
GORGEOUS,
RESPLENDENT,
RIAL, SUBLIME,
SUPERB
splendor—ECLAT, GLORY,
POMP
splicing pin—FID
splinter—FLINDER,
SHATTER, SLIVER,
SHIVER, SPALE
split—CHAP, CLEAVE,
DISRUPT, REND,
RIFT, RIVET, RIVE,

SCHISM, SLICE,
TEAR

spoil—ADDLE, BOOTY,
IMPAIR, LOOT, MAR,
PAMPER, PELF
PLUNDER, ROT,
TAINT

spoiled—BAD, DECAYED,
IMPAIRED, ROTTEN,
WASTED

spoke—BAR, PIN, RAY,
ROD, RUNG, SAID,
UTTERED

sponge—BADIAGA,
CADGE, EFFACE,
ERASE, EXPUNGE,
PARASITE, WIPE,
ZIMOCCA

sponger—BEGGAR,
CADGER, PARASITE,
SORN

spongy—BIBULOUS,
PITHY, POROUS

sponsorship—AEGIS, EGIS

spooky—EERIE,
GHOSTLY, SPIRITED,
WEIRD

spool—BOBBIN, COP,
CYLINDER, REEL,
WIND

spoon—CHIP, BAIT,
IMPLEMENT, LABIS,
OAR, PEN, LURE,
TROLL, UTENSIL

spore—CARPEL, GERM,
SEED

sporty—FLASHY, GAY,
JOCUND, MERRY,
PLAYFUL, RORTY

spot—BLEMISH, BLOT,
DAPPLE, DOT,
FLAW, FLECK,
LOCALITY, MACLE,
MACULA, NOTICE,
PLACE, SPECK,
TARNISH

spout—DISCHARGE,
EJECT, GARGOYLE,
GEAT, JET, SPILE

spread—BROADEN,

BRUIT, COVER,
DELATE, DIFFUSE,
EXTEND, FEAST,
FLARE, SET, TED

spreader—SPATULA,
TEDDER

spree—BEANO, BENDER,
BINGE, FROLIC,
LARK, ORGY,
WASSAIL

sprightly—AIRY, ALIVE,
BUOYANT, CHIPPER,
GAY, NIMBLE, PERT,
TID

spring—ARISE, BOLT,
CEE, COME,
DARTLE, LEAP,
RAMP, SALTATION,
SPA, VAULT

springs—BATHS, FONTS,
SPAS, THERMAE

sprinkle—ASPERGE,
BEDEW, BEDROP,
DEG, FLOUR,
SPARGE, SPATTER,
STREW, WET

sprite—ARIEL, BROWNIE,
DEMON, ELF, ELVE,
FAIRY, FAY,
GOBLIN, HOB, IMP,
PIXIE

sprocket—PROJECTION,
TOOTH

sprout—BUD, BURGEON,
CHIT, CROP, CION,
GERMINATE, GROW,
SCION, SHOOT,
SPRIT

sprouts—ACROSPIRE

spruce—DAPPER, GIM,
NATTY, NEAT,
NOBBY, SMARTEN,
SMUG, TRIG, TRIM

spud—POTATO, TATIE

spume—FOAM, FROTH,
SCUM

spunk—AMADOU, FIRE,
PASSION, PUNK,
SPIRIT, TINDER

spur—ARETE, CALCAR,

DRIVE, GAD, GOAD,
HASTEN, IMPEL,
INCITE, PRICK,
ROWEL, URGE
spurious—BOGUS, FAKE,
FALSE, IMITATION,
PSEUDO, SHAM,
SNIDE
spurn—DECLINE, KICK,
REJECT, SCORN
spurt—BURST, DART,
GUSH, JET, SPOUT,
SQUIRT
spy—DETECT,
DISCOVER,
DISCERN, ESPY,
INFORMER, PRY,
SCOUT, SEE, TOUT,
WORM
squab—CUSHION, SLOP,
SOFA, UNFLEDGED
squad—GANG, GROUP,
TEAM
squall—CRY,
DISTURBANCE,
GALE, GUST, MEWL
squander—DISSIPATE,
MISSPEND, SACK,
SPEND, WASTE
square—AREA, EVEN,
QUADRATE
squatter—MULL, NESTER,
NESTLER, PRESS,
ZEST
squeeze—COMPRESS,
CRUSH, EXTORT,
GRIPE, HUG, JAM,
MURE, NIP, PINCH,
PRESS
squire—BEAU, ESCORT,
GALLANT, KNIGHT,
LOVER
squirrel—CALABAR,
CHIPMUNK,
GOPHER, MINIVER,
PHALANGER, SISEL
Afr.—XERUS
fish—SERRANO
flying, Amer.—ASSAPAN
flying, E.

Ind.—TAGUAN
ground—GOPHER,
SISEL, SUSLIK
nest—DRAY
shrew—TANA
skin—VAIR
stab—ATTEMPT, GORE,
PAUNCH, PIERCE,
PINK, PUNCTURE,
WOUND
stable—BARN,
CONSTANT,
FIRMLY, FIXED,
LASTING, MEW,
PADDOCK, STALLS
stack—CHIMNEY, HEAP,
PILE, RICK,
SCINTLE, SHOCK
staff—BATON, CUDGEL,
MACE, POLE, ROD,
TRUNCHEON,
WAND
stag—COLT, DEER, ELK,
HART, MALE,
POLLARD, SPADE,
SPY, TAIL, TRAIL
stage—APRON, LEGIT,
PHASE, PLATFORM,
STEP, THEATER
stagger—HESITATE,
LURCH, REEL,
REELING, STOT,
STUN, SWAY,
TOTTER, WAVER
staid—DECOROUS,
DEMURE, GRAVE,
SEDATE, SERIOUS,
SOBER
stain—BLEMISH, BLOT,
COLOR, DISCOLOR,
DYE, FOUL, SMEAR,
SMUDGE, TINGLE
stair—ASCEND, STEP,
STILE, STAIRCASE,
stake—ANTE, BET,
HAZARD, PALE,
PICKET, PILE, POLE,
POST, RISK, WAGER
stale—BANAL, FUSTY,
INSIPID, OLD,

TRITE, VAPID
stalemate—CHECK,
DEADLOCK, DRAW,
IMPASSE, TIE
stalk—PEDICEL,
PEDUNCLE,
PETIOLE, STEM,
STIPE
stall—BOOTH
CAVESSON,
COMPARTMENT,
CRIB, DELAY,
EXCUSE, LOGE,
MIRE, PEW, SEAT,
STABLE
stammer—HEM, MANT,
STUTTER
stammering—APHASIA,
PSELLISM
stamp—BRAND, DIE,
IMPRESS, PESTLE,
POSTAGE, PRINT
stampede—DEBACLE,
ROUT, RUN
stanch—FAITHFUL,
LOYAL, QUELL,
STEM, STEADY,
STOP, TRUE
stand—ABIDE, BEAR,
BOOTH, EASEL,
ENDURE, HALT,
LAST, POSITION,
TABORET, TRIVET
standard—CANON,
CLASSIC, CRITERIA,
CRITERION,
ENSIGN, FLAG,
GONFALON, NORM,
PAR, RULE
standing—ERECT, GRADE,
PRESTIGE, STATUS
stanza—STROPHE, VERSE
star—ASTERISK,
BESPANGLE,
CELEBRITY,
FEATURE,
LUMINARY, MAE,
RIGEL, SPICA
starch—AMYL,
ARROWROOT,
ARUM, CASSAVA,

FARINA, SAGO
starchy—AMYLOID,
FORMAL, STIFF
stare—AGAPE, GAPE,
GAZE, GLARE,
LOOK, WONDER
starlike—ASTRAL,
PLANETOID,
STELLAR
starry—ASTRAL,
SIDEREAL,
SPARKLING,
STELLAR
start—BEGIN,
COMMENCE,
INITIATE, ONSET,
OPEN, LOOSEN,
MOVE, DART, JUMP
started—ORIGINATED,
SPRANG
starting point—DATA,
SCRATCH
startle—ALARM, FEAR,
FRIGHTEN, SHOCK,
SURPRISE
stately—AUGUST,
MAJESTIC, REGAL,
TOGATED
statement—ACCOUNT,
ASSERTION,
DICTUM, DIXIT,
FACT, OPINION
station—BASE, DEPOT,
DEGREE, PLACE,
POST, RANK, SET,
STOP
stationary—FIXED,
NAILED, RIVETED,
STATIC, STILL,
TRAPPED
statue—ACROLITH, BUST,
IMAGE, SCULPTURE
statute—ACT, DOOM,
EDICT, LAW,
TREATY
stave—BREAK, CASK,
COVERING,
CUDGEL, LAG,
POLE, STAFF, STICK,
VERSE
stay—ABIDE, BRACE,

GUY, LINGER, PROP,
REMAIN, STOP,
TARRY, WAIT

stead—ADVANTAGE,
AVAIL, LIEU,
PLACE, SERVICE

steady—FIRM, FIXED,
CONSTANT, GRAVE,
EVEN, EQUABLE,
GUY, REGULAR,
STAID

steal—CRIB, FILCH,
GLOM, LOOT, NIM,
PILFER, PURLOIN,
ROB, RUSTLE,
SNITCH

stealing—LOOTING,
PIRACY, RAPINE,
RUSTLING,
SNITCHING, THEFT

stealthy—CATTY,
FURTIVE, SECRET,
SLY

steam—ENERGY, FUME,
FORCE, OAM,
POWER, PUTHER,
REEK, VAPOR

steamer—LINER,
STEAMSHIP, VESSEL

steed—CHARGER, COB,
HORSE, NAG,
PEGASUS

steel—HARD, HARDEN,
IRON, STRONG

steep—ABRUPT, BREW,
CLIFTY, HIGH,
HILLY, IMBUTE,
LOFTY, RET, SHEER,
SOAK, SOP

steeple—EPI, FLECHE,
HENNIN, MINARET,
SPIRE

steer—BOVINE, BULL,
BULLOCK, CON,
CONTROL, GUIDE,
HELM, OX, PILOT,
PLY, PURSUE

steeve—CRAM, LADE,
PACK, SPAR, STORE,
STOW, STUFF

stein—FLAGON, MUG,
NOGGIN

stellar—ASTRAL, STARRY

stem—ARREST, BINE,
CION, CORM,
CHECK, PEDICEL,
PEDUNCLE,
PETIOLE, PROW,
REED, SCAPE,
STALK, STANCH,
STRAW

stentorian—CLARION,
LOUD

step—DEGREE, GAIT,
PACE, PAS, PHASE,
RACE, STAIR,
STRIDE, TRAMPLE,
TREAD, WALK

stepped—ACTED, TROD,
PACED, WALKED

sterile—ACARPOUS,
BARREN,
EXIGUOUS,
INFERTILE,
IMPOTENT,
UNFRUITFUL

stern—AUSTERE,
FORBIDDING, GRIM,
HARSH, RIGOROUS,
SEVERE

stertor—SNORE, SNORING

stevedore—LADER,
LOADER, STOWER,
UNLOADER

stew—BOIL, FRET,
HARICOT, OLLA,
POT, RAGOUT,
SEETHE, SIMMER,
WORRY

steward—ECONOME,
ERENACH, REEVE,
SENESCHAL

stewardly—FRUGAL,
SPARING

stick—ADHERE, BAR,
BAT, BATON, CANE,
COHERE, PASTE,
POLE, ROD, STALL,
WAND

sticky—GOO, LIMY,

PASTY, TACKY,
TREACLY, VISCID
stiff—INFLEXIBLE,
RIGID, FORMAL,
FRIGID, STARK,
STARCHY, STILTED
stigma—BLOT, BRAND,
PORE, STAIN, TAINT
stiletto—BODKIN, STYLET
still—BUT, COSH, DUMB,
EVEN, IMMOBILE,
IMMOVABLE, MUM,
QUIET, SILENT, YET
stimulate—AROUSE, FAN,
INCITE,
INNERVATE, JOY,
PIQUE, STIR, URGE,
WHET
stimulus—GOAD,
IMPETUS,
INCENTIVE, SPUR
sting—BITE, GOAD,
INCITE, PRICK,
SMART, TANG
stinging—BITING,
CAUSTIC, SHARP
stingy—CLOSE, MEAN,
MISERLY, NEAR,
NIGGARDLY,
SCALY, SCANTY
stint—CHORE, CRIMP,
DESIST, DULL,
DUTY, RESTRAIN,
RESTRICT, SCRIMP,
TASK
stipend—ANN, PAY,
PENSION,
PREBEND, SALARY,
WAGE, WAGES
stir—ADO, AGITATE,
AROUSE, BUSTLE,
DISTURB, EXCITE,
FUSS, MIX, MOVE,
ROUSE, URGE
stitch—ACHE, CRICK,
KNIT, PAIN, SEW,
SUTURE
stoat—ERMINE, WEASEL
stock—BLOCK, BRACE,
BUTT, FRAME, PILE,

POST, RACE, STORE,
STUMP
stockade—CORRAL,
ENCLOSURE, ETAPE,
KRAAL, PEN,
RAMPART,
REDOUBT
stocking—HOSE, SHINNER
stocky—FAT, CHUBBY,
PLUMP, STOUT,
STUB
stoker—FIREMAN
stole—BOA, GARMENT,
LOOTED, ORARY,
PIRATED,
VESTMENT
stomach—CRAW, MAW,
RESENT, RUMEN
stone—AGATE, DRUPE,
FLINT, GEM, JEWEL,
LAPIS, MARBLE,
PEBBLE, PIT, SLATE,
TALUS
stony—NIOBEAN,
PETRIFIED,
PETROUS, PITILESS,
ROCKY
stool—CROCK, STUMP,
TABOURET
stop—ARREST, AVAST,
BALK, BAR, CEASE,
CESSATION, DAM,
DESIST, DETER,
HALT
stoppage—ARRESTING,
BLOCK, CESSATION,
DAM, HALT,
OBSTRUCTION
stopper—BUNG, CAP,
CORK, PLUG, SPILE
store—ACCUMULATE,
AMASS, BIN, CACHE,
FUND, HUSBAND,
MARKET, MART,
SHOP, STOCK
stork, genus—ERODIUM
large—ADJUTANT,
JABIRU, MARABOU
rel. to—HERON, IBIS,
PELARGIC

storm—BESIEGE,
DISTURB, FUME,
OUTBREAK, RAGE,
RAMPAGE, RAVE,
TEMPEST
stormy—INCLEMENT,
SEVERE,
TURBULENT,
VIOLENT
story—ANALOGY,
FABLE, FLOOR,
JEREMIAD,
LEGEND, LORE,
MYTH, NOVEL,
SAGA, TALE, YARN
stout—BRAVE, BOLD,
FIRM, SOLID,
STRONG, STURDY
stove—ETNA, HEATER,
KILN, OVEN, RANGE
stow—BOX, CRATE,
LODGE, PACK,
HIDE, HOLD, STORE,
TRIM
straggler—LAGGER,
NOMAD, STRAY,
WANDERER
straight—ARROW,
CANDID, DIRECT,
EVEN, FLAT,
FRANK, LEVEL,
LINED
strain—BEND, BREED,
EXERT, FILTER,
HEAVE, PROGENY,
RACE, SIFT, STRESS,
TAX
strainer—SIEVE, SIFTER,
SYTH, TAMIS
strait—AREA, ANGUST,
CHANNEL,
ISTHMUS, KERSEY,
NARROW, NECK,
PHARE
strange—ALIEN,
FOREIGN, NOVEL,
ODD, QUAINT,
RARE,
TRAMONTANE
stranger—ALIEN,

FOREIGNER,
INTRUDER,
NEWCOMER
strangle—CHOKE,
GARROTE, STIFLE
strap—BELT, CINCH,
GIRT, LEASH, REIN,
STROP, THONG
stratagem—ARTIFICE,
COUP, FINESSE,
RUSE, TRAP, TRICK,
WILE
strategic—ARTIFICE,
PLAN, WESEL
stratum—BED, DEPOSIT,
LAY, LAYER, SEAM,
TIER
straw—CULM, MOTE,
SHIV, STALK
stray—ABERRANT,
DEVIATE, ERR,
GAD, LOSE, SIN,
WANDER
streak—BAR, BRINDLE,
LINE, ROW, STRIA,
STRIPE, TRACE,
TRAIT, VEIN
stream—ARROYA,
BROOK, CREEK,
FLOW, FRESHET,
POUR, RILL, RIVER,
RUN, SPRUIT,
TORRENT
streamer—FLAG,
PENNANT,
STANDARD
street—AVENUE,
FOOTPATH, ROAD,
THOROUGHFARE
strength—FORCE,
INTENSITY, MAIN,
POWER, SINEW,
SOUNDNESS,
STAMINA, THEW,
VIGOR
strengthening—BRACING,
PROP, SOBORANT
stress—ACCENT, ARSIS,
EMPHASIS, ICTUS,
PRESSURE, STRAIN,

TENSION
stretch—COURSE,
DIRECTION,
ELASTIC,
EXAGGERATE,
EXPAND, EXTEND,
FLEX, PULL
stretcher—LITTER,
RACKER, STEND
strict—DRAWN, EXACT,
PRECISE, RIGID,
RIGOROUS, STERN,
STRAIT
strife—BATTLE, BATE,
COMBAT, CONTEST,
DISCORD, FEUD,
FIGHT, SPAT, WAR
strigil—CLEANER,
GRAZE, SCRAPER
strike—ATTACK, BANG,
BATTLE, BEAT,
BLAST, BLOW,
CANCEL, CAST,
CAROME, DART,
DAUB, DASH,
DOWN, ELIDE,
FORCE, FIGHT,
FRACAS, GARROTE,
GNASH, GOAD,
GRASP, HARM, HIT,
HURL, IMPOSE,
INFLICT, JAB,
KNOCK, LACE, LICK,
LOWER, MASH,
MISS, NAB, NICK,
NIP, NUDGE,
OFFEND, OPPOSE,
OUTRAGE, PAIN,
PANG, PANIC,
PASTE, PICK,
PICKET, PLUG,
POKE, POP, POUNCE,
PRICK, PROD,
PUNCH, PUNISH,
RAP, RAM, REJECT,
REMOVE, REPULSE,
REVENGE, RIB,
RILE, RIP, ROB,
ROUT, ROW,
RUFFLE, SAP,

SLAP,
SLUG, SMACK,
SMITE, STRICLE,
STROKE, TAP, TEAR,
TRIP, UPEND,
UPON, UPPERCUT,
VILLAIN, WAGE,
WALLOP, WAR,
WHACK, WHALE,
WHANG, WHIP,
WHOP, WRECK
string—CORD, LINE,
ROPE, STRAND,
TWINE
stringed instrument—ASOR,
BANJO, CELLO,
GUITAR, HARP,
LUTE, LYRE, PIANO,
REBEC, UKE, VIOL,
VIOLA, VIOLIN
ancient—BANDORE,
MANDOLA, REBEC,
STRAD
device—CLAVIA,
ELECTRUM,
KEYBOARD, MUTE
strip—BAND, BARE,
DENUDE, DIVEST,
DISMANTLE,
FILLET, REMOVE,
SKIN, TAPE
stripe—BAR, BRAID,
CHEVRON, FILLET,
RIDGE, STRIP,
WALE, WEAL, WELT
stripling—LAD, STRIP
stripper—ECDYSIAST,
PARER, PEELER,
PICKER, SHEDDER
strive—ATTEMPT,
BATTLE, CONTEND,
CONTEST, EFFORT,
ENDEAVOR, LABOR,
STRUGGLE, TRY,
VIE
stroke—ATTACK, BEAT,
BLOW, COUP, FIT,
ICTUS, MOVEMENT,
PARALYSIS, SHOCK
stroll—PROMENADE,

RAMBLE, ROVE,
SAUNTER, WANDER
strong—COGENT, FIRM,
HALE, INTENSE,
POWERFUL,
ROBUST, STOUT,
STURDY, TOUGH
stronghold—CITADEL,
FORT, FORTRESS,
GARRISON, KEEP,
MUNIMENT, POST
struggle—ATTEMPT,
CONTEST, COPE,
EFFECT, EFFORT,
LABOR, STRIFE, VIE,
WRESTLE
stub—COUNTERFOIL,
COUPON, RECEIPT,
STUMP, TAB
stubble—EDDISH, STUMP
stubborn—DIFFICULT,
OBSTINATE,
ORNERY,
REFRACTORY,
RESOLUTE,
UNYIELDING
stud—BOSS, BUTTON,
KNOB, NAIL,
ORNAMENT,
STALLION
student—DISCIPLE,
LEARNER, PLEBE,
PORER, PUPIL,
SCHOLAR, TOSHER
studio—ATELIER,
WORKSHOP
study—CON, CONSIDER,
EYE, ENDEAVOR,
MEDITATE, PERUSE,
PORE, SCAN, WEIGH
stuff—CRAM, FABRIC,
FILL, GORGE, PAD,
PRESS, RAM, SATE,
SATIATE, STEEVE,
STOW, WAD
stulm—ADIT, PASSAGE,
PASSAGEWAY
stump—BUTT,
CHALLENGE,
CLUMP, DARE, FOIL,

LOP, PLATFORM,
SKEG, SNAG, STOCK
stun—ASTOUND, BESOT,
BRUISE, DAUNT,
DAZE, DOZEN,
DRUG, FOOLISH,
OVERPOWER,
STUPEFY
stunning—BEAUTIFUL,
EXCELLENT,
DAZING, FINE
stunt—ATROPHY,
CHECK, CROWL,
DULL, DWARF,
EXPLOIT, FEAT,
STINT, TRICK
stupefy—BEMUSE, BESOT,
DAZE, DOPE, DRUG,
DULL, MAZE,
PALL, STUN, TORPID
stupid—ASININE, CRASS,
DOLTISH, DUMB,
INANE, INEPT
stupor—COMA,
DROWSINESS,
LETHARGY,
NARCOMA, SOPOR,
TORPOR, TRANCE
sturgeon, genus—
ACIPENSER
large—HAUSEN
roe—CAVIAR
small—STERLET
species of—OSSETER
white—BELUGA
style—DUB, FASHION,
MANNER, MODE,
TECHNIC, TYPE,
VOGUE, WAY
stylet—DAGGER, DIRK,
STILETTO
stylish—ALAMODE, CHIC,
DRESSY, NIFTY,
TOPPY
styptic—ALUM,
AMADOU,
ASTRINGENT
suave—BLAND,
DIPLOMATIC,
SMOOTH, URBANE

subdue—AWE, CALM,
CENSOR, CONQUER,
CRUSH, QUASH,
QUELL, SOBER,
TAME

subject—CITIZEN,
ENTHRALL, LIABLE,
LIEGE, PRONE,
TEXT, THEME,
TOPIC

submerged—AWASH,
INUNDATED, SUNK

submit—BOW, CEDE,
OBEY, RESIGN,
STAND, STOOP,
YIELD

subordinate—INFERIOR,
MINOR,
SECONDARY,
SUBALTERN

subside—ABATE,
FALL, DESCEND,
EBB, LANGUISH,
RELAPSE, SETTLE,
SINK, WANE

substance—BODY,
COMPONENT,
ELEMENT, ESSENCE,
GIST, IMPORT,
MATERIAL, OBJECT

substitute—AGENT,
ALTERNATE,
COMMUTE,
DEPUTY, ERSATZ,
EXCHANGE,
REPLACE

subterfuge—DECEPTION,
ESCAPE, EVASION,
FLEE, RUSE, SHIFT

subterranean—
ABYSMAL,
HIDDEN,
PLUTONIC, SECRET,
SUNK, VAULT

subtle—ARTFUL,
CRAFTY, DELICATE,
NICE, SLY, WISE

suburb—ENVIRONS,
PURLIEU, TOWN,
URBAN, VILLAGE

subway—METRO, TUBE

success—DEGREE, FAME,
GO, HIT, MEASURE,
VICTORY

succession—AROW,
ORDINAL, SERIES

succinct—BRIEF,
CONCISE, GIRDED,
SHORT, TERSE,
TUCKED

succor—AID, ASSIST,
HELP, NURSE,
RELIEF, RESCUE

succulent—JUICE, JUICY,
LUSH, PAPPY,
PULPY

sudden—ABRUPT,
HASTINESS, QUICK,
PRECIPITATE

suet—FAT, TALLOW

suffer—ACHE, AGONIZE,
AIL, BEAR, DREE,
LET, PERMIT,
SMART, STARVE,
TOLERATE

suffice—AVAIL,
CAPABLE,
CONTENT, DO,
SATISFY, SERVE

sufficient—ADEQUATE,
AMPLE, BASTANT,
COMPETENT,
ENOUGH, ENOW,
FIT, FULL

sugar—DEXTROSE,
MANNOSE, OSE,

suggest—CUE, HINT,
INTIMATE, PROPOSE

suggestion—CLUE, HINT,
TRACE, WRINKLE

suit—AGREE, ADAPT,
BECOME, BEFIT, FIT,
HIT, PETITION,
PLEASE, SATISFY,
WOOING

suitable—ADAPTED, APT,
BEFITTING, DUE,
FIT, IDONEOUS,
MEET, PAT, PROPER

suitcase—BAG, SATCHEL,

VALISE
suite—RETINUE, STAFF,
TRAIN
suitor—AMOROSO, BEAU,
SWAIN, WOOER
summary—BRIEF,
COMPEND,
COMPREHENSIVE,
CONCISE, PRECIS
summit—ACME, APEX,
CLIMAX,
CULMINATION,
KNAP, MERIDIAN,
PEAK, TOP, SPIRE,
VERTEX
summon—ACCITE, BID,
CALL, CITE,
CONVENE,
EVOCATE, EVOKE,
MUSTER, PAGE,
WARN
sump—BOG, PIT, POOL,
WELL
sun—HELIOS, SOL, STAR
sunder—CUT, DIVIDE,
PART, REND, RIVE,
SEVER
sunstroke—
CALENTURE,
ICTUS,
INSOLATION,
SIRIASIS
superhighway—
EXPRESSWAY,
FREEWAY
superintend—BOSS,
OVERSEE
superior—ABOVE, FINER,
MISTRESS,
PALMARY, UPPER
superiority—MASTERY,
ODDS
supernatural—
ABNORMAL,
EERIE,
HYPERPHYSICAL
supine—BENT, INERT,
LAZY, LISTLESS,
PRONE, SLUGGISH
supple—COMPLIANT,

LISSOME, LITHE,
PLIANT
supplement—ADD, EKE,
FILL
supplies—
AMMUNITION,
ESTOVERS,
MATERIAL,
RATIONS, STORES
supply—AFFORD, CATER,
FUND, PURVEY,
STORE
support—ABET, AID,
BACK, BASE,
BEHALF, GUY, LEG,
LIMB, PEG, PROP,
PIER, TENON,
PEDESTAL, SECOND,
SIDE
supporter—
ADVOCATE, FAN
suppose—ASSUME, DEEM,
BELIEVE, OPINE,
PRESUME, WEEN,
WIS
supposed—PUTATIVE,
SURMISED
supreme—CHIEF,
GREATEST,
HIGHEST, LAST,
PARAMOUNT,
ULTIMATE, UTMOST
surd—DISC,
IRRATIONAL,
RADICAL, VOICELESS
surface—EXTERIOR,
FACE, MEROS,
NAPPE, PLAT
surfeit—CLOY, GLUT,
JADE, REPLETE,
SATIATE
surgeon—LEECH,
PHYSICIAN,
SAWBONES
surly—ABRUPT,
ARROGANT,
CRABBED, CROSS,
CRUSTY, GRUM,
GRUFF, RUDE,
SULLEN

surname—AGNOMEN,
COGNOMEN, DOE,
EPONYM,
PATRONYMIC
surpass—BEAT, BEST,
CAP, EXCEED,
EXCEL, OUTCLASS,
OUTDO, OUTSHINE,
TRANSCEND
surplice—COTTA, PELISSE
surplus—EXCESS, OVER,
REST, SPARE
surrender—CEDE,
CESSION, DEDITION,
RELINQUISH,
REMIT, YIELD
surround—BELAY, BELT,
BESET, ENCASE,
ENCLOSE,
ENCIRCLE,
HEM
surrounding—AMBIENT,
BESET,
ENTOURAGE,
ENVIRON
suspended—DEFERRED,
EXCLUDED, HELD,
HUNG, PENSILE,
SUPPORTED
suspension—DELAY,
FAILURE, PENALTY,
HINT, RESPITE
suspicious—DOUBTFUL,
LEARY, LEERY,
QUESTIONABLE,
SKEPTICAL
suture—JUNCTION,
PTERION, RAPHE,
SEAM, SEW,
STITCHING
swab—EPAULET, LOUT,
MALKIN, MOP,
SPONGE, WIPE
swag—BOOTY, BOODLE,
LURCH, PLUNDER,
SAG, SPOILS, SWAY
swagger—BRAG, BOAST,
BLUSTER, PRANCE,
STRUT, SWELL
swain—BEAU, DAMON,

FLAME, GALLANT,
LAD, LOVER,
RUSTIC
swallow—MARTIN, TERN
swamp—BOG,
EVERGLADE, FEN,
MARSH, MORASS,
OVERWHELM, SLUE
swampy—PALUDAL,
ULIGINOUS, UVID
swan—LEDA,
TRUMPETER
female—PEN
genus—OLOR
male—COB
young—CYGNET
swap—BARTER,
EXCHANGE, TRADE
sward—GRASS, LAWN,
LEA, SOD, TURF
swarm—BIKE, FRY,
HERD, HIVE,
MIGRATE,
NEST, SNEE,
TEEM, THRONG
sway—BEND,
FLUCTUATE,
GOVERN, INCLINE,
POWER, REEL,
ROCK, TEETER,
WAVER
swear—CURSE, OATH,
VOW
sweat—EXUDE,
HIDROSIS, PERSPIRE
sweater—CARDIGAN,
PULLOVER, SLIPON,
SUDORIFIC
sweet—DEAR, DOUCE,
DULCET, FRESH,
HONEY, MAPLE,
SUGARY
sweetbread—RIS, RUSK
sweetbrier—
EGLANTINE,
HIP
sweetheart—BEAU,
LADYLOVE, LEMAN,
LOVER, PARAMOUR,
VALENTINE

sweetsop—ATES, ATTA
ATES, ATTA
swell—BULB, BULGE,
DILATE, DISTEND,
EXPAND, FOP, NOB,
RISE, SURF, SURGE,
STRUT, TUFF
swelling—BLAIN, BUBO,
DROPSY, EDEMA,
LUMP, NODE, RISE,
RISING, STYE
swerve—CAREEN,
DEVIATE, SHIFT,
SHY, SKEW, VEER
swift—FAST, FLYING,
HASTY, JET, RAPID,
RACY, QUICK,
READY, SPEEDY
swimming—NATANT,
VERTIGO
swindle—BAM, BILK,
BUNCO, CHEAT,
CON, DUPE,
FLEECE, FRAUD,
GYP, IMPOSTURE,
HUMBUG, HOAX,
MISCHIEF, SCHEME,
SHAM, TRICK,
WANGLE
swindler—CHEATER,
DUPER, FRAUD,
GYP, SCHEMER,
SHARK
swine—BOAR, HOG, PIG,
PORCINE, SHOAT,
SOW, TAPIR
swinelike—PORCINE
swing—BRANDISH,
FLOURISH, FLY,
FLUTTER,
OSCILLATE, SWAY,
THRASH, WAVE
swirl—EDDY, GURGE,
WHIRL
switch—FLOG, LASH,
SHIFT, SHUNT,

TRANSFER
swivel—PIVOT, SWING,
TRAVERSE, TURN
swollen—BLOATED,
BOLLEN, TUMID
sword—BADELAIRE,
BILBO, DIRK, EPEE,
GLAIVE, KUKRI,
RAPIER, SABER,
TOLEDO
broad—CUTLASS
case—SCABBARD,
SHEATH
fencing—EPEE, FOIL
handle—HAFT, HILT
Oriental—SCIMITAR
swordfish—AUS, DORADO,
ESPADON
sycophant—FLUNKY,
PARASITE, SPANIEL,
TOADEATER,
TOADY
sylvan—FOREST, GROVE,
RUSTIC, WOODEN,
WOODS
symbol—EMBLEM,
IMAGE, OM, PALM,
SIGN, TOKEN,
TOTEM
sympathy—CONDOLE,
CONSOLE,
CONSENT, PITY
symptom—ALARM,
MARK, NOTE, SIGN,
TOKEN, WARNING
synopsis—ABSTRACT,
CONSPECTUS,
DIGEST, EPITOME,
OUTLINE, TABLE
synthetic—ARTIFICIAL,
NYLON
syrup—MAPLE,
SORGHUM,
TREACLE
system—ISM, METHOD,
ORDER, REGIMEN

TAB 207 TALENTED

-T-

tab—ACCOUNT, FLAP, LABEL, MARK, PAN, STRIP, TAG, TALLY

tabernacle—CHURCH, HABITATION, HILET, KIRK, SHELTER, TEMPLE, TENT

tableau—PICTURE, PORTRAIT, REPRESENTATION, SCENE

tableland—MESA, PLATEAU

tablet—BRED, FACIA, PAD, PILL, TROCHE

taboo—BAN, DEBAR, FORBID, INTERDICT, RESTRICT

tacit—INDICATED, IMPLIED, SILENT, UNSPOKEN

taciturn—QUIET, RETICENT, SILENT

tack—BASTE, BRAD, FASTEN, GEAR, NAIL, ROPE, SECURE

tackle—APPARATUS, CAT, EQUIPMENT, GARNET, GEAR, PULLEY, HARNESS, RIGGING, SEIZE, YOKE

tact—ADDRESS, FEELING, POISE,

tadpole—POLLIWOG, SALIENTIA

tag—FLAP, FLY, FRAZZLE, GAME, LABEL

tail—BACK, BOTTOM, CODA, END, ESCAPE, FLEE, LAST, REAR,

RETINUE, SHADOW

tailless—ACAUDAL, ACAUDATE, ANURIA, ANUROUS

tailor—DRAPER, SARTOR, SYNDER

taint—BLEMISH, CORRUPT, DEFILE, INFECT, POISON, POLLUTE, VITIATE

tainted—BAD, IMBUED, PINDY, POLLUTED

take—ABSTRACT, ADMIT, ADOPT, ASSUME, AVAIL, BUY, CAPTURE, CARRY, CAST, CATCH, CHOOSE, CONSIDER, CONSUME, DEDUCE, DERIVE, EMPLOY, EXTRACT, FEED, FINGER, FISH, FRISK, GRASP, GRIP, HOLD, INFER, JOCKEY, LAY, LEAD, OBTAIN, OCCUPY, PICK, RECEIVE, RECORD, REMOVE, REPRESENT, SEIZE, SELECT, SNATCH, SUBTRACT, TOTE, UNDERGO, UNDERTAKE

talc—AGALITE, POWDER, SOAPSTONE

tale—ANECDOTE, FALSEHOOD, GESTE, LEGEND, LIE, MYTH, SAGA, STORY

talent—APTITUDE, DOWER, FLAIR, GIFT, VERVE

talented—ABLE, APT,

CLEVER, GENIUS,
GIFTED
talisman—AMULET,
CHARM, FETISH,
KARMA
talk—ADDRESS, CHAT,
CONVERSE, CRACK,
GAB, GAS, HARP,
ORATE, PRATE,
SPEAK
talker—MAGPIE,
ORATOR, PROSER,
STENTOR
talking bird—MAGPIE,
MINA, MINAH,
MYNA, MYNAH,
PARROT
tall—ACTIVE, BRAVE,
COMELY,
COURAGEOUS,
EXCELLENT, FINE,
HIGH, LARGE
tallow—FAT, SUET
tally—COUNT, NOTCH,
RECKON, REGISTER,
RUN, SCORE,
SQUARE
tambourine—DAIRA,
TAAR, TABOR,
TIMBREL
tame—CONQUER,
DOCILE, GENTLE,
MILD, HARMLESS,
INSIPID, SUBDUED,
TRACTABLE
tan—BEIGE, BRONZE,
BUFF, ECRU,
BROWN, SUNBURN,
TAW
tangle—MAT, SHAG,
SLEAVE, WEAVE
tank—BASIN, CISTERN,
POND, POOL, TUB,
VAT
tap—OPEN, PLUG,
SOUND, SPILE
taper—CANDLE,
DIMINISH, LIGHT,
PYRAMIDICAL,
SPIRY

tapestry—ARRAS,
DOSSER, TAPIS
tar—GOB, JACKY,
MARINER, SALT,
SAILOR
tarboosh—FEZ, TURBAN
tardy—BUSTARD,
DILATORY, LATE,
LAG, SLOW, TARRY
target—AIM, AMBITION,
BUTT, BIRD, GOAL,
MARK, OBJECT,
SHIELD, SIGHT,
VANE
tarnish—DESTROY,
DULL, MAR, SOIL,
SMIRCH, SULLY
tarry—ABIDE, BIDE, LAG,
LINGER, LOITER,
REMAIN, STAY,
WAIT
tarsus—ANKLE
tart—ACID, ACRID,
ACUTE, CAUSTIC,
SHARP, SOUR,
SUBACID
tartan—PLAID, SETT
task—CHORE, DUTY,
JOB, LABOR,
PENSUM, STINT,
TAX
taste—FLAVOR, FREE,
PALATE,
PENCHANT, RELISH,
SAPOR, SAVOR, SIP,
TANG
tasteless—FADED, FLAT,
INSIPID, PALL,
SAPID, VAPID,
WATERY
tasty—NEAT, SAPOROUS,
SAVORY
tatter—PATCH, RAG,
REMNANT, SHRED
tattle—BLAB, BLABBER,
DIVULGE, GOSSIP,
TELL
tattler—CHATTER,
GOSSIP, LAB,
PRATER,

QUIDNUNC,
TALEBEARER
tattoo—BUGLE, CALL,
COLOR, MARK,
PRICKING
taunt—DERIDE, FLOUT,
GIBE, INSULT, JEER,
QUIP, QUIRK,
RIDICULE, SNEER
taut—FIRM, SNUG,
TENSE, TIGHT, TIDY
tavern—CABARET, INN,
PUB, SALOON
tawny—BROWN, DUSKY,
RUBIATE, TAN,
TIGRENE
tax—ASSESS, CESS,
DUTY, EXCISE,
GELD, IMPOST,
LEVY, SCAT, SCOT,
TOLL, TRIBUTE
tea—CAMBRIC, CHA,
HYSON, MATE,
OOLONG, PEKOE,
TISANE, YERBA
teach—COACH, CRAM,
DRILL, EDIFY,
EDUCATE, ENDUE,
MONITOR, PRIME,
SCHOOL, TUTOR
teacher—INSTRUCTOR,
PEDAGOGUE,
PUNDIT, SCRIBE
teaching—DOCENT,
INSTRUCTING,
PEDAGOGY,
PRECEPT
team—CREW, GROUP,
JOIN, PAIR,
SPAN, SQUAD,
YOKE
teamster—BEARER,
CARRIER, CARTER,
TOTER
tear—CLEAVE,
LACERATE, REND,
RIP, RIVE, SPLIT
tearful—MAUDLIN,
WEEPING
tease—ANNOY, BANTER,

COAX, HECTOR,
MOLEST, NAG,
PESTER, PLAGUE,
TANTALIZE
ted—SCATTER, SPREAD
tedious—DREARY,
ELENGE,
FATIGUING,
IRKSOME, NOXIOUS,
PROSE, TIRESOME
tedium—BOREDOM,
ENNUI
teeter—JIGGLE, ROCK,
SEESAW, SWAY,
WAVER
teeth—BITERS, FANGS,
INCISORS, MOLARS
tela—MEMBRANE,
TISSUE, WEB
telegraph—WIRE
code—MORSE
instrument part—ANVIL,
KEY
recorder—SIPHON
tell—DISCLOSE, INFORM,
NARRATE, RECITE,
RECOUNT, RELATE,
SAY
telling—COGENT,
DISCLOSING,
INFORMING,
POTENT, RELATING
temper—ANNEAL,
DANDER, METAL,
METTLE, MITIGATE,
MOOD, QUALIFY,
TANTRUM, TONE
temperament—ACTION,
CRASIS,
DISPOSITION,
INTERNAL, HUMOR,
MIND
temperate—MODERATE,
SOBER
tempest—BLAST, ORAGE,
SAMIEL, STORM,
TUMULT
temple—CHURCH, COVIL,
FANE, HUACA,
SANCTUARY,

PAGODA
tempo—METER,
   RHYTHM, TIME
temporal—CIVIL, LAY,
   WORLDLY
temporary—
   EPHEMERAL,
   INTERIM, NONCE,
   TRANSITORY
tempt—ALLURE, BAIT,
   DECOY, ENTICE,
   INCITE, LURE,
   PROVOKE, TEST,
   URGE
ten—DECADE, DENARY,
   TENFOLD
tend—CARE, CONDUCE,
   GUARD, INCLINE,
   LEAN, MIND,
   TREND
tender—GENTLE, HEART,
   KIND, OFFER,
   PRESENT, PROFFER,
   SENSITIVE, SOFT,
   SORE
tendon—MUSCLE, SINEW,
   STIPULE
tendril—CURL, PLANT,
   STIPULE, TENACLE
tenet—BELIEF, CREED,
   DOCTRINE, DOGMA,
   ISM, MAXIM,
   PRINCIPLE
tenon—COG, MORTISE,
   TOOTH, TUSK
tenor—COURSE, DRIFT,
   EFFECT, INTENT,
   PURPORT, TREND
tent—CAMP, ENCAMP,
   PROBE, TEPEE
tent, Indian—PAWL,
   TEPEE, WIGWAM
tentacle—FEELER, HAIR
tenure—HOLDING,
   LEASE, TERM
term—AGE, CALL,
   DURATION, EPOCH,
   ERA, LIMIT, PERIOD,
   SEMESTER, TIME
terminal—BOUNDARY,

CONCLUDING,
DEPOT, END,
EXTREMITY, LAST,
STATION, YARD
termination—
   AMEN, BOUND,
   CONCLUSION, END,
   EXTENT, FINAL,
   FINIAL, LAST
termite—ANAI, ANY,
   ANT, WHITEANT
terrace—BALCONY,
   BERM, DIAS,
   PLATEAU
terrapin—CODDLE,
   EMYD, POTTER,
   SLIDER
terrestrial—EARTHLY,
   GEAL, TERRENE
terrible—AWFUL, DIRE,
   DREADFUL, GAST,
   GRIM, FEARFUL,
   TERROR, TRAGIC
terrier—
   kind of—FOX,
   MANCHESTER,
   SEALYHAM, SKYE
terrify—ABAST, ALARM,
   APPALL, DAUNT,
   SHOCK
territory—DEMESNE,
   DISTRICT, DOMAIN,
   REGION, ACREAGE,
   BOUNDARIES
terror—DREAD, FEAR,
   FRIGHT, HORROR,
   NUISANCE, PITY,
   TRAGIC
terse—COMPACT, CRISP,
   CONCISE, LACONIC,
   PITHY, SUCCINCT
test—CHECK,
   CRITERION, ASSAY,
   EXAMINE, PROOF,
   STANDARD, TRIAL,
   TRY
tester—ASSAYER,
   CHECKER, CIEL,
   TRYER
testify—ATTEST, AVER,

AVOW, DEPONE,
DEPOSE, DECLARE,
MANIFEST, PROOF,
TESTIMONY

tether—BIND, CONFINE,
FASTEN, LEASH,
LONGE, RESTRAIN,
TIE

text—COMPOSE,
PASSAGE, SUBJECT,
THEME, TOPIC,
VERSE

texture—WALE, WEAVE,
WEB, WOOF

thatched—COVERING,
PALMED, REEDED,
STRAWED

theater—ARENA. DRAMA,
ODEA, ODEON,
ODEUM, STAGE

theme—ESSAY, MOTIF,
SUBJECT, TEMA,
TEXT, THESIS, TOPIC

theory—DOCTRINE,
HYPOTHESIS, ISM

therefore—ALSO, AND,
ERGO, HENCE, SO,
THUS, TOO

thicken—CAKE, CLOT,
CURDLE,
INSPISSATE, LYE,
SOLIDIFY

thicket—BOSCAGE, BOSK,
BOSKET, BUSH,
COPPICE, COPSE,
COVERT, HEDGE,
RONE, SHRUB

thief—FAGIN, FILCHER,
GANEF, GANOF,
LOOTER, PIKER,
PIRATE, ROBBER,
YEGG

thimble—CAP, RING,
SPUT

thin—BONY, DILUTED,
FINE, GAUNT,
LANK, LEAN,
MEAGRE, SHEER,
SLIM, SPARSE,
SVELTE, WATERY

thing—ENTITY,
EXISTENCE, IT,
MATTER

think—BELIEVE,
COGITATE,
CONSIDER, DEEM,
MULL, MUSE,
OPINE, PONDER,
WIS

thinness—RARITY,
SLENDER, TENUITY

thither—TO, TOWARD,
THERE ,YON, YOND

thole—BEAR, ENDURE,
FULCRUM,
OARLOCK

thong—AMENTA,
AMENT, KNOUT,
ROMAL, STRAP,
WHIP

thorn—BRIAR, BRIER,
PRICKLE, SETA,
SPINE, STOB

thousand—CHILIAD,
CHILIARCH, MIL,
MILLE

thrall—BONDMAN, ESNE,
SERF, SLAVE

thrash—BELABOR, BLESS,
CANE, DRUDGE,
FLAIL, FLOG, LAM,
TAN, TROUNCE,
URTICATE

thread—FILAMENT,
FIBER, HAIR, LINE,
LISLE, REEVE,
STAMEN, TWINE

threadlike—FIBROID,
FILAR,
FILOSE, LINEAR

three—TER, THRIN, TRI,
TRIA, TRIO, TRIAD

threshing tool—FLAIL

threshold—DEARN, EVE,
ENTRANCE, GATE,
LIMEN, SILL

thrill—DINDLE, FLUSH,
SHIVER, THROB,
TINGLE, TIRL,
TREMBLE, TREMOR,

VIBRATE
thrilling—
  ELECTRIC,
  SHOCKING
thrive—ADDLE,
  BATTEN,
  GROW, PROSPER,
  PROVE
throat—GULA, MAW
throbbing—PALPITANT,
  PATTERING,
  PITAPAT
throe—ACHE, AGONY,
  PAIN, PANG, RACK,
  SUFFERING
throne—ASANA, EXALT,
  SOVEREIGNTY
throng—CREW, CROWD,
  HORDE, HOST,
  MASS, MOB, PRESS
throttle—GAG, LEVER,
  STRANGLE,
  SUFFOCATE
through—BY, DIA, PER,
  TRUG
throw—CAST, COP,
  FLING, HEAVE,
  HURL, PITCH, TOSS,
  YEND
thrush—FAUCES, MAVIS,
  MISSEL, OMAO,
  OUSEL, OUZEL,
  ROBIN, SHAMA,
  SPREW, SPRUE,
  VERRY
thrust—ALLONGE,
  DARTLE, DIG,
  LUNGE, ONSET,
  POKE, PROD,
  SHOVE, STAB
thud—BEAT, BLOW,
  BUMP, KNOCK, RAP
thug—CUTTLE, GOON,
  GUNMAN,
  ROUGHNECK,
  RUFFIAN, YEGG
thumb—POLLEX
thunder—ROAR, SOUND
thus—HENCE, SIC, SO,
  THEREFORE

thwart—BAFFLE, BALK,
  BRAIN, FOIL,
  FRUSTRATE, SPITE
thymus—GLAND, MINT,
  SWEETBREAD
tiara—CORONET,
  CROWN, DIADEM,
  FRONTLET,
  GARLAND
tick—ACARID, BOLSTER,
  CREDIT, DOT,
  HEART, MARK,
  MITE, PILLOW,
  RECORD
ticket—ADMISSION,
  CERTIFICATE,
  DUCAT, NOTE,
  PERMIT, SLIP,
  SLATE, TOKEN
tickle—EXCITE, PLEASE,
  TITILLATE
tidal flow—BORE, EAGRE,
  EBB, ESTUARY,
  NEAP, SURGE
tide—BEFALL, CURRENT,
  EBB, NEAP, SEASON,
  SURGE
tidewater—SEACOAST
tiding—ADVICE, NEWS,
  REPORT, SLOGAN,
  WORD
tidy—FLAWLESS,
  IMMACULATE,
  NEAT, PURE, SNOD,
  SPRUCE, TED, TRIM,
  TRIG
tie—BIND, BOND,
  CRAVAT, DRAW,
  EQUAL, FASTEN,
  KNOT, LACE, LINK,
  SCARF, TETHER
tier—BANK, CHESS,
  LAYER, RANK, ROW,
  SERIES, STORY
tighten—FASTEN, LACE,
  STRETCH, TAUTEN
tightwad—FIST, MISER,
  NIGGARD, PIKER,
  SKINFLINT, STINGY
tile—DOMINO,

FIRECLAY, HAT,
PIPE, SLATE

tillable—ARABLE

tilt—ASLANT, DISPUTE,
JOUST, LEAN, HEEL,
LIST, OBLIQUELY,
SLANT, TIP

timber—LUMBER, TREES,
WOOD

time—DURATION,
EPOCH, ERA,
LEISURE,
OCCASION, PERIOD,
SCHEDULE, TEMPO

timeless—AGELESS,
ETERNAL,
EVERLASTING,
PERPETUAL

timely—APT, EARLY,
OPPORTUNE, PAT,
PROMPT

timepiece—
CHRONOSCOPE,
CLOCK,
HOROLOGE,
HOURGLASS,
INDICATOR,
SUNDIAL, WATCH

timorous—AFRAID,
FEARFUL,
SHRINKING,
SHY, TIMID, TREPID

tin—STANNUM

tincture—DASH, IMBUE,
MODICUM, TRACE,
TINT

tinder—AMADOU,
KINDLING, PUNK

tine—BIT, PRONG, SPIKE,
TYNE

tinge—CAST, COLOR,
DYE, HUE, IMBUE,
SHADE, STAIN,
TINT, TRACE

tint—DYE, HUE,
NUANCE, STAIN,
SHADE, TINCTURE,
TINGE, TONE

tiny—ATOMIC, LITTLE,
MINUTE, PETIT,

PETITE, SMALL,
TEENY, WEE

tip—APICAL, CANT,
CAREEN, COCK,
HEEL, HINT, LEAN,
LIST, POINT,
OVERTURN, TILT

tippet—ALMUCE, BOA,
FUR, MUFFLER,
SCARF

tippler—DRINKER,
DRUNKARD,
PIGEON, SOT,
TOPER, TUMBLER,
WINER, WINO

tirade—PHILIPPIC,
SCREED, SPEECH

tire—BORE, FAG, IRK,
JADE, SHOE,
TUCKER

tiresome—BORING,
DREARY, TEDIOUS,
WEARISOME

tissue—BAST, FABRIC,
FAT, FIBER,
TELA, TELAR, TELO

titanic—ENORMOUS,
GIGANTIC,
POWERFUL

title—CAPTION, CLAIM,
HEADING,
MUNIMENT, NAME,
OWNERSHIP, SIR,
TERM

titmouse—BLUECAP,
GOOSANDER,
JACKSAW, MAG,
OXEYE, PARUS, TAT,
TOMTIT, VERDIN

titter—GIGGLE, LAUGH,
SNICKER, TEHEE

to—FOR, FORWARD,
INTO, ONTO,
TOWARD, UNTIL

toad—AGUA, LIZARD,
PIPA

toady—FAWN, PARASITE

toast—BROWN,
PROSIT, SCORCH,
SKOAL, SUN, TAN

tobacco—CAPA,
CAPORAL, CUBAN,
KNASTER, LATAKIA,
ORONOCO,
UPPOWOC, VUELTA

tocsin—ALARM, BELL,
WARNING

toe—DACTYL, DIGIT,
TAE

together—ALONG,
GROUPED,
HARMONY, MASS,
SAMEN, UNION

toil—DRAG, EXERT,
LABOR, NET,
SNARE, STRUGGLE,
WORK

token—AMULET, BADGE,
EARNEST, INDEX,
SCRIP, SIGN, RELIC

toll—DUES, IMPOST,
KNELL, PEAL,
RESOUND, RING,
STRIVE, TAILAGE

tomboy—HOYDEN,
ROMP, TOMRIG

tomb—GRAVE,
MASTABA, VAULT

tone—ACCENT, AIR,
ENERGY, METER,
PITCH, SOUND,
VIGOR

tongue—DIALECT,
LANGUAGE, PATOIS

tonic—BRACER,
INVIGORATING,
REFRESHING

tonsil—AMYGDALA

too—ALSO, AND, ELSE,
LIKEWISE, OVER,
OVERLY

tool—CHASER, CONER,
DUPE, IMPLEMENT,
INSTRUMENT,
MACHINE

tools—DOLLY, KIT,
INSTRUMENTS,
MATTOCKS

tooth—BICUSPID, COG,
CROWN, CUSPID,
FANG, INCISOR,
MOLAR, PREMOLAR,
TUSK

toothache—
ODONTALGIA

toothless—DENTALGIA,
EDENTATE

top—ACE, ACME, APEX,
CAP, COP, EXCEL,
HEAD, LID,
SUMMIT,
SURMOUNT,
SURPASS, VERTEX

toper—BOOZER,
DRINKER, DRUNK,
SOT, TOSSPOT

topic—HEAD, SUBJECT,
TEXT, THEME

topical—LOCAL,
THEMATIC

topnotch—ACE, AONE,
CREST

topsy turvy—ASKEW,
INVERTED

torch—CRESSET, FLAME,
FLAMBEAU, LAMP,
LANTERN,
FLASHLIGHT

torment—BADGER, BAIT,
DEVIL, PLAGUE,
RACK, TEASE,
TORTURE

tormentor—BAITER,
STRIGIL, TEASER

torpedo—DETONATOR,
FISH, MISSILE

torrent—DOWNPOUR,
FLOOD, GLOW,
SPATE, STREAM

torrid—HOT, PARCHING
TROPICAL

tortoise—EMYD
Cent. Amer.—HICATEE
order—CHELONIA
shell—CARAPACE,
SCUTE
So. Amer.—
MATAMATA

torture—FLAY, MARTYR,
PAIN, RACK

toss—CAST, FLIP,
HEAVE, HURL, LOB,
PELT, THROW
total—ENTIRE, UTTER,
WHOLE
touch—ADJOIN,
CONTACT, FEEL,
FINGER, IMPINGE,
MEET, PALM,
SHAVE, TIG,
TWIDDLE
tough—COHESIVE,
LEATHERY, WIRY
tow—DRAW, HALE, PULL
toward—FACING, GAIN,
IMMINENT,
OBLIGING,
PROGRESS, TO,
TRACTABLE
towel—CLEAN, CLOTH,
DRY, MOP, WIPER
tower—BABEL, CITADEL,
BELFRY, MINARET,
PYLON, TOR,
TORRION, TURRET
town—DISTRICT,
MUNICIPALITY,
VILLAGE, URBAN
townsman—CAD, CIT,
RESIDENT,
SELECTMAN
toy—BAUBLE, BALL,
BALLOON, DALLY,
DOLL, GEWGAW,
PLAY, SPORT,
TRINKET
trace—CLEW, DERIVE,
FOLLOW, PRINT,
PATH, RAIL, RUT,
TRAIL
trade—BARTER, CRAFT,
DEAL, EXCHANGE,
SELL, SWAP, SWOP,
TRAFFIC
trademark—BRAND,
LABEL, SYMBOL
trading—BARTERING,
EXCHANGING,
SWAP, VENAL
traduce—ASPERSE,

DEBASE, REVILE,
SLUR
trail—ABATURE,
COURSE, DRAG,
FOIL, FOLLOW,
HUNT, LAG, PATH,
ROUTE, RUN,
SPOOR, TRACK,
WAY
train—BREED, CHAIN,
COACH, CORTEGE,
DRESS. DRILL, EL,
INSTRUCT, LOCAL,
LORRY
tramp—BO, BUM, HIKE,
HOBO, LANDLOPER,
NOMAD, PAD, SLOG,
TREAD, VAGRANT
trance—DAZE, PASSAGE,
SPELL, HYPNOSIS,
STUPOR, SWOON,
TRANSIENT
transaction—ACTUM,
DEAL, SALE,
TRAFFIC
transcript—APOGRAPH,
DOCUMENT,
LETTER,
REPRESENTATION
transfer—CEDE, CONVEY,
DEPUTE, GRANT,
LET, PASS, REMOVE,
TRANSMIT,
TRANSPOSE
transfix—EMPALE,
IMPALE, NAIL, PIN,
STAB
transform—CHANGE,
CONVERT, RENEW,
TRANSMUTE
transparent—CLEAR,
CRYSTAL,
DIAPHANOUS,
PELLUCID, SHEER
transport—CARRY, CART,
CONVEY, FERRY,
RAPT, RAPTURE,
SHIP, TRUCK
trap—AMBUSH,
ENSNARE, GIN,

GRAB, NAIL, NET,
NOOSE, PIT,
PITFALL, SNARE,
WEB

trapper—DECOYER,
LURER, SNARER

trash—DISCARD,
LOPPINGS, REFUSE,
RUBBISH,
RIFFRAFF, TRAMP

travel—JOURNEY, MUSH,
PEREGRINATE,
TOUR, TRAVERSE,
TREK, TRIP, WEND

traveler—ITINERANT,
MOTORIST,
PASSENGER,
TOURIST, VIATOR,
WAYFARER

trawl—DRAGNET, FISH,
NET, TROLL

tray—SALVER, SERVER

treacherous—
FAITHLESS,
UNRELIABLE

treasure—APPRECIATE,
CHERISH, PRIZE,
GEM, HOARD,
STORE, VALUABLES

treasury—BURSE, CHEST,
EXCHEQUER, FISC,
REPOSITORY,
THESAURUS

treat—HANDLE,
MANAGE,
MANIPULATE,
NEGOTIATE,
REGALE, SHOUT,
TEND, USE

treatise—ESSAY, THESIS,
TRACT

treaty—ALLIANCE, MISE,
NEGOTIATION,
PACT, PROTOCOL

trefoil—ARCH, CLOVER,
LOTUS

trellis—ARBOR,
ESPALIER, LATTICE,
PERGOLA

tremble—DODDER, JAR,

QUAKE, QUIVER,
SHAKE, SHIVER,
THRILL

trench—FOSS, GAW,
LEAT, MOAT, SAP

trend—BENT, DRIFT,
INCLINE,
MOVEMENT, TEND,
SWING, TENDENCY,
TENOR

trespass—DEBT,
ENCROACH,
INTRUDE, POACH,
VENTURE

tress—BRAID, CURL,
LOCK, PLAIT,
RINGLET

triad—TERNARY,
TRINARY, TRINE,
TRINITY,
TRIVALENT

trial—ATTEMPT, DOOM,
ESSAY, HARDSHIP,
ORDEAL, TEST

triangle—TRIGON

tribe—CLAN, FAMILY,
GENS, GROUP,
HORDE, RACE, SECT

tribunal—BAR, COURT,
FORA, FORUM, SEAT

tribute—ALMS, ALLOT,
BESTOW,
ENCOMIUM, GIFT,
HOMAGE, OVATION,
PAYMENT, TAX

trick—ANTIC, ARTIFICE,
BAM, DECEIT,
DEFRAUD, DUPE,
FLAM, FRAUD,
GULL, JAPE, PRANK,
RUSE, STUNT

trickster—DEFRAUDER,
FINAGLER

tricky—CRAFTY,
QUIRKY, SNIDE

tried—ETTLED,
FAITHFUL, PROVED,
RENDERED, TESTED

trifle—ACE, BAGATELLE,
DALLY, DOIT, FICO,

FRIVOL, FLIRT,
MONKEY, POTTER
trim—ADORN,
DECORATE, LOP,
NEAT, NIFTY, PERK,
PREEN, PRUNE,
SPRUCE
trimming—EDGING,
RUCHE
trinket—BIBELOT, BIJOU,
GAUD, TAHLI,
TRIFLE
triple—THREEFOLD,
TRIN
triplet—TERCET, TRINE
tripod—EASEL, SPIDER,
THEODOLITE,
TRIVET
trismus—LOCKJAW,
TETANUS
trite—BANAL, BETIDE,
PASSE, STALE,
THREADBARE
triton—EFT, NEWT,
SALAMANDER
triumph—EXULT,
PREVAIL, VICTORY,
WIN
trivial—DOGGEREL,
NICE, NOMINAL,
PETTY, SLIGHT,
SMALL
trombone—SACKBUT,
SAMBUKE
troop—BAND, COMPANY,
PARTY, DIVISION,
TROUPE
troops—ARMY, BATTERY,
COMPANY,
DIVISION,
REGIMENT,
SQUADRON
trophy—AWARD, CUP,
PRIZE, SPOILS
tropic—CIRCLE, SOLAR
tropical—SULTRY,
TORRID, WARM
trouble—ADO, AGITATE,
AIL, BOTHER, IRK,
MOLEST, SORE

trough—CHUTE, DALE,
HOD, MANGER,
SLUICE, STRAKE,
TOM
trout—CHAR, CHARR,
GULL, KELT,
LONGE. SEWEN,
SEWIN
true—ACCURATE, ALINE,
FACE, FACT,
FAITHFUL,
GERMANE, HONEST,
LEAL, LOYAL
truly—AMEN, DULY,
INDEED, RIGHTLY,
VERILY, YEA, YES
trumpet—BUGLE,
CLARION, LURE,
TUBA
  blare—TANTARA
  blast—BLARE
  flourishes—
    FANFARES
trunk—BOLE, BOX,
CHEST, COFFER,
PROBOSCIS, SHORT,
STOCK
trust—BELIEF, CREDIT,
DEPEND, FAITH,
HOPE, LEAN, LIEGE,
MERGER, RELY
truth—FACT, FEALTY,
FIDELITY,
GENUINENESS,
VERACITY, VERITY
try—ATTEMPT,
ENDEAVOR, ESSAY,
ETTLE, PUT,
SAMPLE, SAY,
STRIVE, TEST, TRIAL
tub—CASK, PIGGIN,
TUN, VAT
tube—BOUCH, DUCT,
HOSE, PIPE,
PIPETTE, REED,
TELESCOPE
tuber—EDDO, JALAP,
OCA, POTATO,
TARO, YAM
tuck—FOLD, PRESS,

PLEAT, RAPIER,
WRAP
tufa—LIMESTONE
tuft—BUNCH, CLUMP,
CLUSTER, CREST,
GOATEE, TASSEL,
TUSSOCK
tufted—COMOSE,
CRESTED
tule—BULRUSH, SCIRPUS
tumor—ADENOMA,
BOTCH, GLIOMA,
OMA, WEN
tumult—BEDLAM, DIN,
HUBBUB, FRAY,
RIOT, TEMPEST,
UPROAR
tune—ADAPT, AIR, ARIA,
LILT, MELODY,
SONANCE, SOUND,
TONE
tunic—ACTON, BLOUSE,
CHITON, STOLA,
TOGA
tunnel—BURROW,
FUNNEL,
SUBPASSAGEWAY
turban—MUDIL, PATTA
turbid—DISTURB,
FECULENT,
MUDDY, ROILED,
ROILY, TUMULT,
TURGID
turbulent—VIOLENT,
WILD
tureen—LADLE, VESSEL
turf—DIVOT, GRASS,
PEAT, SOD,
SWARD,
turgid—INFLATED,
POMPOUS,
SWOLLEN
turn—BEND, GYRATE,
PIVOT, REVOLVE,
ROTATE, TWIST,
VERT
turnip—NAPE, NEEP,
RUTABAGA
turret—BUTTE, CUPOLA,
TOREL, TOWER

turtle—ARRAU, CARET,
COOTER, EMYD,
EMYS, JURARA,
SNAPPER,
TERRAPIN,
TORTOISE
delicacy—CALIPEE
freshwater—EMYD
giant—ARRAU
pert. to—CHELONIAN
shell—CARAPACE
tusk—FANG, IVORY,
RAZOR, TOOTH
tutor—DOCENT,
GOVERNOR,
INSTRUCTOR,
MENTOR, TEACHER
twaddle—DRIVEL,
FLAPDOODLE,
FUSTIAN, GABBLE,
PRATTLE
twenty—CORGE, SCORE
twice—BIS, DOUBLY, DIS
twig—CION, ROD, SPRIG,
SWITCH, WITHE
twilight—
CREPUSCULAR,
CREPUSCLE, DUSK,
EVE, GLOAM,
GLOAMING
twin—COUPLE, DOUBLE,
DUPLICATE,
GEMEL, MATCH,
SIAMESE, TWO,
YOKE
twine—CORD, LINE,
STRING, WREATHE
twist—BEND, COIL,
CONTORT, QUIRK,
SKEW, SLUE,
SNAKE, TIRL, TURN,
WARP, WRING
twisted—CUED, SLEWED,
SLUED, TIRLED,
WRY
twit—BANTER, BLAME,
DEFECT, JOSH,
RIDICULE, TAUNT,
UPBRAID
twitching—TIC, TWINGE

twitter—CHITTER,
GIGGLE, TITTER
two—BOTH, BRACE,
COUPLE, DUET,
DUO, PAIR,
TWINS, YOKE
twofold—BINAL, BINARY,
DIDYMOUS,
DOUBLE, DUPLE,
DUAL, TWIN
tycoon—BARON,
MASTER, MAGNATE,
MOGUL, PEER,
SHOGUN
type—EMBLEM, GENRE,
ITALIC, KIND,
MODEL, NORM,
SORT, TOKEN,
VARIETY
tyrant—DESPOT,
MONARCH, RULER,
TSAR

-U-

unclean—FILTHY, FOUL,
IMPURE, OBSCENE,
UNCHASTE, VILE
uncommon—
INFREQUENT,
NICE, RARE
SPECIAL, UNUSUAL
unconscious—OUT,
UNAWARE
unconsciousness—
NARCOSIS
uncouth—AWKWARD,
BORING, BOORISH,
HARSH, RUDE,
RUGGED,
UNREFINED
uncover—BARE,
DISCLOSE, EXPOSE,
REMOVE, REVEAL
unction—OINTMENT,
SALVE, SOOTHING,
UNGUENT
unctuous—FATTY,
GREASY, OILY,
SALVY
under—BELOW,
BENEATH,
INFERIOR, LOWER,
NEATH, SHORT, SUB
underdone—PARTIAL,
RARE, REAR
underhand—COVERT,
DERN,
FRAUDULENT,
SECRET, SLY

undermine—EXCAVATE,
SAP, WEAKEN
understanding—BRAIN,
DIG, DISCERNMENT,
ENTENTE,
KNOWING
understood—ASSUMED,
IMPLIED, SAVVY,
TACIT
undertake—ENGAGE,
ENTER, EXECUTE,
GUARANTEE,
PROMISE, TRY
undertaker—CERER,
ENTREPRENEUR,
MORTICIAN
undertaking—ACT,
ENGAGING, MOOD
underwear—BVD,
LINGERIE, SLIP,
UNDERCLOTHES,
UNDERSHIRT
underworld—EREBUS,
HADES, SHEOL,
TARTARUS
underwrite—FINANCE,
INSURE
undeveloped—EMBRYO,
RUDIMENTARY
undo—ANNUL, COOK,
DESTROY, LOOSEN,
NEGLECT, OFFSET,
RELEASE, RUIN
undraped—BARE, NUDE,
STRIPPED,

UNVEILED

undulating—ARIPPLE,
BILLOWY, SURGING,
SWELLING, WAVY

undulation—CRIMP,
HEAVE, SURGE,
VIBRATION, WAVE

undyed—CORAH, ECRU,
PLAIN, RAW

unemployed—IDLE, LAZY,
OTIOSE

unexpected—ABRUPT,
SUDDEN

unfit—AWKWARD,
DISABLE,
DISQUALIFY,
FOOLISH. INEPT

unfledged—CALLOW,
IMMATURE

unfold—DEPLOY,
DEVELOP,
DISCLOSE, DISPLAY,
EVOLVE, OPEN,
REVEAL, SPREAD,
UNFURL, UNWRAP

unfriendly—OPPOSED,
HOSTILE,
INIMICAL,
UNPROPITIOUS

ungrateful—
DISAGREEABLE,
THANKLESS,
UNPLEASING

unhappiness—GRIEF,
PAIN, SADNESS,
SORROW, WOE

uniform—CONSISTENT,
EQUAL, EVEN,
LEVEL, SIMILAR,
STEADY,
UNCHANGING

union—ALLIANCE,
COALITION,
FUSION, JUNCTION,
LEAGUE, LIAISON,
MARRIAGE,
MERGER

unique—ALONE, ODD,
SINGLE, SOLE,
STRANGE, RARE

unison—AGREEMENT,
ACCORD, CONCORD,
HARMONY,
TUNED

unit—ACE, MONAD, ONE,
SYLLABLE

unite—ALLY, CEMENT,
COALESCE,
COMBINE, CONJOIN,
CONNECT, FAY,
FUSE, JOIN, LINK,
MERGE, WED, YOKE

united—COMBINED,
CONNECTED,
JOINED, MERGED,
TIED, WEDDED,
WELDED

unity—AGREEMENT,
INTEGRITY, ONE,
ONENESS,
SOLIDARITY

unjust—DISHONEST,
FAITHLESS,
PARTIAL, UNFAIR,
WRONGFUL

unkempt—ROUGH,
SEEDY, SHAGGY,
UNTIDY

unkind—BRUTAL,
CRUEL, HARSH,
INHUMAN,
MERCILESS,
SAVAGE

unlawful—
CONTRABAND,
ILLEGAL,
ILLEGITIMATE,
ILLICIT, ILLOGICAL,
IMPROPER

unless—EXCEPT, NISI,
OTHERWISE

unlike—DISSIMILAR,
DIVERSE,
MULTIFORM,
SEPARATE

unmarried—CELIBATE,
SINGLE, SOLE

unmoved—DEAD, INERT,
POWERLESS,
SERENE

unproductive—BARREN,
DRY, STERILE
unreal—ARTIFICIAL,
CHAOTIC,
FANCIFUL,
ILLUSIVE,
VISIONARY
unrefined—CRASS,
CRUDE, GROSS,
RAW, WILD
unruffled—CALM, COOL,
SERENE, STILL
unruly—DISORDERLY,
LAWLESS, RESTIVE,
TURBULENT
unspoken—INEFFABLE,
TACIT
unstable—ERRATIC,
INCONSTANT,
IRREGULAR,
UNSTEADY,
VACILLATING
untidy—CARELESS,
MESSY, MUSSY,
SLOVENLY
unusual—EXOTIC,
NOVEL, ODD,
RARE,
UNCOMMON
unwilling—AVERSE,
ESCHEW, LOATH,
NILL, RELUCTANT
unwritten—BLANK, ORAL,
PAROL,
TRADITIONAL
unyielding—ADAMANT,
GRIM, HARD,
OBDURATE, RIGID,
SET, STERN, STIFF
up—ABOVE, ALOFT,
ATOP, HIGHER,
UPON
upbraid—BERATE,
CHARGE,
REPROACH,
REPROVE, SCOLD
upright—
CONSCIENTIOUS,
ERECT, HONEST,
CORRECT, JUST,

VERTICAL
uproar—DIN, HUBBUB,
NOISE, RIOT,
TUMULT
upset—COUP,
DISCOMPOSE, KEEL,
OVERTHROW,
TOPPLE
upshot—CONCLUSION,
FINAL, RESULT,
SEQUEL
upstart—PARVENUE,
SNOB, SNUB
urbane—BLAND, POLITE,
SUAVE
urchin—ARAB, ELFIN,
GAMIN, IMP,
HEDGEHOG, TAD
urge—ABET, ACTUATE,
DRIVE, DUN, EGG,
GOAD, INCITE, PLY,
PROD, SPUR
urn—KIST, PIG, STEIN
usage—CUSTOM, HABIT,
MANNERS,
TREATMENT, WONT
use—AVAIL, CONSUME,
CUSTOM, EMPLOY,
EXHAUST, OCCUPY,
PRACTICE, TREAT
used—CONSUMED,
EATEN,
EXHAUSTED,
OCCUPIED,
SECONDHAND
useful—BENEFICIAL,
HELPFUL, UTILE
useless—FRUITLESS,
FUTILE, IDLE,
INUTILE, NULL,
OTIOSE, VAIN
usher—DOORKEEPER,
ESCORT, FOREARM,
FORERUN,
INTRODUCE, SHOW,
SEATS
usual—AVERAGE,
COMMON,
CUSTOMARY,
HABITUAL,

WONTED
utmost—BEST, EXTREME,
GREATEST,
HIGHEST, LAST,
MAXIMUM
utopian—IDEALISTIC,

VISIONARY
utter—ABSOLUTE, AVER,
BRAY, DRAWL,
EMIT, INTONATE,
MOOT, SAY, STARK,
STATE, VOICE

-V-

vacancy—BLANK, EMPTY,
GAP, OPENING,
VACUUM, VOID
vacant—EMPTY, FREE,
IDLE, HOLLOW,
UNOCCUPIED, VOID
vacation—HOLIDAY,
INTERMISSION,
RECESS, RESPITE,
SPELL
vagabond—BUM, HOBO,
RODNEY, TRAMP,
TRUANT, VAGRANT,
WASTREL
vague—DIM, HAZY,
LOOSE, OBSCURE,
SKETCHY
vain—EMPTY, FUTILE,
IDLE, HOWWOW,
NUGATORY,
OTIOSE, PETTY,
USELESS, VOID
vale—DALE, DELL,
DINGLE, GLEN
valentine—GIFT,
GREETING, LOVE,
SWEETHEART, TOKEN
valet—ATTENDANT,
CRISPIN,
MANSERVANT,
SQUIRE
valiant—BRAVE,
COURAGEOUS,
HEROIC, ROBUST,
VALOROUS
valid—COGENT, LEGAL
SOUND, TELLING
valley—CANYON, COMB,
COOMB, DALE,
DELL, DINGLE,
GLADE, GLEN,

SWALE, VALE
value—ADMIRE,
APPRAISE, CARAT,
ESTEEM, PAR,
PRICE, PRIZE, RATE,
STERLING,
TREASURE, WORTH
vamoose—DECAMP, GO,
LAM, SCAT. SCRAM
vampire—BAT, FLIRT,
LAMIA.
BLOODSUCKER
vandal—HUN
vane—BANNER, FAN,
FLAG, PHANEKILL,
WEATHERCOCK
vanish—DISAPPEAR,
EVANESCE, FADE,
FLEE, FLY, PASS,
RECEDE
vanity—CONCEIT,
EGOISM, SHAM
vapid—DULL, FLAT,
INANE, INSIPID,
POINTLESS,
SPIRITLESS, STALE,
TRITE
vapor—AIR, FOG, GAS.
MIST, RACK, REEK,
STEAM
variable—MOBILE,
MUTABLE, PROTEAN
variegated—DAPPLED,
MOTLEY, PAINTED,
PIED, PINTO,
STRIPED, TISSUED
variety—CLASS,
DIVERSITY, FIRM,
GENUS, SORT,
SPECIE, TYPE
various—DIFFERENT,

DIVERSE,
MANIFOLD, MANY,
SEVERAL, SUNDRY
varnish—ADORN, JAPAN
LAC, SHELLAC
vas—DUCT, VESSEL
vase—DIOTA, JAR, URN
vassal—BONDMAN,
LIEGE, SERF,
SLAVE, SUBJECT
vast—GREAT, HUGE,
IMMENSE, UNTOLD
vat—BAC, CISTERN,
GYLE, KEEVE,
TANK, TUB
vault—CRYPT, FORNIX,
LEAP, SPRING,
TOMB
vaulted—ARCHED,
CONCAVE, DOMED,
ROUNDED
vector—FORCE, ROTOR,
VELOCITY
vegetable—HERB, PLANT,
ROOT, SEED, TARO,
UDO
vehicle—BUS, CAB,
CALECHE, CAR,
DRAY, GOCART,
LANDAU, LORRY,
SLEDGE, TAXI
veil—NET, CONCEAL,
CURTAIN,
DISGUISE, HIDE,
MASK, PRETENSE
vein—NERVURE, RENAL,
RIB, STREAK,
TENOR, VENA,
VENULE
velocity—CELERITY,
HASTE, SPEED,
SWIFT
velvet—PANNE,
VELVETEEN,
VELURE
vendor—ALIENOR,
PEDDLER, SELLER,
VENDOR
venerable—AGED,
AUGUST, HOAR,

OLD, OLDEN,
PROTEAN
venerate—ADORE,
HONOR, LOVE,
RESPECT, REVERE,
REVERENCE,
WORSHIP
veneration—AWE,
RESPECT, WORSHIP
venom—GALL, MALICE,
POISON, SPITE,
VIRUS
vent—AIRHOLD,
APERTURE,
EXPRESS, OPENING,
OUTLET, SAY
ventriloquism—
HARIOLATE
venture—BRAVE, BOLD,
DARE, ENTERPRISE,
PRESUME, RISK,
WAGE
veranda—LANAI, PYAL,
STOA, STOOP
verge—APPROACH,
BRINK, EDGE,
MARGIN, TIP
verily—AMEN, AVER,
INDEED, TRULY,
YEA
verse—CANTO,
CONSIDER, FIT,
POEM, POETRY,
RIME, STANZA
version—EDITION,
TRANSLATION
vertebra—APOPHYSIS,
SPONDYL
vertical—PLUMB,
UPRIGHT
verve—ARDOR, ELAN,
PEP, SPIRIT
very—ACTUAL,
GENUINE,
IDENTICAL,
LAWFUL, MUCH,
REAL, SAME, TOO,
TRUE, WELL
vessel—BASIN, BARQUE,
BOAT, CRAFT,

DIOTA, DUBBER,
KETCH, LINER, PAN,
POT, PINNACE,
OILER. SHIP, SLOOP,
STEAMER, TANKER,
TUG, TUB, URN,
VAT

vest—ARRAY, DRESS,
GARB, ROBE,
WESKIT

vestal—CHASTE, NUN,
VIRGINAL

vestibule—ENTRY,
FOYER, HALL,
LOBBY, NARTHEX

vestige—IOTA, MARK,
RELIC, SIGN,
SHRED, TINCTURE,
TRACE. TRACK

vestment—ALB, AMICE,
COPE, DRESS,
EPHOD, GARB,
STOLE, SURPLICE

vestry—CHAPEL,
SACRISTY,
WARDROBE

vetch—AKRA, ERS,
FITCH, TARE

vex—AGITATE, ANNOY,
CARK, FRET, GALL,
HARASS, IRK,
IRRITATE, NETTLE,
PEEVE, RILE, ROIL

vexation—CHAFE,
CHAGRIN,
IRRITATION, PEST,
PIQUE

vexed—IRKED,
PESTED, SPITED

viaduct—BRIDGE, SPAN,
TRESTLE

vial—AMPULE, BOTTLE,
CRUET, PHIAL

viand—CATE, EATS,
FARE, FOOD,
EDIBLES,
PROVISIONS

vibrate—DINDLE, JAR,
QUAVER,
RESONATE, THROB,

TIRL, TREMOR

vicar—DEPUTY, PASTOR,
PRIEST

vice—EVIL, FAULT,
INIQUITY, SIN

vicious—CORRUPT,
CRUEL,
DEGENERATE,
FAULTY, IMPURE,
INFAMOUS, MEAN,
WICKED

victim—CULLY, DUPE,
GULL, PREY

victor—CONQUEROR,
MASTER, WINNER

victory—CONQUEST,
NIKE, PALM,
SUCCESS, TRIUMPH

victual—EAT, FEED,
FOOD, KAI, MEAT,
NOURISHMENT,
NUTRIMENT,
PROTEINS

vie—CHALLENGE,
COMPETE,
CONTEND, FAY,
LIFE

view—EYE, GLIMPSE,
KEN, INSPECT,
OPINION,
PERCEPTION,
SEE. SCOPE,
VISTA

vigilant—ALERT, AWAKE,
AWARE,
CIRCUMSPECT,
WARY, WATCHFUL

vigor—ENERGY, ELAN,
FORCE, LIFE, PEP,
STAMINA,
STRENGTH,
VALIDITY, VIM

vigorous—ANIMATED,
COGENT,
ENERGETIC,
FETTLE, HALE,
LUSTY, ROBUST,
STURDY

vile—ABJECT, BASE,
LOW, MEAN,

ODIOUS, SINFUL,
SORDID, VULGAR
vilify—ASPERSE,
DEBASE, DEGRADE,
DEFAME, MALIGN,
REVILE, TRADUCE
village—COMMUNITY,
DORP, HAMLET,
THORPE, TOWN
villain—BOOR, GIANT,
KNAVE,
SCOUNDREL
villein—CARL, CEORL,
CHURL, ESNE, SERF,
SERI
vim—ENERGY, ELAN,
FORCE, GIMP, PEP,
SPIRIT, VIGOR, ZIP
vindicate—ASSERT,
AVENGE, DEFEND,
DELIVER,
EXCULPATE,
JUSTIFY, PUNISH
vine—BINE, CREEPER,
GRAPEVINE, HOP,
IVY, LIANA, PEA,
WISTERIA
vinegar—ACETA,
AECTATE, ACETUM,
EISEL
vineyard—CRU,
PLANTATION
viol—CONTRABASS,
ROPE, RUANA,
SARINDA, VIOLA,
VIOLIN,
VIOLONCELLO
violent—EXTREME,
INTENSE, RABID
violet—MAUVE, VIOLA,
WISTERIA
blue—INDIGO
dye—ARCHIL
ketone—IRONE
violin—FIDDLE, STRAD,
VIOL
virago—AMAZON, FURY,
TERMAGANT,
VIXEN
virgin—GIRL, MAID,

PURE, VESTAL
virile—CAPABLE,
FORCEFUL, MALE,
MASCULINE,
MASTERFUL,
MANHOOD
virulent—BITTER,
POISON, RABID
virus—POISON, VENOM
viscid—ADHERING,
GLUTINOUS, LIMY,
STICKY, VISCOUS
visible—EXPOSED,
MANIFEST,
OBVIOUS, OPEN,
PATENT, SEE
vision—DREAM, EYE,
MIRAGE, REVERIE,
SIGHT
visionary—AERY,
DREAMER, FEY,
IDEAL, UTOPIAN
visit—BLESS, CALL,
INSPECT, HAUNT,
INFLICT, SEE, STAY
vital—INHERENT,
MORTAL, ORGANIC,
SOULED
vitreous—BRITTLE,
GLASS, LUSTER
vixen—SHREW, SHEFOX,
VIRAGO
vocal—ORAL
vocation—CALLING,
CAREER, METIER,
PROFESSION,
TRADE
voice—ALTO, BASS, EMIT,
SAY, SOPRANO,
TENOR
voiceless—ANAUDIA,
SPIRATE, SURD
void—ABOLISH, ANNUL,
EGEST, EMPTY,
NUL, NULL, SPACE
volume—BULK, CUBAGE,
CUBATURE, MO,
TOME
volution—SPIRAL, TURN,
WHORL

voracious—EDACIOUS,
GLUTTONOUS,
GREEDY,
IMMODERATE,
RAVENOUS
vortex—EDDY, GYRE,
VACUUM,
WHIRLPOOL
vote—BALLOT, ELECT,
LOGROLL, POLL,
STRAW
vouchsafe—BESTOW,
CONCEDE, DEIGN,
GUARANTEE,
GRANT, YIELD
vow—ASSEVERATION,
OATH, PLEDGE,
PROMISE, SWEAR,
TROW, VOTARY
voyage—CRUISE,
JOURNEY, TOUR,
TRIP, TRAVEL
vulgar—COARSE,
COMMON, DOWDY,
LEWD, LOW,
OFFENSIVE,
PROFANE, RIBALD,
VILE
vulture—AURA, CONDOR,
EAGLE, FALCON,
HAWK, URUBU

-W-

wabble—TITTER,
VACILLATE,
WAVER, WOBBLE
wad—BAT, CRAM, HEAD,
LUMP, MASS, PAD,
PLUMBAGO, STUFF
wade—FORD, GO, PASS,
PLODGE
wader—CRANE, HERON,
SANDPIPER, SNIPE
wadi—CHANNEL,
STREAM
wading bird—AVOCET,
CRANE, EGRET,
FLAMINGO, HERON,
GREBE, IBIS, SNIPE,
STILT, STORK
wag—FARCEUR, JOKER,
OSCILLATE, ROGUE,
SWAY, SWING,
WIT,
wage—ENGAGE,
EMPLOY FEE, HIRE,
PAY, STIPEND
wager—ANTE, BET,
GAMBLE, PARLAY,
PLEDGE, RISK,
STAKE, VENTURE,
WIT
wagon—CAISSON, CAR,
CART, CHARIOT,
COACH, DRAY,
LORRY, TONGA,
TRAM, TRUCK, VAN,
WAIN
waif—GAMIN, LOST,
STRAY
wail—BEMOAN, HOWL,
LAMENT, MOAN,
SOB, ULULATE
wainscot—CEILING,
PANEL, WALL
waist—BASQUE, BODICE,
GARIBALDI
waistcoat—DOUBLET,
GILET, VEST,
VESTEE
walk—AMBULATE,
DADDLE, GAD,
HIKE, MUSH, PACE,
PLOD, STEP, STRIDE,
TRAMP
wall—DEFENSE, LEVEE,
FORTIFY, PANEL,
RAMPART,
SEPARATE
wan—ASHEN, ASHY,
COLORLESS, FADE,
LANGUID, PALE,
PALLID, SICKLY

wand—BATON,
CADUCEUS, OSIER,
ROD, SCEPTER,
STAFF, VERGE

wander—DIGRESS,
DIVAGATE, ERR,
GAD, MEANDER,
RAMBLE, ROAM,
ROVE, STRAY,
STROLL

wanderer—ARAB, GYPSY,
NOMAD, ROVER,
TRUANT, VAG,
VAGRANT,
VAGABOND

wandering—ASTRAY,
ERRANT, ERRING,
NOMADIC,
ODYSSEY,
VAGRANT

wane—DECREASE, EBB,
FADE, FAINT, FALL,
SHRINK

wangle—FINAGLE,
SHAKE, WAG,
WIGGLE

want—ABSENCE,
DEFICIENCY,
DESIRE, LACK,
NEED, PENURY,
POVERTY, WISH

wanted—LACK, NEED,
WISH

wanton—FREE,
RAMPANT, RANK,
WILD

war—BATTLE,
CONFLICT,
HOSTILITY, STRIFE,
STRUGGLE

warble—CAROL, SING,
TRILL, YODEL

warden—GATEKEEPER,
GUARDIAN,
GOVERNOR,
KEEPER

wardrobe—ALMIRAH,
AMBRY, CABINET,
CLOSET, CLOTHING

warehouse—DEPOT,
ETAPE

warfare—CRUSADE,
CONFLICT,
DISCORD, ENMITY,
HOSTILITY,
POLEMY, STRIFE

warm—GENIAL, HOT,
HUMID, MUGGY,
PASSIONATE, TEPID,
THERMAL

warn—ADVISE,
CAUTION, FLAG,
FOREWARN, HEED,
INFORM, SIGNAL

warning—ALERT,
CAVEAT, NOTICE,
OMEN, SIGNAL,
SIREN

warp—BIAS, DISTORT,
DEFORM, SWAY,
TWIST

warrant—ABLE, DEFEND,
ENSURE,
GUARANTEE,
PLEVIN, PRECEPT,
SECURE, SECURITY

warrior—BATTLER,
COHORT, FIGHTER,
SOLDIER

wary—ALERT, CANNY,
CAREFUL,
GUARDED, FOXY,
SHY, WATCHFUL,
WISE

wash—CLEANSE,
DRENCH, FLUSH,
LAVE, POUR,
PURIFY, RENCH,
RINSE, TYE

washing—BATH,
CLEANSING,
LAVAGE, RINSING,
SLUICE

wasp—HORNET, JIGA,
WHAMP

waste—BANGLE, CHAFF,
DROSS, EMACIATE,
EXHAUST, FRITTER,
LOSE, RAVAGE,
SPILL

wasteful—LAVISH,
PRODIGAL
wastrel—ARAB, LOSER,
PROFLIGATE,
SPENDTHRIFT,
VAGABOND, WAIF
watch—EYE, GUARD,
PATROL, TEND,
VIGIL
watchful—ALERT,
VIGILANT, WARY
water—AQUA, EAU,
DILUTE, IRRIGATE,
RAIN, SEA,
SPRINKLE, WASH
waterfall—CASCADE,
CATARACT, LIN,
LINN
waterless—ANHYDROUS
watery—AQUEOUS,
SEROUS, SOGGY
TEARFUL, THIN,
VAPID, WET
wattle—BIND, DEWLAP,
FENCE, LAPPET
wave—BLESS, BREAKER,
COMBER, CRIMP,
FLUTTER, FLY,
FLAP, RIPPLE,
ROLLER, SEA
wavelet—RIPPLE
waver—FALTER
FLICKER, HESITATE,
LISP, STAGGER,
SWAY, TEETER,
TOTTER, VEER
wavy—ONDY, UNDATE,
UNDE
wax—CERATE, CERE,
CERIN, GROW,
INCREASE, PELA
waxy—CERAL, FICTILE
way—COURSE, LANE,
MANNER, METHOD,
MODE, PASSAGE,
PATH, ROAD,
ROUTE, VIA, WONT
weak—DEBILE, FADE,
FAINT, FRAIL,
PECCABLE, PUNY,

SIMPLE, SLIGHT,
THIN
weaken—ATTENUATE,
CRAZE, DILUTE,
ENERVATE, PETER,
SAP, UNNERVE,
VITIATE
weakness—ASTHENIA,
FAULT, FOIBLE,
SOFT
weal—STATE, STRIPE,
SUCCESS, WALE,
WELFARE, WELT
wealth—AFFLUENCE,
FORTUNE, RICHES
weapon—ARM, BOMB,
CLUB, DAGGER,
FIREARM, GAT,
GUN, MUSKET,
PISTOL, RIFLE,
SPEAR, SWORD,
TORPEDO
wear—CARRY, CHAFE,
DISPLAY, EXHIBIT,
FRAY. FRET,
IMPAIR. SHOW, USE
wearied—BORED,
EXHAUSTED,
FAGGED,
FATIGUED, IRKED,
JADED, SAPPED
weasel—ERMINE,
FERRET, MUSTELLE,
OTTER, SABLE,
STOAT. VARE
weave—ENTWINE,
INTERLACE, MAT,
PLAIT, REEL, SPIN
web—CAUL, FABRIC,
NETWORK, SNARE,
TELA, TEXTURE,
TISSUE, TRAP, WEFT
wed—ESPOUSE, MARRY,
MATED
wedge—CAM, CLEAT,
COTTER, COIGN,
GIB, KEY, QUOIN,
SHIM
weed—DANDELION,
DOCK, DARNEL,

KNAWEL,
PLANTAIN, TARE
weekly—AWEEK,
HEBDOMADAL
weep—BLUBBER, CRY,
LAMENT, LERM,
ORP, SOB
weevil—BILLBUG, BOUD,
CURCULIO. KIS
weighing—BALANCING,
CONSIDERING,
MEASURING,
TARING
weir—BARRIER,
DAM, GARTH,
NET, SEINE
weird—EERIE. EERY,
ELDRITCH
well—BIEN, FIT, GAY,
HALE, HARDY,
HEALTHY, SPRING,
TRIG
wen—MOLE, TALPA
western—HESPERIAN
wet—ASOP, DAMP,
DANK, MOIST,
RAINY, SOAK,
SOPPING, WATERY
wether—CALF, SHEEP
whale—BELUGA, CET,
CETE. CETACEAN,
ORC, SPERM
  Arctic—NARWHAL,
  ORC
  female—COW
  killer—GRAMPUS,
  ORC
  school—GAM, POD
  skin—FLENSE, SCULP
  sperm—CACHALOT
wharf—DOCK, JETTY,
KEY, PIER, QUAI,
QUAY
wheat—DURRA, DURUM,
EMMER, SPELT
wheedle—BAM,
BLANDISH, CAJOLE,
COAX, ENTICE,
FLATTER, GAIN
wheel—CASTER, HELM,

ROTA
wheeze—GAG, HISS,
JOKE, TRITE
whelk—GASTROPOD,
PIMPLE, PUSTULE,
SNAIL
whelp—CUB, CHILD,
PUPPY, YOUTH
when—ALTHOUGH,
CONDITIONAL,
AS, WHEREAS,
WHILE, THOUGH
where—AS, PLACE
SITUATION, SPOT,
STAGE, WHITHER
whet—GRIND, HONE,
KEEN, SHARPEN,
STIMULATE
while—AS, DURING,
FILLING, UNTIL
whim—CAPRICE, DRUM,
FAD, FANCY,
FREAK, HUMOR,
MAGGOT, NOTION,
TOY
whimper—CRY, MEWL,
PULE, SNIFF
whine—GROWL, PULE,
SNIVEL, YAUP
whip—BEAT, CANE, CAT,
DEFEAT, FLAY,
FLOG, FROTH,
LASH, OVERLAY,
SCOURGE, WALE
whirl—EDDY, GYRATE,
PIRL, REEL,
REVOLVE, SPIN,
SWIRL, TWIRL
whirling—PIROUETTE,
SPINNING,
TWIRLING
whirlpool—EDDY,
GURGE, SWIRL,
VORTEX
whiskey—MOONSHINE,
POTEEN, SPIRITS
whit—ATOM, BIT. DOIT,
IOTA, JOT, MITE,
PARTICLE, SPECK
white—ALABASTER,

ASHY, HOAR, PALE,
SNOWY
whiten—BLANCH,
BLEACH, ETIOLATE
whitish—ALBESCENT,
CHALKY,
MOONSTONE
whittle—CUT, DESTROY,
PARE, REMOVE,
TRIM
whiz—HUM, PIRR, WHIR,
WHIRR, ZIZZ
whole—AGGREGATE,
ALL, COMPLETE,
ENTIRE, GROSS,
PURE, SUM, TOTAL,
UNCUT
wholly—ALL,
COMPLETELY,
EXCLUSIVELY,
FULLY, QUITE,
SOLELY, TOTALLY
wide—BROAD,
DISTENDED,
EXTENSIVE,
ROOMY, RANGY,
SPACY
widen—BROADEN, FLUE,
SCATTER, SPREAD
wife—BRIDE, FRAU,
MATE, RIB, SPOUSE
wig—HAIRPIECE, JASEY,
PERIWIG, PERUKE,
TETE, TOUPEE, TUFT
wigwam—TEEPEE,
TEPEE, TIPI
wild—FERAL, FIERCE,
FERINE,
FEROCIOUS,
SAVAGE, STORMY
wilderness—DESERT,
FOREST,
MOUNTAINS,
PLAINS, WASTE,
WILDS
wile—ART, DECEIT,
RUSE, SORCERY,
TOY, TRICK,
TRICKERY
will—BEHEST, CHOICE,

DECREE, DESIRE,
INCLINATION,
SETTLEMENT, WISH
willing—BAIN, DESIROUS,
FAIN, MINDED,
PRONE, READY,
VOLUNTARY
willow—ITEA, OSIER,
SALIX, TEASER,
WOLF
wilt—DROOP, FLACCID,
FLAG, LANGUISH,
LOWER
wily—ARTFUL, ASTUTE,
CRAFTY, FOXY, SLY
win—ACQUIRE, EARN,
GAIN, GET, OBTAIN,
PREVAIL, TRIUMPH
wind—AIR, BREATH,
CHINOOK, COIL,
GALE, MONSOON,
SIMOOM, SORNADO,
SIROCCO
windlass—CRAB,
CAPSTAN, REEL,
WINCH
wine—ASTI, BARBERA,
BORDEAUX,
BURGUNDY,
CABERNET,
CATAWBA,
CHABLIS,
CHAMPAGNE,
CHIANTI,
CLARET, GRAVE,
HOCK, MADEIRA,
MALAGA, MEDOC,
MOSELLE,
MUSCATEL, NEGUS,
PORT, RHINE,
RIESLING, SACK,
SAUTERNE,
SHERRY, TINTA,
TOKAY, TORAN,
VIN, VINO
wing—ALA, ALULA,
PENNA, PINNA,
PINION
winged—ALATED, FLEW,
PENNATE

wingless—APTERAL,
DEALATE, EXALATE
wink—BAT, BLINK,
NICTATE,
NICTITATE,
TWINKLE
winner—ACE, EARNER,
CHAMPION,
CONQUEROR,
VICTOR
winnow—FAN, BLOW,
DISPERSE, SIFT,
STIR, WIM
winsome—BONNY,
CHEERFUL, GAY,
MERRY, PLEASANT,
WINNING
wipe—CLEAN, EFFACE,
GIBE, MOP, SWAB,
TAUNT
wire—TELEGRAM,
TELEGRAPH
wireless—PHONE, RADIO,
TELEGRAPH
wise—ERUDITE,
INFORMED,
JUDICIOUS,
PRUDENT, SAGE,
SANE, SAPIENT
wish—ASPIRE, DESIRE,
INVOKE, LONG,
REQUEST, VOTE
wisp—BUNCH, BUNDLE,
FRAGMENT,
RUMPLE, TAIT
wit—BANTER,
CLEVERNESS,
HUMOR, SATIRE,
SENSE, WAG,
WAGGERY
witch—CRONE, HAG,
HEX, LAMIA, SIREN
witchcraft—BROOM,
MAGIC, SORCERY
withdraw—AVOID,
DETRACT,
DISAVOW, QUIT,
RETIRE, RETRACT,
RETREAT
wither—DECAY, DROOP,

DRY, FADE, SERE,
SHRINK, SHRIVEL,
WILT
within—INNER, INTO, ON
without—EXTERNALLY,
LACKING
withstand—BIDE, LAST,
OPPOSE, RESIST
witness—ATTEST,
COGNIZANCE,
OBSERVE, TESTE,
TESTIFY
witticism—JEST, MOT,
SALLY
witty—DROLL, FACETE,
FACETIOUS,
HUMOROUS,
JOCOSE, SHARP
wizard—ENCHANTER,
FIEND, SHAMAN,
SORCERER
wolf—COYOTE, LOBO
wolverine—CARCAJOU
wonder—AWE, MARVEL,
MUSE, PRODIGY,
RARITY
wonderful—
ASTONISHING,
MARVELOUS,
UNIQUE
wont—DESIRE, HABIT,
HAUNT, CUSTOM,
USAGE, USE
woo—COURT, ENTREAT,
SOLICIT, SPARK,
SUE
woods—FOREST, GROVE,
MOTTE, SYLVA
woodwind—BASSOON,
OBOE
woody—BOSKY,
LIGNEOUS, SYLVAN,
XYLOID
wooly—FLEECY,
FLOCCULENT,
LANATE, LANOSE
word—ADAGE,
COMMAND,
INFORMATION,
MESSAGE, PARLE,

TALK, TERM,
TIDINGS
wordiness—PLEONASM,
PROLIXITY,
VERBIAGE
work—ACT, CHARE,
COACT, DRUDGERY,
EFFORT, ERGON,
JOB, LABOR, MOIL,
OPERATE, OPUS,
PEG, PLY, SLAVE,
TOIL, TRAVAIL
workshop—ATELIER,
LAB, PLANT,
STUDIO
world—COSMOS, EARTH,
GLOBE, REALM
worldly—EARTHLY,
MUNDANE,
SECULAR, TERRENE
worm—ANNELID,
CADEW, ESS, ERIA,
LEECH, LOA,
MAGGOT, NAID,
NEMATODE
worn—CHAFED,
FRAYED, SERE,
SHABBY,
TATTERED, TRITE,
USED
worry—BAIT, CARE,
CARK, FRET,
HARASS, HARRY,
STEW, VEX
worship—ADORE,
HONOR, IDOLIZE,
RESPECT, REVERE,
SERVE, VENERATE
worst—BAD, DEFEAT,
INFERIOR, LOWER,
POORER, ROUT,
UNPLEASANT
worth—BETIDE, CARAT,
MERIT, PRICE,
RICHES, VALUE,
WEALTH
worthless—BAD, FUTILE,
PALTRY, RACA,
RAP, TRASHY,
USELESS, WASTE

wound—CUT, INJURY,
LESION, MAUL,
PIERCE, RUPTURE,
STAB, SCATHE,
TRAUMA
wrangle—BICKER,
BRAWL, DISPUTE,
MELL, QUARREL
wrap—CAPE, CERE,
ENSWATHE,
ENVELOPE, INFOLD,
SHAWL, STOLE,
SWATHE
wreath—ANADEM,
CIRCLET, CROWN,
GARLAND, LEI
wreck—DESTRUCTION,
INJURE, RAZE,
RUIN, SMASH
wren—KINGLET, REED,
SEDGE, STAG
wrench—DISTORTION,
SPANNER, SPRAIN,
TWIST, WREST
wrest—ELICIT, GARBLE,
REND, SNATCH,
TURN, TWIST
wrestling hold—
HEADLOCK,
NELSON, TOEHOLD
wretch—EXILE, PUNISH,
SINNER, VAGRANT
wretched—FORLORN,
ILL, MISERABLE,
PALTRY, SAD
wrinkle—CREASE,
FURROW, PUCKER,
RIDGE, RIPPLE,
RUCK, RUGA, SEAM
wrist—CARPUS, CARPI
writ—PONE, PROCESS,
VENIRE
write—COMPOSE,
INDITE, INSCRIBE,
PEN, SCRIBE,
TRANSCRIBE
writer—AUTHOR,
PENMAN, SCRIBE
writing cipher—
CRYPTOGRAPHY

wrong—AMISS, CHEAT,
ERR, EVIL, FAULTY,
INJURE, SIN, VICE,
WRY
wrongdoing—CRIME,
EVIL, FELONY,
INJURE, SIN, VICE,
WRY
wry—CONTORT,
DISTORTED,
PERVERSITY, TURN,
TWIST, WRITHE
wryneck—SNAKEBIRD,
TORTICOLLIS

-X-

X-ray—ROENTGEN
xenodochy—
HOSPITALITY
xenos—ALIEN, STRANGE
xeres—JEREZ, SHERRY
xerophyte—CACTUS
xerotic—DRY
xylem—HADROME
xylite—ASBESTOS
xylonite—CELLULOID
xylophone—GIGELIRA,
MARIMBA, SARON
xyst—PORTICO, STOA
xyster—SCRAPER

-Y-

yaffle—WOODPECKER
yahoo—BRUTE,
BUMPKIN, COURSE,
ROUGH, SAVAGE
yak—SARLAK, SARLYK
yakin—BUDORCAS
yam—HOI, UBE, UVE,
UVI
yap—BARK, YELP
yard—CROFT,
ENCLOSURE,
GARTH
yarn—CLEW, CREWEL,
FLAX, STORY, TALE,
THREAD
yawn—CHASM, GAPE,
OSCITATE
yawning—AGAPE,
OSCITANT
year—ANNUM
yearly—ANNUAL,
ANNUALLY,
ETESIAN
yearn—CRAVE, DESIRE,
EAGER, HANKER,
LONG, PINE, WISH
yeast—BARM, BEES,
FERMENT,
FOMENT, FROTH,
KOJI, LEAVEN
yell—CHEER, RAH,
ROAR, SHOUT,
SHRIEK
yellow—GULL,
JAUNDICED,
SALLOW, XANTHIC,
YOLK
brown pigment—SIENNA
coloration—ICTERINE
deep—SAFFRON
dyestuff—ANNATTO,
MARTIUS, MORIN
ochre—LIMONITE,
SIL
yellowhammer—FINCH,
FLICKER, SKITE,
YITE
yellowish—CATECHU,
GAMBIER
yeoman—FREEHOLDER
yew—CONIFER,
HEMLOCK
yield—BOW, CEDE, CROP,
GIVE, LOSE, NET,
OBEY, PRODUCE,
RELENT, SOFTEN,

SUBMIT
yielding—RELENTING,
    SOFT
yogi—ASCETIC, FAKIR
yoke—COUPLE, JOIN,
    LINK, SERVITUDE,
    TEAM
yokel—BOOR, BUMPKIN,
    HICK, OAF,
    PLOWBOY, RUBE,
    RUSTIC
young—BABE, BABY,
    CHILD, CHILDISH,
    IMMATURE,
    JUNIOR, JUVENILE,
    OFFSPRING
youngster—BABY, KID,
    LAD, MOPPET,
    SHAVER, TAD, TOT,
    YOUTH
youth—ALADDIN, KID,
    LAD, SHAVER,
    TEEN, TAD

-Z-

zany—BUFFOON,
    CLOWN, FOOL,
    GABY, POOP,
    SAWNEY
zeal—ARDOR, ELAN,
    FERVOR, INTEREST,
    MOOD, PASSION
zealot—DEVOTEE,
    ENTHUSIAST,
    FANATIC, PARTISAN
zebra, extinct
    variety—QUAGGA
zenana—HAREM,
    SERAGLIO
zenith—ACME, APEX,
    MERIDIAN, PEAK,
    SUMMIT, TOP
zero—BLANK, CIPHER,
    HOUR, NAUGHT,
    NIL, NOTHING
zest—FLAVOR, GLEE,
    GUSTO, RELISH,
    RAPTURE, SPICE,
    TASTE
zigzag—AWRY,
    CHEVRON,
    CRANKLE, TACK
zinc—SPELTER,
    TUTENAG
zither—ROTA
zodiac sign—1st—ARIES,
    2nd—TAURUS,
    3rd—GEMINI,
    4th—CANCER,
    5th—LEO,
    6th—VIRGO,
    7th—LIBRA,
    8th—SCORPIO,
    9th—SAGITTARIUS,
    10th—CAPRICORN,
    11th—AQUARIUS,
    12th—PISCES
zone—BELT, CLIME,
    GIRDLE, GIRTH,
    ISLE, REGION
zoril—MARIPUT,
    POLECAT, ZORILLA
zyme—FERMENT,
    LEAVEN, YEAST

PART II: INFORMATION BY SUBJECT

Geographical Gazetteer	236
Coins, Money	260
Weights and Measures	261
The Bible	263
Mythological Terms	266
Prefixes	269
Suffixes	270
Names of Famous Persons	272
Nobel Prizes	279
Religious Terms	284
Heraldic Terms	285
Chemical Elements	287
Presidents of the United States	289

GAZETTEER

ABYSSINIA (see Ethiopia)

ADRIATIC
City—VENICE
Gulf—TRIESTE
Island—ESO, LAGOSTA, LIDO
Seaport—BARI, FIUME, POLA
Wind—BORA

AEGEAN
Peoples—LELEGES, PSARA, PSYRA, SAMIAN, SAMIOTE
Arm—SAROS
Island—COS, DELOS, IOS, NIO, PSARA, SAMOS

AFGHANISTAN
City—HERAT, KABUL (c.), KANDAHAR
River—HARI RUD, INDUS
Tribe—SAFI, ULUS

AFRICA
City—ACCRA, BANGUI, CAIRO, DAKAR, KHARTOUM, MONROVIA, ORAN, PRETORIA, RABAT, TUNIS
Country—(see individual countries in gazetteer)
Desert—KALAHARI, LIBYAN, SAHARA
District—NUBIA, RAND, RUANDA
Headland—KOP, RAS

Island—AZORES, CANARIES, DJERBA, MADAGASCAR, MADEIRA
Lake—ASAL, CHAD, DILOLO, MWERU, NYASA, RUDOLF, SHIRWA, TCHAD
Mountain—ATLAS, KILIMANJARO, NATAL
Tribe—ABO, BANTU, BONI, BARI, BERBER, GOLO, KAFFIR, LURI, MADI, RIFF, ZULU

AKIMOLINSK
City—OMSK (c.)

ALABAMA
City—BIRMINGHAM, MOBILE, MONTGOMERY (c.), SELMA
Flower—GOLDENROD, CAMELIA
Nickname—COTTON, HEART OF DIXIE
Motto—WE DARE DEFEND OUR RIGHTS

ALASKA
City—JUNEAU (c.), NOME, SITKA
Flower—FORGET-ME-NOT
Nickname—THE LAST FRONTIER
River—YUKON

ALBANIA
City—DURRES,
   SHKODER, TIRANA
   (c.), VIORE
Lake—OHRID, PRESPA,
   SCUTARI
River—BIJOSE, DRIN,
   SEMENI, SHKUMBI

ALEUTIAN
Island—ADAK, ATKA,
   ATTU, KISKA,
   UMNAK

ALGERIA
City—ALGIERS (c.),
   BONA, MEDIA,
   ORAN
Department—ALGIERS,
   CONSTANTINE,
   ORAN
Mountain—ATLAS
River—SHELIF

ALPS
Mountain—BLANC,
   JUNGFRAU,
   MATTERHORN
Pass—CENIS, COL,
   SIMPLON

AMAZON
Cetacean—INIA
Estuary—PARA

ANATOLIA—ARMENIA

ANDORRA
City—ANDORRA LA
   VELLA (c.),
River—RUI VALIRA
Mountain—COMA
   PEDROSA

ANNAM
City—HUE
Division—COCHIN
   CHINA
Tribe—MOIS

ANTARCTIC
Coastal region—ADELIE
Sea—ROSS

ARABIAN
Gulf—ADEN, OMAN
City—ADEN, MECCA,
   MEDINA
Desert—DAHNA,
   NEFUD, SYRIAN
Mountain—NEBO, SINAI
Tribe—ASIR, AUS,
   IRAD, KEDAR
Wind—SIMOOM,
   SIMOON

ARCTIC
Current—LABRADOR
Base—ETAH
Plain—TUNDRA

ARGENTINA
City—BAHIA BLANCA
   BUENOS AIRES (c.),
   CORDOBA,
   MENDOZA, ROSARIO
District—CHACO,
   CHUBUT, JUJUY, LA
   PAMPA, MENDOZA,
   TUCUMAN
River—NEGRO,
   PARAGUAY,
   PARANA, URUGUAY

ARIZONA
City—NOGALES,
   PHOENIX (c.),
   TEMPE, TUCSON,
   YUMA
Flower—SAGUARO
Nickname—GRAND
   CANYON, SUNSET
   LAND
Motto—DITAT DEUS;
   GOD ENRICHES
River—GILA

ARKANSAS
City—LITTLE ROCK (c.)
Flower—APPLE

BLOSSOM
Nickname—LAND OF
OPPORTUNITY,
WONDER
Motto—REGNAT
POPULUS: LET THE
PEOPLE RULE

ARMENIA
City—ERIVAN (c.)
Mountain—ARARAT
River—ARAS

ASIA
City—AMOY,
BAGHDAD,
BOMBAY,
SINGAPORE
Desert—GOBI
Island—JAPAN, LUZON,
MALAY, SUMATRA
River—AMUDARYA,
AMUR, ARA, ILI,
INDUS, LENA, OB,
ONON, PEI, SI,
TIGRIS, WEI
Mountain—ALTAI,
EVEREST,
HIMALAYAS, HINDU-
KUSH

ASIA MINOR
City—ILION, ISSUS,
MYRA, SARDIS,
TROY, USHAK
Island—SAMOS
Mountain—IDA
River—HALYS
Sea—AEGEAN

ASSAM
City—SHILLONG (c.)
Tribe—AHOM, AKA,
AO, GARO, NAGA

ASSYRIA
City—ASSHUR,
ANTIOCH, HARA,
NINEVEH
River—ADHIAN, ZAB

ATHENS
Hill—ACROPOLIS
Mountains—PARNES
Port—PIRAEUS
Territory—ATTICA

ATLANTIC
Island—AZORES,
BERMUDA, CANARY
CUBA, GREENLAND,
ICELAND

AUSTRALIA
City—BRISBANE,
CANBERRA (c.),
HOBART,
MELBOURNE,
PERTH, SYDNEY
Districts—
QUEENSLAND,
TASMANIA,
VICTORIA
Rivers—DARLING,
MURRAY,
MURRUMBIDGEE,
SWAN
Lakes—COWAN,
DUNDAS, EYRE,
EVERARD, FROME,
DISAPPOINTMENT

Mountains—
CAPOOMPETA,
DALRYMPLE,
KOSCIUSKO,
SEAVIEW,
ULAWUM

AUSTRIA
City—GRAZ, LINZ,
SALZBURG, VIENNA
(c.)
Districts—BOHEMIA
CARINTHIA,
GALICIA, SILESIA
STYRIA, TIROL
Rivers—DANUBE,
DRAVA, ENNS, INN,
LEITHA, PIAVE,
TRAUN

Mountains—CARNIC,
KAPAWANKEN,
OTZTALER,
RHAETIAN,
SEMMERING

AZORES
Town—HORTA

BABYLONIA
City—AKKAD,
CUNAXA
Division—ELAM,
SUMER
Mountain—ARARAT
River—EUPHRATES,
TIGRIS

BAHAMA
Island—ABACO,
ANDROS, BIMINI
Cap.—NASSAU

BALEARIC ISLAND
Island—CABRERA,
MAJORCA,
MINORCA

BALKAN
Country—ALBANIA,
RUMANIA, SERBIA,
YUGOSLAVIA

BALTIC
Island—ALSEN, DAGO,
OSEL
Port—REVAL, RIGA

BARBADOS
City—BRIDGETOWN
(c.)
Towns—HASTINGS,
HOLETOWN,
PORTLAND

BARBARY
States—ALGIERS,
MOROCCO, TRIPOLI,
TUNIS

BAVARIA
City—HOF
River—ISAR

BELGIUM
City—ANTWERP,
BRUSSELS (c.),
GHENT, LIEGE, SPA,
YPRES
Commune—AATH,
ALOST, ANS, ATH,
BRUGES, BRUGGE,
DUERNE, EVERE,
IEPER, LOUVAIN,
OSTEND
Rivers—MEUSE,
OURTHE, SAMBRE,
SEMOY
Mountains—
ARDENNES

BENGAL
Town—BARISAL,
CALCUTTA. DACCA
(c.), MADRAS
District—NADIA
Native—BANIAN, KOL

BERMUDA
Cap.—HAMILTON

BOEOTIA
Cap.—THEBES
Region—IONIA

BOHEMIA
City—PILSEN, PRAGUE
River—ELBE, ISER

BOLIVIA
Cap.—SUCRE, LA PAZ
City—COCHABAMBA,
LA PAZ (c.),
ORURO, POTOSI,
SUCRE (c)
Districts—ALTIPLANO,
YUNGAS
Lake—CAIPASA,
CONCEPCION,

POPPO, TITICACA,
UINAMARCA
River—ABUNA, BENI,
BLANCO,
DESAGUADERO,
GRANDE, GUAPORE,
LAUCA, AMAORE,
NEGRO
Mountain—ANDES,
BALA CORDILLERA,
NEUVO MUNDO,
OLLAGUE, REAL,
SAJAMA, YUNGAS

BOMBAY
City—SURAT
Town—POONA

BORNEO
Port—BALIK, MIRI,
PAPAN
River—BRUNI, KAJAN

BRAZIL
City—BRASILIA (c.),
MACEIO, NATAL,
RECIFE, "RIO" (RIO
DE JANEIRO),
SANTOS, SAO PAULO
Districts—AMAZONAS,
BAHIA, PARAIBA
Rivers—APORE,
CANOAS, CAPIM,
AMAZON, IJUI,
IRIRI, IVAI, JURUA,
PARA, PARANA,
PEIXE, POTI,
PARAGUAY,
URUGUAY, XINGU
Mountains—ACARAI,
CAIAPO, PARECIS,
XAVANTES

BULGARIA
City—BURGAS,
PLOVDIV, RUSE,
SOFIA (c.), VARNA
Districts—KHASKOVD,
PLEVEN, VIDIN,
VRATSA

Rivers—ARDA, CERRA
LOM, DANUBE,
GOLEM ISKER,
KAMCHIYA, LUDA,
MARITSA, OGOSTA
SAZLE, STROMA,
TUNDZAH, VIT
Mountains—BALKAN,
RHODOPE

BURMA
City—AKYAB,
MANDALAY,
MOULMEIN
RANGOON (c.)
Districts—
TENASSERIM,
PEGU, BASSEIN,
TOUNGOO, ARAKAN
River—CHINDWIN,
IRRAWADDY,
SITTANG
Mountain—ARAKAN
YOMA, NAMKIN

CALEDONIA—
SCOTLAND

CALIFORNIA
City—ALAMEDA,
FRESNO, NAPA,
SACRAMENTO (c.)
Flower—GOLDEN
POPPY
Nickname—GOLDEN,
GRAPE
Motto—EUREKA, I
HAVE FOUND IT
Lake—BUENA, CLEAR,
EAGLE, SODA,
TAHOE
Mountain—PALOMAR

CAMBODIA
City—KOMPONG
CHAM, KOMPONG
District—PARROT'S
BEAK
Lake—TONLE SAP

River—MEKONG

CAMEROON
River—SHARI

CANADA
City—CALGARY,
EDMONTON,
MONTREAL,
OTTAWA (c.),
SASKATOON,
TORONTO,
VANCOUVER,
VICTORIA
Province—ALBERTA,
BRITISH COLUMBIA,
MANITOBA, NEW
BRUNSWICK,
NEWFOUNDLAND,
NOVA SCOTIA,
ONTARIO, PRINCE
EDWARD ISLAND,
QUEBEC,
SASKATCHEWAN
Lakes—GRAND
MANAN,
NIPIGON,
UPPER SEAL,
WINNIPEG, GREAT
SLAVE, GREAT
BEAR, LOUISE
River—BATTLE,
BEAVER,
CHURCHILL,
FRASER, KAZAN,
NELSON, PEACE,
EASTMAIN,
MISSINAIBI, SEVERN
Mountain—CARIBOO,
CHURCHILL,
MICHELSON,
ROBSON

CARIBBEAN
Gulf—DARIEN
Islands—CUBA,
JAMAICA, NASSAU

CAROLINE ISLANDS
Islands—PALU, TRUK,

YAP

CASPIAN SEA
River—ARAS, KUMA,
URAL, VOLGA

CASTILE
Province—AVILA,
SORIA
River—EBRO, ESLA

CEYLON
City—COLOMBO (c.)
Port—GALLE

CHANNEL ISLAND
Islands—GUERNSEY,
JERSEY, SARK

CHILE
City—CALDERA,
CABIJA, LOTA,
SANTIAGO (c.),
TALCA
Province—ARAUCO,
ATACAMA,
MAULE, NUBLE,
VALDIVIA
Desert—ATACAMA
River—BIO-BIO, ITATA,
LOA, MAIPU,
VALDIVIA
Mountain—MAIPU,
PULAR

CHINA
City—AMOY, CANTON,
CHANGSHA,
CHUNGKING,
FOOCHOW,
HANKOW,
NANKING, PEKING
(c.), TIENTSIN,
YENPING
Province—AMUR,
FUKIEN, HONAN,
SHANSI, SHENSI,
YUNNAN
Lake—BUUR, NAM,

POYANG
River—ILI, MIN PEI,
TUNG TARIM, YUAN
Mountain—ALTAI,
ALASHAN, JARA,
OMEI, SUNG, TSINS

COLOMBIA
City—BOGOTA (c.),
CALI, CUCUTA,
NEIVA, PASTO,
TUNJA
Lake—TOTA
Province—BOLIVAR,
CAUCA CHOCO,
NARINA, VALLE
River—ATRATO,
GUAVIARA,
MAGDALENA, SINU,
TOMO

COLORADO
City—ASPEN,
BOULDER,
DENVER (c.),
GREELEY
County—ADA, BACA,
CROWLEY, DOLORES,
MESA, MONTEZUMA,
PARK
Flower—COLUMBINE
Nickname—
CENTENNIAL,
ROVER
Motto—NIL SINE
NUMINE: NOTHING
WITHOUT DEITY
River—BEAR, DOLORES,
GRAND, LARAMIE
Mountain—MASSIVE,
OSO

CONGO
Town—BOMA, MATADI
Lake—TUMBA
River—ZAHIR, ZAIRE

CONNECTICUT
City—AVON,
BRIDGEPORT,

HARTFORD (c.), NEW
HAVEN, MERIDEN
County—FAIRFIELD,
LITCHFIELD,
MIDDLESEX, NEW
HAVEN
Flower—MOUNTAIN
LAUREL
Nickname—
CONSTITUTION,
NUTMEG
Motto—QUI
TRANSTULIT,
SUSTINET: HE WHO
TRANSPLANTED,
SUSTAINS

COSTA RICA
City—ALAJUELA,
SAN JOSE (c.)
Mountain—BLANCO

CRETE
City—CANEA (c.),
CANDIA
Mountain—IDA

CRIMEA
City—SEVASTOPOL,
YALTA
River—ALMA
Sea—AZOF, AZOV

CROATIA
City—AGRAM, FIUME,
ZAGREB (c.)

CUBA
City—CIENFUEGO,
GUINES, HAVANA
(c.), SANTIAGO
Province—CAMAGUEY,
ORIENTE, PINAR
DEL RIO
Mountain—COPPER

CYCLADES ISLANDS
Islands—ANDROS,
IOS, MELOS, NAXOS,
PAROS, SYROS,

TENOS

County—KENT, SUSSEX

CYPRUS
City—LIMASOL,
NICOSIA (c.)
Mountain—TROODOS

CZECHOSLAVAKIA
City—BRNO, BUDWEIS,
BRATISLAVA,
OPAVA, PRAGUE (c.)
Province—BOHEMIA,
MORAVIA
River—EGER, GRAN,
HRON, ISER,
MOLDAU, NIYRA,
ODER, WAAG
Mountain—TATRA

DALMATIA
City—SPALATO

DAMASCUS
River—ABANA,
BARADA

DANUBE
Tributary—ARGES,
DRAVA, ILLER,
RABA, SAVA
Town—ULM

DARDANELLES—
HELLESPONT

DEAD SEA
City—SODOM
River to—JORDAN
Mountain—PISGAH

DELAWARE
City—CHESTER,
DOVER (c.),
WILMINGTON
Flower—PEACH
BLOSSOM
Nickname—FIRST,
DIAMOND
Motto—LIBERTY AND
INDEPENDENCE

DENMARK
City—AARHUS,
COPENHAGEN,
(c.), ODENSE
County—SORO
Island—AERO, FAROE
River—ASA, GUDEN,
HOLM

DODECANESE ISLANDS
Island—COO, COS,
LEROS, NISIRO,
PATMOS

**DUTCH (SEE
NETHERLANDS)**

EAST INDIA
Island—BALI, BORNEO,
CELEBES, SUMATRA

ECUADOR
City—LOJA, MANTO,
NAPO, QUITO (c.),
SALCEDO
Province—EL ORO,
GUAYAS,
IMBABURA,
MANABI
River—AMBATO,
GUAYAQUIL, NAPO
Mountain—ANTISANA,
CAYAMBE,
COTOPAXI

EGYPT
City—ALEXANDRIA
(c.), ASWAN, GIZA,
CAIRO (c.),
KARNAK
Desert—LIBYAN,
NUBIAN, SAHARA
Lake—MENZALEH,
MOERIS
River—NILE
Oasis—KHARGA, SIWA
Wind—KHAMSIN

EL SALVADOR
 City—SAN SALVADOR
 (c.)

ELAM
 City—SUSA (c.)

ELBE
 Tributary—EGER, ISER

ENGLAND
 City—BATH, DERBY,
 EXETER, GRIMSBY,
 HALIFAX,
 HASTINGS,
 LIVERPOOL,
 LONDON (c.),
 NORWICH,
 PLYMOUTH,
 SHEFFIELD,
 SOUTHAMPTON,
 TOTTENHAM
 County—DEVON,
 ESSEX, HANTS,
 KENT, SUSSEX
 Island—MAN, WIGHT
 Lake—CONISTON,
 ULLSWATER
 Mountain—PENNINE,
 SCAWFELL
 River—AIRE, AVON,
 DEE, EDEN, ESK,
 NEN, OUSE, THAMES

ESTONIA
 City—MARVA, MUHU,
 REVEN (c.) TALLINN
 (c.)
 Island—DAGO, OESEL

ETHIOPIA
 City—AXUM, ADDIS
 ABABA (c.), GONDAR
 District—DEMBEA,
 HARAR, SHOA,
 TIGRE
 Lake—DEMBEL, TANA,
 TSANA, TZANA
 River—BARO, JUBA,
 OMO

ETRUSCAN
 City—VEII
 Land—ETRURIA

EUROPE
 Country—AUSTRIA,
 BELGIUM,
 BULGARIA,
 DENMARK,
 FINLAND, FRANCE,
 GERMANY,
 HOLLAND,
 HUNGARY, ITALY,
 LATVIA,
 LUXEMBOURG,
 NORWAY, POLAND,
 RUMANIA, SPAIN,
 SWEDEN,
 SWITZERLAND

FIJI ISLANDS
 Island—LAU, VITA,
 VITI
 Cap—SUVA

FINLAND
 City—ABO, HELSINKI
 (c.), OULU, PORI
 Island—ALAND
 Lake—ENARE

FLANDERS
 City—GHENT (c.) LILLE

FLORENCE
 River—ARNO

FLORIDA
 City—MIAMI,
 ORLANDO,
 PENSACOLA,
 TALLAHASSEE (c.)
 Flower—ORANGE
 BLOSSOM
 Nickname—SUNSHINE
 Motto—IN GOD WE
 TRUST
 County—DADE,
 BROWARD, GULF

FORMOSA
City—DAI-HOKU,
TAIPEI, TAIWAN

FRANCE
City—ALX, BREST,
CAEN, DIJON,
LE HAVRE, LILLIE,
LYONS, NANCE,
ORLEANS, PARIS (c.),
REIMS, ROUEN,
TOURS, VICHY
Department—AUBE,
CHER, EURE, GARD,
INDRE, LOIRE,
MARNE, NIEVRE,
OISE, SEINE,
VAUCLUSE
Mountain—ALPS,
CEVENNES,
PYRENEES, VOSGES
River—LOIRE, MARNE,
RHONE, SEINE
Wine
District—
BURGUNDY,
CHAMPAGNE

GALILEE
Town—CANA,
NAZARETH

GEORGIA
City—ATLANTA (c.),
ATHENS, MACON
County—CLAY, COBB,
DADE, PIKE, TIFE,
WARE
Flower—CHEROKEE
ROSE
Nickname—EMPIRE
STATE OF THE
SOUTH, PEACH
STATE
Motto—WISDOM,
JUSTICE,
MODERATION

GERMANY
City—BONN (c.),
BERLIN (c.), CASSEL,
COLOGNE,
DRESDEN,
HAMBURG,
POTSDAM
Mountain—ALPS, BERG,
River—ELBE, ISAR,
ODER, SAAR, RHINE

GOBI DESERT
Lake—HARA
Site—ASIA

GREAT LAKE
Lakes—ERIE, HURON,
MICHIGAN,
ONTARIO, SUPERIOR

GREECE
City—ATHENS (c.),
BARCA, EDESSA,
CORINTH, LACONIA,
SALONIKA,
THESSALY
Areas—ATTICA,
HELLAS, SPARTA,
PELOPONNESUS
Island—CRETE, DELOS,
MELOS, LESBOS,
RHODES, CYCLADES
Mountain—ETA, OSSA,
PELION, OLYMPUS

GREENLAND
Town—ETAH,
JULIANEHAAB
Base—ETAH

GUATEMALA
City—GUATEMALA,
SALAMA
Lake—ATITLAN,
DULCE
River—CHIXOY, SAN
PEDRO
Volcano—AGUA,
ATITLAN

GUINEA
Port—BATA

HAITI
City—PORT-AU-
PRINCE (c.)
Island—GONAVE

HAWAII
City—HILO,
HONOLULU (c.)
Flower—HIBISCUS
Nickname—ALOHA
Motto—THE LIFE OF
THE LAND IS
PERPETUATED
IN RIGHTEOUSNESS
District—KONA
Island—HAWAII,
KAUAI, LANAI,
MOLOKAI, OAHU
Mountain—KILAUEA,
MAUNA KEA,
MAUNA LOA

HEBRIDES
Islands—BARRA,
IONA, LEWIS,
MULL, SKYE

HOLLAND (see
Netherlands)

HONDURAS
City—CEDROS,
GRACIAS,
TEGUCIGALPA
(c.)
Mountain—CEIBA
River—AGUAN,
NEGRO, PATUCA

HONG KONG
City—VICTORIA
Bay—MIRS

HUNGARY
City—BUDAPEST (c.),
DEBRECEN, GYOR,
KECSKEMET, MAKO
Lake—BALATON
Mountains—ALPS,
CARPATHIAN
River—DANUBE,
DRAVE, MAROS,
VISTULA

ICELAND
City—REYKJAVIK
(c.)
Mountain—JOKUL
Volcano—HEKLA

IDAHO
City—BOISE (c.),
NAMPA,
POCATELLO
Flower—LEWIS MOCK
ORANGE
Nickname—GEM STATE
Motto—ESTO,
PERPETUA: EXIST,
FOREVER
County—ADA, BUTTE,
GEM, KATAH, LEWIS
River—KOOTENAY
SNAKE

ILLINOIS
City—ALTON,
CHICAGO,
DECATUR, ELGIN,
JOLIET, MOLINE,
SPRINGFIELD (c.)
Flower—VIOLET
Nickname—PRAIRIE
STATE
Motto—STATE
SOVEREIGNTY,
NATIONAL UNION
County—COOK, FORD,
KANE, LEE, OGLE,
POLK

INDIA
City—AGRA, DELHI
(c.), GAYA, MADRAS,
PATNA, SIMLA

District—DAYA,
  MALABAR
State—ASSAM, BIHAR,
  DELHI, GUJARAT,
  MANIPUR, SIKKIM
Desert—THAR
Mountain—GHAT,
  TRISUL

INDIANA
  City—BRAZIL,
    FOWLER,
    HAMMOND,
    INDIANAPOLIS
    (c.), MUNCIE, PERU
  Flower—PEONY
  Nickname—HOOSIER
  Motto—CROSSROADS
    OF AMERICA
  County—CASS, JAY,
    LAKE, OWEN, PIKE
  River—WABASH

INDO-CHINA
  City—HANOI, SAIGON,
    VINH
  County—CAMBODIA,
    LAOS, THAILAND,
    VIETNAM
  River—TE
  Region—ANNAM

INDONESIA
  City—JAKARTA (c.)
  Island—BALI, BORNEO,
    JAVA, SUMATRA,
    TIMOR
  Lake—TOBA

IONIA
  City—TEOS
  Island—ITHACA,
    ZANTE
  Gulf—ARTA

IOWA
  City—AMES,
    DAVENPORT, DES
    MOINES (c.)

Flower—WILD ROSE
Nickname—HAWKEYE
Motto—OUR LIBERTIES
  WE PRIZE, OUR
  RIGHTS WE WILL
  MAINTAIN
County—ADAIR, LYON,
  ONAWA

IRAN
  City—BASRA,
    ISPAHAN, JASK,
    MOGUL, TEHERAN
    (c.)
  River—KARUN, MAND,
    TIGRIS
  Mountain—HINDU,
    KUSH,
    PARAPANISUS

IRAQ
  City—BAGHDAD (c.)
  Town—ANA, BASRA

IRELAND
  City—CORK, DUBLIN
    (c.), ENNIS,
    KILKENNY, TARA
  County—CORK, DOWN,
    GALWAY, MAYO,
    TIPPERARY
  Island—ARAN
  Lake—DERG, ERNE,
    LOUGH
  Mountain—
    DONEGAL,
    WICKLOW
  River—BOYNE, FOYLE,
    SHANNON

ISRAEL
  City—AQABA,
    JERUSALEM (c.),
    TEL AVIV
  Desert—NEGEB
  Plain—SHARON

ISTANBUL
  Constantinople
  Foreign quarter—PERA

ITALY
City—ASTI, FIUME,
GENOA, MILAN,
ROME (c.), TURIN
Dept.—APULIA,
LIGURIA,
SARDINIA, SICILIA,
SALERNO, VENICE
Gulf—GENOA,
SELERMO, VENICE
Lake—ALBANO, COMO,
GARDA, MAGGIORE
Mountain—ALPS,
APENNINES,
VESUVIUS
River—ARNO, PO
RUBICON, TIBER

JAPAN
City—AKITA,
HIROSHIMA, LIDA,
NAGASAKI, TOKYO
Prov.—IWAKI,
SATSUMA
Island—BONIN,
HONSHU, KYUSHU,
NIPPON
Mountain—ASAMA,
FUJI, HONDO
River—TONEGAWA

JAVA
City—BATAVIA,
JAKARTA,
SURAKARTA
Island—BALI
Mountain—LAWOE,
RAOENG

JERUSALEM
Mountain—OLIVET,
SION, ZION

JORDAN
Region—PEREA
Mountain—HOR,
PISGAH

KANSAS
City—ABILENE,
DODGE,
LEAVENWORTH,
SALINA, TOPEKA (c.)
Flower—SUNFLOWER
Motto—AD ASTRA PER
ASPERA: TO THE
STARS THROUGH
DIFFICULTIES
Nickname—
SUNFLOWER
County—ELK, GOVE,
LYON, RENO
River—OSAGE

KENT
District—PENGE

KENTUCKY
City—FRANKFORT
(C.), LOUISVILLE
Flower—GOLDENROD
Nickname—
BLUEGRASS
Motto—UNITED WE
STAND, DIVIDED
WE FALL
County—KNOX, OWEN,
PIKE

KENYA
City—NAIROBI (c.)

KOREA
City—ANJU, PUSAN,
SEOUL (c.)
River—KUN, YALU

LACONIA
Cap.—SPARTA

LADRONE ISLANDS
Islands—GUAM,
MARIANAS, SAIPAN

LAPLAND
City—KOLA

LATVIA
City—DVINSK, LIBAU,
RIGA (c.)

River—AA

LEBANON
City—ARCA, BEIRUT
(c.), SAIDA, TYRE
Mountain—MZAR,
SANNINE
River—LITANI, LYCOS

LEEWARD ISLANDS
Islands—ANTIGUA,
BARBUDA,
DOMINICA,
MONTSERRAT,
NEVIS

LIBERIA
City—MARSHALL,
MONROVIA (c.)
River—SAN PEDRO

LIBYA
City—BENGAZI,
TRIPOLI
Port—DERNA

LITHUANIA
City—KOVNO, MEMEL,
VILNYUS

LOIRE
Tributary—INDRE

LORRAINE
City—METZ (c.)
River—SAAR

LOUISIANA
City—BATON ROUGE
(c.), NEW ORLEANS,
SHREVEPORT
Flower—MAGNOLIA
Nickname—PELICAN
Motto—UNION,
JUSTICE,
CONFIDENCE
County (Parish)—
ACADIA, CADDO,
SABINE

LUXEMBOURG
River—MOSELLE

LUZON (see Philippines)

MACEDONIA
City—BEREA, EDESSA,
PELLA (ancient cap.)
Mountain—OLYMPUS

MADAGASCAR (see
MALAGASY
REPUBLIC)

MAINE
City—AUGUSTA (c.),
BANGOR, BATH,
ORONO
Flower—PINE CONE
AND TASSEL
Nickname—PINE TREE
STATE
Motto—DIRIGO: I
DIRECT
County—KNOX,
WALDO
Lake—MOOSE, SEBAGO
River—KENNEBEC

MALAGASY REPUBLIC
City—MOJANGO,
TANANARIVE

MALAYSIA
City—KUALA LUMPUR
(c.)
States—JOHORE,
KEDAH,
KELANTAN,
MALACCA,
PAHANG,
SELANGOR
Island—BALI, JAVA,
TIMOR
Mountain—GUNUNG

MALTA
City—VALETTA (c.)
Island—MELITA

MANCHURIA
  City—HARBIN, HULAN
  River—AMUR, YALU

MARIANAS
  Islands—SAIPAN,
    TINIAN

MARYLAND
  City—ANNAPOLIS
    (c.), BALTIMORE,
    BETHESDA
  Flower—BLACKEYED
    SUSAN
  Nickname—OLD LINE,
    FREE
  Motto—MANLY
    DEEDS, WOMANLY
    WORDS
  County—CECIL,
    HOWARD

MASSACHUSETTS
  City—AMHERST,
    BOSTON (c.), LYNN,
    NORTHAMPTON,
    SPRINGFIELD
  Flower—MAYFLOWER
  Nickname—BAY, OLD
    COLONY
  Motto—BY THE SWORD
    WE SEEK PEACE,
    BUT PEACE ONLY
    UNDER LIBERTY
  County—ESSEX,
    HAMPSHIRE,
    SUFFOLK

MEDITERRANEAN
  Country—ALGERIA,
    FRANCE, GREECE,
    ITALY, SPAIN
  Island—CRETE,
    CYPRUS, ELBA,
    MAJORCA, MALTA,
    SARDINIA

MESOPOTAMIA (see Iraq)

MEXICO
  City—ACAPULCO,
    GUADALAJARA,
    JALAPA, JUAREZ,
    MEXICO CITY (c.),
    TAMPICO
  State—COLIMA,
    HIDALGO,
    TABASCO,
    YUCATAN
  Lake—CHAPALA
  River—TABASCO,
    YAQUI
  Mountain—
    POPOCATEPETL

MICHIGAN
  City—DETROIT, FLINT,
    LANSING (c.)
  Flower—APPLE
    BLOSSOM
  Nickname—
    WOLVERINE
  Motto—IF YOU SEEK A
    PLEASANT
    PENINSULA, LOOK
    ABOUT YOU
  County—BAY, CLARE,
    DELTA, LAKE

MINNESOTA
  City—DULUTH,
    MINNEAPOLIS,
    ST. PAUL (c.),
    ROCHESTER
  Flower—SHOWY
    LADY'S-SLIPPER
  Nickname—NORTH
    STAR, GOPHER
  Motto—L'ETOILE DU
    NORD: STAR OF THE
    NORTH
  County—CASS, LYON,
    PINE, RICE
  Lake—MINNEWASKA,
    RED

MISSISSIPPI
  City—BILOXI,
    GULFPORT,

JACKSON (c.)
Flower—MAGNOLIA
Nickname—
MAGNOLIA
Motto—VIRTUTE ET
ARMIS: BY VIRTUE
AND ARMS
County—CLAY, PIKE,
YAZOO

MISSOURI
City—
INDEPENDENCE,
JEFFERSON CITY
(c.), ST. LOUIS
Flower—HAWTHORN
Nickname—SHOW ME
Motto—THE WELFARE
OF THE PEOPLE
SHALL BE THE
SUPREME LAW
County—ADAIR, DENT,
LINN, OZARK

MONGOLIA
City—URGA (c.)
Desert—GOBI
River—PEI

MONTANA
City—BILLINGS,
BUTTE, HELENA (c.)
Flower—BITTERROOT
Nickname—TREASURE
Motto—ORO Y PLATA:
GOLD AND SILVER
County—BLAINE, HILL,
TETON
River—SUN, TETON,
WILLOW

MOROCCO
City—ASSA, RABAT (c.)
Island—MADEIRA

NEBRASKA
City—LINCOLN (c.),
OMAHA
Flower—GOLDENROD
Nickname—BEEF.

CORNHUSKER
Motto—EQUALITY
BEFORE THE LAW
County—BOYD, GAGE,
OTOE

NEPAL
City—K(H)ATMANDU
(c.), PALAN
Mountain—EVEREST
River—KUSI

NETHERLANDS
City—AMSTERDAM
(c.), BREDA, HAGUE,
ROTTERDAM,
UTRECHT
Commune—EDE,
BREDE, DELFT,
SNEEK
Island—SHELLING,
TEXEL
Province—DRENTE,
HOLLAND,
ZEELAND
River—EMS, LE(C)K,
SCHELDT

NEVADA
City—CARSON CITY
(c.), LAS VEGAS,
RENO
Flower—SAGEBRUSH
Motto—ALL FOR OUR
COUNTRY
Nickname—
SAGEBRUSH, SILVER
County—ELKO, NYE,
WASHOE

NEW CALEDONIA
City—NUMEA

NEW GUINEA
City—LAE, SORON
River—FLY, SEPIK
Island—PAPUA
Mountain—VICTORIA

NEW HAMPSHIRE
City—CONCORD (c.),
DOVER, HANOVER,
MANCHESTER,
NASHUA
Flower—PURPLE LILAC
Nickname—GRANITE
Motto—LIVE FREE OR
DIE
County—COOS
Lake—SUNAPEE

NEW JERSEY
City—BAYONNE,
CAMDEN, TRENTON
(c.)
Flower—PURPLE
VIOLET
Nickname—GARDEN
Motto—LIBERTY AND
PROSPERITY
County—BERGEN,
ESSEX, PASSAIC,
SUSSEX
River—TOMS

NEW MEXICO
City—
ALBUQUERQUE,
ROSWELL,
SANTA FE (c.)
Flower—YUCCA
Nickname—LAND OF
ENCHANTMENT
Motto—CRESCIT
EUNDO: IT GROWS
AS IT GOES
County—TAOS, MORA
River—GILA

NEW YORK
City—ALBANY (c.),
ELMIRA, GOTHAM,
ITHACA, OLEAN,
SARATOGA
Flower—ROSE
Nickname—EMPIRE
Motto—EXCELSIOR:
EVER UPWARD

County—CAYUGA,
ERIE, GENESEE,
NIAGARA, ONTARIO
Lake—CAYUGA,
ONEIDA, SARANAC
River—EAST, HARLEM,
HUDSON

NEW YORK CITY
Island—BEDLOES,
ELLIS, MANHATTAN
River—EAST, HARLEM

NEW ZEALAND
City—AUCKLAND,
CHRISTCHURCH,
DUNEDIN,
HAMILTON,
QUEENSTOWN,
WELLINGTON (c.)
Island—OTEA
Lake—GUNN, HAWEA,
TAUPO
Mountain—COOK,
EGMONT,
MESSENGER
River—TARAMAKAU,
WAIMAKARIRI

NICARAGUA
City—GRANADA,
LEON, MANAGUA
(c.)
Lake—MANAGUA,
NICARAGUA
River—SAN JUAN,
WANHO

NIGERIA
City—EDE, LAGOS (c.),
OFFA
Province—ISA, NUPE
River—NIGER

NILE
Town on—ASYUT,
CAIRO
Island—RODA

NORMANDY

Cap.—ROUEN
Dept.—CALVADOS,
   EURE, MANCHE,
   ORNE

NORTH ATLANTIC
Island—ICELAND,
   IRELAND

NORTH CAROLINA
City—DURHAM,
   EDENTON, RALEIGH
   (c.)
Flower—DOGWOOD
Nickname—TAR HEEL,
   OLD NORTH
Motto—TO BE,
   RATHER THAN TO
   SEEM
County—ASHE,
   LENOIR, NASH
River—NEUSE, PEE
   DEE, TAR
Cape—FEAR,
   HATTERAS

NORTH DAKOTA
City—BISMARCK (c.),
   FARGO
Flower—WILD PRAIRIE
   ROSE
Nickname—SIOUX,
   FLICKERTAIL
Motto—LIBERTY AND
   UNION, NOW AND
   FOREVER, ONE AND
   INSEPARABLE
County—CASS, TRAILL

NORWAY
City—BERGEN, OSLO
   (c.)
Mountain—
   BLADFJELL, KJOLEN,
   NUMEDAL,
   TELEMARK
River—ENA, GLOMMA

NOVA SCOTIA
Cape—BRETON,

GEORGE
Port—TRURO
City—HALIFAX (c.),
   DARTMOUTH

OCEANIA
Countries—
   AUSTRALIA, MALAYA,
   MELANESIA,
   MICRONESIA, NEW
   ZEALAND,
   POLYNESIA

OHIO
City—ATHENS,
   COLUMBUS (c.),
   DAYTON,
   SANDUSKY,
   TOLEDO
Flower—SCARLET
   CARNATION
Nickname—BUCKEYE
Motto—WITH GOD,
   ALL THINGS ARE
   POSSIBLE
County—ADAMS, ERIE,
   ROSS

OKLAHOMA
City—ADA, ALVA,
   ENID, LAWTON,
   OKLAHOMA CITY
   (c.), STILLWELL
Flower—MISTLETOE
Nickname—SOONER
Motto—LABOR OMNIA
   VINCIT: LABOR
   CONQUERS ALL
County—CADDO,
   ELLIS, LOVE, OSAGE
River—RED
Mountain—OZARK

ONTARIO
Cap.—TORONTO

OREGON
City—MEDFORD,
   PORTLAND, SALEM
   (c.)

Flower—OREGON
GRAPE
Nickname—BEAVER
Motto—THE UNION
County—COOS,
GILLIAM, GRANT,
WALLOWA, WASCO
River—COLUMBIA,
WILLAMETTE
Mountain—CASCADE,
HOOD

ORKNEY ISLANDS
Cap.—KIRKWALL
Islands—ITOY,
POMONA

PACIFIC ISLANDS
Islands—ARU, BALI,
DUCIE, FIJI, GUAM,
KOMODO, LIFU,
OKINAWA, SAIPAN,
SAMOA, TAHITI,
WAKE

PALESTINE
Town—CANA, ENDOR,
GAZA
Mountain—EBOL,
NEBO, PISGAH, ZION
Lake—MEROM,
GALILEE
Port—ACRE, HAIFA

PANAMA
City—COLON,
CRISTOBAL,
PANAMA CITY (c.)
Gulf—DARIEN
River—CHAGRES
Lake—GATUN

PARAGUAY
City—ASUNCION (c.),
BELEM, ITA
River—APA, PARANA

PARIS
District—AUTEUIL,
MONTMARTRE
Airport—ORLY
River—SEINE

PELOPONNESUS
City—SPARTA
District—LACONIA

PENNSYLVANIA
City—CHESTER, ERIE,
HARRISBURG (c.),
LEBANON,
PHILADELPHIA,
READING
Flower—MOUNTAIN
LAUREL
Nickname—KEYSTONE,
QUAKER
Motto—VIRTUE,
LIBERTY, AND
INDEPENDENCE
County—BUCKS, ERIE,
TIOGA
River—BEAVER,
CONEMAUGH,
LEHIGH,
SCHUYKILL

PERSIA (see Iran)

PERU
City—CUZCO, ICA,
LIMA (c.), PAITA
Province—LORETO,
PIURA, TACNA
Lake—TITICACA
River—ACARA,
MARANON, RIMAC,
SANTA
Mountain—MISTI

PHILIPPINES
City—ALBAY, CEBU,
IRIGA, MANILA (c.)
Island—LEYTE, LUZON,
MINDANAO, SAMAR
Province—ABRA,
ILOILO, LEYTE,
TARLAC

River—ARBA,
CAGAYAN, PASIG
Lake—TAAL
Mountain—APO, IBA

POLAND
City—DANZIG,
LODZ, GDYNIA,
WARSAW (c.)
Island—WOLIN
River—DNIESTER,
VISTULA

POLYNESIA
Island—FIJI,
PHOENIX, SAMOA

POMERANIA
City—ANKLAM,
STETTIN (c.)
Island—RUGEN,
USEDOM
River—ODER

PORTUGAL
City—BRAGA, EVORA,
LISBON (c.), OPORTO
Province—ALGARVE,
BEIRA, MINHO
River—DOURO, TAGUS

PRUSSIA
City—AACHEN,
BRESLAU,
HALLE, KIEL
Province—BERLIN,
HANOVER,
POMERANIA
SILESIA
River—ALLE, ELBE,
ODER, SAAR

PUERTO RICO
City—ARECIBO,
DORADO, SAN JUAN
(c.)
Island—MONA

PUNJAB
Cap.—LAHORE

PYRENEES
Mt. peak—ANETO

QUEBEC
City—MONTREAL,
QUEBEC CITY,
SOREL
Peninsula—GASPE

QUEENSLAND
River—BRISBANE

RED SEA
Gulf—AQABA,
SUEZ
Peninsula—SINAI
Island—PERIM

RHINE
Tributary—AAR, LAHN,
RUHR

RHODE ISLAND
City—KINGSTON,
NEWPORT,
PROVIDENCE (c.)
Flower—VIOLET
Nickname—LITTLE
RHODY
Motto—HOPE
County—KENT

RHONE
Tributary—GARD,
ISERE, SAONE

ROCKY MOUNTAINS
Range—TETON

ROME
Dist.—PAGUS,
PONTINE
Hill—AVENTINE,
CAELIAN,
CAPITOLINE,
ESQUILINE,
PALATINE,
QUIRINAL, VIMINAL

RUMANIA

City—AIUD, BACAU,
BUCHAREST,
GALATI,
HUSI,
SEVERIN
Mountain—NEGOI
River—ARGES, SIRET

RUSSIA
City—AKA,
ARCHANGEL, KIEV,
MOSCOW (c.), PENZA,
TASHKENT,
VLADIVOSTOK
Region—ARMENIA,
GALICIA, GEORGIA,
KIRGHIZ, SIBERIA,
UKRAINE
River—AMUR, DNEPR,
DON, LENA, NEVA,
VOLGA
Sea—ARAL, AZOV,
BAIKAL
Mountain—ALAI, URAL
Peninsula—CRIMEA

SAMOA
Cap.—APIA
Island—MANUA,
SAVAII

SCANDINAVIA
Country—DENMARK,
NORWAY, SWEDEN

SCOTLAND
City—ABERDEEN,
ALLOWAY, AYR,
EDINBURGH (c.),
GLASGOW,
INVERNESS
County—ANGUS,
BANFF,
KINCARDINE,
MIDLOTHIAN,
WIGTOWN
River—DEE, NITH,
NORN, TEVIOT
Lake—NEVIS, RYAN,
NESS

SIBERIA
City—OMSK,
VLADIVOSTOK
Mountains—ALTAI
River—MAYA, OLENEK

SICILY
City—AETNA,
MARSALA,
MESSINA, PALERMO
(c.)
Volcanic
Mountain—ETNA
River—BELICE,
PLATANI

SOMALIA
City—BERBERA,
MOGADISHU (c.)

SOUTH AFRICA
City—CAPE TOWN (c.),
DURBAN,
JOHANNESBURG,
PRETORIA
Province—NATAL,
TRANSVAAL
Mountain—
DRAKENSBURG

SOUTH CAROLINA
City—CHARLESTON,
COLUMBIA (c.)
Flower—YELLOW
JESSAMINE
Nickname—
PALMETTO
Motto—DUM SPIRO,
SPERO: WHILE I
BREATHE, I HOPE
County—AIKEN,
HORRY, SALUDA
Mountain—BLUE
RIDGE

SOUTH DAKOTA
City—PIERRE (c.)
Flower—PASQUE
FLOWER
Nickname—COYOTE,

SUNSHINE
Motto—UNDER GOD,
THE PEOPLE RULE
Mountain—
RUSHMORE

SOUTH PACIFIC
Island—FIJI, SAMOA
Sea—CORAL, TASMAN

SOUTH SEA
Island—BALI, SULU

SPAIN
City—BARCELONA,
CADIZ, GIJON,
LEON, MADRID (c.),
TOLEDO, VALENCIA
Province—ALAVA,
AVILA, GERONA,
NAVARRA
Island—BALEARIC,
CANARY

SUDAN
City—KHARTOUM
(c.)
Desert—LIBYAN,
NUBIAN

SUMATRA
City—ACHIN,
BENCOOLEN,
PALEMBANG
River—JANBI, ROKAN
Lake—TOBA

SWEDEN
City—FALUN,
GOTEBORG,
MALMO,
STOCKHOLM (c.)
Gulf—BOTHNIA
Lake—ASNEN, MALAR
River—GOTA, LAINIO

SWITZERLAND
City—BERNE (c.),
GENEVA, LUCERNE,
NEUCHATEL,

ZURICH
Canton—BASEL,
GRISONS,
UNTERWALDEN
Lake—BIENNE,
LUGANO, THON
Mountains—ALPS, DOM,
JURA

SYRIA
City—ALEPPO,
BEIRUT,
SELEUCIA
Lake—TIBERIAS
Mountain—CARMEL

TAHITI
Cap.—PAPEETE

TANZANIA
Mountain—MERU

TASMANIA
Cap.—HOBART
Cape—GRIM
Lake—
WESTMORELAND
Mountain—DROME,
GREY, NEVIS,
WELLINGTON
River—ARTHUR,
TAMAR

TENNESSEE
City—
CHATTANOOGA,
KNOXVILLE,
MEMPHIS,
NASHVILLE (c.)
Flower—IRIS
Nickname—
VOLUNTEER
Motto—AMERICA
AT ITS BEST
County—CLAY, GILES,
RHEA
Mountain—
CUMBERLAND

TEXAS
City—ABILENE,
AUSTIN (c.),
DENISON,
HOUSTON,
LUBBOCK
Flower—BLUEBONNET
Nickname—LONE STAR
Motto—FRIENDSHIP
County—ANGELINA,
CHEROKEE, NOLAN,
RUSK, WALKER
River—PECOS, RED,
RIO GRANDE

THAILAND
City—BANGKOK (c.)
River—MEKONG,
MENAM
Isthmus—KRA

THAMES
Other name—ISIS

TIBET
Cap.—LHASA
River—INDUS

TROY
Mountain—IDA

TUNISIA
City—BIZERTE, GABES,
TUNIS (c.)
Gulf—HAMMAMET

TURKEY
City—ANKARA (c.),
EDESSA, ISTANBUL,
SMYRNA
District—ORDU, PERA
Gulf—COS
Mountain—ARARAT
River—MESTA, SARUS

TUSCANY
City—PISA
Island—ELBA

UGANDA
Cap.—KAMPALA
Lake—VICTORIA

UKRAINE
City—ODESSA, ROVNO

URUGUAY
City—MELO,
MONTEVIDEO (c.),
RIVERA
Dept.—ARTIGAS,
ROCHA
Lake—MERIN
River—NEGRO,
ULIMAR

UTAH
City—OGDEN, SALT
LAKE CITY (c.)
Flower—SEGO LILY
Nickname—BEEHIVE
Motto—INDUSTRY
Lake—SALT, SEVIER
Mountain—WASATCH
River—GRAND,
JORDAN, WEBER

VENEZUELA
City—ATURES,
BARQUISTIMETO,
CARACAS (c.),
MATURIN,
VALENCIA
State—COJEDES,
GUARICO, ZAMORA
River—ARAUSA,
ORINOCO
Mountain—ANDES,
CONCHA, IMUTACA

VENICE
Island—RIALTO
Resort—LIDO
River—BRENTA

VERMONT
City—BARRE,
MONTPELIER

Flower—RED CLOVER
Nickname—GREEN
  MOUNTAIN
Motto—FREEDOM
  AND UNITY
County—ESSEX,
  ORLEANS
Mountain—TACONIC

VIRGINIA
City—DANVILLE,
  RICHMOND (c.)
Flower—DOGWOOD
Nickname—OLD
  DOMINION
Motto—SIC SEMPER
  TYRANNIS: THUS
  ALWAYS TO
  TYRANTS
County—BATH, CRAIG,
  HENRICO
River—JAMES,
  POTOMAC
Mountain—CEDAR

WALES
City—BANGOR,
  CARDIFF,
  PEMBROKE
River—SNOQUALMIE
Lake—BALA

WASHINGTON
City—ABERDEEN,
  OLYMPIA (c.),
  TACOMA, WALLA
  WALLA
Flower—
  RHODODENDRON
Nickname—
  EVERGREEN
Motto—BY AND BY
County—ADAMS,
  KING, YAKIMA
River—SNOQUALMIE
Mountain—RAINIER

WEST INDIES
Island—ARUBA,
  BAHAMA,
  BARBADOS, CUBA,

JAMAICA, NEVIS,
  TRINIDAD

WEST VIRGINIA
City—CHARLESTON
  (c.), LOGAN
Flower—
  RHODODENDRON
Nickname—
  MOUNTAIN
Motto—MONTANI
  SEMPER LIBERI:
  MOUNTAINEERS
  ALWAYS FREE
County—CLAY, MINGO,
  ROANE

WISCONSIN
City—BELOIT,
  KENOSHA,
  MADISON (c.),
  OSHKOSH, RACINE
Flower—BUTTERFLY
  VIOLET
Nickname—BADGER
Motto—FORWARD

WYOMING
City—CHEYENNE
  (c.), JACKSON,
  LARAMIE
Flower—WYOMING
  PAINT BRUSH
Nickname—EQUALITY
Motto—EQUAL RIGHTS
River—TETON
Mountain—MORAN,
  TETON

YEMEN
Cap.—SANA
Port—MOCHA

YORKSHIRE
River—URE
District—SELBY

YUGOSLAVIA
City—BELGRADE (c.),
  CATTARO, SENTA,
  VARSAC
River—DRINA,
  VARDAR

MONEY AND COINS

AFGHANISTAN—abbasi, afghani, anania, pul
ALBANIA—franc, lek, qintar
ANGLO-SAXON—mancus, ora, sceat
ANGOLA—angolar, macuta
ARGENTINA—centavo, peso
ATHENS—chalcus, obol
AUSTRIA—ducat, florin, krone, schilling
BELGIUM—belga, centime, franc
BIBLE—beka, drachma, mite, shekel, talent
BOLIVIA—boliviano, bolivar, centavo
BRAZIL—cento, dobra, milreis, reis
BULGARIA—dinar, lev, lew
BURMA—kyat
CANADA—dollar
CHILE—condor, peso
CHINA—cash, cent, li, tael, yuan
COLOMBIA—condor, peso, real
COSTA RICA—centimo, colon
CUBA—centavo, peso
CZECHOSLOVAKIA—ducat, haler, heller
DENMARK—krone, ore
ECUADOR—condor, sucre
EGYPT—girsh, pound
ENGLAND—florin, groat, guinea, pound, pence
ESTONIA—kroon, sent
ETHIOPIA—besa, girsh, harf, talari
FINLAND—markka, penni
FRANCE—centime, ecu, franc, liard, livre, obole, sol, sou
GENOA—jane

GERMANY—krone, mark, pfennig, thaler
GREECE—lepton, nomas, obol, stater
HAITI—gourde
HOLLAND—daalder, doit, florin, gulden
HONDURAS—centavo, peso
HUNGARY—giller, gara, pengo
ICELAND—aurar, eyrir, krona
INDIA—anna, fels, lac, pice, pie, rupee, tara
IRAN—daric, dinar, pul, rial, shahi
IRAQ—dinar
IRELAND—rap
ITALY—lira, scudo, soldo
JAPAN—bu, ickibu, itzebu, rin, sen, yen
KOREA—hwan, won
LATVIA—lat, latu
LITHUANIA—lit
MACAO—avo
MALAYA—tra
MEXICO—centavo, peso
MONGOLIA—tugrik
MONTENEGRO—florin, para, perpera
MOROCCO—okia, rial
NEPAL—mohar
NICARAGUA—coroloba, peso
NORWAY—krone, ore
OMAN—gaz, goz, shazi
PANAMA—balboa
PARAGUAY—guarani
PERU—centavo, dinero, libra, sol
POLAND—ducat, grosz, marka, zloty
PORTUGAL—conto, dobra, escudo, rei
ROME—as, aes, denarius,

dinder, semis, sesterce
RUMANIA—ban, lei, leu
RUSSIA—altin, copec,
  kopek, ruble
SOMALIA—besa
SOUTH AFRICA—cent,
  florin, pound, rand
SPAIN—alfonso, centimo,
  cuarto, dobla, piaster
SWEDEN—krone, ore
SWITZERLAND—batz,
  franc, rappe

THAILAND—att, bhat,
  fuang, tical
TURKEY—asper, lira,
  mahbub, para
UNITED STATES—bit,
  cent, dime, dollar, eagle,
  nickel, penny, quarter
VENEZUELA—bolivar,
  centimo, fuerto, medio,
  real
VENICE—betso, bezzo
YUGOSLAVIA—dinar

WEIGHTS AND MEASURES

ANNAM—binh, dong, fan,
  gon, hao, ly, mau, that
ALGERIA—pik, rotl, tarri
ARABIA—chekl, covido,
  den, kella, nevat
ARGENTINA—grano,
  quintal, sino
AUSTRIA—fass, seidel,
  unze
BIBLE—beka, cubit, digit,
  shekel
BOLIVIA—celemin, libra
BRAZIL—arratel, arroba,
  libra, moio, onca, pe,
  pipa
BULGARIA—krine, oka,
  ore, tovar
BURMA—byee, dain, kait,
  voo, vis
CALCUTTA—kunk, pank,
  raik
CHINA—bu, catty, fen, hao,
  ho, li, picul, sheng, yin
COLOMBIA—carga, quilate,
  saco, vara
COSTA RICA—caja, tercia
CUBA—tercio, vara
CZECHOSLOVAKIA—
  lan, mira, sah
DENMARK—album, es,
  fod, lod, mil, ort, pot,
  vog

ECUADOR—fanega, libra
EGYPT—apt, ardab, cubit,
  heml, khar, khet, oka
ENGLAND—cran, pin,
  stone, virgate
ESTONIA—liin, nael, puud
ETHIOPIA—cuba, kasm,
  natr, oket, tat
FINLAND—tunna
FRANCE—arpen, aune,
  gros, kilo, marc, minot,
  once, pot, tonne
GERMANY—aam, eimer,
  kette, lot, stein
GREECE—borile, bema,
  cotula, pous
HOLLAND—aam, duim,
  kan, lood, stoop, wichtje
HUNGARY—ako, hold
  joch, yoke
ICELAND—alin, fet, pund
INDIA—chittak, drona,
  kunk, masha, para, raik,
  tank
IRAN—charac, dang, guz,
  jerib, miskal, mou,
  pinar, zar
IRELAND—bandle
ITALY—braccia, canna,
  denaro, oncia, palmo,
  punto, tavola
JAPAN—fun, hiro, kin, mo,

se, shaku, tan
KOREA—kon
LATVIA—kanne
LIBYA—bozze
MALAYA—pau
MEXICO—labor
MOROCCO—artel, fanega,
  sahh
NICARAGUA—manzana,
  suerte
NORWAY—fot, lod, mark,
  pot, pund
PERU—galon, topo
POLAND—cal, funt, lut,
  mila, morg, pret
PORTUGAL—bota, grao,
  marco, meio, onca, vara
ROME—as, bes, clima,
  cuella, juger, libra,
  modius, palmus, saltus,
  urna
RUSSIA—dola, foute, funt,
  loof, lot, pajak, paletz,
  pud, verst
SPAIN—adarme, arroba,

codo, estadel, grano,
milla, onza, pie, tomin,
vara
SWEDEN—aln, am, famn,
  fot, mil, ort, pund, ref,
  sten, tum
SWITZERLAND—elle,
  imi, maass, saum, setier,
  viertel
THAILAND—catty, coyan,
  fuang, kwien, rai,
  salung, sat, sen, sok, yot
TURKEY—almud, arshin,
  batman, cequi, fortin,
  kerat, oka, rotl
UNITED STATES—acre,
  bag, barrel, bolt, bushel,
  carat, cord, dram, drum,
  flask, foot, grain, hank,
  inch, keg, mil, ounce,
  peck, pint, pound,
  prime, quarter, rod, ton
YUGOSLAVIA—akov,
  dramm, rif

THE BIBLE

Books of the Bible

Old Testament

Genesis	Chronicles II	Daniel
Exodus	Ezra	Hosea
Leviticus	Nehemiah	Joel
Numbers	Esther	Amos
Deuteronomy	Job	Obadiah
Joshua	Psalms	Jonah
Judges	Proverbs	Micah
Ruth	Ecclesiastes	Nahum
Samuel I	Song of Solomon	Habakkuk
Samuel II	Isaiah	Zephaniah
Kings I	Jeremiah	Haggai
Kings II	Lamentations	Zechariah
Chronicles I	Ezekiel	Malachi

Apocrypha

Tobit	Wisdom
Baruch	Susanna
Esdras (1)	Maccabees I, II
Esdras (2)	Bel and the Dragon
Esther	Song of the Three Children
Judith	Prayer of Manasses
Sirach (Ecclesiasticus)	

New Testament

Matthew	Ephesians	Hebrews
Mark	Philippians	James
Luke	Colossians	Peter I
John	Thessalonians I	Peter II
The Acts	Thessalonians II	John I
Romans	Timothy I	John II
Corinthians I	Timothy II	John III
Corinthians II	Titus	Jude
Galatians	Philemon	Revelation

Biblical Kings

Agag	David
Ahab	Herod
Ahaz	Omri
Bera	Saul
Birsha	Solomon

Biblical Prophets

Amos	Jeremiah
Daniel	Joel
Elijah	Jonah
Elisha	Micah
Ezekiel	Moses
Haggai	Nahum
Hosea	Obadiah
Isaiah	

Biblical Peoples

Amorite	Hivite
Arkite	Kenite
Dan	Moabite
Dodanim	Phut
Edomite	Rephaim
Enim	Semite
Hamite	Sinite
Hittite	

Biblical Mountains

Ararat	Nebo
Ebal	Peor
Gilead	Pisgah
Hermon	Seir
Hor	Sinai
Horeb	Tabor
Moriah	Zion

Biblical Cities and Towns

Ain	Dan	Joppa
Akkad	Elim	Nazareth
Arad	Gadara	Nineveh
Arvad	Gath	Sidon
Ashur	Gaza	Sodom
Bethel	Geba	Tarsus
Biblos	Gomorrah	Tyre
Bozra	Jericho	
Cana	Jerusalem	

Biblical Lands

Canaan	Moab
Elam	Nod
Judah	Zobah

Biblical Names

Abel	Eve	Obal
Adam	Gog	Omar
Ahi	Hadad	Oreb
Amasa	Iram	Oren
Cain	Isaac	Reba
Caleb	Ivah	Seth
Ebal	Jael	Ucal
Enos	Jared	Vashti
Eran	Mary	Zaham
Esau	Merab	

MYTHOLOGY

Greek Gods

AEOLUS—winds
APOLLO—youth, sun
ARES—war
AUSTER—south wind
BACCHUS—wine
BOREAS—north wind
CHAOS—first god
COMUS—mirth
CRONUS—crops
DIONYSUS—wine, vegetation
EROS—love
EURUS—southeast wind

HADES—underworld
HELIOS—sun
HERMES—herald
HYMEN—marriage
KRONOS (CRONUS)
MOMUS—ridicule
MORPHEUS—sleep
NEREUS—sea
PONTUS—sea
POSEIDON—sea
POTHOS (EROS)
THANATOS—death
URANUS—heaven

Greek Goddesses

APHRODITE—beauty
ARA—vengeance
ARTEMIS—moon
ASTARTE (ARTEMIS)
ATE—mischief
ATROPOS—fate, thread cutter
ATHENA—arts
CHLORIS—flowers
CHLOTHO—Fate, spinner
COTYS—vegetation
CYBELE—nature
DEMETER—agriculture
DICE (DIKE)
DIKE—Hora: Justice
ENYO—war
EOS—dawn
ERIS—discord
GAEA (GE)
GAIA (GE)
GE—earth

HEBE—youth
HECATE—moon
HERA—queen
HESTIA—hearth
HORA—one of Horae
HORAE—one of seasons
HYGEIA—health
IRENE—Hora: peace
LACHESIS—Fate: thread length
MNEMOSYNE—memory
MOIRA—fate
MUSES—arts
NEMESIS—revenge
NIKE—victory
NYX—night
PALLAS—wisdom
RHEA—god's mother
SELENA (SELENE)
SELENE—moon

Roman Gods

AMOR—love
BACCHUS—wine
CUPID—love
DIS—underworld
FAUNUS—rural god
JOVE (JUPITER)
JUPITER—chief god
LARES—house gods
MARS—war
MERCURY—thieves
MORS—death

NEPTUNE—sea
ORCUS—orcus
PAN—flocks
PENATES—household
PLUTO—hades
QUIRINUS—war
SOL—sun
SOMNUS—sleep
SYLVANUS—woods
VULCAN—fire

Roman Goddesses

ANNONA—crops
AURORA—dawn
CERES—grain
DIANA—moon, hunting
DECUMA—Fate
EPONA—horses
FAUNA—fields
FERONIA—fountain
FIDES—faith
FLORA—flowers
FORTUNA—fortune
JUNO—womanhood
LUCINA—childbirth
LUNA—moon
MINERVA—peace

MORTA—fate
NONA—fate
OPS—harvest
PARCAE—Fates
PAX—peace
PHOEBUS—moon
PROSERPINA—
    underworld
SALUS—health, prosperity
SPES—hope
TELLUS—earth
TERRA—earth
VACUNA—hunting
VENUS—love
VESTA—hearth

Egyptian Gods

AMEN—king of gods
AMMON (AMEN)
ANUBIS—underworld
ATEN—solar disk
ATMU—sun
ATUM—sun
BES—pleasure
GEB—earth
HAPI—Nile
HORUS—day (hawk head)
KHEM—procreation
MIN—procreation
OSIRIS—underworld

PTAH—Memphis
RA—sun
SEB—earth
SEBEK—evil (crocodile
    head)
SERAPIS (OSIRIS)
SET—war, evil
SETH (SET)
SHU—sun
SU—sun
TEM—sun
THOTH—wisdom, magic
TUM (TEM)

Egyptian Goddesses

APET—maternity
ATHOR (HATHOR)
BAST—lion head
BUTO—serpent
HATHOR—love (cow head)
ISIS—fertility, life

MA (MAAT)
MAAT—truth, law
NUT—heavens
SATI—queen
SEKHET—cat head
SESHAT—learning

Norse Gods

AEGIR—sea
AESIR—chief gods
ALCIS—twin gods
BALDER—light
BALDR (BALDER)
BRAGE—poetry
BRAGI (BRAGE)
DONAR (THOR)
EAR (TIU)
ER (TIU)
FREY—fertility
HIER—sea
HODER—blind god
LOK (LOKI)
LOKI—mischief

ODIN—chief, war, wisdom,
    slew ymir
THOR—thunder
TIU—sky, war
TIW (TIU)
TYR (TIU)
ULL—bow skill
VANIR—early race of gods
VANS (VANIR)
VILI—Odin's brother
WODAN (ODIN)
WODEN (ODIN)
WOTAN (ODIN)
ZIO (TIU)

Norse Goddesses

EIR—healing
FREA (FRIGG)
FREYA—beauty
NANNA—flowers
NERTHUS—peace
FRIA (FRIGG)—marriage
HEL—death
HELA (HEL)

NORN—destiny
RAN—sea
SAGA—history
SIF—earth
URD (NORN)
URTH (URD)
VOR—betrothal

Hindu Gods

AGNI—fire, lightning
AKAL—immortal one
BHAGA—love
CIVA (SIVA)
DEVA (DEWA)
DEWA—divinity
DYAUS—sky
GANESHA—wisdom

KA—unknown god
KAMA—love
KRISHNA—fire
SIVA—supreme
VARUNA—sea, sun
VAYU—wind
VISHNU—supreme
YAMA—judge of dead

Hindu Goddesses

DEVI—mother goddess
KALI—death
LAKSHMI (SRI)
SHREE (SRI)
SHRI (SRI)
SRI—beauty

UMA—splendor
USHAS—dawn
USAS (USHAS)
VAC—speech
VACH (VAC)

PREFIXES

across—DIA, TRANS
after—MET, META, METH
again—ANA, ANTI, OB,
 RE
against—ANTI
air—AERO
all—OMNI, TOTI
alone—SOLI
alongside—PARA
animal—ZO
antitoxin—SERO
apart—DIA, DIS
around—AMPHI, PERI
Austria—AUSTRO
away from—AB, APO
back—ANA, UN
bad—DYS, MAL, MIS
before—ANTE, AVANT,
 OB, PRAE, PRE
below—INFRA
beside—PAR, PARA
between—INTER, META,
 DIA
beyond—PARA
bird—ORNI
blood—HEMA, HEMO
bone—OSSE
bright—HELI
broad—PLATY
chief—ARCH, ARCHI
children—PEDO
Chinese—SINO
color—CHROM
Cornish town—TRE
dark—MELANO
difficult—DYS
disease—PATHO
distant—TELE
double—DIS, DI
down—CATA, DE
ear—OTO
early—EO
earnest—SERIO
earth—GEO

egg—OO, OVI
eight—OCTI, OCTO
English—ANGLI, ANGLO
equal—ISO, EQUI, PARI
equality—EQUI
eye—OCULO
facing—OB
false—PSEUDO
father—PATRI
faulty—MIS
feet—PED, PEDI
female—GYN, GYNO
few—OLIG
field—AGRI
fire—PYR, PYRO
fish—PISCI
flesh—SARCO
foreign—XENO
form—MORPH
four—TETRA
from—AB, DE, EC, EX,
 APO, FRO
god—THEO
great—MEGA
Greek—GRECO
groin—ILEO
half—BI, DEMI, SEMI,
 HEMI
hard—DYS, SCLERO
hate—MISO
heart—CARDI
hidden—CRYPTO
high—ACRO
ideas—IDEO
image—ICONO
in—EN
intestinal—ILEO
joint—CO
kidney—RENI
large—MACRO, MAGNI
life—BIO
love—PHILO
lung—PNEUMO
many—MULT, MULTI

middle—MES, MESO
milk—LACTO
moon—LUNI
mother—MATRI
mountain—ORO
much—POLY
muscle—MYO
near—PARA, JUXTA
new—NE, NEO
night—NOCTI, NYCT
nose—NASO, RHIN
not—IL, IR, NON, UN, IM, DIS
off—AB, DE
oil—OLEO
on—EPI
on this side—CIS
out of—EC, EX
over—EPI, HYPER
oxygen—OXA, OXY
people—DEMO
personal—IDIO
place—LOCO
poisonous—TOX, TOXI
priority—PRE
pus—PY, PYO
race—ETHNO
round—ROTA
Russia—RUSSO
sacred—HAGIO
same—HOMO
seed—SPORO
seven—SEPT
short—BREVI
single—MONO
six—HEXA
small—MICRE, MICRO
spine—MYEL
star—ASTRO

stones—LITHO
straight—RECT, ORTHO
son of—MAC
sound—PHON
sun—HELI, HELIO
tail—URO
ten—DEC, DECA, DEKA
thousand—KILO
thread—NEMATO
three—TRI
through—DIA
throughout—ANA
time—CHRON
to—AP, AC
together—SYN, CO, COM, JUXTA
tooth—DENTI, ODONT
toward—OC, AD, OB
turning—ROTO
twice—BI, DI, DIS, BIN, BIS
two fold—DI, BI
under—SUB, HYP, HYPO
union—GAMO
up—ANA
upon—EPI, EP, SUR
water—HYDRO
well—EU
wheel—ROTO
whole—UDINE, HOLO
wind—ANEMO
with—COL, COM, SYL, SYM, SYN
within—ENDO, ENTO, INTRA
womb—UTERO
wood—HYLO
word—LOGO
wrong—MIS

SUFFIXES

action—ENCE, URE
alky—OL
away from—AP, APH, APO
animal life—ALIA, ZOA
belief—ISM
believer—IST
belonging to—ISH
blood—EMIA

chemical—ANE, OL, OLE, OSE
city—POLIS
condition—ANCE, ESIS, ERY, ISE, OSIS
craze—ITIS
disease—PATHIC
district—RIC

divided—FID
equality—ENT
fear—PHOBE
female—STER, GYNE
feminine—ETTE, ETTES,
INE
full—OSE, OSES, ULOUS
geometrical figures—GON
heat—THERMY
inflammation—ITIS
inhabitant—ITE
killer—CIDE
knowledge—SOPHY
leading—AGOGUE
leaf—PHYL
like—ACEOUS, INE, ISH,
OID, AL, LY, ESQUE
make—IZE
murder—CIDE
native of—ESE, ITE
new—CENE
of action—SION
one who—IST, STER
origin—OTE, GENIC
pain—ALGIA
paralysis—PLEGIA,
PLEGY
past tense—PRET

pertaining—AC, AR, IC,
ILE, INE
practitioner—ICIAN
process—URE
quality—CY, ACY
relating to—AC, ANE, ARY
resembling—ISH, OID,
PHANE
ruler—CRAT
science—LOGY
separate—APO
sight—OPSIS
skin—DERM
small one—ULE
somewhat—ISH
state of being—URE
superlative—EST
swelling—OSIS
tens—TY
tending to—IVE
those who—STERS
treat—IZE
treatment—IATRY
tribe—INI
tumor—OMA
turning—TROPE, TROPY
worship—LATRY
violent attack—LEPSY

FAMOUS NAMES

Aaron—BURR, HANK, COPLAND
Abbott—BUD
Abner—LIL
Acheson—DEAN
Adams—JOHN, MAUDE
Adolph—OCHS
Alan—LADD, PATON
Albert—CAMUS
Aldous—HUXLEY
Alexander—FLEMING, POPE
Alfred—DRAKE, LUNT, NOBEL, SMITH
ali—KHAN MOHAMMED
Alighieri—DANTE
Allen—ETHAN, MEL, STEVE
Aleksei—KOSYGIN
Ambrose—BIERCE
Amelia—EARHART
Anatole—FRANCE
Andersen—HANS
Andre—GIDE
Andrew—JACKSON, JOHNSON
Andrews—DANA
Anita—LOOS
Anna—HELD, PAVLOVA
Anne—BOLEYN
Anthony—EDEN, SUSAN
Anton—DVORAK
Antony—MARK
Arden—EVE
Arnaz—DESI
Artemus—WARD
Arthur—CONAN DOYLE, CHESTER A.
Ataturk—KEMAL
Attlee—CLEMENT
Auguste—RODIN
Autry—GENE
Baba—ALI

Babe—RUTH
Bailey—PEARL, BILL
Bainter—FAYE
Balzac—HONORE
Barkley—ALBEN
Bartok—BELA
Barton—CLARA
Basie—COUNT
Baxter—ANNE
Beau—GESTE
Becky—SHARP
Bede—ADAM
Ben—HOGAN, HUR, JONSON
Bennett—CERF
Bergson—HENRI
Berlin—IRVING
Bernard—SHAW, BARUCH
Bernhardt—SARAH
Berra—YOGI
Bert—LAHR
Bette—DAVIS
Billy—ROSE, SUNDAY
Blas—GIL
Blum—LEON
Boleyn—ANNE
Bolger—RAY
Bolivar—SIMON
Bonheur—ROSA
Boone—DANIEL
Booth—EDWIN, JOHN WILKES
Boss—TWEED
Boswell—JAMES
Bradley—OMAR
Brendan—BEHAN
Bret—HARTE
Brigham—YOUNG
Bruce—CABOT
Brynner—YUL
Buck—PEARL
Buffalo Bill—CODY
Bunche—RALPH
Burbank—LUTHER

Burl—IVES
Burr—AARON
Burrows—ABE
Calloway—CAB
Cantor—EDDIE, IDA
Captain—AHAB
Carney—ART
Carnegie—ANDREW,
    DALE
Carnera—PRIMO
Carpenter—SCOTT
Carroll—BAKER, LEWIS
Carson—JOHNNY, KIT
Carrie—NATION
Casals—PABLO
Cassius—CLAY
Castle—IRENE, VERNON
Cather—WILLA
Catherine—PARR
Cecil—RHODES
Celeste—HOLM
Cesare—BORGIA
Chagall—MARC
Chaney—LON
Channing—CAROL
Chaplin—CHARLIE,
    OONA
Charles—DANA, LAMB
Charlotte—BRONTE,
    CORDAY
Chase—ILKA
Chekhov—ANTON
Chico—MARX
Chou—EN LAI
Christie—AGATHA
Clare—BOOTH LUCE
Clarence—DARROW,
    DAY
Clark—GABLE, MARK
Claude—RAINS
Cliburn—VAN
Clifton—WEBB
Cobb—TY
Cole—NAT "KING",
    PORTER
Como—PERRY
Connie—MACK
Cooper—GARY
Copland—AARON
Cordell—HULL

Coward—NOEL
Cox—WALLY
Crane—HART
Cronyn—HUME
Crockett—DAVY
Curie—MARIE
Custis—MARTHA
Dailey—DAN
Dale—EVANS
Daniel—DEFOE, BOONE
Davis—JEFF, BETTE
Day—DORIS, LARAINE,
    DENNIS
Dean—DIZZY, MARTIN,
    RUSK
Defoe—DANIEL
De l'Enclos—NINON
De Leon—PONCE
De Maupassant—GUY
De Valera—EAMON
Debs—EUGENE
Descartes—RENE
Devine—ANDY
Dewey—TOM, JOHN
Dickinson—EMILY
Dionne—ANNETTE,
    CECILE, EMILIE,
    MARIE, OLIVA,
    YVONNE
Disney—WALT
Dolly—MADISON
Donlevy—BRIAN
Doone—LORNA
Dorian—GRAY
Doris—DAY, DUKE
Dorothy—DIX, GISH
Dors—DIANA
Doyle—ARTHUR CONAN
Dreyfus—ALFRED
Duke—DORIS
Dunne—IRENE
Durocher—LEO, LIP
Duryea—DAN
Dvorak—ANTON
Dylan—THOMAS
Eamon de—VALERA
Earhart—AMELIA
Eartha—KITT
Eddie—FOY
Edgar—POE, BERGEN

Edith—PIAF
Edna—BEST, FERBER,
  MILLAY
Edouard—MANET
Edvard—GRIEG
Edward—ELGAR, HALE
Edwin—BOOTH
Einstein—ALBERT
Elbridge—GERRY
Eleanora—DUSE
Elias—HOWE
Elihu—ROOT, YALE
Ellington—DUKE
Ellery—QUEEN
Elmer—GANTRY
Emerson—RALPH WALDO
Emile—ZOLA
Emily—BRONTE, POST
Enoch—ARDEN
Enrico—FERMI, CARUSO
Ericson—LEIF
Ernie—FORD
Ethan—ALLEN, FROME
Ethel—WATERS,
  KENNEDY
Eugene—DEBS, O'NEILL
Eva—GABOR
Eyre—JANE
Ezra—POUND
Ferber—EDNA
Fernando—LAMAS
Ferrer—JOSE, MEL
Fibber—MCGEE
Fillmore—MILLARD
Fitz—HONEY
Fitzgerald—ELLA
Flanders—MOLL
Foch—NINA
Ford—HENRY, EDSEL
France—ANATOLE
Frances—ALDA
Francis—BACON, DRAKE
Franchot—TONE
Franck—CESAR
Frankie—LAINE
Franklin—PIERCE,
  ROOSEVELT
Franz—KAFKA, LEHAR,
  LISZT
Frome—ETHAN

Gabler—HEDDA
Gabor—EVA, MAGDA,
  ZSA ZSA
Gagarin—YURI
Gantry—ELMER
Garbo—GRETA
Gardner—AVA, ERLE
  STANLEY
Gary—COOPER
Gene—AUTRY, KELLY,
  TIERNEY, TUNNEY
George—ELIOT, PATTON,
  LLOYD, SAND,
  CUSTER
Gehrig—LOU
Gershwin—IRA, GEORGE
Gertrude—BERG, STEIN
Geste—BEAU
Gide—ANDRE
Gil—BLAS
Glenn—FORD, JOHN
Goldberg—RUBE, MOLLY
Goodman—BENNY
Goriot—PERE
Gould—JAY
Graham—BILLY, GREENE
Gray—DORIAN
Greco—JOSE
Greeley—HORACE
Gregor—MENDEL
Greta—GARBO
Grey—ZANE
Guiseppe—VERDI
Gypsy Rose—LEE
Hale—NATHAN
Hammarskjold—DAG
Hanks—NANCY
Harding—WARREN
Harold—ICKES
Harriet—STOWE
Harris—PHIL
Harry—TRUMAN,
  HOPKINS, HOUDINI
Hart—CRANE
Hayes—HELEN
Hayward—SUSAN
Hayworth—RITA
Hedda—GABLER
Heifetz—JASCHA
Heinrich—HEINE

Held—ANNA
Helen—HAYES, KELLER
Henrik—IBSEN
Henry—HUDSON, FORD
Herbert—HOOVER,
    VICTOR
Hercule—POIROT
Heyerdahl—THOR
Heywood—BROUN
Hitler—ADOLF
Hogan—BEN
Hoover—HERBERT
Horace—MANN
Horatio—ALGER
Horne—LENA
Hopkins—HARRY
Houdini—HARRY
Houston—SAM
Howe—ELIAS
Hunter—KIM, TAB
Hur—BEN
Hus—JAN
Huxley—ALDOUS
Ian—FLEMING
Igor—STRAVINSKY
Ilka—CHASE
Immanuel—KANT
Irene—CASTLE, DUNNE
Irving—BERLIN
Isaac—STERN, NEWTON
Isadora—DUNCAN
Iturbi—JOSE
Ives—BURL
Izaak—WALTON
Jack—LONDON, PAAR
Jackson—ANDREW
Jacob—RIIS
James—AGEE, FARLEY,
    JESSE, JOYCE,
    WATT
Jan—HUS
Jane—AUSTEN, EYRE
Janet—GAYNOR, LEIGH
Jay—GOULD
Jean—HARLOW
Jean-Paul—MARAT
Jefferson—DAVIS,
    THOMAS
Jeffreys—ANNE
Jenny—LIND

Jerome—KERN
Jesse—JAMES
Jessica—TANDY
Johann Sebastian—BACH
John—ALDEN, BROWN,
    DEWEY, KEATS,
    KENNEDY, SMITH
John Philip—SOUSA
John Wilkes—BOOTH
Johnny—CARSON
Johnson—ANDREW,
    LYNDON, VAN
Jolson—AL
Jonas—SALK
Jonathan—SWIFT
Jonson—BEN
Jose—GRECO, ITURBI
Joyce—JAMES, KILMER
Juan—PERON
Jules—VERNE
Julie—ANDREWS
Kafka—FRANZ
Karel—CAPEK
Karenina—ANNA
Karl—MARX
Kazan—ELIA
Keller—HELEN
Kelly—GENE, GRACE,
    EMMETT
Kemal—ATATURK
Kern—JEROME
Khachaturian—ARAM
Khan—AGA, ALI
Khayyam—OMAR
Klee—PAUL
Knute—ROCKNE
Kovacs—ERNIE
Lagerlof—SELMA
Lahr—BERT
Lanchester—ELSA
Lanza—MARIO
Lardner—RING
Laurel—STAN
Laurence—OLIVIER
Lazarus—EMMA
Learned—HAND
Legree—SIMON
Leif—ERICSON
Lena—HORNE
Leonardo—DAVINCI

Levant—OSCAR
Lew—AYRES
Lewis—JOHN, TED
Lil—ABNER
Lillie—BEA
Lily—PONS
Linkletter—ART, JACK
Liszt—FRANZ
Lombardo—GUY
Long—HUEY
Lonigan—STUDS
Loren—SOPHIA
Lorna—DOONE
Lorre—PETER
Louis—JOE, PASTEUR
Lowell—AMY
Lucrezia—BORGIA
Lugosi—BELA
Lupino—IDA
Luther—MARTIN,
    BURBANK
Mack—CONNIE, TED
Magnani—ANNA
Mailer—NORMAN
Mann—HORACE
Mantle—MICKEY
Marco—POLO
Marie—CURIE
Marilyn—MONROE
Mario—LANZA
Mark—TWAIN,
    ANTHONY, CLARK
Marner—SILAS
Martha—MITCHELL,
    RAYE
Martin—LUTHER
Mary—ASTOR, TODD
Marx—CHICO, GROUCHO,
    HARPO, KARL,
    ZEPPO
Masaryk—JAN
Mata—HARI
Maude—ADAMS
Maurice—RAVEL
Maxwell—ELSA
Mel—ALLEN, OTT
Melville—HERMAN
Mendel—GREGOR
Menuhin—YEHUDI
Meriwether—LEWIS

Merman—ETHEL
Mickey—MANTLE
Miller—ARTHUR
Monroe—MARILYN
Moorehead—AGNES
Moss—HART
Mostel—ZERO
Mundt—KARL
Muni—PAUL
Murray—DON, JAN
Musial—STAN
Nancy—HANKS
Nash—OGDEN
Nathan—HALE
Nation—CARRIE
Nelson—BARRY, OZZIE
Nero—WOLFE
Newton—ISAAC
Nikolai—LENIN
Nilsson—BIRGIT
Noel—COWARD
Norman—MAILER
O'Casey—SEAN
Ogden—NASH
Oliver—HARDY
Omar—BRADLEY
O'Neill—EUGENE
Orville—WRIGHT
Orson—WELLES
Oscar—LEVANT, WILDE
Ott—MEL
Pablo—PICASSO
Page—PATTI
Paine—TOM
Pancho—VILLA
Pasternak—BORIS
Pasteur—LOUIS
Paton—ALAN
Patrick—HENRY
Paul—MUNI
Pauling—LINUS
Pavlova—ANNA
Peron—EVA, JUAN
Perry—COMO, MASON
Peter—LORRE
Phileas—FOGG
Philip—NERI
Picasso—PABLO
Pierre—CURIE
Pinza—EZIO

Polo—MARCO
Ponce de—LEON
Pons—LILY
Porter—COLE
Post—EMILY
Pound—EZRA
Priscilla—ALDEN
Proust—MARCEL
Rains—CLAUDE
Ralph—BUNCHE
Rathbone—BASIL
Rayburn—SAM
Rebecca—WEST
Reed—DONNA
Rex—STOUT
Rhodes—CECIL
Rice—ELMER
Richard—BYRD
Ring—LARDNER
Rip—TORN
Robert—BURNS, FULTON,
  KENNEDY, TAFT
Robinson—CRUSOE,
  JACKIE
Rockne—KNUTE
Rockwell—NORMAN
Rogers—ROY, WILL
Romero—CESAR
Root—ELIHU
Rose—BILLY
Roy—ROGERS
Rudy—VALLEE
Runyon—DAMON
Rusk—DEAN
Ruth—BABE
Rutledge—ANNE
Salvador—DALI
Sam—HOUSTON, SNEAD
Samuel—MORSE
Sancho—PANZA
Sand—GEORGE
Sawyer—TOM
Schulberg—BUDD
Schweitzer—ALBERT
Seeger—ALAN
Sevareid—ERIC
Sharp—BECKY
Shelley—PERCY BYSSHE
Sigmund—FREUD
Sigrid—UNDSET

Silas—MARNER
Silvers—PHIL
Simon—LEGREE,
  BOLIVAR
Sinclair—LEWIS, UPTON
Skinner—OTIS
Smith—AL
Snead—SAM
Sonja—HENIE
Sophia—LOREN
Sothern—ANN
Standish—MILES
Stanford—WHITE
Stengel—CASEY
Stephen—BENET
Stevenson—ADLAI
Stravinsky—IGOR
Sullivan—ED
Sunday—BILLY
Susan B.—ANTHONY
Syngman—RHEE
Tarkington—BOOTH
Taylor—ZACHARY,
  ELIZABETH
Teasdale—SARA
Templar—SIMON
Templeton—ALEC
Thatcher—BECKY
Theda—BARA
Thomas—DYLAN,
  HARDY, MANN,
  WOLFE
Thornton—WILDER
Tito—BROZ
Tocqueville—ALEXISDE
Tolstoy—LEO
Tom—MIX, PAINE
Torme—MEL
Toscanini—ARTURO
Truman—CAPOTE,
  HARRY
Trygve—LIE
Tse-tung—MAO
Tunney—GENE
Turpin—BEN
Twain—MARK
Tweed—BOSS
Ty—COBB
Tyler—JOHN
Uncle—SAM

Undset—SIGRID
Uriah—HEEP
Vallee—RUDY
Van Buren—MARTIN
Verdon—GWEN
Verdugo—ELENA
Verne—JULES
Vernon—CASTLE
Victor—BORGE,
   HERBERT, HUGO
Villa—PANCHO
Vincent—PRICE, VAN
   GOGH
Virginia—WOOLF
Vivien—LEIGH
Wallace—GEORGE,
   HENRY
Wallach—ELI
Walt—DISNEY,
   WHITMAN
Walton—IZAAK
Warren—EARL,
   HARDING
Ward—ARTEMUS
Webster—NOAH, DANIEL
Welles—ORSON, H. G.
Wharton—EDITH

White—WILLIAM ALLEN
Whiteman—PAUL
Whitman—WALT
Whitney—ELI
Wilbur—CROSS
Wilder—THORNTON
Wiley—POST
Will—ROGERS
Willa—CATHER
William—HART,
   HOLDEN, INGE,
   PENN, PITT
Williams—TED
Winterhalter—HUGO
Wolfe—TOM
Woolf—VIRGINIA
Wright—ORVILLE,
   WILBUR
Wynn—ED
Yale—ELIHU
Young—CY, ALAN,
   BRIGHAM
Yuri—GAGARIN
Zane—GREY
Zanuck—DARRYL
Zeppo—MARX
Zola—EMILE

NOBEL PRIZES

PHYSICS

Anderson	1936	Kusch	1955
Appleton	1947	Lamb	1955
Bardeen	1956	Landau	1962
Barkia	1917	Lawrence	1939
Basov	1964	Lee	1957
Becquerel	1903	Lenard	1905
Bethe	1967	Lippmann	1908
Blackett	1948	Lorentz	1902
Bloch	1952	Marconi	1909
Bohr	1922	Mayer	1963
Born	1954	Michelson	1907
Bothe	1954	Millikan	1923
Bragg, W.H.	1915	Mossbauer	1961
Bragg, W.L.	1915	Nirenberg	1968
Brattain	1956	Pauli	1945
Braun	1909	Perrin	1926
Brigman	1946	Planck	1918
Chadwick	1935	Powell	1950
Chamberlain	1959	Prochorov	1964
Cherenkov	1958	Purcell	1952
Cockcroft	1951	Rabi	1944
Compton	1927	Raman	1930
Curie, M.	1903	Rayleigh	1904
Curie, P.	1903	Richardson	1928
Dalen	1912	Roentgen	1901
Davisson	1937	Schroedinger	1933
de Broglie	1929	Schwinger	1965
Dirac	1933	Segre	1959
Einstein	1921	Shockley	1956
Fermi	1938	Siegbahn	1924
Feynman	1965	Stark	1919
Franck	1925	Stern	1943
Frank	1958	Tamm	1958
Glaser	1960	Thomson, G.P.	1937
Guillaume	1920	Thomson, J.J.	1906
Heisenberg	1932	Tomonaga	1965
Hertz	1925	Townes	1964
Hess	1936	van der Waals	1910
Hofstadter	1961	von Laue	1914
Holley	1968	Walton	1951
Jensen	1963	Wien	1911
Kamerlingh-Onnes	1913	Wigner	1963
Kastler	1966	Wilson	1927
Khorana	1968	Yang	1957

Yukawa	1949	Perutz	1962
Zeeman	1902	Porter	1967
Zernike	1953	Pregl	1923
		Ramsay	1904

CHEMISTRY

		Richards	1914
		Robinson	1947
Alder	1950	Rutherford	1908
Aston	1922	Ruzicka	1939
Arrhenius	1903	Sabatier	1912
Bergius	1931	Sanger	1958
Bosch	1931	Seaborg	1951
Butenandt	1939	Semenov	1956
Buchner	1907	Soddy	1921
Calvin	1961	Stanley	1946
Curie	1911	Staudinger	1953
Debye	1936	Sumner	1946
Diels	1950	Svedberg	1926
du Vigneaud	1955	Synge	1952
Eigen	1967	Tiselius	1948
Euler-Chelpin	1929	Todd	1957
Fischer, E.	1902	Urey	1934
Fischer, H.	1930	van't Hoff	1901
Giauque	1949	Virtanen	1945
Grignard	1912	von Baeyer	1905
Haber	1918	von Hevesy	1943
Hahn	1944	Wallach	1910
Harden	1929	Werner	1913
Haworth	1937	Wieland	1927
Heyrovsky	1959	Willstatter	1915
Hinselwood	1956	Windans	1928
Hodgkin	1964	Woodward	1965
Joliot-Curie, F.	1935	Ziegler	1963
Joliot-Curie, I.	1935	Zsigmondy	1925
Karrer	1938		
Kendrew	1962		

MEDICINE-PHYSIOLOGY

Kuhn	1938		
Langmuir	1932		
Libby	1960	Adrian	1932
Martin	1952	Alvarez	1968
McMillan	1951	Bantling	1923
Moissan	1906	Barany	1914
Mulliken	1966	Beadle	1958
Natta	1963	Bloch	1964
Nernst	1920	Bordet	1920
Norris	1967	Bovet	1957
Northrop	1946	Burnet	1960
Onsager	1968	Cajal	1906
Ostwald	1909	Carrel	1912
Pauling	1954	Chain	1945

Cori, C.F.	1947	Macleod	1923
Cori, G.T.	1947	Medawar	1960
Cournand	1956	Metchnifoff	1908
Crick	1962	Meyerhof	1922
Dale	1936	Minot	1934
Dam	1943	Moniz	1949
Doisy	1943	Monod	1965
Domagk	1939	Morgan	1933
Eccles	1963	Mueller	1948
Ehrlich	1908	Muller	1946
Eijkman	1929	Murphy	1934
Einthoven	1924	Nicolle	1928
Enders	1954	Ochoa	1959
Erlanger	1944	Pavlov	1904
Fibiger	1926	Reichstein	1950
Finsen	1903	Richards	1956
Fleming	1945	Richet	1913
Florey	1945	Robbins	1954
Forssmann	1956	Ross	1902
Gasser	1944	Rous	1966
Golgi	1906	Sherrington	1935
Granit	1967	Szent-Gyorgi	1937
Gullstrand	1911	Tatum	1958
Hartline	1967	Theiler	1951
Hench	1950	Theorell	1955
Hess	1949	von Behring	1901
Heymans	1938	von Bekesy	1961
Hill	1922	Waksman	1952
Hodgkin	1963	Wald	1967
Hopkins	1929	Warburg	1931
Houssay	1947	Watson	1962
Huggins	1966	Weller	1954
Huxley	1963	Whipple	1934
Jacob	1965	Wilkins	1962
Jauregg	1927		
Kendall	1950	LITERATURE	
Koch	1905		
Kocher	1909	Agnon	1966
Kornberg	1959	Andric	1961
Kossel	1910	Asturias	1967
Krebs	1953	Benavente	1922
Krogh	1920	Bergson	1927
Landsteiner	1930	Bjornson	1903
Laveran	1907	Buck	1938
Lederberg	1958	Bunin	1933
Lipman	1953	Camus	1957
Loewi	1936	Carducci	1906
Lwoff	1965	Churchill	1953
Lynen	1964	Deledda	1926

du Gard	1937	Undset	1928
Echegaray	1904	von Heidenstam	1916
Eliot	1948	Yeats	1923
Eucken	1908		
Faulkner	1949	**PEACE**	
France	1921		
Galsworthy	1932	Addams	1931
Gide	1947	Angell	1933
Gjellerup	1917	Arnoldson	1908
Hamsun	1920	Asser	1911
Hauptmann	1912	Bajer	1908
Hemingway	1954	Balch	1946
Hesse	1946	Beerhaert	1909
Heyse	1910	Bourgeois	1920
Jensen	1944	Branting	1921
Jimenez	1956	Briand	1926
Karlfeldt	1931	Buisson	1927
Kawabata	1968	Bunche	1950
Kipling	1907	Butler	1931
Lagerkvist	1951	Cassin	1968
Lagerlof	1909	Chamberlain	1925
Laxness	1955	Chelwood	1937
Leger	1960	Cremer	1903
Lewis	1930	Dawes	1925
Maeterlinck	1911	d'Estournelles	1909
Mann	1929	Ducommun	1902
Mauriac	1952	Dunant	1901
Mistral, F.	1904	Fried	1911
Mistral, G.	1945	Gobat	1902
Mommsen	1902	Hammerskjold	1961
O'Neill	1936	Henderson	1934
Pasternak	1958	Hull	1945
Pirandello	1934	Jouhaux	1951
Pontoppidan	1917	Kellogg	1929
Prudhomme	1901	King	1964
Quasimodo	1959	La Fontaine	1913
Reymont	1924	Lamas	1936
Rolland	1915	Lange	1921
Russell	1950	Luthuli	1959
Sachs	1967	Marshall	1953
Sartre	1964	Moneta	1907
Seferis	1963	Mott	1946
Shaw	1925	Nansen	1922
Sholokhov	1965	Noel-Baker	1959
Sienkiewicz	1905	Orr	1949
Sillanpaa	1939	Passy	1901
Spitteler	1919	Pauling	1962
Steinbeck	1962	Pearson	1957
Tagore	1913	Pire	1958

Quidde	1927	Söderblom	1930
Renault	1907	Stresemann	1926
Roosevelt	1906	von Ossietzky	1935
Root	1912	von Suttner	1905
Schweitzer	1952	Wilson	1919

RELIGIOUS TERMS

assistant—ACOLYTE,
    ALTARBOY
belief—CREED, DEISM,
    DHARMA, SECT,
    SUNNAN, TENET
book—AVESTA, BIBLE,
    KORAN, SASTRA,
    SUTRA, TRIPITAKA,
    VEDA
brotherhood—SODALITY
chief—DATTO, EMIR,
    IMAM, MAHDI, RAIS,
    SAYID
clothing—ABNET, ALB,
    AMICE, CASSOCK,
    CHASUBLE, COPE,
    COTTA, CROSIER,
    EPHOD, FEZ,
    KULAH, MANIPLE,
    MANTLE, ORALE,
    RABAT, SCAPULAR,
    SOUTANE, STOLE,
    TAJ, TIARA
council—CURIA,
    SANHEDRIN,
    SYNOD, ULEMA
devotee—FAKIR
evil spirit—ASMODEUS,
    DAEVA, DEMON,
    DEVIL, EBLIS,
    JINNI, LUCIFER,
    SATAN
fast—LENT, RAMADAN

festival—CHANUKAH,
    CHRISTMAS,
    DASAHARA,
    DEWALI, DIVALI,
    EASTER, EED, HOLI,
    PURIM
image—ICON, IKON
journey—HEGIRA,
    PILGRIMAGE
law—ADAT, CANON,
    MANUS, TALMUD,
    TORAH
minister—ABBE, BISHOP,
    CARDINAL, CURE,
    LAMA, PADRE,
    PASTOR,
    PRESBYTER, PRIEST,
    RABBI
offering—ALMS,
    DEODAND,
    OBLATION, TITHE
order—CENOBITE,
    JESUIT, MARIST,
    TEMPLAR
prayer—NAMAZ,
    NOVENA, SALAT,
    ROSARY
sacred building—
    CATHEDRAL,
    CHAPEL
    CHURCH, KAABA,
    TEMPLE
song—CHANT, PSALM

HERALDIC TERMS

Lines of Partition

ANNULET
BEND
BILLET
BORDURE
CANTON
CHEVRON
CHIEF
CROSS
FESS
FLANCHES
FUSIL
GYRON
INESCUTCHEON
LOZENGE
PALE
PALL
PILE
QUARTER
ROUNDEL
SALTIRE

Colors

ARGENT—silver
AZURE—blue
GULES—red
MURREY—dark red
OR—gold
SABLE—black
TENNE—orange
VERT—green
PURPURE—purple

Furs

ERMINE
POTENT
VAIR

Terms of Succession
(Ordinaries and Sub-
 Ordinaries)

LABEL	first son
CRESCENT	second son
MULLET	third son
MARTLET	fourth son
ANNULET	fifth son
FLEURDELIS	sixth son
ROSE	seventh son
CROSSMOLINE	eighth son
DOUBLEQUATREFOIL	ninth son

Miscellaneous Terms

BREY	barnacle
MARTLET	bird
LAVER	colter
PALY	division

WYVERN	dragon
GUTTAE	drops of seme
CANNET	duck
FLOTANT	floating
ENTE	grafted
SINISTER	left-side
SEME	sown, sprinkled
ASSIS	sitting
TREFLE	three-lobed
TIERCE	three parts
PASSANT	walking
AILE	winged
VULN	wound

CHEMICAL ELEMENTS

ACTINIUM—Ac
ALUMINUM—Al
AMERICIUM—Am
ANTIMONY—Sb
ARGON—A
ARSENIC—As
ASTATINE—At
BARIUM—Ba
BERKELIUM—Bk
BERYLLIUM—Be
BISMUTH—Bi
BORON—B
BROMINE—Br
CADMIUM—Cd
CALCIUM—Ca
CALIFORNIUM—Cf
CARBON—C
CERIUM—Ce
CESIUM—Cs
CHLORINE—Cl
CHROMIUM—Cr
COBALT—Co
COLUMBIUM—Cb
COPPER—Cu
CURIUM—Cm
DYSPROSIUM—Dy
EINSTEINIUM—E
ERBIUM—Er
EUROPIUM—Eu
FLUORINE—F
FRANCIUM—Fr
GADOLINIUM—Gd
GALLIUM—Ga
GERMANIUM—Ge
GOLD—Au
HAFNIUM—Hf
HELIUM—He
HOLMIUM—Ho
HYDROGEN—H
INDIUM—In
IODINE—I
IRIDIUM—Ir
IRON—Fe
KRYPTON—Kr

LANTHANUM—La
LAWRENCIUM—Lw
LEAD—Pb
LITHIUM—Li
LUTETIUM—Lu
MAGNESIUM—Mg
MANGANESE—Mn
MENDELEVIUM—Mv
MERCURY—Hg
MOLYBDENUM—Mo
NEODYMIUM—Nd
NEON—Ne
NEPTUNIUM—Np
NICKEL—Ni
NIOBIUM—Nb
NITROGEN—N
NOBELIUM—No
OXYGEN—O
OSMIUM—Os
PALLADIUM—Pd
PHOSPHORUS—P
PLATINUM—Pt
PLUTONIUM—Pu
POLONIUM—Po
POTASSIUM—K
PRASEODYMIUM—Pr
PROMETHIUM—Pm
PROTACTINIUM—Pa
RADIUM—Ra
RADON—Rn
RHENIUM—Re
RHODIUM—Rh
RUBIDIUM—Rb
RUTHENIUM—Ru
SAMARIUM—Sm
SCANDIUM—Sc
SELENIUM—Se
SILICON—Si
SILVER—Ag
SODIUM—Na
STRONTIUM—Sr
SULPHUR—S
TANTALUM—Ta

TECHNETIUM—Tc
TELLURIUM—Te
TERBIUM—Tb
THALLIUM—Tl
THORIUM—Th
THULIUM—Tm
TIN—Sn
TITANIUM—Ti
TUNGSTEN—W

URANIUM—U
VANADIUM—V
WOLFRAM—W
XENON—Xe
YTTERBIUM—Yb
YTTRIUM—Y
ZINC—Zn
ZIRCONIUM—Zr

PRESIDENTS OF
THE UNITED STATES
1789–1972

President	Vice-President	Party
GEORGE WASHINGTON	John Adams	
JOHN ADAMS	Thomas Jefferson	Fed.
THOMAS JEFFERSON	Aaron Burr George Clinton	Dem. Rep.
JAMES MADISON	George Clinton Elbridge Gerry	Dem. Rep.
JAMES MONROE	Daniel D. Tompkins	Dem. Rep.
JOHN QUINCY ADAMS	John C. Calhoun	Nat. Rep.
ANDREW JACKSON	Martin Van Buren	Dem.
MARTIN VAN BUREN	Richard M. Johnson	Dem.
WILLIAM HENRY HARRISON	John Tyler	Whig
JOHN TYLER		Whig
JAMES KNOX POLK	George M. Dallas	Dem.
ZACHARY TAYLOR	Millard Fillmore	Whig
MILLARD FILLMORE		Whig
FRANKLIN PIERCE	William R. King	Dem.

Opp. Candidate	Sec'y of State	Wife
	Jefferson Randolph Pickering	Martha Dandridge Custis
Thomas Jefferson	Pickering Marshall	Abigail Smith
Aaron Burr Charles Pinckney	Madison	Martha Wayles Skelton
Charles Pinckney DeWitt Clinton	Smith Monroe	Dorothea (Dolly) Todd
Rufus King John Quincy Adams	J. Q. Adams	Elizabeth Kortwright
Andrew Jackson Henry Clay William H. Crawford	Clay	Louisa Catherine Johnson
J. Q. Adams Henry Clay	Van Buren Livingston McLane Forsyth	Rachel Robards
W. H. Harrison	Forsyth	Hannah Hoes
Martin Van Buren	Daniel Webster	Anna Symmes
	Webster Upshur Calhoun	Letitia Christian Julia Gardner
Henry Clay	Calhoun Buchanan	Sarah Childress
Lewis Cass	Buchanan Clayton	Margaret Smith
	Clayton Webster Everett	Abigail Powers Caroline (Carmichael) McIntosh
Winfield Scott	March	Jane Means Appleton

JAMES BUCHANAN	John C. Breckinridge	Dem.
ABRAHAM LINCOLN	Hannibal Hamlin Andrew Johnson	Rep.
ANDREW JOHNSON		Dem.
ULYSSES S. GRANT	Schuyler Colfax Henry Wilson	Rep.
RUTHERFORD B. HAYES	William A. Wheeler	Rep.
JAMES GARFIELD	Chester A. Arthur	Rep.
CHESTER A. ARTHUR		Rep.
GROVER CLEVELAND	Thomas A. Hendricks	Dem.
BENJAMIN HARRISON	Levi P. Morton	Rep.
WILLIAM MCKINLEY	Garret A. Hobart Theodore Roosevelt	Rep.
THEODORE ROOSEVELT	Charles W. Fairbanks	Rep.
WILLIAM H. TAFT	James S. Sherman	Rep.
WOODROW WILSON	Thomas R. Marshall	Dem.
WARREN G. HARDING	Calvin Coolidge	Rep.

John C. Fremont	Marcy Cass Black	
Douglas Breckinridge Bell McClellan	Black Seward	Mary Todd
	Seward Washburn	Eliza McCardle
Horatio Seymour Horace Greeley	Washburn Fish	Julia Dent
Samuel J. Tilden	Fish Evarts	Lucy Ware Webb
Winfield S. Hancock	Evarts Blaine	Lucretia Rudolph
	Blaine Frelinghuysen	Ellen Lewis Herndon
James G. Blaine Benjamin Harrison James Weaver	Frelinghuysen Bayard Gresham Olney	Frances Folsom
Grover Cleveland	Bayard Blaine Foster	Caroline Lavinia Scott Mary Scott Dimmock
William J. Bryan	Olney Sherman Day Hay	Ida Saxton
Alton B. Parker	Hay Root Bacon	Alice Hathaway Lee Edith Kermit Carow
William J. Bryan	Bacon Knox	Helen Herron
Theodore Roosevelt	Knox Bryan	Ellen Louise Axson Edith Bolling Galt
James M. Cox	Hughes	Florence Kling DeWolfe

CALVIN COOLIDGE	Charles G. Dawes	Rep.
HERBERT HOOVER	Charles Curtis	Rep.
FRANKLIN D. ROOSEVELT	John N. Garner Henry A. Wallace Harry S. Truman	Dem.
HARRY S. TRUMAN	Alben W. Barkley	Dem.
DWIGHT D. EISENHOWER	Richard M. Nixon	Rep.
JOHN F. KENNEDY	Lyndon B. Johnson	Dem.
LYNDON B. JOHNSON	Hubert H. Humphrey	Dem.
RICHARD M. NIXON	Spiro Agnew	Rep.

John W. Davis	Hughes	**Grace** Anna Goodhue
Robert M. LaFollette	Kellogg	
Alfred E. Smith	Kellogg	**Lou** Henry
	Stimson	
Herbert Hoover	Hull	**Anna** Eleanor Roosevelt
Alfred Landon	Stettinius	
Wendell Willkie		
Thomas E. Dewey		
Thomas E. Dewey	Stettinius	Elizabeth (Bess) Wallace
J. Strom Thurmond	Byrnes	
Henry A. Wallace	Marshall	
	Acheson	
Adlai E. Stevenson	Dulles	**Mamie** Geneva Doud
Richard M. Nixon	Rusk	**Jacqueline** Lee Bouvier
Barry M. Goldwater	Rusk	**Claudia** Alta (Ladybird) Taylor
Hubert H. Humphrey	Rogers	**Thelma** Patricia Ryan

PART III: WORD FINDER

In this section you will find two, three, and four letter words listed and defined for easy reference. The words are defined in one list and arranged in a variety of ways to enable you to refer back to the defined list. The three letter words are arranged in A — — to Z — —, — A — to — Z —, and — AA to — ZZ lists, with definitions to be found in the A — — to Z — — list. Four letter words are organized into A — — A to Z — — Z, AA — — ZY — —, — AA — to — ZU —, and — — AA to — — ZZ lists, with definitions following the A — — A to Z — — Z list.

An example will help illustrate use of the word finder. Suppose, with the word "bishop" for a clue, you have A — — A. In the A — — A to Z — — Z list you will find ANBA defined as bishop. If you have AN — —, check the AA — — to ZY — — list and jot down the AN — — words. Referring to the A — — A to Z — — Z list, the AN — — words (ANAM to ANZU) can be looked up until you reach ANBA, defined as "bishop". With — NB —, do the same thing, using the — AA — to — ZU — list. Then check the words (ANBA through UNBE) against the A — — A to Z — — Z list. The same procedure is to be followed with the last two letters filled in: — — BA. Again, referral would be made to the A — — A to Z — — Z list, checking the words ABBA through YABA until ANBA with the definition "bishop" is reached.

TWO LETTER WORDS

A TO Z

AA—lava
AB—prefix: from; immortal heart (Egypt), Jewish month
AC—current
AD—notice; toward
AE—Ir. Poet, G. Russell; digraph
AH—exclamation
AI—diphthong; exclamation; sloth
AL—nickname; Indian mulberry
AM—part of "to be"
AN—article
AO—Assam tribe; personification of light
AP—prefix: to; Associated Press
AR—measure; Moab city
AS—like; since; thus; qua; coin; weight
AT—prep.: near, by
AU—with the (Fr.); gold symbol
AW—exclamation
AX—cutting tool; fell
AY—exclamation; yes vote

BA—Bachelor of Arts; bleat; soul
BB—rifle shot; chess move
BE—exist
BI—prefix: twice
BK—chess move
BO—monk (Buddhist); chief (Burma); sacred tree (Hindu)
BQ—chess move
BR—chess move
BU—coin (Jap.)
BY—pass; beside; near; with

CE—Civil Engineer; this (Fr.)
CH—digraph
CO—prefix: together

DA—yes (Russ.); prosecutor
DC—current
DD—Doctor of Divinity
DE—prefix: from; of; with
DI—prefix: away; twice
DM—music: right hand
DO—first note of scale; perform; act

EA—chief god (Babyl.), river
EC—prefix: from
ED—verb ending; nickname
EE—Electrical engineer
EF—F
EG—that is; for example
EH—exclamation
EI—diphthong
EL—L; elevated train; Syrian god
EM—M; type measure; electrical unit
EN—N; half em; suffix: made of
EO—prefix: dawn; early time
ER—stammer; Judah's son
ES—suffix: weight
ET—and; diminutive
EX—prefix: without, from; former

FA—fourth note of the scale
FB—fullback
FE—musical syllable
FF—size of shot
FI—musical note
FO—Buddha

FU—Chin. department

GA—Gold Coast Negro
GE—earth goddess
GI—Liberian tribe; enlisted
    man, U.S. Army
GO—move; leave; energy

HA—exclamation
HB—halfback
HE—man
HI—salutation; greeting
HO—listen; cry; Kol dialect
HU—Mongol; northern tribe
    in China

IA—Iowa (abbr.)
IC—suffix
ID—self; carp
IE—that is; diphthong
IF—providing; condition
IL—the (It.); prefix: not
IM—prefix: not; contraction
IN—prep.: among
IO—hawk; Inachus's
    daughter
IQ—intelligence quotient
IR—Irish ancester
IS—part of "to be"
IT—pronoun; player
IU—diphthong
IY—diphthong

JA—yes (Ger.)
JO—love; sweetheart
JU—diphthong; Chin.
    porcelain

KA—double (Egypt);
    unknown god (Hindu)
KB—chess move
KK—chess move
KO—knockout; Chin.
    porcelain
KP—kitchen police
KY—Kentucky (abbr.)

LA—sixth note of scale;
    Louisiana (abbr.)

LE—football position; article
    (Fr.)
LF—left field (baseball)
LI—Chin. coin; Chin. mile;
    Chin. correct behavior
LO—behold
LT—shavetail (abbr.);
    football position
LU—game card; nickname

MA—Master of Arts;
    mother
MD—Doctor of Medicine
ME—Middle English;
    pronoun: I; Maine
    (abbr.)
MI—third note of scale
MO—book; instant; Mossi
    lang.
MR.—title
MU—Greek M; forty;
    electronic term
MY—poss. pronoun;
    exclamation

NA—continent
NE—compass point
NO—negative
NU—Greek N; chaos
NW—compass point

OA—digraph; diphthong
OB—prefix: to; before;
    against
OD—alleged force
OE—digraph; wind
OF—prep.: about
OG—Bashan king
OH—exclamation
OK—correct; affirmation
OM—mystic sound; Hindu
    mantra
ON—prep.: along; forward;
    near to
OO—prefix: egg; bird
OR—conjunction; alternative

PA—father; N.Z. native fort
PH—digraph

PI—P, Greek; math. ratio
PS—postscript
PU—Chinese coin
PY—prefix: pus

QB—quarterback; chess
   move
QK—chess move
QQ—chess move
QR—chess move
QV—which see (abbr.)

RA—sun god (Egypt),
   second note of scale
RB—chess move
RE—regarding; football
   position, musical note
RF—right field (baseball)
RH—digraph; RH
   factor—blood substance
RI—measure; Rhode Island
   (abbr.)
RK—chess move
RN—Registered Nurse
RO—artificial language;
   right hand page
RQ—chess move
RR—chess move; railroad
   (abbr.)
RT—football position

SA—continent
SE—compass point
SH—digraph; quiet!
SI—note of scale; yes (Sp.,
   It.)
SO—thus; ever; very;
   musical note
SS—shortstop
ST—quiet; saint (abbr.);
   street (abbr.)
SU—son of RA
SW—compass point
SY—scythe

TA—pagoda; article; toe
   (Swedish)
TD—clay pipe

TE—"- - Deum," thee;
   musical note
TH—digraph; suffix
TI—note of scale; palm lily
TO—prep.: as far as
TS—digraph
TT—rifle shot size
TU—you: It., thou: Fr.
TY—suffix: quality; tens

UG—exclamation
UM—word of hesitation
UN—prefix: not; United
   Nations
UO—diphthong
UP—prep.: raise; newspaper
   service; wire service
UR—Chaldean city;
   Abraham's birthplace
US—pronoun; United States
UT—Utah (abbr.); Guido's
   note
UW—diphthong

VA—Virginia (abbr.);
   Veterans
   Administration; music:
   it proceeds
VE—Frigg's brother-in-law;
   Odin's brother
VT—Vermont (abbr.)
VU—deja—; Fr.: seen

WA—measure; Burmese
   lang., native
WE—pronoun; editorial
   and papal I
WI—with: Scot.
WO—woo; woe
WU—Chinese dialect

YA—diphthong
YE—you; yea
YO—exclamation

ZA—Tartini's B-Flat
ZO—zebra—yak hybrid
ZU—storm god

THREE LETTER WORDS

A — to Z—

ABA—Arab cloak; camel hair

ADA—fem. name

AEA—candlenut tree bark

AGA—Moslem commander; Eastern title; Turkish officer

AHA—exclamation; hidden fence

AKA—Assam language; tribesman; N. Z. vine

ALA—Alabama (abbr.); according to

AMA—chalice; Oriental maid; American Medical Association; candlenut tree

ANA—collection; prefix; track; Celtic goddess

APA—wallaba tree, Braz.

ARA—palm; Braz. parrot; screw pine; constellation; goddess of vengeance

ASA—masc. name; king of Judah

ATA—Mindanao native; flour; sweetsop

AVA—Burm. cap.; ancient; fem. name; kava; Poly. drink

AWA—milkfish; away: Scot.

ABB—yarn for warp; poorest fleece

ALB—priest's garment; vestment

ABC—rudiments; basics

AEC—Atomic Energy Commission

ARC—curved part

ADD—annex; join

AID—help; helper; succor

AND—conjunction

ABE—Lincoln; masc. nickname

ACE—air hero; expert; a-one; card

ADE—drink

AGE—ripen; era; period

AKE—forever; Maori; N.Z. tree

ALE—beer-like drink

AME—soul: Fr.

ANE—donkey; one; chem. suffix

APE—monkey; mimic; simian

ARE—part of "to be"; land measure

ASE—Peer Gynt's mother (Ibsen); enzyme, ashes

ATE—consumed; impulse to ruin; goddess of mischief

AVE—"hail"; greeting

AWE—intimidate; millwheel bucket; reverence

AXE—tool; destroy

AYE—yes (vote)

AEF—WW I—American Expeditionary Force

ALF—masc. nickname; Landon, pres. candidate

ACH—Germ. exclam.: Alas!; E. Indian timber tree

AKH—spirit of man: Egypt

ASH—tree; fire residue; pallor

AUH—exclamation

ABI—Hezekiah's mother

ACI—chem. prefix

AHI—Vedic cloud serpent

ALI—Mohammed's son; Arab name; boxer; Caliph
AMI—friend: Fr.
ANI—blackbird
API—comb. form: bee
ARI—Biblical lion
ATI—N.Z. aborigine
ACK—antiaircraft
AIK—oak: Scot.
ALK—turpentine resin
ARK—Arkansas (abbr.); boat;—of the Covenant
ASK—question; beg; seek
AUK—diving bird
AAL—Indian mulberry; red dye
AFL—American Federation of Labor; American Football League
AIL—be sick
ALL—whole; totality
AWL—shoemaker's tool
AAM—liquid measure
AIM—goal; direction; end
ARM—limb; branch; sleeve; inlet; projection
AUM—Dutch liquid measure
AIN—wellspring, Bib.; Heb. letter
ANN—fem. name
ARN—alder tree
AWN—beard of grain; arista
ABO—tribe
ADO—stir; fuss; trouble
AGO—past
AKO—Hung. liquid measure
AMO—"I love"; Lat.
ANO—tropical black bird
APO—prefix: away; P. I. volcano
ARO—Nigerian Negro
ASO—Jap. volcano; Jap. national park
AZO—nitrogen
ALP—mountain
AMP—unit of electricity

ASP—adder; snake of Cleopatra
AAR—Rhine tributary; underground river
AER—air; chalice veil
AFR—Africa (abbr.)
AIR—breath; breeze; tune; manner
AES—bronze; Rom. money
ALS—than: Ger.
ANS—town near Liege; commune
ARS—art: Lat.
ASS—donkey
AUS—out of; Arab
ABT—Ger. composer
ACT—deed; play a part; do
AET—aged: Lat.
AFT—back, toward the stern
AIT—island; islet
ALT—old: Ger.; high in pitch: music
AMT—county: Dan.
ANT—insect; emmet; formic acid source
APT—fit; proper; ready
ART—skill; trade; craft
ATT—Siam. coin
AUT—prefix: self
ABU—Ir. battle cry; Sumerian god
ACU—needle
AHU—Poly. burial place; Asian deer
AKU—Hawaiian fish
ANU—Baby. god
ARU—indeed: Ir.; South Sea island
AYU—sweetfish
AEX—duck genus
AIX—duck genus
AUX—according to
ACY—suffix: quality
ADY—length measure
ALY—pert. to malt drink
AMY—fem. name; - - - Lowell

ANY—some; - - - one;
- - - thing
ADZ—cutting tool

BAA—sheep's bleat
BOA—constrictor; python;
scarf
BRA—underwear; brassiere
(abbr.)
BSA—Boy Scouts of
America
BAB—founder of Babism
BIB—apron
BKB—chess move
BOB—haircut; Robert
(abbr.); fish line cork;
weight
BQB—chess move
BUB—boy
BAC—cistern; vat
BSC—science degree
BAD—evil; malicious; ill;
wrong
BED—bottom; base; cot
BID—offer; invite
BUD—lad; develop
BEE—insect; drone; letter B
BYE—aside; run in cricket
BAG—sack; purse; capture
BEG—plead; ask
BIG—large; enormous
BOG—marsh; swamp
BUG—insect; defect; listen
in
BAH—exclamation
BOH—Burmese chief
BOK—American editor;
Harvard president
BAL—Fr: ball; Cornish:
mine
BEL—Indian fruit; log. unit;
Baby. chief god
BUL—Canaanite month
BAM—cheat
BIM—Barbados native
BUM—hobo; tramp;
borrow; Levantine boat
BAN—forbid; interdict

BEN—masc. nickname;
mountain: Scot.
BIN—crib; Indian flute
BON—good: Fr.; kidney
bean
BUN—roll; hair knot;
chignon
BOO—hoot; scary yell
BAP—Baptist (abbr.); small
leaf
BAR—forbid; obstruct; legal
association; counter;
crosspiece
BER—jujube
BKR—chess move
BOR—neighbor
BQR—chess move
BUR—prickly seed coat
BAS—low, Fr., - - - re-
lief
BES—god to ward off evil
BIS—encore; twice
BOS—cattle genus
BUS—vehicle
BAT—club; stake; mammal;
cudgel
BET—wager
BIT—drill; mite; iota; bridle
part
BKT—chess move
BOT—kind of fly
BUT—conjunction: unless,
except, only
BAW—exclamation
BOW—Apollo's instrument;
weapon; yield; bend,
curtsey; prow
BOX—package; spar; fight;
confine; evergreen shrub
BAY—window; inlet; bark;
compartment
BEY—Turkish governor
BLY—Nellie—
BOY—lad; servant
BUY—purchase
BIZ—business (slang)
BOZ—Dickens' pseudonym

CHA—tea; --- Cha, dance
CIA—Central Intelligence Agency
CAB—taxi; Civil Aeronautics Board
COB—horse; male swan
CUB—young animal; --- scout
CCC—Civilian Conservation Corps
CAD—bounder
CID—Spanish epic
COD—fish; Cape - - -
CUD—quid; rumen
CEE—letter C
CHE—Asian shrub
CIE—business house; Fr.
CLE—suffix; diminutive
COE—Iowa college; sheep disease
CUE—hint; signal; Q; line; billiard stick
CAG—insult
CIG—cigarette
COG—gear; cockboat
CHI—Greek letter; Gold Coast tongue
CAL—wolframite; California (abbr.); pres. nickname
COL—mountain pass; Colorado (abbr.)
CUL— - - - de sac
CAM—rotating gear; come: Scot.; sliding part
COM—prefix: together
CUM—with: Lat.
CWM—cirque; geol.
CAN—tin - - -; preserve; fire; jail
CON—deceive; against
CHO—Jap. length measure
CIO—Congress of Industrial Organizations
COO—bird cry; island
CRO—murder fine: Scot.; --- Magnon

CAP—hat; cover; top; explosive
COP—policeman; catch; thicket
CUP—vessel; prize; liquid measure
CYP—tree; Trinidad
CAR—automobile; balloon basket; for: Fr.; lobster box
COR—main star of constellation; heart
CUR—mongrel dog; mutt
CES—French pronoun
CIS—prefix: on this side
COS—type of lettuce; romaine
CAT—feline animal; anchor tackle; grimalkin
CET—that: Fr.
CIT—inhabitant of a town
COT—bed
CUT—chop; carve; sever; slight; hew
CRU—vineyard: Fr.
CAW—crow's cry
COW—bovine; intimidate
COX—steersman
CAY—islet; island
COY—shy; bashful; demure
CRY—weep; call
COZ—cousin

DEA—goddess: Lat.
DHA—Burmese distance measure
DIA—prefix: across, through
DRA—distance measure
DUA—two
DAB—touch; tap; dress; flat fish
DEB—debutante (abbr.)
DIB—dibble; pool: Scot.
DUB—call; rub smooth; dress leather
DEC—prefix: ten; December (abbr.)
DOC—doctor (abbr.)
DUC—duke: Fr.

DAD—father
DID—acted
DOD—annular die; molding plate
DUD—defective bomb; clothes
DAE—do: Scot.
DEE—D; Scot. river
DIE—expire; vanish; tool
DOE—female deer; John —
DUE—owed; debt
DYE—color
DAG—Hammarskjold; antler; pistol
DEG—sprinkle; dampen
DIG—excavate; verbal thrust
DOG—canine; andiron
DUG—excavated; searched
DAH—Burmese knife
DOH—palm fiber
DEI—god
DII—gods
DUI—twosomes
DAK—mail, India
DAL—pigeon pea
DEL—Delaware (abbr.)
DAM—obstruct; wall; embankment; female parent
DEM—Democrat (abbr.)
DIM—darken; obscure
DOM—priestly title; Port. man
DUM—doom palm: Afr.; gingerbread
DAN—buoy, Eng.; masc. nickname; master, Archaic
DEN—lair: haunt; scout pack
DIN—uproar; stir; noise
DON—teacher; tutor; Sp. man; river
DUN—brown; demand payment; cure
DAO—P. I. tree
DJO—Jap. distance measure
DSO—Distinguished Service Order

DUO—twosome; pair
DAP—dibble; dip; drop a fish line; skip a stone
DIP—swim; immerse; ladle; pickpocket
DOP—gem cutting cup
DAR—Daughters of the American Revolution; oriental dwelling; Indian tree
DER—Germ. article
DOR—beetle; bumblebee; drone
DUR—C major: music
DAS—Germ. article; badger
DDS—Doctor of Dental Surgery
DES—Fr. article, preposition
DIS—prefix: apart; god of Hades, Pluto
DOS—dowry; back: Fr.
DDT—insecticide
DIT—surnamed: Fr.; poem: old Fr.
DOT—dowry; music char.; speck; point
DHU—dagger, Ir.; black: Celt; outlaw in "Lady of the Lake"
DEV—Buddhist deity
DIV—do: Scot.
DAW—kind of crow; grackle
DEW—dawn moisture
DOW—behoove: Burmese knife; lateen-rigged boat
DIX—pinochle score; Fort---
DUX—Eng. class leader; fugue theme
DAY—date; lifetime
DEY—Alger. governor; pasha
DRY—arid; plain; dull; jejune

ECA—Economic Cooperation Administration

ELA—bombast; extravagance; highest note
ENA—Alfonso's queen; last queen of Spain
ERA—epoch; time division; geol.
ESA—Economic Stability Administration
ETA—Greek E; Jap. outcast
EVA—Little --- (Uncle Tom's Cabin); fem. name
EBB—tide; recede
ELB—jujube
ETC—and so on
EED—Moslem Easter
ELD—ancient times
END—finish; aim; goal; limit
ERD—earth; plowed field
EAE—combining form in geology
EDE—Dutch commune
EKE—augment; piece out
ELE—eel: Old English
EME—crony; gossip; uncle: Scot.
ENE—compass point; chem. suffix
ERE—before
ESE—compass point; suffix
ETE—summer: Fr.
EVE—fem. name; first woman: Bible; twilight; dusk
EWE—female sheep
EXE—Devon river
EYE—view; look at; scan; organ
ELF—dwarf; fairy; pixie
EGG—germ cell; size of coal; incite; urge; ovum
ENG—E. Indian wood; Siamese twin
ERG—work unit
EDH—Anglo-Saxon letter
ETH—Anglo-Saxon letter; suffix: ordinal number

ELI—Bib. judge; high priest; teacher of Samuel
EPI—finial ornament; ear of grain: Fr.; suffix: outer skin
ERI—Bib. character; Assam silkworm; Bombyx
ELK—B.P.O.E. member; kind of leather; wapiti
EEL—conger; elver; elongated fish; lamprey
ELL—annex; wing; cloth measure
ELM—tree
EAN—beget; sire
EEN—even; level; eyes: Scot.
EIN—Germ. article
EON—time period; forever
ERN—bird of prey; eagle
EBO—Nigerian tribe; Cent. Amer. tree
EDO—taro root; Nigerian tribe
EGO—I; self; entire man
ESO—comb. form: within
ETO—WWII area: European Theatre of Operations
EXO—prefix: outer, outside
ESP—Extrasensory Perception
EAR—attention; auditory organ; stalk; front page weather box
EER—always
EIR—goddess of healing
ERR—mistake, fault
EUR—Europe (abbr.)
EES—eyes: Scot.
EIS—ice, Germ.
ELS—otherwise: Scot.
EMS—Prussian spa
ENS—being; entity
EOS—aurora; dawn
ERS—bitter vetch
ESS—S; curve
EAT—consume
ECT—combin. form: without

EFT—small lizard
ELT—knead; young pig
ENT—comb. form: within
ERT—urge: Scot.
EST—is: Fr.; Eastern
Standard Time; suffix:
superlative
EAU—water: Fr.
ECU—five franc coin; shield
EMU—Austral. bird
ELY—Eng. cathedral city
ERY—suffix: state of

FHA—Federal Housing
Administration
FLA—Florida (abbr.)
FRA—monk; brother
FIB—lie; untruth
FOB—cheat; foist; palm;
watch chain
FUB—cheat; plump child
FCC—Federal
Communications
Commission
FAD—craze; novelty
FED—nourished; gave food;
sustained
FID—supporting bar; wood
fastener
FOD—dist. measure:
Denmark
FEE—charge; cost; debit
FIE—exclamation
FOE—enemy; protagonist;
adversary
FAG—cigarette; fatigue
FIG—fruit
FOG—obscurity; mist;
vapor; daze
FUG—reek; fume
FOH—exclamation
FBI—Federal Bureau of
Investigation
FEI—Poly. banana
FUL—Sudanese person
FAN—devotee; spread out;
stimulate
FEN—bog; mire; marsh

FIN—fish part; kind of keel;
five dollar bill
FON—Dahomey Negro
FUN—amusement
FLO—fem. nickname
FOO—Chin. department
FRO—from; away
FOP—coxcomb; dandy
FAR—long; distant
FIR—tree; evergreen
FOR—because; to
FUR—pelt; coat; hair
FAS—Roman divine law
FAT—stout; obese
FIT—proper; apropos;
suitable; spell; attach
FOT—Norwegian distance
measure
FUT—Russian dist. measure
FEU—benefice; fire: Fr.
FLU—influenza (abbr.);
grippe
FOU—fool: Fr.; bushel:
Scot.
FEW—not many
FIX—mend; fasten; adjust;
difficulty
FOX—vixen; rope; naut
FAY—close to; fit; fem.
name; fairy
FEY—elfin
FLY—flit; gad; insect; tent
flap
FRY—pan cook; young fish
FEZ—Turk. headdress;
tarboosh
FIZ—hissing sound

GOA—gazelle; mugger;
Aust. tribe; Port. colony
GRA—Ir. sweetheart; love
GAB—talk; chatter; engine
hook; E. Indian
persimmon
GEB—Eg. earth god
GIB—bearing plate; crane
arm; male cat

GOB—mass; wad; sailor
GAD—exclamation; flit; mining tool; oath; Jacob's son
GED—oath
GID—sheep disease
GOD—deity; Jehovah
GEE—command to horse; G; oath
GIE—give: Scot.; present: Scot.
GUE—viol: Shetlands
GAF—Arabic letter
GAG—joke; choke; wisecrack
GEG—Albanian dialect
GIG—carriage; chaise; fish hook
GOG—ruler of Magog
GHI—Indian butter
GRI—gypsy horse
GAJ—coin
GAL—female
GEL—coagulate; harden; set
GUL—rose
GAM—leg; herd of whales; visit at sea
GEM—muffin; jewel
GUM—resin; tissue in jaw; adhesive; exudate
GYM—sports arena
GAN—Roland's destroyer
GEN—clan; hereditary factor
GIN—liquor; cotton machine; against: Scot.
GON—measure
GEO—prefix: earth; George (abbr.)
GOO—sticky substance
GAP—aperture; hiatus; hole; breach
GIP—cheat; swindle
GOP—Grand Old Party: Republican Party
GUP—gossip: India
GYP—cheat; swindle
GAR—long-nosed or needlefish

GER—alien (Heb.); convert to Judaism
GOR—Indies tribesman
GRR—growl
GUR—crude sugar
GAS—fuel; anesthetic; chatter
GES—S. American Indian
GUS—masc. nickname
GAT—channel; medium; gun
GET—Jewish divorce bill; gain; win
GIT—get; hole in casting mold
GOT—get (past tense)
GUT—intestine; passage; eviscerate
GAU—old Germ. district
GNU—antelope
GAV—gypsy village
GAW—trench: Scot:
GAY—Begger's Opera author; merry; glad
GEY—pretty
GOY—non-Jew
GRY—gypsy horse
GUY—masc. name; fellow; lad; chap; ridicule
GAZ—Persian and Indian measure; coin
GUZ—Persian and Indian measure

HEA—Baby. chief god
HIA—parrot; hawk
HOA—cry
HOB—cutting tool; fireplace side shelf; mischief
HUB—wheel center; pipe
HIC—exclamation; hiccough
HAD—possessed; owned
HID—secreted; concealed
HOD—brick carrier
HAE—have: Scot.
HIE—hurry; hasten
HOE—tool; dig; plow
HUE—shout; disturbance; color; shade

HAG—quagmire: Scot.;
  witch; shrew
HOG—pig; shoat; swine
HUG—keep close; embrace
HAH—exclamation
HEH—Chin. tribe: Miao
HOH—Indian whaler
HSH—hush
HUH—exclamation
HAI—fencer's cry
HEI—Hawaiian game
HOI—haw, as cattle;
  Hawaiian yam
HUI—Chinese assembly;
  guild
HAK—due, India
HAL—masc. nickname;
  Good King; Prince ---
HEL—goddess; Loki's
  daughter
HAM—cut of meat; radio
  buff; Shem's brother
HEM—border; confine;
  edge; hesitate
HIM—pronoun
HUM—buzz; sing; to be
  busy
HAN—Jap. barony; Chin.
  dynasty; Yangtze
  tributary
HEY—call; yell; to attract
  attention
HOY—barge

IBA—P. I. tree
IDA—fem. name; mountain;
  Asia Minor
ILA—Bantu language; labor
  union
INA—fem. suffix; fem.
  name
IRA—Biblical char.; one of
  David's rulers
ITA—Eskimo; Malay
  Negrito; labor union
IVA—herb eve; marsh elder
IWA—Hawaiian frigate bird
IYA—Oriental maid

ICC—Interstate Commerce
  Commission
IND—Indiana (abbr.); poet:
  India
ICE—chill; diamonds; frost
IDE—fish; cyprinoid; chem.
  suffix
IFE—hemp: Afr.
IKE—pres. nickname
ILE—island: Fr.; suffix:
  condition
INE—suffix: chem.; Saxon
  king
IRE—anger; wrath
ISE—Danish fjord; suffix:
  condition; verb
ITE—suffix: follower;
  adherent
IVE—suffix
ING—suffix; Anglo-Saxon
  god of peace
ICH—I: German
ISH—adjec. suffix
ITH—Irish ancestor;
  legendary Celt
ICI—here: Fr.
IHI—N. Z. fish; stitchbird
INI—suffix: order
IRI—son of Bela
ICK—fish disease
ILK—kind; class; caste;
  genus
INK—blacken; fluid;
  cuttlefish fluid
IRK—annoy; vex; rile
IAL—adjec. suffix
ILL—sick; Illinois (abbr.)
ISM—creed; belief; doctrine
IAN—masc. name; John:
  Scot., Gaelic
INN—lodge; hotel
ION—charged molecule;
  Apollo's son
IAO—honey eater bird
IBO—Nigerian tribe
IDO—artificial language
ILO—world workers group:
  International Labor
  Org.

INO—Athamas' wife;
 Cadmus' daughter
ISO—comb. form: equal
ITO—Jap. admiral; Zionist
 group
IWO— - - - Jima; Pacific Island
IYO—African bass; P. I.
 vine
IMP—urchin; rascal
IER—comparative ending
IHR—yours: Germ.
IOR—comparative ending
ICS—suffix: science of
IHS—symbol of Jesus
ILS—Fr. pronoun: they
INS—incumbents;
 International News
 Service
IOS—hawks
ITS—poss. pronoun
IST—practitioner
IMU—baking pit
IOU—statement of debt
ICY—frosty; chilled
IVY—vines; climbing plant

JAB—poke: punch
JIB—crane arm; triangular
 sail
JOB—chore; work; Biblical
 character
JOE—masc. nickname
JAG—protuberance; crying
 —; slash
JIG—dance; hop
JOG—trot; jostle; elbow
JUG—pitcher; ewer; prison;
 - jail
JAH—Jehovah
JAM—preserve; stoppage;
 fix
JIM—masc. nickname
JUM—cultivation method
JIN—demon, Oriental
JAP—Japanese; Nipponese
JAR—collide; grate; shock;
 jolt
JUR—Nilotic Negro
JUS—Fr.: gravy; Lat.: law

JAT—Punjab native
JET—plane; --- set; gush;
 spurt
JOT—note; iota; particle;
 mite
JUT—project; extend
JEU—Fr.: game
JAW—maxilla; scold; talk
JEW—Hebrew; Semite
JOW—distance measure,
 India
JAY—masc. name; blue bird
JOY—bliss; exultation;
 happiness; fem. name

KEA—large N. Z. parrot
KHA—Laotian native;
 Nepal native
KOA—Hawaiian tree
KRA—long tailed ape
KAB—Hebrew measure
KEB—Eg. earth god
KOB—African antelope
KTB—chess move
KED—Scot: sheep tick
KID—leather; rib; josh:
 youngster; tot; young
 goat
KAE—jackdaw: Scot.: serve
KEG—cask; tub; 100 lbs. of
 nails
KAJ—Poly. food: Aust.
 food; Jap. province
KOI—Jap. carp
KYI—Kandh language;
 Siamese group
KIL—Irish church
KOL—Bengal native
KYL—Himal. ibex
KIM—Kipling child hero
KAN—Dutch measure
KEN—masc. nickname;
 knowledge; Jap.
 prefecture
KIN—Chin. dynasty;
 relatives; Chin.
 instrument
KEP—Scot.: catch

KIP—bed; gym feat; undressed hide; weight
KOP—S. Afr. hill
KUP—Dutch dry measure
KTQ—chess move
KER—ghost; malignant spirit
KOR—Hebrew measure
KTR—chess move
KAS—Dutch clothespress
KOS—island
KAT—narcotic shrub
KIT—outfit; rig; small violin
KOU—Pacific tree
KRU—Liberian language and tribe
KAY—fem. nickname; K
KEY—attune; island

LEA—meadow; field; yarn measure
LIA— - - - Fail (Ir. crowning stone)
LOA—Afr. worm; eye insect
LAB—laboratory (abbr.)
LLB—Bachelor of Laws
LOB—brewers ferment; manner of hitting ball
LAC—milk: pharm.; resin; gum; 100,000 rupees
LAD—boy; tad; youth
LED—guided
LID—cover; hat
LLD—Doctor of Laws
LTD—limited (abbr. for a company)
LUD—legendary Br. king
LEE—shelter; haven; Amer. general
LIE—extend; fib; untruth; golf term
LOE—Scot: love
LUE—sift
LYE—alkaline solution
LOF—measure
LAG—linger; loiter; barrel stave
LEG—limb; part of course; cut of meat; support

LOG—fuel; diary
LUG—carry; tote; worm; Celtic god; ear
LAI—medieval tale
LEI—garland; anadem; wreath
LOI—Fr.: law
LAK—grouse's courting strut
LEK—gather
LOK—Balder's killer; god of discord
LIL—gypsy's paper; books; fem. nickname
LAM—escape; elude; loom lever
LIM—blue pine
LUM—chimney
LAN—Cornish name prefix; Swed. county
LIN—tree
LON—masc. nickname
LYN—Scot: waterfall
LAO—Indo-Chin. native and language
LEO—masc. name; constellation; pope
LOO—card game
LUO—Nilotic Negro
LWO—Nilotic Negro
LAP—circuit; fold; drink eagerly
LIP—rim; edge; impudence; cheek
LOP—chop; axe; droop; wilt
LAR—Burmese gibbon; Etruscan god
LER—Brythonic god; Celtic god
LUR—Persian native
LAS—Sp.: article
LES—Fr.: article
LIS—fairy fort; fleur de ---
LOS—Sp.: article
LYS—Fr.: lily
LAT—Buddhist pillar
LET—allowed; permitted; lease; rent; tennis term
LIT—drunk; lighted

LOT—building site; fate; share
LST—landing ship
LUT—Polish weight
LEU—Rumanian coin
LOU—fem. nickname
LEV—coin
LIV—Livonian
LAW—canon; rule; code; statute
LEW—masc. nickname; Bulg. coin
LOW—base; vile; soft; weak
LAX—loose; remiss
LEX—Rom: law
LOX—smoked salmon
LUX—unit of light
LAY—medieval poem; secular; reclined
LEY—Rumanian coin
LOY—post-hole digger; slick
LAZ—Caucasian Moslem
LIZ—fem. nickname

MAA—maw; sheep's bleat
MIA—mine: It.
MNA—mina: Greek weight
MOA—extinct bird
MYA—clam genus
MAB—fairy queen
MIB—marble
MOB—crowd; rabble
MAC—son of: Ir., Scot.
MAD—insane; angry; irate
MID—central; half-way point
MOD—fad; Scot. congress
MUD—abusive charges
MAE—fem. name
MME—fem. title of address; Madam
MOE—masc. nickname
MAG—Brit. halfpenny; bird; titmouse
MEG—feminine nickname; Alcott heroine
MIG—marble; plane
MUG—cup; face; gangster
MAH—angel

MAI—Fr.: May
MOI—Indo-Chin. tribes; Fr.: me
MAL—prefix: evil; ill; disease; low caste Hindu
MEL—masc. nickname; honey
MIL—.001 of inch; wire measure
MOL—gram molecule
MUL—Danish measure
MAM—Mayan Indians
MEM—Hebrew letter
MOM—mother
MUM—chrysanthemum; hush; quiet; madam
MAN—male; anyone; person; furnish crew; game piece
MEN—crew; gang; troops; lunar god
MIN—chief deity; Eg. god of procreation
MON—Burmese; Jap. family badge
MUN—roisterer
MAO—peacock; Chin. Communist leader
MEO—agricultural caste: India
MHO—elec. unit
MIO—Sp.: my
MOO—low; cow's sound
MAP—cartograph; chart; plan; survey
MOP—swab
MAR—damage; impair
MER—Fr.: sea
MIR—chief; Russian community
MUR—Fr.: wall
MAS—suffix: feast day
MES—pronoun: Fr.
MIS—prefix: bad; faulty; wrong
MOS—folkway
MRS.—title; feminine
MUS—mouse genus

MAT—dull color; entangle; picture border
MET—happened upon; convened
MIT—glove; Ger.: with
MOT—Fr.: word; mark of quoits; witty remark
MUT—cur; Amen's wife
MAU—measure
MEU—spicknel
MRU—Indo-Chin. native
MAW—craw; crop; gullet; opium poppy seed
MEW—cage; cat cry; enclose; feathers
MOW—cut down (esp. grass, hay)
MAX—masc. nickname
MIX—stir; mingle; blend
MAY—fem. name; hawthorn
MUY—Sp.: very

NAA—no
NEA—National Education Association
NOA—common; profane: Hawaiian
NRA—National Recovery Administration
NAB—arrest; halt; capture
NEB—Nebraska (abbr.); beak
NIB—beak; pen point
NOB—head; cribbage term; society person
NUB—pith; gist: knot
NED—masc. nickname
NID—brood; nest
NOD—beckon; drowse
NAE—Scot.: no
NEE—Fr.: born; maiden name
NIE—eyes; Germ.: never
NNE—compass point
NYE—brood; humorist
NEF—clock in form of a ship

NAG—harass; beset; horse; annoy
NIG—cut edge of coin; dress (as stone)
NOG—black (wood); egg drink
NTH—indefinite power
NAK—stigmatic point of mango
NIL—nothing
NUL—nothing
NIM—margosa tree; Eng.: steal
NOM—Fr.: name
NYM—Falstaff's follower
NAN—fem. nickname
NON—prefix: not
NUN—kind of buoy; Hebrew letter; pigeon; sister; chaos
NEO—prefix: recent, new
NOO—n w
NAP—game; doze; rest; pile
NEP—catnip; tuft; knot in fiber
NIP—check; bracer
NAR—Scot.: near
NER—relative of Saul
NOR—and not
NAS—has not
NIS—brownie; gnome; Constantine's birthplace
NOS—Fr.: our; Lat.: we
NAT—Burmese devil; Burmese sprite
NET—snare; mesh; capture; clear; fabric
NIT—insect egg
NOT—hornless; negative
NUT—crackpot; fastener; hard-shelled fruit
NGU—distance measure
NEV—Nevada (abbr.)
NEW—fresh; late; recent
NNW—compass direction
NOW—presently
NIX—gnome; nothing
NOX—goddess of night
NYX—goddess of night

NAY—denial
NEY—Fr.: marshal
NEZ—Fr.: nose

OCA—edible root; oxalis; wood sorrel
ODA—harem room
OKA—oca: Turk. weight
OLA—palm leaf
OMA—suffix: tumor
ONA—Cape Horn native
OPA—WWII agency
ORA—money
OVA—eggs
OXA—chemical prefix
ORB—encircle; eye; sphere
ORC—grampus; cetacean; whale
ODD—droll; spare; strange
OID—suffix: like
OLD—aged; passe; hoary
ORD—fort
OBE—clan division
ODE—lyric; hymn
OKE—Turk. weight
OLE—bullfight cry; palm leaf
ONE—identical; same; individual; person
OPE—unclose; unlock
ORE—crude metal; Oregon (abbr.); mineral
OSE—simple sugar; suffix: carbohydrate; full of
OTE—suffix: origin
OWE—indebted
OYE—Scot.: grandchild
OAF—boor; lout; dolt
OFF—absent; away; at a distance; erring
ORP—fish; yellow ide
OUF—exclamation
OCH—alas!
OBI—Japanese sash
OII—muttonbird
ONI—any
ORI—boundary
OVI—egg
OAK—tree; hardwood

OCK—Turk. weight
ORK—whale
OUK—Scot.: week
OIL—anoint; fuel; lard
OWL—bird
OHM—elec. unit
OLM—amphibian
OWN—possess; have
ODO—William I's half-brother
OHO—exclamation
OMO—prefix: shoulder
ONO—Biblical name
ORO—gold; mountain
OTO—prefix: ear
OOP—Scot.: bird
ORP—Scot.: weep
OAR—blade; propeller
OER—poetic: over
ORR—hockey player; novelist
OUR—possessive pronoun
OAS—Organization of American States
ODS—oath
OES—plural of O
ONS—field parts in cricket
OPS—Ceres' mother; goddess of harvest; of plenty
OSS—Office of Strategic Services
OUS—adjective suffix
OAT—avena, cereal grain; shepherd's pipe
OCT—October (abbr.); combin. form for eight
OFT—frequently
OLT—Danube tributary
OOT—Scot.: out
OPT—choose; elect
ORT—food bit; morsel; leftover
OUT—absent; at odds; on strike
ONY—any
ORY—like ore

PEA—size of coal; legume, seed
PIA—arrowroot; brain part
POA—bluegrass
PTA—Parent-Teacher Association
PUA—hemp shrub
PWA—Public Works Administration
PAB—flax refuse
POB—porridge; Post Office Box (abbr.)
PUB—tavern; bar
PAC—half-boot; moccasin
PIC—Eg. measure
PAD—cushion; tablet; animal's foot; robber
PED—basket; combining form for foot; child
POD—legume; group of seals
PUD—forefoot; hand
PIE—tart; pastry; dessert; jumble; bird
POE—Amer. poet; Edgar Allen ---; parson bird
PRE—prefix: before; ere
PUE—exclamation
PYE—engraver
PEG—fem. nickname; cribbage pin; small drink; support
PIG—ingot; pork; ham; shoat
PUG—dog; molded clay; snub nose
PAH—exclamation; N. Z. fort
POH—exclamation
PHI—Greek letter
POI—Hawaiian dish
PSI—Greek letter
PIK—dist. measure
PAL—companion; mate; crony
PIL—combining form for hair
PUL—Persian money; Assyrian king

PAM—card game
POM—small dog (Pomeranian)
PAN—combining form for all; field deity; cooking dish; tub
PEN—confine; writing instrument; jail
PIN—dowel; fastener; secure; skittle
PUN—play on words
PRO—for; expert
PWO—Indo-Chin. language
PAP—soft food; medical test
PEP—vigor; vim
PIP—apple seed; fowl disease; spot on a card
POP—explode; burst; soft drink
PUP—young seal or dog
PAR—average; norm; golf term
PER—by means of; through
PIR—Moslem holy person; saint
POR—Sp.: for
PUR—cat sound
PYR—fire; heat; light unit
PAS—dance step
PES—foot part
PUS—suppuration
PAT—stroke; apropos; fitting; tap
PET—fondle; favorite; caress; cosset
PIT—excavation; mine; seed; theatre floor
POT—poker stake; shoot; cooking vessel
PST—call to attract attention
PUT—card game; golf shot; lay
PAU—Edomite city; birthplace of Henry IX; Fr. resort
PEU—Fr.; little
PHU—Cretan spikenard
PIU—It.: more
PAW—foot; handle

PEW—bench; exclamation; fish-prong
POW—prisoner of war; exclamation
PAX—peace
PIX—church vessel; ciborium
POX—disease
PYX—church vessel; ciborium
PAY—wages; compensation; fee
PLY—fold; layer; plait; thickness; twist; practice (a trade)
PRY—gaze; examine; scan; lever; meddle
PUY—Fr.: hill
PAZ—Sp.: peace

QUA—as; like; so far as
QKB—chess move
QQB—chess move
QUE—Fr.: that
QUF—myth. mountain
QUI—Fr.: that; who
QUO—measure
QKR—chess move
QQR—chess move
QKT—chess move

REA—turmeric
RIA—creek; kill; estuary
ROA—brown kiwi
RUA—Bantu
RAB—mortar beater; Hebrew teacher
REB—Confederate soldier
RIB—costa; joke; leaf vein
RKB—chess move
ROB—steal; plunder; masc. nickname
RQB—chess move
RUB—polish; annoy
ROC—myth. bird
RAD—energy unit; Scot.: afraid
RED—color; crimson; --- river; --- sea; flushed

RID—clear; disencumber; dispose
ROD—stick; bar; gun; land measure
RUD—red-eyed carp; fish
RAE—Scot. explorer
REE—arikara; female ruff
RHE—fluidity unit
RIE—cereal grass
ROE—fish eggs; caviar; deer
RUE—herb; regret
RYE—cereal grain
RAF—Royal Air Force
REF—referee; official
RIF—measure
RAG—fog; roofing piece; shred
RIG—equip; fit; outfit
RUG—carpet; mat
RAH—cheer
REH—alkali
RAI—measure
REI—Lat.: event; Port. coin; Biblical name
RII—Venice canals
ROI—N. Z. fern; Fr.: king
RAJ—India: reign
ROK—Korean soldier
REL—elec. unit of resistance
RAM—batter; sheep; pump; constellation
RIM—edge; border; hem
ROM—gypsy
RUM—liquor
RAN—hank of twine; Aegir's wife; sea goddess
RIN—coin
RON—King Arthur's lance
RUN—train; brook; flow; operate
REO—car
RHO—Greek R; 100
RIO—coffee; river; canal
RAP—talk, discuss, knock, least bit; coin
REP—fabric (twilled or corded)
RIP—tear; lacerate; rend
RKR—chess move

RQR—chess move
RAS—cape; Eastern title; fabric
RES—Lat.: thing
ROS—Cornish prefix; rulers
RUS—Scandinavians in Russia
RAT—bandicoot; deserter; fake hair; rodent
RET—to prepare flax
RIT—scratch; split
RKT—chess move
ROT—corrode; rust; decay
RUT—groove; habit
REU—Peleg's son
REV—speed a motor
RAW—uncooked; crude; cold; naked
REW—Scot.: village
ROW—argument; fight; series; line; use oars
REX—Lat.: king
RUX—sport; worry
RAY—cowfish; skate; sunshine; masc. nickname
REY—Sp.: king
ROY—masc. name

SAA—measure
SEA—waters; ocean; expanse
SHA—wild Asian sheep; oorial
SIA—Keresan Indian
SMA—Scot.: small
SNA—Scot.: snow
SPA—mineral spring; health resort
STA—mus.: as written
SUA—Latin pronoun: hers
SEB—Eg. earth god
SIB—kindred; sister; brother
SOB—cry; wail; lament
SUB—Lat.: under; abbr.: substitute
SAC—pouch; bag; Indian; Strategic Air Command

SEC—dry; arid; Securities and Exchange Commission
SIC—Lat.: thus
SOC—Old English court district
SAD—depressed; drab; cheerless; gloomy; dull
SID—masc. nickname
SOD—sward; turf
SUD—foam
SAE—Scot.: so
SEE—observe; perceive; bishopric; eye
SHE—fem. pronoun; novel by H. R. Haggard
SIE—Germ.: you; Scot.: drip
SOE—tub; pail
SSE—compass point
STE—Fr.: Sainte
SUE—plead; entreat; take court action; fem. nickname
SYE—cutting tool; drop
SIF—Thor's wife
SAG—droop; wilt
SOG—soak
SAH—measure
SOH—exclamation; gutta mixture
SAI—monkey
SKI—snow runner
SRI—Hindu title
SUL—Chin. dynasty
SAJ—E. Indian tree
SAK—Eg. cotton
SOK—measure
SUK—Nilotic Negro
SAL—salt; E. Indian tree; fem. nickname
SEL—Fr.: salt; Scot.: self
SIL—Chin. yellow; yellow ochre
SOL—mus. note; sun god
SAM—masc. nickname; Uncle ---
SIM—masc. nickname
SUM—total; amount
SAN—Gr. letter; Bushmen

SEN—coin; measure
SIN—moon god; Scot.:
    since; err; vice; Hebrew
    letter
SON—descendant; scion;
    heir
SUN—Helios; Apollo; star;
    sol
SYN—prefix: with
SAO— - - - Paulo, Brazil
SHO—measure
SOO—river rapids; sow
SRO—box office sign:
    Standing Room Only
SAP—drain; deplete; juice;
    foolish person
SIP—taste; drink slowly;
    imbibe
SOP—bribe; soak; steep
SUP—eat; mouthful
SER—Ind. weight; It.:
    gentleman; Pers. weight
SIR—knight; term of address
SUR—comb. form: above;
    Fr.: over
SES—Fr.: his, her
SIS—girl; relative
SOS—distress signal
SSS—Selective Service
    System
SUS—pigs; swine genus
SAT—conferred; Saturday
SET—Eg. evil god; fix;
    adjust; appoint;
    established; rigid
SIT—meet; perch; pose; rest;
    confer
SOT—drunkard
SHU—son of Ra
SMU—Southern Methodist
    University, Dallas
SOU—old Fr. coin
SSU—Chin. weight
SAW—adage; maxim;
    cutting tool; observed;
    cut; blade
SEW—stitch; hem; baste;
    cinch
SOW—pig; plant; scatter

SSW—compass point
SAX—wind instrument
SEX—gender
SIX—card; number
SAY—tell; state; opinion
SEY—pollack fish
SHY—timid; bashful: avoid
SKY—heavens; firmament
SLY—foxy; shrewd; crafty;
    wily
SNY—bend; curved plank;
    knife
SOY—bean; sauce
SPY—discover; agent;
    examine
STY—enclosure; corral; eye
    inflammation

TAA—Chin. pagoda
TEA—drink; infusion
TIA—Sp.: aunt
TOA—beefwood; Samoan
    warrior
TRA—coin
TUA—tree
TVA—Tennessee Valley
    Authority
TWA—Trans World Airlines
TAB—flap; account; check;
    fastener
TUB—vessel; bath; boat;
    keg; cask
TAC—comb. form: touch
TEC—detective
TIC—spasm; jerk; twitch
TAD—urchin
TED—masc. nickname; sow;
    scatter
TOD—bush
TAE—Scot.: accept; Scot.:
    to
TEE—curling mark; golf
    term; T
THE—article
TIE—anchor; fix; moor;
    bind; cravat
TOE—digit; foot; golf club
    part; drive slantingly

TRE—Cornish prefix: town; It.: three
TUE—parson bird
TYE—nautical chain
TAG—saw; child's game; label
TEG—young sheep
TOG—dress up; preen
TUG—pull; boat
TYG—drinking vessel
TCH—exclamation
TAI—Oriental porgy; Indo-Chin. native
TJI—Dutch E. Indies weight
TOI—Fr. pronoun: you
TRI—prefix: three
TUI—dyewood tree; parson bird
TWI—prefix; two
TAJ—dervish hat
TCK—exclamation
TAL—cymbals; palm fiber
TEL—comb. form: communications; prefix: end
TIL—sesame
TOL—Sanskrit school
TAM—Scot. hat
TEM—Eg. sun god
TIM—masc. nickname
TOM—masc. nickname; male cat
TUM—card wool; Eg. sun god
TAN—make leather; color; brown
TEN—big casino; card; decade
TIN—container; metal
TON—suffix: town; weight
TUN—brewer's vat; cask
TAO—Buddhist right conduct; Chin. truth; P. I. peasant
THO—even if
TIO—Sp.: uncle
TKO—boxing term: technical knockout
TOO—also; very

TWO—card; couple; pair
TAP—faucet; spigot; dab; signal; dance; draw
TIP—cant; tilt; upset; end
TOP—crest; peak; pinnacle; better; head; foremost
TUP—mallet; pile driver ram
TAR—pitch; coal; sailor; lute
TER—threefold
TIR—Fr.: hunting match
TOR—craggy hill
TUR—aurochs; wild goat; ibex; pigeon pea
TYR—Aesir; god of Tuesday; Norse sky god
TIS—contraction: it is
TAT—gambling die; make lace; Iranian
TIT—small bird; return blow
TNT—explosive; cap
TOT—youngster; kid
TST—exclamation for quiet
TUT—exclamation
TAU—Greek T; St. Anthony's cross
TIU—Aesir; god of Tuesday
TAV—Heb. letter
TAW—tan; prepare leather; Hebrew letter
TIW—god of Tuesday; Norse sky god
TOW—draw; pull; flax fiber; hemp
TAX—assess; duty; charge; levy; impost
TEX—Texan
TUX—mens' formal wear
THY—poss. pronoun
TOY—plaything; trinket
TRY—attempt; prove; essay; court procedure
TEZ—pungent; spicy

UCA—fiddler crab
ULA—gums; diminutive
UNA—Devi, goddess of splendor
UTA—Jap. verse; lizard

UVA—grape
UND—Germ.: and
URD—East Ind. bean;
    woolly pyrol
UBE—yam
UKE—ukulele
ULE—rubber tree; caucho
    tree
UME—Jap. apricot
UNE—Fr. article
URE—Scot.: mist; suffix:
    state of being
USE—employ; consume;
    advantage; dupe
UTE—Shoshonean Indian
UVE—yam
UGH—exclamation of
    disgust or assent
USH—usher
UBI—Lat.: where; yam
UDI—N. Caucasian lang.
UII—silkworm disease
UNI—prefix: single; plainly
    woven; Juno
UPI—United Press
    International
URI—Swiss canton
UVI—yam
ULL—Aesir; Norse god, son
    of Sif
ULM—Danube city
URN—container; vase
UDO—Chin. plant; Jap.
    shoot
UFO—Unidentified Flying
    Object; flying saucer
ULO—gums; shell currency
UNO—It.: one; Sp. article
URO—S. A. Indian
UMP—referee
UNS—Germ.: us
UIT—Dutch: out
ULU—Eskimo knife
UMU—Poly. oven
URU—S. A. Indian
UTU—Maori compensation

VIA—road; path; Roman
    highway

VAC—speech goddess
VOD—Baltic Finn
VAE—alas!
VEE—five dollar bill; V;
    neckline
VIE—contend; cope; Fr.: life
VOE—inlet; bay
VIF—Fr.: lively
VAG—vagabond; hobo
VOG—weight
VUG—rock cavity; geode
VAI—Liberian native
VEI—Liberian native
VOL—stamp battery block
VIM—vigor; energy
VAN—forefront; bow;
    moving truck
VIN—Fr.: wine
VON—Germ. title
VIP—Very Important
    Person; notable
VIR—Lat.: man
VAS—anat.: duct; Lat.:
    pledge
VIS—force; Lat.: power,
    vigor
VAT—cistern; container
VET—veteran; veterinarian
VOT—Finn in Ingria
VAU—Hebrew letter
VOW—promise; pledge
VEX—annoy; harass
VOX—Lat.: voice
VIZ—namely

WEA—Algonquin Indian
WPA—Works Progress
    Administration
WEB—ensnare; net;
    network; gossamer;
    membrane
WAC—Woman's Army
    Corps
WAD—lump; clod; node;
    gob; black ochre
WED—marry; unite; join
WEE—minute; tiny
WOE—calamity; disaster;
    sorrow

WYE—Y; track
WAG—joker; wit; flap; sway
WIG—toupee; rat; fall
WAH—panda bear
WEI—Chin. dynasty
WAN—ashen; ashy; pale
WEN—cyst; shin growth;
    Old English rune
    (WYN)
WIN—acquire; gain
WON—conquered
WUN—Burmese governor
WYN—Old English rune
WHO—rel. pronoun; World
    Health Organization
WOO—court; pursue
WYO—abbr.: Wyoming
WAP—blow; rap
WAR—strife; battle
WAS—existed; past tense of
    to be; Burmese native
WIS—imagine; think; abbr.
    Wisconsin
WAT—hare; Siam. temple
WET—damp; moist; dank;
    anti-Prohibitionist
WIT—humorist; joker
WAW—Arabic letter
WNW—compass point
WOW—exclamation of
    surprise and/or
    appreciation
WSW—compass point
WAX—grow; increase;
    polish; shine
WAY—course; road; route;
    means; manner;
WEY—unit of weight
WHY—exclamation; reason;
    puzzle
WRY—askew; awry

XER—prefix: dry
XAT—totem pole

YEA—yes (as in voting)
YAH—exclamation
YOI—hunting cry;
    exclamation

YAK—long-haired ox
YOK—Anglo-Saxon G
YAM—edible root; sweet
    potato; batata
YOM—Hebrew day
YEN—coin; desire
YIN—Chin. negative
    principle; Shang dynasty
YON—far; remote; over
    there
YUN—Laos tribal native
YAO—Chin. aborigine;
    Chin. ruler
YAP—bark; bay; chatter;
    prate
YEP—affirmative answer,
    slang
YIP—bark; squeal
YAR—growl; snarl
YES—affirmative
YET—though; but; besides
YOU—pronoun
YAW—steering term; pitch
    and ---; deviate; err
YEW—coniferous tree
YOW—exclamation; yelp
YEZ—you

ZEA—maize genus; Indian
    corn
ZOA—Blake's symbolic
    figure
ZAC—Caucasian ibex
ZED—French Z
ZEE—Z; Dutch inlet
ZOE—fem. name
ZIF—Jewish month
ZAG—jagged line; zig - - -
ZIG—jagged line; - - - zag
ZOH—zebu-yak hybrid
ZAK—measure
ZAL—Rustum's father
ZEL—cymbal, Oriental
ZAN—Zeus
ZEN—Buddhist sect
ZIO—Norse sky god
ZOO—menagerie; collection
    of animals
ZEP—airship; zeppelin

ZIP—energy; vigor; bullet
    sound
ZAR—measure
ZER—measure

ZAT—slate trimming tool
ZIY—Norse sky god
ZAX—slate trimming tool

THREE LETTER WORDS --A-- --Z--

BAA	MAE	SAI	EAN	DAR	SAT
MAA	NAE	TAI	FAN	EAR	TAT
NAA	RAE	VAI	GAN	FAR	VAT
TAA	SAE	GAJ	HAN	GAR	WAT
BAB	TAE	RAJ	IAN	JAR	UAT
CAB	VAE	SAJ	KAN	LAR	ZAT
DAB	GAF	TAJ	LAN	MAR	EAU
GAB	KAF	DAK	MAN	NAR	GAU
JAB	OAF	HAK	NAN	OAR	MAU
KAB	QAF	LAK	PAN	PAR	PAU
LAB	GAB	NAK	RAN	SAR	TAU
MAB	CAG	OAK	SAN	TAR	VAU
NAB	DAG	SAK	TAN	WAR	GAV
PAB	FAG	YAK	VAN	YAR	TAV
RAB	GAG	ZAK	WAN	ZAR	BAW
TAB	HAG	BAL	ZAN	BAS	CAW
BAC	JAG	CAL	DAO	DAS	DAW
FAC	LAG	DAL	GAO	FAS	FAW
LAC	MAG	GAL	HAO	GAS	GAW
MAC	NAG	HAL	IAO	HAS	HAW
PAC	RAG	IAL	LAO	KAS	JAW
SAC	SAG	MAL	MAO	LAS	LAW
TAC	TAG	PAL	SAO	MAS	MAW
VAC	VAG	SAL	TAO	NAS	NAW
WAC	WAG	TAL	YAO	OAS	PAW
ZAC	ZAG	ZAL	BAP	PAS	RAW
BAD	BAH	AAM	CAP	RAS	SAW
CAD	DAH	BAM	DAP	VAS	TAW
DAD	HAH	CAM	GAP	WAS	WAW
FAD	JAH	DAM	HAP	BAT	YAW
GAD	MAH	GAM	JAP	CAT	LAX
HAD	PAH	HAM	LAP	EAT	MAX
LAD	RAH	JAM	MAP	FAT	PAX
MAD	SAH	LAM	NAP	GAT	SAX
PAD	VAH	MAM	PAP	HAT	TAX
RAD	WAH	PAM	RAP	JAT	WAX
SAD	YAH	RAM	SAP	KAT	ZAX
TAD	HAI	SAM	TAP	LAT	BAY
WAD	KAI	TAM	WAP	MAT	CAY
DAE	LAI	YAM	YAP	NAT	DAY
EAE	MAI	BAN	AAR	OAT	FAY
HAE	PAI	CAN	BAR	PAT	GAY
KAE	RAI	DAN	CAR	RAT	HAY

JAY	TCK	ZEA	PEG	NEO	LET
KAY	ECO	DEB	REG	REO	MET
LAY	ICS	GEB	SEG	YEO	NET
MAY	ACT	KEB	TEG	HEP	PET
NAY	OCT	NEB	VEG	KEP	RET
PAY	ACU	REB	HEH	NEP	SET
RAY	ECU	SEB	REH	PEP	VET
SAY	CCV	WEB	DEI	REP	WET
WAY	DCV	AEC	FEI	YEP	YET
GAZ	CCX	DEC	HEI	ZEP	FEU
LAZ	ACY	SEC	LEI	AER	HEU
PAZ	ICY	TEC	REI	BER	LEU
		BED	VEI	DER	MEU
ABA	ADA	EED	WEI	EER	PEU
IBA	IDA	FED	LEK	GER	DEV
ABB	ODA	GED	BEL	HER	LEV
EBB	ADD	KED	DEL	IER	NEV
ABC	ODD	LED	EEL	KER	REV
ABE	ADE	NED	GEL	LER	DEW
OBE	EDE	PED	HEL	MER	FEW
UBE	IDE	RED	MEL	NER	HEW
ABI	ODE	SED	PEL	OER	JEW
FBI	EDH	TED	REL	PER	LEW
UBI	UDI	WED	SEL	SER	MEW
ABO	ADO	ZED	TEL	TER	NEW
EBO	EDO	BEE	ZEL	VER	PEW
IBO	IDO	CEE	DEM	WER	REW
ABT	ODO	DEE	GEM	XER	SEW
ABU	UDO	FEE	HEM	ZER	YEW
	DDS	GEE	JEM	AES	AEX
ECA	ODS	LEE	MEM	BES	HEX
OCA	DDT	NEE	SEM	CES	LEX
UCA	CDV	PEE	TEM	DES	REX
CCC	CDX	REE	DEN	EES	SEX
DCC	ADY	SEE	EEN	FES	TEX
FCC	ADZ	TEE	FEN	GES	VEX
ICC		VEE	GEN	LES	BEY
MCC	AEA	WEE	HEN	MES	DEY
ACE	DEA	ZEE	KEN	OES	FEY
ICE	HEA	AEF	MEN	PES	GEY
ACH	KEA	KEF	PEN	RES	HEY
ICH	LEA	NEF	SEN	SES	KEY
OCH	NEA	REF	TEN	YES	LEY
TCH	PEA	BEG	WEN	AET	NEY
ACI	REA	DEG	YEN	BET	REY
ICI	SEA	GEG	ZEN	CET	SEY
ACK	TEA	KEG	GEO	GET	WEY
ICK	WEA	LEG	LEO	JET	FEZ
OCK	YEA	MEG	MEO	KET	GEZ

NEZ	PHU	NIE	NIM	SIR	VIZ
TEZ	SHU	PIE	RIM	TIR	
YEZ	SHY	RIE	SIM	VIR	TJI
	THY	SIE	TIM	BIS	UJI
MFA	WHY	TIE	VIM	CIS	DJO
IFE		VIE	AIN	DIS	
OFF	CIA	RIF	BIN	EIS	AKA
AFL	DIA	SIF	DIN	HIS	OKA
UFO	HIA	VIF	EIN	LIS	BKB
AFR	LIA	ZIF	FIN	MIS	OKB
AFT	MIA	BIG	GIN	NIS	RKB
EFT	PIA	CIG	HIN	SIS	AKE
OFT	RIA	DIG	JIN	TIS	EKE
AGA	SIA	FIG	KIN	VIS	IKE
AGE	TIA	GIG	LIN	WIS	OKE
EGG	VIA	JIG	MIN	AIT	UKE
UGH	BIB	MIG	PIN	BIT	AKH
AGO	DIB	NIG	RIN	CIT	SKI
EGO	FIB	PIG	SIN	DIT	AKO
NGU	GIB	RIG	TIN	FIT	TKO
	JIB	WIG	VIN	GIT	BKR
AHA	MIB	ZIG	WIN	HIT	QKR
CHA	NIB	CII	YIN	KIT	RKR
DHA	RIB	DII	ZIN	LIT	BKT
FHA	SIB	LII	CIO	MIT	QKT
KHA	HIC	MII	MIO	NIT	RKT
SHA	PIC	OII	RIO	PIT	AKU
THA	SIC	RII	TIO	RIT	AKY
CHE	TIC	VII	ZIO	SIT	
RHE	AID	AIK	DIP	TIT	ALA
SHE	BID	PIK	GIP	UIT	ELA
THE	CID	AIL	HIP	WIT	FLA
AHI	DID	KIL	KIP	PIU	ILA
CHI	FID	LIL	LIP	TIU	OLA
GHI	GID	MIL	NIP	ZIU	ULA
IHI	HID	NIL	PIP	CIV	ALB
PHI	KID	OIL	RIP	DIV	ELB
OHM	LID	PIL	SIP	LIV	LLB
CHO	MID	SIL	TIP	TIW	ELD
MHO	NID	TIL	VIP	AIX	LLD
OHO	OID	AIM	YIP	DIX	OLD
RHO	RID	BIM	ZIP	FIX	ALB
SHO	SID	DIM	AIR	MIX	CLE
THO	CIE	GIM	DIR	NIX	ELE
WHO	DIE	HIM	EIR	PIX	ILE
IHR	FIE	JIM	FIR	SIX	OLE
IHS	GIE	KIM	HIR	BIZ	ULE
AHU	HIE	LIM	MIR	FIZ	ALF
DHU	LIE	MIM	PIR	LIZ	ELF
					ALI

ELI	AMT	ONY	FOE	HOL	LOP
ALK	EMU	SNY	HOE	KOL	MOP
ELK	IMU		JOE	MOL	OOP
ALL	SMU	BOA	LOE	POL	POP
ELL	UMU	GOA	MOE	SOL	SOP
ILL	CMV	HOA	POE	TOL	TOP
ULL	AMY	IOA	ROE	VOL	BOR
ELM		KOA	SOE	COM	COR
OLM	ANA	LOA	TOE	DOM	DOR
ULM	INA	MOA	VOE	MOM	FOR
ALN	MNA	NOA	WOE	NOM	GOR
FLO	ONA	POA	HOF	POM	HOR
ILO	SNA	ROA	LOF	ROM	IOR
ULO	UNA	SOA	BOG	TOM	KOR
ALP	AND	TOA	COG	YOM	MOR
ALS	END	ZOA	DOG	BON	NOR
ELS	IND	BOB	FOG	CON	POR
ILS	UND	COB	GOG	DON	TOR
ALT	ANE	FOB	HOG	EON	COS
ELT	ENE	GOB	JOG	FON	DOS
OLT	INE	HOB	LOG	GON	EOS
FLU	NNE	JOB	NOG	ION	IOS
ULU	ONE	KOB	SOG	LON	KOS
CLV	UNE	LOB	TOG	MON	LOS
ALY	ENG	MOB	VOG	NON	MOS
BLY	ING	NOB	ZOG	PON	NOS
ELY	ANI	POB	BOH	RON	ROS
FLY	INI	ROB	DOH	SON	SOS
PLY	ONI	SOB	FOH	TON	BOT
SLY	UNI	DOC	HOH	VON	COT
	INK	ROC	POH	WON	DOT
AMA	ANN	SOC	SOH	YON	FOT
IMA	INN	COD	ZOH	BOO	GOT
OMA	ANO	DOD	GOI	COO	HOT
SMA	INO	FOD	HOI	FOO	JOT
UMA	UNO	GOD	KOI	GOO	LOT
AME	ANS	HOD	LOI	LOO	MOT
EME	ENS	JOD	MOI	MOO	NOT
MME	INS	LOD	POI	NOO	OOT
UME	ONS	MOD	ROI	SOO	POT
AMI	UNS	NOD	TOI	TOO	ROT
IMI	ANT	POD	YOI	WOO	SOT
AMO	ENT	ROD	BOK	ZOO	TOT
OMO	TNT	SOD	LOK	BOP	VOT
AMP	ANU	TOD	ROK	COP	YOT
IMP	GNU	VOD	SOK	FOP	FOU
UMP	NNW	YOD	YOK	GOP	IOU
EMS	WNW	COE	COL	HOP	KOU
HMS	ANY	DOE	GOL	KOP	LOU

SOU	OPS	KRK	ISH	ATT	PUG
YOU	PPS	ORK	USH	ITU	TUG
SOV	APT	ARM	PSI	UTU	VUG
BOW	OPT	ARN	ASK	STY	AUH
COW	SPY	ERN	ISM		HUH
DOW		URN	ASO	DUA	DUI
HOW	BQB	ARO	DSO	KUA	HUI
JOW	QQB	CRO	ESO	PUA	KUI
LOW	RQB	FRO	ISO	QUA	QUI
MOW	BQR	ORO	ASP	RUA	SUI
NOW	QQR	PRO	ESP	SUA	TUI
POW	RQR	SRO	ASS	TUA	AUK
ROW		URO	ESS	BUB	OUK
SOW	ARA	ORP	OSS	CUB	SUK
TOW	BRA	GRR	SSS	DUB	BUL
VOW	DRA	ORR	EST	FUB	CUL
WOW	ERA	ARS	IST	HUB	FUL
YOW	FRA	ERS	LST	NUB	GUL
BOX	GRA	IRS	PST	PUB	MUL
COX	IRA	MRS	TST	RUB	NUL
FOX	KRA	ART	SSU	SUB	PUL
HOX	NRA	ERT	SSW	TUB	AUM
LOX	ORA	ORT	WSW	DUC	BUM
NOX	TRA	ARU		BUD	CUM
POX	ARC	CRU	ATA	CUD	DUM
VOX	ORC	KRU	ETA	DUD	GUM
BOY	ERD	MRU	ITA	LUD	HUM
COY	ORD	URU	PTA	MUD	JUM
GOY	URD	CRY	STA	PUD	LUM
HOY	ARE	DRY	UTA	RUD	MUM
JOY	ERE	ERY	KTB	SUD	RUM
LOY	IRE	FRY	ETC	CUE	SUM
ROY	ORE	GRY	LTD	DUE	TUM
SOY	PRE	ORY	ATE	GUE	BUN
TOY	TRE	PRY	ETE	HUE	DUN
BOZ	URE	TRY	ITE	LUE	FUN
COZ	ORF	WRY	OTE	PUE	GUN
GOZ	ERG		STE	QUE	HUN
POZ	ARI	ASA	UTE	RUE	MUN
	ERI	ESA	ETH	SUE	NUN
APA	GRI	BSC	ITH	TUE	PUN
SPA	IRI	ASE	NTH	OUF	RUN
WPA	KRI	ESE	ATI	BUG	SUN
APE	ORI	ISE	ETO	DUG	TUN
OPE	SIR	OSE	ITO	FUG	WUN
API	TRI	SSE	KTO	HUG	YUN
EPI	URI	USE	OTO	JUG	DUO
UPI	ARK	ASH	KTR	LUG	LUO
APO	IRK	HSH	ITS	MUG	PUO

QUO	AUS	AUX	OVE	OXA	WYE
CUP	BUS	DUX	UVE	AXE	TYG
GUP	GUS	LUX	OVI	EXE	HYL
HUP	JUS	RUX	UVI	EXO	KYL
KUP	MUS	TUX	IVY	CXV	GYM
PUP	OUS	BUY		DXV	NYM
SUP	PUS	GUY	AWA	LXX	LYN
TUP	RUS	MUY	IWA		SYN
SUQ	SUS	PUY	PWA	AYA	WYN
BUR	AUT	BUZ	TWA	IYA	IYO
CUR	BUT	GUZ	AWE	MYA	OYO
DUR	CUT	HUZ	EWE	PYA	WYO
EUR	FUT		OWE	AYE	CYP
FUR	GUT	AVA	TWI	BYE	GYP
GUR	HUT	EVA	AWL	DYE	PYR
HUR	JUT	IVA	OWL	EYE	TYR
JUR	LUT	OVA	CWM	LYE	LYS
LUR	MUT	TVA	AWN	NYE	TYT
MUR	NUT	UVA	OWN	OYE	AYU
OUR	OUT	MVD	IWO	PYE	NYX
PUR	PUT	AVE	LWO	RYE	PYX
SUR	RUT	EVE	TWO	SYE	
TUR	TUT	IVE		TYE	AZO

ORD	DAE	NAE	UKE	DUG	WAG
PAD	DEE	NEE	ULE	EGG	WIG
PED	DIE	NIE	UME	ENG	ZAG
POD	DOE	NNE	UNE	ERG	ZIG
PUD	DUE	NYE	URE	FAG	
RAD	DYE	OBE	USE	FIG	ACH
RED	EAE	ODE	UTE	FOG	AKH
RID	EDE	OKE	UVE	FUG	ASH
ROD	EKE	OLE	VAE	GAG	AUH
RUD	ELE	ONE	VEE	GEG	BAH
SAD	EME	OPE	VIE	GIG	BOH
SED	ENE	ORE	VOE	GOG	DAH
SID	ERE	OSE	WEE	HAG	DOH
SOD	ESE	OTE	WOE	HOG	EDH
SUD	ETE	OVE	WYE	HUG	ETH
TAD	EVE	OWE	ZEE	ING	FOH
TED	EWE	OYE		JAG	HAH
TOD	EXE	PEE	AEF	JIG	HEH
UND	EYE	PIE	ALF	JOG	HOH
URD	FEE	POE	ELF	JUG	HSH
VOD	FIE	PRE	GAF	KEG	HUH
WAD	FOE	PUE	HOF	LAG	ICH
WED	GEE	PYE	KAF	LEG	ISH
ZED	GIE	QUE	KEF	LOG	ITH
	GUE	RAE	LOF	LUG	JAH
ABE	HAE	REE	NEF	MAG	MAH
ACE	HIE	RHE	OAF	MEG	NTH
ADE	HOE	RIE	OFF	MIG	OCH
AGE	HUE	ROE	ORF	MUG	PAH
AKE	ICE	RUE	OUF	NAG	POH
ALE	IDE	RYE	QAF	NIG	RAH
AME	IFE	SAE	REF	NOG	REH
ANE	IKE	SEE	RIF	PEG	SAH
APE	ILE	SHE	SIF	PIG	SOH
ARE	INE	SIE	VIF	PUG	TCH
ASE	IRE	SOE	ZIF	RAG	UGH
ATE	ISE	SSE		RIG	USH
AVE	ITE	STE	BAG	RUG	WAH
AWE	IVE	SUE	BEG	SAG	YAH
AXE	JOE	SYE	BIG	SOG	ZOH
AYE	KAE	TAE	BOG	TAG	
BEE	LEE	TEE	BUG	TEG	ABI
BYE	LIE	THE	CAG	TOG	ACI
CEE	LOE	TIE	CIG	TUG	AHI
CHE	LUE	TOE	COG	TYG	ALI
CIE	LYE	TRE	DAG	VAG	AMI
CLE	MAE	TUE	DEG	VEG	ANI
COE	MME	TYE	DIG	VOG	API
CUE	MOE	UBE	DOG	VUG	ARI

THREE LETTER WORDS -- A to -- Z

ABA	IOA	SEA	DUB	SOB	BUD
ADA	IRA	SHA	EBB	SUB	CAD
AEA	ITA	SIA	ELB	TAB	CID
AGA	IVA	SMA	FIB	TUB	COD
AHA	IWA	SNA	FOB	WEB	CUD
AKA	IYA	SOA	FUB		DAD
ALA	KEA	SPA	GAB		DID
AMA	KHA	STA	GEB	ABC	DOD
ANA	KOA	SUA	GIB	AEC	DUD
APA	KRA	TAA	GOB	ARC	EED
ARA	KUA	TEA	HOB	BAC	ELD
ASA	LEA	TIA	HUB	BSC	END
ATA	LIA	TOA	JAB	CCC	ERD
AVA	LOA	TRA	JIB	DEC	FAD
AWA	MAA	TUA	JOB	DOC	FED
BAA	MFA	TVA	KAB	DUC	FID
BOA	MIA	TWO	KEB	ETC	FOD
BRA	MNA	UCA	KOB	FAC	GAD
CHA	MOA	ULA	KTB	FCC	GED
CIA	MYA	UMA	LAB	HIC	GID
DEA	NAA	UNA	LLB	ICC	GOD
DHA	NEA	UTA	LOB	LAC	HAD
DIA	NOA	UVA	MAB	MAC	HID
DRA	NRA	VIA	MIB	ORC	HOD
DUA	OCA	WEA	MOB	PAC	IND
ECA	ODA	WPA	NAB	PIC	KED
ELA	OKA	YEA	NEB	ROC	KID
ERA	OLA	ZEA	NIB	SAC	LAD
ESA	OMA		NOB	SEC	LED
ETA	ONA		NUB	SIC	LID
EVA	ORA	ABB	ORB	SOC	LLD
FHA	OVA	ALB	PAB	TAC	LTD
FLA	OXA	BAB	POB	TEC	LUD
FRA	PEA	BIB	PUB	TIC	MAD
GOA	PIA	BKB	QKB	VAC	MID
GRA	POA	BOB	QOB	WAC	MOD
HEA	PTA	BQB	RAB	ZAC	MUD
HIA	PUA	BUB	REB		MVD
HOA	PWA	CAB	RIB	ADD	NED
IBA	QUA	COB	RKB	AID	NID
IDA	REA	CUB	ROB	AND	NOD
ILA	RIA	DAB	RUB	BAD	ODD
IMA	ROA	DEB	SEB	BED	OID
INA	RUA	DIB	SIB	BID	OLD

ATI	SKI	OAK	PAL	KIM	DON
CHI	SRI	OCK	PEL	LAM	DUN
CMI	SUI	ORK	PIL	LIM	EAN
COI	TAI	OUK	POL	LUM	EEN
CRI	TJI	PIK	PUL	MAM	EIN
CUI	TOI	ROK	REL	MEM	EON
CVI	TRI	SAK	SAL	MIM	ERN
DEI	TUI	SOK	SEL	MOM	FAN
DIL	TWI	SUK	SIL	MUM	FEN
DUI	UBI	TCK	SOL	NIM	FIN
ELI	UDI	YAK	TAL	NOM	FON
EPI	UJI	YOK	TEL	NYM	FUN
ERI	UNI	ZAK	TIL	OHM	GAN
FBI	UPI		TOL	OLM	GEN
FEI	URI	AFL	ULL	PAM	GIN
GHI	UVI	AIL	VOL	POM	GON
GOI	VAI	ALL	ZAL	RAM	GUN
GRI	VEI	AWL	ZEL	RIM	HAN
HAI	WEI	BAL		ROM	HEN
HEI	XII	BEL	AIM	RUM	HIN
HOI	XLI	BUL	ARM	SAM	HUN
HUI	XVI	CAL	AUM	SEM	IAN
ICI	YOI	COL	BAM	SIM	INN
IHI		CUL	BIM	SUM	ION
INI	GAJ	DAL	BUM	TAM	JIN
IRI	RAJ	DEL	CAM	TEM	KAN
KAI	SAJ	EEL	COM	TIM	KEN
KOI	TAJ	ELL	CUM	TOM	KIN
KRI		FUL	CWM	TUM	LAN
KUI	ACK	GAL	DAM	ULM	LIN
LAI	AIK	GEL	DEM	VIM	LON
LEI	ALK	GUL	DIM	YAM	LYN
LOI	ARK	HAL	DOM	YOM	MAN
MAI	ASK	HEL	DUM		MEN
MOI	AUK	IAL	ELM	AIN	MIN
OII	BOK	ILL	GAM	ALN	MON
OMI	DAK	KIL	GEM	ANN	MUN
ONI	ELK	KOL	GIM	ARN	NAN
ORI	HAK	KYL	GUM	AWN	NON
OVI	ICK	LIL	GYM	BAN	NUN
PHI	ILK	MAL	HAM	BEN	OWN
POI	INK	MEL	HEM	BIN	PAN
PSI	IRK	MIL	HIM	BON	PEN
QUI	KRK	MOL	HUM	BUN	PIN
RAI	KTK	MUL	ISM	CAN	PON
REI	LAK	NIL	JAM	CON	PUN
RII	LEK	NUL	JEM	DAN	RAN
ROI	LOK	OIL	JIM	DEN	RIN
SAI	NAK	OWL	JUM	DIN	RON

RUN	EBO	TAO	LOP	DAR	POR
SAN	ECO	THO	MAP	DER	PUR
SEN	EDO	TIO	MOP	DIR	PYR
SIN	EGO	TKO	NAP	DOR	QKR
SON	ESO	TOO	NEP	DUR	QQR
SUN	ETO	TWO	NIP	EAR	RKR
SYN	EXO	UDO	OOP	EER	RQR
TAN	FLO	UFO	ORP	EIR	SAR
TEN	FOO	ULO	PAP	EUR	SER
TIN	FRO	UNO	PEP	FAR	SIR
TON	GEO	URO	PIP	FIR	SUR
TUN	GOO	WHO	POP	FOR	TAR
URN	HAO	WOO	PUP	FUR	TER
VAN	IAO	WYO	RAP	GAR	TIR
VIN	IBO	YAO	REP	GER	TOR
VON	IDO	ZIO	RIP	GOR	TUR
WAN	ILO	ZOO	SAP	GRR	TYR
WEN	INO		SIP	GUR	VIR
WIN	ISO	ALP	SOP	HAR	WAR
WON	ITO	AMP	SUP	HER	XER
WUN	IWO	ASP	TAP	HIR	YAR
WYN	IYO	BAP	TIP	HOR	ZAR
YEN	LAO	BOP	TOP	HUR	ZER
YIN	LEO	CAP	TUP	IER	
YON	LOO	COP	UMP	IHR	ABS
YUN	LUO	CUP	VIP	IOR	AES
ZAN	LWO	CYP	WAP	JAR	ALS
ZEN	MAO	DAP	YAP	JUR	ANS
ZIN	MEO	DIP	YEP	KER	ARS
	MHO	ESP	YIP	KOR	ASS
ABO	MIO	FOP	ZEP	KTR	AUS
ADO	MOO	GAP	ZIP	LAR	BAS
AGO	NEO	GIP		LER	BES
AKO	NOO	GOP	KTQ	LUR	BIS
AMO	ODO	GUP	SUQ	MAR	BOS
ANO	OHO	GYP		MER	BUS
APO	OMO	HAP	AAR	MIR	CES
ARO	ORO	HEP	AER	MOR	CIS
ASO	OTO	HIP	AFR	MUR	COS
AZO	PRO	HOP	AIR	NAR	DAS
BOO	PUO	HUP	BAR	NER	DDS
CHO	QUO	IMP	BER	NOR	DES
CIO	REO	JAP	BKR	OAR	DIS
COO	RHO	KEP	BOR	OER	DOS
CRO	RIO	KIP	BQR	ORR	EES
DAO	SAO	KOP	BUR	OUR	EIS
DJO	SHO	KUP	CAR	PAR	ELS
DSO	SOO	LAP	COR	PER	EMS
DUO	SRO	LIP	CUR	PIR	ENS

EOS	SES	GAT	RET	LEU	DOW
ERS	SIS	GET	RIT	LOU	FEW
ESS	SOS	GIT	RKT	MAU	GAW
FAS	SSS	GOT	ROT	MEU	HAW
GAS	SUS	GUT	RUT	MRU	HEW
GES	TIS	HAT	SAT	NGU	HOW
GUS	UNS	HIT	SET	PAU	JAW
HAS	VAS	HOT	SIT	PEU	JEW
HIS	VIS	HUT	SOT	PHU	JOW
HMS	WAS	IST	TAT	PIU	LAW
ICS	WIS	JAT	TIT	REU	LEW
IHS	YES	JET	TNT	SHU	LOW
ILS		JOT	TOT	SMU	MAW
INS	ABT	JUT	TST	SOU	MEW
IOS	ACT	KAT	TUT	SSU	MOW
IRS	AET	KET	UIT	TAU	NAW
ITS	AFT	KIT	VAT	TIU	NEW
JUS	AIT	LAT	VET	ULU	NNW
KAS	ALT	LET	VOT	UMU	NOW
KOS	AMT	LIT	WAT	URU	PAW
LAS	ANT	LOT	WET	UTU	PEW
LES	APT	LST	WIT	VAU	POW
LIS	ART	LUT	YET	YOU	RAW
LOS	ATT	MAT	YOT	ZIU	REW
LYS	AUT	MET	ZAT		ROW
MAS	BAT	MIT		CCV	SAW
MES	BET	MOT	ABU	CDV	SEW
MIS	BIT	MUT	ACU	CIV	SOW
MOS	BKT	NAT	AHU	CLV	SSW
MRS	BOT	NET	AKU	CMV	TAW
MUS	BUT	NIT	ANU	CXV	TIW
NAS	CAT	NOT	ARU	DCV	TOW
NIS	CET	NUT	AYU	DEV	VOW
NOS	CIT	OAT	CRU	DIV	WAW
OAS	COT	OCT	DHU	DXV	WNW
ODS	CUT	OFT	EAU	GAV	WOW
OES	DDT	OLT	ECU	LEV	WSW
ONS	DIT	OOT	EMU	LIV	YAW
OPS	DOT	OPT	FEU	NEV	YEW
OSS	EAT	ORT	FLU	REV	YOW
OUS	EFT	OUT	FOU	SOV	
PAS	ELT	PAT	GAU	TAV	AEX
PES	ENT	PET	GNU		AIX
PPS	ERT	PIT	HEU	BAW	AUX
PUS	EST	POT	IMU	BOW	BOX
RAS	FAT	PST	IOU	CAW	CCX
RES	FIT	PUT	ITU	COW	CDX
ROS	FOT	QKT	KOU	DAW	COX
RUS	FUT	RAT	KRU	DEW	DIX

DUX	ERY	WRY
FIX	FAY	
FOX	FEY	ADZ
HEX	FLY	BIZ
HOX	FRY	BOZ
LAX	GAY	BUZ
LEX	GEY	COZ
LOX	GOY	FEZ
LUX	GRY	FIZ
LXX	GUY	GAZ
MAX	HAY	GEZ
MIX	HEY	GOZ
NIX	HOY	GUZ
NOX	ICY	HUZ
NYX	IVY	LAZ
PAX	JAY	LIZ
PIX	JOY	NEZ
POX	KAY	PAZ
PYX	KEY	POZ
REX	LAY	TEZ
RUX	LEY	VIZ
SAX	LOY	YEZ
SEX	MAY	
SIX	MUY	
TAX	NAY	
TEX	NEY	
TUX	ONY	
VEX	ORY	
VOX	PAY	
WAX	PLY	
ZAX	PRY	
	PUY	
ACY	RAY	
ADY	REY	
ALY	ROY	
AMY	SAY	
ANY	SEY	
BAY	SHY	
BEY	SKY	
BLY	SLY	
BOY	SOY	
BUY	SPY	
CAY	STY	
COY	THY	
CRY	TOY	
DAY	TRY	
DEY	WAY	
DRY	WEY	
ELY	WHY	

FOUR LETTER WORDS

A — — A to Z — — Z

ABBA—bishop's title; father
ABIA—biblical name; Samuel's son
ABRA—mouth of canyon
ACCA—fabric
ACTA—deeds; proceedings
ADDA—skink; god
AERA—age
AETA—Luzon native
AFRA—fem. name
AGHA—Moslem commander
AGLA—acrostic
AGRA—Indian carpet, comb. form
AGUA—Sp.: water; toad
AIDA—opera; Verdi heroine
AIRA—grass genus
AKHA—Kaw: Burmese
AKIA—Hawaiian shrub
AKKA—pygmy
AKRA—vetch; Gold Coast tribe
AKUA—Poly. deity
ALBA—medieval lyric poem; brain matter
ALCA—auk
ALDA—Sp.: hamlet; soprano
ALEA—Athena
ALFA—grass
ALGA—sea plant
ALIA—Lat.: other
ALLA—according to
ALMA—dancing girl; fabric; fem. name
ALTA—Lat.: high
ALVA—Sp. duke

ALYA—star
AMBA—mountain
AMIA—bowfin
AMLA—tanning tree
AMMA—abbess
AMRA—plum
ANBA—bishop
ANDA—Brazil tree
ANNA—coin; fem. name
ANOA—Celebes ox
ANSA—handle
ANTA—nut; pier; porch
APIA—Samoan port
AQUA—water; green-blue
ARBA—vehicle
ARCA—alms box
AREA—district; zone; region
ARIA—tune; melody
ARNA—buffalo
AROA—Venezuela copper center
ARPA—It.: harp
ARRA—exclamation
ARTA—Ionian gulf
ARYA—Indo-European
ASEA—at sea; muddled
ASHA—tribe
ASIA—East; Orient; continent
ASTA—measure; fictional dog
ATMA—Hindu soul
ATTA—flour; meal; sweetsop; Luzon native
ATUA—Poly. deity
AUCA—Indian
AULA—hall
AURA—distinctive air

AUSA—Sp. commune
AZHA—star
ABIB—Jewish month
ADIB—star
AGIB—dervish
AHAB—Biblical king; ship's captain
ARAB—urchin; horse; Semite
ALEC—masc. nickname; anchovy sauce
AMIC—pert. to amide
AVEC—Fr.: with
ABED—resting
ACID—sour; tart
ADAD—exclamation; coarse fiber
AGED—old
ALOD—estate
AMID—among
APOD—footless
ARAD—flower
ARID—dry; sec
ARND—Ger. theologian
AULD—Scot.: old
AVID—eager; greedy
AARE—river
ABBE—Fr. priest
ABIE—masc. nickname; ----'s Irish Rose
ABLE—capable; fit
ACHE—hurt; pain
ACLE—Asiatic tree
ACME—peak; culmination; apex
ACNE—skin disease
ACRE—measure of land; city
ADZE—cutting tool
AGEE—askew; awry; crooked
AGUE—fever
AIDE—helper
AINE—eldest; Fr.: senior
AIRE—Ir. nobleman
AJEE—awry
AKEE—tree
ALAE—wing-like part
ALBE—album
ALEE—away from weather;
to shelter
ALLE—auk
ALME—dancing girl
ALOE—Afr. plant; drug
ALTE—Ger.: old
AMIE—Fr.: friend
ANCE—suffix
ANDE—Indian tribe
ANGE—Fr.: angel
ANNE—fem. name; Eng. queen
ANTE—stake; prefix: before
A-ONE—excellent
APSE—church part; bishop's throne
ARME—Fr.: weapon
ARNE—Eng. composer
ASSE—fox; caama
ATLE—salt tree
AUDE—river
AUGE—Ger. priestess
AUNE—measure
AXLE—spindle
ALEF—Heb. letter
ALIF—Arab. letter
ATEF—crown of Osiris
AZOF—arm of Black Sea
AGAG—Bib. king
AGOG—eager; excited
AJOG—jogging
AREG—deserts; shifting sands
ACTH—medicine; hormone
ADAH—fem. name; Esau's wife
AICH—yellow alloy
ALPH—river in "Kubla Khan"
AMAH—Oriental nurse
ANKH—cross
ARAH—exclamation
ARCH—chief; support
AYAH—nurse
AANI—ape; dog-faced
ABRI—dugout
ABSI—tribe
ADMI—Afr. gazelle
AERI—prefix: air
AGNI—Lat.: lamb; fire god
AGRI—Lat.: fields

AIPI—cassava
ALAI—Turk. regiment; jai
—; mountain
ALBI—flagellants
ALII—royal chief (Hawaii)
AMBI—prefix: both
AMLI—tanning tree
AMMI—herb genus
AMOI—Fr.: mine
ANAI—termite
ANDI—Caucasian language
ANNI—Lat.: years
ANTI—prefix: opposed;
Indian
APII—starchy plant
ARNI—buffalo; India
ARUI—Afr. sheep
ASCI—spore sacs
ASSI—holly
ASTI—It. wine
ATLI—Gudrun's husband;
Attila
ATRI—It. town
AURI—prefix: ear
ADAK—Aleut. island
AMOK—berserk; frenzy
ANAK—Bibl. giants
ASAK—Asiatic tree
ASOK—Asiatic tree
ATIK—star
ABEL—Adam's son; Cain's
brother
ACYL—acid part
AGAL—Headband cord
AKAL—god
AMIL—vine; yellow dye
plant
AMYL—starch
ANAL—pert. to anus
ANIL—indigo dye
AOUL—Nepalese
ARAL—Russ. sea
ARIL—seed covering
AVAL—grandparental
AWOL—absent without
leave
AXAL—from pole to pole
AXIL—leaf angle
AZUL—Sp.: blue
ADAM—masc. name; first

man
AHEM—interjection for
attention
AHOM—Indo-Chin.
language
AHUM—humming sound
AKIM—Gold Coast tribe
ALEM—fruit shrub
ALIM—Moslem teacher
ALUM—astringent; styptic
ANAM—sumac tree
ARAM—Bibl. region; Eng.
murderer
ARUM—plant genus
ASEM—gold-silver alloy
ATOM—monad; particle
ATUM—Eg. sun god
AZAM—Pers. title
ACON—Fr.: boat; scow
ADAN—Moslem prayer call
ADEN—comb. form: gland;
country
AEON—age; era
AGON—argument; hassle
AKAN—Gold Coast tribe
AKIN—related
ALAN—dog; masc. name
ALEN—Danish measure
ALIN—measure
AMEN—so be it; solemn
assent; Eg. god
AMIN—ammonia
compound
AMON—Eg. god
AMUN—Eg. god
ANAN—interjection; tree
ANON—now, soon, after a
while
ARAN—Bibl. name
ASIN—Hindu month
ATEN—solar disk
ATON—solar disk
AVON—Shakespeare home;
river
AWAN—tribe
AXON—nerve cell process
AYIN—Heb. letter
AZAN—Moslem prayer call
AZON—radio guided bomb
ABOO—battle cry

ACTO—Sp.: legal action
AERO—airplane
AGAO—Hamitic language
AGIO—exchange premium; fee
AGRO—prefix: soil
AINO—Jap. aborigine
ALBO—prefix: white
ALCO—tropical dog
ALLO—prefix: reversal
ALSO—besides; too
ALTO—voice range
AMBO—pulpit
AMMO—abbr.: ammunition
ANGO—tumeric
ANNO—Lat.: year; —— Domini
APIO—plant
AREO—prefix: Mars
ARGO—Jason's ship: constellation
ARNO—cartoonist; river
AROO—indeed
ARTO—prefix: bread
ASNO—Sp.: donkey; ass
ATEO—Poly. god
ATMO—prefix: vapor; steam
AUTO—prefix: self
AAUP—American Association of University Professors
ALOP—awry; askew
APAP—Eg. month
ASOP—wet; moist
ATAP—palm
ATIP—on tiptoe
ATOP—over; above; at the apex
ABIR—Indian red powder
ACER—maple genus
ACOR—acidity
ADAR—Jew. month
ADER—Bibl. name
ADOR—spelt
AFAR—far off; distant; Hamite
AGAR—agalloch wood
AGER—dyeing apparatus; enclosed field

AHIR—caste
AJAR—slightly open
ALAR—pert. to axilla; winglike
ALUR—East African people
AMAR—measure
AMER—Fr.: bitter
AMIR—prince
AMOR—Fr.: love
ANER—Bibl. name; city
APAR—armadillo
APER—mimic
ARAR—sandarac tree
ASAR—glacial ridge
ASER—Jacob's son
ASKR—Norse Adam
ASOR—lyre
ASUR—war god
ATAR—flower extract; perfume
AUER—Hung. violinist
AVAR—Caucasian language
AVER—affirm; assert
AZUR—Cote d'——; Riviera site
ABAS—Fr.: down; low
ABCS—basics; first principles
ACIS—Galatea's beloved
ACTS—book of Bible
ACUS—Lat.: pin
ADES—Hades
AGIS—Spartan king
AIRS—pretensions
ALAS—cry of despair
ALMS—charity
ALPS—mountains
ALYS—fem. name; Alice
AMES—Amer. author; city
AMOS—masc. name; shepherd prophet
ANAS—duck
ANES—once
ANIS—fennel
ANUS—end of alimentary canal
APIS—honey bee genus; sacred Eg. bull
APUS—constellation
ARAS—river

ARES—Zeus' eldest son; Eri's brother; Gr. god of war
ARIS—edge of molding
ARMS—weapons; limbs
ARTS—sciences; skills
ATES—sweetsop
ATIS—monkshood
AVES—Lat.: birds
AVIS—Lat.: bird
AVUS—Lat.: grandfather
AXIS—central line; alliance; deer
AYES—yes votes
ABET—aid; assist
ABOT—Mishnah section
ABUT—border on; touch
ACHT—Ger.: eight
ADAT—E. Indies law
ADIT—entrance
AHET—Eg. season
AINT—contraction
ALIT—dismounted; descended
ANAT—abbr.: scientific study; Assyr. sky god
ANET—dill herb
APET—maternity goddess
ARNT—contraction
AUNT—parent's sister; relative
AALU—Eg. abode of dead
AARU—Eg. abode of dead
ABOU—Arab. father
ACLU—American Civil Liberties Union
ACTU—Lat.: act
ADDU—god of storm
AGAU—Hamitic language
AINU—Jap. aborigine
AMMU—abbr.: ammunition
ANSU—Korean apricot
ANZU—Korean apricot
APSU—Babylon. chaos
ATMU—sun god
ATTU—Aleut. island
AULU—tree
AUSU—tree
AUZU—tree
AKOV—measure

AZOV—arm of Black Sea
ALOW—naut.: below
ANEW—afresh; over again
AROW—in a line
AVOW—promise; declare
ABOX—naut.: braced
AJAX—Gr. hero
ALIX—fem. name
AMEX—American Expeditionary Force
ANAX—Castor or Pollux
APEX—zenith; top; summit
ABBY—fem. nickname
ABLY—skillfully
ACHY—painful
ADDY—fem. nickname
ADRY—thirsty
AERY—eagle's nest; ethereal
AFFY—betroth
AHEY—exclamation
AHOY—naut. exclamation; ship ----
AIRY—bright; light
AKEY—weight
ALAY—marble
ALGY—masc. nickname
ALKY—alcohol
ALLY—confederate; friend
ANAY—Guat. fruit
ANCY—noun sufixx
ANDY—masc. nickname
ARMY—force; men at arms
ARTY—artistic
ASHY—gray; pale; wan
ATRY—kept bow on sea
AWAY—absent; gone; far; off
AWRY—askew, distorted
AGAZ—Indian
AHAZ—king of Judah

BABA—nurse; cake; title
BAGA—turnip
BAKA—evil spirit
BALA—geol. epoch
BANA—giant; titan
BARA—measure
BATA—child; servant
BAYA—weaverbird
BEGA—measure

BEJA—Hamite
BEKA—weight
BELA—jasmine; Benjamin's
    first born; king
BEMA—part of chancel
BENA—vetiver; grass
BERA—king of Sodom
BESA—god
BETA—Greek B; two
BIGA—two-horse chariot
BIJA—tree
BINA—Hindu guitar
BISA—antelope
BIWA—loquat tree
BIXA—shrub genus
BL'AA—sound of disgust;
    ridicule
BOBA—chicken snake
BOCA—Sp.: harbor entrance
BOGA—fish
BOLA—ball-rope missile
BOMA—Afr. stockade
BONA—Lat.: good
BORA—Adriatic wind
BOSA—Arab drink
BOTA—measure
BOZA—Arab drink
BREA—mineral tar
BUBA—tropical disease
BUDA—It. millet
BUNA—synthetic rubber
BURA—Asian windstorm
BADB—Ir. goddess
BARB—fish; sharp point;
    pigeon
BIBB—mast; support
BLAB—talk; tattle
BLEB—blister
BLOB—drop; mass; daub
BLUB—swell
BODB—Ir. goddess
BOMB—shell; explosive
BOOB—simpleton; fool
BRAB—palymra palm
BROB—spike
BULB—corm; tuber; bud
BANC—Fr.: bench
BLOC—political union
BOSC—autumn pear
BALD—bare; hairless

BAND—group; crew;
    orchestra; sash
BARD—armor; poet
BAUD—telegraphic speed
    unit
BEAD—bauble; drop
BEID—star
BEND—arch; curve; turn
BIND—cohere; join; tie
BIOD—life force
BIRD—avian; fowl
BLED—past tense of bleed
BOLD—brave; valiant;
    daring
BOND—money certificate;
    union; tie; captivity
BORD—mining road
BRAD—fastener; nail
BRED—brought up; raised
BUND—embankment;
    Ger.: league
BYRD—Amer. explorer
BABE—baby
BADE—invited; commanded
BAKE—dry cooking; biscuit
BALE—bundle; pack; woe;
    harm
BANE—harm; damage;
    curse
BARE—naked; exposed
BASE—bottom; diamond
    corner; dishonorable;
    low
BATE—diminish; lessen
BAVE—silk; Fr.: froth
BEDE—Adam ----; monk
    wild hog
BENE—It.: well; Lat.: well;
BETE—Fr.: beast; ---- noire
BICE—blue; green
BIDE—dwell; live; wait
BIKE—bicycle
BILE—choler
BINE—plant shoot
BISE—cold wind
BITE—chew; gnaw; cut;
    sting
BIZE—cold wind
BLAE—livid
BLUE—color; ocean; sky;

sad
BOCE—colored fish
BODE—augur; portend
BOLE—clay; tree trunk
BONE—cram; study
BORE—dullard; pierce; hole
BOSE—test ground
BRAE—hillside; slope
BRIE—cheese
BUBE—W. African tribe
BURE—coarse cloth
BYEE—measure
BYRE—court house
BAFF—stroke
BEEF—meat; cow; steer
BIFF—blow
BUFF—rub to polish; tan;
    beige
BANG—beat; slam
BENG—Gypsy devil
BERG—ice mass; floe
BING—sharp sound
BONG—bell sound
BORG—Dan. borough
BRAG—boast
BRIG—sailing ship; jail
BUNG—plug; cork
BURG—borough
BACH—composer
BASH—smash
BATH—tub; resort
BETH—fem. nickname;
    Heb. letter
BIKH—poison
BINH—weight
BISH—poison
BLAH—nonsense
BOOH—exclamation
BOSH—nonsense
BOTH—two
BRUH—macaque Indian
BUKH—prate
BUSH—shrub
BABI—Pers. sect
BAHI—fortune
BALI—island
BANI—coins
BARI—hut; It. city
BELI—legendary Brit. king
BENI—sesame

BIBI—lady, India
BINI—Nigerian
BITI—blackwood
BNAI— ---- B'rith (Jewish
    organization)
BOII—Celtic tribe
BONI—Fr. Guiana
    tribesman
BORI—soprano
BUBI—W. Afr. tribe
BUGI—Celebes, Malayan
BURI—tree
BACK—help; aid; hind;
    rear; posterior
BALK—pitcher's false move;
    stop; hesitate
BANK—bench; flock of
    swans; deposit
BARK—peel; rind; skin
BASK—luxuriate; sunbathe
BEAK—bill; neb
BECK—nod; bow; summons
BILK—cheat; gyp
BISK—prison
BOCK—beer; leather
BONK—money
BOOK—tome; volume
BOSK—thicket
BOWK—steep in lime
BUCK—male deer; dollar
BUKK—prate
BULK—mass; wad
BUNK—nonsense
BUSK—beat about
BAAL—deity
BAIL—dip out; security;
    bond
BALL—game; sphere; dance
BAUL—Bengal singer
BAWL—cry
BEAL—river mouth
BELL—kind of buoy; gong;
    Amer. inventor
BHEL—quince
BHIL—Indian people
BILL—beak; debt; masc.
    nickname; poster
BIRL—spin; floating log
BOIL—bubble; agitate; heat
BOLL—plant pod

BOOL—curved handle
BOWL—dish
BUAL—wine
BUHL—inlaid decoration
BULL—papal letter; male cow
BURL—knot in wood
BALM—soothe; oil
BARM—brewer's yeast
BAUM—Am. author; Oz creator
BEAM—timber; bar; smile
BERM—canal bank; ledge
BOOM—spar; explosive sound
BRAM—masc. nickname
BRIM—edge; rim
BROM— ---- Bones (Ichabod Crane's rival)
BAIN—Fr.: bath
BARN—bin; silo; storage place
BAWN—Ir.: white
BEAN—legume; pea; head
BEEN—snake charmer's clarinet; participle
BEHN—tree
BERN—Swiss capital
BIEN—Fr.: well
BINN—box; case; chest
BION—physiological individual
BIRN—clarinet socket
BONN—Germ. city; Beethoven's birthplace
BOON—benefit; avail
BORN—nee; birthed
BRAN—legendary Brit. king; chaff
BREN—gun
BRIN—fan's stick; silk filament
BUNN—small cake
BURN—be on fire; exhaust; waste
BAGO—Asiatic shrub
BAHO—prayer stick
BARO—Gypsy: great; big; prefix: atmospheric pressure

BENO—palm liquor
BILO—Balkan ridged area
BINO—palm liquor
BITO—Afr. shrub
BOBO—owala tree
BODO—Indo. Chin. language
BOGO—tree; Hamite
BOHO—grass
BOJO—grass
BOKO—evil spirit
BOLO—knife
BORO—spring rice; Peruvian Indian
BOTO— ---- Voto, Indian
BOZO—fellow
BRIO—con ----, with spirit
BROO—Scot.: broth
BUBO—eagle owl
BUFO—toad genus
BUTO—Eg. serpent goddess
BUYO—betel leaf
BYGO—pass by
BIAS—diagonal; prejudice; slant
BIOS—life
BLAS—"Gil ---," Le Sage novel
BOIS—Fr.: wood
BORS—finder of Holy Grail
BOSS—employer; stud
BRAS—Fr.: arm
BUSS—kiss; smack
BAFT—astern
BAHT—Siam. money
BAIT—lure; badger
BALT—Lithuanian; Lett
BANT—diet
BART—masc. nickname
BAST—woody fiber; phloem
BATT—cotton batting
BEAT—throb; strike; defeat
BEET—vegetable
BELT—band; strip; strike
BENT—inclination; curved
BERT—masc. nickname
BEST—most excellent
BHAT—minstral
BHUT—ghost
BITT—naut. fastener

BKKT—chess move
BLAT—calf's cry
BLET—fruit decay
BLOT—stain; erase
BLUT—Ger.: blood
BOAT—to go by ship
BOLT—shaft; arrow; rifle part; flight
BOOT—shoe; recruit
BORT—diamond fragments; Round Table Knight
BOTT—clay plug; larva of fly
BOUT—contest
BQKT—chess move
BRAT—child
BRIT—herring
BRUT—dry wine; legendary Brit. king
BULT—hill
BUNT—ball (to hit); wheat disease
BUST—statue; bosom; break; destroy
BUTT—cask; hinge; ram; target
BABU—Hindu gentlemen
BAJU—malay jacket
BAKU—carpet; hat; tree
BALU—Sumatra wildcat
BARU—tree
BEAU—lover; boyfriend
BENU—sacred bird
BLEU—Fr.: blue
BLEW—stormed
BLOW—stroke; disaster; move air
BOUW—measure
BREW—plot; concoct; drink
BROW—forehead
BABY—infant
BEVY—flock; brood
BHOY—rowdy
BODY—group; anatomy; structure
BOGY—spectre
BONY—skeletal
BOXY—like a box
BRAY—donkey's sound
BREY—barnacle

BUOY—channel marker; float
BURY—inter
BUSY—active
BUXY—paymaster
BAEZ—Joan ----, singer
BATZ—coin
BOAZ—Ruth's husband
BUZZ—hum; fly near

CACA—Rom. giant
CAJA—Sp.: funds
CANA—Galilee town; site of first miracle
CAPA—Sp.: cloak
CARA—It.: dear
CASA—Sp.: house
CATA—prefix: down
CAVA—pepper shrub; vein
CAZA—Turk. district
CEBA—tree
CELA—Fr.: that
CENA—Last Supper picture
CEPA—onion
CERA—wax
CHAA—tea
CHIA—salvia
CIMA—It.: mountain peak
CIVA—Hindu fire god
COCA—leaf to chew; cocaine source
CODA—musical close; finale
COJA—Moslem teacher
COLA—tree; drink
COMA—torpor; state of unconsciousness
COPA—landmark; tree
CORA—gazelle; fem. name; goddess; Indian
COTA—P. I. fort
COXA—hip
CREA—linen
CUBA—measure; W. I. Island
CUCA—cocaine source
CUNA—Panama Indian
CURA—Sp.: priest
CUYA—timber tree
CYMA—molding

CHAB—woodpecker
CHIB—tongue; language
CHOB—broken spike of grain
CHUB—fish
CLUB—cudgel; stick; organization
COBB—Am. humorist; Am. baseball star
COMB—crest; rake
CRAB—crustacean; apple; complain
CRIB—manger; creche; pony; trot
CURB—rein; restrain; sidewalk edge
CHIC—stylish
CIRC—circle
CRIC—lamp condensing ring
CROC—harquebus support
CAID—fort commander
CARD—comb wool; pasteboard
CHAD—lake; country; masc. nickname
CHUD—Mongol
CLAD—dressed
CLOD—boor; lout; lump
COED—girl student
COLD—gelid; icy; chill
COND—direct ship's steering
CORD—cubic measure; string; ribbed fabric
CURD—coagulated milk
CADE—cask; juniper; pet
CAFE—restaurant
CAGE—confine; pen
CAKE—harden; confection
CALE—Gypsy
CAME—arrived; window lead; Braz. Indian
CANE—sugar ----; stem; stick
CAPE—cloak; headland; mantle
CARE—anxiety; caution; heed
CASE—box; chest; problem; legal action
CATE—tidbit
CAVE—cavern; grotto
CEDE—yield; grant
CENE—comb. form: recent
CEPE—edible fungus
CERE—wax; beak part
CETE—whale
CHEE—weight
CINE—Sp.: movie
CISE—dice term: six
CITE—quote; summon
CIVE—onionlike plant
CLEE—bird
CLOE—fem. name
CLUE—hint; guide
CODE—body of law; signal system
COKE—coal remains; popular beverage
COLE—cabbage; ---- Porter, composer
COME—arrive
CONE—geometric solid; ice cream ----; strobile
COPE—contend; canopy; priestly garment
CORE—center; heart
COSE—friendly chat
COTE—Fr.: coast; bird house
COVE—bay; inlet
CUZE—friendly chat
CREE—Indian
CUBE—square solid
CUKE—cucumber
CURE—Fr.: priest; heal; preserve
CUTE—cunning; foxy; attractive
CYKE—cyclorama
CYME—flower cluster: gold
CALF—young bovine; lower leg
CHEF—cook
CLEF—music character
COIF—hairdressing
CUFF—blow; manacle; end of sleeve
CANG—wooden collar

CHUG—explosive sound
CLOG—impede; stop; choke off; dance
COAG—dowel
CRAG—cliff; promontory
CRIG—blow
CAPH—Hebr. letter
CASH—money
CHIH—Chin. measure
COBH—port in Cork County
COSH—snug; comfortable; moth term
CUSH—money; Ethiopia; Ham's son
CADI—judge
CAXI—snapper (fish)
CAZI—Moslem judge
CHAI—gypsy girl
COLI—intestinal bacterium
CONI—Nobel winners
CUBI—measure
CALK—fill seams; make watertight
CARK—care; trouble
CASK—barrel; keg
CAUK—tenon
CAWK—rook's cry
CHEK—Chin. fort
COAK—dowel; wooden pin; tenon
COCK—bird; male fowl; hay pile
CONK—decay; nose; stop; hit
COOK—chef; prepare food
CORK—plug; stopper; tree bark; Ir. county
CUSK—fish
CALL—shout; beckon; summon; visit
CARL—masc. name; peasant; yeoman
CAUL—basket; covering membrane
CEIL—line; overlay
CELL—cubicle; unit
CHIL—kite
CHOL—Asian plain
CIEL—Fr.: sky

CIRL—bunting bird
COAL—ember; fuel
COEL—cuckoo
COIL—curl; twist; rope
COOL—calm; chill
COWL—monk's hood; shawl
CRAL—hut
CULL—pick out; glean
CURL—lock of hair; coil
CAAM—loom; heddles
CALM—unmoved; cool; quiet
CHAM—bite; morsel; Alban. dialect
CHUM—pal; buddy
CLAM—mollusk
CLEM—fight; starve
CLIM—archer in Eng. ballad
CLYM—archer in Eng. ballad
COOM—coal dust
CORM—tuber; bulb
CRAM—press; study
CROM—Irish idol
CULM—coal refuse; grass stem
CAEN—city
CAIN—Gaelic tribute; slayer of Abel
CARN—stone heap
CERN—decide
CHAN—caravansary; resthouse
CHEN—snow goose genus
CHIN—lower jaw; dynasty
CHUN—Chin. pottery
CION—descendant; graft; plant shoot
CLAN—tribe; folk; race; family
COAN—pert. to Cos Island
COIN—money; invent (as in "---- a phrase")
CONN—direct steering of boat; abbr.: Connecticut
COON—possum
CORN—kernel; grain; ear; banality
COYN—cornerstone

CRIN—fine silk
CYAN—green-blue
CACO—bandit
CALO—Gypsy
CANO—Sp.: canal
CARO—It.: dear
CASO—Dodecanese Island
CATO—Roman statesman
CAYO—Sp. reef
CERO—mackeral-like fish
CETO—prefix: cetacean
   (whale)
CIPO—liana
CITO—It.: quickly
CLEO—Cleopatra (Queen of
   Egypt)
CLIO—Muse of history
COCO—palm; nut
CODO—measure
COHO—silver salmon
COMO—It. lake
COSO—Sp.: open space
COTO—medicinal bark
COYO—avocado
CALP—limestone
CAMP—tents; military base
CAPP—Al ----, Amer.
   cartoonist (L'il Abner)
CARP—cavil; complain; fish
CAUP—Scot.: tribute
CHAP—fellow
CHIP—golf shot; fragment
CHOP—cut of meat; crack;
   jaw
CLAP—applaud; thunder
   sound
CLIP—clasp; fastener; shear;
   gait
CLOP—hobble
COOP—confine; pen
COUP—blow; stroke; cut;
   ---- d'etat
CROP—harvest; trim
CUSP—crescent moon's
   point
CINQ—Fr.: five
CARR—Scot.: pool
CHAR—burn; scorch; brook
   trout
CHER—Fr.: dear

CHIR—pine; pheasant
CHOR—Gypsy thief
COIR—coconut fiber
CUIR—dorado; Fr.: leather
CURR—museum
CZAR—dictator; ruler, esp.
   in Russia
CATS— ---- cradle, child's
   string game
CENS—payment to owner
CESS—tax
CITS—citizens
COOS—Indian
COSS—dist. measure
COUS—cowlike
CRIS—dagger
CRUS—leg-like part
CUSS—swear; curse
CANT—change direction;
   contraction; jargon
CART—two-wheeled vehicle
CAST—throw; pitch; toss;
   actors
CELT—Irish; Scotch; Welsh
CENT—coin; penny
CEST—belt; sash
CHAT—talk; bird
CHIT—child; girl; voucher
CHUT—nonsense
CIST—box; chest
CLOT—coagulate; mass
COAT—cover; outerwear
COLT—young horse; gun
COOT—bird; duck-like
COPT—Egypt. Christian
CULT—sect; system of
   worship
CURT—short; terse
CYST—abnormal skin sac
CHOU—cabbage; Chin.
   dynasty
CLOU—Fr.: nail
CHAW—masticate
CHEW—masticate
CHOW—dog
CLAW—nail; hammer;
   scratch
CLEW—yarn ball; sail loop
CLOW—floodgate
CRAW—crop

CREW—gang; group
CROW—raven; bird (black)
CALX—hell; broken glass to
   remelt
CEYX—Halcyon's husband
COAX—wheedle; cajole
COIX—grass genus; Job's-
   tears
CRAX—bird genus;
   curassow
CREX—corn crake (bird)
CRUX—crucial point; pivot;
   Southern Cross
CADY—golf attendant
CAGY—shrewd
CAKY—crusty; hard
CAVY—guinea pig; stray
   animal
CAZY—Moslem judge
CHAY—herb root; red dye
CHOY—herb root; red dye
CITY—urban area
CLAY—earth; Henry ——,
   Am. statesman
CLOY—satiate; glut
CODY—Buffalo Bill ——
COKY—dirty
COLY—mousebird
CONY—rabbit
COPY—duplicate
COSY—snug
COTY—Fr. statesman
COZY—snug
CUVY—sea girdles
CHEZ—Fr.: at the home of

DADA—art style; father
DAMA—gazelle
DANA—Celtic goddess;
   masc. name; author
DATA—facts
DAZA—Berber
DECA—prefix: ten
DEJA—Fr.: already
DEPA—measure
DERA—suffix: neck types
DEVA—Buddhist angel;
   Zoroastrian demon
DEWA—deity
DIKA—bread tree seeds

DISA—orchid
DITA—tree
DIVA—opera star; prima
   donna
DOLA—weight
DONA—It. lady
DOPA—pigment test
DORA—grain; fem. name
DOSA—hatred
DOXA—E. Church
   doxology
DRAA—measure
DUMA—Russ. parliament
DURA—spinal membrane
DYNA—prefix: power
DARB—language group
DAUB—smear on
DIEB—jackal
DOAB—tract of land
DOOB—Burmuda grass
DOUB—Burmuda grass
DRAB—brown; dull;
   colorless; fabric
DRIB—drop; globule
DRUB—beat (with stick)
DUAB—tract of land
DUBB—Syrian bear
DUMB—speechless; mute
DISC—circular plate;
   record; spine part
DOUC—monkey
DEAD—deceased
DEED—act; legal document
DIAD—pair
DOWD—shabby woman
DRED— ———— Scott (slave; S.
   C. decision)
DUAD—pair
DYAD—pair
DACE—fish
DALE—dell; glen
DAME—girl; woman; title
DANE—Scandanavian
DARE—challenge; defy
DATE—fruit tree;
   appointment
DAVE—masc. nickname
DAYE—first colonial printer
DAZE—stupefy
DELE—erase

DEME—Greek town or commune
DENE—sand hill; dune
DICE—gaming cube; cut into cubes
DIKE—embankment; goddess - one of Horae
DIME—coin; ten cents
DINE—eat dinner
DIRE—dreadful; evil
DIVE—plunge; duck; low haunt
DOBE—sun-dried brick (building)
DOGE—It. magistrate
DOLE—ration; parcel out; relief
DOME—cupola; roof
DONE—carried out; completed; all through
DOPE—drug; jerk; information
DORE—gold; gilt
DOSE—prescribed quantity
DOTE—be overfond; timber rot
DOVE—bird; plunged
DOZE—drowse; sleep
DREE—Scot.: endure
DUCE—It.: leader; chief; Mussolini
DUDE—city person; dandy
DUNE—sand hill
DUPE—catspaw; tool
DUSE—It. actress
DYKE—embankment; levee
DYNE—unit of force
DAFF—put aside
DEAF—hard of hearing; inattentive
DOFF—take off; remove (as one's hat)
DUBB—pudding
DAGG—pistol
DANG—mild curse
DING—sound
DOEG—Saul's chief herdsman
DONG—bell sound

DRAG—harrow; haul; car race
DREG—residue
DRUG—medicine; pharmaceutical; dope
DAGH—hill
DASH—punctuation mark; spring
DISH—plate; receptacle for food
DOTH—does
DRAH—measure
DALI—tree; Salvador ——
DARI—grain; sorghum
DASI—female slave
DECI—prefix: tenth
DEFI—challenge; defy
DEMI—prefix: half
DESI—jute
DEVI—Siva's wife
DIVI—divine ones
DIXI—Lat.: I have spoken
DONI—boat
DREI—German: three
DANK—damp
DARK—dim; unlighted
DAUK—relay mail, India
DAWK—relay mail, India
DECK—adorn; ship's floor; cards
DESK—table; work place
DHAK—tree
DICK—detective; fellow; masc. nickname
DIRK—dagger
DISK—circular plate
DOCK—curtail; pier
DOOK—wooden brick
DUCK—canvas; dodge; wild fowl
DUNK—immerse
DUSK—eve; twilight
DYAK—Borneo native
DYCK—Van ——, painter
DAIL—Eire legislature
DEAL—apportion; mete; bargain; transaction
DEIL—Scot.: devil
DELL—glen; valley
DEUL—Hindu temple

DIAL—face; call
DILL—herb (used in pickling)
DOLL—puppet; plaything
DOWL—down
DUAL—double; twin
DUEL—combat (fight between two)
DULL—drab; tedious; blunt
DAWM—coin
DEEM—consider; rate
DERM—combining form: skin
DEUM—Te ---- (hymn)
DIEM—Lat.: day
DOOM—condemn; fate
DORM—dormitory; campus building
DOUM—tree
DRAM—small drink; measure
DRUM—musc. instrument; tympanum
DUIM—measure
DAIN—measure
DAMN—curse
DARN—mend; sew; mild oath
DAWN—daybreak; Aurora; fem. name
DEAN—university officer; clergyman
DEIN—Ger.: your
DHAN—India: property
DIAN—reveille, call to
DION—masc. name
DOMN—Rumanian king's title
DOON—tree
DORN—thornback ray
DOWN—soft feathers; below; defeat; depressed
DUAN—Gaelic poem
DADO—decorated wall part; border
DAGO—tribe
DATO—Malay tribal chief
DEDO—measure
DEMO—prefix: people
DHAO—knife

DIDO—caper; antic; Carthage queen
DILO—poon tree
DINO—prefix: fearful
DODO—extinct bird
DOKO—Afr. pygmy
DOTO—sea slug genus
DUCO—lacquer
DURO—Sp. money
DAMP—moist; wet; press down
DEEP—profound
DOPP—ladle; dip
DORP—hamlet; town
DRAP—Fr.: cloth
DRIP—globule; fall slowly
DROP—discard; let fall; globule
DUMP—junkyard; unload
DAER—borrowed stock
DARR—black tern (bird)
DEAR—loved one; expensive
DEER—cervine animal; ruminant
DHAR—Ind. state, town
DIER—one who died
DIOR—clothes designer
DOER—actor; agent; performer
DOOR—gate; portal; entrance
DOUR—sullen
DUAR—mountain pass
DUHR—star
DURR—grain sorghum
DYER—tinter
DAIS—platform
DANS—Fr.: in
DAYS—by day
DEBS—Eugene ---- (socialist)
DENS—Lat.: troth
DEUS—Lat.: god
DIBS—grape juice
DIES—Lat.: days
DISS—Medit. grass
DOES—performs
DOSS—bed
DUDS—clothing; failures

DUNS—dull
DUOS—duets
DYAS—geol. period
DAFT—foolish; zany
DART—arrow; bolt; missile;
 run swiftly
DEBT—liability; obligation
DEFT—skillful
DENT—depression
DIET—synod; assembly;
 fare; food
DINT—effort; force
DIRT—earth; soil
DOAT—be overfond
DOIT—bit
DOLT—ass; blockhead;
 dunce
DONT—contraction
DOST—do
DRAT—mild oath
DUAT—underworld
DUCT—tube
DUET—done by two; music
 for two
DUIT—Columbian Indian
DUNT—split
DUST—powdery matter; dirt
DANU—goddess
DATU—tribal chief
DEGU—S. Am. rodent
DIAU—Indian
DIEU—Fr.: god
DUKU—lanseh tree
DAUW—zebra
DHAW—knife
DHOW—lateen-rigged
 boat
DRAW—depict; sketch; pull;
 attract; tie
DREW—sketched; pulled
DEUX—Fr.: two
DAVY—masc. nickname;
 safety lamp
DAZY—confused
DEFY—challenge; dare
DEMY—paper size
DENY—refuse; contradict;
 negate
DEWY—moist; wet
DOBY—sun-dried brick

 (building)
DOGY—duck; calf
DOMY—domelike
DORY—small boat
DOTY—discolored
DOXY—religious opinion
DOZY—drowsy
DRAY—squirrel's nest; cart
DREY—squirrel's nest
DUFY—Fr. artist
DUTY—tax; obligation
DAEZ—daze
DIAZ—Bartholomew (Port.
 explorer)

ECCA—geol. epoch
EDDA—heroic song; epic
EDNA—fem. name
EGBA—Afr. native
EKKA—India: carriage
ELBA—island of exile for
 Napoleon
ELIA—Lamb's pen name
ELLA—fem. name; Sp.: she;
 fem suffix
ELSA—Lohengrin's wife
EMMA—fem. name
ENNA—Sicilian resort
EPHA—Hebrew measure
ERDA—Brunnhilde's
 mother; earth goddess
ERIA—Assam silkworm
ERMA—fem. name
ERUA—mother goddess
ESCA—plant apoplexy
ESTA—Sp.: this
ETNA—volcano
ETTA—fem. name
EVEA—ipecac source
EYRA—wild cat
EZBA—measure
EZRA—masc. name
EPIC—heroic poem
ERIC—masc. name
ERUC—cordage fiber
ECAD—habitat plant form;
 modified plant form
EGAD—oath
EILD—Scot.: age
ELOD—force

EMYD—terrapin
ENID—fem. name;
   Geraint's wife
EYED—looked at; observed
EASE—comfort; rest;
   facilitate
EAVE—roof edge
EBOE—tree; Negrito
ECCE—Lat.: behold
EDGE—brink; rim;
   advantage
EIDE—ideas
EINE—Ger.: one
EIRE—Ireland
ELBE—river
ELLE—Fr.: she
ELSE—besides; otherwise
ENCE—suffix
ENNE—prefix: nine
ENSE—suffix
ENTE—Her.: grafted; Sp.:
   being
EPEE—fencing sword
ERIE—Iroquoian; lake
ERNE—bird of prey
ERSE—Celt
ESCE—verb suffix
ESNE—slave
ESSE—existence; Lat.: to be
ESTE—Sp.: this; Ital. family
ETRE—Fr.: to be
ETTE—feminine suffix
EUGE—bravo
EVOE—bacchanal's cry
EYRE—circuit judge; Jane
   —— (Bronte heroine)
ELEF—Heb. letter
ENIF—star
EACH—every one
ELAH—Biblical king
ESTH—Balt.; Estonian
ETAH—Eskimo settlement
ETCH—engrave
EYAH—Oriental maid
EKOI—W. Afr. native
ENKI—Babylonian god
EQUI—prefix; same
ETUI—small vanity case
EFIK—W. Afr. native
ESEK—Biblical well

EARL—nobleman; masc.
   name
EDEL—Ger.: noble
EGAL—Fr.: equal
EGIL—Norse hero
EGOL—antiseptic
ELUL—month
EMIL—masc. name
ENOL—chem. suffix
ERAL—epochal
ETAL—Lat.: and others
EVIL—bad; malevolent
EZEL—juniper tree
EDAM—city; cheese
EDOM—Biblical country
ELAM—Biblical kingdom
EMIM—giants
ENAM—land grant
ETYM—abbr.: word roots
EXAM—test
EARN—deserve; merit
EBEN—masc. nickname
EBON—jet; black
EDEN—paradise; heaven
ELAN—dash; spirit
ELON—Biblical man
ENIN—blue grape pigment
ENON—Biblical country;
   town
EOAN—pert. to dawn
EOIN—John; Sean
ERIN—Ireland
ETON—school; collar;
   jacket
EVAN—masc. name
EVEN—equal; tie
EWAN—masc. name
EBRO—Sp. river
ECHO—repeat; iterate;
   reverberate; Narcissis'
   lover
ECTO—prefix: outside
EDDO—taro root
EGBO—secret society
EJOO—feather palms
ENDO—prefix: within
ENTO—inner
ENYO—Ares' mother
ERGO—hence; therefore
EBER—ancestor

EBUR—Lat.: ivory
EDAR—Bib. town
EDER—river
EGER—river
EMER—Cuchulain's wife
EMIR—Arab chieftain
ERER—sooner
ESER—weight
EUER—Ger.: your
EVER—always
EWER—pitcher
EYER—needle maker
EADS—bridge; Am.
　　engineer
EATS—food; consumes
EDES—Gr. resistance group
EGGS—ova
EGIS—symbol of Athena;
　　auspices; patronage;
　　shield protection
ELIS—Gr. city-state (anc.)
EMYS—tortoise
ENNS—river
ENOS—Adam's grandson;
　　Seth's son
EPOS—epic poetry
ERIS—Ares' sister; goddess
　　of discord
EROS—god of love; Cupid
ESUS—Gaulish god
ETES—Fr.: (you) are
EYAS—nestling
EAST—direction; Orient
EDIT—correct; blue pencil
EMIT—send forth; issue
ERAT—Lat.: he was
ERST—former; first
ETAT—Fr.: state
EVET—eft; newt
EXIT—departure;
　　leavetaking
EYOT—island
ECRU—beige
EHEU—exclamation
EMEU—ostrichlike bird
ENZU—moon god (Babyl.)
ESAU—Jacob's twin; Isaac's
　　son
ENOW—enough
EAUX—Fr.: water

ERYX—sand snake
ESOX—fresh water fish
EASY—simple; not difficult;
　　unruffled
EDDY—whirlpool
EDGY—nervous
EELY—wriggling
EERY—uncanny; weird
EGGY—yolky
ELMY—many elms
EMMY—television award
ENVY—to be jealous; covet
ESAY—Isaiah
ESPY—behold; see
EWRY—linen closet
EYEY—having holes
EYRY—bird's nest

FABA—vetch
FALA—refrain; dog
FAMA—rumor
FLEA—insect
FORA—Roman markets
FREA—Frigg (Odin's wife)
FRIA—Frigg (Odin's wife)
FUGA—It.: fugue
FLUB—blunder; make a
　　mistake
FRAB—scold
FRIB—dirty wool
FISC—exchequer
FLOC—wisp
FARD—face paint
FEED—nourish; fodder
FEND—restrain; parry
FEOD—feudal estate
FEUD—vendetta
FIND—discover
FLED—ran away
FOLD—fall; bend; plait
FOND—loving
FOOD—nourishment
FORD—wade across;
　　crossing place
FOUD—judge
FRED—masc. nickname
FUAD—Arab king;
　　Farouk's father
FUND—supply; money
FYRD—old English army

FACE—surface; visage
FADE—wilt; droop
FAKE—sham; pretend; cheat
FAME—renown; eminence
FANE—temple
FARE—menu; price; fee
FATE—destiny; kismet
FAZE—bother; disturb
FEKE—trick
FEME—wife
FETE—festival
FIDE—trust; faith
FIFE—small flute
FILE—tool; rasp; line; column
FINE—elegant; posh; end; thin
FIRE—arouse; stir; discharge; combustion
FIVE—number; card
FLEE—run away
FLOE—floating ice; berg
FLUE—air passage; chimney pipe
FORE—van; front; golf cry
FREE—disengage; gratuitous; unfettered; independent
FROE—cleaving tool
FUME—reek; smoke; rage
FUSE—melt together
FUTE—Eskimo curlew
FUZE—melt together
FYKE—bag net
FIEF—feudal estate
FANG—tooth
FLAG—banner; ensign; standard; signal; dwindle
FLOG—whip
FONG—Dahomey Negro
FROG—amphibian
FRUG—contemporary dance
FUNG—Bantu
FASH—vex
FISH—piscine; probe
FOCH—Fr. general
FAVI—tile

FIJI—Islands
FOCI—center points
FUCI—rockweed
FUJI—Jap. cherry; Jap. volcano
FUNJ—Negroid
FEAK—tress; twist
FECK—amount
FINK—bird; strikebreaker; scab
FISK—exchequer
FLAK—antiaircraft shells
FOLK—people; customs
FORK—pronged implement
FULK—unfair shove in marbles
FUNK—fright; panic
FAIL—err
FALL—drop; sink; descend
FARL—scone
FEEL—sense; grope
FILL—occupy; pack
FOAL—young horse
FOIL—baffle; elude; balk; fencing sword
FOOL—clown; jester; buffoon
FOUL—rotten
FOWL—poultry
FUEL—gas; combustible
FULL—adequate; replete
FURL—roll up
FAAM—tea leaves
FARM—plow; land
FILM—thin layer; photograph
FIRM—stable; solid; company
FLAM—trick; ruse
FOAM—froth; spume
FORM—shape; mold
FROM—out of
FAIN—desirous; gladly
FAMN—measure
FAON—fawn color
FAUN—field deity
FAWN—color; brown; deer
FERN—seedless plant
FINN—person from Finland
FIRN—glacial snow field

FLAN—custard
FOHN—warm dry wind
FADO—folk tune
FANO—Eucharist cloth;
   maniple
FARO—card game
FICO—trifle
FIDO—dog's name
FILO—silk thread
FONO—Samoan council
FLAP—beat; slap; flutter;
   sway
FLIP—toss; overturn
FLOP—failure; slump down
FRAP—draw tight
FAIR—bazaar; festival; just
FEAR—fright
FOUR—number; card
FASS—measure
FEES—charges
FEIS—Irish meeting
FELS—coin
FESS—broad band (her.)
FILS—Fr.: son
FONS—fountain
FOSS—ditch; trench
FUSS—ado; bother; bustle
FACT—reality; deed
FAIT—Fr.: fact
FAST—speedy; abstain
   (from food); firmly
   fixed
FAUT—Fr.: proper
FEAT—accomplishment
FELT—fabric; sensed
FEST—festival; gathering
FIAT—It. car; sanction;
   command
FIOT—Congo tribe
FIST—grasp
FLAT—level; dull
FLIT—dart along
FONT—basin; type
   collection
FOOT—paw; base; bottom
FORT—frontier post;
   stronghold
FRAT—fraternity
FRET—worry
FRIT—fuse partly

FROT—chafe; rub
FUST—mustiness; shaft of
   column
FERU—cordage fiber
FRAU—Ger.: wife; Mrs.
FUGU—fish
FLAW—defect
FLEW—aviated
FLOW—stream; gush
FROW—Dutch woman
FAEX—dregs
FALX—Roman sword
FLAX—plant; fiber
FLEX—bend
FLIX—down; fur
FLUX—change; flow
FADY—weakening
FAKY—spurious
FLAY—strip off skin
FLEY—frighten
FOGY—dull
FOXY—cunning; shrewd;
   wily
FRAY—fight; melee; wear
   off
FREY—Aesir; god; Norse
   god of fertility
FUMY—vaporous
FURY—rage
FIZZ—hissing sound
FRIZ—curl
FUZZ—down; police

GAEA—earth goddess
GAIA—earth goddess
GALA—festival; tribe
GAMA—Vasco de ----, Port.
   navigator
GARA—coin
GATA—nurse shark
GAZA—Israel city; ---- Strip
GENA—cheek
GETA—Jap. clogs
GIGA—medieval fiddle
GILA— ---- monster; lizard
GJOA—1st Northwest
   Passage ship
GLIA—neuroglia (nerve)
GOLA—caste; cyma;
   granary

GOMA—Bantu
GONA—New Guinea
  victory
GORA—reed instrument
GOYA—Sp. painter
GUFA—boat
GUHA—Bantu
GULA—Lat.: throat;
  molding
GUNA—Sankhya phil. term
GARB—apparel
GAUB—persimmon
GERB—firework
GLIB—fluent; flippant
GLUB—make swallowing
  sound
GRAB—nab; arrest
GRUB—larva
GUIB—Afr. antelope
GAUD—ornament
GAWD—ornament
GELD—castrate; tax
GERD—Frey's wife
GILD—adorn with gold
GIRD—clothe; vest
GLAD—pleased
GLED—bird; kite
GOAD—incentive; urge;
  spur
GOLD—precious metal
GOND—Indian
GOOD—able; sound
GRAD—centesimal unit
GRID—grating
GABE—taro
GADE—fish
GAGE—measure; gauge;
  pledge; plum
GALE—wind
GAME—gamble; sport
GANE—yawn
GAPE—yaw; stare
GARE—Fr.: beware, station
GATE—entrance; portal
GAUE—German region
GAVE—donated
GAZE—stare
GENE—masc. nickname;
  hereditary factor
GHEE—butter

GIBE—agree; deride; jeer
GIDE—Andre ----, author
GITE—Fr.: lodging place
GIVE—impart; donate;
  bestow
GLEE—happiness
GLUE—adhesive
GONE—absent; departed
GORE—penetrate; stab
GUZE—red circle (Her.)
GYBE—agree; deride; jeer
GYLE—brewing; beer vat
GYNE—prefix; female
GYRE—circular motion
GYVE—fetter; iron
GAFF—spear; spar (for
  fishing)
GOAF—mow of hay; rick
GOFF—clown
GOLF—sport; game
GOOF—mistake; dolt
GRAF—Ger. count;
  Zeppelin
GUFF—humbug
GULF—abyss; chasm; bay
GANG—crew; team
GHEG—Albanian
GLUG—liquid sound
GONG—bell
GRIG—cricket
GROG—liquor drink
GASH—cut; incision
GATH—Philistine city
GISH—Moroccan public
  land
GOGH—Van ----, painter
GOSH—oath
GOTH—barbarian; Hun
GUSH—jet; spew
GABI—taro
GALI—abuse
GAZI—warrior
GERI—Odin's wife
GOAI—shrub
GOBI—desert in Mongolia
GOLI—musket ball
GUTI—Kurd
GYRI—brain ridges
GUNJ—granary
GAWK—stare

GINK—eccentric person
GOWK—simpleton
GAAL—brewing
GAEL—Celt
GAGL—sweet gale
GAIL—brewing; fem. name
GALL—bile; venom; chafe;
   cheek; nerve
GAOL—jail
GAUL—Celt; France (anc.)
GEAL—pert. to earth
GILL—branchia; breathing
   device
GIRL—young female
GOAL—aim; end; purpose;
   score
GOEL—avenger
GOLL—Irish hero
GOUL—monster
GOWL—monster; yell
GULL—coast bird; deceive;
   trick
GARM—Hel's watchdog
GERM—seed; microbe
GEUM—herb
GLIM—light
GLOM—steal; watch
GLUM—morose; blue
GRAM—chick-pea;
   measure; sword; small
   weight
GRIM—stern; harsh
GRUM—morose
GUAM—Mariana Island
GAIN—acquire; earn; profit;
   benefit
GAON—Jewish title of
   honor
GARN—go on; yarn
GEAN—cherry
GEIN—glucoside root
GLEN—dell
GMAN—U.S. government
   agent
GOAN—pert. to Goa
GOON—thug
GOWN—dress; formal wear
GRAN—weight
GRIN—smile
GUAN—S. Amer. bird

GWYN—deity
GAJO—non-Gypsy
GANO—Roland's destroyer
GAPO—partly inundated
   forest
GARO—Indo-Chin.
   language
GILO—E. Ind. vine
GIRO—credit system; tour
GOBO—Jap. vegetable
GOGO—Bantu nation;
   bugaboo; soap vine;
   contemporary dance
GOLO—Sudanese
GRAO—weight
GUAO—tree
GULO—wolverine genus
GYRO—prefix: spiral; circle
GAMP—umbrella; Sairey
   —— (Dickens' char.)
GASP—pant
GAUP—gape
GAWP—gape
GIMP—dress trimming
GOOP—nonsense creature
GRIP—valise; grasp
GULP—drink; swig; swallow
GUMP—silly ones; cartoon
   characters
GAUR—wild ox
GEAR—clothing;
   equipment; notched
   wheel
GHOR—Jordan valley
GIER—eagle
GNAR—growl
GOER—runner
GOOR—sugar
GOUR—wild ox
GUAR—forage plant
GUHR—earth deposit
GAUS—Ger. region
GENS—clan; family
GHES—Tapuyan Indian
GLIS—dormouse genus
GOES—proceeds
GRAS—horse
GRES—Fr.: stoneware
GRIS—Fr.: gray
GROS—fabric; weight

GRUS—constellation
GAIT—manner of walking
GALT—clay bed
GAUT—landing place
GEAT—Scandanavian
GELT—money
GENT—gentleman
GEST—adventure; deed
GETT—divorce bill
GHAT—landing place
GIFT—present; talent
GILT—gold; female hog
GIRT—encircle
GIST—main point; pith
GLUT—fill to excess
GNAT—fly
GOAT—ruminant
GOUT—disease; Fr.: taste
GRIT—sand; bravery
GROT—cave
GUST—burst of wind
GENU—Lat.: knee
GUGU—P.I. soldier
GURU—teacher
GLOW—glisten; shine
GNAW—chew
GREW—increased
GROW—wax; increase;
    develop
GABY—fool
GAPY—full of holes
GARY—city
GOBY—fish
GORY—bloody
GRAY—color; dull; Eng.
    poet
GREY—color; dull
GEEZ—Ethiopic
GHUZ—Turkish tribesman
HABA—Sp. bean
HAHA—laugh
HALA—pine tree
HELA—Loke's daughter
HERA—goddess queen
HILA—eye of bean
HIMA—Hamitic tribe
HOGA—hill pasture
HOJA—title
HOLA—herb; hello
HORA—book of hours;
    Israeli dance
HOVA—Madagascar native
HOYA—plant
HSIA—Chin. dynasty
HUIA—bird
HULA—Hawaiian dance
HUPA—Athapascan Indian
HURA—bishop's hat;
    sandbox tree
HYLA—amphibian
HAAB—Mayan year
HARB—Bedouin
HERB—flavoring plant
HOBB—fireplace projection
HUBB—pipe end
HAEC—Lat.: this one
HAND—measure; pass;
    penmanship; worker;
    cards
HARD—set; obstinate
HEAD—chief; skull; brain
HEED—notice; listen to
HELD—retained
HERD—crowd
HIND—rear; posterior; deer
HOLD—maintain; assert;
    grasp
HOOD—cowl; head covering
HUED—tinged
HABE—tribe
HADE—angle
HAKE—fish
HALE—healthy; hearty;
    Nathan ----, Amer.
    patriot
HARE—Lepus genus;
    rodent; rabbit
HASE—cobra
HATE—abhor; loathe
HAVE—possess
HAZE—mist; harass
HEBE—cupbearer of gods
HEHE—Bantu tribe
HERE—present
HIDE—external covering;
    secrets
HIKE—walk; raise
HIPE—wrestling throw
HIRE—employ
HIVE—bee house; apiary

HOHE—Indian tribe
HOLE—gulf; chasm; pit
HOME—domicile; habitat
HONE—sharpen
HOPE—trust; expect
HOSE—stockings; pipe
HOVE—lifted with effort
HOWE—hollow; empty
HUGE—enormous; large
HULE—rubber tree
HUME—Eng. philosopher
HUSE—whale
HYDE—measure; ---- Park
HYLE—matter: philos.
HYPE—wrestling throw
HAAF—fishing grounds
HALF—moiety
HEAF—pasture
HOOF—ungula; foot; dance
HUFF—sulking
HAGG—demoness
HANG—suspend
HING—asafetida
HOGG—unshorn sheep
HONG—Chin. guild
HUNG—suspended
HAKH—due (India)
HASH—mixture
HATH—has
HEGH—exclamation
HETH—Hittite ancestor
HIGH—elevated; tipsy;
    noble
HISH—hiss
HOCH—Ger. exclamation
HOTH—blind god
HUGH—masc. nickname
HUNH—questioning
    exclamation
HUSH—quiet; silence!
HAGI—Jap. clover
HAMI—hooks
HAPI—Nile, as god
HATI—heart
HEII—Hawaiian fern
HEMI—half
HEVI—apple
HIFI—kind of recorded
    sound
HOLI—festival

HOPI—color; Indian
HADJ—pilgrimage to Mecca
HAAK—food fish; wander
HACK—cut; chop; taxi;
    writer
HAIK—garment
HANK—skein; coil; masc.
    nickname
HARK—listen
HAWK—bird of prey;
    peddle; sell
HECK—oath
HICK—yokel; rube
HOCK—animal leg-joint
HOEK—curve in a stream
HONK—goose cry; toot
HOOK—catch; snag; trap
HUCK—towel fabric
HULK—wrecked ship
HUNK—lump; piece
HUSK—external covering
HAIL—greet; salute; ice
HALL—corridor;
    passageway
HARL—barb; filament
HAUL—catch; pull; drag;
    loot
HEAL—cure
HEEL—back part of foot;
    rascal
HELL—Hades; underworld
HERL—feather barb
HILL—mound
HOWL—cry; moan
HULL—husk; ship's body
HURL—toss; pitch
HAEM—prefix: blood
HALM—plant stems
HARM—injure; maim
HELM—tiller
HOLM—holly
HEIN—Fr.: exclamation
HEWN—felled
HOEN—weight
HOON—coin
HORN—antenna; prong;
    trumpet; instrument
HYMN—religious song
HAKO—Indian rite
HALO—circle; crown

HANO—Indian
HEMO—prefix: blood
HERO—protagonist;
  sandwich; Leander's
  love
HILO—Hawaiian grass
HINO—timber tree
HOBO—tramp
HOMO—man; prefix: some
HUGO—Fr. author
HUSO—whale
HYPO—photo solution;
  injection
HARP—musical instrument;
  refer to repeatedly
HASP—clasp
HEAP—pile
HEEP—Dickens' character
HELP—aid; support
HEMP—cannabis; rope;
  hashhish
HOOP—wicket; circle
HUMP—protuberance
HAAR—fog
HAIR—filament; fiber;
  Broadway show
HEAR—harken; attend
HEER—Dutch mister
HEIR—inheritor
HERR—Ger. form of
  address
HIER—Fr.: yesterday
HOAR—frost; rime
HOER—scraper
HOUR—time unit
HALS—Dutch painter
HANS—Ger. John
HENS—fowl
HERS—possessive pronoun
HISS—sibilant sound
HOPS—beer ingredient
HORS—Fr.: out
HAFT—handle; hilt
HALT—stop; cease; lame
HANT—haunt; ghost
HART—deer
HAST—contraction
HAUT—Fr.: high
HEAT—warmth; pressure;
  strain

HEFT—weight
HEST—command
HILT—handle
HINT—allusion
HIST—call to attract
  attention
HOLT—copse; plantation
HOOT—owl's cry
HOST—army; troops; person
  having guests
HUNT—seek; search for
HURT—harmed; injured
HAKU—kingfish
HAPU—N.Z. clan
HIKU—fish
HOJU—Jap. army reserve
HULU—feathers of owl
HOAX—trick; deception
HAZY—vague; dim
HOEY—Hawaiian
  partnership
HOLY—sacred
HOMY—intimate
HAYZ—pert. to zodiac
HUZZ—murmur

IDEA—whim; fancy;
  concept
IJMA—Moslem principle
IKRA—caviar
ILIA—bones
INCA—Peruvian Indian
INGA—shrub
INIA—Amazon celacean
INKA—Peruvian Indian
IOLA—Kansas town
IONA—Celt. Church;
  college
IOTA—Greek I; ten
IOWA—state
IRMA—fem. name
IRRA—Babyl. war god
ISBA—log hut
ISHA—Upanishad
ITEA—shrub genus
ITZA—Indian
IXIA—corn lily
IAMB—poetic foot
IDIC—pert. to ids
IBAD—Arab

IBID—in same place; **P.I.**
　　lizard
ICED—frozen; chilled
IMID—chem. compound
IRAD—Bib. name
IRID—crocus
IDEE—Fr.: idea
IDLE—lazy; not working
ILLE—Lat.: he
IMBE—cordage fiber
INDE—blue
INEE—arrow poison
INGE—playwright
INRE—concerning
IOLE—Eurytus' daughter
IONE—Bulwer-Lytton
　　heroine
IPSE—"---- dixit" Lat.; Lat.:
　　himself
IRAE—"Dies ----" (Days of
　　Wrath)
ISLE—ait; eyot; insulate;
　　island
IXLE—fiber plant
ILOG—river (Tagalog)
INCH—measure
INVH—Supreme Being
ITCH—skin irritation
IVAH—Bib. name
IIWI—bird
IMMI—measure
IMPI—Kaffir warrior
INTI—Inca sun god
IONI—Caddoan Indian
IRAK—country;
　　Mesopotamia
IROK—feather palm
ICAL—compound
IDOL—effigy; image; god
IDYL—pastoral poem
IFIL—P. I. tree
IPIL—P. I. tree
ITOL—chem. suffix
IXIL—Indian
IDEM—Lat.: same
IMAM—Caliph
ITEM—article; entry; detail
IBAN—dyak
ICON—image; statue
IDEN—Henry VI character

IDUN—Norse mythical
　　woman
IKON—icon
IRAN—country; Persia
IRON—metal; press; golf
　　club; shackle
ITEN—Bolivian Indian
IVAN—Czar; masc. name;
　　John
IAGO—Othello villain;
　　traitor
ICHO—gingko tree
IDEO—comb. form: idea
IDIO—prefix; peculiar
IDJO—Nigerian tribe
IDYO—Nigerian tribe
IDZO—Nigerian tribe
IKMO—betel pepper
INRO—Jap. box
INTO—preposition
IPSO—Lat.: itself
ITMO—betel pepper
IRAQ—country;
　　Mesopotamia
ICER—freezer
IGOR—Russ. name
IMER—Caucasian
ISAR—Danube tributary
ISER—river
ITER—brain passage
IYAR—Jewish month
IZAR—star; Moslem
　　garment
IBIS—Egypt. bird
IDAS—Castor's killer
IDES—Roman date
ILLS—troubles; difficulties
IRAS—character in *Antony
　　and Cleopatra*
IRIS—part of eye; flower;
　　blue
IRUS—Odyssey beggar
ISIS—goddess; Horus'
　　mother
ITYS—Tereus' son
IVES—American inventor
IBIT—P. I. lizard
IKAT—silk fabric
ILOT—island; ait
IALU—Egypt. heaven

ICHU—Andes grass
IGLU—Eskimo house
IBEX—wild goat
IDLY—lazily
INKY—black
INLY—within
ISMY—doctrinaire
INEZ—Don Juan's mother

JACA—jack tree
JAGA—Bantu
JAMA—Moslem tunic
JAVA—coffee; island
JENA—Napoleonic victory
JIVA—Hindu life energy
JOTA—Sp. dance
JOVA—Pimian Indian
JUBA—dance
JUCA—cassova
JUDA—James' brother
JUGA—carrot ridges
JURA—mountain range
JUZA—star
JAMB—leg armor
JIBB—sail
JOAB—David's captain
JOAD—Steinbeck character;
  Eng. philosopher
JADE—color; gem; peridot;
  tire
JAKE—masc. nickname
JANE—old money; fem.
  name
JAPE—jest
JAVE—Jehovah
JEFE—Sp.: chief
JETE—ballet jump
JIBE—agree; deride; mock;
  shift position
JIVE—swing music
JOIE—spirit; zest; ---- de
  vivre
JOKE—wisecrack; quip
JOLE—jowl; cheek
JOSE—masc. name
JOVE—Jupiter
JUBE—chancel screen
JUDE—Apostle
JUKE—partridge call
JULE—name

JUNE—month; fem. name
JUPE—Fr.: petticoat
JURE—law
JUTE—cordage fiber; E.
  Ind. plant
JEFF—rope; masc.
  nickname
JIFF—moment; trice
JAGG—slash
JOUG—pillory
JUNG—psychiatrist
JETH—Hindu month
JHVH—Hebrew Supreme
  Being
JHWH—Hebrew Supreme
  Being
JOSH—kid; make fun; tease
JAMI—central mosque
JATI—caste
JOGI—Hindu ascetic
JOLI—Fr.: pretty
JACK—nickname; tool;
  card; ensign; raising
  device
JERK—spasm; boor; twist;
  pull
JOCK—jockey; masc.
  nickname
JONK—jonquil
JUCK—partridge
JUNK—trash; garbage;
  Oriental ship
JAEL—Sisera's killer
JAIL—prison
JARL—Danish chieftain
JEEL—marsh
JELL—harden; solidify
JILL—fem. name
JOEL—OT prophet; masc.
  name
JOWL—cheek
JHUM—cultivation method
JOOM—cultivation method
JAIN—Hindu relig. sect
JANN—Moslem deity
JAUN—palanquin
JEAN—name; cotton fabric
JINN—Arab demon
JOAN—fem. name; St. ----,
  Maid of Orleans

JOHN—name; saint
JOIN—connect; unite
JUAN—man's name
JAKO—parrot
JATO—unit of jet
  propulsion
JOBO—hog plum, W. Ind.
JODO—Buddhist paradise
JUDO—Jap. art of self-
  defense
JUNO—goddess, Queen
JEEP—vehicle
JUMP—leap
JEER—taunt
JOAR—Ind. millet
JOUR—Fr.: day
JUAR—Ind. millet
JASS—Swiss card game
JESS—strap on falcon's leg
JOSS—Chin. deity
JEST—trick; ruse
JILT—betray (in romance)
JOLT—shake; jar
JUST—fair; exact
JACU—bird
JADU—magic
JEHU—Biblical driver
JESU—Jesus
JOCU—dog snapper fish
JUJU—charm
JEUX—Fr.: game
JINX—hoodoo
JYNX—hoodoo
JADY—like jade
JAWY—talkative
JOEY—young kangaroo;
  name
JOKY—jocular
JOSY—nickname
JOZY—nickname
JUDY—famous puppet;
  name
JULY—month
JURY—court panel
JAZZ—dance; music
JUEZ—judge

KADA—measure
KAFA—Abyssinian
KAHA—proboscis monkey
KAKA—parrot
KALA—bird
KAMA—fire god
KANA—Jap. writing
KAPA—Hawaiian cloth
KARA—river
KASA—E. Ind. grass
KAVA—pepper shrub
KAWA—pepper shrub
KELA—measure
KETA—dog salmon
KINA—quinine
KIVA—ceremonial chamber
KOBA—antelope
KOLA—caffeine nut; jackal;
  Russ. town; peninsula
KONA—Hawaiian
  windstorm
KORA—bird
KOTA—P. I. fort; Dravidian
  language
KUBA—carpet; measure
KUFA—boat
KULA—measure
KERB—sidewalk edge
KNAB—nibble
KNOB—handle; node
KNUB—waste silk
KTKB—chess move
KTQB—chess move
KAID—chief; general
KELD—spring
KIND—sort; species; variety
KURD—Turk. tribesman;
  Iranian
KADE—sheep tick
KALE—cabbage
KAME—glacial ridge
KANE—Hawaiian god
KATE—Shakespearian
  shrew; fem. nickname
KERE—Heb.: Bib.
  pronunciation aid
KILE—measure
KINE—cows
KITE—bird of prey; flying
  toy
KIVE—brewer's vat

KLEE—Paul (painter)
KNEE—joint
KOAE—red-tailed, Hawaiian bird
KOBE—Honshu port
KOME—Greenland geol. division
KORE—myth. chaos; Demeter's daughter
KUGE—Jap. nobleman
KURE—Jap. naval station
KAIF—lanquor; hemp
KEEF—hemp
KEIF—hemp
KERF—cut; notch
KIEF—hemp
KIFF—languor
KOFF—Dutch two-masted vessel
KING—monarch; ruler; card
KNAG—peg
KRAG—rifle
KUNG—public
KAPH—Heb. letter
KATH—astringent
KISH—basket; graphite
KITH—friends
KOCH—Ger. bacteriologist, Robert ----
KOPH—Hebrew letter
KUSH—Ham's son
KYAH—bird
KADI—Moslem judge
KALI—carpet; glasswort; tongue of Agni
KAMI—Jap. gods; Indo.- Chin. language
KARI—gum tree
KASI—tile
KAVI—Japanese language
KAWI—Japanese language
KAZI—Moslem judge
KEPI—military cap
KERI—Heb.: Bib. pronunciation aid
KIKI—castor oil plant
KIRI—knobkerrie; paulownia tree
KIWI—apteryx; flightless bird
KIYI—yelp
KOBI—Jap. army second line
KOJI—Jap. yeast cake
KOLI—low caste
KOPI—N.Z. tree
KORI—bustard; low caste
KUEI—disembodied spirit
KUKI—Burmese tribe
KULI—low caste
KURI—tribesman
KWEI—disembodied spirit
KAIK—Maori village
KEEK—spy in fashion trade
KIAK—canoe
KICK—hit with foot; excitement
KINK—cramp; twist
KIRK—church: Scot.
KONK—tree decay
KUNK—measure
KURK—church: Scot.
KYAK—canoe
KAIL—pine tree
KARL—masc. name
KEAL—cabbage
KEEL—ocher; ship's bottom; rudder
KIEL—ocher; rudder
KILL—slay; creek
KOEL—bird
KOHL—eye cosmetic
KRAL—hut; village
KUHL—eye cosmetic
KASM—measure
KHEM—chief god
KLAM—weight
KLOM—weight
KAAN—title; Pers. lord
KARN—stone heap
KAUN—Pers. lord
KAWN—Pers. lord
KEEN—avid; eager
KERN—type part; composer
KHAN—title; caravansary
KILN—oast; oven
KLAN—Ku Klux ----
KRAN—coin
KUAN—Chin. official;

Chin. pottery
KALO—taro root
KANO—Jap. school of
    painting
KARO—N.Z. plant
KAYO—knock out
KENO—game
KIHO—butterfly
KILO—measure
KINO—resin; prefix: moving
KOKO—parson bird;
    Mikado
KOLO—folk dance
KOSO—Panamint Indian
KOTO—Jap. harp
KOZO—paper mulberry
KROO—Liberian tribe
KEEP—preserve; last
KELP—iodine source;
    seaweed
KIPP—peak
KLOP—sound
KNAP—hilltop; nibble; tip
KNIP—bite; peck
KNOP—projection; stud
KOOP—bargain
KAAR—weight
KEIR—bleaching vat
KERR—physicist; drama
    critic
KIER—bleaching vat
KNAR—knot in wood
KNOR—knot in wood
KNUR—knot in wood
KTKR—chess move
KTQR—chess move
KUAR—month
KYAR—coconut fiber
KEYS—Florida islands
KIDS—children
KISS—smack; buss
KOSS—measure
KRAS—wild goat
KRIS—Malay dagger
KVAS—Russ. beer
KAAT—narcotic shrub
KANT—change direction;
    Immanuel ----
KEET—guinea fowl

KELT—Celt
KENT—Lear's follower
KEPT—retained
KHET—measure
KILT—Scottish skirt
KIST—antique chest; fixed
    payment
KNIT—unite; loop
KNOT—tie; loop; problem
KNUT—king
KOPT—Copt
KTKT—chess move
KYAT—weight
KADU—tribe
KAGU—bird
KAHU—harrier hawk
KIKU—chrysanthemum
KIVU—tsetse fly
KOBU—seaweed food
KUDU—Afr. antelope
KUKU—bird
KIEV—Russ. city
KNEW—was aware
KNOW—understand
KATY—fem. nickname
KAZY—Moslem judge
KNEZ—Slavic prince

LAMA—Buddhist monk
LANA—flannel; wood
LARA—Byron poem
LATA—jumping disease
LAVA—molten rock
LEDA—Castor's mother;
    Helen's mother;
    Pollux' mother
LENA—firewood; Conrad
    heroine
LIDA—fem. nickname
LIJA—fish
LILA—fem. name
LIMA—bean; city
LINA—fem. name
LIPA—fat
LIRA—money; hurdy-gurdy
LISA—fem. nickname
LOKA—universe
LOLA—fem. name
LOMA—fringe; flop

LORA—fem. name; tree-snake
LOTA—burbot genus; pot
LOWA—bird
LUBA—Bantu
LUNA—moth; moon
LURA—brain opening
LYRA—constellation
LAMB—Charles ----; Elia; essayist; amateur
LIMB—arm; branch
LOBB—brewer's vat; tread heavily; tennis stroke
LAIC—secular
LAID—put down
LAND—disembark
LARD—fat; bacon
LAUD—praise; extol
LEAD—conduct; metal; bullets
LEND—grant; loan
LEWD—obscene
LIED—Ger.: song
LIND—Jenny ----, singer
LOAD—burden; onus
LOOD—weight
LORD—nobleman
LOUD—noisy
LACE—flavor; netting
LADE—dip
LAKE—red pigment; pool; inland sea
LAME—crippled; halt; fabric
LANE—plane's fixed route; narrow street
LATE—tardy; dead
LAVE—bathe; wash
LAZE—to be idle
LENE—consonant; smooth
LICE—insects
LIFE—existence; biography
LIKE—as; similar; quo; while
LIME—calcium oxide; caustic; fruit; color
LINE—row; wire; track; boundary
LIRE—Fr.: read
LITE—suffix: mineral, rock

LIVE—dwell; exist; alert
LOBE—leaf division
LODE—mineral deposit
LOGE—theatre box
LOKE—Balder's killer; god of discord
LONE—single
LOPE—easy gait
LORE—history; knowledge
LOSE—forfeit; fail
LOTE—poet.: lotus
LOVE—tennis score; affection; Eros; zero
LUBE—oil
LUCE—pike; Clare Boothe ----; Henry ----
LUGE—sled
LUKE—name; evangelist
LUNE—crescent-shaped; hawk's leash
LUPE—bird
LURE—tempt
LUTE—Apollo's instrument; cement; jar ring
LUXE—elegance
LYRE—harp
LEAF—plant part; page; sheet
LEIF—Norse explorer, ---- Ericson
LIEF—willingly
LOAF—bread; be idle
LOOF—sponge gourd
LUFF—sail nearer wind
LING—burbot; fish
LONG—crave; desire
LUNG—air bladder
LURG—marine annelid
LAKH—100,000 rupees
LASH—whip; stroke; part of eye
LATH—strip of wood
LEAH—fem. name; Jacob's wife; Laban's daughter
LECH—monument
LITH—comb. form: stone
LOCH—Scot.: lake
LOSH—wash leather
LOTH—averse
LUGH—Celtic sun god

LUSH—luxuriant
LARI—gull genus; hook money
LASI—tribe
LAZI—tribe
LETI—island of Timor
LEVI—Jacob's son; Leah's son
LITI—medieval peasant
LOCI—Lat.: places
LODI—Napoleonic victory
LOKI—Aesir; god of discord; Balder's killer
LORI—lemur
LOTI—Fr. author
LUDI—Roman public games
LURI—Cent. Afr. Negro
LACK—need; desire
LANK—slender; lean
LARK—bird
LEAK—ooze; crack
LEEK—flavoring plant; onion-like plant
LICK—tongue stroke; defeat
LINK—join; unite; chain part
LOCK—fasten; bolt; piece of hair
LONK—Eng. black-faced sheep
LOOK—appear; glance; see
LUCK—chance; lot; fortune
LURK—skulk
LEAL—Scot.: faithful
LILL—small pin
LOLL—lounge
LULL—calm; quiet spell
LIAM—Ir.: William
LOAM—kind of earth
LOOM—appear; seem
LYAM—bloodhound
LAIN—reclined
LAUN—sieve
LAWN—bishop's office; grass; fabric
LEAN—rawboned; skinny; lank
LEON—masc. name
LIEN—attachment;

garnishment
LIIN—measure
LIMN—draw; portray
LINN—Scot.: pool, waterfall
LION—cat
LLYN—pool
LOAN—lend
LOIN—cut of meat; body part
LOON—bird
LORN—desolate
LOUN—bird; loon
LOWN—dolt
LYON—Fr. city
LAGO—lake
LAZO—lariat
LENO—cotton fabric
LERO—Dodecanese Island
LETO—Apollo's mother
LEVO—prefix: left
LIDO—It. resort
LINO—measure; kind of type
LOBO—wolf
LOCO—mad; weed
LOLO—Caucasian race in China
LORO—bird; parrot-fish
LOTO—game; pot
LUDO—dice game
LAAP—eucalyptus secretion
LAMP—light; bulb
LAPP—northern Scandinavian
LARP—eucalyptus secretion
LEAP—jump; skip
LERP—eucalyptus secretion
LIMP—flaccid; loose
LISP—speech defect; stammer
LOOP—circular turn; noose
LOUP—half-mask; Pawnee Indian
LUMP—swelling; node
LAIR—den; haunt
LEAR—Shakespearean king
LEER—ogle; stare; oven
LEHR—oven

LIAR—falsifier
LOIR—dormouse
LOUR—frown; scowl
LAIS—Grk. beauty
LAOS—S.E. Asian country
LARS—Porsena
LASS—girl
LAWS—rules; regulations
LEES—dregs
LENS—magnifying glass
LESS—minus; fewer
LIAS—geol. division
LISS—fairy fort; fleur-de-lis; relieve
LOIS—fem. name
LOOS—Anita ----, writer
LOSS—deprivation; waste; forfeiture
LOTS—quantities; a great deal
LUBS—pert. to Lubeck
LYAS—geol. period
LACT—prefix: milk
LAET—freedman
LAIT—Fr.: milk
LAST—final; endure
LEET—candidates list; old Eng. court
LEFT—departed
LENT—fasting period; loaned
LEST—for fear that
LETT—Latvian; Balt.
LIFT—Brit.: elevator; raise; elevate
LILT—lively song
LINT—yarn fluff
LIST—careen; tip; record; catalogue
LOFT—attic; garret
LOOT—plunder; booty
LOST—misplaced; defeated; confused
LOUT—dolt; boor
LUST—desire
LATU—Latvian money
LIEU—place; stead
LIMU—edible seaweed
LUAU—Hawaiian cook-out
LULU—bird

LLEW—deity
LWOW—Polish city
LANX—Rom. dish
LYNX—wildcat
LACY—netty; like lace
LADY—title; woman
LAZY—idle
LELY—Dutch painter
LEVY—tax; assess
LILY—flower
LIMY—viscous
LINY—streaky
LIVY—Roman historian
LOGY—dull; boring; heavy
LORY—bird
LUCY—fem. name
LUNY—crazy
LINZ—city of Danube
LITZ—radio wire
LODZ—Polish city

MABA—Moslem Negroes; tree genus
MAHA—Ceylon ape; deer
MAIA—Hermes' mother; star; crab genus
MAJA—crab genus
MALA—evil; wrong; bird's jaw
MAMA—mother
MANA—Chin. letter; nature's power
MARA—Buddhist demon; Naomi
MASA—corn meal
MATA— ----Hari (spy)
MAYA—Hindu magic; weaverbird; Buddha's mother
MEDA—secret order
MEGA—prefix: great
MELA—prefix: black; relig. festival
MESA—flat elevated ground
META—Rom. circus post; goal post
MICA—isinglass
MILA—measure
MINA—anc. weight; woman's nickname

MIRA—variable star
MOHA—delusion; It. millet
MOLA—sunfish genus
MONA—monkey
MORA—delay; Spartan
army division
MOTA—Moslem marriage
MOXA—cautery plant
MUGA—silk
MURA—Indian
MUSA—banana genus
MUTA—change: music;
Moslem marriage
MYNA—talking bird
MYRA—ancient city; name
MYXA—tree
MOAB—Bib. kingdom; Lot's
son
MARC—grape refuse; name
MAID—domestic; girl
MAND—grass
MAUD—plaid fabric; shawl;
fem. name
MEAD—fermented drink;
meadow; Lake ——
MEED—recompense
MELD—canasta play; merge
MEND—repair; darn
MILD—calm; soft
MIND—care for; tend;
brain; dislike
MOED—Mishnah festivals
MOLD—fashion; shape;
fungus
MOOD—disposition; temper
MUDD—measure
MUND—protection right
MACE—staff; chemical;
spice
MADE—fashioned;
manufactured
MAGE—magician
MAKE—create; produce;
identify
MALE—manly; gender
MANE—hair
MARE—fem. horse; sea
MAZE—labyrinth
MEDE—anc. Asiatic
MELE—Hawaiian chant

MENE—Bib. word; —— tekel
upharsin (handwriting
on the wall)
MERE—only; simple;
boundary
MESE—Grk. musical term
METE—allot; grant
MICE—rodents
MIDE—Ojibway secret
order
MIKE—masc. nickname
MILE—dist. measure
MIME—clown; actor; Gr.
drama
MINE—poss. pronoun; ore
deposit; explosive
MIRE—fen; marsh
MISE—stake; grant
MITE—arachnid; insect
MIXE—Mexican Indian
MODE—manner; method;
fashion
MOKE—donkey
MOLE—birthmark; Mossi
language; nevus,
burrowing animal
MOPE—be listless; sulk
MORE—greater
MOSE—masc. nickname
MOTE—particle
MOUE—Fr.: grimace
MOVE—excite; act; stir
MULE—slipper; spinning
jenny; animal
MURE—squeeze against
wall
MUSE—ponder; meditate;
goddess
MUTE—silent; mum
MIFF—offend
MOFF—fabric
MUFF—woolen or fur
warmer for hands
MAGG—bird; magpie
MIGG—marble
MING—Chin. dynasty;
pottery
MORG—measure
MUNG—grass
MAGH—Hindu month

MASH—crush; mixture; hammer
MATH—school subject; Hindu monastery
MESH—entangle; netting
MOTH—insect; page in Shakespeare
MUCH—a great deal
MUSH—boiled meat; proceed!
MUTH—measure
MYTH—legend
MABI—tree
MADI—Upper Nile Negro
MAGI—priestly caste; wise men
MAKI—lemur
MALI—country; caste
MANI—peanut
MARI—Fr.: husband; prefix: sea
MAUI—Polynesian hero
MEDI—prefix: middle
MIDI—Southern France
MIMI—opera heroine; fem. nickname
MOKI—Maori raft
MUNJ—rope-making grass
MARK—sign; stamp; notice; money; evangelist; man's name
MASK—disguise; domino
MEEK—timid
MICK—Irishman
MILK—exploit; white fluid; drain
MINK—furry animal
MIRK—darkness
MOCK—ridicule; deride
MONK—cenobite; friar
MOSK—Masjid; moslem temple
MUCK—mess
MULK—freehold land
MURK—darkness
MUSK—perfume base
MAAL—measure
MAIL—chain armor; post; send
MALL—mallet; promenade

MARL—clayey soil; fertilizer
MAUL—hammer; attack; mangle
MEAL—ground grain; repast
MERL—blackbird
MEWL—whimper
MILL—quern; grinder
MOIL—drudge; work
MOLL—girl; fem. nickname
MULL—fabric; ponder
MAAM—madam
MAIM—injure; harm; mutilate
MALM—clayey soil; limestone
MARM—school ——; ma'am
MEUM—carrotlike herb genus; Lat.: mine
MIAM—Australian hut
MAIN—chief; head; conduit
MANN—Am. educator; Ger. writer
MAUN—must
MEAN—unkind; nasty; denote; middle; average
MEIN—Chin. noodles
MIAN—master
MIEN—bearing; manner
MOAN—groan
MORN—a.m., dawn; morning
MOWN—trimmed
MADO—fish
MAKO—shark; bird
MALO—breechcloth
MAMO—bird
MANO—grindstone
MAPO—goby fish
MARO—Jap. ship
MAYO—Indian; —— Clinic
MAZO— ——dela Roche (author); *Jalna* series
MEIO—measure
MEMO—note
MERO—grouper
MIAO—Chinese aborigine
MICO—marmoset
MILO—grain

MINO—Jap. outer garment
MIRO—bird; timber tree
MOGO—stone hatchet
MOHO—bird
MOIO—measure
MOJO—voodoo charm
MOKO—Maori tattooing
MONO—prefix: one; monkey; Indian
MORO—bird; Mindanao native
MOTO—music: movement
MOXO—Indian
MOZO—Sp.: manservant
MUSO—Indian
MYXO—mold
MUMP—cheat; sponge on
MAHR—Moslem marriage settlement
MEER—Ger.: sea
MOHR—Afr. gazelle
MOOR—heath; Moslem: to anchor
MAAS—river
MAIS—Fr.: but
MANS—Chin. aborigine
MARS—planet; war god
MASS—aggregate; populace; rite; service
MESS—botch; disorder; meal
MEWS—royal stables
MIAS—orangutan
MISS—girl; failure; omit
MONS—Lat.: mountain
MORS—death deity
MOSS—lichen; parasitic plant
MUSS—rumple
MAAT—goddess
MALT—barley; beer ingredient
MART—store; market; masc. nickname
MAST—beechnuts; pole
MATT—without shine; masc. nickname
MEAT—food; flesh
MEET—encounter; contest
MELT—dissolve; liquefy

MENT—falcon-headed god
MILT—spleen; masc. nickname
MINT—aromatic herb; candy; coin
MIST—drizzle; fog
MITT—glove
MOAT—trench
MOLT—to shed hair
MONT—Fr.: mountain
MOOT—undecided
MORT—death; the kill; salmon
MOST—greatest; largest number
MUST—necessity; staleness
MUTT—cur; mongrel
MYST—Grk. priest
MAKU—Indian
MANU—prefix: hand; Hindu ancestor
MARU—Jap. ship name
MASU—fish
MENU—bill of fare
MEOU—cat's cry
MERU—Hindu "Olympus"
MIAU—cat's cry
MITU—curassow
MUAV—geol. epoch
MEOW—cat's cry
MIAW—cat's cry
MANX—tailless cat; Celtic
MINX—pert girl
MANY—numerous
MARY—fem. name; Christ's mother
MATY—India: native servant
MIRY—boggy; marshy
MITY—insect infected
MOLY—herb
MOSY—shuffle along
METZ—city

NAGA—snake; cobra
NAIA—cobra genus
NAJA—cobra genus
NALA—legendary hero
NAMA—Hottentot

NANA—nurse; Aztec hero's wife
NAPA—Calif. wine region; glove leather
NASA—National Aeronautics & Space Administration
NEMA—prefix: thread; eelworm
NEPA—needle bug; water scorpion
NERA—Tiber tributary
NEVA—river in Leningrad
NINA—Columbus' ship; goddess
NIPA—atap palm; palm drink
NOLA—fem. name
NONA—fate; music: ninth
NORA—fem. name; Ibsen heroine
NOTA—geology: back; observe
NOVA—blaze star; new
NOXA—something harmful
NUBA—Nubian
NUDA—ctenphores
NUMA—Roman legendary king
NAAB—river
NIMB—circle of light; halo
NUMB—deadened
NAID—worm
NARD—herb-plant
NEED—demand; claim; lack; want
NEJD—kingdom
NKVD—Russian secret police
NUDD—legendary Brit. king
NAME—title; cite
NANE—Scot.: none
NAPE—neck back
NARE—Loki's son
NASE—cape; headland
NATE—born
NAVE—church part
NAZE—cape; headland
NETE—Grk. music. term

NEUE—Ger.: new
NEVE—firn; snow field
NICE—Riviera port; good; pleasing
NIDE—brood; covey
NIFE—core material of earth
NIKE—goddess of victory
NILE—river
NINE—card; the Muses
NIUE—Savage Island language
NODE—joint; knot; lump
NOME—city in Alaska
NONE—not any; ninth hour
NORE—Thames estuary
NOSE—plane part; pry; sniff; proboscis
NOTE—memo; observe; record
NOVE—It.: nine
NUDE—naked; type of art work
NUPE—Nigerian native
NAIF—having true luster
NIOG—coconut palm
NOGG—egg drink
NASH—American humorist
NATH—star
NIGH—near
NISH—Constantine's birthplace
NOAH—Bib. ark builder
NASI—combin. form: nose; patriarch's title
NAZI—fascist
NERI—It.: blacks
NETI—thatch grass
NGAI—E. Afr. spiritual power
NIDI—nest
NISI—Lat.: unless
NODI—complications
NORI—alga; seaweed
NABK—thorny shrub
NAIK—leader
NARK—informer
NECK—isthmus; body part
NICK—chip; notch
NOCK—fit string to arrow

NOOK—corner; cranny
NAEL—weight
NAIL—claw; talon; fasten
NEAL—masc. name
NEIL—masc. name
NELL—fem. nickname
NILL—refuse; be unwilling
NOEL—Christmas; carol
NOIL—waste fiber
NOLL—nickname: Oliver
NOYL—waste fiber
NULL—zero; naught
NURL—to mill; knot in
    wood
NAAM—distraint
NEEM—margosa tree
NORM—masc. nickname;
    average
NEIN—Ger.: no
NEON—kind of light; gassy
    element
NOON—midday
NORN—goddess of fate
NOUN—part of speech
NABO—P.I. shrub
NAIO—N. Z. tree
NATO—North Atlantic
    Treaty Organization
NEBO—god of wisdom
NEMO—prefix: glade; Jules
    Verne character
NERO—Roman emperor
NINO—Sp.: boy
NITO—climbing fern
NOIO—noddy tern
NOLO— ---- contendere,
    defendant's plea
NONO—It.: ninth
NEAP—lowest high tide;
    wagon tongue
NEEP—turnip
NOUP—promontory
NATR—weight
NEAR—close to
NEER—poet.: never; kidney
NOIR—Fr.: black
NURR—gnarl
NAIS—river nymph
NAOS—star
NESS—cape; suffix

NEWS—tidings; word
NIAS—island
NIBS—personage
NOBS—cribbage term
NOES—votes
NOUS—Fr.: we; intellect
NAST—cartoonist
NAUT—sea mile
NEAT—tidy; straight
NEST—den; cozy place
NEWT—eft; salamander
NEXT—following;
    subsequent
NOTT—Norse night
NOWT—neat cattle
NUIT—Fr.: night
NABU—god of wisdom
NAPU—Indo-Malayan
    animal
NIOU—measure
NOSU—Caucasian race in
    China
NOIX—edible gland
NAGY—Hungarian premier
NARY—not one
NAVY—color; fleet
NOSY—prying
NOWY—curved

OBRA—Sp.: work
OCHA—weight
OCRA—vegetable; gumbo
OCTA—prefix: eight
ODEA—theatre
OFFA—Teutonic legendary
    hero
OHIA—timber tree
OKIA—Moroccan money
OKRA—vegetable; gumbo
OLEA—olive
OLGA—fem. name
OLLA—cooking pot; highly
    seasoned dish; jar
ONCA—ounce
ONZA—Sp.: ounce
ORCA—killer whale
ORNA—measure
ORRA—Scot.: odd
OSSA—bones; mountain
OTEA—Great Barrier Island

OTRA—Sp.: other
OXEA—sponge spicule
ODIC—of a poem
OLIC—chem. suffix
OTIC—auditory
OLID—fetid
OOID—egg shaped
OORD—coin
ORAD—toward the mouth
OVID—poet
OXID—oxygen compound
OBOE—woodwind; music.
　　instrument
OESE—bacteriologist's
　　wire
OGEE—molding; cyma;
　　pointed arch
OGLE—gaze; stare
OGRE—monster
OHNE—Ger.: without
OIME—Alas!
OISE—Fr. river
OKIE—migrating worker
ONCE—one time; in the
　　past
ONDE—Fr.: wave
OOZE—slimy mud; seep
ORFE—fish; yellow ide
ORLE—fillet; heraldic
　　bearing
ORNE—measure; Caen's
　　river
OSTE—prefix: bone
OTOE—Sioux Indian
OUSE—river
OLAF—viking; Norweg.
　　saint
OATH—pledge; vow; curse
OKEH—all right; o.k.
OPAH—bright colored fish
OUCH—exclamation
OUGH—exclamation
OMEI—Buddhist sacred
　　mountain
OMNI—prefix: all
OMRI—king of Israel
OMSK—Siberian city
OBOL—coin
ODAL—E. Ind. vine; land
ODEL—E. Ind. vine

ODYL—alleged force
OPAL—Oct. birthstone; gem
ORAL—aloud; spoken
OREL—Russian city
OVAL—egg-shaped;
　　elliptical
OXYL—oxygen radical
ODUM—tree
OGAM—Ir. alphabet
OGUM—Ir. alphabet
OLAM—eon; eternity
ONYM—tech. name (biol.)
OVUM—egg cell; germ cell
OBAN—coin
ODIN—Aesir; chief Norse
　　god; Frigg's husband
OLAN—Pearl Buck heroine
OMAN—sultanate
OMEN—augury; portent
ONAN—Judah's son
OPEN—candid; frank;
　　honest; bare; unfold
ORAN—seaport
OVEN—kiln; stove for
　　baking
OWEN—masc. name
OXAN—gas
OXEN—draft animals;
　　bovines
OCTO—prefix: eight
ODIO—It.: hatred
OHIO—Buckeye State
OKRO—gumbo; vegetable
OLEO—margarine
OLIO—medley
OMAO—Hawaiian thrush
ONTO—hep; wise to
ORDO—rel. book of feasts
ORLO—plinth
OSLO—Norweg. city
OTHO—Roman emperor
OTRO—Sp.: another
OTTO—flower extract;
　　Germ. emperor; masc.
　　name
ODER—river
ODOR—smell
OGOR—Turkic person
OLOR—swan genus
OMAR—Pers. poet; caliph;

masc. name
OMER—measure
ONER—blow; individual
OSAR—eskers; glacial ridge
OSER—Fr.: dare
OVER—above; done;
    beyond
OWER—debtor
OXER—fence
OYER—court hearing
OAKS—horse race; trees
OCHS—publisher; Adolph

ODDS—chances; advantage
OFFS—cricket field sides
ONES—persons; individuals
ONUS—responsibility;
    burden
OONS—minced oath
OPUS—work
ORAS—Danish money
OTIS—general; inventor;
    bustard genus
OTUS—giant slain by
    Apollo
OURS—poss. pronoun
OVIS—sheep genus
OYES—court cry
OAST—kiln
OBIT—death notice
OKET—ounce
OMIT—neglect
OONT—camel
OUST—cast out; eject
OAHU—Hawaiian island
OGPU—Russ. secret police
ORDU—Turk. army corps
OBEX—layer in the brain
ODAX—rock whiting genus
OLAX—evergreen
ONYX—cameo stone; gem
ORYX—antelope
OAKY—oaklike
OARY—oarlike
OBEY—submit
OHOY—nautical cry
OILY—unctuous
OKAY—all right
OLAY—palm
ONLY—single; exclusively

OOZY—slimy
ORGY—carousal
ORLY—Paris airport
OYEZ—court cry

PACA—rodent
PAGA—rice
PAHA—glacial hill
PALA—weight
PANA—city
PAPA—father
PARA—Belem; coin
PASA—dried berry; raisin
PATA—sword; cloth strip
PAWA—weight
PEBA—armadillo; Peruvian
    Indian
PECA—coin
PEDA—pastoral staff
PEGA—fish
PELA—wax insect
PERA—district of
    Constantinople
PESA—coin
PEVA—armadillo; Peruvian
    Indian
PICA—magpie; type size
PIKA—little chief hare
PIMA—Indian; cotton fabric
PINA—cone of silver;
    pineapple
PIPA—Surinam toad
PISA—city; tower
PITA—aloe fiber
PLEA—request; prayer
POHA—gooseberry
POLA—city
POOA—hemp shrub
PROA—Malay boat
PUCA—goblin
PUJA—Hindu festival
PUKA—N.Z. tree
PUMA—Amer. cat
PUNA—high region of
    Andes
PUPA—chrysalis; instar
PUYA—brain opening
PYLA—brain opening
PLEB—plebian; ordinary
    person; freshman

PARC—Fr.: park
PAID—reimbursed; compensated
PARD—spotted cat; leopard
PEND—suspend; be delayed
PHAD—star
PIED—many-colored
PLOD—trudge
POND—lake; water
POOD—weight
PROD—goad; urge
PUND—weight
PUUD—weight
PACE—horse's gait; measure; speed
PAGE—attendant; summon; leaf (of a book)
PALE—wan; ashy
PANE—glass panel
PAPE—bird
PARE—peel; skin
PATE—crown; head; paste
PAVE—jewelry setting; cover
PEKE—small dog
PELE—volcano goddess, Hawaii
PENE—head
PERE—Fr.: father; priest
PETE—masc. nickname; safe
PICE—weight
PIKE—fish; highway; pointed staff
PILE—fuzz
PINE—coniferous tree; yearn for
PIPE—music. instrument; whistle; hose
PISE—building material
PLIE—fold
POKE—nudge
POLE—rod; wand; staff; shaft
POME—apple; fruit
PONE—cornbread
POPE—bishop of Rome; pontiff
PORE—opening; ponder
POSE—posture; baffle

POWE—weight
PUCE—color; eureka red
PUKE—vomit
PULE—whimper
PUME—language
PURE—chaste
PYLE—Am. author, illustrator
PYRE—funeral pile
PELF—booty
PIAF—Fr. singer
PIFF—bullet sound
POUF—exclamation
PUFF—whiff
PANG—throe
PEAG—wampum; money
PING—sound
PLUG—stopper
PONG—sound
PUNG—box sleigh
PATH—road; lane; track
PISH—contemptuous exclamation
PITH—heart; core
POOH—bosh!
POSH—elegant
PRAH—Malay boat
PTAH—god
PUGH—exclamation
PUSH—shove
PADI—rice
PAHI—Malay boat
PALI—precipice; Buddhist language
PANI—Polish form of address
PASI—low caste Hindu
PEAI—medicine man
PEDI—prefix: foot
PERI—fairy
PICI—bird
PIKI—maize bread
PILI—comb. form: hair; P.I. nut
PIPI—mollusk
PULI—Hungarian dog
PURI—Indian yellow
PACK—bundle; scout unit; crowd
PANK—weight

PARK—green; common
  grounds
PEAK—apex; summit
PECK—1/4 bushel; kiss; nip
PEEK—peer; look slyly
PERK—make lively
PICK—choose; tool
PINK—carnation; color;
  healthy condition
PISK—nighthawk
POLK—Cossack regiment;
  President
POOK—goblin
PORK—meat; swine
PUCK—ice hockey disc;
  sprite
PULK—Cossack regiment
PUNK—tinder; touchwood
PAAL—measure
PAIL—bucket
PALL—cloy; become insipid
PAUL—Apostle; masc.
  name
PAWL—detent
PEAL—ring; sound
PEEL—external covering;
  strip; skin
PHIL—masc. nickname
PILL—tablet; medicine
POLL—head; survey; take a
  vote
POOL—game; pond; stake;
  fund
POUL—Russian coin
PULL—draw; tow; drag
PURL—knitting stitch;
  murmur
PYAL—veranda
PALM—tree; part of hand;
  foist
PERM—elec. unit; hair
  curling treatment
PLUM—fruit; tree
POEM—epode; verse
PRAM—baby carriage
PRIM—stiffly nice; proper
PROM—promenade; ball;
  dance
PAIN—afflict; ache; trouble
PAON—peacock blue

PAUN—betel leaf
PAWN—chessman; pledge
PEAN—song of praise
PEEN—hammer head
PENN—William ----
PEON—slave; laborer
PERN—honey buzzard
PHON—measurement of
  loudness
PIEN—arris
PION—excavate; dredge
PIRN—bobbin; reel
PLAN—method; order;
  design
POON—wood for mast
PACO—alpaca
PAHO—prayer stick
PAJO—prayer stick
PALO—Sp.: wooden pole
PATO—Muscovy duck
PAVO—constellation;
  peacock
PECO—black tea
PEDO—combining form:
  foot
PEHO bird (morepork)
PELO—It.: hair
PEPO—squash; cucumber;
  fleshy fruit
PERO—Sp.: but
PESO—Sp. coin; dollar
PETO—Henry IV
  character; fish
PHOO—sound of disgust
PICO—game; peak
PINO—pine
PIRO—Indian
PISO—weight
PITO—aloe fiber
POCO—slightly; little
POGO—comic strip
  character; jumping stick
POLO—game; Marco ----,
  explorer
POMO—Indian
PORO—secret society of
  Sierra Leone
PRAO—Malay boat
PUNO—Andes wind
PYRO—prefix: fire

PALP—antenna; feeler
PEEP—look narrowly; bird's chirp
PIMP—procurer
PLAP—fall; spill
PLOP—fall; spill
PLUP—sound of a fall
POMP—splendor; formality
POOP—ship's deck
PREP—prepare; kind of school
PROP—brace; support
PULP—pith; paper
PUMP—draw out; kind of shoe
PAAR—sandstone
PAIR—brace; two
PARR—young salmon; Catherine ----, wife of Henry VIII
PEAR—fruit
PEER—equal; stare
PEUR—Fr.: fear
PIER—breakwater
PIRR—whiz
POOR—codfish; indigent
POUR—teem; rain; Fr.: for
PURR—cat's sound
PACS—lumberman's boots
PAIS—Fr.: country
PARS—Lat.: part
PASS—omit; opening; go through
PHOS—phosphorus
PIUS—Pope ----
PLUS—and; also; more
PONS—Lat.: bridge, Lily ----, singer
POUS—measure
PRES——Fr.: near
PUSS—cat; face
PACT—treaty; agreement
PANT—gasp
PART—divide; separate; split
PAST—by; ago; after
PEAT—turf; fuel
PEET—turf; fuel
PELT—skin; covering; hurl
PENT—confined

PERT—saucy; bold; lively
PEST—nuisance; insect
PHIT—bullet sound
PHOT—unit of illumination
PHUT—bullet sound
PIAT—antitank gun
PICT—ancient inhabitant of Britain
PIET—chatterbox; magpie
PINT—measure
PIOT—magpie
PIST—call to attract attention
PITT—Eng. statesman
PLAT—braid; map; land parcel
PLET—Russ. whip
PLOT—plan; design; land parcel
POET—versifier; elegist
PONT—Afr. ferryboat; Fr.: bridge
POOT—sound of disgust
PORT—harbor; bay; wine; naut.: left side
POST—Lat.: after; pillar; to mail
POTT—paper size
POUT—be sullen
PRET—measure
PUNT—boat; football kick
PUTT—golf stroke
PYAT—magpie
PYET—magpie
PATU—Maori weapon
PEGU—Burmese language
PELU—timber tree
PERU—country
POKU—Afr. antelope
PRAU—Malay boat
PUDU—Chilean deer
PUKU—Afr. antelope
PULU—Hawaiian tree fern
PURU—Braz. Indian
PHEW—exclamation
PLEW—beaver skin
PLOW—hoe; till; implement
PROW—boat front
PLEX—form a network
PNYX—Gr. voters' meeting

place
PRIX—Fr.: price
PALY—heraldic design
PAVY—clingstone peach
PEVY—lumberman's hook
PIAY—medicine man
PIKY—full of fish
PILY—pilelike
PINY—pinelike
PIPY—shrill
PITY—compassion; mercy
PIXY—sprite; elf
PLAY—frisk; romp; drama
PLOY—coup; strategem
POGY—fish
POKY—slow
POLY—prefix: many; herb
PONY—trot; small horse
POSY—flower
PRAY—beseech; entreat
PREY—plunder; pillage
PULY—complaining
PUNY—feeble; weak
PUXY—ill-tempered
PHIZ—face

QAID—fortress commander
QUAD—quadrangle; college
    area
QUID—cud; pound
QUOD—prison
QERE—Hebrew Bible
    pronunciation aid
QUAE—"---- vide", which
    see
QUAG—bog; marsh
QUNG—Afr. Bushman
QOPH—Hebrew letter
QERI—Hebrew Bible
    pronunciation aid
QUAI—landing place; pier
QUEI—measure
QUAN—money
QUIP—wisecrack; joke
QUAS—Russian beer
QKKT—chess move
QQKT—chess move
QUIT—stop; end
QUAY—landing place; pier
QUIZ—exam; test; question

RABA—river
RACA—Bibl. reproach
RADA—Russ. convention;
    legislature
RAIA—non-Moslem of
    Ottoman empire
RAJA—Hindu prince
RAMA—Hindu deity;
    Vishnu Incarnation
RANA—frog genus; Hindu
    prince
RARA— ---- avis (rare bird)
RASA—essence
RATA—chestnut; pro ----
RAYA—bird
REBA—Hebrew weight
REJA—Sp.: grille
RENA—Calif. fish
RHEA—bird genus; mother
    of gods; Krono's wife
RIGA—city
RIMA—breadfruit; chink;
    fissure
RIPA—river bank
RITA—fem. name
RODA—Nile Island
ROKA—mafura tree
ROMA—Lat.: Rome
ROPA—Sp.: clothes
ROSA—flower genus
ROTA—Catholic tribunal;
    court; hurdy-gurdy
RUGA—wrinkle
RUPA—Buddhism: form
RUSA—deer genus
RUTA—rue herb genus
RHOB—fruit jelly
RUMB—compass point
RAAD—Dutch assembly;
    fish
RAID—foray
RAND—basket strip;
    border; Afr. gold field
READ—peruse; study; pore
REED—bamboo; coarse
    grass; musical
    instrument
REND—cleave; tear
RETE—network
REVE—Fr.: dream

RIBE—lean animal
RICE—cereal; Elmer ----
RIDE—drive; urge; journey
RIFE—abundant; ample
RILE—anger; rage; irritate
RIME—chink
RINE—ditch; hemp
RIPE—mature
RIRE—Fr.: to laugh
RISE—emerge; emanate
RITE—ceremony
RIVE—cleave; rend
ROBE—garment
RODE—herd; measure
ROLE—actor's part
ROME—city
RONE—thicket
ROPE—cord; lime; cable
ROSE—flower; color; fem.
  name; stood up
ROTE—repetition; routine
ROUE—rake
ROVE—ramble; wander
RUBE—yokel; rustic
RUDE—rough; discourteous
RULE—law; canon; reign
RUNE—old letter; character
RUSE—trick; deception
RUTE—measure
RYME—water surface
RYPE—ptarmigan
REEF—reduce sail; shoal;
  sand bar
RIFF—ripple; Berber
ROOF—cover; top of a
  house
RUFF—bird; collar
RANG—sounded (as a bell
  or alarm)
RING—encircle; arena
RONG—Indo-Chin.
  language
RUNG—chair part; ladder
  part
RASH—hasty; skin irritation
RATH—chariot; hill fort
RESH—Heb. letter
RICH—wealthy; full
ROCH—14th Cent. Saint
RUKH—fabled bird

RUSH—hurry
RUTH—pity; compassion;
  Old Testament Book
RABI—spring crop; atomic
  physicist
RAGI—cereal grass
RAMI—branch
RANI—gypsy lady; princess
RATI—weight
RAVI—Bartu tribe
REKI—Baluchistan tribe
REMI—ancient people of
  Gaul
RENI—It. painter
RODI—Med. Island
ROMI—gypsy wife
RORI—Bantu tribe
ROTI—Fr.: roast
RACK—clouds; gait
RAIK—weight; measure
RANK—classify; rate; fetid
RECK—care for
REEK—exude; smell
RICK—haystack
RIKK—Eg. tambourine
RINK—skating arena
RISK—peril; hazard; danger
ROCK—roll; sway; stone;
  diamond
ROOK—bird; chessman
RUCK—crows; wrinkle
RUSK—Dean ----, Am.
  statesman; bread
RAIL—bird; scoff
REAL—actual; true
REEL—bobbin; spool
RIAL—coin
RIEL—Rebel leader (Red
  River)
RILL—small brook
ROIL—disturb
ROLL—rotate; drumbeat;
  bread
ROTL—weight
RULL—to trundle
RYAL—coin
RYEL—coin
REAM—bevel out; paper
  quantity
REEM—wild ox

REIM—oxhide strap
RHUM—alcoholic drink
RIEM—thongs of hide
ROAM—wander
ROOM—chamber
RAIN—teem; pour; shower
RANN—Ir. verse
REIN—check
RHIN—river; strap
RIEN—Fr.: nothing
ROAN—horse, parti-colored
ROON—Ir.: darling
RUIN—despoil
RALO—measure
REDO—make over
RENO—Nevada city
ROJO—Sp.: red
ROTO—Sp.: ragged person
RAIP—cord; rope
RAMP—gangplank
RASP—coarse file; grate
REAP—acquire; harvest
REPP—fabric
RISP—metal bar
ROMP—play; frisk
RSVP—Fr.: answer please
RUMP—sirloin part
REAR—hind; back
RIDD—Lorna Doone character
RIND—skin; bark; Odin's wife
ROAD—way; route; track
RODD—crossbow
ROED—filled with roe
ROOD—crucifix; land measure
ROUD—fish
RUDD—carp (fish)
RYND—millstone support
RACE—people; contest
RAGE—anger; fury
RAKE—tool; roue
RALE—lung sound
RAME—branch
RAPE—ravish
RARE—scarce; underdone
RASE—demolish
RATE—estimate; tax; price
RAVE—rant

RAZE—demolish
REDE—counsel
RESE—rage
RIER—whale oil cask
ROAR—loud sound
ROER—gun
RUER—repenter
RUHR—Ger. district
RAIS—Nile captain; Nepalese
RATS—exclamation of disgust
REIS—Nile captain
REMS—river
REVS—revolutions per minute
RHUS—sumac genus
RIIS—Am. journalist
RISS—geol. stage
ROOS—Ger. painter
ROSS—bark; Eng. explorer
RUSS—Russian
RAFT—boat; float
RANT—declaim; rave
RAPT—absorbed; attentive
RECT—philos. element
REFT—cleft; deprived
RENT—fissure; hire; let
REST—leisure; pause; remainder
RIFT—quarrel; split
RIOT—disturbance; row; tumult
RKKT—chess move
ROOT—base; extirpate
ROUT—defeat completely; flight
RQKT—chess move
RUNT—dwarf; small animal
RUST—corrode; eat away
RYOT—Indian peasant
RAHU—demon
RIMU—imou pine
RURU—N.Z. bird
ROUX—thickener; paste
RACY—spicy
RELY—depend
RILY—vexed; irritated
RIMY—frosty
ROEY—mottled

ROPY—stringy
ROSY—blushing; optimistic
ROWY—streaky
ROXY—fem. nickname
RUAY—weight
RUBY—gem; fem. name
RAZZ—ridicule; deride

SABA—textile fiber
SAGA—narrative; legend
SALA—Sp.: dining hall
SAMA—fish
SANA—fiber plant; Yemen's capital
SAPA—grape juice or jelly
SARA—fem. name
SASA—fencer's cry
SAYA—skirt
SEBA—Bib. country
SERA—antitoxin; blood part
SETA—bristle; caterpillar hair
SHEA—butter tree
SHOA—Abyssinian tribesman
SIDA—hemp; tree
SIKA—Jap. deer
SIMA—igneous rock
SINA—Bibl. mountain; drug
SITA—Ramachandra's wife
SIVA—dance
SKUA—bird
SODA—bicarbonate
SOFA—divan; couch
SOGA—Sp.: grass rope
SOJA—soybean
SOKA—drought blight
SOLA—alone; herb
SOMA—animal body; vine
SORA—bird
SOYA—soybean
STOA—colonnade; portico
SULA—genus
SUPA—tree
SURA—chapter in Koran
SUSA—cap. of Elam
SYRA—island
SCAB—encrustation; strikebreaker

SCOB—defect in fabric
SERB—Balkan; Servian
SLAB—thick slice; rock
SLEB—Arab nomad
SLOB—slovenly person
SLUB—twist of fiber
SNAB—brow of hill
SNIB—to escape logging work
SNOB—supercilious person
SNUB—rebuff
SORB—apple tree; Slav
STAB—attempt; pierce
STIB—bird
STUB—stocky; stump; bump
SWAB—mop
SWEB—swoon
SWOB—mop
SAIC—ketch
SPEC—speculation; specification
SADD—damm; waste matter on the Nile
SAID—uttered; spoke
SAND—grit; silica
SARD—carnelian; red
SCAD—fish
SCUD—wind-driven clouds
SEED—grain; germ; plant
SEID—Moslem lord; chief
SEND—transmit; dispatch
SHAD—fish
SHED—molt; cast off; hut
SHOD—wearing shoes
SIND—river
SKID—slide
SLED—cutter; snow vehicle
SLID—past tense of slide
SNED—lop; prune
SNOD—trim
SOLD—vended
SPAD—nail
SPED—hurried; hastened
SPUD—potato
STAD—S. Afr. town
STOD—Danish speech sound
STUD—button; breeding stock
SUDD—Eg. dam

SULD—measure
SURD—irrational number
SWAD—lump
SYED—Moslem title
SYUD—Moslem title
SABE—know
SADE—Heb. letter
SAFE—secure
SAGE—herb
SAKE—Jap. beer
SALE—auction; bargain;
    Fr.: dirty; salted
SAME—ditto; identical
SANE—rational
SATE—fill to excess; glut
SAVE—only; but; preserve
SAXE—greenish blue
SEME—dotted pattern
SERE—burn; wither; Sudan
    Negroid
SEVE—Fr.: delicacy of wine
SHEE—Irish fairies
SHOE—tire casing; boot
    covering
SICE—six
SIDE—aspect; facet; lateral
SIME—monkey
SINE—trig. function; Lat.:
    without
SIRE—beget
SISE—six
SITE—locale; scene
SIVE—sickle
SIZE—bulk; mass
SKEE—ski
SKYE—isle; kind of terrier
SLEE—sly
SLOE—black haw; plumlike
    fruit
SLUE—marsh; swamp; lot
SMEE—bird; duck
SNEE—cut
SOIE—silk
SOKE—court district
SOLE—exclusive; fish
SOME—part; any
SORE—deer; sensitive;
    painful; angry
SPAE—foretell
SPEE—Graf ----; German

count
STYE—disease of eyelid
SUPE—theatre extra
SURE—certain; firm
SYCE—groom
SYKE—fountain
SYNE—Scot.: since
SYPE—ooze
SELF—ego; identity
SERF—slave; peasant
SOUF—sigh
STOF—liquid measure
SURF—waves; swell of the
    sea
SANG—did sing
SARG—puppet maker
SHAG—hair; nap; tobacco
SING—carol; vocalize
SKAG—ship's keel part
SKEG—keel part
SLAG—dross
SLOG—strike; hit
SLUG—small drink; metal
    spacer
SMOG—fog; smoke; haze
SMUG—priggish
SNAG—obstacle; catch;
    knot
SNIG—drag
SNUG—comfortable; cozy
SONG—aria; tune; melody
STAG—deer; men's party
STOG—stall in mud
SUNG—Chin. dynasty;
    made vocal music
SWAG—booty; loot
SWIG—drink; gulp
SAAH—measure
SADH—holy man
SAHH—measure
SASH—belt; part of
    window
SEAH—measure
SETH—Adam's son;
    merchant
SHAH—ruler (Iran)
SHIH—measure
SIGH—lament
SIKH—Hindu
SINH—math term

SISH—slushy ice
SOPH—sophomore; 2nd
    year student
SOSH—drunk
SUCH—similar; same; like
SAFI—Afghan
SAKI—monkey; Jap. beer
SARI—garment
SATI—Eg. queen of gods
SEBI—prefix: fat
SEMI—half
SERI—betel nut; Mex.
    Indian
SESI—black-fin snapper
SETI—pharaoh
SHRI—goddess
SIDI—Moslem title
SIMI—Dodecanese isle
SIRI—betel nut
SISI—porkfish
SOLI—single performances
SORI—fern spore
SUFI—mystic
SUGI—Jap. cedar
SUJI—wheat
SUSI—fabric
SACK—discharge; pillage;
    wine; bag
SANK—immersed
SARK—Channel Island
SAUK—Indian
SAWK—measure
SECK—unprofitable
SEEK—search for; hunt
SEIK—Hindu sect
SHIK—Turkoman
SICK—ill
SILK—fabric
SINK—immerse; descend;
    fall; basin
SOAK—sot; saturate; imbue
SOBK—deity
SOCK—strike; foot covering
SOOK—market booth; hog
    call
SOUK—market booth
SUCK—draw in
SULK—be sullen
SUNK—immersed
SAAL—Ger.: hall

SAIL—ship canvas
SAUL—timber tree; King
    ----; St. Paul
SEAL—aquatic animal;
    fasten
SEEL—blind
SELL—vend; mart
SHUL—synagogue
SIAL—outer part of earth
SILL—window part; door
    part
SIOL—Irish tribe
SKIL—fish
SOIL—stain; spot; earth; dirt
SOUL—spirit; principle;
    person
SAUM—weight
SEEM—appear
SEIM—Polish assembly
SEJM—Polish assembly
SHAM—deceit; fraud
SHEM—Noah's son
SHIM—leveling ship; shingle
SIAM—Thailand
SKIM—glide; slip
SLAM—bridge term; bang
SLIM—slender; slight
SLUM—downtrodden area
STEM—check; stalk
STOM—prefix: mouth
STUM—grape juice
SWAM—past tense of swim
SWIM—move in water
SWUM—swim participle
SAAN—Bushmen
SAIN—bless; consecrate
SAWN—saved
SCAN—examine
SCON—teacake
SEAN—John
SEEN—observed
SENN—Swiss herdsman
SEWN—sewed; stitched
SHAN—Indo-Chin. native
SHEN—god
SHIN—front of leg
SHUN—avoid
SIGN—omen; portent
SION—purple seaweed

SKEN—squint
SKIN—hide; external covering; rind
SOON—presently
SPAN—bridge
SPIN—turn; rotate; revolve
SPUN—whirled
STEN—gun
STUN—shock; daze
SUNN—fiber plant
SVAN—Caucasian
SWAN—bird
SACO—weight
SADO—carriage
SAGO—starchy food
SAHO—language
SAPO—soap; toadfish
SEGO—edible bulb
SERO—prefix: thin; late student
SHOO—scram!; begone!; frighten off
SILO—place for fodder storage
SINO—prefix: Chinese
SITO—prefix: food
SKEO—fisherman's hut
SLOO—swamp
SOCO—heron
SOHO—London district; exclamation
SOLO—perform alone
SOSO—middling
SALP—marine animal
SAMP—grain
SCOP—poet
SCUP—fish
SEEP—ooze; leak
SEIP—ooze; leak
SHIP—vessel
SHOP—store; buy
SIMP—idiot; fool
SKEP—basket; beehive
SKIP—omit; pass; jump
SLAP—strike
SLIP—slide; glide; error; mistake
SLOP—slush
SNAP—break; cookie; cinch; fastener
SNIP—clip; shear; cut
SNUP—snap up a bargain
SOAP—cleanser
SOUP—broth
STEP—grade; rank; pace
STOP—cease; desist; halt; arrest
SUMP—tank; pump; cesspool
SWAP—trade; barter
SWOP—trade
SHOQ—tree
SAAR—Fr.-Ger. river region
SADR—lotus tree
SAER—tenant
SCAR—cicatrix; wound mark
SCUR—horn tissue
SEAR—cauterize; gun lock catch
SEER—foreteller; prophet
SEHR—Germ.: very
SEIR—Bib. place; Esau's home
SHIR—cook; gather
SHOR—Tatar tribe
SIER—fish
SKYR—sour curdled milk
SLUR—defame; disparage; murmur
SOAR—fly high; glide
SOIR—Fr.: evening
SOUR—bitter; acid
SPAR—mast; box; gaff; mineral
SPUR—animal track; goad; incite
STAR—asterisk; luminary; heavenly body
STER—suffix: agent, condition
STIR—agitate; dither; ado
SUER—prosecutor; claimant
SAIS—city; groom; Fr.: know
SANS—Fr.: without
SEIS—Fr.: six
SEPS—lizard
SESS—soap frame bar

SISS—hissing sound
SORS—divination by lot
SOUS—Fr.: under
SPES—goddess of hope
SUDS—foam; lather
SALT—condiment; season;
    sodium chloride; NaCl
SART—Iranian Turk
SCAT—begone!; scram!
SCOT—Celt; assessment
SCUT—short tail
SEAT—chair; membership
SECT—denomination
SEIT—measure
SEPT—clan; Fr.: seven
SERT—Sp. painter
SETT—paving stone
SEXT—canonical hour;
    organ stop
SHAT—Afr. salt lake
SHOT—ammunition;
    discharged
SHUT—close
SIFT—screen; separate
SILT—mud deposit;
    sediment
SKAT—card game; star
SKIT—short sketch
SKYT—scoot
SLAT—flap; slab; lath
SLIT—cut; slash
SLOT—animal track;
    aperture
SLUT—slattern
SMUT—coal dust; soot;
    plant disease
SOFT—easy; mild; malleable
SOOT—black; carbon
SOPT—Dog Star
SORT—classify; rank; grade
SPAT—oyster; quarrel
SPET—barracuda
SPIT—point of land;
    roasting rod;
    expectorate
SPOT—location; place; stain
SPUT—boiler plate
STAT—copy
STET—let it stand!
STOT—stumble

SUET—fat
SUIT—court action;
    costume; fit
SWAT—to hit a ball
SAHU—Eg. spiritual body
SHOU—Tibetan deer
SUKU—Bantu
SULU—Moro
SUSU—blind dolphin
SKIV—sovereign (coin)
SLAV—Eastern European
STEV—stanza
SCOW—flat-bottomed
    boat
SHAW—thicket; George
    Bernard ----, playwright
SHEW—display
SHOW—come in third;
    denote; indicate;
    exhibition
SKEW—slanting; distorted
SLAW—cabbage
SLEW—killed; swamp
SLOW—dilatory; tardy
SMEW—diving duck
SNOW—ice crystals
SPEW—emanate
STEW—boil; seethe; ragout
STOW—pack; store
SWOW—oath
SPEX—spectacles
STYX—river of Charon;
    river of the underworld
SAGY—wise
SHAY—one-horse carriage
SIDY—pretentious
SIZY—viscous
SKEY—yoke bar
SLAY—kill; murder
SLEY—weaver's reed
SORY—vitriolic earth
SPAY—castrate
SPEY—river
SPRY—perky; vigorous;
    nimble
STAY—rope; endure;
    remain; last
SUSY—nickname: Susan
SUZY—nickname: Susan
SWAY—flap; move to and

fro
SIZZ—hiss
SUEZ—canal
SWIZ—swindle; gyp

TAHA—bird
TALA—basin; palm tree
TAMA—Indian
TANA—lake (Blue Nile
source); shrew
TAPA—bark; cloth
TARA—ancient Ir. city;
palm
TAWA—tree
TCHA—rolled tea
TECA—Indian
TEDA—Berber
TELA—brain tissue; banana
part
TEMA—music: theme; Arab
TERA—Buddhist monastery
TESA—Indian buzzard
TEWA—Indian
THEA—tea genus
TINA—fem. nickname
TIZA—ulexite
TOBA—Choco Indian
TOGA—Roman cloak
TOLA—weight
TOMA—Afr. Negro
TOOA—beefwood
TORA—Torah; hartebeeste
TOTA—grivet monkey
TOXA—sponge spicule
TSIA—rolled tea
TUBA—saxhorn
TUFA—porous rock
TULA—metal alloy; city
TUNA—food fish; pear
TUZA—pocket gopher
THEB—measure
THOB—rationalize
TOMB—grave
TALC—chalky powder
TEND—care for; incline
THUD—dull sound
TIED—united; joined
TIND—kindle
TOAD—amphibian
TOED—stepped

TOLD—recounted; narrated
TROD—walked
TUND—pound
TACE—steel splint
TAKE—acquire; seize
TALE—legend; saga; story
TAME—docile; subdue
TANE—Polynesian god
TAPE—band; fillet; tie
TARE—allowance; vetch
TATE—lock of hair
TAVE—fem. nickname
TCHE—Asian shrub; Chin.
flute
TELE—prefix: far
TENE—comb. form: ribbon
TETE—Fr.: head
THEE—you
TICE—lure; cricket term
TIDE—current; drift
TIGE—firing pin
TIKE—child; toddler
TILE—baked clay
TIME—meter; rhythm;
speed; hour; minute
TINE—prong; tooth
TIPE—rabbit trap
TIRE—wheel covering; shoe
TOBE—cotton garment
TODE—sled to haul logs
TOLE—allure; entice;
metalware
TOME—book
TONE—accent
TOPE—drink; fish; shark
TORE—ripped
TOTE—carry; haul
TREE—wood; plant
TRUE—loyal; honest;
factual
TUBE—cylinder; subway
TUKE—canvas
TULE—bulrush; cattail
TUNE—air; melody; song
TUTE—tutor
TWEE—bird's cry
TYEE—chief
TYKE—child
TYNE—Eng. river
TYPE—classify; rank; grade;

standard

TYRE—Phoenician city;
    wheel covering
TEFF—grain
TIFF—quarrel
TOFF—dandy
TUFF—rock
TURF—peat; sod
TANG—Chin. dynasty;
    flavor; zest
TEGG—sheep in 2nd year
TEIG—masc. nickname
TENG—measure
THUG—criminal; hoodlum
TING—Chin. pottery; tinkle
TONG—Chin. secret society
TOUG—standard
TRIG—neat; trim; math
    course
TUNG—oil-bearing tree
TWIG—branch
TANH—math term
TECH—technical school
TETH—Hebrew letter
TOPH—Hebrew drum
TUSH—long tooth
TABI—sock
TALI—weight
TARI—earth goddess
TAXI—comb. form:
    arrangement; cab
TELI—low caste
THAI—Siamese
TIKI—Poly. first man
TIPI—wigwam
TITI—petrel; monkey
TOPI—helmet
TORI—molding
TSHI—Gold Coast tongue
TUPI—Braz. Indian
TURI—tribe in India
TUWI—P. I. dyewood tree
TYBI—Eg. month
TACK—change direction;
    veer; course
TALK—converse; chat; talk
TANK—war vehicle; basin
TASK—chore; job;
    assignment
TEAK—dark wood

TECK—ready made tie
TICK—arachnid; mattress
    cover
TOCK—hornbill
TONK—clang
TOOK—seized
TOSK—Albanian dialect
TREK—journey; hike
TUCK—fold
TURK—Mongoloid;
    Ottoman
TUSK—long tooth
TAAL—S. Afr. language
TAEL—weight
TAIL—end; caudal
    appendage; plane part
TALL—high
TEAL—bird; duck
TEEL—sesame
TEIL—tree
TELL—narrate; inform;
    William ----
TEYL—tree
TILL—harrow; cultivate
TOIL—labor; drudge
TOLL—ring; sound
TOOL—implement
TEAM—group; crew
TEEM—abound
TERM—time period; word;
    phrase
THEM—pronoun
TRAM—trolley
TRIM—fit; neat; adorn
TURM—cavalry troop
TAIN—tin plate
TARN—lake
TAUN—measure
TEAN—Scot.: tone
TEEN—age: 13-19; damage
TERN—gull; bird
THAN—comparative term
THEN—at a former time;
    therefore
THIN—slender; skinny; lean
TIEN—Chin. sky
TION—suffix
TMEN—treasury agents
TOON—mahogany tree
TORN—ripped; rent

TOWN—hamlet; burg; city; village
TRIN—triplet
TSIN—Chin. dynasty
TSUN—Chin. measure
TUAN—title
TURN—veer; tack; corner
TWIN—match; double
TAJO—Sp.: trench
TANO—Indian
TARO—root; poi
TAXO—comb. form: arrangement
TECO—Indian
TINO—Sambal language
TIRO—amateur
TITO—Yugo. leader
TOCO—bird
TODO—bustle; stir
TOHO—hunting cry
TOKO—Chin. shop
TORO—N.Z. tree
TOTO—Lat.: all; Fr.: baby animal
TRIO—set of three
TUNO—gum tree
TYPO—printing error
TYRO—amateur; novice
TYTO—barn owl
TAMP—pound down
TARP—piece of canvas
TERP—archeo. mound
TORP—Swed. small farm
TOUP—Malay lugger
TRAP—catch; snare; net
TRIP—journey; tour; travel
TROP—Fr.: too much
TRYP—parasite in blood
TUMP—mound
TURP—turpentine
TYMP—blast furnace stone
TYPP—yarn count
TAAR—tambourine
TAHR—goat
TAIR—goat
TEAR—weep; rip
TEER—mix colors
TEHR—goat
THAR—goat
THOR—thunder god

TIAR—crown; headgear
TIER—row; layer
TOUR—circuit; journey
TSAR—dictator; czar; ruler
TYER—one who ties
TYRR—war god
TZAR—tsar
TAOS—Indian
TAPS—sundown; evening call
TASS—Soviet News Agency
TEES—river into North Sea
TEOS—Ionian city
TESS—Hardy heroine
THIS—demonstrative pronoun
THOS—jackal
THUS—so; therefore
TOGS—clothes
TOPS—most superior; best
TOSS—buffet; throw; fling
TRES—Fr.: very
TRIS—prefix: thrice
TACT—diplomacy; discernment
TAFT—Repub. President; Repub. senator
TAIT—marsupial
TAKT—musical beat
TART—pastry
TATT—knot lace
TAUT—tense
TEAT—nipple
TENT—canvas shelter
TEST—exam; try; shell
TEXT—body of writing
THAT—demonstrative pronoun
TILT—incline; tip; joust
TINT—color; hue; shade
TOOT—sound horn
TORT—civil wrong
TOUT—Fr.: all; tipster
TRET—allowance
TRIT—prefix: third
TROT—jog; gait
TUFT—bunch; clump
TWIT—taunt; mock
TABU—taboo
TAKU—Indian

TAPU—taboo
TATU—armadillo
TCHU—exclamation
TEJU—lizard
THOU—you
TIBU—Berber
TIOU—Indian
TOLU—balsam
TULU—Dravidian
TUNU—gum tree
TUTU—poisonous N.Z. shrub; ballet skirt
THAW—melt
THEW—muscle; sinew
TROW—believe; fishing boat
TAKY—taking
TAVY—fem. nickname
THEY—pronoun
TIDY—neat
TINY—small; little
TOBY—mug; dog; masc. name
TODY—bird
TONY—nickname; stage award
TORY—conservative
TOTY—low caste laborer
TOWY—like flax
TRAY—platter; salver
TREY—card; three
TROY—system of weights; city
TUNY—melodious
TYPY—typical

UEBA—measure
ULNA—arm bone
ULUA—fish
ULVA—sea lettuce
UNCA—eighth note
UPLA—fuel
URFA—city
URIA—auk
URNA—measure
URSA—bear constellation
URVA—mongoose
USHA—Bana's daughter
UVEA—eye layer
UDIC—Caucasian language
UDAD—sheep

USED—accustomed
UVID—moist; wet
ULME—elme
UNDE—wavy
UNIE—unicorn fish
URDE—key-shaped
URGE—desire; goad; prod; impel
USEE—future user
UANG—beetle
UMPH—grunt
URTH—one of Norn
UTAH—state
UBII—Teutonic tribe
UNCI—claws
UDAL—land
URAL—Russian mountain range
UVAL—grapelike
URIM—Bib. instruments
UTUM—bird; owl
ULAN—cavalryman
UPON—above; over
URAN—lizard
USUN—North China
UZAN—weight
ULLO—shell money
UMBO—boss on shield
UNCO—strange; uncanny
UNDO—unfasten
UNIO—mussel
UNTO—to; for
UPGO—ascent; climb
UBER—Ger.: above
ULLR—son of Sif; Thor's stepson
USAR—alkali
USER—employer
USSR—Soviet Union
UTOR—to use
UNIS—Fr.: Les Etats —— (United States)
UPAS—poison tree
UPIS—artemis
URUS—wild ox
USAS—goddess of dawn
USES—beneficiary law
UTAS—eight days after a feast
UNIT—one; monad; single

thing
UNAU—sloth
URDU—Hindustani
ULEX—spiny shrub
UGLY—bad looking;
　unpleasant
UNDY—wavy
URDY—key-shaped
UREY—physicist
UNTZ—weight

VARA—measure
VASA—duct
VEDA—sacred Hindu books
VEGA—plain; meadow
VELA—membranes; "Sails"
　of constellation Argo
VENA—Lat.: vein
VERA—fem. name
VETA—mountain sickness
VIDA—fem. name
VILA—fairy
VINA—guitar
VIRA—Bantu
VISA—passport
　endorsement
VITA—Lat.: life
VIVA—long live!
VOLA—palm
VOTA—Roman festivals
VERB—action word
VELD—So. Afr. grassland
VEND—market; sell
VERD—green
VOID—empty
VADE—leave
VALE—farewell
VANE—weathercock
VARE—weasel
VASE—vessel
VICE—sin; fault
VIDE—Lat.: see
VILE—base
VINE—climbing plant
VIRE—arrow
VITE—Fr.: quick
VIVE—long live!
VOCE—It.: voice
VOLE—mouse
VOTE—choice; ballot; Finn

in Ingria
VANG—rope
VOOG—rock cavity
VUGG—rock cavity
VACH—goddess
VOTH—Finn in Ingria
VUGH—rock cavity
VAGI—cranial nerve
VALI—viceroy
VARI—comb. form: various
VERI—centipede
VILI—Odin's brother
VLEI—creek
VOLK—Germ.: people
VAIL—gain
VEAL—calf; meat
VEIL—head covering;
　cloistered life
VIAL—small vessel
VILL—village
VIOL—musical instrument
VAIN—ineffectual; futile;
　proud
VEIN—blood vessel
VULN—wound
VELO—velocity per
　second
VETO—no vote
VINO—liquor
VIVO—lively
VOTO—Indian
VAMP—shoe part; flirt
VEEP—vice president
VAIR—fur
VEER—turn; change
　direction

VIER—Ger.: four
VOIR—Fr.: see
VANS—gods
VEPS—tribe
VISS—weight
VAST—huge; enormous
VENT—air passage; flue; let
　out
VERT—green
VEST—clothe; empower
VINT—card game
VOET—measure
VOLT—elec. force unit;
　sideway's tread

VASU—nephew
VAYU—Vishnu god
VEAU—Fr.: veal
VIEW—look at
VAUX—Fr. fort (battle of
Verdun)
VARY—change; alter
VERY—so; true; same
VILY—fairy
VINY—like vines
VLEY—swamp; marsh

WAKA—canoe
WEGA—star
WEKA—flightless bird
WETA—locust
WHOA—stop! (to a horse)
WAAC—woman soldier
WAAD—black ochre
WAFD—Egyptian
WAND—pointer; rod; staff
WARD—political division;
guard (against)
WEED—plant
WELD—unite; join; link
WEND—go; travel; Slav
WILD—crazy; rough; unruly
WIND—coil; twist
WOLD—upland plain
WOOD—forest; timber
WORD—promise; tidings;
term
WYRD—Norn
WADE—walk in water
WAGE—carry on; pay
WAIE—sea demon
WAKE—rouse; stir; track of
ship
WALE—welt; ridge;
texture
WANE—decline; ebb
WARE—cautious;
commodity
WAVE—billow; swell;
flutter
WERE—contraction: we are;
be (past tense)
WEVE—contraction
WHEE—sound of whistle
WIDE—roomy; broad

WIFE—mate; spouse
WILE—artiface; ruse
WINE—fermented juice
WIPE—rub off
WIRE—cable
WISE—sage; astute
WIVE—marry; wed
WOKE—roused
WORE—past tense of wear
WOTE—Finn in Ingria
WAIF—stray
WAKF—grant of property
WAQF—grant of property
WELF—princely family
WERF—farmyard
WOLF—animal; bolt food;
flirtatious man
WOOF—crossthreads
WRAF—air force
WUFF—bark sound
WUKF—grant of property
WAAG—monkey; grivet
WAEG—bird
WANG—weight
WEGG—Dickens character -
ballad seller
WHIG—political party
WING—annex; faction
WONG—field
WASH—launder; bathe
WISH—desire; want
WITH—and; including
WABI—Indian
WADI—dry river bed; oasis
WALI—governor; prefect
WEKI—fern
WERI—aweto
WALK—go on foot
WEAK—feeble; puny
WEEK—time period
WELK—snail
WICK—candle; lamp
WILK—snail
WINK—blink
WORK—toil; operate;
function
WAIL—cry; weep
WALL—fence
WEAL—body politic;
common ----

WEFL—fish basket; trap
WELL—watering place; sound
WIEL—whirlpool
WILL—testament; volition
WOOL—fleece
WARM—affectionate; hot
WHAM—strike; exclamation
WHIM—fancy
WHOM—demonstrative pronoun
WORM—crawler
WURM—glacial state
WAIN—wain
WARN—caution
WEAN—alienate; detach
WHEN—as; while; how soon
WHIN—gorse; rock
WHUN—gorse; rock
WOON—Burmese governor
WORN—shabby; used
WREN—bird; Eng. architect
WYNN—timber truck
WACO—city
WHOO—exclamation
WHYO—foot pad
WAPP—nautical rope
WARP—contort; twist; threads
WASP—yellow jacket
WEEP—wail; cry; lament
WHIP—flog; beat; lash
WISP—tuft; bunch; lack of hair
WRAP—cloak; mantle
WAER—dam
WEAR—deteriorate; clothe
WEIR—dam
WHIR—buzzing sound
WAYS—methods
WIES—y's
WAFT—float; whiff
WAIT—delay; attend
WALT—masc. nickname
WANT—desire; wish; lack
WART—protuberance
WATT—inventor
WEET—bird's cry

WEFT—crossthreads
WELT—ridge; beat; wale
WENT—departed
WEPT—cried
WERT—were
WEST—direction; author; painter
WHAT—pronoun
WHET—sharpen
WHIT—iota
WILT—droop; sag
WIST—know
WONT—contraction; will not
WORT—herb
WRIT—legal order
WHAU—tree
WIDU—Moslem ablution
WUDU—Moslem ablution
WUZU—Moslem ablution
WHEW—exclamation
WADY—oasis
WAKY—alert
WANY—diminished
WARY—cautious
WAVY—sinuous; undulating
WAXY—pliable
WHEY—watery part of milk
WILY—sly; artful
WINY—vinous
WIRY—sinewy
WHIZ—buzzing sound

XEMA—gull
XINA—nickname
XOSA—Kaffir language
XOVA—Pimian Indian
XIPE—Aztec god
XENO—prefix: strange, foreign
XERO—copy
XMAS—Christmas

YAKA—Bantu
YAMA—first mortal
YANA—tribe
YAPA—palm leaf mat
YAYA—tree
YETA—Jap. outcast
YIMA—Pers. demigod

YMCA—Young Men's
  Christian Association
YOGA—philosophy
YUCA—cassava
YUGA—Hindu age cycle
YUMA—city
YWCA—Young Woman's
  Christian Association
YARD—spar; measure; 3
  feet
YOND—past
YAGE—plant
YAJE—plant
YALE—university; lock
YARE—manageable; ready
YATE—eucalyptus
YIPE—cry
YOKE—join; merge; link
YORE—ancient times
YULE—Christmas
YANG—philo. principle
YEGG—burglar
YEAH—yes
YHVH—Heb. supreme being
YHWH—Heb. supreme
  being
YODH—Heb. letter
YOGH—Anglo-Saxon
  letter
YALI—govt. residence;
  mansion
YATI—ascetic
YENI—bird
YOGI—ascetic; disciple of
  yoga
YANK—American; New
  Englander; jerk; tug
YOLK—yellow of egg
YORK—Eng. cathedral city;
  royal house
YARL—chieftain
YAWL—sailboat
YELL—shout; call
YOWL—howl
YPIL—tree
YARN—spun wool; tale
YAWN—gape
YEAN—lamb
YUAN—Chin. money
YEDO—Tokyo

YESO—gypsum
YAPP—bookbinding style
YAUP—yawn
YAWP—yawn
YELP—bark
YOUP—yelp; bark
YARR—growl
YEAR—time period; 12
  months
YMER—giant
YMIR—giant
YOUR—possessive pronoun
YSER—river
YAWS—skin disease
YEAS—yes votes
YELT—sow
YUFT—Russ. leather
YUIT—Eskimo
YURT—tent
YALU—river
YARU—heaven
YUTU—bird
YUNX—woodpecker genus

ZAMA—Hannibal's defeat
ZETA—Greek Z
ZIPA—Chibcha chief
ZIRA—Turk: measure
ZOLA—author
ZONA—shingles
ZUZA—weight
ZYGA—rowers' bench
ZIMB—Abyssin. fly
ZINC—metal
ZEKE—masculine nickname
ZEME—fetish
ZONE—area
ZYME—ferment
ZARF—cup stand
ZING—vim; vigor
ZACH—masculine nickname
ZATI—bonnet monkey
ZEMI—fetish
ZUNI—Indian
ZEAL—ardor, zest
ZOOM—approach quickly
ZAIN—horse
ZEIN—protein
ZION—heaven
ZOON—developed

compound animal
ZENO—philosopher
ZERO—cipher; nothing;
  nought
ZOBO—yak hybrid
ZOGO—sacred object
ZARP—policeman
ZOAR—town
ZEUS—head of the gods

ZIPS—Czech.
ZOAS—Blake's symbolic
  figures
ZEST—ardor, relish
ZEBU—Brahman bull
ZENU—African sheep
ZULU—ship
ZANY—buffoon; clown
ZIZZ—whiz; whirring sound

FOUR LETTER WORDS AA -- to ZY --

AALU	ACTU	AGIO	AKHA	ALLO	AMOI
AANI	ACUS	AGIS	AKIA	ALLY	AMOK
AARE	ACYL	AGLA	AKIM	ALMA	AMON
AARU	ADAD	AGNI	AKIN	ALMS	AMOR
ABAS	ADAH	AGNO	AKKA	ALME	AMOS
ABBA	ADAK	AGOG	AKOV	ALOD	AMRA
ABBE	ADAM	AGON	AKRA	ALOE	AMUN
ABBY	ADAN	AGRA	AKUA	ALOP	AMYL
ABCS	ADAR	AGRI	ALAE	ALOW	AMAI
ABED	ADAT	AGRO	ALAI	ALPH	AMAK
ABEL	ADDA	AGUA	ALAN	ALPS	AMAL
ABET	ADDU	AGUE	ALAR	ALSO	ANAM
ABIA	ADDY	AHAB	ALAS	ALTA	ANAN
ABIB	ADEN	AHAZ	ALAY	ALTE	ANAS
ABIE	ADER	AHEM	ALBA	ALTO	ANAT
ABIR	ADES	AHET	ALBE	ALUM	ANAX
ABLE	ADIB	AHEY	ALBI	ALUR	ANAY
ABLY	ADIN	AHIO	ALBO	ALVA	ANBA
ABOO	ADIT	AHIR	ALCA	ALYA	ANCE
ABOT	ADMI	AHOM	ALCO	ALYS	ANCY
ABOU	ADOR	AHOY	ALDA	AMAH	ANDA
ABOX	ADRY	AHUM	ALEA	AMAR	ANDE
ABRA	ADZE	AICH	ALEC	AMBA	ANDI
ABRI	AEON	AIDA	ALEE	AMBI	ANDY
ABSI	AERA	AIDE	ALEF	AMBO	ANER
ABUT	AERI	AILE	ALEM	AMEN	ANES
ACCA	AERO	AINE	ALEN	AMER	ANET
ACER	AERY	AINO	ALEP	AMES	ANEW
ACHE	AETA	AINT	ALES	AMEX	ANGE
ACHT	AFAR	AINU	ALEY	AMIA	ANGO
ACHY	AFFY	AIPI	ALFA	AMIC	ANIL
ACID	AFRA	AIRA	ALGA	AMID	ANIS
ACIS	AGAG	AIRE	ALGY	AMIE	ANKH
ACLE	AGAL	AIRS	ALIA	AMIL	ANNA
ACME	AGAO	AIRT	ALIF	AMIN	ANNE
ACNE	AGAR	AJAR	ALII	AMIR	ANNI
ACON	AGAU	AJAX	ALIM	AMIS	ANNO
ACOR	AGAZ	AJEE	ALIN	AMLA	ANOA
ACRE	AGED	AJOG	ALIT	AMLI	ANON
ACTA	AGEE	AKAL	ALIX	AMMA	ANSA
ACTH	AGER	AKAN	ALKY	AMMI	ANSU
ACTO	AGHA	AKEE	ALLA	AMMO	ANTA
ACTS	AGIB	AKEY	ALLE	AMMU	ANTE

ANTI	AROD	ATRI	AZOV	BANS	BEID
ANUS	AROO	ATRY	AZUL	BANT	BEJA
ANZU	AROW	ATTA	AZUR	BARA	BEKA
AONE	ARPA	ATTU		BARB	BELA
AOUL	ARRA	ATUA	BAAL	BARD	BELI
APAP	ARTA	ATUM	BAAR	BARE	BELL
APAR	ARTO	ATWO	BAAS	BARI	BELT
APER	ARTS	AUCA	BABA	BARK	BEMA
APET	ARTY	AUDE	BABE	BARM	BENA
APEX	ARUI	AUER	BABI	BARN	BEND
APIA	ARUM	AUGE	BABU	BARO	BENE
APII	ARYA	AULA	BABY	BARR	BENG
APIO	ASAK	AULD	BACH	BART	BENI
APIS	ASAR	AULU	BACK	BARU	BENJ
APOD	ASCI	AUNE	BADB	BASE	BENO
APSE	ASEA	AUNT	BADE	BASH	BENT
APSU	ASEM	AURA	BAEL	BASK	BENU
AQUA	ASER	AURI	BAER	BASS	BERA
ARAB	ASHA	AUSA	BAEZ	BAST	BERG
ARAD	ASHY	AUSU	BAFF	BATA	BERM
ARAH	ASIA	AUTO	BAFT	BATE	BERN
ARAL	ASIN	AUZU	BAGA	BATH	BERT
ARAM	ASKR	AVAL	BAGO	BATT	BESA
ARAN	ASNO	AVAR	BAHI	BATZ	BESS
ARAR	ASOK	AVEC	BAHO	BAUD	BEST
ARAS	ASO	AVER	BAHT	BAUL	BETA
ARBA	ASOR	AVES	BAIL	BAUM	BETE
ARCA	ASSE	AVID	BAIN	BAVE	BETH
ARCH	ASSI	AVIS	BAIT	BAWL	BEVY
AREA	ASTA	AVON	BAJU	BAWN	BHAR
AREG	ASTI	AVOW	BAKA	BAYA	BHAT
AREO	ASUR	AVUS	BAKE	BEAD	BHEL
ARES	ATAP	AWAN	BAKU	BEAK	BHIL
ARGO	ATAR	AWAY	BALA	BEAL	BHOY
ARGY	ATEF	AWOL	BALD	BEAM	BHUT
ARIA	ATEN	AWRY	BALE	BEAN	BIAS
ARID	ATEO	AXAL	BALI	BEAR	BIBB
ARIL	ATES	AXIL	BALK	BEAT	BIBI
ARIS	ATIK	AXIS	BALL	BEAU	BICE
ARME	ATIP	AXLE	BALM	BECK	BIDE
ARMS	ATIS	AXON	BALT	BEDE	BIEN
ARMY	ATLE	AYAH	BALU	BEEF	BIER
ARNA	ATLI	AYES	BANA	BEEN	BIFF
ARND	ATMA	AYIN	BANC	BEEP	BIGA
ARNE	ATMO	AZAM	BAND	BEER	BIJA
ARNI	ATMU	AZAN	BANE	BEES	BIKE
ARNO	ATOM	AZHA	BANG	BEET	BIKH
ARNT	ATON	AZOF	BANI	BEGA	BILE
AROA	ATOP	AZON	BANK	BEHN	BILK

BILL	BLUT	BORD	BROO	BUZZ	CART
BILO	BNAI	BORE	BROW	BYEE	CASA
BINA	BOAR	BORG	BROZ	BYGO	CASE
BIND	BOAT	BORI	BRUH	BYRD	CASH
BINE	BOAZ	BORN	BRUT	BYRE	CASK
BING	BOBA	BORO	BUAL		CASO
BINH	BOBO	BORS	BUBA	CAAM	CAST
BINI	BOCA	BORT	BUBE	CACA	CASY
BINN	BOCE	BOSA	BUBI	CACO	CATA
BINO	BOCK	BOSC	BUBO	CADE	CATE
BIOD	BODB	BOSE	BUCK	CADI	CATO
BION	BODE	BOSH	BUDA	CADY	CATS
BIOS	BODO	BOSK	BUDE	CAEN	CAUK
BIRD	BODY	BOSS	BUFF	CAFE	CAUL
BIRL	BOER	BOTA	BUFO	CAGE	CAUP
BIRN	BOGA	BOTH	BUGI	CAGN	CAVA
BIRR	BOGO	BOTO	BUHL	CAGY	CAVE
BISA	BOGY	BOTT	BUHR	CAID	CAVY
BISE	BOHO	BOUT	BUKH	CAIN	CAWK
BISH	BOHR	BOUW	BUKK	CAJA	CAWL
BISK	BOII	BOWK	BULB	CAKE	CAXI
BITE	BOIL	BOWL	BULK	CAKY	CAYO
BITI	BOIS	BOXY	BULL	CALE	CAZA
BITO	BOJO	BOZA	BULT	CALF	CAZI
BITT	BOKO	BOZO	BUMP	CALK	CAZY
BIUR	BOLA	BQKT	BUNA	CALL	CEBA
BIWA	BOLD	BRAB	BUND	CALM	CEDE
BIXA	BOLE	BRAD	BUNG	CALO	CEIL
BIZE	BOLL	BRAE	BUNK	CALP	CELA
BKKT	BOLO	BRAG	BUNN	CALX	CELL
BLAA	BOLT	BRAM	BUNT	CAME	CELT
BLAB	BOMA	BRAN	BUOY	CAMP	CENA
BLAE	BOMB	BRAS	BURA	CANA	CENE
BLAH	BONA	BRAT	BURE	CANE	CENS
BLAS	BOND	BRAY	BURG	CANG	CENT
BLAT	BONE	BREA	BURI	CANO	CEPA
BLEB	BONG	BRED	BURL	CANT	CEPE
BLED	BONI	BREN	BURN	CAPA	CERA
BLET	BONK	BRER	BURP	CAPE	CERE
BLEU	BONN	BREW	BURR	CAPH	CERN
BLEW	BONY	BREY	BURY	CAPP	CERO
BLIP	BOOB	BRIE	BUSH	CARA	CESS
BLOB	BOOK	BRIG	BUSK	CARD	CEST
BLOC	BOOH	BRIM	BUSS	CARE	CETE
BLOT	BOOL	BRIN	BUST	CARK	CETO
BLOW	BOOM	BRIO	BUSY	CARL	CEYX
BLUB	BOON	BRIT	BUTO	CARN	CHAA
BLUE	BOOR	BROB	BUTT	CARO	CHAB
BLUP	BOOT	BORH	BUXY	CARP	CHAD
BLUR	BORA	BORM	BUYO	CARR	CHAI

CHAM	CIVE	COJA	COXA	CUBY	DATO
CHAN	CLAD	COKE	COYN	CUYA	DATU
CHAP	CLAM	COKY	COYO	CXIX	DAUB
CHAR	CLAN	COLA	COZE	CYAN	DAUK
CHAT	CLAP	COLD	COZY	CYKE	DAUW
CHAW	CLAW	COLE	CRAB	CYLE	DAVE
CHAY	CLAY	COLI	CRAG	CYMA	DAVY
CHEE	CLEE	COLP	CRAL	CYME	DAWK
CHEF	CLEF	COLT	CRAM	CYST	DAWM
CHEK	CLEM	COLY	CRAP	CYTE	DAWN
CHEN	CLEO	COMA	CRAW	CZAR	DAYE
CHER	CLEW	COMB	CRAX		DAYS
CHEW	CLIM	COME	CREA	DACE	DAZA
CHEZ	CLIO	COMO	CREE	DADA	DAZE
CHIA	CLIP	COND	CREW	DADO	DAZY
CHIB	CLOD	CONE	CREX	DAER	DEAD
CHIC	CLOE	CONI	CRIB	DAEZ	DEAF
CHIH	CLOG	CONK	CRIC	DAFF	DEAL
CHIL	CLOP	CONN	CRIG	DAFT	DEAN
CHIN	CLOT	CONY	CRIN	DAGG	DEAR
CHIP	CLOU	COOK	CRIS	DAGH	DEBS
CHIR	CLOW	COOL	CROC	DAGO	DEBT
CHIT	CLOY	COOM	CROM	DAIL	DECA
CHOB	CLUB	COON	CROP	DAIN	DECI
CHOL	CLUE	COOP	CROW	DAIS	DECK
CHOP	CLYM	COOS	CRUS	DALE	DEDO
CHOR	COAG	COOT	CRUX	DALI	DEED
CHOU	COAK	COPA	CUBA	DALL	DEEM
CHOW	COAL	COPE	CUBE	DAMA	DEEP
CHUB	COAN	COPT	CUBI	DAME	DEER
CHUD	COAT	COPY	CUCA	DAMN	DEFI
CHUG	COAX	CORA	CUFF	DAMP	DEFT
CHUM	COBB	CORD	CUIR	DANA	DEFY
CHUN	COBH	CORE	CUKE	DANE	DEGU
CHUT	COCA	CORK	CULL	DANG	DEIL
CIEL	COCK	CORM	CULM	DANK	DEIN
CIMA	COCO	CORN	CULT	DANS	DEJA
CINE	CODA	COSE	CUNA	DANU	DELE
CINQ	CODE	COSH	CURA	DARD	DELL
CION	CODO	COSO	CURB	DARE	DEME
CIPO	CODY	COSS	CURD	DARI	DEMI
CIRC	COED	COSY	CURE	DARK	DEMO
CIRL	COEL	COTA	CURL	DARN	DEMY
CISE	COEN	COTE	CURR	DARR	DENE
CIST	COHO	COTO	CURT	DART	DENS
CITE	COIF	COTY	CUSH	DASH	DENT
CITO	COIL	COUP	CUSK	DASI	DENY
CITS	COIN	COUS	CUSP	DASS	DEPA
CITY	COIR	COVE	CUSS	DATA	DERA
CIVA	COIX	COWL	CUTE	DATE	DERM

DESI	DIVA	DOTE	DUEL	EBUR	ELLA
DESK	DIVE	DOTH	DUET	ECAD	ELLE
DEUL	DIVI	DOTO	DUFF	ECCA	ELMY
DEUM	DIXI	DOTY	DUFY	ECCE	ELOD
DEUS	DOAB	DOUB	DUHR	ECHO	ELON
DEUX	DOAT	DOUC	DUIM	ECHT	ELSA
DEVA	DOBE	DOUM	DUIT	ECRU	ELSE
DEVI	DOBY	DOUR	DUKU	ECTO	ELUL
DEWA	DOCK	DOVE	DULL	EDAM	EMER
DEWY	DODO	DOWD	DUMA	EDAR	EMEU
DHAK	DOEG	DOWL	DUMB	EDDA	EMIL
DHAN	DOER	DOWN	DUMP	EDDO	EMIM
DHAO	DOES	DOXA	DUNE	EDDY	EMIR
DHAR	DOFF	DOXY	DUNG	EDEL	EMIT
DHAW	DOGE	DOZE	DUNK	EDEN	EMMA
DHOW	DOGS	DOZY	DUNS	EDER	EMMY
DIAD	DOGY	DRAA	DUNT	EDGE	EMPT
DIAL	DOIT	DRAB	DUOS	EDGY	EMYD
DIAN	DOKO	DRAG	DUPE	EDIT	EMYS
DIAU	DOLA	DRAH	DURA	EDNA	ENAM
DIAZ	DOLE	DRAM	DURO	EDOM	ENCE
DIBS	DOLI	DRAP	DURR	EELY	ENDO
DICE	DOLL	DRAT	DUSE	EERY	ENID
DICK	DOLT	DRAW	DUSK	EFIK	ENIF
DIDO	DOME	DRAY	DUST	EGAD	ENIN
DIEB	DOMN	DRED	DUTY	EGAL	ENKI
DIEM	DOMY	DREE	DYAD	EGBA	ENNA
DIER	DONA	DREG	DYAK	EGBO	ENNE
DIES	DONE	DREI	DYAS	EGER	ENNS
DIET	DONG	DREW	DYCK	EGGS	ENOL
DIEU	DONI	DREY	DYER	EGGY	ENON
DIKA	DONT	DRIB	DYKE	EGIL	ENOS
DIKE	DOOB	DRIP	DYNA	EGIS	ENOW
DILL	DOOK	DROP	DYNE	EGOL	ENSE
DILO	DOOM	DRUB		EHEU	ENTE
DIME	DOON	DRUG	EACH	EIDE	ENTO
DINE	DOOR	DRUM	EADS	EINE	ENVY
DING	DOPA	DUAB	EARL	EILD	ENYO
DINO	DOPE	DUAD	EARN	EIRE	ENZU
DINT	DOPP	DUAL	EASE	EJOO	EOAN
DION	DORA	DUAN	EAST	EKKA	EOIN
DIRE	DORE	DUAR	EASY	EKOI	EPEE
DIRK	DORM	DUAT	EATS	ELAH	EPHA
DIRT	DORN	DUBB	EAUX	ELAM	EPIC
DISA	DORP	DUCE	EAVE	ELAN	EPOS
DISC	DORY	DUCK	EBEN	ELBA	EQUI
DISH	DOSA	DUCO	EBER	ELBE	ERAL
DISK	DOSE	DUCT	EBOE	ELEF	ERAT
DISS	DOSS	DUDE	EBON	ELIA	ERDA
DITA	DOST	DUDS	EBRO	ELIS	ERER

ERGO	EWER	FAUN	FISH	FORA	FUSS
ERIA	EWRY	FAUT	FISK	FORD	FUST
ERIC	EXAM	FAVI	FIST	FORE	FUTE
ERIE	EXIT	FAVN	FIVE	FORK	FUZE
ERIN	EYAH	FAWN	FIZZ	FORM	FUZZ
ERIS	EYAS	FAZE	FLAG	FORT	FYKE
ERMA	EYED	FEAK	FLAK	FOSS	FYRD
ERNE	EYER	FEAR	FLAM	FOUD	
EROS	EYEY	FEAT	FLAN	FOUL	
ERSE	EYOT	FECK	FLAP	FOUR	GAAL
ERST	EYRA	FEED	FLAT	FOWL	GABE
ERUA	EYRE	FEEL	FLAW	FOXY	GABI
ERUC	EYRY	FEES	FLAX	FRAB	GABY
ERYX	EZBA	FEET	FLAY	FRAP	GADE
ESAU	EZEL	FEIS	FLEA	FRAT	GAEA
ESAY	EZRA	FEKE	FLED	FRAU	GAEL
ESCA		FELD	FLEE	FRAY	GAFF
ESCE		FELL	FLEM	FREA	GAGE
ESEK	FAAM	FELS	FLEW	FRED	GAGL
ESER	FABA	FELT	FLEX	FREE	GAIA
ESNE	FACE	FEME	FLEY	FRET	GAIL
ESOX	FACT	FEND	FLIP	FREY	GAIN
ESPY	FADE	FEOD	FLIT	FRIA	GAIT
ESSE	FADO	FERN	FLIX	FRIB	GAJO
ESTA	FADY	FERU	FLOC	FRIT	GALA
ESTE	FAEX	FESS	FLOE	FRIZ	GALE
ESTH	FAIL	FEST	FLOG	FROE	GALI
ESUS	FAIN	FETE	FLOP	FROG	GALL
ETAH	FAIR	FEUD	FLOW	FROM	GALT
ETAL	FAIT	FIAT	FLUB	FROT	GAMA
ETAT	FAKE	FICO	FLUE	FROW	GAME
ETCH	FAKY	FIDE	FLUX	FRUG	GAMP
ESES	FALA	FIDO	FOAL	FUAD	GANE
ETNA	FALL	FIEF	FOAM	FUCI	GANG
ETON	FALX	FIFE	FOCH	FUEL	GANO
ETRE	FAMA	FIJI	FOCI	FUGA	GAOL
ETTA	FAME	FILE	FOGO	FUGU	GAON
ETTE	FAMN	FILL	FOGY	FUJI	GAPE
ETUI	FANE	FILM	FOHN	FULA	GAPO
ETYM	FANG	FILO	FOIL	FULK	GAPY
EURE	FANO	FILS	FOLD	FULL	GARA
EUGE	FAON	FIND	FOLK	FUME	GARB
EVAN	FARD	FINE	FOND	FUMY	GARE
EVEA	FARE	FINK	FONG	FUND	GARM
EVEN	FARL	FINN	FONO	FUNG	GARN
EVER	FARM	FIOT	FONT	FUNJ	GARO
EVET	FARO	FIRE	FONS	FUNK	GARY
EVIL	FASH	FIRM	FOOD	FURL	GASH
EVOE	FASS	FIRN	FOOL	FURY	GASP
EWAN	FAST	FISC	FOOT	FUSE	GATA
	FATE				GATE

GATH	GIGA	GOLA	GROW	HAHA	HEAR
GAUB	GILA	GOLD	GRUB	HAIK	HEAT
GAUD	GILD	GOLF	GRUM	HAIL	HEBE
GAUE	GILL	GOLI	GRUS	HAIR	HECK
GAUL	GILO	GOLL	GUAM	HAJE	HEED
GAUP	GILT	GOLO	GUAN	HAKE	HEEL
GAUR	GIMP	GOMA	GUAO	HAKH	HEEP
GAUS	GINK	GONA	GUAR	HAKO	HEER
GAUT	GIRD	GOND	GUFA	HAKU	HEFT
GAVE	GIRL	GONE	GUFF	HALA	HEGH
GAWD	GIRO	GONG	GUGU	HALE	HEHE
GAWK	GIRT	GOOD	GUHA	HALF	HEII
GAWN	GISH	GOOF	GUHR	HALL	HEIN
GAUP	GIST	GOOM	GUIB	HALM	HEIR
GAZA	GITE	GOON	GULA	HALO	HELA
GAZE	GIVE	GOOP	GULF	HALS	HELD
GAZI	GJOA	GOOR	GULL	HALT	HELL
GEAL	GLAD	GORA	GULO	HAMI	HELM
GEAN	GLED	GORE	GULP	HAND	HELP
GEAR	GLEN	GORY	GIMP	HANG	HEMI
GEAT	GLIA	GOSH	GUNA	HANK	HEMO
GEEZ	GLIB	GOTH	GUNJ	HANO	HEMP
GEIN	GLIM	GOUL	GURU	HANS	HENS
GELD	GLIS	GOUR	GUSH	HANT	HERA
GELT	GLOM	GOUT	GUST	HAPU	HERB
GENA	GLOW	GOWK	GUTI	HARB	HERD
GENE	GLUB	GOWL	GUZE	HARD	HERE
GENS	GLUE	GOWN	GWYN	HARE	HERL
GENT	GLUG	GOYA	GYBE	HARK	HERO
GENU	GLUM	GRAB	GYLE	HARL	HERR
GEON	GLUT	GRAD	GYNE	HARM	HERS
GERB	GMAN	GRAF	GYRE	HARP	HEST
GERD	GNAR	GRAM	GYRI	HART	HETH
GERI	GNAT	GRAN	GYRO	HASH	HETT
GERM	GNAW	GRAO	GYVE	HASP	HEVI
GEST	GOAD	GRAS		HAST	HEWN
GESU	GOAF	GRAY	HAAB	HATE	HICK
GETA	GOAI	GRES	HAAF	HATH	HIDE
GETT	GOAL	GREW	HAAK	HATI	HIEL
GEUM	GOAN	GREY	HAAR	HAUL	HIEN
GHAT	GOAT	GRID	HABA	HAUT	HIER
GHEE	GOBI	GRIG	HABE	HAVE	HIFI
GHEG	GOBO	GRIM	HACK	HAWK	HIGH
GHES	GOBY	GRIN	HADE	HAYZ	HIKE
GHOR	GOEL	GRIP	HADJ	HAZE	HIKU
GHUZ	GOER	GRIS	HAEC	HAZY	HILA
GIBE	GOES	GRIT	HAEM	HEAD	HILL
GIDE	GOFF	GROG	HAFT	HEAF	HILO
GIER	GOGH	GROS	HAGG	HEAL	HILT
GIFT	GOGO	GROT	HAGI	HEAP	HIMA

HIND	HYLE	HOST	IMAM	ISIS	JAZZ
HING	HYMN	HOTH	IMBE	ISLE	JEAN
HINO	HYPE	HOUR	IMER	ISMY	JEEL
HINT	HYPO	HOVA	IMID	ITCH	JEEP
HIPE		HOVE	IMMI	ITEA	JEER
HIRE	IAGO	HOWE	IMPI	ITEM	JEFE
HISH	IALU	HOWL	INCA	ITEN	JEFF
HISS	IAMB	HOYA	INCH	ITER	JEHU
HIST	IBAD	HSIA	INDE	ITMO	JELL
HIVE	IBAN	HUBB	INEE	ITOL	JENA
HOAR	IBEX	HUCK	INEZ	ITYS	JERK
HOAX	IBID	HUED	INGA	ITZA	JESS
HOBB	IBIS	HUFF	INGE	IVAH	JEST
HOBO	IBIT	HUGE	INIA	IVAN	JESU
HOCH	ICAL	HUGH	INKA	IVES	JETE
HOCK	ICED	HUGO	INKY	IXIA	JETH
HOEK	ICER	HUIA	INLY	IXIL	JEUX
HOEN	ICHO	HULA	INRE	IXLE	JHUM
HOER	ICHU	HULE	INRO	IYAR	JHVH
HOEY	ICON	HULK	INTI	IZAR	JHWH
HOGA	IDAS	HULL	INTO		JIBE
HOGG	IDEA	HULU	IOLA	JACA	JIFF
HOHE	IDEE	HUME	IOLE	JACK	JILL
HOJA	IDEM	HUMP	IONA	JACU	JILT
HOJU	IDEN	IDIO	IONE	JADE	JINN
HOLA	IDEO	IDJO	IONI	JADU	JINX
HOLD	IDES	IDLE	IOTA	JADY	JIVA
HOLE	IDIC	IDLY	IOWA	JAEL	JIVE
HOLI	HOME	IDOL	IPIL	JAGA	JOAB
HOLM	HOMO	IDUN	IPSE	JAGG	JOAD
HOLT	HOMY	IDYL	IPSO	JAIL	JOAN
HOLY	HONE	IDYO	IRAD	JAIN	JOAR
HUND	HONG	IDZO	IRAE	JAKE	JOBO
HUNG	HONI	IFIL	IRAK	JAKO	JOCK
HUNH	HONK	IGLU	IRAN	JAMA	JOCU
HUNK	HOOD	IGOR	IRAQ	JAMB	JODO
HUNT	HOOF	IHVH	IRAS	JAMI	JOEL
HUPA	HOOK	IIWI	IRID	JANE	JOEY
HURA	HOON	IJMA	IRIS	JANN	JOGI
HURL	HOOP	IKAT	IRMA	JAPE	JOHN
HURT	HOOT	IKMO	IROK	JARL	JOIE
HUSE	HOPE	IKON	IRON	JASS	JOIN
HUSH	HOPI	IKRA	IRRA	JATI	JOKE
HUSK	HOPS	ILIA	IRUS	JATO	JOKY
HUSO	HORA	ILLE	ISAR	JAUN	JOLE
HUZZ	HORN	ILLS	ISBA	JAVA	JOLI
HYDE	HORS	ILOG	ISER	JAVE	JOLL
HYLA	HOSE	ILOT	ISHA	JAWY	JOLT

JONK	KAFA	KEIR	KISH	KONA	KYAR
JOOM	KAGU	KELA	KISS	KONK	KYAT
JORD	KAHA	KELD	KIST	KOOP	
JOSE	KAHU	KELL	KITE	KOPH	LAAP
JOSH	KAID	KELP	KITH	KOPI	LABE
JOSS	KAIF	KELT	KIVA	KOPT	LACE
JOSY	KAIK	KENO	KIVE	KORA	LACK
JOTA	KAIL	KENT	KIVU	KORE	LACT
JOUG	KAKA	KEPI	KIWI	KORI	LACY
JOUR	KALA	KEPT	KIYI	KOSO	LADE
JOVA	KALE	KERB	KLAM	KOSS	LADY
JOVE	KALI	KERE	KLAN	KOTA	LAET
JOWL	KALO	KERF	KLEE	KOTO	LAGO
JOZY	KAMA	KERI	KLIP	KOZO	LAIC
JUAN	KAME	KERN	KLOM	KRAG	LAID
JUAR	KAMI	KERR	KLOP	KRAL	LAIN
JUBA	KANA	KETA	KNAB	KRAN	LAIR
JUBE	KANE	KEYS	KNAG	KRAS	LAIS
JUCA	KANO	KHAN	KNAP	KRIS	LAIT
JUCK	KANT	KHAR	KNAR	KROO	LAKE
JUDA	KAPA	KHAS	KNEE	KTKB	LAKH
JUDE	KAPH	KHEM	KNEW	KTKR	LAMA
JUDO	KARA	KHET	KNEZ	KTKT	LAMB
JUDY	KARI	KHOR	KNIP	KTQB	LAME
JUEZ	KARL	KIAK	KNIT	KTQR	LAMP
JUGA	KARN	KICK	KNOB	KUAN	LANA
JUJU	KARO	KIDS	KNOP	KUAR	LAND
JUKE	KASA	KIEF	KNOR	KUBA	LANE
JULE	KASI	KIEL	KNOT	KUDU	LANK
JULY	KASM	KIER	KNOW	KUEI	LANX
JUMP	KATE	KIEV	KNUB	KUFA	LAOS
JUNE	KATH	KIFF	KNUR	KUGE	LAPP
JUNG	KATY	KIHO	KNUT	KUHL	LARA
JUNK	KAUN	KIKI	KOAE	KUKI	LARD
JUNO	KAVA	KIKU	KOBA	KUKU	LARI
JUPE	KAVI	KILE	KOBE	KULA	LARK
JURA	KAWA	KILL	KOBI	KULI	LARP
JURE	KAWI	KILN	KOBU	KULM	LARS
JURY	KAWN	KILO	KOCH	KULU	LASH
JUST	KAYO	KILT	KOEL	KUNG	LASI
JUTE	KAZI	KINA	KOFF	KUNK	LASS
JUZA	KAZY	KIND	KHOL	KURD	LAST
JYNX	KEAL	KINE	KOIL	KURE	LATA
	KEEF	KING	KOJI	KURI	LATE
KAAN	KEEK	KINK	KOKO	KURK	LATH
KAAT	KEEL	KINO	KOKU	KUSH	LATU
KADA	KEEN	KIPE	KOLA	KVAS	LAUD
KADE	KEEP	KIPP	KOLI	KWEI	LAUN
KADI	KEET	KIRI	KOLO	KYAH	LAVA
KADU	KEIF	KIRK	KOME	KYAK	LAVE

LAWN	LIEF	LOAN	LOTH	MARC
LAWS	LIEN	LOBB	LOTI	MAAL	MARE
LAZE	LIER	LOBE	LOTO	MAAM	MARI
LAZI	LIEU	LOBO	LOTS	MAAN	MARK
LAZO	LIFE	LOCH	LOUD	MAAS	MARL
LAZY	LIFO	LOCI	LOUN	MAAT	MARM
LEAD	LIFT	LOCK	LOUP	MABA	MARO
LEAF	LIIN	LOCO	LOUR	MABI	MARS
LEAH	LIJA	LODE	LOUT	MACE	MART
LEAK	LIKE	LODI	LOVE	MADE	MARU
LEAL	LILA	LODZ	LOWA	MADI	MARY
LEAN	LILL	LOFT	LOWN	MADO	MASA
LEAP	LILT	LOGE	LUAU	MAGE	MASH
LEAR	LILY	LOGY	LUBA	MAGG	MASK
LECH	LIMA	LOIN	LUBE	MAGH	MASS
LEDA	LIMB	LOIR	LUBS	MAGI	MAST
LEEK	LIME	LOIS	LUCE	MAHA	MASU
LEER	LIMN	LOKA	LUCK	MAHR	MATA
LEES	LIMP	LOKE	LUCY	MAIA	MARE
LEET	LIMU	LOKI	LUDI	MAID	MATH
LEFT	LIMY	LOLA	LUDO	MAIL	MATT
LEHR	LINA	LOLL	LUES	MAIM	MAUD
LEIF	LIND	LOLO	LUFF	MAIN	MAUI
LELY	LINE	LOMA	LUGE	MAIS	MAUL
LENA	LING	LONE	LUGH	MAJA	MAUN
LEND	LINK	LONG	LUKE	MAKE	MAYA
LENE	LINN	LONK	LULL	MAKI	MAYO
LENO	LINO	LOOD	LULU	MAKO	MAZE
LENS	LINT	LOOF	LUMP	MAKU	MAZO
LENT	LINY	LOOK	LUNA	MALA	MEAD
LEON	LINZ	LOOM	LUNE	MALE	MEAL
LERO	LION	LOON	LUNG	MALI	MEAN
LERP	LIPA	LOOP	LUNY	MALL	MEAT
LESS	LIRA	LOOS	LUPE	MALM	MEDA
LEST	LIRE	LOOT	LURA	MALO	MEDE
LETI	LISA	LOPE	LURE	MALT	MEDI
LETO	LISP	LORA	LURG	MAMA	MEED
LETT	LISS	LORD	LURI	MAMO	MEEK
LEVI	LIST	LORE	LURK	MANA	MEER
LEVO	LITE	LORI	LUSH	MAND	MEET
LEVY	LITH	LORN	LUST	MANE	MEGA
LEWD	LITI	LORO	LUTE	MANI	MEIN
LIAM	LITZ	LORS	LUXE	MANN	MEIO
LIAR	LIVE	LORY	LWOW	MANO	MELA
LIAS	LIVY	LOSE	LYAM	MANS	MELD
LICE	LLEW	LOSH	LYAS	MANU	MELE
LICK	LLYN	LOSS	LYNX	MANX	MELT
LIDA	LOAD	LOST	LYON	MANY	MEMO
LIDO	LOAF	LOTA	LYRA	MAPO	MEND
LIED	LOAM	LOTE	LYRE	MARA	MENE

MENS	MIRA	MORO		NECK	NIUE
MENT	MIRE	MORS	NAAB	NEED	NKVD
MENU	MIRK	MORT	NAAM	NEEM	NOAH
MEOU	MIRO	MOSE	NABK	NEEP	NOAP
MEOW	MIRY	MOSK	NABO	NEER	NOBS
MERE	MISE	MOSS	NABU	NEIL	NOCK
MERL	MISS	MOST	NACH	NEIN	NODE
MERO	MIST	MOSY	NAEL	NEIR	NODI
MEUR	MITE	MOTA	NAGA	NEJD	NOEL
MESA	MITT	MOTE	NAGY	NELL	NOGG
MESE	MITU	MOTH	NAHA	NEMA	NOIL
MESH	MITY	MOTO	NAIA	NEMO	NOIO
MESS	MIXE	MOUE	NAID	NEON	NOIX
META	MOAB	MOVE	NAIF	NEPA	NOLA
METE	MOAN	MOWN	NAIL	NERA	NOLL
METZ	MOAT	MOXA	NAIO	NERI	NOLO
MEUM	MOCK	MOXO	NAIS	NERO	NOME
MEWL	MODE	MOZO	NAJA	NESH	NONA
MEWS	MOED	MUAV	NALA	NESS	NONE
MIAM	MOFF	MUCH	NAMA	NEST	NONO
MIAN	MOGO	MUCK	NAME	NETE	NOOK
MIAO	MOHA	MUDD	NANA	NETI	NOON
MIAS	MOHO	MUFF	NAAE	NEUE	NORA
MICA	MOHR	MUGA	NAOS	NEVA	NORE
MICE	MOIL	MULE	NAPA	NEVE	NORI
MICK	MOIO	MULK	NAPE	NEWS	NORM
MICO	MOJO	MULL	NAPU	NEWT	NORN
MIDE	MOKE	MUMP	NARD	NEXT	NOSE
MIDI	MOKI	MUND	NARE	NGAI	NOSU
MIEN	MOKO	MUNG	NARK	NIAS	NOSY
MIFF	MOLA	MUNJ	NARY	NIBS	NOTA
MIGG	MOLD	MURA	NASA	NICE	NOTE
MIKE	MOLL	MURE	NASE	NICK	NOTT
MILA	MOLT	MURK	NASH	NIDE	NOUN
MILD	MOMO	MUSA	NASI	NIDI	NOUP
MILE	MONA	MUSE	NAST	NIFE	NOUS
MILK	MONG	MUSH	NATE	NIGH	NOVA
MILL	MONK	MUSK	NATH	NIKE	NOVE
MILO	MONO	MUSO	NATO	NILE	NOWT
MILT	MONS	MUSS	NATR	NILL	NOWY
MIMB	MONT	MUST	NAUT	NIMB	NOXA
MIMI	MOOD	MUTA	NAVE	NINA	NOYL
MINA	MOON	MUTE	NAVY	NINE	NUBA
MIND	MOOR	MUTH	NAZE	NINO	NUDA
MINE	MOOT	MUTT	NAZI	NIOG	NUDD
MING	MOPE	MYNA	NEAL	NIOU	NUDE
MINK	MORA	MYRA	NEAP	NIPA	NUIT
MINO	MORE	MYST	NEAR	NISH	NULL
MINT	MORG	MYTH	NEAT	NISI	NUMA
MINX	MORN	MYXO	NEBO	NITO	NUMB

NUPE	OIME	OONT	OVUM	PAON	PEHO
NURL	OISE	OORD	OWEN	PAPA	PEKE
	OKAY	OOZE	OWER	PAPE	PELA
OAHU	OKEE	OOZY	OXAN	PARA	PELF
OAKS	OKEH	OPAH	OXEA	PARC	PELO
OAKY	OKET	OPAL	OXEN	PARD	PELT
OARY	OKIA	OPEN	OXER	PARE	PELU
OAST	OKIE	OPUS	OXID	PARK	PEND
OATH	OKRA	ORAD	OXIM	PARR	PENE
OATY	OKRO	ORAL	OXYL	PARS	PENN
OBAN	OLAF	ORAN	OYER	PART	PENT
OBEX	OLAM	ORAS	OYES	PASA	PEON
OBEY	OLAN	ORCA	OYEZ	PASI	PEPO
OBIT	OLAX	ORDO	OZEM	PASS	PERA
OBOE	OLAY	ORDU		PAST	PERE
OBOL	OLEA	OREL		PATA	PERI
OBRA	OLEO	OREN	PAAL	PATE	PERK
OCHA	OLGA	ORFE	PAAN	PATH	PERM
OCHS	OLIC	ORGY	PAAR	PATO	PERN
OCRA	OLID	ORLE	PACA	PATU	PERO
OCTA	OLIO	ORLO	PACE	PAUL	PERT
OCTO	OLLA	ORLY	PACK	PAUN	PERU
ODAL	OLOR	ORNA	PACO	PAVE	PESA
ODAX	OLPE	ORNE	PACT	PAVO	PESO
ODDS	OLPH	ORRA	PADI	PAVY	PESS
ODEA	OMAN	ORYX	PAGA	PAWA	PEST
ODEL	OMAO	OSAR	PAGE	PAWL	PETE
ODER	OMAR	OSER	PAHA	PAWN	PETO
ODIC	OMEI	OSLO	PAHI	PEAG	PEUR
ODIN	OMEN	OSSA	PAHO	PEAI	PEVA
ODIO	OMER	OSTE	PAID	PEAK	PEVY
ODOR	OMIT	OTEA	PAIL	PEAL	PHAD
ODUM	OMNI	OTHO	PAIN	PEAN	PHEW
ODYL	OMRI	OTIC	PAIR	PEAR	PHIL
OESE	OMSK	OTIS	PAIS	PEAT	PHIT
OEUF	ONAN	OTOE	PAJO	PEBA	PHIZ
OFFA	ONCA	OTRA	PALA	PECA	PHON
OFFS	ONCE	OTRO	PALE	PECK	PHOO
OGAM	ONDE	OTTO	PALI	PECO	PHOS
OGEE	ONDY	OTUS	PALL	PEDA	PHOT
OGLE	ONER	OUCH	PALM	PEDI	PHUT
OGOR	ONES	OUGH	PALO	PEDO	PIAT
OGPU	ONLY	OURS	PALP	PEEK	PIAY
OGRE	ONTO	OUSE	PALY	PEEL	PICA
OGUM	ONUS	OUST	PANA	PEEN	PICE
OHIA	ONYM	OVAL	PANE	PEEP	PICI
OHIO	ONYX	OVEN	PANG	PEER	PICK
OHNE	ONZA	OVER	PANI	PEET	PICO
OHOY	OOID	OVID	PANK	PEGA	PICT
OILY	OONS	OVIS	PANT	PEGU	PIED

PIEN	PLET	**POOP**	PULI	QUAS	**RASH**
PIER	PLEW	**POOR**	PULK	QUAY	**RASP**
PIET	PLEX	**POOT**	PULL	QUEI	**RATA**
PIFF	PLIE	**POPE**	PULP	QUID	**RATE**
PIKA	PLOD	**PORE**	PULU	QUIP	**RATH**
PIKE	PLOP	**PORK**	PULY	QUIT	**RATI**
PIKI	PLOT	**PORO**	PUMA	QUIZ	**RATS**
PIKY	PLOW	**PORT**	PUME	QUNG	**RAVE**
PILE	PLOY	**POSE**	PUMP	QUOD	**RAVI**
PILI	PLUG	**POSH**	PUNA		**RAYA**
PILL	PLUM	**POST**	PUND	RAAD	**RAZE**
PILY	PLUP	**POSY**	PUNG	RABA	**RAZZ**
PIMA	PLUS	**POTE**	PUNK	RABI	**READ**
PIMP	PNYX	**POTT**	PUNO	RACA	**REAL**
PINA	POBS	**POUF**	PUNT	RACE	**REAM**
PINE	POCK	**POUL**	PUNY	RACK	**REAP**
PING	POCO	**POUR**	PUPA	RACY	**REAR**
PINK	PODA	**POUS**	PURE	**RADA**	**REBA**
PINO	PODE	**POUT**	PURI	**RAFT**	**RECK**
PINT	POEM	**POWE**	PURL	**RAGE**	**RECT**
PINY	POET	PRAH	PURR	**RAGI**	**REDE**
PION	POGO	PRAM	PURU	**RAHU**	**REDO**
PIOT	POGY	PRAO	PUSH	**RAIA**	**REED**
PIPA	POHA	PRAT	PUSS	**RAID**	**REEF**
PIPE	POIL	PRAU	PUTT	**RAIK**	**REEK**
PIPI	POKE	PRAY	PUUD	**RAIL**	**REEL**
PIPY	POKU	PREP	PUXY	**RAIN**	**REEM**
PIRN	POKY	PRES	PUYA	**RAIP**	**REFT**
PIRO	POLA	PRET	PYAL	**RAIS**	**REIM**
PIRR	POLE	PREY	PYAT	**RAJA**	**REIN**
PISA	POLK	PRIM	PYET	**RAKE**	**REIS**
PISE	POLL	PRIX	PYIC	**RALE**	**REJA**
PISH	POLO	PROA	PYLA	**RALO**	**REKI**
PISK	POLY	PROD	PYLE	**RAMA**	**RELY**
PISO	POMA	PROM	PYOT	**RAME**	**REMI**
PIST	**POMB**	PROP	PYRE	**RAMI**	**REMS**
PITA	**POMO**	PROW	PYRO	**RAMP**	**RENA**
PITH	**POMP**	PSHA		**RANA**	**REND**
PITO	**POND**	PTAH	QAID	**RAND**	RENI
PITT	**PONE**	PUCA	QAIS	**RANG**	RENO
PITY	**PONG**	PUCE	QERE	**RANI**	RENT
PIUS	**PONS**	PUCK	QERI	**RANK**	REPP
PIXY	**PONT**	PUDU	QKKT	**RANN**	RESE
PLAN	**PONY**	PUFF	QOPH	**RANT**	RESH
PLAP	**POOA**	PUGH	QQKT	**RAPE**	REST
PLAT	**POOD**	PUJA	QUAD	**RAPT**	RETE
PLAY	**POOH**	PUKA	QUAE	**RARA**	REVE
PLEA	**POOK**	PUKE	QUAG	**RARE**	REVS
PLEB	**POOL**	PUKU	QUAI	**RASA**	RHEA
PLED	**POON**	PULE	QUAN	RASE	RHIN

RHOB	RODA	RUBE	SAER	SAXE	SEMO
RHEM	RODD	RUBY	SAFE	SAYA	SEND
RHUS	RODE	RUCK	SAFI	SCAB	SENN
RIAL	RODI	RUDD	SAGA	SCAD	SEPS
RICE	ROED	RUDE	SAGE	SCAN	SEPT
RICH	ROER	RUER	SAGO	SCAP	SERA
RICK	ROEY	RUFF	SAGY	SCAR	SERB
RIDD	ROIL	RUGA	SAHA	SCAT	SERE
RIDE	ROJO	RUHR	SAHH	SCOB	SERF
RIEL	ROKA	RUIN	SAHO	SCON	SERI
RIEM	ROLE	RUKH	SAHU	SCOP	SERO
RIEN	ROLL	RULE	SAIC	SCOT	SERT
RIER	ROMA	RULL	SAID	SCOW	SESI
RIFE	ROME	RUMB	SAIL	SCUD	SESS
RIFF	ROMI	RUMP	SAIN	SCUG	SETA
RIFT	ROMP	RUNE	SAIS	SCUM	SETH
RIGA	RONE	RUNG	SAKE	SCUP	SETI
RIIS	RONG	RUNT	SAKI	SCUR	SETT
RIKK	ROOD	RUPA	SALA	SCUT	SEVE
RILE	ROOF	RURU	SALE	SEAH	SEWN
RILL	ROOK	RUSA	SALP	SEAL	SEXT
RILY	ROOM	RUSE	SALT	SEAM	SHAD
RIMA	ROON	RUSH	SAMA	SEAN	SHAG
RIME	ROOS	RUSK	SAME	SEAR	SHAH
RIMU	ROOT	RUSS	SAMP	SEAT	SHAM
RIMY	ROPE	RUST	SANA	SEBA	SHAN
RIND	ROPY	RUTA	SAND	SEBI	SHAT
RINE	RORI	RUTE	SANE	SECK	SHAW
RING	RORY	RUTH	SANG	SECT	SHAY
RINK	ROSA	RYAL	SANK	SEED	SHEA
RIOT	ROSE	RYAZ	SANS	SEEK	SHED
RIPA	ROSS	RYEL	SAPA	SEEL	SHEE
RIPE	ROSY	RYME	SAPO	SEEM	SHEM
RIRE	ROTA	RYND	SARA	SEEN	SHEN
RISE	ROTE	RYPE	SARD	SEEP	SHER
RISK	ROTI		SARG	SEER	SHEW
RJSP	ROTL	SAAH	SARI	SEGO	SHIS
RISS	ROTO	SAAL	SARK	SEHR	SHIK
RITA	ROUD	SAAN	SART	SEID	SHIM
RITE	ROUE	SAAR	SASA	SEIK	SHIN
RIVE	ROUT	SABA	SASH	SEIM	SHIP
RKKT	ROUX	SABE	SATE	SEIP	SHIR
ROAD	ROVE	SACK	SATI	SEIR	SHOA
ROAM	ROWY	SACO	SAUK	SEIT	SHOD
ROAN	ROXY	SADD	SAUL	SEJM	SHOE
ROAR	RYOT	SADE	SAUM	SELF	SHOG
ROBE	RQKT	SADH	SAVE	SELL	SHOO
ROCH	RSVP	SADO	SAWK	SEME	SHOP
ROCK	RUAY	SADR	SAWN	SEMI	SHOR

SHOT	SIZE	SLUG	SOOK	STEN	SUSI
SHOU	SIZY	SLUM	SOON	STEP	SUSU
SHOW	SIZZ	SLUR	SOOT	STER	SUSY
SHRI	SKAG	SLUT	SOPH	STET	SUZY
SHUE	SKAT	SMEE	SOPT	STEV	SVAN
SHUL	SKEE	SMEW	SORA	STEW	SWAB
SHUN	SKEG	SMOG	SORB	STIB	SWAD
SHUT	SKEN	SMUG	SORE	STIR	SWAG
SIAL	SKEO	SMUR	SORI	STOA	SWAM
SIAM	SKEP	SMUT	SORS	STOD	SWAN
SICE	SKEW	SNAB	SORT	STOF	SWAP
SICK	SKEY	SNAG	SORY	STOG	SWAT
SIDA	SKID	SNAP	SOSH	STOM	SWAY
SIDE	SKIL	SNED	SOSO	STOP	SWEB
SIDI	SKIM	SNEE	SOUD	STOT	SWIG
SIDY	SKIN	SNIB	SOUF	STOW	SWIM
SIER	SKIP	SNIG	SOUK	STUB	SWIZ
SIFT	SKIT	SNIP	SOUP	STUD	SWOB
SIGH	SKIV	SNOB	SOUR	STUM	SWOP
SIGN	SKUA	SNOD	SOUS	STUN	SWOW
SIKA	SKUN	SNOW	SOYA	STUT	SWUM
SIKH	SKYE	SNUB	SPAD	STYE	SYCE
SILK	SKYR	SNUG	SPAE	STYX	SYED
SILL	SKYT	SNUP	SPAN	SUCH	SYKE
SILO	SLAB	SNUR	SPAR	SUCK	SYNE
SILT	SLAG	SOAK	SPAT	SUDD	SYPE
SIMA	SLAM	SOAP	SPAY	SUDS	SYRA
SIME	SLAP	SOAR	SPEC	SUER	SYUD
SIMI	SLAT	SOBK	SPED	SUET	
SIMP	SLAV	SOCK	SPEE	SUEZ	TAAL
SINA	SLAW	SOCO	SPES	SUFI	TAAR
SIND	SLAY	SODA	SPET	SUGI	TABI
SINE	SLEB	SOFA	SPEW	SUIT	TABU
SING	SLED	SOFT	SPEX	SUJI	TACE
SINH	SLEE	SOGA	SPEY	SUKU	TACK
SINK	SLEW	SOHO	SPIN	SULA	TACT
SINO	SLEY	SOIA	SPIT	SULD	TAEL
SIOL	SLID	SOIE	SPOT	SULK	TAFT
SION	SLIM	SOIL	SPRY	SULU	TAHA
SIRE	SLIP	SOIR	SPUD	SUMP	TAHR
SIRI	SLIT	SOKA	SPUN	SUNG	TAIL
SISE	SLOB	SOKE	SPUR	SUNK	TAIN
SISH	SLOE	SOLA	SPUT	SUNN	TAIR
SISI	SLOG	SOLD	STAB	SUPA	TAIT
SISS	SLOO	SOLE	STAD	SUPE	TAJO
SITA	SLOP	SOLI	STAG	SURA	TAKE
SITE	SLOT	SOLO	STAR	SURD	TAKT
SITO	SLOW	SOMA	STAT	SURE	TAKU
SIVA	SLUB	SOME	STAY	SURF	TAKY
SIVE	SLUE	SONG	STEM	SUSA	TALA

TALC	TECO	THIS	TOED	TRAM	TURK
TALE	TEDA	THOB	TOFF	TRAP	TURM
TALI	TEEL	THOR	TOGA	TRAY	TURN
TALK	TEEM	THOS	TOGO	TREE	TURP
TALL	TEEN	THOU	TOGS	TREK	TUSH
TAMA	TEER	THUD	TOHO	TRES	TUSK
TAME	TEES	THUG	TOIL	TRET	TUTE
TAMP	TEFF	THUS	TOKO	TREY	TUTU
TANA	TEGG	TIAR	TOLA	TRIG	TUWI
TANE	TEHR	TIBU	TOLD	TRIM	TUZA
TANG	TEIG	TICE	TOLE	TRIN	TWEE
TANH	TEIL	TICK	TOLL	TRIO	TWIG
TANK	TEJU	TIDE	TOLU	TRIP	TWIN
TANO	TELA	TIDY	TOMA	TRIS	TWIT
TAOS	TELE	TIED	TOMB	TRIT	TYBI
TAPA	TELI	TIEN	TOME	TROD	TYEE
TAPE	TELL	TIER	TONE	TROP	TYER
TAPS	TEMA	TIFF	TONG	TROT	TYKE
TAPU	TEND	TIGE	TONK	TROW	TYMP
TARA	TENE	TIKE	TONY	TROY	TYNE
TARE	TENG	TIKI	TOOA	TRUE	TYPE
TARI	TENT	TILE	TOOK	TRYP	TYPO
TARN	TEOS	TILL	TOOL	TSAR	TYPP
TARO	TERA	TILT	TOON	TSHI	TYPY
TARP	TERM	TIME	TOOT	TSIA	TYRE
TART	TERN	TINA	TOPE	TSIN	TYRO
TASK	TERP	TIND	TOPH	TSUN	TYRR
TASS	TESA	TINE	TOPI	TUAN	TYTO
TATE	TESS	TING	TOPS	TUBA	TZAR
TATT	TEST	TINO	TORA	TUBE	
TATU	TETE	TINT	TORE	TUCK	UANG
TAUN	TETH	TINY	TORI	TUFA	UBER
TAUT	TEWA	TION	TORN	TUFF	UDIC
TAVE	TEXT	TIPE	TORO	TUFT	UDAD
TAVY	TEYL	TIPI	TORP	TUKE	UDAL
TAWA	THAI	TIRE	TORT	TULA	UBII
TAXI	THAN	TIRO	TORY	TULE	UEBA
TAXO	THAR	TITI	TOSK	TULU	UGLY
TCHA	THAT	TITO	TOSS	TUMP	ULAN
TCHE	THAW	TIZA	TOTA	TUNA	ULEX
TCHU	THEA	TMAN	TOTE	TUND	ULLO
TEAK	THEB	TOAD	TOTO	TUNE	ULLR
TEAL	THEE	TOBA	TOTY	TUNG	ULME
TEAM	THEM	TOBE	TOUG	TUNO	ULNA
TEAN	THEN	TOBY	TOUP	TUNU	ULUA
TEAR	THEO	TOCK	TOUR	TUNY	ULVA
TEAT	THEW	TOCO	TOUT	TUPI	UMBO
TECA	THEY	TODE	TOWN	TUPY	UMPH
TECH	THIN	TODO	TOWY	TURF	UNAU
TECK	THIO	TODY	TOXA	TURI	UNBE

UNCA		VIDE	WADY	WEFT	WILK
UNCI	VACH	VIER	WAEG	WEGA	WILL
UNCO	VADE	VIEW	WAER	WEGG	WILT
UNDE	VAGI	VILA	WAFD	WEIR	WILY
UNDO	VAIL	VILE	WAFT	WEKA	WIND
UNDY	VAIN	VILI	WAGE	WEKI	WINE
UNIE	VAIR	VILL	WAIF	WELD	WING
UNIO	VALE	VILY	WAIL	WELF	WINK
UNIS	VALI	VINA	WAIN	WELK	WINY
UNIT	VAMP	VINE	WAIT	WELL	WIPE
UNTO	VANE	VINO	WAKA	WELS	WIRE
UNTZ	VANG	VINT	WAKE	WELT	WIRY
UPAS	VANS	VINY	WAKF	WEND	WISE
UPGO	VARA	VIOL	WAKY	WENT	WISH
UPIS	VARE	VIRA	WALE	WEPT	WISP
UPLA	VARI	VIRE	WALI	WERE	WIST
UPON	VARY	VISA	WALK	WERF	WITH
URAL	VASA	VISE	WALL	WERI	WIVE
URAN	VASE	VISS	WALT	WERT	WOKE
URAO	VAST	VITA	WAND	WEST	WOLD
URDE	VASU	VITE	WANE	WETA	WOLF
URDU	VAUX	VIVA	WANG	WEVE	WONG
URDY	VAYU	VIVE	WANT	WHAM	WONT
UREY	VEAL	VIVO	WANY	WHAT	WOOD
URFA	VEAU	VLEI	WAPP	WHAU	WOOF
URGE	VEDA	VLEY	WAQF	WHEE	WOOL
URIA	VEEP	VOCE	WARD	WHEN	WOON
URIM	VEER	VOET	WARE	WHET	WORD
URNA	VEGA	VOID	WARM	WHEW	WORE
URSA	VEIL	VOIR	WARN	WHEY	WORK
URTH	VEIN	VOLA	WARP	WHIG	WORM
URUS	VELA	VOLE	WART	WHIM	WORN
URVA	VELD	VOLK	WARY	WHIN	WORT
USAR	VELO	VOLT	WASH	WHIP	WOTE
USED	VENA	VOOG	WASP	WHIR	WOVE
USEE	VEND	VOTA	WATE	WHIT	WRAF
USER	VENT	VOTE	WATT	WHIZ	WRAP
USES	VEPS	VOTH	WAVE	WHOA	WREN
USHA	VERA	VOTO	WAVY	WHOO	WRIT
USUN	VERB	VUGG	WAXY	WHOM	WUDU
USUS	VERD	VUGH	WAYS	WHUN	WUFF
UTAH	VERI	VULN	WEAK	WHYO	WUKF
UTAS	VERT		WEAL	WICK	WURM
UTOR	VERY	WAAC	WEAN	WIDE	WUZU
UTUM	VEST	WAAG	WEAR	WIDU	WYNN
UVAL	VETA	WABI	WEED	WIEL	WYRD
UVEA	VETO	WACO	WEEK	WIES	
UVID	VIAL	WADD	WEEL	WIFE	XEMA
UZAN	VICE	WADE	WEEP	WILD	XENO
	VIDA	WADI	WEET	WILE	XERO

XINA	YARL	YENI	YOUP	ZARF	ZIRA
XIPE	YARN	YESO	YOUR	ZARP	ZIZZ
XMAS	YARR	YETA	YOWL	ZATI	ZOAR
XOSA	YARU	YHVD	YPIL	ZEAL	ZOAS
XOVA	YATE	YHVH	YSER	ZEBU	ZOBO
	YATI	YIMA	YUAN	ZEIN	ZOGO
YABA	YAUP	YIPE	YUCA	ZEKE	ZOLA
YAGE	YAWL	YITE	YUFT	ZEME	ZONA
YAJE	YAWN	YMCA	YUGA	ZEMI	ZONE
YAKA	YAWP	YMER	YUIT	ZENO	ZOOM
YALE	YAWS	YMIR	YULE	ZENU	ZOON
YALI	YAYA	YNCA	YUMA	ZERO	ZULU
YALU	YEAH	YODH	YUNX	ZEST	ZUNI
YAMA	YEAN	YOGA	YURT	ZETA	ZUZA
YANA	YEAR	YOGH	YUTU	ZEUS	ZYGA
YANG	YEAS	YOGI	YWCA	ZIMB	ZYME
YANK	YEDO	YOKE		ZINC	
YAPA	YEGG	YOLK	ZACH	ZING	
YAPP	YELL	YOND	ZAIN	ZION	
YARD	YELP	YORE	ZAMA	ZIPA	
YARE	YELT	YORK	ZANY	ZIPS	

BAAL	MABI	TACK	WADY	DAGO	SAHU
BAAS	NABK	TACT		GAGE	TAHA
CAAM	NABO	VACH	BAEL	GAGL	TAHR
FAAM	NABU	WACO	BAER	HAGG	
GAAL	RABA	ZACH	BAEZ	HAGI	BAIL
HAAB	RABI		CAEN	IAGO	BAIN
HAAF	SABA	BADB	DAER	JAGA	BAIT
HAAK	SABE	BADE	DAEZ	JAGG	CAID
HAAR	TABI	CADE	FAEX	KAGU	CAIN
KAAN	TABU	CADI	GAEA	LAGO	DAIL
KAAT	WABI	CADY	GAEL	MAGE	DAIN
LAAP	YABA	DADA	HAEC	MAGG	DAIS
MAAL		DADO	HAEM	MAGH	FAIL
MAAM	BACH	EADS	JAEL	MAGI	FAIN
MAAN	BACK	FADE	LAET	NAGA	FAIR
MAAS	CACA	FADO	NAEL	NAGY	FAIT
MAAT	CACO	FADY	SAER	PAGA	GAIA
NAAB	DACE	GADE	TAEL	PAGE	GAIL
NAAM	EACH	HADE	WAEG	RAGE	GAIN
PAAL	FACE	HADU	WAER	RAGI	GAIT
PAAN	FACT	JADE		SAGA	HAIK
PAAR	HACK	JADU	BAFF	SAGE	HAIL
RAAD	JACA	JADY	BAFT	SAGO	HAIR
SAAH	JACK	KADA	CAFE	SAGY	JAIL
SAAL	JACU	KADE	DAFF	VAGI	JAIN
SAAN	LACE	KADI	DAFT	WAGE	KAID
SAAR	LACK	KADU	GAFF	YAGE	KAIF
TAAL	LACT	LADE	HAFT		KAIK
TAAR	LACY	LADY	KAFA	BAHI	KAIL
WAAC	MACE	MADE	SAFI	BAHO	LAIC
WAAG	NACH	MADI	RAFT	BAHT	LAID
BABA	PACA	MADO	SAFE	HAHA	LAIN
BABE	PACE	PADI	TAFT	KAHA	LAIR
BABI	PACK	RADA	WAFD	KAHU	LAIS
BABU	PACO	SADD	WAFT	MAHA	LAIT
BABY	PACT	SADE		MAHR	MAIA
FABA	RACA	SADH	BAGA	OAHU	MAID
GABE	RACE	SADO	BAGO	PAHA	MAIL
GABY	RACK	SADR	CAGE	PAHI	MAIM
HABA	RACY	VADE	CAGN	PAHO	MAIN
HABE	SACK	WADD	CAGY	RAHU	MAIS
LABE	SACO	WADE	DAGG	SAHH	NAIA
MABA	TACE	WADI	DAGH	SAHO	NAID

NAIF	BAKU	CALX	TALI	TAME	MANA
NAIK	CAKE	DALE	TALK	TAMP	MAND
NAIL	CAKY	DALI	TALL	VAMP	MANE
NAIO	FAKE	DALL	VALE	YAMA	MANI
NAIS	FAKY	FALA	VALI	ZAMA	MANN
PAID	HAKE	FALL	WALE		MANO
PAIL	HAKH	FALX	WALI	AANI	MANS
PAIN	HAKO	GALA	WALK	BANA	MANU
PAIR	HAKU	GALE	WALL	BANC	MANX
PAIS	JAKE	GALI	WALT	BAND	MANY
QAIS	JAKO	GALL	YALE	BANE	NANA
QAID	KAKA	GALT	YALI	BANG	NANE
RAIA	LAKE	HALA	YALU	BANI	PANA
RAID	LAKH	HALE		BANK	PANE
RAIK	MAKE	HALF	CAME	BANS	PANG
RAIL	MAKI	HALL	CAMP	BANT	PANI
RAIN	MAKO	HALM	DAMA	CANA	PANK
RAIP	MAKU	HALO	DAME	CANE	PANT
RAIS	OAKS	HALS	DAMN	CANG	RANA
SAIC	OAKY	HALT	DAMP	CANO	RAND
SAID	RAKE	IALU	FAMA	CANT	RANG
SAIL	SAKE	KALA	FAME	DANA	RANI
SAIN	SAKI	KALE	FAMN	DANE	RANK
SAIS	TAKE	KALI	GAMA	DANG	RANN
TAIL	TAKT	KALO	GAME	DANK	RANT
TAIN	TAKU	MALA	GAMP	DANS	SANA
TAIR	TAKY	MALE	HAMI	DANU	SAND
TAIT	WAKA	MALI	IAMB	FANE	SANE
VAIL	WAKE	MALL	JAMA	FANG	SANG
VAIN	WAKF	MALM	JAMB	FANO	SANK
VAIR	WAKY	MALO	JAMI	GANE	SANS
WAIF	YAKA	MALT	KAMA	GANG	TANA
WAIL		NALA	KAME	GANO	TANE
WAIN	AALU	PALA	KAMI	HAND	TANG
WAIT	BALA	PALE	LAMA	HANG	TANH
ZAIN	BALD	PALI	LAMB	HANK	TANK
	BALE	PALL	LAME	HANO	TANO
	BALI	PALM	LAMP	HANS	UANG
BAJU	BALK	PALO	MAMA	HANT	VANE
CAJA	BALL	PALP	MAMO	JANE	VANG
GAJO	BALM	PALY	NAMA	JANN	VANS
HAJE	BALT	RALE	NAME	KANA	WAND
MAJA	BALU	RALO	RAMA	KANE	WANE
NAJA	CALE	SALA	RAME	KANO	WANG
PAJO	CALF	SALE	RAMI	KANT	WANT
RAJA	CALK	SALP	RAMP	LANA	WANY
TAJO	CALL	SALT	SAMA	LAND	YANA
YAJE	CALM	TALA	SAME	LANE	YANG
	CALO	TALC	SAMP	LANK	YANK
BAKA	CALP	TALE	TAMA	LANX	ZANY
BAKE					

	BARM	KARN	VARE	LASI	GATA
FAON	BARN	KARO	VARI	LASS	GATE
GAOL	BARO	LARA	VARY	LAST	GATH
GAON	BARR	LARD	WARD	MASA	HATE
LAOS	BART	LARI	WARE	MASH	HATH
NAOS	BARU	LARK	WARM	MASK	HATI
PAOS	CARA	LARP	WARN	MASS	JATI
TAOS	CARD	LARS	WARP	MAST	HATO
	CARE	MARA	WART	MASU	KATE
CAPA	CARK	MARC	WARY	NASA	KATH
CAPE	CARL	MARE	YARD	NASE	KATY
CAPH	CARN	MARI	YARE	NASH	LATA
CAPP	CARO	MARK	YARL	NASI	LATE
GAPE	CARP	MARL	YARN	NAST	LATH
GAPO	CARR	MARM	YARR	OAST	LATU
GAPY	CART	MARO	YARU	PASA	MATA
HAPU	DARD	MARS	ZARF	PASI	MATE
JAPE	DARE	MART	ZARP	PASS	MATH
KAPA	DARI	MARU		PAST	MATT
KAPH	DARK	MARY	BASE	RASA	MATY
LAPP	DARN	NARD	BASH	RASE	NATE
MAPO	DARR	NARE	BASK	RASH	NATH
NAPA	DART	NARK	BASS	RASP	NATO
NAPE	EARL	NARY	BAST	SASA	NATR
NAPU	EARN	OARY	CASA	SASH	OATH
PAPA	FARD	PARA	CASE	TASK	OATY
PAPE	FARE	PARC	CASH	TASS	PATA
RAPE	FARL	PARD	CASK	VASA	PATE
RAPT	FARM	PARE	CASO	VASE	PATH
SAPA	FARO	PARK	CAST	VAST	PATO
SAPO	GARA	PARR	CASY	VASU	PATU
TAPA	GARB	PARS	DASH	WASH	RATA
TAPE	GARE	PART	DASI	WASP	RATE
TAPS	GARM	RARA	DASS		RATH
TAPU	GARN	RARE	EASE	BATA	RATI
WAPP	GARO	SARA	EAST	BATE	RATS
YAPA	GARY	SARD	EASY	BATH	SATE
YAPP	HARB	SARG	FASH	BATT	SATI
	HARD	SARI	FASS	BATZ	TATE
WAQF	HARE	SARK	FAST	CATA	TATT
	HARK	SART	GASH	CATE	TATU
AARE	HARL	TARA	GASP	CATO	WATE
AARU	HARM	TARE	HASH	CATS	WATT
BARA	HARP	TARI	HAST	DATA	YATE
BARB	HART	TARN	JASS	DATE	YATI
BARD	JARL	TARO	KASA	DATO	ZATI
BARE	KARA	TARP	KASI	DATU	
BARI	KARI	TART	KASM	EATS	BAUD
BARK	KARL	VARA	LASH	FATE	BAUL

BAUM	JAVA		OBAN		ACRU
CAUK	JAVE	CAXI		ECAD	OCRA
CAUL	KAVA	SAXE	ABBA	ICAL	
CAUP	KAVI	TAXI	ABBE	SCAB	ACTA
DAUB	VALA	TAXO	ABBY	SCAD	ACTH
DAUK	LAVE	WAXY		SCAN	ACTO
DAUW	NAVE		ABCS	SCAP	ACTS
EAUX	NAVY	BAYA		SCAR	ACTU
FAUN	PAVE	CAYO	ABED	SCAT	ECTO
FAUT	PAVO	DAYE	ABEL		OCTA
GAUB	PAVY	DAYS	ABET	ACCA	OCTO
GAUD	RAVE	HAYZ	EBEN	ECCA	
GAUE	RAVI	KAYO	EBER	ECCE	ACUS
GAUL	SAVE	MAYA	IBEX		SCUD
GAUP	TAVE	MAYO	OBEX	ACER	SCUG
GAUR	TAVY	RAYA	OBEY	ICED	SCUM
GAUS	WAVE	SAYA	UBER	ICER	SCUP
GAUT	WAVY	VAYU			SCUR
HAUL		WAYS	ABIA	ACHE	SCUT
HAUT	BAWL	YAYA	ABIB	ACHT	
JAUN	BAWN		ABIE	ACHY	ACYL
KAUN	CAWK	CAZA	ABIR	ECHO	
LAUD	CAWL	CAZI	IBID	ECHT	ADAD
LAUN	DAWK	CAZY	IBIS	ICHO	ADAH
MAUD	DAWM	DAZA	IBIT	ICHU	ADAK
MAUI	DAWN	DAZE	OBIT	OCHA	ADAM
MAUL	FAWN	DAZY	UBIT	OCHS	ADAN
MAUN	GAWD	FAZE	UBII	TCHA	ADAR
NAUT	GAWK	GAZA		TCHE	ADAT
PAUL	GAWN	GAZE	ABLE	TCHU	EDAM
PAUN	GAWP	GAZI	ABLY		EDAR
SAUK	HAWK	HAZE		ACID	IDAS
SAUL	JAWY	HAZY	ABOO	ACIS	ODAL
SAUM	KAWA	JAZZ	ABOT		ODAX
TAUN	KAWI	KAZI	ABOU	ACLE	UDAD
TAUT	KAWN	KAZY	ABOX		UDAL
VAUX	LAWN	LAZE	EBOE	ACME	
YAUP	LAWS	LAZI	EBON		ADDA
	PAWA	LAZO	OBOE	ACNE	ADDU
	PAWL	LAZY	OBOL		ADDY
BAVE	PAWN	MAZE		ACON	EDDA
CAVA	SAWK	MAZO	ABRA	ACOR	EDDO
CAVE	SAWN	NAZE	ABRI	ICON	EDDY
CAVY	TAWA	NAZI	EBRO	SCOB	ODDS
DAVE	YAWL	RAZE	OBRA	SCON	
DAVY	YAWN	RAZZ		SCOP	ADEN
EAVE	YAWP		ABSI	SCOT	ADER
FAVI	YAWS	ABAS		SCOW	ADES
FAVN		IBAD	ABUT		EDEL
GAVE		IBAN	EBUR	ACRE	EDEN
HAVE					

EDER		PEAR	NECK	JEER	WEET
IDEA	BEAD	PEAT	PECA	KEEF	
IDEE	BEAK	READ	PECK	KEEK	DEFI
IDEM	BEAL	REAL	PECO	KEEL	DEFT
IDEN	BEAM	REAM	RECK	KEEN	DEFY
IDEO	BEAN	REAP	RECT	KEEL	HEFT
IDES	BEAR	REAR	SECK	KEEN	JEFE
ODEA	BEAT	SEAH	SECT	KEEP	JEFF
ODEL	BEAU	SEAL	TECA	KEET	LEFT
ODER	DEAD	SEAM	TECH	LEEK	REFT
	DEAF	SEAN	TECK	LEER	TEFF
EDGE	DEAL	SEAR	TECO	LEES	WEFT
EDGY	DEAN	SEAT		LEET	
	DEAR	TEAK	BEDE	MEED	BEGA
ADIB	FEAK	TEAL	CEDE	MEEK	DEGU
ADIT	FEAR	TEAM	DEDO	MEER	HEGH
EDIT	FEAT	TEAN	LEDA	MEET	MEGA
IDIC	GEAL	TEAR	MEDA	NEED	PEGA
IDIO	GEAN	TEAT	MEDE	NEEM	PEGU
ODIC	GEAR	VEAL	MEDI	NEEP	SEGO
ODIN	GEAT	VEAU	PEDA	NEER	TEGG
ODIO	HEAD	WEAK	PEDI	PEEK	VEGA
ODIC	HEAF	WEAL	PEDO	PEEL	WEGA
UDIC	HEAL	WEAN	REDE	PEEN	WEGG
	HEAP	WEAR	REDO	PEEP	YEGG
IDJO	HEAR	YEAH	REDA	PEER	
	HEAT	YEAN	VEDA	PEET	BEHN
IDLE	JEAN	YEAR	YEDO	REED	HEHE
IDLY	KEAL	YEAS		REEF	JEHU
	LEAD	ZEAL	BEEF	REEK	LEHR
ADMI	LEAF		BEEN	REEL	PEHO
	LEAH	CEBA	BEEP	REEM	SEHR
EDNA	LEAK	DEBS	BEER	SEED	TEHR
	LEAL	DEBT	BEES	SEEK	
ADOR	LEAN	HEBE	BEET	SEEL	BEID
EDOM	LEAP	NEBO	DEED	SEEM	CEIL
IDOL	LEAR	PEBA	DEEM	SEEN	DEIL
ODOR	MEAD	REBA	DEEP	SEEP	DEIN
	MEAL	SEBA	DEER	SEER	FEIS
ADRY	MEAN	SEBI	FEED	TEEL	GEIN
	MEAT	UEBA	FEEL	TEEM	HEII
IDUN	NEAL	ZEBU	FEES	TEEN	HEIN
ODUM	NEAP		FEET	TEER	HEIR
	NEAR	BECK	GEEZ	TEES	KEIF
IDYL	NEAT	DECA	HEED	VEEP	KEIR
IDYO	PEAG	DECI	HEEL	VEER	LEIF
ODYL	PEAI	DECK	HEEP	WEED	MEIN
	PEAK	FECK	HEER	WEEK	MEIO
ADZE	PEAL	HECK	JEEL	WEEL	NEIL
IDZO	PEAN	LECH	JEEP	WEEP	NEIN

NEIR	HELL	MEMO	PEND	AERY	PERT
REIM	HELM	NEMA	PENE	BERA	PERU
REIN	HELP	NEMO	PENN	BERG	QERE
REIS	JELL	REMI	PENT	BERM	QERI
SEID	KELA	REMS	RENA	BERN	SERA
SEIK	KELD	SEME	REND	BERT	SERB
SEIM	KELL	SEMI	RENI	CERA	SERE
SEIP	KELP	SEMO	RENO	CERE	SERF
SEIR	KELT	TEMA	RENT	CERN	SERI
SEIT	LELY	XEMA	SEND	CERO	SERO
TEIG	MELA	ZEME	SENN	DERA	SERT
TEIL	MELD	ZEMI	TEND	DERM	TERA
VEIL	MELE		TENE	KERY	TERM
VEIN	MELT	BENA	TENG	FERN	TERN
WEIN	NELL	BEND	TENT	FERU	TERP
WEIR	PELA	BENE	VENA	GERB	VERA
	PELE	BENG	VEND	GERD	VERB
BEJA	PELF	BENI	VENT	GERI	VERD
DEJA	PELO	BENO	WEND	GERM	VERI
NEJD	PELT	BENT	WENT	HERA	VERT
REJA	PELU	BENU	XENO	HERB	VERY
SEJM	RELY	CENA	YENI	HERD	WERE
TEJU	SELF	CENE	ZENO	HERE	WERF
	SELL	CENS	ZENU	HERL	WERI
BEKA	TELA	CENT		HERO	WERT
FEKE	TELE	DENE	AEON	HERR	XERO
PEKE	TELI	DENS	FEOD	HERS	ZERO
REKI	TELL	DENT	GEON	JERK	
WEKA	VELA	DENY	LEON	KERB	BESA
WEKI	VELD	FEND	MEOU	KERE	BESS
ZEKE	VELO	GENA	MEOW	KERF	BEST
	WELD	GENE	NEON	KERI	CESS
BELA	WELF	GENS	PEON	KERN	CEST
BELI	WELK	GENT	TEOS	KERR	DESI
BELL	WELL	GENU	CEPA	LERO	DESK
BELT	WELS	HENS	CEPE	LERP	FESS
CELA	WELT	JENA	DEPA	MERE	FEST
CELL	YELL	KENO	KEPI	MERL	GEST
CELT	YELP	KENT	KEPT	MERO	GESU
DELE	YELT	LENA	NEPA	MERU	HEST
DELL		LEND	PEPO	NERA	JESS
EELY	BEMA	LENE	REPP	NERI	JEST
FELD	DEME	LENO	SEPS	NERO	JESU
FELL	DEMI	LENS	SEPT	PERA	LESS
FELS	DEMO	LENT	VEPS	PERE	LEST
FELT	DEMY	MEND	WEPT	PERI	MESA
GELD	FEME	MENE		PERK	MESE
GELT	HEMI	MENS	AERA	PERM	MESH
HELA	HEMO	MENT	AERI	PERN	MESS
HELD	HEMP	MENU	AERO	PERO	NESH

NESS	TETH			SHAT	
NEST	VETA	CEYX	AGNI	SHAW	AHIQ
OESE	VETO	KEYS		SHAY	AHIR
PESA	WETA	TEYL	AGOG	THAI	BHIL
PESO	YETA		AGON	THAN	CHIA
PESS	ZETA	AFAR	EGOL	THAR	CHIB
PEST		AFFY	IGOR	THAT	CHIC
RESE	DEUL	OFFA	OGOR	THAW	CHIH
RESH	DEUM	OFFS		WHAM	CHIL
REST	DEUS		OGPU	WHAT	CHIN
SESI	DEUX	EFIK		WHAU	CHIP
SESS	FEUD	IFIL	AGRA		CHIR
TESA	GEUM		AGRI	AHEM	CHIT
TESS	JEUX	AFRA	AGRO	AHET	OHIA
TEST	MEUM		OGRE	AHEY	OHIO
VEST	NEUE	AGAG		BHEL	PHIL
WEST	OEUF	AGAL	AGUA	CHEE	PHIT
YESO	PEUR	AGAO	AGUE	CHEF	PHIZ
ZEST	ZEUS	AGAR	OGUM	CHEK	RHIN
		AGAU		CHEN	SHIH
AETA	BEVY	AGAZ	AHAB	CHER	SHIK
BETA	DEVA	EGAD	AHAZ	CHEW	SHIM
BETE	DEVI	EGAL	BHAR	CHEZ	SHIN
BETH	HEVI	NGAI	DHAT	EHEU	SHIP
CETE	LEVI	OGAM	CHAA	GHEE	SHIR
CETO	LEVO		CHAB	GHEG	THIN
FETE	LEVY	EGBA	CHAD	GHES	THIO
GETA	NEVA	EGBO	CHAI	KHEM	THIS
GETT	NEVE		CHAM	KHET	WHIG
HETH	PEVA	AGED	CHAN	PHEW	WHIM
HETT	PEVY	AGEE	CHAP	RHEA	WHIN
JETE	REVE	AGER	CHAR	SHEA	WHIP
JETH	REVS	EGER	CHAT	SHED	WHIR
KETA	SEVE	OGEE	CHAW	SHEE	WHIT
LETI	WEVE		CHAY	SHEM	WHIZ
LETO		EGGS	DHAK	SHEN	
LETT	DEWA	EGGY	DHAN	SHEW	OHNE
META	DEWY		DHAO	THEA	
METE	HEWN	AGHA	DHAR	THEB	AHOM
METZ	LEWD		DHAW	THEE	AHOY
NETE	MEWL	AGIB	GHAT	THEM	BHOY
NETI	MEWS	AGIO	KHAN	THEN	CHOB
PETE	NEWS	AGIS	KHAR	THEO	CHOL
PETO	NEWT	EGIL	KHAS	THEW	CHOP
RETE	SEWN	EGIS	PHAD	THEY	CHOR
SETA	TEWA		SHAD	WHEE	CHOU
SETH		AGLA	SHAG	WHEN	CHOW
SETI	NEXT	IGLU	SHAH	WHET	DHOW
SETT	SEXT	OGLE	SHAM	WHEW	GHOR
TETE	TEXT	UGLY	SHAN	WHEY	KHOR

OHOY	JHVH	MICO	BIER	NIFE	
PHON	YHVH	NICE	CIEL	PIFF	AILE
PHOO		NICK	DIEB	RIFE	BILE
PHOS	WHYO	PICA	DIEM	RIFF	BILK
PHOT		PICE	DIER	RIFT	BILL
RHOB	BIAS	PICI	DIES	SIFT	BILO
SHOA	DIAD	PICK	DIET	TIFF	DILL
SHOD	DIAL	PICO	DIEU	WIFE	DILO
SHOE	DIAN	PICT	FIEF		EILD
SHOO	DIAU	RICE	GIER	BIGA	FILE
SHOP	DIAZ	RICH	HIEL	GIGA	FILL
SHOQ	FIAT	RICK	HIEN	HIGH	FILM
SHOR	KIAK	SICE	HIER	MIGG	FILO
SHOT	LIAM	SICK	KIEF	NIGH	FILS
SHOU	LIAR	TICE	KIEL	RIGA	GILA
SHOW	LIAS	TICK	KIER	SIGH	GILD
THOB	MIAM	VICE	KIEV	SIGN	GILL
THOR	MIAN	WICK	LIED	TIGE	GILO
THOS	MIAO		LIEF		GILT
THOU	MIAS	AIDA	LIEN	KIHO	HILA
WHOA	NIAS	AIDE	LIEU		HILL
WHOM	PIAT	BIDE	MIEN	LIIN	HILO
WHOO	PIAY	DIDO	PIED	RIIS	HILT
	RIAL	EIDE	PIEN		JILL
SHRI	SIAL	FIDE	PIER	BIJA	JILT
	SIAM	FIDO	PIET	FIJI	KILE
AHUM	TIAR	GIDE	RIEL	LIJA	KILL
BHUT	VIAL	HIDE	RIEM		KILN
CHUB		KIDS	RIEN	BIKE	KILO
CHUD	BIBB	LIDA	RIER	BIKH	KILT
CHUG	BIBI	LIDO	SIER	DIKA	LILA
CHUM	DIBS	MIDE	TIED	DIKE	LILL
CHUN	GIBE	MIDI	TIEN	HIKE	LILT
CHUT	JIBE	NIDE	TIER	HIKU	LILY
GHUZ	NIBS	NIDI	VIER	KIKI	MILA
JHUM	TIBU	RIDD	VIEW	KIKU	MILD
PHUT		RIDE	WIEL	LIKE	MILE
RHUM	AICH	SIDA	WIES	MIKE	MILK
RHUS	BICE	SIDE		NIKE	MILL
SHUE	DICE	SIDI	BIFF	PIKA	MILO
SHUL	DICK	SIDY	FIFE	PIKE	MILT
SHUN	FICO	TIDE	GIFY	PIKI	NILE
SHUT	HICK	TIDY	HIFI	PIKY	NILL
THUD	KICK	VIDA	JIFF	PIKK	OILY
THUG	LICE	VIDE	KIFF	SIKA	PILE
THUS	LICK	WIDE	LIFE	SIKH	PILI
WHUN	MICA	WIDU	LIFO	TIKE	PILL
	MICE		LIFT	TIKI	PILY
IHVH	MICK	BIEN	MIFF		RILE

RILL
RILY
SILK
SILL
SILO
SILT
TILE
TILL
TILT
VILA
VILE
VILI
VILL
VILY
WILD
WILE
WILK
WILL
WILT
WILY

CIMA
CIME
GIMP
HIMA
LIMA
LIMB
LIME
LIMN
LIMP
LIMU
LIMY
MIME
MIMI
NIMB
OIME
PIMA
PIMP
RIMA
RIME
RIMU
RIMY
SIMA
SIME
SIMI
SIMP
TIME
YIMA
ZIMB

AINE
AINT
AINU
BINA
BIND
BINE
BING
BINH
BINI
BINN
BINO
CINE
CINQ
DINE
DING
DINO
DINT
EINE
FIND
FINE
FINK
FINN
GINK
HIND
HING
HINO
HINT
JINN
JINX
KINA
KIND
KINE
KING
KINK
KINO
LINA
LIND
LINE
LING
LINK
LINN
LINO
LINT
LINY
LINZ
MINA
MIND
MINE
MING

MINK
MINO
MINT
MINX
NINA
NINE
NINO
PINA
PINE
PING
PINK
PINO
PINT
PINY
RIND
RINE
RING
RINK
SINA
SIND
SINE
SING
SINH
SINK
SINO
TINA
TIND
TINE
TING
TINO
TINT
TINY
VINA
VINE
VINO
VINT
VINY
WIND
WINE
WING
WINK
WINY
XINA
ZINC
ZING

BIOD
BION
BIOS
CION

DION
FIOT
LION
NIOG
NIOU
PION
PIOT
RIOT
SIOL
SION
TION
TIOU
VIOL
ZION

AIPI
CIPO
HIPE
KIPE
KIPP
LIPA
NIPA
PIPA
PIPE
PIPI
PIPY
RIPA
RIPE
TIPE
TIPI
WIPE
XIPE
YIPE
ZIPA
ZIPS

AIRA
AIRE
AIRS
AIRT
BIRD
BIRL
BIRN
BIRR
CIRC
CIRL
DIRE
DIRK
DIRT
EIRE

FIRE
FIRM
FIRN
GIRD
GIRL
GIRO
GIRT
HIRE
KIRI
KIRK
LIRA
LIRE
MIRA
MIRE
MIRK
MIRO
MIRY
PIRN
PIRO
PIRR
RIRE
SIRE
SIRI
TIRE
TIRO
VIRA
VIRE
WIRE
WIRY
ZIRA

BISA
BISE
BISH
BISK
CISE
CIST
DISA
DISC
DISH
DISK
DISS
FISC
FISH
FISK
FIST
GISH
GIST
HISH
HISS

HIST
KISH
KISS
KIST
LISA
LISP
LISS
LIST
MISE
MISS
MIST
NISH
NISI
OISE
PISA
PISE
PISH
PISK
PISO
PIST
RISE
RISK
RISP
RISS
SISE
SISH
SISI
SISS
VISA
VISE
VISS
WISE
WISH
WISP
WIST

BITE
BITI
BITO
BITT
CITE
CITO
CITS
CITY
DITA
GITE
KITE
KITH
LITE
LITH

LITI	BIWA	ADHA	BLAH		VLEY
LITZ	IIWI		BLAS	ALCA	
MITE	KIWI	AKIA	BLAT	ALCO	ALFA
MITT		AKIM	CLAD		
MITU	BIXA	AKIN	CLAM	ALDA	ALGA
MITY	DIXI	OKIA	CLAN		ALGY
NITO	MIXE	OKIE	CLAP	ALEA	OLGA
PITA	PIXY	SKID	CLAW	ALEC	
PITH		SKIL	CLAY	ALEE	ALIA
PITO	KIYI	SKIM	ELAH	ALEF	ALIF
PITT		SKIN	ELAM	ALEM	ALII
PITY	BIZE	SKIP	ELAN	ALEN	ALIM
RITA	FIZZ	SKIT	FLAG	ALEY	ALIN
RITE	SIZE	SKIV	FLAK	BLEB	ALIT
SITA	SIZY		FLAM	BLED	ALIX
SITE	SIZZ	AKKA	FLAN	BLET	BLIP
SITO	TIZA	BKKT	FLAP	BLEU	CLIM
TITI	ZIZZ	EKKA	FLAT	BLEW	CLIO
VITA		QKKT	FLAW	CLEE	CLIP
VITE	AJAR	RKKT	FLAX	CLEF	ELIA
WITH	AJAX		FLAY	CLEM	ELIS
YITE		IKMO	GLAD	CLEO	FLIP
	AJEE		KLAM	CLEW	FLIT
BIUR		AKOV	KLAN	ELEF	FLIX
NIUE	IJMA	EKOI	OLAF	FLEA	GLIA
PIUS		IKON	OLAM	FLED	GLIB
	AJOG		OLAN	FLEE	GLIM
CIVA	EJOO	AKRA	OLAX	FLEM	GLIS
CIVE	GJOA	IKRA	OLAY	FLEW	ILIA
DIVA		OKRA	PLAN	FLEX	KLIP
DIVE	AKAL	OKRO	PLAP	FLEY	OLIC
DIVI	AKAN		PLAT	GLED	OLID
FIVE	IKAT	AKUA	PLAY	GLEN	OLIO
GIVE	OKAY	SKUA	SLAB	DLEE	PLIE
HIVE	SKAG		SLAG	LLEW	SLID
JIVA	SKAT	NKVD	SLAM	OLEA	SLIM
JIVE			SLAP	OLEO	SLIP
KIVA	AKEE	SKYE	SLAT	PLEA	SLIT
KIVE	AKEY	AKYR	SLAV	PLEB	
KIVU	OKEE	SKYT	SLAW	PLED	ALKY
LIVE	OKEH		SLAY	PLET	
LIVY	OKET	ALAE	ULAN	PLEW	ALLA
RIVE	SKEE	ALAI		PLEX	ALLE
SIVA	SKEG	ALAR	ALBA	SLEB	ALLO
SIVE	SKEN	ALAN	ALBE	SLED	ALLY
VIVA	SKEO	ALAS	ALBI	SLEE	ELLA
VIVE	SKEP	ALAY	ALBO	SLEW	ELLE
VIVO	SKEW	BLAA	ELBA	SLEY	ILLE
WIVE	SKEY	BLAB	ELBE	ULEX	ILLS
		BLAE		VLEI	OLLA

ULLO
ULLR

ALMA
ALME
ALMS
ELMY
ULME
ULNA

ALOD
ALOE
ALOP
ALOW
BLOB
BLOC
BLOT
BLOW
CLOD
CLOE
CLOG
CLOP
CLOT
CLOU
CLOW
CLOY
ELOD
ELON
FLOC
FLOE
FLOG
FLOP
FLOW
GLOM
GLOW
ILOG
ILOT
KLOM
KLOP
OLOR
PLOD
PLOP
PLOT
PLOW
PLOY
SLOB
SLOE
SLOG
SLOO
SLOP

SLOT
SLOW

ALPH
ALPS
OLPE
OLPH

ALSO
ELSA
ELSE

ALTA
ALTE
ALTO

ALUM
ALUR
BLUB
BLUE
BLUP
BLUR
BLUT
CLUB
CLUE
ELUL
FLUB
FLUE
FLUX
GLUB
GLUE
GLUG
GLUM
GLUT
PLUG
PLYM
PLUP
PLUS
SLUB
SLUE
SLUG
SLUM
SLUR
SLUT
ULUA

ALVA
ULVA

ALYA

ALYS
CLYM
LLYN

AMAH
AMAR
GMAN
IMAM
OMAN
OMAO
OMAR
XMAS

AMBA
ABMI
AMBO
IMBE
UMBO

YMCA

AMEN
AMER
AMES
AMEX
EMER
EMEU
IMER
OMEI
OMEN
OMER
SMEE
SMEW
TMEN
YMER

AMIA
AMIC
AMID
AMIE
AMIL
AMIN
AMIR
AMIS
EMIL
CMIM
EMIR
EMIT
IMID
OMIT

YMIR

AMLA
AMLI

AMMA
AMMI
AMMO
AMMU
EMMA
EMMY
IMMI

OMNI

AMOI
AMOK
AMON
AMOR
AMOS
SMOG

EMPT
IMPI
UMPH

AMRA
OMRI

AMSK

AMUN
SMUG
SMUR
SMUT

AMYL
EMYD
EMYS

ANAI
ANAK
ANAL
ANAM
ANAN
ANAS
ANAT
ANAX
ANAY
BNAI

ENAM
GNAR
GNAT
GNAW
KNAB
KNAG
KNAP
KNAR
ONAN
SNAB
SNAG
SNAP
UNAU

ANBA
UNBE

ANCE
ANCY
ENCE
INCA
INCH
ONCA
ONCE
UNCA
UNCI
UNCO
YNCA

ANDA
ANDE
ANDI
ANDY
ENDO
INDE
ONDE
ONDY
UNDE
UNDO
UNDY

ANER
ANES
ANET
ANEW
INEE
INEZ
KNEE
KNEW
KNEZ

ONER
ONES
SNED
SNEE

ANGE
ANGO
INGA
INGE

ANIL
ANIS
ENID
ENIF
ENIN
INIA
KNIP
KNIT
SNIB
SNIG
SNIP
UNIE
UNIO
UNIS
UNIT

ANKH
ENKI
INKA
INKY

INLY
ONLY

ANNA
ANNE
ANNI
ANNO
ENNA
ENNE
ENNS

ANOA
ANON
ENOL
ENON
ENOS
ENOW
KNOB
KNOP

KNOR	COAK	HOBB	BODY		TOHO
KNOT	COAL	HOBO	CODA	DOFF	
KNOW	COAN	JOBO	CODE	GOFF	BOII
SNOB	COAT	KOBA	CODO	KOFF	BOIL
SNOD	COAX	KOBE	CODY	LOFT	BOIS
SNOW	DOAB	KOBI	DODO	MOFF	COIF
	DOAT	KOBU	JODO	SOFA	COIL
INRE	EOAN	LOBB	LODE	SOFT	COIN
INRO	FOAL	LOBO	LODI	TOFF	COIR
	FOAM	NOBS	LODZ		COIX
ANSA	GOAD	POBS	MODE	BOFY	DOIT
ANSU	GOAF	ROBE	NODE	BOGA	EOIN
ENSE	GOAI	SOBK	NODI	BOGO	FOIL
	GOAL	TOBA	RODA	DOGE	JOIE
ANTA	GOAN	TOBE	RODD	DOGS	JOIN
ANTE	GOAT	TOBY	RODE	DOGY	KOIL
ANTI	HOAR	ZOBO	RODI	FOGO	LOIN
ENTE	HOAX		SODA	FOGY	LOIR
ENTO	JOAB	BOCA	TODE	GOGH	LOIS
INTI	JOAD	BOCE	TODO	GOGO	MOIL
INTO	KOAE	BOCK	TODY	HOGA	MOIO
ONTO	LOAD	COCA	YODH	HOGG	NOIL
UNTO	LOAF	COCK		JOGI	NOIO
UNTZ	LOAM	COCO	BOER	LOGE	NOIX
	LOAN	DOCK	COED	LOGY	OOID
ANUS	MOAB	FOCH	COEL	MOGO	POIL
KNUB	MOAN	FOCI	COEN	NOGG	ROIL
KNUR	MOAT	HOCH	DOEG	POGO	SOIA
KNUT	NOAH	HOCK	DOER	POGY	SOIE
ONUS	NOAP	JOCK	DOES	SOGA	SOIL
SNUB	ROAD	JOCU	GOEL	TOGA	SOIR
SNUG	ROAM	KOCH	GOER	TOGO	TOIL
SNUP	ROAN	LOCH	GOES	TOGS	VOID
SNUR	ROAR	LOCI	HOEK	YOGA	VOIR
	SOAK	LOCK	HOEN	YOGH	
ENVY	SOAP	LOCO	HOER	YOGI	BOJO
	SOAR	MOCK	HOEY	ZOGO	COJA
ENYO	TOAD	NOCK	JOEL		HOJA
ONYM	ZOAR	POCO	JOEY	BOHO	HOJU
ONYX	ZOAS	ROCH	KOEL	BOHR	KOJI
PNYX		ROCK	MOED	COHO	MOJO
	BOBA	SOCK	NOEL	FOHN	ROJO
ANZU	BOBO	SOCO	POEM	HOHE	
ENZU	COBB	TOCK	POET	JOHN	BODO
ONZA	COBH	TOCO	ROED	KOHL	COKE
	DOBE	VOCE	ROER	MOHA	COKY
BOAR	DOBY		ROEY	MOHO	DOKO
BOAT	GOBI	BODB	TOED	MOHR	JOKE
BOAZ	GOBO	BODE	VOET	POHA	JOKY
COAG	GOBY	BODO		SOHO	KOKO

KOKU	HOLM		DONI	YOND	MOON
LOKA	HOLT	BOMA	DONT	ZONA	MOOR
LOKE	HOLY	BOMB	FOND	ZONE	MOOT
LOKI	IOLA	COMA	FONG		NOOK
MOKE	IOLE	COMB	FONO	BOOB	NOON
MOKI	JOLE	COME	FONS	BOOH	POOA
MOKO	JOLI	COMO	FONT	BOOK	POOD
POKE	JOLL	DOME	GONA	BOOL	POOH
POKU	JOLT	DOMN	GOND	B_OM	POOK
POKY	KOLA	DOMY	GONE	BOON	POOL
ROKA	KOLI	GOMA	GONG	BOOR	POON
SOKA	KOLO	HOME	HONE	BUOT	POOP
SOKE	LOLA	HOMO	HONG	COOK	POOR
TOKO	LOLL	HOMY	HONI	COOL	POOT
WOKE	LOLO	KOME	HONK	COOM	ROOD
YOKE	MOLA	LOMA	IONA	COON	ROOF
TOKO	MOLD	MOMO	IONE	COOP	ROOK
WOKE	MOLE	NOME	IONI	COOS	ROOM
YOKE	MOLL	POMA	JONK	COOT	ROON
	MOLT	POME	KONA	DOOB	ROOS
BOLA	NOLA	POMO	KONK	DOOK	ROOT
BOLD	NOLL	POMP	LONE	DOOM	SOOK
BOLE	NOLO	ROMA	LONG	DOON	SOON
BOLL	POLA	ROME	LONK	DOOR	SOOT
BOLO	POLE	ROMI	MONA	FOOD	TOOA
BOLT	POLK	ROMP	MONG	FOOL	TOOK
COLA	POLL	SOMA	MONK	FOOT	TOOL
COLD	POLO	SOME	MONO	GOOD	TOON
COLE	POLY	TOMA	MONS	GOOF	TOOT
COLI	ROLE	TOMB	MONT	GOOM	VOOG
COLP	ROLL	TOME	NONA	GOON	WOOD
COLT	SOLA		NONE	GOOP	WOOF
COLY	SOLD	AONE	NONO	GOOR	WOOL
DOLA	SOLE	BONA	OONS	HOOD	WOON
DOLE	SOLI	BOND	OONT	HOOF	ZOOM
DOLI	SOLO	BONE	POND	HOOK	ZOON
DOLL	TOLA	BONG	PONE	HOON	
DOLT	TOLD	BONI	PONG	HOOP	COPA
FOLD	TOLE	BONK	PONS	HOOT	COPE
FOLK	TOLL	BONN	PONT	JOOM	COPT
GOLA	YOLU	BONY	PONY	KOOP	COPY
GOLD	VOLA	COND	RONE	LOOD	DOPA
GOLF	VOLE	CONE	RONG	LOOF	DOPE
GOLI	VOLK	CONI	SONG	LOOK	DOPP
GOLL	VOLT	CONK	TONE	LOOM	HOPE
GOLO	WOLD	CONN	TONG	LOON	HOPI
HOLA	WOLF	CONY	TONK	LOOP	HOPS
HOLD	YOLK	DONA	TONY	LOOS	KOPH
HOLE	ZOLA	DONE	WONG	LOOT	KOPI
HOLI		DONG	WONT	MOOD	KOPT

LOPE	LORA		XOSA		
MOPE	LORD	BOSA		AOUL	COVE
POPE	LORE	BOSC	BOTA	BOUT	DOVE
QOPH	LORI	BOSE	BOTH	BOUW	HOVA
ROPE	LORN	BOSH	BOTO	COUP	HOVE
ROPY	LORO	BOSK	BOTT	COUS	JOVA
SOPH	LORS	BOSS	COTA	DOUB	JOVE
SOPT	LORY	COSE	COTE	DOUC	LOVE
TOPE	MORA	COSH	COTO	DOUM	MOVE
TOPH	MORE	COSO	COTY	DOUR	NOVA
TOPI	MORG	COSS	DOTE	FOUD	NOVE
TOPS	MORN	COSY	DOTH	FOUL	ROVE
	MORO	DOSA	DOTO	FOUR	WOVE
BORA	MORS	DOSE	DOTY	GOUL	XOVA
BORD	MORT	DOSS	GOTH	GOUR	
BORE	NORA	DOST	HOTH	GOUT	BOWK
BORG	NORE	FOSS	IOTA	HOUR	BOWL
BORI	NORI	GOSH	JOTA	JOUG	COWL
BORN	NORM	HOSE	KOTA	JOUR	DOWD
BORO	NORN	HOST	KOTO	LOUD	DOWL
BORS	OORD	JOSE	LOTA	LOUN	DOWN
BORT	PORE	JOSH	LOTE	LOUP	FOWL
CORA	PORK	JOSS	LOTH	LOUR	GOWK
CORD	PORO	JOSY	LOTI	LOUT	GOWL
CORE	PORT	KOSO	LOTO	MOUE	GOWN
CORK	RORI	KOSS	LOTS	NOUN	HOWE
CORM	RORY	LOSE	MOTA	NOUP	HOWL
CORN	SORA	LOSH	MOTE	NOUS	IOWA
DORA	SORB	LOSS	MOTH	POUF	JOWL
DORE	SORE	LOST	MOTO	POUL	LOWA
DORM	SORI	MOSE	NOTA	POUR	LOWN
DORN	SORS	MOSK	NOTE	POUS	MOWN
DORP	SORT	MOSS	NOTT	POUT	NOWT
DORY	SORY	MOST	POTT	ROUD	NOWY
FORA	TORA	MOSY	ROTA	ROUE	POWE
FORD	TORE	NOSE	ROTE	ROUT	ROWY
FORE	TORI	NOSU	ROTI	ROUX	TOWN
FORK	TORN	NOSY	ROTL	SOUD	TOWY
FORM	TORO	POSE	ROTO	SOUF	YOWL
FORT	TORP	POSH	SOTO	SOUK	
GORA	TORT	POST	SOTS	SOUP	BOXY
GORE	TORY	POSY	TOTA	SOUR	COXA
GORY	WORD	ROSA	TOTE	SOUS	DOXA
HORA	WORE	ROSE	TOTO	TOUG	DOXY
HORN	WORK	ROSS	TOTY	TOUP	FOXY
HORS	WORM	ROSY	VOTA	TOUR	MOXA
JORD	WORN	SOSH	VOTE	TOUT	MOXO
KORA	WORT	SOSO	VOTH	YOUP	NOXA
DORE	YORE	TOSK	VOTO	YOUR	ROXY
DORI	YORK	TOSS	WOTE		

TOXA		BRAB	KRAS	DREG	CRIN
	EPHA	BRAD	ORAD	DREI	CRIS
COYN		BRAE	ORAL	DREW	DRIB
COYO	APIA	BRAG	ORAN	DREY	DRIP
GOYA	APII	BRAM	ORAS	ERER	ERIA
HOYA	APIO	BRAN	PRAH	FREA	ERIC
NOYL	APIS	BRAS	PRAM	FRED	ERIE
SOYA	EPIC	BRAT	PRAO	FREE	ERIN
	IPIL	BRAY	PRAT	FRET	ERIS
BOZA	SPIN	CRAB	PRAU	FREY	FRIA
BOZO	SPIT	CRAG	PRAY	GRES	FRIB
COZE	UPIS	CRAL	TRAM	GREW	FRIT
COZY	YPIL	CRAM	TRAP	GREY	FRIZ
DOZE		CRAP	TRAY	OREL	GRID
DOZY	UPLA	CRAW	URAL	OREN	GRIG
JOZY		CRAX	URAN	PREP	GRIM
KOZO	APOD	DRAA	URAO	PRES	GRIN
MOZO	EPOS	DRAB	WRAF	PRET	GRIP
OOZE	SPOT	DRAG	WRAP	PREY	GRIS
OOZY	UPON	DRAH		TREE	GRIT
		DRAM	ARBA	TREK	IRID
APAP	SPRY	DRAP		TRES	IRIS
APAR		DRAT	ARCA	TRET	KRIS
OPAH	APSE	DRAW	ARCH	TREY	PRIM
OPAL	APSU	DRAY	ORCA	UREY	PRIX
SPAD	IPSE	ERAL		WREN	TRIG
SPAE	IPSO	ERAT	ERDA		TRIM
SPAN		FRAB	ORDO	ORFE	TRIN
SPAR	APUS	FRAP	ORDU	URFA	TRIO
SPAT	OPUS	FRAT	URDE		TRIP
UPAS	SPUD	FRAU	URDU	ARGO	TRIS
UPDP	SPUN	FRAY	URDY	ARGY	TRIT
	SPUR	GRAB		ERGO	URIA
	SPUT	GRAD	AREA	ORGY	URIM
APER	BQKT	GRAF	AREG	URGE	WRIT
APET	QQKT	GRAM	AREO		
APEX	RQKT	GRAN	ARES	ARIA	ORLE
EPEE		GRAO	BREA	ARID	ORLO
OPEN		GRAS	BRED	ARIL	ORLY
SPEC	AQUA	GRAY	BREN	ARIS	ARME
SPED	EQUI	IRAD	BRER	BRIE	ARMS
SPEE		IRAE	BREW	BRIG	ARMY
SPES	ARAB	IRAK	BREY	BRIM	ERMA
SPET	ARAD	IRAN	CREA	BRIN	IRMA
SPEW	ARAH	IRAQ	CREE	BRIO	ARNA
SPEX	ARAL	IRAS	CREW	BRIT	ARND
SPEY	ARAM		CREX	CRIB	ARNE
	ARAN	KRAG	DRED	CRIC	ARNI
UPGO	ARAR	KRAL	DREE	CRIG	ARNO
	ARAS	KRAN			

ARNT		ESCA	OSSA	STEV	OTRA
ERNE	ERSE	ESCE		STEW	OTRO
ORNE	ERST		ASTA		
URNA	URSA	ASEA	ASTI	OTHO	ATTA
		ASEM	ESTA		ETTA
AROA	ARTA	ASER	ESTE	ATIK	ETTE
AROD	ARTO	ESEK	ESTH	ATIP	OTTO
AROO	ARTS	ESER	OSTE	ATIS	ATUA
AROW	ARTY	ISER		OTIC	ATUM
BROB	URTH	OSER	ASUR	OTIS	ETUI
BROH		USED	ESUS	STIB	OTUS
BROM	ARUI	USEE	TSUN	STIR	STUB
BROO	ARUM	USER	USUN		STUD
BROW	BRUH	USES	USUS	KTKB	STUM
BROZ	BRUT	YSER		KTKR	STUN
CROC	CRUS		RSVP	KTKT	STUT
CROM	CRUX	ASHA	ATAP		UTUM
CROP	DRUB	ASHY	ATAR	ATLE	
CROW	DRUG	ISHA	ETAH	ATLI	ATWO
DROP	DRUM	PSHA	ETAL		
EROS	ERUA	TSHI	ETAT	ATMA	ETYM
FROE	ERUC	USHA	PTAH	ATMO	ITYS
FROG	FRUG		STAB	ATMU	STYE
FROM	GRUB	ASIA	STAD	ITMO	STYX
FROT	GRUM	ASIN	STAG		
FROW	GURS	HSIA	STAR	ETNA	ITZA
GROG	IRUS	ISIS	STAT		
GROS	TRUE	TSIA	STAY	ATOM	BUAL
GROT	URUS	TSIN	UTAH	ATON	DUAB
GROW			UTAS	ATOP	DUAD
IROK	URVA	ASKR		ETON	DUAL
IRON		ISLE	ETCH	ITOL	DUAN
KROO	ARYA	OSLO	ITCH	TOTE	DUAR
PROA	ERYX			STOA	DUAT
PROD	ORYX	ISMY	ATEF	STOD	FUAD
PROM	TRYP		ATEN	STOF	GUAM
PROP		ASNO	ATEO	STOG	GUAN
PROW	ASAK	ESNE	ATES	STOM	GUAO
TROD	ASAR		ETES	STOP	GUAR
TROP	ESAU	ASOK	ITEA	STOT	JUAN
TROT	ESAY	ASOP	ITEM	STOW	JUAR
TROW	ISAR	ASOR	ITEN	UTOR	KUAN
TROY	OSAR	ESOX	ITER		KUAR
	TSAR		OTEA	KTQB	LUAU
ARPA	USAR	ESPY	STEM	KTQR	MUAV
			STEN		QUAD
ARRA	ISBA	ASSE	STEP	ATRI	QUAE
IRRA		ASSI	STER	ATRY	QUAG
ORRA	ASCI	ESSE	STET	ETRE	QUAI

QUAN	SUCK	KUFA	QUIT	JULE	RUMP
QUAS	TUCK	LUFF	QUIZ	JULY	SUMP
QUAY	YUCA	MUFF	RUIN	KULA	TUMP
RUAY		PUFF	SUIT	KULI	YUMA
TUAN	AUDE	RUFF	YUIT	KULM	
YUAN	BUDA	SUFI		KULU	AUNE
	BUDE	TUFA	FUJI	LULL	AUNT
BUBA	DUDE	TUFF	JUJU	LULU	BUNA
BUBE	DUDS	TUFT	PUJA	MULE	BUND
BUBI	JUDA	WUFF	SUJI	MULK	BUNG
BUBO	JUDE	YUFT		MULL	BUNK
CUBA	JUDO		BUKH	NULL	BUNN
CUBE	JUDY	AUGE	BUKK	PULE	BUNT
CUBI	KUDU	BUGI	CUKE	PULI	CUNA
DUBB	LUDI	EUGE	DUKU	PULK	DUNE
HUBB	LUDO	FUGA	JUKE	PULL	DUNG
JUBA	MUDD	FUGU	KUKI	PULP	DUNK
JUBE	NUDA	GUGU	KUKU	PULU	DUNS
KUBA	NUDD	HUGE	LUKE	PULY	DUNT
LUBA	NUDE	HUGH	PUKA	RULE	FUND
LUBE	PUDU	HUGO	PUKE	RULL	FUNG
LUBS	RUDD	JUGA	RUKH	SULA	FUNJ
NUBA	RUDE	KUGE	SUKU	SULD	FUNK
RUBE	SUDD	LUGE	TUKE	SULK	GUNA
RUBY	SUDS	LUGH	WUKF	SULU	GUNJ
TUBA	WUDU	MUGA		TULA	HUND
TUBE		OUGH	AULA	TULE	HUNG
	AUER	PUGH	AULD	TULU	HUNH
AUCA	DUEL	RUGA	AULU	VULN	HUNK
BUCK	DUET	SUGI	BULB	YULE	HUNT
CUCA	EUER	VUGG	BULK	ZULU	JUNE
DUCE	FUEL	VUGH	BULL		JUNG
DUCK	HUED	YUGA	BULT	BUMP	JUNK
DUCO	JUEZ		CULL	DUMA	JUNO
DUCT	KUEI	BUHL	CULM	DUMB	KUNG
FUCI	LUES	BUHR	CULT	DUMP	KUNK
HUCK	QUEI	DUHR	DULL	FUME	LUNA
JUCA	RUER	GUHA	FULA	FUMY	LUNE
JUCK	SUER	GUHR	FULK	GUMP	LUNG
LUCE	SUET	KUHL	FULL	HUME	LUNY
LUCK	SUEZ	RUHR	GULA	HUMP	MUND
LUCY			GULF	JUMP	MUNG
MUCH	BUFF	CUIR	GULL	LUMP	MUNJ
MUCK	BUFO	DUIM	GULO	MUMP	PUNA
OUCH	CUFF	DUIT	GULP	NUMA	PUND
PUCA	DUFF	GUIB	HULA	NUMB	PUNG
PUCE	DUFY	HUIA	HULE	PUMA	PUNK
PUCK	GUFA	NUIT	HULK	PUME	PUNO
RUCK	GUFF	QUID	HULL	PUMP	PUNT
SUCH	HUFF	QUIP	HULU	RUMB	PUNY

QUNG	CURR	BUSK	BUTT	KVAS	TWEE
RUNE	CURT	BUSS	CUTE	OVAL	
RUNT	DURA	BUST	DUTY	SVAN	SWIG
RUNG	DURO	BUSY	FUTE	UVAL	SWIM
	DURR	CUSH	GUTI		SWIZ
SUNG	FURL	CUSK	JUTE	AVEC	TWIG
SUNK	FURY	CUSP	LUTE	AVER	TWIN
SUNN	GURU	CUSS	MUTA	AVES	TWIT
TUNA	HURA	DUSE	MUTE	EVEA	
TUND	HURL	DUSK	MUTH	EVEN	AWOL
TUNE	HURT	DUST	MUTT	EVER	LWOW
TUNG	JURA	FUSE	PUTT	EVET	SWOB
TUNO	JURE	FUSS	RUTA	IVES	SWOP
TUNU	JURY	FUST	RUTE	OVEN	SWOW
TUNY	KURD	GUSH	RUTH	OVER	
YUNX	KURE	GUST	TUTE	UVEA	AWRY
ZUNI	KURI	HUSE	TUTU		EWRY
	KURK	HUSH	YUTU	AVID	
BUOY	LURA	HUSK		AVIS	SWUM
DUOS	LURE	HUSO	PUUD	EVIL	
QUOD	LURG	JUST		OVID	SWYN
	LURI	KUSH	CUVY	OVIS	AXAL
DUPE	LURK	LUSH		UVID	EXAM
HUPA	MURA	LUST	TUWI		OXAN
JUPE	MURE	MUSA		AVON	
LUPE	MURK	MUSE	BUXY	AVOW	OXEA
NUPE	NURL	MUSH	LUXE	EVOE	OXEN
PUPA	OURS	MUSK	PUXY		OXER
RUPA	PURE	MUSO		AVUS	
SUPA	PURI	MUSS	BUYO	OVUM	AXIL
SUPE	PURL	MUST	CUYA		AXIS
TUPI	PURR	OUSE	PUYA	AWAN	CXIX
TUPY	PURU	OUST		AWAY	EXIT
	RURU	PUSH	AUZU	EWAN	IXIA
AURA	SURA	PUSS	BUZZ	SWAB	IXIL
AURI	SURD	RUSA	FUZE	SWAD	OXID
BURA	SURE	RUSE	FUZZ	SWAG	OXIM
BURE	SURF	RUSH	GUZE	SWAM	
BURG	TURF	RUSK	HUZZ	SWAN	
BURI	TURI	RUSS	JUZA	SWAP	AXLE
BURL	TURK	RUST	SUZY	SWAT	IXLE
BURN	TURM	SUSA	TUZA	SWAY	
BURP	TURN	SUSI	WUZU		AXON
BURR	TURP	SUSU	ZUZA	YWCA	
BURY	WURM	SUSY			OXYL
CURA	YURT	TUSH	AVAL	EWER	
CURB		TUSK	AVAR	KWEI	AYAH
CURD	AUSA		EVAN	OWEN	CYAN
CURE	AUSU	AUTO	IVAH	OWER	DYAD
CURL	BUSH	BUTO	IVAN	SWEB	DYAK

DYAS	DYER			LYRA	
EYAH	EYED	GYLE	EYOT	LYRE	AZAM
EYAS	EYER	HYLA	LYON	MYRA	AZAN
IYAR	EYEY	MYLE	PYOT	PYRE	CZAR
KYAH	OYER	PYLA	RYOT	PYRO	IZAR
KYAK	OYES	PYLE		SYRA	TZAR
KYAR	OYEZ		HYPE	TYRE	UZAN
KYAT	PYET	CYMA	HYPO	TYRO	
LYAM	RYEL	CYME	RYPE	TYRR	EZBA
LYAS	SYED	CYMN	SYPE	WYRD	
PYAL	TYEE	RYME	TYPE		EZEL
PYAT	TYER	TYMP	TYPO	CYST	OZEM
RYAL		ZYME	TYPP	MYST	
			TYPY		AZHA
	BYGO			CYTE	
GYBE	ZYGA	DYNA		MYTH	AZOF
TYBI		KYNE	BYRD	TYTO	AZON
	AYIN	GYNE	BYRE		AZOV
DYCK	PYIC	JYNX	EYRA		
SYCE		LYNX	EYRE	SYUD	
	CYKE	MYNA	EYRY		EZRA
HYDE	DYKE	RYND	FYRD	GYVE	
	FYKE	SYNE	GYRE		AZUL
AYES	SYKE	TYNE	GYRI	MYXA	AZUR
BYEE	TYKE	WYNN	GYRO	MYXO	

BLAA	IRAD	QUAG	COAK	ODAL	KLAM
CHAA	JOAD	SHAG	DHAK	OPAL	LIAM
DRAA	LEAD	SKAG	DYAK	ORAL	LOAM
AHAB	LOAD	SLAG	FEAK	OVAL	LYAM
ARAB	MEAD	SNAG	FLAK	PAAL	MAAM
BLAB	ORAD	STAG	HAAK	PEAL	MIAM
BRAB	PHAD	SWAG	IRAK	PYAL	NAAM
CHAB	QUAD	WAAG	KIAK	REAL	OGAM
CRAB	RAAD	ADAH	KYAK	RIAL	OLAM
DOAB	READ	AMAH	LEAK	RYAL	PRAM
DRAB	ROAD	ARAH	PEAK	SAAL	REAM
DUAB	SCAD	AYAH	SOAK	SEAL	ROAM
FRAB	SHAD	BLAH	TEAK	SIAL	SEAM
GRAB	SPAD	DRAH	WEAK	TAAL	SHAM
HAAB	STAD	ELAH	AGAL	TEAL	SIAM
JOAB	SWAD	ETAH	AKAL	UDAL	SLAM
KNAB	TOAD	EYAH	ANAL	URAL	SWAM
MOAB	UDAD	IVAH	ARAL	UVAL	TEAM
NAAB	ALAE	KYAH	AVAL	VEAL	TRAM
SCAB	BLAE	LEAH	AXAL	VIAL	WHAM
SLAB	BRAE	NOAH	BAAL	WEAL	ADAN
SNAB	IRAE	OPAH	BEAL	ZEAL	AKAN
STAB	KOAE	PRAH	BUAL	ADAM	ALAN
SWAB	QUAE	PTAH	COAL	ANAM	ANAN
WAAC	SPAE	SAAH	CRAL	ARAM	ARAN
ADAD	DEAF	SEAH	DEAL	AZAM	AWAN
ARAD	GOAF	SHAH	DIAL	BEAM	AZAN
BEAD	GRAF	UTAH	DUAL	BRAM	BEAN
BRAD	HAAF	YEAH	EGAL	CAAM	BRAN
CHAD	HEAF	ANAI	ERAL	CHAM	CHAN
CLAD	LEAF	BNAI	ETAL	CLAM	CLAN
DEAD	LOAF	CHAI	FOAL	CRAM	COAN
DIAD	OLAF	GOAI	GAAL	DRAM	CYAN
DUAD	WRAF	ILAI	GEAL	EDAM	DEAN
DYAD	AGAG	NGAI	GOAL	ELAM	DHAN
ECAD	BRAG	PEAI	HEAL	ENAM	DIAN
EGAD	COAG	QUAI	ICAL	EXAM	DUAN
FUAD	CRAG	THAI	KEAL	FAAM	ELAN
GLAD	DRAG	TYAI	KRAL	FLAM	EOAN
GOAD	FLAG	ADAK	LEAL	FOAM	EVAN
GRAD	KNAG	ANAK	MAAL	GRAM	EWAN
HEAD	KRAG	ASAK	MEAL	GUAM	FLAN
IBAD	PEAG	BEAK	NEAL	IMAM	GEAN

GMAN	GRAO	FEAR	EYAS	PIAT	CLAY
GOAN	GUAO	GEAR	GRAS	PLAT	DRAY
GRAN	MIAO	GNAR	IDAS	PRAT	ESAY
GUAN	OMAO	GUAR	IRAS	PYAT	FLAY
IBAN	PRAO	HAAR	KHAS	SCAT	FRAY
IRAN	URAO	HEAR	KRAS	SEAT	GRAY
IVAN	APAP	HOAR	KVAS	SHAT	OKAY
JEAN	ATAP	ISAR	LIAS	SKAT	OLAY
JOAN	CHAP	IYAR	LYAS	SLAT	PIAY
JUAN	CLAP	IZAR	MAAS	SPAT	PLAY
KAAN	CRAP	JOAR	MIAS	STAT	PRAY
KHAN	DRAP	JUAR	NIAS	SWAT	QUAY
KLAN	FLAP	KHAR	ORAS	TEAT	RUAY
KRAN	FRAP	KNAR	QUAS	THAT	SHAY
KUAN	HEAP	KUAR	UPAS	WHAT	SLAY
LEAN	KNAP	KYAR	UTAS	AGAU	SPAY
LOAN	LAAP	LEAR	XMAS	BEAU	STAY
MAAN	LEAP	LIAR	YEAS	DIAU	SWAY
MEAN	NEAP	NEAR	ZOAS	ESAU	TRAY
MIAN	NOAP	OMAR	ADAT	FRAU	AGAZ
MOAN	PLAP	OSAR	ANAT	LUAU	AHAZ
OBAN	REAP	PAAR	BEAT	PRAU	BOAZ
OLAN	SCAP	PEAR	BHAT	UNAU	DIAZ
OMAN	SLAP	REAR	BLAT	VEAU	
ONAN	SNAP	ROAR	BOAT	WHAU	ABBA
ORAN	SOAP	SAAR	BRAT	MUAV	ALBA
OXAN	SWAP	SCAR	CHAT	SLAV	AMBA
PAAN	TRAP	SEAR	COAT	CHAW	ANBA
PEAN	WRAP	SOAR	DOAT	CLAW	ARBA
PLAN	IRAQ	SPAR	DRAT	CRAW	BABA
QUAN	ADAR	STAR	DUAT	DHAW	BOBA
ROAN	AFAR	TAAR	ERAT	DRAW	BUBA
SAAN	AGAR	TEAR	ETAT	FLAW	CEBA
SCAN	AJAR	THAR	FEAT	GNAW	CUBA
SEAN	ALAR	TIAR	FIAT	SHAW	EGBA
SHAN	AMAR	TSAR	FLAT	SLAW	ELBA
SPAN	APAR	TZAR	FRAT	THAW	EZBA
SVAN	ARAR	USAR	GEAT	AJAX	FABA
SWAN	ASAR	WEAR	GHAT	ANAX	HABA
TEAN	ATAR	YEAR	GNAT	COAX	ISBA
THAN	AVAR	ZOAR	GOAT	CRAX	JUBA
TUAN	BEAR	ABAS	HEAT	FLAX	KOBA
ULAN	BHAR	ALAS	IKAT	HOAX	KUBA
URAN	BOAR	ANAS	KAAT	ODAX	LUBA
UZAN	CHAR	ARAS	KYAT	OLAX	MABA
WEAN	CZAR	BAAS	MAAT	ALAY	NUBA
YEAN	DEAR	BIAS	MEAT	ANAY	PEBA
YUAN	DHAR	BLAS	MOAT	AWAY	RABA
AGAO	DUAR	BRAS	NEAT	BRAY	REBA
DHAO	EDAR	DYAS	PEAT	CHAY	SABA

SEBA	TYBI	ESCA	ETCH	MUCK	JACU
TOBA	WABI	INCA	FOCH	NECK	JOCU
TUBA	NABK	JACA	HOCH	NICK	ANCY
UEBA	SOBK	JUCA	INCH	NOCK	LACY
YABA	ALBO	MICA	ITCH	PACK	LUCY
BIBB	AMBO	ONCA	KOCH	PECK	RACY
COBB	BOBO	ORCA	LECH	PICK	
DUBB	BUBO	PACA	LOCH	PUCK	ADDA
HOBB	EGBO	PECA	MUCH	RACK	AIDA
HUBB	GOBO	PICA	NACH	RECK	ALDA
LOBB	HOBO	PUCA	OUCH	RICK	ANDA
ABBE	JOBO	RACA	RICH	ROCK	BUDA
ALBE	LOBO	TECA	ROCH	RUCK	CODA
BABE	NABO	UNCA	SUCH	SACK	DADA
BUBE	NEBO	YMCA	TECH	SECK	EDDA
CUBE	UMBO	YNCA	VACH	SICK	ERDA
DOBE	ZOBO	YUCA	ZACH	SOCK	JUDA
ELBE	DEBS	YWCA	ASCI	SUCK	KADA
GABE	DIBS	ANCE	DECI	TACK	LEDA
GIBE	LUBS	BICE	FOCI	TECK	LIDA
GYBE	NIBS	BOCE	FUCI	TICK	MEDA
HABE	NOBS	DACE	LOCI	TOCK	NUDA
HEBE	POBS	DICE	PICI	TUCK	PEDA
IMBE	TIBS	DUCE	UNCI	WICK	RADA
JIBE	URBS	ECCE	BACK	ALCO	RODA
JUBE	DEBT	ENCE	BECK	CACO	SIDA
KOBE	BABU	ESCE	BOCK	COCO	SODA
LABE	KOBU	FACE	BUCK	DUCO	TEDA
LOBE	NABU	LACE	COCK	FICO	VEDA
LUBE	TABU	LICE	DECK	LOCO	VIDA
ROBE	TIBU	LUCE	DICK	MICO	BADB
RUBE	ZEBU	MACE	DOCK	PACO	BODB
SABE	ABBY	MICE	DUCK	PECO	MUDD
TOBE	BABY	NICE	DYCK	PICO	NUDD
TUBE	DOBY	ONCE	FECK	POCO	RIDD
UNBE	GABY	PACE	HACK	SACO	RODD
COBH	GOBY	PICE	HECK	SOCO	RUDD
ALBI	RUBY	PUCE	HICK	TECO	SADD
AMBI	TOBY	RACE	HOCK	TOCO	SUDD
BABI		RICE	HUCK	UNCO	WADD
BIBI	ACCA	SICE	JACK	WACO	AIDE
BUBI	ALCA	SYCE	JOCK	ABCS	ANDE
CUBI	ARCA	TACE	JUCK	DUCT	AUDE
GABI	AUCA	TICE	KICK	FACT	BADE
GOBI	BOCA	VICE	LACK	LACT	BEDE
KOBI	CACA	VOCE	LICK	PACT	BIDE
MABI	COCA	AICH	LOCK	PICT	BODE
RABI	CUCA	ARCH	LUCK	RECT	BUDE
SEBI	DECA	BACH	MICK	SECT	CADE
TABI	ECCA	EACH	MOCK	TACT	CEDE

CODE	PADI	JUDY	FLED	TREE	GAEL
DUDE	PEDI	LADY	FRED	TWEE	GOEL
EIDE	RODI	ONDY	GLED	TYEE	HEEL
FADE	WADI	SIDY	HEED	USEE	HIEL
FIDE	HADJ	TIDY	HUED	WHEE	JAEL
GADE	BODO	TODY	ICED	ALEF	JEEL
GIDE	CODO	UNDY	LIED	ATEF	JOEL
HADE	DADO	URDY	MEED	BEEF	KEEL
HIDE	DEDO	WADY	MOED	CHEF	KIEL
HYDE	DIDO	LODZ	NEED	CLEF	KOEL
INDE	DODO		PIED	ELEF	NAEL
JADE	EDDO	ALEA	PLED	FIEF	NOEL
JUDE	ENDO	AREA	REED	KEEF	ODEL
KADE	FADO	ASEA	ROED	KIEF	OREL
LADE	FIDO	BREA	SEED	LIEF	PEEL
LODE	JODO	CREA	SHED	REEF	REEL
MADE	JUDO	EVEA	SLED	AREG	RIEL
MEDE	LIDO	FLEA	SNED	DOEG	RYEL
MIDE	LUDO	FREA	SPED	DREG	SEEL
MODE	MADO	GAEA	SYED	CHEG	TAEL
NIDE	ORDO	IDEA	TIED	SKEG	TEEL
NODE	PEDO	ITEA	TOED	WAEG	WEEL
NUDE	REDO	ODEA	USED	OKEH	WIEL
ONDE	SADO	OLEA	WEED	DREI	AHEM
REDE	TODO	OTEA	AGEE	KUEI	ALEM
RIDE	UNDO	OXEA	AJEE	KWEI	ASEM
RODE	YEDO	PLEA	AKEE	OMEI	CLEM
RUDE	SADR	RHEA	ALEE	OUEI	DEEM
SADE	DUDS	SHEA	BYEE	VLEI	DIEM
SIDE	EADS	THEA	CHEE	CHEK	FLEM
TIDE	KIDS	UVEA	CLEE	ESEK	HAEM
TODE	ODDS	BLEB	CREE	HOEK	IDEM
UNDE	SUDS	DIEB	DREE	KEEK	ITEM
URDE	ADDU	PLEB	EPEE	LEEK	KHEM
VADE	JADU	SLEB	FLEE	MEEK	NEEM
VIDE	KADU	SWEB	FREE	PEEK	OZEM
WADE	KUDU	THEB	CHEE	REEK	POEM
WIDE	ORDU	ALEC	IDEE	SEEK	REEM
SADH	PUDU	AVEC	INEE	TREK	RIEM
YODH	URDU	HAEC	KLEE	WEEK	SEEM
ANDI	WIDU	SPEC	KNEE	ABEL	SHEM
CADI	WUDU	ABED	OGEE	BAEL	STEM
KADI	ADDY	AGED	OKEE	AHEL	TEEM
LODI	ANDY	BLED	SHEE	CIEL	THEM
LUDI	BODY	BRED	SKEE	COEL	ADEN
MADI	CADY	COED	SLEE	DUEL	ALEN
MEDI	CODY	DEED	SMEE	EDEL	AMEN
MIDI	EDDY	DRED	SNEE	EZEL	ATEN
NIDI	FADY	EYED	SPEE	FEEL	BEEN
NODI	JADY	FEED	THEE	FUEL	BIEN

BREN	SKEP	OMER	TEES	KNEW	JUEZ
CAEN	STEP	ONER	TRES	LLEW	KNEZ
CHEN	VEEP	OSER	USES	PHEW	OYEZ
COEN	WEEP	OVER	WIES	PLEW	SUEZ
EBEN	ACER	OWER	ABET	SHEW	
EDEN	ADER	OXER	AHET	SKEW	ALFA
EVEN	AGER	OYER	ANET	SLEW	GUFA
GLEN	AMER	PEER	APET	SMEW	KAFA
HIEN	ANER	PIER	BEET	SPEW	KUFA
HOEN	APER	RIER	BLET	STEW	OFFA
IDEN	ASER	ROER	DIET	THEW	SOFA
ITEN	AUER	RUER	DUET	VIEW	TUFA
KEEN	AVER	SAER	EVET	WHEW	URFA
LIEN	BAER	SEER	FEET	AMEX	WAFD
MIEN	BEER	SIER	FRET	APEX	CAFE
OMEN	BIER	STER	KEET	CREX	FIFE
OPEN	BOER	SUER	KHET	FAEX	JEFE
OREN	BRER	TEER	LAET	FLEX	LIFE
OVEN	CHER	TIER	LEET	IBEX	NIFE
OWEN	DAER	TYER	MEET	OBEX	ORFE
OXEN	DEER	UBER	OKET	PLEX	RIFE
PEEN	DIER	USER	PEET	SPEX	SAFE
PIEN	DOER	VEER	PIET	ULEX	WIFE
RIEN	DYER	VIER	PLET	AHEY	BAFF
SEEN	EBER	WAER	POET	AKEY	BIFF
SHEN	EDER	YMER	PRET	ALEY	BUFF
SKEN	EGER	YSER	PYET	BREY	CUFF
STEN	EKER	ADES	SPET	DREY	DAFF
TEEN	EMER	AMES	STET	EYEY	DOFF
THEN	ERER	ANES	SUET	FLEY	DUFF
TIEN	ESER	ARES	TRET	FREY	GAFF
TMEN	EUER	ATES	VOET	GREY	GOFF
WHEN	EVER	AVES	WEET	HOEY	GUFF
WREN	EWER	AYES	WHET	JOEY	HUFF
AREO	EYER	BEES	BLEU	OBEY	JEFF
ATEO	GIER	DIES	DIEU	PREY	JIFF
CLEO	GOER	DOES	EHEU	ROEY	KIFF
IDEO	HEER	ETES	EMEU	SKEY	KOFF
OLEO	EIER	FEES	LIEU	SLEY	LUFF
SKEO	HOER	GHES	KIEV	SPEY	MIFF
THEO	ICER	GOES	STEV	THEY	MOFF
BEEP	IMER	GRES	ANEW	TREY	MUFF
DEEP	ISER	IDES	BLEW	UREY	PIFF
HEEP	ITER	IVES	BREW	VLEY	PUFF
JEEP	JEER	LEES	CHEW	WHEY	RIFF
KEEP	KIER	LUES	CLEW	BAEZ	RUFF
NEEP	LEER	ONES	CREW	CHEZ	TEFF
PEEP	MEER	OYES	DREW	DAEZ	TIFF
PREP	NEER	PRES	FLEW	GEEZ	TOFF
SEEP	ODER	SPES	GREW	INEZ	TUFF

WUFF	RUGA	SIGH	LOGY	TOHO	TSIA
DEFI	SAGA	VUGH	NAGY	BOHR	URIA
FUFI	SOGA	YOGH	ORGY	BUHP	ABIB
HIFI	TOGA	BUGI	POGY	DUHR	ADIB
SAFI	VEGA	HAGI	SAGY	GUHR	AGIB
SUFI	WEGA	JOGI		LEHR	CHIB
BUFO	YOGA	MAGI	AGHA	MAHR	CRIB
LIFO	YUGA	RAGI	AKHA	MOHR	DRIB
OFFS	ZYGA	SUGI	ASHA	RUHR	FRIB
BAFT	ANGE	VAGI	AZHA	SEHR	GLIB
DAFT	AUGE	YOGI	EPHA	TAHR	GUIB
DEFT	CAGE	GAGL	GUHA	TEHR	SNIB
GIFT	DOGE	CAGN	HAHA	OCHS	STIB
HAFT	EDGE	SIGN	ISHA	ACHT	AMIC
HEFT	EUGE	ANGO	KAHA	BAHT	CHIC
LEFT	GAGE	ARGO	MAHA	ECHT	CRIC
LIFT	HUGE	BAGO	MOHA	ICHU	EPIC
LOFT	INGE	BOGO	OCHA	JEHU	ERIC
RAFT	KUGE	BYGO	PAHA	KAHU	IDIC
REFT	LOGE	DAGO	POHA	OAHU	LAIC
RIFT	LUGE	ERGO	PSHA	RAHU	ODIC
SIFT	MAGE	FOGO	TAHA	SAHU	OLIC
SOFT	PAGE	GOGO	TCHA	TCHU	OTIC
TAFT	RAGE	HOGO	USHA	ACHY	PYIC
TUFT	SAGE	HUGO	ACHE	ASHY	SAIC
WAFT	TIGE	IAGO	HEHE		UDIC
WEFT	URGE	LAGO	HOHE	ABIA	ACID
YUFT	WAGE	MOGO	TCHE	AKIA	AMID
AFFY	YAGE	POGO	SAHH	ALIA	ARID
DEFY	DAGG	SAGO	BAHI	AMIA	AVID
DUFY	HAGG	SEGO	PAHI	APIA	BEID
	HOGG	TOGO	TSHI	ARIA	CAID
ALGA	JAGG	UPGO	BUHL	ASIA	ENID
BAGA	MAGG	ZOGO	KOHL	CHIA	GRID
BEGA	MIGG	DOGS	KUHL	ELIA	IBID
BIGA	NOGG	EGGS	BEHN	ERIA	IMID
BOGA	TEGG	TOGS	FOHN	FRIA	IRID
FUGA	VUGG	DEGU	JOHN	GAIA	KAID
GIGA	WEGG	FUGU	BAHO	GLIA	LAID
HOGA	YEGG	GUGU	BOHO	HSIA	MAID
INGA	DAGH	KAGU	COHO	HUIA	NAID
JAGA	GOGH	PEGU	ECHO	ILIA	OLID
JUGA	HEGH	ALGY	ICHO	INIA	OOID
MEGA	HIGH	ARGY	KIHO	IXIA	OVID
MUGA	HUGH	BOGY	MOHO	MAIA	OXID
NAGA	LUGH	CAGY	OTHO	NAIA	PAID
OLGA	MAGH	DOGY	PAHO	OHIA	QAID
PAGA	NIGH	EDGY	PEHO	OKIA	QUID
PEGA	OUGH	EGGY	SAHO	RAIA	RAID
RIGA	PUGH	FOGY	SOHO	SOIA	SAID

SEID	AXIL	MAIM	SPIN	COIR	QAIS
SKID	BAIL	OXIM	TAIN	CUIR	RAIS
SLID	BHIL	PRIM	THIN	EMIR	REIS
UVID	BOIL	REIM	TRIN	FAIR	RIIS
VOID	CEIL	SEIM	TSIN	HAIR	SAIS
ABIE	CHIL	SHIM	TWIN	HEIR	THIS
AMIE	COIL	SKIM	VAIN	KEIR	TRIS
BRIE	DAIL	SLIM	VEIN	LAIR	UNIS
ERIE	DEIL	SWIM	WAIN	LOIR	UPIS
JOIE	EGIL	TRIM	WHIN	NEIR	ADIT
OKIE	EMIL	URIM	ZAIN	PAIR	ALIT
PLIE	EVIL	WHIM	ZEIN	SEIR	BAIT
POIE	FAIL	AKIN	AGIO	SHIR	BRIT
SOIE	FOIL	ALIN	AHIO	SOIR	CHIT
UNIE	GAIL	AMIN	APIO	STIR	COIT
ALIF	HAIL	ASIN	BRIO	TAIR	CUIT
COIF	IFIL	AYIN	CLIO	VAIR	EDIT
ENIF	IPIL	BAIN	IDIO	VOIR	EMIT
KAIF	IXIL	BRIN	MEIO	WEIR	EXIT
KEIF	JAIL	CAIN	MOIO	WHIR	FAIT
LEIF	KAIL	CHIN	NAIO	YMIR	FLIT
NAIF	KOIL	COIN	NOIO	ACIS	FRIT
WAIF	MAIL	CRIN	ODIO	AGIS	GAIT
BRIG	MOIL	DAIN	OHIO	AMIS	GRIT
CRIG	NAIL	DEIN	OLIO	ANIS	IBIT
GRIG	NEIL	ENIN	THIO	APIS	KNIT
SNIG	NOIL	EOIN	TRIO	ARIS	LAIT
SWIG	PAIL	ERIN	UNIO	ATIS	NUIT
TEIG	PHIL	FAIN	ATIP	AVIS	OBIT
TRIG	POIL	GAIN	BLIP	AXIS	OMIT
TWIG	RAIL	GEIN	CHIP	BOIS	PHIT
WHIG	ROIL	GRIN	CLIP	CRIS	QUIT
CHIH	SAIL	HEIN	DRIP	DAIS	SEIT
SHIH	SKIL	JAIN	FLIP	EGIS	SKIT
ALII	SOIL	JOIN	GRIP	ELIS	SLIT
APII	TAIL	LAIN	KLIP	ERIS	SPIT
BOII	TEIL	LIIN	KNIP	FEIS	SUIT
HEII	TOIL	LOIN	QUIP	GLIS	TAIT
UBII	VAIL	MAIN	RAIP	GRIS	TRIT
ATIK	VEIL	MEIN	SEIP	IBIS	TWIT
EFIK	WAIL	NEIN	SHIP	IRIS	UNIT
HAIK	YPIL	ODIN	SKIP	ISIS	WAIT
KAIK	AKIM	PAIN	SLIP	KRIS	WHIT
NAIK	ALIM	RAIN	SNIP	LAIS	WRIT
RAIK	BRIM	REIN	TRIP	LOIS	YUIT
SEIK	CLIM	RHIN	WHIP	MAIS	SKIV
SHIK	DUIM	RUIN	ABIR	NAIS	ALIX
AMIL	EMIM	SAIN	AHIR	OTIS	COIX
ANIL	GLIM	SHIN	AMIR	OVIS	CXIX
ARIL	GRIM	SKIN	CHIR	PAIS	FLIX

NOIX	ROKA	BUKH	FAKY	SALA	DOLE
PRIX	SAKA	HAKH	INKY	SOLA	ELLE
FRIZ	SIKA	LAKH	JOKY	SULA	FILE
PHIZ	SOKA	RUKH	OAKY	TALA	GALE
QUIZ	WAKA	SIKH	PIKY	TELA	GYLE
SWIZ	WEKA	ENKI	POKY	TOLA	HALE
WHIZ	YAKA	KIKI	TAKY	TULA	HOLE
	KTKB	KUKI	WAKY	UPLA	HULE
BEJA	BAKE	LOKI		VELA	HYLE
BIJA	BIKE	MAKI	AGLA	VILA	IDLE
CAJA	CAKE	MOKI	ALLA	VOLA	ILLE
COJA	COKE	PIKI	AMLA	ZOLA	IOLE
DEJA	CUKE	REKI	AULA	BULB	ISLE
HOJA	CYKE	SAKI	BALA	TALC	IXLE
LIJA	DIKE	TIKI	BELA	AULD	JOLE
MAJA	DYKE	WEKI	BOLA	BALD	JULE
NAJA	FAKE	BUKK	CELA	BOLD	KALE
PUJA	FEKE	RIKK	COLA	COLD	KILE
RAJA	FYKE	BOKO	DOLA	EILD	LILE
REJA	HIKE	DOKO	ELLA	FELD	MALE
NEJD	JAKE	HAKO	FALA	FOLD	MELE
HAJE	JOKE	JAKO	FULA	GELD	MILE
YAJE	JUKE	KOKO	GALA	GILD	MOLE
FIHI	LAKE	MAKO	GILA	GOLD	MULE
FUJI	LIKE	MOKO	GOLA	HELD	NILE
KOJI	LOKE	TOKO	GULA	HOLD	OGLE
SUJI	LUKE	ASKR	HALA	KELD	ORLE
SEJM	MAKE	KTKR	HELA	MELD	PALE
BOJO	MIKE	OAKS	HILA	MILD	PELE
GAJO	MOKE	BKKT	HOLA	MOLD	PILE
IDJO	NIKE	BOKT	HULA	SOLD	POLE
MOJO	PEKE	KTKT	HYLA	SULD	PULE
PAJO	PIKE	QKKT	IOLA	TOLD	PYLE
ROJO	POKE	QQKT	KALA	VELD	RALE
TAJO	PUKE	RKKT	KELA	WELD	RILE
BAJU	RAKE	RQKT	KOLA	WILD	ROLE
HOJU	SAKE	TAKT	KULA	WOLD	RULE
JUJU	SOKE	BAKU	LILA	ABLE	SALE
TEJU	TYKE	DUKU	LOLA	ACLE	SOLE
	TAKE	HAKU	MALA	AILE	TALE
AKKA	TIKE	HIKU	MELA	ALLE	TELE
BAKA	TYKE	KUKU	MILA	ATLE	TILE
BEKA	WAKE	MAKU	MOLA	AXLE	TOLE
DIKA	WOKE	POKU	NALA	BALE	TULE
EKKA	YOKE	PUKU	NOLA	BILE	VALE
HAKA	ZEKE	SUKU	OLLA	BOLE	VILE
KAKA	WAKF	TAKU	PALA	CALE	VOLE
LOKA	WUKF	ALKY	PELA	COLE	WALE
PIKA	ANKH	CAKY	POLA	DALE	WILE
PUKA	BIKH	COKY	PYLA	DELE	YALE

YULE	WELK	RULL	VELO	BALU	FAMA
CALF	WILK	SELL	CALP	HULU	GAMA
GOLF	YOLK	SILL	COLP	IALU	GOMA
GULF	BALL	TALL	GULP	IGLU	HIMA
HALF	BELL	TELL	HELP	KULU	IJMA
PELF	BILL	TILL	KELP	LULU	IRMA
SELF	BOLL	TOLL	PALP	PELU	JAMA
WELF	BULL	VILL	PULP	PULU	KAMA
WOLF	CALL	WALL	SALP	SULU	LAMA
AMLI	CELL	WELL	YELP	TOLU	LIMA
ATLI	CULL	WILL	ULLR	TULU	LOMA
BALI	DALL	YELL	FELS	YALU	MAMA
BELI	DELL	BALM	FILS	ZULU	NAMA
COLI	DILL	CALM	HALS	CALX	NEMA
DALI	DOLL	CULM	ILLS	FALX	NUMA
DOLI	DULL	FILM	WELS	ABLY	PIMA
GALI	FALL	HALM	BALT	ALLY	POMA
GOLI	FELL	HELM	BELT	COLY	PUMA
HOLI	FILL	HOLM	BOLT	EELY	RAMA
JOLI	FULL	KULM	BULT	HOLY	RIMA
KALI	GALL	MALM	CELT	IDLY	ROMA
KOLI	GILL	PALM	COLT	INLY	SAMA
KULI	GOLL	KILN	CULT	JULY	SIMA
MALI	GULL	VULN	DOLT	LELY	SOMA
PALI	HALL	ALLO	FELT	LILY	TAMA
PILI	HELL	BILO	GALT	OILY	TEMA
PULI	HILL	BOLO	GELT	ONLY	TOMA
SOLI	HULL	CALO	GILT	ORLY	XEMA
TALI	JELL	DILO	HALT	PALY	YAMA
TELI	JILL	FILO	HILT	PILY	YIMA
VALI	JOLL	GILO	JILT	POLY	YUMA
VILI	KELL	GOLO	JOLT	PULY	ZAMA
WALI	KILL	GULO	KELT	RELY	BOMB
YALI	LILL	HALO	KILT	RILY	COMB
BALK	LOLL	HILO	LILT	UGLY	DUMB
BILK	LULL	KALO	MALT	VILY	IAMB
BULK	MALL	KILO	MELT	WILY	JAMB
CALK	MILL	LOLO	MILT		LAMB
FOLK	MOLL	MALO	MOLT	ALMA	LIMB
FULK	MULL	MILO	PELT	AMMA	NIMB
HULK	NELL	NOLO	SALT	ATMA	NUMB
MILK	NILL	ORLO	SILT	BEMA	RUMB
MULK	NOLL	OSLO	TILT	BOMA	TOMB
POLK	NULL	PALO	VOLT	CIMA	ZIMB
PULK	PALL	PELO	WALT	COMA	ACME
SILK	PILL	POLO	WELT	CYMA	ALME
SULK	POLL	RALO	WILT	DAMA	ARME
TALK	PULL	SILO	YELT	DUMA	CAME
VOLK	RILL	SOLO	AALU	EMMA	COME
WALK	ROLL	ULLO	AULU	ERMA	CYME

DAME	DAMN	LIMU	PINA	SIND	MANE
DEME	DOMN	RIMU	PUNA	TEND	MENE
DIME	FAMN	ARMY	RANA	TIND	MINE
DOME	HYMN	DEMY	RENA	TUND	NANE
FAME	LIMN	DOMY	SANA	VEND	NINE
FEME	AMMO	ELMY	SINA	WAND	NONE
FUME	ATMO	EMMY	TANA	WEND	OHNE
GAME	COMO	FUMY	TINA	WIND	ORNE
HOME	DEMO	HOMY	TUNA	YOND	PANE
HUME	HEMO	ISMY	ULNA	ACNE	PENE
KAME	HOMO	IIMY	URNA	AINE	PINE
KOME	IKMO	RIMY	VENA	ANNE	PONE
LAME	ITMO		VINA	AONE	RINE
LIME	MAMO	ANNA	XINA	ARNE	RONE
MIME	MEMO	ARNA	YANA	AUNE	RUNE
NAME	MOMO	BANA	ZONA	BANE	SANE
NOME	NEMO	BENA	BANC	BENE	SINE
OIME	POMO	BINA	ZINC	BINE	SYNE
POME	SEMO	BONA	ARND	BONE	TANE
PUME	BUMP	BUNA	BAND	CANE	TENE
RAME	CAMP	CANA	BEND	CENE	TINE
RIME	DAMP	CENA	BIND	CINE	TONE
ROME	DUMP	CUNA	BOND	CONE	TUNE
RYME	GAMP	DANA	BUND	DANE	TYNE
SAME	GIMP	DONA	COND	DENE	VANE
SEME	GUMP	DYNA	FEND	DINE	VINE
SIME	HEMP	EDNA	FIND	DONE	WANE
SOME	HUMP	ENNA	FOND	DUNE	WINE
TAME	JUMP	ETNA	FUND	DYNE	ZONE
TIME	LAMP	GENA	GOND	EINE	BANG
TOME	LIMP	GONA	HAND	ENNE	BENG
ULME	LUMP	GUNA	HIND	ERNE	BING
ZEME	MUMP	IONA	HUND	ESNE	BONG
ZYME	PIMP	JENA	KIND	FANE	BUNG
ADMI	POMP	KANA	LAND	FINE	CANG
AMMI	PUMP	KINA	LEND	GANE	DANG
DEMI	RAMP	KONA	LIND	GENE	DING
HAMI	ROMP	LANA	MAND	GONE	DONG
HEMI	RUMP	LENA	MEND	GYNE	DUNG
IMMI	SAMP	LINA	MIND	HONE	FANG
JAMI	SIMP	LUNA	MUND	IONE	FONG
KAMI	SUMP	MANA	PEND	JANE	FUNG
KOMI	TAMP	MINA	POND	JUNE	GANG
MIMI	TUMP	MONA	PUND	KANE	GONG
RAMI	VAMP	MYNA	RAND	KINE	HANG
REMI	ALMS	NANA	REND	LANE	HING
ROMI	ARMS	NINA	RIND	LENE	HONG
SEMI	REMS	NONA	RYND	LINE	HUNG
SIMI	AMMU	ORNA	SAND	LONE	JUNG
ZEMI	ATMU	PANA	SEND	LUNE	KING

KUNG	PANI	MANN	LENS	BENU	SNOB
LING	RANI	PENN	MANS	DANU	SWOB
LONG	RENI	RANN	MENS	GENU	THOB
LUNG	YENI	SENN	MONS	MANU	BLOC
MING	ZUNI	SUNN	NUNS	EMNU	CROC
MONG	FUNJ	WYNN	OONS	TUNU	FLOC
MUNG	GUNJ	ANNO	PONS	ZENU	ALOD
PANG	MUNJ	ARNO	SANS	JINX	APOD
PING	BANK	ASNO	VANS	JYNX	AROD
PONG	BONK	BENO	AINT	LANX	BIOD
PUNG	BUNK	BINO	ARNT	LYNX	CLOD
QUNG	CONK	CANO	AUNT	MANX	ELOD
RANG	DANK	DINO	BANT	MINX	FEOD
RING	DUNK	FANO	BENT	YUNX	FOOD
RONG	FINK	FONO	BUNT	BONY	GOOD
RUNG	FUNK	GANO	CANT	CONY	HOOD
SANG	GINK	HANO	CENT	DENY	LOOD
SING	HANK	HINO	DENT	LINY	MOOD
SONG	HONK	JUNO	DINT	LUNY	POLD
SUNG	HUNK	KANO	DONT	MANY	POOD
TANG	JONK	KENO	DUNT	PINY	PROD
TENG	JUNK	KINO	FONT	PONY	QUOD
TING	KINK	LENO	GENT	PUNY	ROOD
TONG	KONK	LINO	HANT	TINY	SHOD
TUNG	KUNK	MANO	HINT	TONY	SNOD
UANG	LANK	MINO	HUNT	TUNY	STOD
VANG	LINK	MONO	KANT	VINY	TROD
WANG	LONK	NINO	KENT	WANY	WOOD
WING	MINK	NONO	LENT	WINY	ALOE
WONG	MONK	PINO	LINT	ZANY	AROE
YANG	PANK	PUNO	MENT	LINZ	CLOE
ZING	PINK	RENO	MINT		EBOE
BINH	PUNK	SINO	MONT	ANOA	EVOE
HUNH	RANK	TANO	OONT	AROA	FLOE
SINH	RINK	TINO	PANT	GHOA	FROE
TANH	SANK	TUNO	PENT	POOA	OBOE
AANI	SINK	VINO	PINT	PROA	OTOE
AGNI	SUNK	XENO	PONT	SHOA	SHOE
ANNI	TANK	ZENO	PUNT	STOA	SLOE
ARNI	TONK	CINO	RANT	TOOA	AZOF
BANI	WINK	BANS	RENT	WHOA	GOOF
BENI	YANK	CENS	RUNT	BLOB	HOOF
BINI	BINN	DANS	TENT	BOOB	LOOF
BONI	BONN	DENS	TINT	BROB	ROOF
CONI	BUNN	DUNS	VENT	CHOB	STOF
DONI	CONN	ENNS	VINT	DOOB	WOOF
HONI	FINN	FONS	WANT	KNOB	AGOG
IONI	JANN	GENS	WENT	RHOB	AJOG
MANI	JINN	HANS	WONT	SCOB	CLOG
OMNI	LINN	HENS	AINU	SLOB	FLOG

FROG	FROM	ROON	DOOR	RIOT	BUOY
GROG	GLOM	SCON	GHOR	ROOT	CLOY
ILOG	GOOM	SION	GOOR	RYOT	OHOY
NIOG	JOOM	SOON	IGOR	SCOT	PLOY
SLOG	KLOM	TION	KHOR	SHOT	TROY
SMOG	LOOM	TOON	KNOR	SLOT	BROZ
STOG	PROM	UPON	MOOR	SOOT	
VOOG	ROOM	WOON	ODOR	SPOT	ARPA
BOOH	STOM	ZION	OGOR	STOT	CEPA
BROH	WHOM	ZOON	OLOR	TOOT	COPA
POOH	ZOOM	ABOO	POOR	TROT	DEPA
AMOI	ACON	AROO	SHOR	ABOU	DOPA
EKOI	AEON	BROO	THOR	CHOU	GAPA
AMOK	AGON	EJOO	UTOR	CLOU	HUPA
ASOK	AMON	KROO	AMOS	MEOU	KAPA
BOOK	ANON	PHOO	BIOS	NIOU	LIPA
COOK	ATON	SHOO	COOS	SHOU	NAPA
DOOK	AVON	SLOO	DUOS	THOU	NEPA
HOOK	AXON	WHOO	ENOS	TIOU	NIPA
IROK	AZON	ALOP	EPOS	AKOV	PAPA
LOOK	BION	ASOP	EROS	AZOV	PIPA
NOOK	BOON	ATOP	GROS	ALOW	PUPA
POOK	CION	CHOP	LAOS	AROW	RIPA
ROOK	COON	CLOP	LOOS	AVOW	RUPA
SOOK	DION	COOP	NAOS	BLOW	SAPA
TOOK	DOON	CROP	PHOS	BROW	SUPA
AWOL	EBON	DROP	ROOS	CHOW	TAPA
BOOL	ELON	FLOP	TAOS	CLOW	YAPA
CHOL	ENON	GOOP	TEOS	CROW	ZIPA
COOL	ETON	HOOP	THOS	DHOW	CAPE
EGOL	FAON	KLOP	ABOT	ENOW	CEPE
ENOL	GAON	KNOP	BLOT	FLOW	COPE
FOOL	GEON	KOOP	BOOT	FROW	DOPE
GAOL	GOON	LOOP	CLOT	GLOW	DUPE
IDOL	HOON	PLOP	COOT	GROW	GAPE
ITOL	ICON	POOP	EYOT	KNOW	HIPE
OBOL	IKON	PROP	FIOT	LWOW	HOPE
POOL	IRON	SCOP	FOOT	MEOW	HYPE
SIOL	LEON	SHOP	FROT	PLOW	JAPE
TOOL	LION	SLOP	GROT	PROW	JUPE
VIOL	LOON	STOP	HOOT	SCOW	KIPE
WOOL	LYON	SWOP	ILOT	SHOW	LOPE
AHOM	MOON	TROP	KNOT	SLOW	LUPE
ATOM	NEON	SHOQ	LOOT	SNOW	MOPE
BOOM	NOON	ACOR	MOOT	STOW	NAPE
BROM	PAON	ADOR	PHOT	SWOW	NUPE
COOM	PEON	AMOR	PIOT	TROW	OLPE
CROM	PHON	ASOR	PLOT	ABOX	PEPE
DOON	PION	BOOR	POOT	ESOX	PIPE
EDOM	POON	CHOR	PYOT	AHOY	POPE

RAPE	VEPS	GORA	VERB	FARE	SURF
RIPE	ZIPS	HERA	CIRC	FIRE	TURF
ROPE	COPT	HORA	MARC	FORE	WERF
RYPE	EMPT	HURA	PARC	GARE	ZARF
SUPE	KEPT	IKRA	BARD	GORE	BERG
SYPE	KOPT	IRRA	BIRD	GYRE	BORG
TAPE	RAPT	JURA	BORD	HARE	BURG
TIPE	SEPT	KARA	BYRD	HERE	LURG
TOPE	SOPT	KORA	CARD	HIRE	MORG
TYPE	WEPT	LARA	CORD	INRE	SARG
WIPE	HAPU	LIRA	CURD	JURE	ABRI
XIPE	NAPU	LORA	DARD	KERE	AERI
YIPE	OGPU	LURA	FARD	KORE	AGRI
ALPH	TAPU	LYRA	FORD	KURE	ATRI
CAPH	CAPY	MARA	FYRD	LIRE	AURI
KAPH	ESPY	MIRA	GERD	LORE	BARI
KOPH	GAPY	MORA	GIRD	LURE	BORI
OLPH	PIPY	MURA	HARD	LYRE	BURI
QOPH	ROPY	MYRA	HERD	MARE	DARI
SOPH	TUPY	NERA	JORD	MERE	GERI
UMPH	TYPY	NORA	KURD	MIRE	GYRI
AIPI		OBRA	LARD	MORE	KARI
HOPI	KTQB	OCRA	LORD	MURE	KERI
IMPI	WAQF	OKRA	NARD	OGRE	KIRI
KEPI	KTQR	ORRA	OORD	PARE	KORI
KOPI		OTRA	PARD	PERE	KURI
PIPI	ABRA	PARA	SARD	PORE	LARI
TIPI	AERA	PERA	SURD	PURE	LORI
TOPI	AFRA	RARA	VERD	PYRE	LURI
TUPI	AGRA	SARA	WARD	QERE	MARI
CIPO	AIRA	SERA	WORD	RARE	NERI
GAPO	AKRA	SORA	WYRD	RIRE	NORI
HYPO	AMRA	SURA	YARD	SERE	OMRI
MAPO	ARRA	SYRA	AARE	SIRE	PERI
PEPO	AURA	TARA	ACRE	SORE	PURI
SAPO	BARA	TERA	AIRE	SURE	QERI
TYPO	BERA	TORA	BARE	TARE	RORI
CAPP	BORA	VARA	BORE	TIRE	SARI
DOPP	BURA	VERA	BURD	TORE	SERI
KIPP	CARA	VIRA	BYRE	TYRE	SHRI
LAPP	CERA	ZIRA	CARE	VARE	SIRI
REPP	CORA	BARB	CERE	VIRE	SORI
TYPP	CURA	CURB	CORE	WARE	TARI
WAPP	DERA	GARB	CURE	SERE	TORI
YAPP	DORA	GERB	DARE	WIRE	TURI
ALPS	DURA	HARB	DIRE	WORE	VARI
HOPS	EYRA	HERB	DORE	YARE	VERI
SEPS	EZRA	KERB	EIRE	YORE	WERI
TAPS	FORA	SERB	ETRE	KERF	BARK
TOPS	GARA	SORB	EYRE	SERF	CARK

CORK	HARM	GYRO	AIRS	ADRY	SUSA
DARK	MARM	HERO	BORS	AERY	TESA
DIRK	NORM	INRO	HERS	ATRY	URSA
FORK	PERM	KARO	HORS	AWRY	VASA
HARK	TERM	LERO	LARS	BURY	VISA
JERK	TURM	LORO	LORS	DORY	XOSA
KIRK	WARM	MARO	MARS	EERY	BOSC
KURK	WORM	MERO	MORS	EWRY	DISC
LARK	WURM	MIRO	OURS	EYRY	FISC
LURK	BARN	MORO	PARS·	FURY	ANSE
MARK	BERN	NERO	SORS	GARY	APSE
MIRK	BIRN	OKRO	AIRT	GORY	ASSE
MURK	BORN	OTRO	BART	JURY	BASE
NARK	BURN	PERO	BERT	LORY	BISE
PARK	CARN	PIRO	BORT	MARY	BOSE
PERK	CERN	PORO	CART	MIRY	CASE
PORK	CORN	PYRO	CURT	NARY	CISE
SARK	DARN	SERO	DART	OARY	COSE
TURK	DORN	TARO	DIRT	RORY	DOSE
WORK	EARN	TIRO	FORT	SORY	DUSE
YORK	FERN	TORO	GIRT	SPRY	EASE
BIRL	FIRN	TYRO	HART	TORY	ELSE
BURL	GARN	XERO	HURT	VARY	ENSE
CARL	HORN	ZERO	MART	VERY	ERSE
CIRL	KARN	BURP	MORT	WARY	ESSE
CURL	KERN	CARP	PART	WIRY	FUSE
EARL	LORN	DORP	PERT		HOSE
FARL	MORN	HARP	PORT	ANSA	HUSE
FURL	NORN	LARP	SART	AUSA	IPSE
GIRL	PERN	LERP	SERT	BESA	JOSE
HARL	PIRN	TARP	SORT	BISA	LOSE
HERL	TARN	TERP	TART	BOSA	MESE
HURL	TERN	TORP	TORT	CASA	MISE
JARL	TORN	TURP	VERT	DISA	MOSE
KARL	TURN	WARP	WART	DOSA	MUSE
MARL	WARN	ZARP	WERT	ELSA	NASE
MERL	WORN	BARR	WORT	KASA	NOSE
NURL	YARN	BIRR	YURT	LISA	OESE
PURL	YIRN	BURR	AARU	MASA	OISE
YARL	AERO	CARR	BARU	MESA	OUSE
BARM	AGRO	CURR	ECRU	MUSA	PISE
BERM	BARO	DARR	FERU	NASA	POSE
CORM	BORO	DURR	GURU	OSSA	RASE
DERM	CARO	HERR	MARU	PASA	RESE
DORM	CERO	KERR	MERU	PESA	RISE
FARM	DURO	PARR	PERU	PISA	ROSE
FIRM	EBRO	PIRR	PURU	RASA	RUSE
FORM	FARO	PURR	RURU	ROSA	SISE
GARM	GARO	TYRR	PORU	RUSA	VASE
GERM	GIRO	YARR	YARU	SASA	VISE

WISE	NISI	CESS	FAST	CASY	VITA
BASH	PASI	COSS	FEST	COSY	VOTA
BISH	SESI	CUSS	FIST	EASY	WETA
BOSH	SISI	DASS	FUST	JOSY	YETA
BUSH	SUSI	DISS	GEST	MOSY	ZETA
CASH	BASK	DOSS	GIST	NOSY	ZITA
COSH	BISK	FASS	GUST	POSY	ALTE
CUSH	BOSK	FESS	HAST	ROSY	ANTE
DASH	BUSK	FOSS	HEST	SUSY	AUTE
DISH	CASK	FUSS	HIST		BATE
FASH	CUSK	HISS	HOST	ACTA	BETE
FISH	DESK	JASS	JEST	AETA	BITE
GASH	DISK	JESS	JUST	ALTA	CATE
GISH	DUSK	JOSS	KIST	ANTA	CETE
GOSH	FISK	KISS	LAST	ARTA	CITE
GUSH	HUSK	KOSS	LEST	ASTA	COTE
HASH	MASK	LASS	LIST	ATTA	CUTE
HISH	MOSK	LESS	LOST	BATA	CYTE
HUSH	MUSK	LISS	LUST	BETA	DATE
JOSH	OMSK	LOSS	MAST	BOTA	DOTE
KISH	PISK	MASS	MIST	CATA	ENTE
KUSH	RISK	MESS	MOST	COTA	ESTE
LASH	RUSK	MISS	MUST	DATA	ETTE
LOSH	TASK	MOSS	MYST	DITA	FATE
LUSH	TOSK	MUSS	NAST	ESTA	FETE
MASH	TUSK	NESS	NEST	ETTA	FUTE
MESH	KASM	PASS	OAST	GATA	GATE
MUSH	ALSO	PESS	OUST	GETA	GITE
NASH	CASO	PUSS	PAST	IOTA	HATE
NESH	COSO	RISS	PEST	JOTA	JETE
NISH	HUSO	ROSS	PIST	KETA	JUTE
PISH	IPSO	RUSS	POST	KOTA	KATE
POSH	KOSO	SESS	REST	LATA	KITE
PUSH	MUSO	SISS	RUST	LOTA	LATE
RASH	PESO	TASS	TEST	MATA	LOTE
RESH	PISO	TESS	VAST	META	LUTE
RUSH	SOSO	TOSS	VEST	MOTA	MATE
SASH	YESO	VISS	WEST	MUTA	METE
SISH	CUSP	BAST	WIST	NOTA	MITE
SOSH	GASP	BEST	ZEST	OCTA	MOTE
TUSH	HASP	BUST	ANSU	PATA	MUTE
WASH	LISP	CAST	APSU	PITA	NATE
WISH	RASP	CEST	AUSU	RATA	NETE
ABSI	RISP	CIST	GESU	RITA	NOTE
ASSI	WASP	COST	JESU	ROTA	OSTE
DASI	WISP	CYST	MASU	RUTA	PATE
DESI	BASS	DOST	NOSU	SETA	PETE
KASI	BESS	DUST	SUSU	SITA	RATE
LASI	BOSS	EAST	VASU	TOTA	RETE
NASI	BUSS	ERST	BUSY	VETA	RITE

ROTE	HATI	VETO	UNTZ	ROUE	DOUM
RUTE	INTI	VOTO		SHUE	DRUM
SATE	JATI	NATR	AGUA	SLUE	GEUM
SITE	LETI	ACTS	AKUA	TRUE	GLUM
TATE	LITI	ARTS	AQUA	OEUF	GRUM
TETE	LOTI	CATS	ATUA	POUF	JHUM
TOTE	NETI	CITS	ERUA	SOUF	MEUM
TUTE	RATI	EATS	SKUA	CHUG	ODUM
VITE	ROTI	LOTS	ULUA	DRUG	OGUM
VOTE	SATI	RATS	BLUB	FRUG	OVUM
WATE	SETI	BATT	CHUB	GLUG	PLUM
WOTE	TITI	BITT	CLUB	JOUG	RHUM
YATE	YATI	BOTT	DAUB	PLUG	SAUM
YITE	ZATI	BUTT	DOUB	SCUG	SCUM
ACTH	ROTL	GETT	DRUB	SLUG	SLUM
BATH	ACTO	HETT	FLUB	SMUG	STUM
BETH	ALTO	LETT	GAUB	SNUG	SWUM
BOTH	ARTO	MATT	GLUB	THUG	UTUM
DOTH	AUTO	MITT	GRUB	TOUG	AMUN
ESTH	BITO	MUTT	KNUB	BRUH	CHUN
GATH	BOTO	NOTT	SLUB	ARUI	FAUN
GOTH	BUTO	PITT	SNUB	EQUI	IDUN
HATH	CATO	POTT	STUB	ETUI	JAUN
HETH	CETO	PUTT	DOUC	MAUI	KAUN
HOTH	CITO	SETT	ERUC	CAUK	LAUN
JETH	COTO	TATT	BAUD	DAUK	LOUN
KATH	DATO	WATT	CHUD	SAUK	MAUN
KITH	DOTO	ACTU	FEUD	SOUK	NOUN
LATH	ECTO	ATTU	DOUD	AOUL	PAUN
LITH	ENTO	DATU	GAUD	AZUL	SHUN
LOTH	INTO	LATU	LAUD	BAUL	SPUN
MATH	JATO	MITU	LOUD	CAUL	STUN
MOTH	KOTO	PATU	MAUD	DEUL	TAUN
MUTH	LETO	TATU	PYYD	ELUL	TSUN
MYTH	LOTO	TUTU	ROUD	FOUL	USUN
NATH	MOTO	YUTU	SCUD	GAUL	WHUN
OATH	NATO	ARTY	SOUD	GOUL	BLUP
PATH	NITO	CITY	SPUD	HAUL	CAUP
PITH	OCTO	COTY	STUD	MAUL	COUP
RATH	ONTO	DATY	SYUD	PAUL	GAUP
RUTH	OTTO	DOTY	THUD	POUL	LOUP
SETH	PATO	DUTY	AGUE	SAUL	NOUP
TETH	PETO	MATY	BLUE	SHUL	PLUP
URTH	PITO	MITY	CLUE	AHUM	SCUP
VOTH	ROTO	OATY	FLUE	ALUM	SNUP
WITH	SITO	PITY	GAUE	ARUM	SOUP
ANTI	TITO	TOTY	GLUE	ATUM	TOUP
ASTI	TOTO	BATZ	MOUE	BAUM	YAUP
BITI	TYTO	LITZ	NEUE	CHUM	YOUP
GUTI	UNTO	METZ	NIUE	DEUM	ALUR

ASUR	BRUT	VIVA	KAVI	BOWL	TOXA
AZUR	CHUT	XOVA	LEVI	CAWL	LUXE
BIUR	FAUT	NKVD	RAVI	COWL	MIXE
BLUR	GAUT	BAVE	FAVN	DOWL	SAXE
DOUR	GLUT	CAVE	LEVO	FOWL	CAXI
EBUR	GOUT	CIVE	PAVO	GOWL	DIXI
FOUR	HAUT	COVE	VIVO	HOWL	TAXI
GAUR	KNUT	DAVE	RSVP	JOWL	MOXQ
GOUR	LOUT	DIVE	REVS	MEWL	MYXO
HOUR	NAUT	DOVE	KIVU	PAWL	TAXO
JOUR	PHUT	EAVE	BEVY	YAWL	NEXT
KNUR	POUT	FIVE	CAVY	YOWL	SEXT
LOUR	ROUT	GAVE	CUVY	DAWN	TEXT
PEUR	SCUT	GIVE	DAVY	BAWM	BOXY
POUR	SHUT	GYVE	ENVY	DAWM	BUXY
SCUR	SLUT	HAVE	LEVY	DOWN	DOXY
SLUR	SMUT	HIVE	LIVY	FAWN	FOXY
SMUR	SPUT	HOVE	NAVY	GAWN	PIXY
SNUR	STUT	JAVE	PAVY	GOWN	PUXY
SOUR	TAUT	JIVE	PEVY	HEWN	ROXY
SPUR	TOUT	JOVE	TAVY	KAWN	WAXY
TOUR	ROUW	KIVE	WAVY	LAWN	
YOUR	DAUW	LAVE		LOWN	ALYA
ACUS	CRUX	LIVE	BIWA	MOWN	ARYA
ANUS	DEUX	LOVE	DEWA	PAWN	BAYA
APUS	EAUX	MOVE	IOWA	SAWN	CUYA
AVUS	FLUX	NAVE	KAWA	SEWN	GOYA
COUS	JEUX	NEVE	LOWA	TOWN	HOYA
CRUS	ROUX	NOVE	PAWA	YAWN	MAYA
DEUS	VAUX	PAVE	TAWA	ATWO	PUYA
ESUS	GHUZ	RAVE	TEWA	GAWP	RAYA
GAUS		REVE	DOWD	YAWP	SAYA
GRUS	ALVA	RIVE	GAWD	LAWS	SOYA
IRUS	CAVA	ROVE	LEWD	MEWS	YAYA
NOUS	CIVA	SAVE	HOWE	NEWS	EMYD
ONUS	DEVA	SEVE	POWE	YAWS	DAYE
OPUS	DIVA	SIVE	JHWH	NEWT	SKYE
OTUS	HOVA	TAVE	YHWH	NOWT	STYE
PIUS	JAVA	VIVE	IIWI	DEWY	KIYI
PLUS	JIVA	WAVE	KAWI	JAWY	ACYL
POUS	JOVA	WEVE	KIWI	NOWY	AMYL
RHUS	KAVA	WIVE	TUWI	RAWY	IDYL
SOUS	KIVA	WOVE	BOWK	TOWY	NOYL
THUS	LAVA	IHVH	CAWK		ODYL
USUS	NEVA	JHVH	DAWK	BIXA	OXYL
ZEUS	NOVA	YHVH	GAWK	COXA	TEYL
ABUT	PEVA	DEVI	GOWK	DOXA	CLYM
BHUT	SIVA	DIVI	HAWK	MOXA	ETYM
BLUT	ULVA	FAVI	SAWK	MYXA	ONYM
BOUT	URVA	HEVI	BAWL	NOXA	COYN

GWYN	ITYS	DAZA	GAZE	IDZO	KAZY
LLYN	KEYS	GAZA	GUZE	KOZO	LAZY
BUYO	WAYS	ITZA	HAZE	LAZO	OOZY
CAYO	SKYT	JUZA	LAZE	MAZO	SIZY
COYO	VAYU	ONZA	MAZE	MOZO	SUZY
ENYO	CEYX	TIZA	NAZE	ANZU	BUZZ
IDYO	ERYX	TUZA	OOZE	AUZU	FIZZ
KAYO	ONYX	ZUZA	RAZE	ENZU	FUZZ
MAYO	ORYX	ADZE	SIZE	WUZU	HUZZ
WHYO	PNYX	BIZE	CAZI	CAZY	JAZZ
TRYP	STYX	COZE	GAZI	COZY	RAZZ
SKYR	HAYZ	DAZE	KAZI	DAZY	SIZZ
ALYS		DOZE	LAZI	DOZY	ZIZZ
DAYS	BOZA	FAZE	NAZI	HAZY	
EMYS	CAZA	FUZE	BOZO	JOZY